W9-BIY-761

Family BOOK OF CRAFTS

compiled by
LOUISA B. HELLEGERS
and
ANNE E. KALLEM

assisted by
ERIC SMITH
and the
Editors of Sterling

STERLING PUBLISHING CO., INC. NEW YORK
Oak Tree Press Co., Ltd. London & Sydney

OTHER BOOKS OF INTEREST

Practical Encyclopedia of Crafts

LITTLE CRAFT BOOK SERIES

Copyright © 1973 by Sterling Publishing Co., Inc.
419 Park Avenue South, New York, N.Y. 10016
British edition published by Oak Tree Press Co., Ltd., Nassau, Bahamas
Distributed in Australia and New Zealand by Oak Tree Press Co., Ltd.,
P.O. Box 34, Brickfield Hill, Sydney 2000, N.S.W.
Distributed in the United Kingdom and elsewhere in the British Commonwealth
by Ward Lock Ltd., 116 Baker Street, London W 1
Manufactured in the United States of America
All rights reserved
Library of Congress Catalog Card No.: 72-95199
ISBN 0-8069-5250-4   UK 7061- 2439-1
5251-2

CONTENTS

INTRODUCTION

The "Family Book of Crafts," as the title denotes, is a book for the whole family or for any member of it, regardless of age, ability or interest. It presumes no craft knowledge. It starts from the premise that, although the household contains only a limited number of tools and equipment, there is nevertheless a work table and some space that can be converted into a potential craft studio.

Why should a family be interested in crafts? And how can a book be aimed at all members regardless of age? First, the editors feel that your natural creativity can be tapped if the proper suggestions stimulate you, and this event can occur at any age. A parent or grandparent may find most enjoyment in the simplest of crafts, while young children may be challenged by the more technical, involved crafts. Experience has shown us that ability to design, create and produce a craft object with your own hands is not something which is exclusive to any age level.

Some of the crafts and projects in this volume can be performed by a group working together, such as youngster and parent, or several youngsters, or several adults. In general, however, the projects are written for an individual to perform by himself or herself. The handcrafter is given the idea, then taught the technique by copying from the book a particular project or following a pattern so as to become familiar with all of the processes in simple step-by-step fashion. Following the instructions is not for the purpose of simple copying, as from a craft kit or a painting-by-number type of instruction book, but simply for becoming familiar with the process. Immediately after this, you are able to design something similar or something different and, following the same procedures, create your own object.

The idea is to let your imagination be your inspiration for other designs using the same techniques. Any potential handicrafter—experienced or not—can pick up this book and, by flipping through the pages, find dozens of crafts and hundreds of ideas from which to choose. Once having learned the techniques, the user of this book should be able to design and execute some very worthwhile objects and in the process be satisfied. Use your ingenuity and creativity.

No set guide-lines are put down, but the volume is organized in a particular fashion. The projects and sections do not go from easiest to hardest or simplest to most complex. They are arranged somewhat differently.

If you find that a craft which interests you is too technical or is more complex than you thought, there are innumerable others which will satisfy your needs. Simply turn a few pages, and you are bound to find a craft more suitable for you.

Part I is called "The Medium is the thing" — for example, beads, crayons, fabrics, glass, horseshoe nails, natural materials, paint, paper, plastic foam, string, wood and wool. You are supposed to use these specific media to make different things.

Part II is called "The Thing is the thing" and here are included such things as candles, collages, creative gifts, decorative masks, dioramas, flowers of paper or shell, rugs, junk sculptures, knick-knacks, mobiles, model boats, mosaics, musical instruments, picture frames, puppets, silver jewelry and toys, which you can make from different media.

Part III, called "The Process is the thing," includes specific crafts that you use to make different things. The processes include cold enamelling, curling and quilling, lacquer and crackle, macramé with beads and with rope, napkin folding, pebble polishing, printing with potatoes and silk screens, and ceramics by slab.

Within each section the subjects are in alphabetical order by craft. The contents and index will help you to locate the craft you want.

Immediately following Part III is an appendix which begins with a section entitled "Ideas for Designs." If you have tried to create an unusual or striking design that pleases you but feel that you have somehow failed, this section gives you hints of where to look for ideas without telling you exactly what designs to use. Completing the appendix are a Suppliers list to assist you in obtaining any special materials or tools necessary for certain crafts; a Bibliography of the works which have been condensed or adapted for this volume; and a thorough Index which should help you quickly locate any technique, project or process contained in the book.

The "Family Book of Crafts" is a compilation. Some of the articles have been condensed from larger books and others have been written especially for this volume. The illustrations have been numbered separately, starting with Illustration 1 in each article. Each article is self-sufficient and a total entity in itself. How-ever, there is a relationship between the articles and it is the hope of the editors that you will apply the knowledge you have gained in one article to any other article that you work with. In other words, once you learn how to perform one craft, it should be of immense value to you in beginning another craft. Our experience has shown that once a person gets interested in crafting, he or she wants to go on to as many crafts as possible and try to make something out of nothing. How rewarding it is to be able to start from a few pieces of scrap and make an article to hang on the wall that all of your friends and guests admire, or to have a table inlaid with a mosaic that you have made yourself, or to knit or weave a gift which draws the plaudits of the recipient!

In a way this book is a challenge. There are many crafts here that you may not ever have heard of. The immense size of the book itself may give you the feeling that so much is to be known about crafts that you and your family will never get enough energy to pursue even one. Don't be misled. Crafts are easy, following the instructions is easy, and producing the final object gives you a soul-satisfying feeling of accomplishment. Start right now.

THE EDITORS

BEFORE YOU BEGIN

What do you need before you begin to craft? No general list of materials or tools is possible because the specific ones you need vary depending which crafts you decide upon. Each article contains a thorough description of the equipment and supplies you will need, and the Suppliers' list at the back of the book will help you locate any necessary materials.

There are, however, two general processes which you should know before you begin crafting: how to trace and how to enlarge or reduce patterns. You may find designs you like that need to be transferred from a book or that you wish to change to your desired size.

You may, naturally, transfer a design you like freehand to your desired base. Or, you may trace it. To trace a pattern which is the same size as you want it, first see that the book or page with the pattern is flat on your work table. Take a sheet of tracing paper and place it over the page with the pattern. The tracing paper should be at least 3″ larger than the page itself (on the three outside edges if it is a page in a book). Make sure that the tracing paper is free from folds and wrinkles.

You can hold the tracing paper in place with your hand. But, if the paper moves, the parts of your design will not match. It is best, then, to hold the paper in place with pins or cellophane tape which you place at each of the four corners. Tape or pin the paper down to the work table. (Protect the table's surface with newspapers whenever you use pins.) Never pin or tape paper to a book.

When you have the paper in place, use a soft lead pencil to trace over the lines. Do not dig in. Make a line just dark enough to see. Use your ruler to guide you with the straight lines. Trace any markings as well as the pattern.

After you have traced the pattern onto the paper, carefully lift the paper off the book or page. Be sure you do not tear the paper. Next take carbon paper and put it between the tracing paper and the surface to which you would like to transfer the design.

Hold the tracing paper and the carbon paper to the base, flat on the work table, with pins or tape at all four corners. You should always use a soft lead pencil to mark off the patterns. Just follow the lines on the tracings with enough pressure for the carbon to transfer them to the new base. Do not push the pencil hard or you will go through your tracings.

When you are finished, take the tracing paper and the carbon paper away. The pattern should be exactly like that of the original page. Check and see that they are alike.

If the design you have chosen is not the size you want it to be, you may enlarge or reduce it by the grid method. To enlarge a design, for example, draw a $\frac{1}{4}''$-grid, which is simply a series of criss-crossed lines $\frac{1}{4}''$ apart, over the design to be enlarged. On another piece of paper, draw a $1''$-grid—criss-crossed lines $1''$ apart—using the same number of squares as the $\frac{1}{4}''$-grid. Sketching freehand, copy the lines within each of the small squares of the $\frac{1}{4}''$-grid to each of the squares of the $1''$-grid. The $\frac{1}{4}''$- and $1''$-grids increase the original design four times. By varying the size of the grids, you can vary the final size of your design. Reverse the size of the grids—that is, draw a $1''$-grid over the original design and transfer the lines to a $\frac{1}{4}''$-grid—to reduce the design to one quarter the original size.

Believe it or not, there is nothing else you need to know before you begin to craft. This is a reference book, and you should use it as such. You do not need to memorize the articles, but you should turn to various sections or refer to specific techniques as the desire to create strikes you. Simply open the book to any craft which interests you, read through the entire article to set your frame of mind, and begin.

Draw a ¼-inch grid over the original design you wish to enlarge.

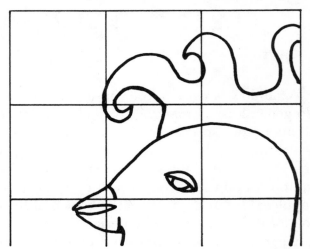

Transfer the design square by square onto a 1-inch grid, thus increasing the design four times.

the
MEDIUM
is
the thing

The Use of
Specific Media to
Make Different Things

BEADCRAFT

Beadcraft—stringing beads, or embroidering or weaving with beads—is creative work. Whoever does it is bound to project his or her personality into it. The techniques of the craft are not difficult, but in order to master them, you need some attention and patience at the start, as beads, especially small ones, are not always easy to handle. For their modest size, however, beads hold great lustre and beauty, and the effort beadcraft requires can be amply rewarded in the results you attain.

Before you start, collect all the beads you like and keep them, preferably, in small glass jars, so that they are fully visible. Then put a piece of felt or velvet of a neutral color in front of you, on a table or—better still—on a low-rimmed tray, which prevents the beads from rolling away. Also, keep close at hand all the materials you may need, so that you will not have to interrupt your work time and again. You need a few cups for selecting the beads, some nylon thread (or stiffer nylon fishing line), string, cord, or other durable filament for threading, and a darning needle or two to start. For embroidering with beads, you also need embroidery floss (a thread with a special sheen, available at needlecraft counters), fabric and an embroidery needle. The eye of the needle must be large enough for the floss, but small enough to go through the holes in the beads you are using.

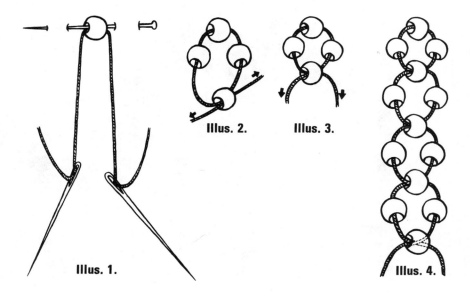

Illus. 2.   **Illus. 3.**

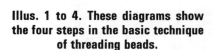

Illus. 1 to 4. These diagrams show the four steps in the basic technique of threading beads.

Illus. 1.

Illus. 4.

Condensed from the books, "Beads Plus Macramé" by Grethe La Croix | © 1971 by Sterling Publishing Co., Inc., New York, and "Creating with Beads" by Grethe La Croix | © 1969 by Sterling Publishing Co., Inc., New York

Medallion Technique

The basic technique upon which this chapter is based is the two-thread technique. Start with a long thread, and run it through one bead. Position this bead at a point halfway down the length of the thread, and keep it in place by fixing it to a sand-filled pincushion (Illus. 1) to hold it while you are doing the rest of the threading. This step forms the looped thread.

Now continue with both ends of the thread (either with two needles—or without needles if you are using a stiff thread such as nylon fishing line). Thread one bead at the left side of the central bead and two at the right. Now cross the threads through the last-threaded bead (Illus. 2), thus connecting the four beads. Pull the two thread-ends downward (Illus. 3).

Continue with three beads each time, until you have attained your desired length (Illus. 4).

You make a medallion or pendant like the ones in Illus. 5 by the two-thread technique with a variation. Start with three beads instead of four, and continue with two instead of three (Illus. 6a and 6b). In this way, the shape becomes round.

Take a long thread and start in the middle of it, as you can see in Illus. 6a. When the string of beads fits around the large bead you will place in the middle, close the circle (Illus. 6c). It is a good idea to start by first putting the loose beads around the central bead, in order to determine the quantity you need. The pendant gets round if you put a round bead in the middle and oval if the central bead is oval.

Illus. 6c shows how you close the circle

Illus. 5. Medallions which are meant to be hung around the neck as pendants or made into brooches are threaded in a slightly different way, as shown in Illus. 6 through Illus. 8.

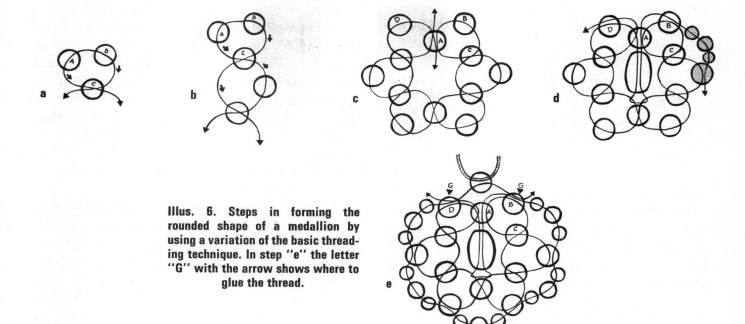

Illus. 6. Steps in forming the rounded shape of a medallion by using a variation of the basic threading technique. In step "e" the letter "G" with the arrow shows where to glue the thread.

around the central bead. The two ends of the thread cross in bead A. You thread the large central bead with the inward-pointing thread, which you then string around the two lower-side threads (Illus. 6d) and return through the large bead and through bead A. You fix the threads as shown in the unshaded parts of Illus. 6d. Glue the thread coming from the central bead into bead B by applying some glue to the threads before you insert them into B. This fixes the thread. Glue the outward-pointing thread from Illus. 6c into bead D in the same way. Where to glue is indicated with arrows in Illus. 6e.

You can cut off both threads now, or use one of the threads to add to the medallion, as shown by the shaded parts of Illus. 6d and by Illus. 6e. To finish the medallion, thread one extra bead at the top as shown in Illus. 6e. (Insert the outside thread which goes through bead D, pull it through the top bead and fix it in bead B.) Use this bead to thread the cord or chain.

For medallions of glass beads, you must use a thin but strong thread (for instance, nylon fishing line) and the beads must have large holes, as some beads are threaded up to four

times. The thread must be pulled taut in order to make the medallion lie perfectly flat.

Illus. 6a to 6e refer to medallions with an even number of three-bead constructions around the central bead. Illus. 7 shows you how to do the threading if you surround the central bead by an *odd* number of three-bead constructions. As is clearly shown in Illus. 7b, you pull the thread used for the central bead up around only one lower-side thread and then return it up through the large bead. Next you run the returned thread through an extra top bead (D), fixing it with glue.

Illus. 7b also shows that you run the outward-

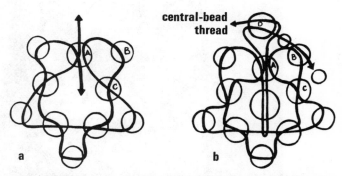

Illus. 7. These are the first two steps for surrounding the central bead with an uneven number of three-bead constructions. The first step uses the same threading as Illus. 6, a–c.

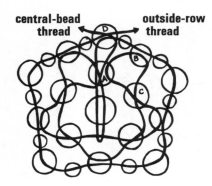

central-bead thread ← → outside-row thread

Illus. 8. The last step for surrounding the central bead with an odd number of three-bead constructions.

pointing thread from Illus. 7a through bead D towards bead B, stringing a small bead between bead D and bead B. Continue threading the outside row of beads, inserting small beads between the big ones, until you have finished, as shown in Illus. 8. Also fix the thread you used for this outside row in bead D, where it crosses the central-bead thread.

Bead Accessories

In some of the following projects, you may want to use metal clasps instead of a beaded loop-and-bar arrangement. There are many kinds of clasps. You can decorate the type pictured here with a medallion. Or, you can attach your medallions to metal discs and thus create a brooch. To a jeweler, these metal accessories are known as "findings," and the most likely source of supply is from companies that manufacture such articles for jewelers.

Illus. 9 shows clasps and discs which are perforated so you can stitch the medallions to the metal. The perforated metal is called a screen or sieve. Screens for brooches (round and rectangular) come provided with a pin and catch and are known as "bar pin plaques." At the top of the photograph is a part for a cuff link. This has a hollow (concave) plate into which you can glue a bead or beadwork. Also, ear clips—flat, hollow, or perforated—are available for making earrings.

In cases where you cannot obtain the finding suggested for the project, you will have to either make your own finding or redesign the project slightly and use a substitute finding. For instance, if you cannot get a perforated clasp, you can wire the back of a perforated disc so it can be joined from the other side of the necklace by a "choker hook." Or you can substitute a "box clasp," and make a necklace without a medallion on the end. See Illus. 14, in the next project.

Crystal Necklace

The necklace shown in Illus. 10 and 13 was threaded with crystal beads. Between the crystals, small, round glass beads were placed. Nylon fishing line was used for the threading, which was done according to the basic technique (see page 14).

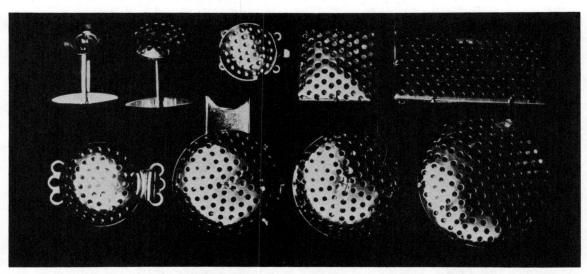

Illus. 9. Metal findings include cuff link holders, clasps, and discs or rectangles to which you can sew or glue your beads.

Illus. 10. This sparkling necklace consists of crystal beads with arches of small round beads.

Notice that you need a metal clasp that has a tongue with eyelets (Illus. 11) and a screen to which you can attach a medallion (Illus. 12). (The tongue fits into the screened part of the clasp for opening and closing.)

First run a thread through two eyelets of the tongue in such a way that the thread-end emerging from the first eyelet and the thread-end emerging from the third eyelet have the same length. String two small beads through each thread-end, run both threads through a crystal bead (A) so they cross and then continue in the basic technique (Illus. 11).

Illus. 11, 12 and 13 show that you thread one small glass bead between each crystal bead. Also, by making use of a separate thread tied to the first eyelet, you add small beads to the top of the necklace. Similarly, a separate thread tied to the bottom eyelet allows you to make little arches of beads at the lower side of the necklace and to attach the medallions (Illus. 13).

The medallions, all of the same size, are made without a central bead. Follow Illus. 13 for threading. Such a medallion is also attached to the screen of the clasp (Illus. 12). But for the clasp medallion, add a small central bead last with the inward-pointing thread, and then glue it into the crystal bead directly opposite.

You must attach the medallion to the screen systematically, with neat stitches that do not pass *through* the beads, but instead pass over the threads of the medallion *between* the beads. In this project, before sewing the medallion on, cover the screen with white leather to hide the metal. (Use glue.)

After you finish threading, attach the thread-ends to the other half of the clasp—the screen, which also has eyelets. Illus. 12 shows the four thread-ends leading to the screen, which is covered by the medallion. Knot the threads after they have been threaded through the eyelets of the screen. Then re-thread the ends (with some glue applied) through a few beads and fix them.

This necklace is threaded in such a way that it

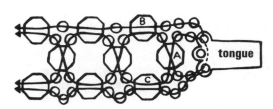

Illus. 11. The dotted line indicates the looped thread behind the tonque of the clasp where the necklace begins.

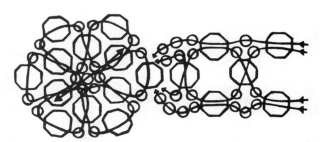

Illus. 12. Four thread-ends of the necklace lead to the screen of the clasp covered by the medallion.

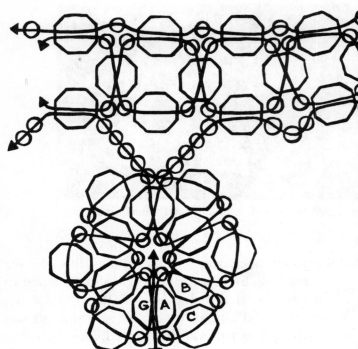

Illus. 13. Thread the crystal necklace in the basic technique with an additional thread on top and one on bottom to add small beads and medallions.

already described. In this case, however, you will have to attach the thread-ends of the finished necklace directly to the perforated disc, which has no eyelets attached. This means that you sew the medallion on to the disc afterwards.

An alternative is to dispense with the medallion-decorated clasp altogether and use a simple "box clasp" (Illus. 14).

Pendant with Glued Beads

If you want to make a piece of jewelry using the glueing method, try the attractive pendant shown here. Trim a piece of wood until it is perfectly round, or have a carpenter do this for you. Mark the wood with a pencil according to the design and colors with which you want to cover the wood. Using your tweezers to pick up the individual beads, place a drop of glue on each bead and then lay it on the wood. Glue the beads in the middle first.

While the glue under the beads is drying, thread a string with beads slightly larger than the others, to fit around the circle. Glue this string of beads to the edge of the wood.

The pendant needs to hang from a cord if you want to wear it around your neck. Decide upon the length of cord you want, and then insert one end of this cord through several of the beads

stands somewhat against the neck, while the medallions lie flat. Of course, you can thread this design with glossy colored beads as well. You can make matching earrings for this necklace by following the medallion design, but using slightly smaller beads. Attach the medallions to ear clips by either sewing them or glueing them on.

As mentioned on page 16, you can make your own sieved clasp if necessary. Fasten wire through perforations of a disc so that the wire forms a vertical bar down the back (Illus. 14). Adjust the tautness of the wire to allow room for a hook to close over it. Begin threading the hook (a "choker hook" with three eyelets) in the same way as you would for the tongue of a screened clasp. Continue with all the steps

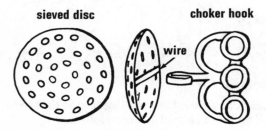

sieved disc   choker hook

box clasp

Illus. 14. Make your own finding with a perforated disc, wired to be joined by a choker hook. Or, substitute a box clasp for a medallion-decorated closure.

Matting Technique

For the matting technique, you again need a long thread (depending on the size of the opening in the beads, a nylon fishing line or a plastic cord). Illus. 16 gives you step-by-step diagrams of how the threads cross each time, how you can widen your work at the end of the row to obtain a kind of "mat," and how you can turn a single row at the corner.

For a hair ornament, fix the beadwork to a rectangular screen, to which a hair clasp is attached.

Illus. 17 pictures some objects—such as table mats, tumbler-holders and frames for a portrait or a mirror—which you can make with the matting technique. The last drawing in Illus. 16 indicates the threading for such a frame. Pay special attention at the corners in order to thread correctly.

Beaded Mats

Here is another way to make beaded mats to add a light, cheerful appearance to your table. Make a set for six or eight to use as individual place mats, or else make just one to use as a centerpiece. Your table will be protected from heat and scratches at the same time that it is enhanced by your beadwork.

Use oval wood beads and strong nylon or plastic cord. Begin your threading as diagrammed in Illus. 6a, making a triangle with three beads. Use both ends of the cord to

Illus. 15. Make a pendant by glueing beads to a wooden circle.

along the outer edge of the pendant. Slip beads of different colors on the ends of the cord. When you have placed as many beads as you want on these cords, tie the ends to a clasp you have purchased. If the beaded cord is long enough to slip over your head without unfastening, you can eliminate the clasp and tie the ends to each other.

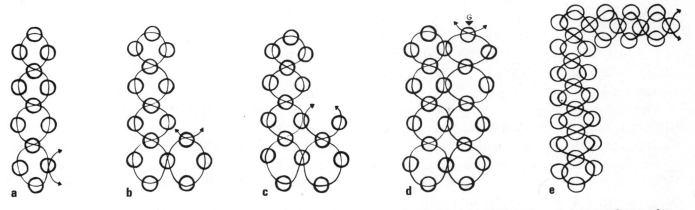

Illus. 16. Matting begins with basic threading, but threads cross in side bead, allowing more beads to be strung. Step e shows how to turn a corner for making frame shapes.

Illus. 17. You can use a mat-like arrangement of beads for picture frames, tumbler-holders and table mats.

thread more beads. When you complete the first hexagon (Illus. 18b), the threads cross in beads 3, 5, 7, 9, 11, and 1. Beads 12, 11, and 10 of the first hexagon form spokes of the second hexagon as well. Beads 19, 10, 9 and 8 become spokes for the third hexagon.

The table mat in Illus. 19 uses beads of different colors: the middle hexagon, made with dark beads, is the first one which you make. The hexagons which surround this first one, the light group in the picture, are made in a circle around this first one. You can make the mat as large as you want simply by adding another round of beads.

The other table mat shown in Illus. 19 uses exactly the same threading procedures as the first one does. It looks a bit fancier because of a simple extra step: before you place an oval bead on the thread, slip a round one on. The result is a mat much lighter in appearance and more ·loosely formed. While it covers the same area as the other mat, fewer hexagons are needed because the round beads expand each small triangle.

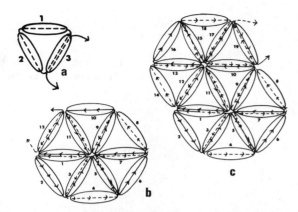

Illus. 18. Diagram for beaded mats. a: the first three beads. b: one completed hexagon. c: two adjacent hexagons.

Embroidery with Beads

It is possible to apply the techniques you have learned to decorate a material (felt, silk, leather) with beads, but you must use small beads for this purpose. You can thread the beadwork separately and then sew it on to the material, or you can embroider the beads directly to the material. The background you embroider on makes it easy to see what you are doing.

Study the illustrations and try to reproduce them. Embroidering on a fabric which is loosely woven or has a regular pattern in it is easier than working on a closely woven material; the threads or lines in the loose fabric act as guides to keep your stitches straight and even. On plain material with no such guides, add light lines with tailor's chalk to help you.

Be sure to use beads which have sufficiently large holes, as sometimes in an intricate pattern the thread passes through the hole several times. The type of bead you use matters also: on tablecloths and other things to be laundered, use only glass, ceramic or plastic beads, never wood ones. The finish on the wood will flake from the heat of the water and detergent. You can use wood beads on other articles, but use thick wool yarn instead of fine silk or cotton thread.

To embroider a design of beads on your material, the following technique is suggested. First draw a circle (with French or tailor's chalk) on the material, making the circle the size you want the finished design to be. Then, by drawing thin lines, divide the circle into eight equal parts. Begin the embroidery in the middle of the circle with a paillette or "sliced" bead and then continue from the middle radially towards the edge. Use the eight lines as a guide to placing eight main beads (the shaded ones in Illus. 20), around which you build your design. As you see in Illus. 20, many variations are possible.

Illus. 19. These two beaded mats are made with the same technique, but the oval beads used in the mat on the right produce a much lighter appearance.

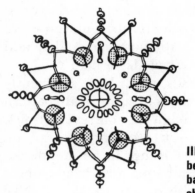

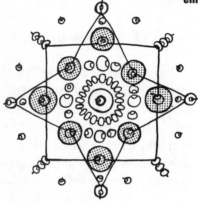

Illus. 20. Eight main beads (shaded) are the basis round which you shape your further embroidery.

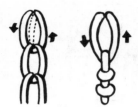

Illus. 21. The Chain stitch on the left, and the Chain with beads on the right.

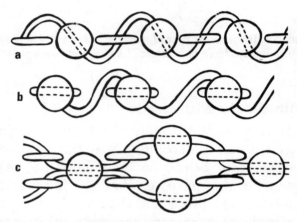

Illus. 22. The Threaded Running stitch (a) and variations.

Some Embroidery Stitches

You can sew separate beads onto the material with any stitch that seems appropriate. However, to secure beads to each other and keep them in the right place, you may find the *Chain stitch* and variations of it (Illus. 21) very helpful.

The *Running stitch* is the most basic stitch, not only in embroidery but in any needlecraft. Bring the needle from the wrong side to the right side of your fabric. Now, take a stitch by inserting the needle in the fabric through to the wrong side and bringing it through to the right side again. Pull the thread through the fabric until it lies flat, and you have made one *Running stitch*. You can vary the *Running stitch* in a number of ways, and add beads to the stitching as you do. The easiest variation is the *Threaded Running stitch*, diagrammed in Illus. 22a. Using a contrasting color for the winding thread, slip the needle—with beads strung on it if you want—under the *Running stitches*. To prevent the beads from sliding around on the thread

after you complete the stitching, make the *Running stitches* close together and use beads which are large enough to fill in the spaces between the running stitches. Or, thread the beads on the *Running stitch* itself (Illus. 22b). The best way to determine which style is best for your threads, beads and fabric is, of course, to make small samples with the materials you plan to use.

Another variation, seen in Illus. 22c, uses two parallel rows of *Running stitches* that are connected by two threads which wind between the rows. Place a bead on the winding thread before you put the needle under each *Running stitch*. Do not make stitches in the fabric with the winding thread; the *Running stitches* hold the thread and beads securely enough, and even small stitches would attach the beads too tightly.

The *Chevron stitch* looks like two parallel rows of *Running stitches* with a third thread winding between the rows. Actually, however, you make this stitch with just one thread. Follow Illus. 23 closely, beginning at A and ending at H. See the illustration for the stringing possibilities and combinations.

The *Y stitch,* so called because it looks like the letter Y, is a stitch you will frequently use. It is very easy to make, and the variations, which depend upon the length of the stem of the Y, are no more complicated than the basic stitch itself.

Follow the diagram in Illus. 24a: starting at A, insert the needle through to the wrong side of the fabric at B, and back to the right side at C. Do not pull stitch A–B tightly; leave it loose enough to form the curved part of the Y. Insert the needle to the wrong side at D, and as you tighten the stitch C–D, pull the loop which extends from A to B so it lies flat on the fabric. Bring the needle up near B at E, and you are ready to make another stitch.

For variety, place a bead on the thread before you make the stem (C–D) of the Y. You can make the stem very long and use two or even three beads, perhaps of different sizes. Or, make the stem very short—just big enough to catch the loop A–B—to make the *Fly stitch.*

When you use the *Y stitch* alone, it makes an attractive border, but you might want to combine it with other stitches to make a more solid and elaborate area.

The *Cross stitch* is one of the most commonly used stitches, because the regularity of the stitches makes it easy to achieve precise, geometric embroidery. To make the basic *Cross stitch,* first work all diagonals in one direction down the row. (See Illus. 25.) Then finish the crosses by turning the work and crossing each diagonal. By stitching all the diagonals in a row at one time, rather than each stitch individually, you are sure to make them evenly. The same half-stitch will be the top stitch on every cross.

To make the *Cross stitch* with beads attached, place a bead on the thread each time you are about to insert the needle through to the wrong side of the fabric while you make the first diagonal stitches. When you return across the row to finish the crosses, insert the needle through the bead again before you put the needle in the fabric.

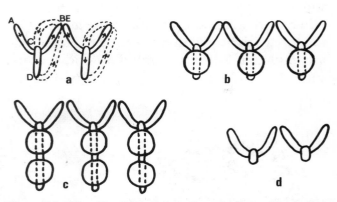

Illus. 24. The Y stitch (a) and variations. The stitch diagrammed in d is called the "Fly stitch."

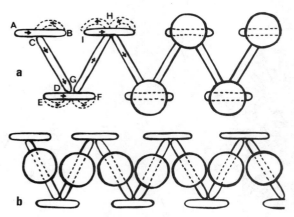

Illus. 23. The Chevron stitch (a) and variations.

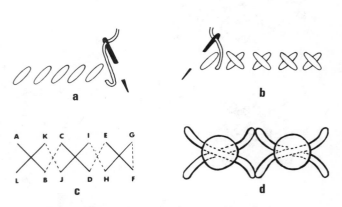

Illus. 25. Steps in making the Cross stitch.

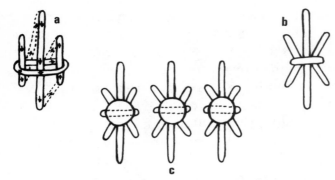

Illus. 26. How to sew the Wheatsheaf stitch.

For all its spectacular effects, the basic *Wheatsheaf stitch* is not hard to do: make three parallel stitches, the middle one longer than the others. Bring the needle up in the center of the longest stitch, but do not split the thread. Then take the needle behind one of the shorter stitches, around and over all three, behind the other short stitch and back into the fabric. Pull the thread tightly so that the stitches on the side are pulled towards the middle. The finished stitch looks like a bundle of wheat tied at the middle. (See Illus. 26.)

A sparkling bead on the horizontal thread changes the whole appearance of this stitch. The pulled side stitches now look like beams radiating from the bead. For extra sheen, use a crystal or glass bead and metallic thread. This stitch makes an elegant edging along a collar or neck, or even along the hem of a garment.

After you have decorated the material, you can use it for covering various articles—a box, for instance—by glueing it on. You should do this carefully and apply very little glue so it will not penetrate the material.

For finishing the edge of a piece of material (for instance the top of the box at the upper right side of Illus. 28), you use a *Buttonhole stitch* with three beads threaded between each stitch (Illus. 29). It is also possible to attach two pieces of material together (the top and the side of the box in Illus. 28). You add a row of *Buttonhole stitches* at the upper edge of the box's side, threading the stitches through the same beads already fixed to the rim (Illus. 30).

Another attractive use for embroidered material is to make a frame around a mirror. First, make a frame of thick cardboard in the

Illus. 27. Here are five interesting ideas for designs.

Illus. 28. You can apply small beads to either felt (top two boxes) or leather (bottom boxes) to create unusual and useful items such as the match-holder shown here.

desired size; then glue on a layer of thin foam rubber. Around this, glue the embroidered material. You can make such a frame for a round as well as for a rectangular mirror.

In all the projects you create with beads, the movement of the color patterns in endless variations on the same theme is not only fascinating to look at, but is also very instructive and inspiring.

At the beginning, aim at playing with beads and color, and by doing so discover some of the joy of the creative artist.

Illus. 29. Use the plain Buttonhole stitch with beads for finishing edges.

Illus. 30. Add another row of the same Buttonhole stitch to sewn beads to join two edges of material.

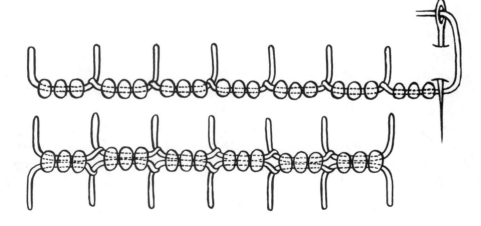

ETCHING WITH CRAYON

Crayon etching is an adaptation of the *sgraffito* process, known since Renaissance times (perhaps before), whereby a surface is scratched or scraped revealing another colored surface below. Each new scratch of the sharp etching tool reveals a line or pattern of bright, warm color. It is the strong contrast—light, warm color beneath an inky blackness—that makes each line so exciting to behold.

Background Paper and Etching Tools

Manila paper works well as a background for crayon etching, but tagboard has the advantage of being smoother and thicker. Also, sharp etching tools will not tear the surface of tagboard quite as easily.

Use an assortment of scratching and scraping tools to get variety in your lines and patterns. Use different tools in a single etching so as to achieve interesting, varied effects. Try working with a section of a hair comb or a silver fork for rhythmic, evenly spaced, flowing lines. Try using the blunt end of a needle, the sharp edge of a narrow-headed screwdriver, a bobby pin, hairpin, a nut pick, the point of a nail file, or a linoleum-block tool for making delicate lines. Search the kitchen and garage for tools. A paring knife or a single-edged razor blade is especially effective in removing large areas of the dark surface.

Preparing the Surface

Creating the base of a crayon etching is simple. There are four surface covers: India ink, crayon, tempera and soft-tip pens. Whatever cover you use, you must first color the entire surface of your background sheet with a layer of crayon, using one or many light, warm colors, juxtaposed. After you paint your cover wash over the crayoned surface and allow it to dry, use a sharp tool, such as a lead pencil point, to etch a design into the dark surface, being careful to reveal but not scratch the crayon color below.

If India ink is your covering medium, occasionally it will be resisted by the crayon so that you have to re-paint a certain area repeatedly before it is properly covered. To speed up the process, pat a blackboard eraser containing chalk dust lightly upon the crayoned surface just prior to adding the India ink. India ink adheres more readily to a non-slick surface.

Experiment with India ink colors other than black, possibly even white, and reverse the usual color scheme of light showing through dark. Use dark colors of crayon on dark paper covered with a light-colored wash of India ink.

Since India ink is a permanent medium, it is difficult to remove from clothing and also a bit expensive. You might substitute black crayon, for example, which will produce a fine

Condensed from the book, "The Complete Crayon Book" by Chester Jay Alkema | © 1969 by Sterling Publishing Co., Inc., New York

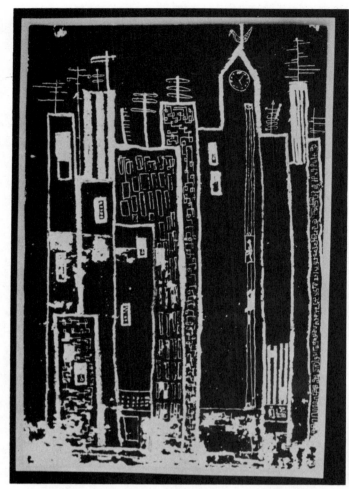

Illus. 1. There are a number of ways to prepare the surface of paper for the etching technique. Here, black tempera over crayon was used to create "The Skyscrapers." Tempera over crayon causes the etched lines to come out ragged.

dark surface and is easy to rub over the lighter crayon colors.

A wash of dark tempera paint may also serve as a substitute for India ink. However, the crayoned surface will resist the tempera paint. To prevent this, powdered tempera of the same color as the liquid wash should first be brushed onto the crayoned surface. Or, use chalk dust once again.

Another remedy for the problem of adherence is soap. First, rub your brush across a wet cake of soap before painting with the liquid tempera. The wash will now spread evenly and effectively.

Liquid or powdered detergent might be added to the liquid tempera to achieve the same results. A raw potato might also come to the rescue. Rub your brush across a sliced potato before painting with it on the crayoned surface.

Using tempera over crayon will cause your etched lines to come out less sharply and distinctly than with India ink, as shown in Illus. 1, although here the somewhat ragged line enhances the etching.

All liquid washes (India ink or tempera) will cause the paper to buckle slightly. This, in turn, causes the wash to run downhill into the recessed areas of the paper. Remove this excess collection of liquid with your brush or else the puddles will crack when dry. It is almost impossible to etch through an extra-thick layer of dry India ink.

Try using a soft-tip pen when covering your waxed crayon surface. You will discover that certain light colors do not cover well, whereas others are truly opaque.

Illus. 2. This artist decided to correlate all her etched lines with the color areas below her covering. The crayon design is carefully made on tagboard with wax crayons. The artist could also have used oil pastels.

ETCHING WITH CRAYON ■ 27

Illus. 3. The artist in Illus. 2 now places tracing paper over the finished crayon design and lightly traces and labels all color shapes in order to remember what is under the black India ink which she has chosen to use for her covering layer.

Illus. 4. Then, the artist pats chalk dust onto the glossy crayon surface so that the India ink will adhere more readily.

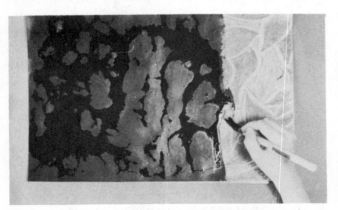

Illus. 5. As you can see, the India ink adheres perfectly because of the dull chalk-dust application.

Correcting Errors

If you feel that you have made an error in etching, it can easily be rectified. India ink, crayon, tempera or the soft-tip pen may be applied a second time to certain areas so as to cover the unwanted etched lines, making possible a second attempt in drawing.

Planned Color-Placement

You might prefer to create an unplanned color design—that is, to etch lines at random, not taking into account which light color shapes lie beneath the dark outer layer. It is possible, however, to directly correlate all etched lines and patterns with certain designated colors. Illus. 2 through 7 show how planned color-placement may be carried out.

Unplanned Color-Placement

The color results in the unplanned color-placement approach are nearly always pleasing when light crayon colors are covered by a dark wash. Colors seldom clash with one another because the dominant black surface subdues the multi-colored surface below.

Illus. 6. The etching begins to appear.

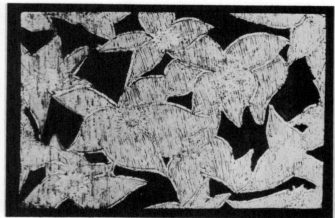

Illus. 7. The finished design. The artist periodically lays the tracing over the design to check which areas are to be left unetched. A second application of India ink can be used to cover any mistakes.

Illus. 8 to 10 show how a fifth-grade student carries out her etching. Pamela leaves the etched patterns surrounded by solid black borders. The pinks and yellows pop up wherever the etched lines allow them to.

As for subject matter for etching, Mother Nature suggests many ideas. Consider trees, flowers and plants, especially leaves and petals, their shapes, their vein patterns, their irregular edges. Consider the bent, curved stems which support blossoms and leaves and cause them to dance about in the breeze. And how interesting the blossom might become when it contains a long, protruding stamen and radiating, patterned petals.

Flying insects are fascinating to depict in a crayon etching. Consider their colorful, patterned wings and long, furry, patterned bodies, protruding antennae, bulging eyes and many crawling legs and feet. Consider the symmetry of an insect's design. Create an imaginary insect design, such as the delicate long-winged butterflies stylistically portrayed in Illus. 11.

Birds, either real or imaginary, provide another fascinating subject for crayon etching.

Illus. 8. Here is the beginning of an unplanned color-placement approach. Shapes in two different colors are juxtaposed for the crayon underlayer.

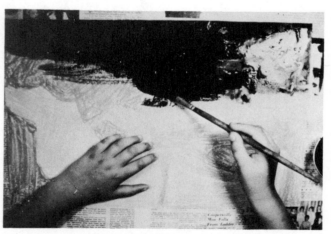

Illus. 9. Now a wash of black India ink is applied to the whole crayoned surface.

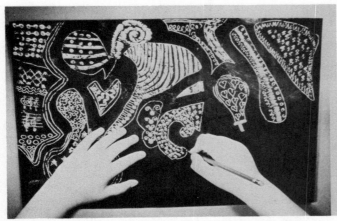

Illus. 10. The sharp point of a pencil scratches into the India ink surface and the colors pop up at random since no attempt is made to correlate the etched lines or shapes with the color shapes underneath.

Illus. 11. Butterflies in flight inspired this abstraction. Notice how the wing shapes in the upper part of the design complement the delicate leaf and flower shapes in the lower part.

Crayon-Etched Containers

Crayon etchings can decorate such useful articles as a vase, wastebasket, scrap box, yarn box or hair-curler box. Select an appropriately sized and shaped cardboard carton, such as a circular oatmeal box, ice-cream carton, or gallon or half-gallon empty milk carton. Cut a large sheet of tagboard to size so that it will completely surround the carton. You may etch the design upon the tagboard while it is around the carton before you put it on.

Illus. 12. This flat design was created to cover quart-sized milk cartons. The design was inspired by the geometric designs found on Indian blankets, jewelry and pottery.

The flat repeat design in Illus. 12, created by a fifth-grade student, was inspired by prints, filmstrips and films displaying American Indian crafts. The Indian designs were geometric and repeated frequently. The finished, flat design here was stapled around an empty milk carton and a coat of clear shellac was added to preserve the etched design.

Crayon-Etched "Stabiles"

You can make "stabiles" such as the two in Illus. 13. The stiff material will stand by itself when creased with vertical folds into a triangular or rectangular shape. It will also stand when rolled into a cylinder. Join the ends of the tagboard with heavy wire or brass paper fasteners.

Crayon-Etched Collages

You can make an interesting collage from your etched designs and patterns. In Illus. B1, for example, various designs were etched on separate sheets of tagboard—one undercolor per sheet—then cut into interesting shapes and glued to a background of black construction paper. The yellow border effectively repeats the yellow colors within the design.

Crayon-Etched Name Designs

Names provide exciting motifs for execution by crayon etching. Decorate the various letters with intricate line designs, and surround the name with patterns, as shown in color Illus. B2.

Simulated Stained-Glass Window Etchings

In using tagboard with the crayon-etching technique to execute a simulated stained-glass window, you will sacrifice the transparent quality of the glass, but you can effectively simulate the design qualities of the window.

The stained-glass window rose in popularity during the 12th century when the Gothic cathedral was at its height. Large architectural openings were filled with brilliantly colored, luminous, transparent glass designs. The earliest windows made use of few colors—blue, yellow, and red. Later, more colors were invented and used, and this started the decline of stained-glass windows. A window design is most pleasing when a few colors are frequently repeated within the composition. A small range of color causes the design to achieve a unity of its parts, while the repetition allows the artist to balance his colors.

Illus. 13. Crayon-etched "stabiles."

Illus. 14 and Illus. 15. You can simulate stained-glass windows with the etching technique. In Illus. 14 (left) the crayoned color areas are placed so that the natural white paper provides a plain border between each shape. Illus. 15 (right) shows the design after the India ink has been applied and the etching completed.

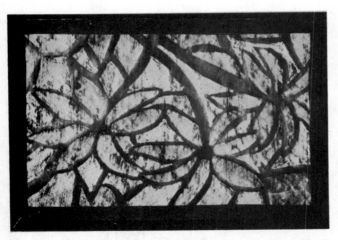

Illus. 16. To make sure his color borders remained black after etching, this artist used a black crayon between the bright colored shapes just prior to applying the India ink. Additional black was added after the etching process.

Illus. 17. After this Madonna was etched on thin white paper, it was coated on the back with linseed oil to make a more transparent etching for a stained-glass window.

The earliest window designs were rather crude in concept. The French artist of the 12th century planned his cathedral window by drawing thin black lines to indicate the iron and lead tracings which held the transparent shapes of glass in place, against wind and storms. The lead and iron tracings usually cut through the faces, hands and legs of figures in a disconcerting way. Through experience, the artist learned to manipulate his framework so that the glass shapes were not sacrificed.

Stained glass has its limitations. It does not allow the artist to achieve the illusion of depth. Photographic likenesses of people, for example, cannot be achieved.

You can use two approaches in simulating stained-glass design. In Illus. 14, the artist applied blue, green and yellow crayons to his tagboard, carefully retaining a border of uncolored paper between each colored shape. When the over-coat of black India ink was dry, he used a sharp pencil point to etch lines across the inked surface, distinctly revealing the solid shapes of colored crayon (Illus. 15). The now-black borders vividly define each color shape.

Using the second approach, in Illus. 16 the artist colored black borders between each light-colored area with a black crayon. India ink was applied over all and partly etched away when dry. The black-crayoned borders remain quite vivid in spite of the etching process. He re-crayoned in black where too much black was etched away by accident.

Colorful stained-glass windows often remind us of the Christmas season. In Illus. 17, the Madonna is surrounded by blue, aqua and purple shades of color. This design was made upon thin white paper and painted (upon the rear side) with a coat of linseed oil, which caused the paper to become more transparent. When placed against a windowpane, the colors of the etched lines became quite intense.

Illus. 18. Four squares were colored on a chalked sheet with different colored crayons (left). When a line design was drawn on the opposite side of an overlaid sheet of paper, a transfer design (right) was obtained.

Crayon-on-Chalk Transfer Etchings

You can make a beautiful negative-positive etching with the use of chalk and crayon, and you can create two designs in one operation.

To begin, take two sheets of manila or white drawing paper identical in size. Cover one of the sheets with a heavy coat of yellow chalk. Next, heavily apply a layer of dark crayon so that the chalk is completely covered. Next, lay your clean sheet over the crayoned sheet. Using a sharp pencil, draw a design upon the uncolored sheet. Press hard and work on a hard-surfaced desk or table so that the transfer etching will be distinct. Create line patterns only, but do not be afraid to shade objects with parallel line patterns or cross-hatch designs.

When you remove the top sheet, you will discover that the pencil drawing has caused the crayon wax to leave the chalk backing, and that delicate crayon lines have been lifted and transferred to the underside of your top sheet (Illus. 19). Mount both parts of your positive-negative design side by side since they have the same colors (but in reverse). (See also Illus. 18.)

Illus. 20 and 21 demonstrate how a complicated folding technique can be used to create a transfer etching upon a single sheet of paper, not upon separate sheets of paper. Vertical, horizontal and diagonal creases were first folded into the paper. Then chalk covered by crayon was applied to alternate triangles

Illus. 19. Here, the bottom sheet has been covered smoothly with a layer of yellow chalk and then a layer of dark crayon. When a clean sheet of paper is placed over this and a pencil sketch is made by pressing hard, two things result. The underside of the top sheet picks up a transfer, and a design in reverse colors is left on the under sheet.

ETCHING WITH CRAYON ■ **33**

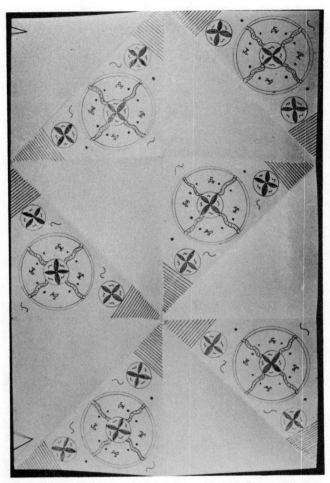

Illus. 20. You can use a complicated folding technique to create a transfer etching, using a single sheet of paper.

Illus. 21. This is the resulting transfer design.

(Illus. 20, left). Using the central, vertical fold as his dividing line, the artist made sure that his crayoned triangles on the left would face an uncrayoned shape on the right, when the paper was again folded in half, along the central vertical crease. A line design was pressed upon the reverse side of the vertically folded sheet now but applied only over those triangles which were covered with chalk and crayon. You can see the results in Illus. 21.

Painted Line Etchings

To paint a line etching, start by covering a smooth sheet of paper completely with a layer of wax crayon or oil pastel. One color or a combination of colors may be used. With a sharp tool, such as the point of a nail file,

scratch a line design through the crayon layer. Press the tool hard enough to remove the crayon film, but not so hard as to tear the paper. Next, paint a wash of black (or other dark color) tempera over the scratched design. The tempera will adhere only to those areas where lines have been scratched through, and will leave a deposit of small bubbles where the wax remains.

While it is usual to paint the black tempera over the entire crayoned area, the tempera in Illus. 23 was painted over the etched lines only, keeping the background as clean as possible.

Embossed Line Etchings

Place your sheet of paper upon a cushion of papers, such as a thin pad of newspaper or a few sheets of manila paper. You are going to imprint an uncolored, embossed line upon your paper, not a pencil line or a crayon line. A nut pick will do nicely as a tool, but any pointed instrument that is sharp enough to press a deep line without leaving a dark line or tearing the paper will do. After completing the embossed line design, rub a dark crayon over the entire surface of the design, *across* your embossed lines and not *with* the lines. Do not press heavily, or the embossed lines will get filled with color. When finished, you will see that the natural color of the paper is retained where the embossed lines have been placed. All other areas will be colored with crayon.

If the strokes of the crayon are too weak to show up the embossed lines distinctly, re-crayon some of the shapes. You will then have a background consisting of two shades of color—a light dark and a darker dark.

Illus. 22. To make an embossed line etching, use a sharp tool to press the design upon a sheet of paper which should be resting on a thick pad of paper. Then, as shown here, rub a dark crayon across the paper's surface to bring out the embossed lines.

Combining Collage and Embossing

Pleased with the tulip design in Illus. 24, the artist decided to make a second similar design which would combine the embossed etching

Illus. 23. In this floral design, black was painted over an etched line design, and care taken not to paint the unlined crayoned areas.

Illus. 24. Green construction paper and white crayon were used to create this embossed line etching. White crayon was rubbed heavily along the side of some of the embossed lines to emphasize them.

Illus. 25. All negative shapes were cut away and the positive forms glued to a contrasting sheet of black construction paper in this combination of collage and embossed line etching.

technique with the collage technique. The embossed line was again pressed onto green construction paper and white crayon was rubbed over the lines. But in Illus. 25 all negative areas of the design were cut away so that the positive shapes might be glued to a contrasting sheet of black construction paper. The etched lines are very much in evidence when viewing the tulip blossoms.

Illus. 26. Two contrasting colored layers of melted wax crayon were painted on tagboard to create this etching. A pencil point was used to etch the design, revealing the darker color below.

Melted Crayon Etchings

Illus. 26 demonstrates what sharp, distinct lines may be achieved when etching with melted wax crayon. Select two contrasting colors of wax crayon and melt each color separately.

Although you can melt crayons over the flame of a burning candle, there is a much safer method. Place peeled crayons in a muffin tin, one color to a compartment. Then either place the muffin tin in a slightly larger tin filled with hot water or put it on top of a large can that has a 100-watt light bulb inside. Either one will keep the crayons in a molten state for quite some time, although you will probably have to replace the hot water from time to time. If you wish, you can place the water-filled tin over a very low flame on the stove, but this is inconvenient.

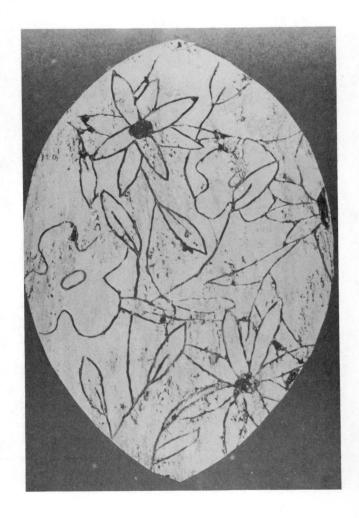

Using a stiff bristle brush, paint one color of melted crayon over tagboard, manila paper, white drawing paper or cardboard, completely covering its surface. When the first layer of wax has hardened, paint on the second color. Next, using a sharp instrument, etch a line design through the top layer so the contrasting color below becomes visible.

Combining Crayon Resist and Etching

In a crayon etching, you use black India ink and bright crayon colors. And when creating a crayon-resist drawing, the desired result is bright color against a dark background. So it would only seem logical that both techniques might be combined within a single composition. And indeed they can, as shown in Illus. 27.

The central rectangular shape in Illus. 27, a tulip design, including decorative leaves and a dotted design surrounding the flower, has been executed by means of the crayon-resist technique. Black tempera was painted over the crayon line design. The colorful border which surrounds the inner rectangle was executed by means of the crayon-etching technique. A solid border of two colors—red and blue—was crayoned on the paper and covered with India ink. Then a ruler and sharp etching tool were used to etch the crossed-line design, revealing the red and blue crayon colors beneath the black ink. The two crayon techniques were beautifully combined to create a single composition.

Preserving Your Crayon Etchings

Finished crayon-etched designs are quite vulnerable to damage. An accidental scratch in the wrong place can easily mar the finished design. To preserve the etching, cover the completed work with a coat of white shellac or light varnish.

Illus. 27. Both the crayon-resist and the crayon-etching techniques were used to execute this design. The etching technique was used to create the colorful border and the resist technique for the central tulip design.

Illus. 28. It is not necessary to have a multi-color underlayer. One single color—white—was placed beneath the India ink covering here.

BATIK

Batik is a dyeing process in which you impregnate cloth fibres with ink. The different areas in batik designs usually fuse together softly, but it is quite possible to make a batik design with sharp outlines which make the design look as if it were printed.

To do batik, you decoratively apply hot wax with a brush or a cup with a spout (called a *tjanting*, purchasable in a craft shop) to thin, light-colored cloth. After the wax layer has hardened, you dampen the entire cloth and then put it into a vat of warm dye. Only the parts not covered by wax absorb the dye. After you rinse the material clean and dry it, you either remove the wax or leave it on and then cover additional areas with wax. Next, you immerse the material in a second dye bath. You can repeat this procedure several times, depending on your desired design.

During the dyeing, the cooled layers of wax usually break and crack in various ways. You can encourage these cracks to appear by crushing the waxed cloth. At these cracks and fractures, the dye penetrates into the cloth, making the "crackle" designs that are typical of batik. This characteristic of the wax guarantees the spontaneous character by which you should be able to recognize batik. It is rarely possible to know in advance what the final batik pattern will be like. The cracks in the wax, the fusion of the different dyes, and the varying depths of color produce a unique, novel charm in each work.

Batik requires quick judgment. The more unhesitatingly and surely you apply the patterns with the wax brush, the more unusual and striking will be their effect.

Large batiked areas seldom give monotonous effects, thanks to the varied crackle designs and the gradations of color.

Not all textiles, however, are equally suitable for batik. The experienced artist in this technique usually restricts himself to pongee and foulard silk, and he may also use a thin, wax-permeable cotton fabric. Heavy linens and cottons are out of the question for batik work. In addition, in batik, the size of the fabric is limited. The piece of material must not be too large to be immersed easily in the dye bath, which must have a fairly low temperature, below the melting point of the wax, which itself is low. You should, therefore, only gently wash batik-treated materials and you should never boil them. Generally, clean batiked silk in dry-cleaning fluid.

The Batik Process

You need the following materials: a spirit lamp (one which burns alcohol), electric hot plate or, if nothing else is available, a thick candle; a metal can in which you can heat the wax, either paraffin or beeswax; a variety of inexpensive brushes with synthetic bristles (animal hair bristles may burn in the hot wax); a tjanting; straight pins; dyes; a large plastic, glass or enamel bowl; tongs or rubber gloves;

Condensed from the book, "Screen Printing" by Heinrich Birkner | © 1971 by Sterling Publishing Co., Inc., New York

Illus. 1. Here are some of the basic materials necessary for batik, listed clockwise: paraffin, beeswax, dry-cleaning solvent, an electric hot plate on which stands a metal can in a pot, dyes, and paint brushes.

an electric iron and ironing board; plain newsprint; waxed paper, and dry-cleaning solvent.

Lay several layers of newsprint on your work table and cover the newsprint with a sheet of waxed paper. Then place the cloth on top of the waxed paper and pin it in place along the sides. The newsprint insulates the work surface and keeps the wax from cooling too quickly, while the waxed paper keeps the batik from sticking to the newsprint when the cloth is waxed. The cloth instead sticks to the waxed paper, which you can later easily peel from the fabric.

Cut the paraffin in small pieces and melt them in the metal can over the hot plate or candle until they are completely liquid. You can also melt them by placing the can in a bath of boiling water, so the aroma of the melting wax is not too pungent. If you use an electric hot plate, place an asbestos sheet under the can to prevent the wax from spurting out onto the heating element, which it might do if there is too much heat. The smell of burning wax is most unpleasant. Adding a little beeswax to the paraffin makes it more elastic and easy to work with, but this is not absolutely necessary.

With a paint brush or your tjanting, deposit hot wax on the cloth in various abstract designs, swirl patterns, or representational

Illus. 2. When you paint wax on the cloth, you might want to raise the cloth from the table with wood laths. The wax can then penetrate the cloth more thoroughly.

Illus. 3. When using a commercial tjanting, place the unmelted wax in the reservoir. As you heat the wax, it will run out the spout. Guide it above the cloth to create finely designed patterns.

designs. But, be careful: painting with wax is very tricky, and your lines will probably not be perfectly even. The imperfections which almost always result appear more attractive when they are part of an abstract pattern than if they are supposed to represent something accurately.

After you have waxed the design, let the wax cool and harden. Turn the fabric over (the waxed paper is attached to it, since the wax you applied to the fabric penetrated and bound the waxed paper) and peel the waxed paper off. Do not peel the *fabric* from the *paper*, as the waxed areas crack when you bend them. Examine the wrong side of the fabric closely to make sure that the wax has penetrated the cloth. If areas need touching up, dab some wax on them.

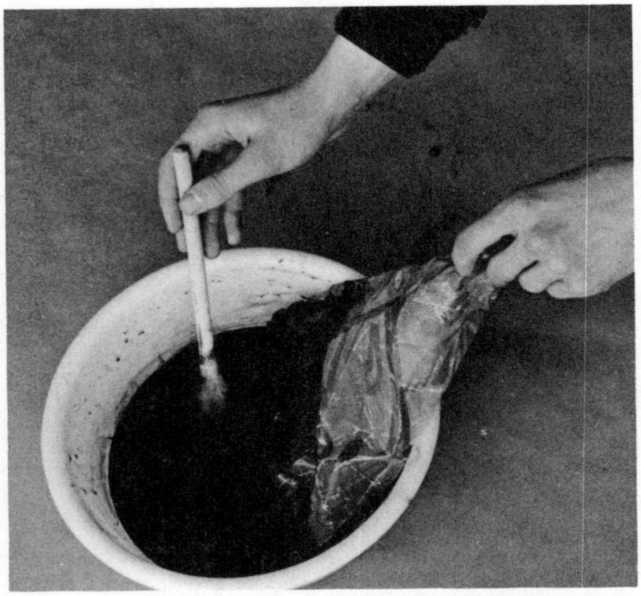

The cloth is now ready for its first dye bath. Almost any dye meant for fabric is suitable; there are several brands which need very little preparation. Prepare the dye according to the directions on the package and, if you prepare it with hot water, allow it to cool until it is lukewarm. (A dye bath which is too hot melts the wax on the cloth.) Unless the dye package advises you differently, add one tablespoon of un-iodized salt for each gallon of liquid dye, or one teaspoon per quart, to help the dye adhere to the fabric.

Wet the cloth before you immerse it in the dye bath. When the cloth is in the dye bath, it looks much darker than it will when it dries. Leave the cloth in the bath for the amount of time that the package directs and then remove it with a pair of tongs or rubber gloves. (Some dyes contain chemicals which may be harsh on your hands.) Do not squeeze or wring the cloth, or the wax will crack. Hang the cloth to dry,

Illus. 4. Since the bowl containing the dyeing liquid is probably not too big, the cloth you dye cannot be too large either. Use a stick or wooden spoon to stir the cloth gently.

but save the dye until you see the finished color. You may want to re-wet and re-dye the fabric to obtain a darker color.

When the cloth is dry, it is ready for the second waxing. In this waxing, which is followed by a second dye bath, cover some of the areas you just dyed, to keep them the color of the first dye bath. Give the cloth a second dye bath in another color exactly as you gave it the first dye bath, remembering that the dye must be lukewarm and that the cloth looks much darker when it is wet. There are no exact instructions for the second waxing, but generally it is best not to introduce new patterns with the wax drawings. Rather, fill in the empty spaces generously and imaginatively with shapes similar to those already batiked. A pointed brush or tjanting is particularly useful for making the designed "handwriting" free and unrestrained. These free lines suit the essential character of the batiked design very well. Make the second dye bath darker and stronger than the first, and the dyeing time longer. Rinse the cloth in lukewarm water until the water runs clear.

After the second dyeing, there are three

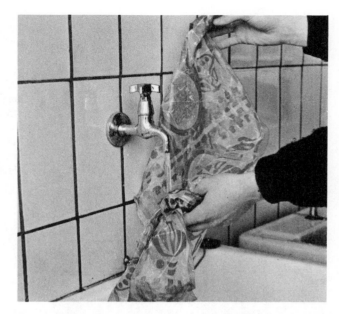

Illus. 5. When the cloth has been in the dye bath long enough (remember that the color looks darker when wet), remove it and rinse it with lukewarm water. Keep rinsing until the water runs clear, but do not squeeze or wring the cloth.

shades on your cloth: the original color of the cloth, preserved on the sections you covered with wax before the first dye bath; the color of the first dye bath, in the areas you covered during the second waxing; and the shade which

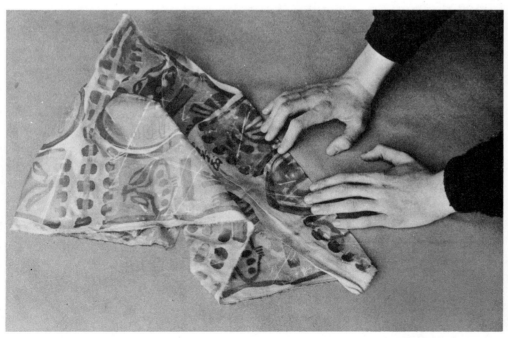

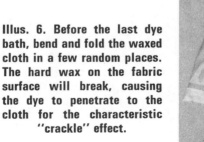

Illus. 6. Before the last dye bath, bend and fold the waxed cloth in a few random places. The hard wax on the fabric surface will break, causing the dye to penetrate to the cloth for the characteristic "crackle" effect.

Illus. 7. To remove the wax from the cloth, place newsprint over the fabric and iron both thicknesses. Remove the newsprint when it becomes saturated and replace it with a new layer. Iron until no more wax goes into the newsprint. Then use dry-cleaning solvent for the remaining wax.

results as a combination of the two dye baths, on those areas which you left completely unwaxed. You can continue to wax and re-dye as many times as you wish, but take into consideration the harmony of colors and amount of detail you want on the cloth.

Removing the Wax

Allow the cloth to dry completely before you remove the wax. Removing the wax while the dye is still wet causes the dye to bleed (that is, run) into the undyed areas, creating blurry lines and indistinct areas of color.

Place many layers of newsprint on your ironing board, cover with the batiked cloth, and then cover the cloth with more newsprint. Set the electric iron at one setting *lower* than that appropriate for the fabric, and iron through all layers with even pressure. The wax melts from the heat of the iron and is absorbed by the newsprint. Remove the layer of newsprint both immediately above and below the cloth every few minutes so that there is a new surface to absorb the wax.

When the newsprint no longer absorbs any wax from the cloth, stop ironing. There is still a dark area around the places where the wax was, since the iron cannot remove all of the wax. To remove these dark spots, you must clean the batik in solvent or dry-cleaning fluid (follow the directions on the package carefully and work in a well-ventilated room), or take the cloth to a dry cleaner.

To avoid the necessity of working with solvent, you might coat the entire cloth with wax, if the area is not too large. When you remove the wax by ironing, the whole piece of fabric is darker, due to the slight amount of wax left clinging to the fibres. There is no difference among the separate areas, though, and thus no reason to remove all the wax completely with solvent.

When the batik is free of all wax, or is uniformly covered with the least amount possible, lay a cloth soaked in white vinegar over the batik and iron it, to set the dye and smooth out any wrinkles. Your batiked cloth is now ready to be mounted, sewn, or made into wall hangings, pillow covers, draperies, room dividers or any other item you can think of.

FELT CRAFTING

The Material

Felt is a soft-textured, colorful material which you will find endless delight in using. Because felt is not woven but is a collection of woollen fibres, it has several advantages over other materials:

1. You can cut it up easily without worrying about the direction of a weave.

2. There is no risk of unravelling.

3. The smooth surface has an especially soft and attractive appearance.

4. You can glue and sew pieces without bordering or hemming them.

5. You need only a strong needle and heavy cotton thread for all stitching.

6. Because it is so flexible, you can manipulate and stuff it easily.

In addition, felt comes in a multitude of different shades.

Begin with a Design

In order to avoid possible loss of material through cutting mistakes, you should first make designs of your project on paper. To reproduce the design the same size as the pattern, place a sheet of transparent paper on top of it, and trace carefully. Unless your design is extremely simple, it is often better to cut out the different parts separately, such as head, feet, wings, and so on, rather than cutting out a whole outline.

If you want your design in a larger or smaller size, use the grid method described on page 10.

Glueing

You can attach cut-up parts to a background with any glue which is recommended for textiles, that is, if the felt does not have its own adhesive backing. Be sure not to put on too much glue since felt sticks very easily, and there is danger of staining if the glue soaks through.

The background you use depends on your purpose and the kind of figure or scene involved. It could be felt of another color, cloth, cardboard, canvas, burlap, or any material you find suitable. It is, however, wise to test the different effects of the glue on these surfaces before you begin a project.

Animals

Once children learn to handle scissors and have succeeded in their first paper cut-outs, they can begin to cut up felt, and they will delight in creating and glueing many interesting, colorful little figures. They will be able to trace patterns, enlarge them, or make them smaller.

Most of the simple animals you will want to make can also be stuffed. The stuffing can be wadding, old rags, or kapok. When making animal patterns, try to achieve shapes and postures that are typical. Sometimes you will be able to cut them out of a single piece as, for example, the bunny rabbit which is shown in Illus. 1 and 2. Sketch the bunny's outline on paper and make him smaller or larger, if you want, by using the grid method.

Condensed from the books, "Felt Crafting" by Jacqueline Janvier | © 1970 by Sterling Publishing Co., Inc., New York, and "Scissorscraft" by Lini Grol | © 1970 by Sterling Publishing Co., Inc., New York. Felt Mosaic section written especially for this volume by Louisa Hellegers from material provided by Phyllis Rosenteur. Felt Mosaic photographs taken especially for this volume by Kal Weyner

Use small scissors to add detail to the bunny's body. Start by making the cuts alongside the bunny's ears. Once you have made this cut, shape the head and neck with your fine scissors. Cut into the body to cut out the inner ears. Lift the felt and pinch it together in the spot where you want to begin your cut. Now cut into the face to make the eyes and nose. In Illus. 2, notice that the fur has been detailed on one side of his body. Naturally, you would use very fine scissors to make these tiny cuts. From the inner ear, make the lines between his eyes to give a cute expression to the bunny's face. When you have added details to your satisfaction, glue this happy hopper onto a different colored piece of felt and hang him in a prominent place.

Illus. 1.

Illus. 2.

Illus. 1 and 2. This bunny rabbit is very cute the way he appears in Illus. 1, but you can add details to make him even more appealing, as in Illus. 2.

Illus. 3. This tree with its heavy trunk of brown felt and many green leaves of different sizes suggests great age and grandeur.

Trees and Flowers

Trees

With felt you can create many fluid, imaginative designs of trees and flowers, in a variety of colors. You can make the tree in Illus. 3 simply by using it as a pattern and making the trunk from a piece of brown felt and the leaves from a green one. Or, make the tree of your dreams!

After designing the outline of the tree you choose, cut out the trunk first, and the branches and leaves separately. Then shuffle these pieces round until you create the effect you like best and glue the parts onto a background.

Flowers

Here is an ideal way to use left-over felt. You can use colors and shapes freely and imaginatively in making felt flowers. Although you may borrow the basic design from nature, these are fantasy flowers, and you do not have to limit yourself to colors existing in nature.

Like all the other figures you have made, you simply cut and glue, and you can use them to decorate almost anything—ladies' blouses, suit lapels, belts, dresses, aprons, handbags, or sweaters.

You can make many different variations of flowers in felt. You might combine the felt with woollen threads, or cut out a simple outline in felt and place a little pearl in the middle. When assembling several flowers into a bouquet, remember to keep a light touch since felt does not have the fragile quality of real flowers.

Cone-Shaped Dolls

This method of making dolls is one of the easiest. For these little figures, a felt cone forms the body on which you place a felt head.

An Angel

Using the pattern "A" in Illus. 6, cut out a half circle about 5″ in diameter from a piece of sky-blue felt. Fold it in half and, starting from the fold, mark a point about $\frac{1}{4}$″ on each side. Cut a small half circle between these two points as shown at "a."

Illus. 4. You can quickly cut out and assemble these red, blue, yellow and green flowers.

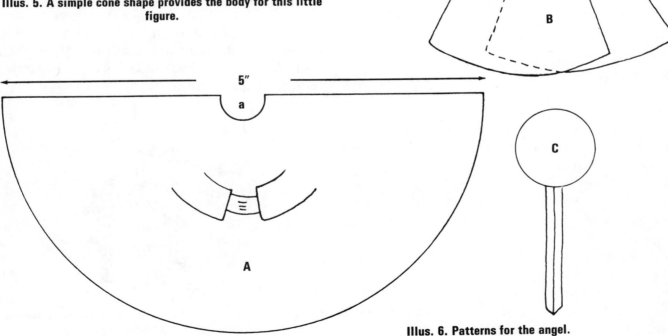

Make slits in the felt for the sleeves as shown in Illus. 6 "A." Cut out little pink felt hands and glue them into the sleeve openings.

Cut out yellow wings from a felt rectangle about $1\frac{1}{2}'' \times \frac{3}{4}''$ and trim the edges as shown in pattern "B." Now form the body into the shape of a cone by joining and overlapping the two ends as shown in pattern "B," and glue them together. Then sew on the wings.

Make the head of the angel from a piece of pink felt about $\frac{3}{4}''$ in diameter. Glue it onto a cardboard rectangle $1\frac{1}{2}''$ long and $\frac{1}{4}''$ wide. Set it into the cone through the small opening remaining on top.

Now create an angelic face with two red felt eyes and a black felt mouth. Glue several yellow felt bands of hair round the head. You might adorn the dress with little scallops round the bottom of the cone.

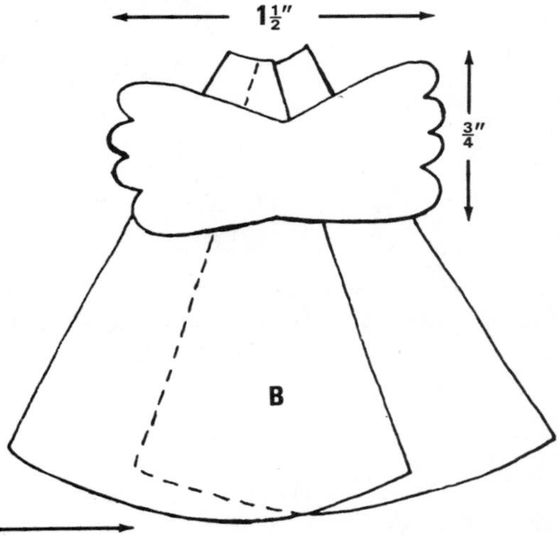

Illus. 5. A simple cone shape provides the body for this little figure.

Illus. 6. Patterns for the angel.

Human Figures

How about trying your hand at cutting human figures to create one-dimensional dolls. The little man in Illus. 7 is shaped like the paper dolls you cut out in school. Cut several figures and decorate each one differently for an entire doll family.

To cut the man in Illus. 7, sketch the figure on paper, using the grid method to make it larger or smaller, and trace it onto a piece of felt. You can dress him in fancy collar and cuffs as shown in Illus. 7a by the method known as *hollow cutting*. Begin by making a hole in the middle of his chest and then cut outwards. Be careful near the edges that you do not cut through them.

You can also add details by cutting in from the outside edge, if you find this technique easier. Now this little man has trousers and buttons on his shirt. The slash on his face was made wide purposely to show you how his facial features were cut from the edge rather than by hollow cutting (Illus. 7b).

The figure has been cut out of one color. If you wish you can cut different colored pieces of felt to make the clothes and glue them on top. If you want to use the hollow cutting technique, you can glue pieces of felt under the cut-out sections to add color and texture.

For some of your felt family, you might want to glue on real buttons instead of cutting them out or you might want to decorate your dolls with bits of lace or ribbon trim. Some of the dolls might enjoy being decorated with beads or sequins. After you have finished dressing them up, glue them to stiff pieces of cardboard so they will be easier to handle.

Illus. 7a.

Illus. 7b.

Felt Mosaic

The special properties of felt, listed on page 43, lend themselves particularly well to this unusual craft. The objects shown in color on page D are just a few of the types of projects you can have fun making with felt mosaics.

Christmas Tree Ornaments

To make Christmas tree balls like the one shown in Illus. 8, you need plastic foam balls of any size. Begin by cutting a small piece of any color felt in any shape you choose. Glue it onto the ball with a dab of a white glue such as Elmer's or Sobo. Next, cut very thin strips of black felt just the length of the sides of the colored felt patch. The nature of felt is such that you do not have to glue these thin strips to the larger piece; if you simply butt them up against the larger piece, they will stay in place. (Hint: An easier way to glue the felt to the ball is to put the glue directly onto the ball rather than onto the small felt pieces.)

Continue in this manner, cutting and glueing oddly shaped pieces of felt and then outlining strips, until you have completely covered the ball. Then, cut a small piece of pipe cleaner, insert one end into the ball between two pieces

Illus. 8. A Christmas tree ornament such as this one is simple and fun to make.

of felt, add a Christmas ball hook, and your first felt mosaic is ready to hang!

For a special friend or relative, try personalizing a ball to give as a gift. Cut felt pieces to spell out the name (even the name can be in mosaics, if you wish) and then fill in the background with a colorful pattern.

Box Covers

Box tops—cardboard, wooden, tin or even glass—are wonderful surfaces on which to felt-mosaic. The cover in Illus. 9 is simply the top of an old, worn tin box, decorated in the

Illus. 9. Old, worn tin box tops are wonderful surfaces to revive with a felt mosaic.

Illus. 10. A geometric pattern is an effective felt design.

same way as the Christmas tree balls. You may plot out a design first (notice the star-like motifs in Illus. 9) or make one up as you work. The special feature of creating this type of top is that you may build the pattern as you have time. You can leave your work at any point and then pick it up when and if you are inspired to add more patches.

Again, you can usually butt thin slivers of felt in between others where glueing would be sloppy because of the small size of the felt pieces.

The box in Illus. 10 was decorated in a slightly different manner. To make a more geometric abstract, decide upon colors and shapes before you cut the felt. Then, plot your pattern on the box top and glue the felt in place.

These are just a few of the many different projects you can easily decorate with felt mosaics. Because you can glue felt to any surface, the creative possibilities are infinite. Use your imagination. Try such items as headbands, pencil holders (mosaic round any cylindrical container), book-marks, eyeglass cases, mirror frames, and wall hangings. You will undoubtedly be proud of the handsome, colorful ornaments you can so easily produce.

LEATHERCRAFTING

Leathers and skins are "in" today and you can use them for many different creative items. Making a project in leather or skin enables you to make it entirely according to your own needs and taste in size, color and quality. Besides, it is worthwhile economically. For the price of an inexpensive, ready-made item in plastic, you can often make a similar one in skin or leather, adding, because it is hand-made, an aesthetic value.

If you have no previous experience or knowledge in the use of these materials and techniques, start out with something simple. Choose an item which you can sew from less expensive skins and then follow closely the technical instructions. If you are already more advanced in leathercrafting, this article should also serve as a starter. You do not have to work only with the measurements and ideas given here; experiment on your own.

Materials

Buy your skins and leathers in a leather or hobby shop. Skins and leathers are sold by the square foot. The measurement includes all irregular shapes, such as the legs and neck of the animal hide. It is important that you buy the right kind of leather, of the correct thickness and pliability, for the article you intend to make.

Use *cow-hide* for soles, cases, bags, belts and similar heavy-duty articles. The middle of the hide, or back of the animal, is the thickest and most attractive part of the skin. The sides are somewhat less uniform in thickness. Cow-hide is either smooth or grained, the grained parts being somewhat more hardy. Cow-hide also comes in various thick and thin *splits* (under-sections of a piece of leather that have literally been split). The lowest layer of split leather, the layer nearest the flesh, is called *cow-hide split*. It is sold with an artificial grain and is inexpensive, but it tears easily. You can also get a suede quality which is inexpensive and good, especially for rustic pieces of clothing.

Calfskin is a close-grained and a very durable leather. It comes in several thicknesses and is well suited for handbags, cases, chair seats, and so on.

Pigskin has a very distinctive grain with wrinkles and holes from the pig's bristles. It is often imitated, but you can easily determine the authenticity of a piece: if the small holes go all the way through the leather, you know it is real. Pigskin is a rather expensive material, but it is strong and pliable.

Sheepskin is an extremely versatile, soft and supple leather to work with. It is available with or without hair, in a natural finish or dyed a different color. Rub lighter shades of sheepskin with talcum powder, which, to some degree, helps protect the delicate surface. Use it for handbags, jackets, carrying cases, and the like.

Goatskin has a delicate surface, but is nevertheless durable. It is very suitable for purses, handbags, gloves, and so on. It, too, is available in natural finishes as well as in many different colors.

Condensed from the book, "Leathercrafting" by Grete Petersen | © 1973 by Sterling Publishing Co., Inc., New York

Nappa leather is a general term for calfskin, sheepskin and goatskin after they have been through the process of tanning, which leaves the skins very soft.

Suede is the flesh side of calfskin, sheepskin and goatskin, and is used for shoes (calfskin) and clothing. It should be soft, even and pliable to touch.

Snakeskin, lizard and *fishskin* have great possibilities for leathercrafting. Snakeskin is available in whole skins or in pieces.

Lining leather or *lining split* is available in several thicknesses and in many colors. It is made mostly from sheepskin.

Leather remnants are excellent for haberdashery, leather mosaics, book-marks and especially for practice work.

Leather lacing is quite expensive, but you can cut laces yourself for far less. Goat splits are perfect for this.

There are many kinds of thread. Choose thread to suit the job at hand. Determine the correct gauge or thickness of thread by considering both its appearance and strength.

Saddler's thread is good for heavy-duty articles such as briefcases, other carrying cases and sandals.

Bookbinder's thread is available in all thicknesses, and is strong and easy to sew with.

Linen thread is decorative and strong.

Carpet yarn is available in several colors and gauges and is strong.

Nylon thread is excellent to use because of its strength.

Buttonhole silk, which you can use for gloves and tote bags, stronger kinds of *machine silk,* linen and nylon threads are well suited for machine sewing. You can sew with quite heavy thread on most machines if you adjust the shuttle and use an appropriate heavy-duty needle. Remember, too, that most sewing machines have a margin attachment, which makes edge-stitching much easier.

Choosing the right kind of needle is essential for you to attain the desired result.

One type of needle is the *saddler's needle,* either straight or curved. This type includes the three-edged or triangular needle *(glover's needle),* available in several sizes, for both hand and machine sewing.

You may also use the *harness needle* which is blunt, though in some cases the eye might be too weak.

For lacing, you may use a *two-prong lacing needle.*

You also need glue. Rubber cement neither stiffens the leather nor penetrates too deeply, and you can easily rub it off if it gets where it is not supposed to be. If necessary, you can thin it with naphtha or cellulose thinner. There is also an excellent leather cement which you can thin with water. This is the easiest glue to work with, but a little more expensive than rubber cement. To glue larger things, a jar of rubber cement, which you spread with a flat paint brush, is most practical.

Use wax to polish your finished project. Either buy a special leather wax, or use paste wax or saddle soap, paraffin wax or a candle. You must wax the thread before you sew.

Use leather dyes and inks for coloring your leather. Follow the directions on the container for the specific product you are using. If you just want to tint the leather, use several thin layers of water colors since one thick layer tends to blotch and discolor the leather. Another coloring agent you can use is India ink, available in many colors. You must, however, thin it with boiled or distilled water before you use it. It also helps to sponge the leather lightly with water before coloring with India ink.

Ammonium chloride, thinned with water in the proportion of 1 part to 3 parts, darkens the leathers and skins and is especially good where the leather has been cut. If you rub cut, darkened areas with candle wax while they are still moist, they will not smear.

Tools

A good pocket knife and cutting board are all you really need for simple leathercrafting.

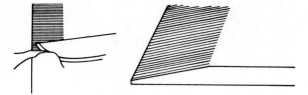

Illus. 1. Use a skiving knife to thin edges.

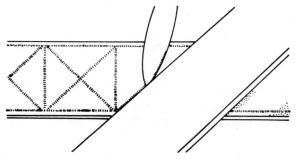

Illus. 2. Use a bone folder to score lines for stitching or decoration.

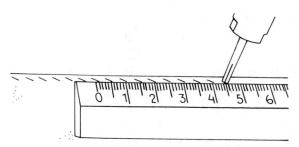

Illus. 3. Use an awl to pierce holes.

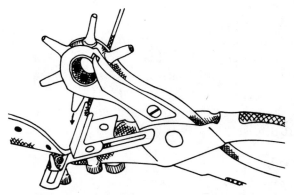

Illus. 4. Use a plier-action hole punch to make evenly spaced holes.

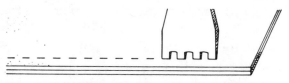

Illus. 5. The slit punch makes slits in the leather.

However, for more complicated work, you should have a few more tools at your disposal:

A *special leather knife* for cutting.

A *skiving knife* for thinning edges.

A *bone folder,* preferably with an *edge creaser* for scoring lines. A clean paper clip can accomplish the same thing.

A *stitch-marking wheel* for making holes.

An *awl* for piercing holes.

Plier-action hole punches. A *rotary,* or revolving, *punch* with a six-tube revolving head is excellent. A *one-hole plier punch* is also very good. You can mount attachments for setting in snap fasteners, eyelets, and so forth, on it. An adjustable gauge is a handy attachment, because it follows the margin of the leather so the holes and eyelets are all equidistant from the edge. Special tools for setting these small attachments into leather are also available. You can make slits with a *slit punch* or *thonging chisel,* which you hit with a mallet.

You need good *leather shears, pinking shears* and a *single-edged razor blade* in a holder.

A *steel ruler, right angle* and *compass* are also very useful items to have.

Headband

Now that you are familiar with the leather-crafting tools, here is a simple first project for you to make.

Before buying or cutting the leather for any project, always draw the pattern on paper or cardboard and cut it out with a paper knife or single-edged razor blade. Using your leather-cutting tools for cutting paper dulls them unnecessarily. Try to work every detail out on paper before starting on the leather. It is also a good idea to take the paper pattern along when you buy the leather.

For a headband, cut out a strip of paper or,

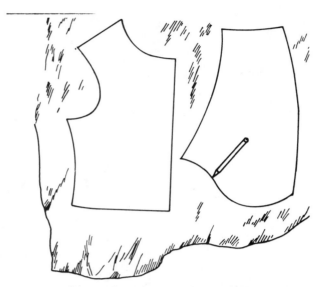

Illus. 6. Placing a pattern on the leather.

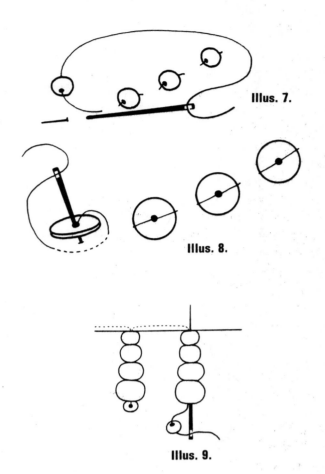

Illus. 7.

Illus. 8.

Illus. 9.

better yet, of cardboard, about 4″ longer than your head measurement. Cut it slightly less than three times the width you want the finished headband.

Next, you must decide carefully where to place the pattern on the leather. For a headband, you need a piece of thin leather. Outline the pattern on the wrong side (the flesh side) of the leather with a pencil, but watch for flaws on the right side. You can cut out this light-weight skin with leather shears. Always make sure you keep your fingers away from the cutting direction.

Sew pearls (as shown in Illus. 7), spangles or flat pearls (Illus. 8) onto the middle third of the leather strip. For thin leather, you do not have to punch holes first to sew. You can also hang pearl fringes from the lower edge of the middle third of the band, as shown in

Illus. 9. Fold the two outer thirds in to the middle.

Spread the glue out evenly, preferably with a flat brush, on the surface of each third. Press the surfaces together, towards the middle. If the edges do not line up, tear the pieces apart immediately and begin again.

Cut out one end of the band as shown in Illus. 10 for a closing mechanism. Make slits on the other end with a slit punch or thonging chisel and a mallet to complete the closing.

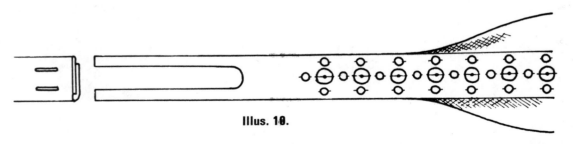

Illus. 10.

Choker

To make a choker with four rows of pearls, cut out six small rectangular pieces, first of cardboard, as a pattern, then of heavy-duty leather. Make the length of each piece the width you want the finished choker to be. Bear in mind that a skin is strongest in the middle, so cut the pieces, which will be exposed to constant wear, from the center. Always cut the less important parts from the sides.

To cut this heavy leather, use a knife, or possibly a razor blade in a holder, and cut the straight lines along a metal ruler. Heavier leather is easier to cut if you moisten it with water before cutting. This also makes it possible for you to straighten or shape it, and hammer it flatter. Hammer from the flesh side, or whichever side will be the inside, with a broad hammer.

Punch four small holes in each rectangular piece, as shown in Illus. 12. Striking a single-hole punch with a mallet is one way to punch holes, but it is easier to use a plier-action hole punch, either a one-hole one or a revolving one, especially if you want several evenly spaced holes. As you go along, a pivot slips into the previous hole punched, thus making the holes equal distance from one another.

Now, take four pieces of linen thread, each about 28" long. Tie the threads together with a knot about 8" in from one end and lace them onto a leather rectangle, by pulling each thread through a hole in the leather. Measure your neck, and space pearls and the remaining leather rectangles equally around (Illus. 13). Braid the left-over strings on each end, tie a knot, and don your creation.

Illus. 11. After you make a headband or a choker, see if you can make an attractive necklace using the same methods.

Bracelet

A bracelet with sewn-in pearls is another lovely item you can create. Make a pattern by drawing a circle with a radius of about 16" (use a thumb-tack, a piece of string 16" long and a pencil). Measure the length for the upper edge of the bracelet on your arm, and mark off this measurement on the circle. Draw two lines from the center of the circle to the two end points you marked on the circle.

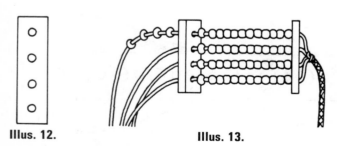

Illus. 12.   Illus. 13.

Illus. 14. This technique makes the decorative pearls an actual part of the rustic leather bracelet.

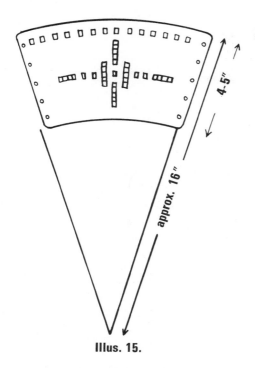

Illus. 15.

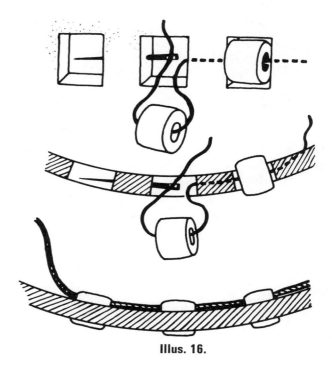

Illus. 16.

Make a smaller inside circle, using as the center the same center you used for the larger circle. The width of the bracelet is the distance you make this smaller circle from the larger one (see Illus. 15). Mark off the bracelet on heavy-duty leather (see page 54) and cut it out according to the directions above. Round off the corners.

To place the pearls, cut or punch out holes in the leather just the size of the pearls, or the size of several pearls together, if that is how you wish to place them. Sew on the pearls, preferably with a glover's needle. Start out by putting the needle through the leather on a slant into the first hole (see Illus. 16). Put the pearl or pearls on a piece of string and stick the needle back into the hole. Press the pearl(s) into the hole (see Illus. 16). Continue in this manner until you have placed all the pearls into the leather.

Lining

You may line the back of the bracelet. Cut a piece of lining leather or lining split a little smaller than the bracelet. When you snip or cut the corner, include enough lining for folding over a margin (Illus. 17). Skive the margin, if necessary. Skiving is the term for paring down some of the thickness at the edge of a piece of leather. Whenever you intend to glue, turn or hem the edges of a heavy piece of leather, you will probably have to skive

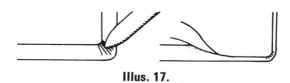

Illus. 17.

them. A real skiving knife is best for this, but you may also use a razor blade in a holder. Hold the knife at a very narrow angle against the wrong side (inside) of the leather and guide it carefully forward and out (see Illus. 1).

Glue the margin down. Push the pleats at the corner down firmly with a lacing needle or paper knife. Cut the lining (for some projects, the lining may be paper) a little smaller than the underlayer and glue it down (Illus. 17). To do this, spread glue with a flat brush evenly on

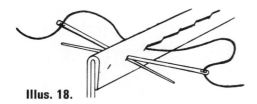

Illus. 18.

Illus. 19.

the surface of both the lining and the bracelet. Press the two pieces together, from the center out towards the edges. If the edges are not even, tear the pieces apart and begin again, as you did for the headband.

Sometimes, you may have to line a project with a turned edge. Skive the outer leather if it requires it. After glueing the lining on, fold the edge over and glue it down tightly. Then, you may sew the hem by hand or machine (see Illus. 18 and page 58).

Lacing

To finish, you should make slits or holes so that the bracelet can be braided or laced together. Whenever you plan to lace two pieces of leather together, you should punch the holes or slits together. If this is impractical, due to either the thickness or the shape of the leather, punch one side first, and then mark the other piece through the punched holes or slits on the first piece.

If you want the lacing to go round several similar corners on the same piece of work, do the corners first so they will be identical. Adjust the distance between the holes round the curve, and mark the same number of holes on

each side. This is not really necessary for this project.

To make slits, use a slit punch with four or more prongs. With it, you can conveniently punch several slits at a time. Or, punch holes as you did for the pearls in the bracelet. Use leather lacing or string to lace together the bracelet ends. You can buy both leather and plastic strips (laces) in many different colors and widths, but they are rather expensive. Instead, you can easily cut your own. If the strips are not long enough, lengthen them. Illus. 19 shows how to join longitudinal sections of leather strips or straps. Simply cut the surfaces that you want to join together at the same angle, smear them with glue and push them evenly together.

You can also cut leather lace or thongs from a piece of round or oval leather by following a spiral pattern (see Illus. 20).

Laces go through the holes easily if you cut the ends diagonally to a point. If this does not help, buy a special lacing needle.

The best way to lace pieces of leather together is with two laces, in shoelace fashion. If you cast over with only one lace, you can easily pull the pieces apart. Lace the bracelet in this way (Illus. 21).

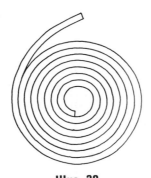

Illus. 20.

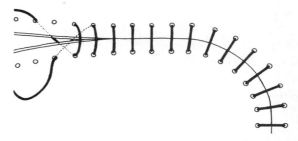

Illus. 21. Lace pieces of leather in the same way you lace shoes. Although your bracelet does not need this much lacing, proceed in this manner until you reach your desired length.

Braided Headband with Three Strands

Cut two slits in a narrow, solid strap of leather with a knife or razor blade. The strap should be about 2″ longer than your head measurement, depending upon how wide it is and how tight you braid. Make two holes in one end of the strap and four holes in the other with a single-hole punch, as described on page 54 (see Illus. 22). Braid with the three com-

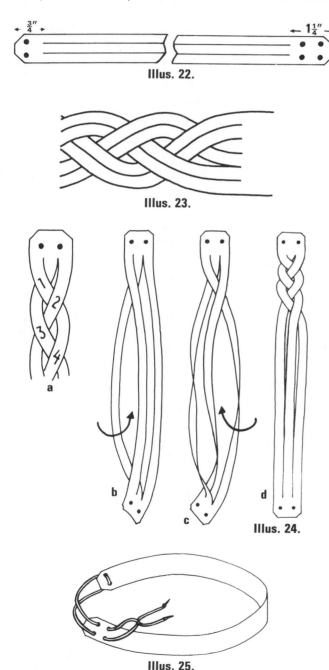

Illus. 22.

Illus. 23.

Illus. 24.

Illus. 25.

Illus. 26. Try your skill at making a three-strand braided bracelet to match your headband.

ponent strands (see Illus. 24a). (You can make a braided band or belt more flexible by separating the individual strands as in Illus. 22.) If you want to keep both ends of a band or belt intact, braid the following way: take the first strand (strand 1) and push it between the two other strands from the front towards the back (Illus. 24b). Then, push the second strand (2) through the two other strands towards the back (Illus. 24c), and so on. ·By every sixth move, you should be back to where you started. To end up with an even braid, you have to braid rather tightly, and smooth out the braiding after the last six moves. Put a leather lace or string through the holes to tie the belt (Illus. 25).

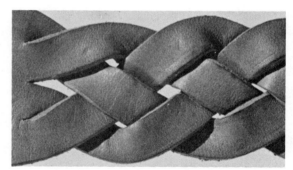

Illus. 27. A four-strand braid.

Braided Belt with Four Strands

To make this belt, you need leather and a buckle which you can buy at a sewing shop. First, measure your waist. To that measurement, add extra for the buckle—cut out the piece for the buckle double the finished length

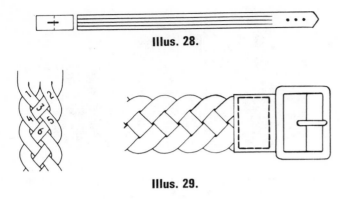

Illus. 28.

Illus. 29.

you want it (Illus. 28)—plus about 2″ extra for the braiding. Cut the strap as shown in Illus. 28, making sure to add holes for the buckle, and a slit in the buckle piece. Braid as shown in Illus. 29. You must skive the ends of the braided belt before you sew them together with the buckle piece (see page 55).

Stitching

Attach the buckle onto the leather buckle piece by looping the leather round the buckle, with the metal prong of the buckle through the slit you made in the leather (see Illus. 29). Fold the leather piece so that the ends meet. Place the ends of the braided belt between these ends. Now, you are ready to sew along the dotted lines indicated in Illus. 29. Before you sew, however, it is a good idea to mark off a line for the stitching with a bone folder. This provides a sewing guide and, at the same time, a trough or groove for the stitches to lie in so they are not so exposed to wear. A bone folder with an edge creaser is good for making decorative lines. It is also useful for toughening a skin —you can dampen the leather and knead in the moisture with the bone folder.

For easier sewing, use waxed thread, which also holds better. Use ordinary paraffin wax or a candle to wax each length of thread before using it.

To make a seam like the one in Illus. 30, use a single running stitch. You may use this same stitch for a lapped seam as shown in Illus. 31.

If your belt is made of light-weight leather, simply use a glover's needle—one with a triangular cross-section, sharpened on three sides so that it cuts through the leather. If the leather is too heavy for this needle, some preparation is necessary—you must pierce holes for the stitches first. If the leather is not too heavy, use a sewing machine without thread to make the holes. Otherwise, use an awl with a square or rectangular point to make holes, piercing them at an angle so the stitches lie flat. To make the stitches regular, pierce along a ruler or use an old saw blade or a stitch-marking wheel, which makes uniformly spaced holes, instead. Of course, if you are sewing with leather lacing or thongs, you have to punch holes first with punch pliers (see page 54). Sew with a blunt needle. It goes through holes easily and does not enlarge them.

Besides the single running stitch, there are a variety of others you can use to sew your leather. One such stitch is the double running stitch, pictured in Illus. 32. Sew with a running stitch along the length of the leather once, with a leather needle. Sew back, filling in the alternating stitches, with an ordinary needle. Do not use a leather needle the second time because it cuts the first thread in two.

Another possibility is the saddler's stitch in Illus. 33. Sew with two needles at a time through holes pierced at an angle. Put the needles through in opposite directions, and then pull the two threads simultaneously for uniform stitches. If you do not think it is necessary to pierce holes, use one sharp needle, which you poke through first, and one blunt needle.

You can get a better hold on heavy work by

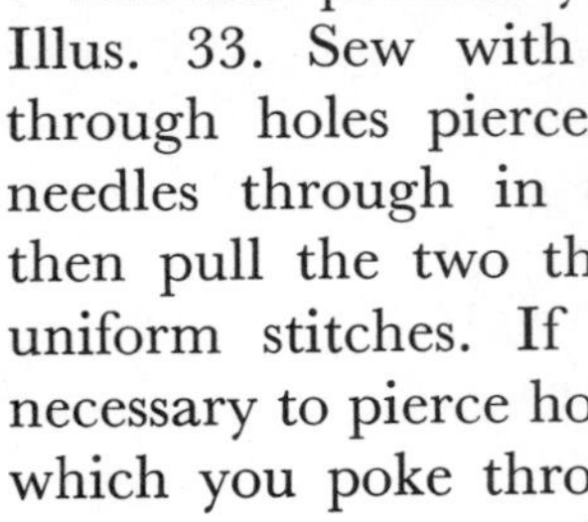

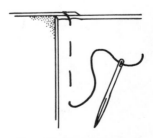

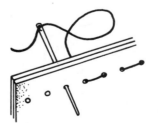

Illus. 30. Single running stitch.

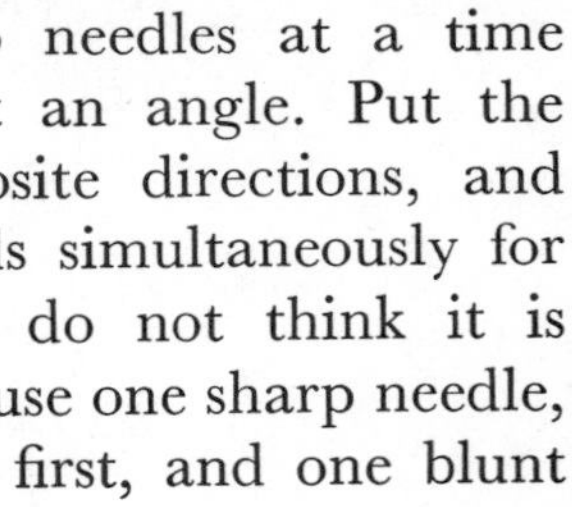

Illus. 31. Lapped seam.

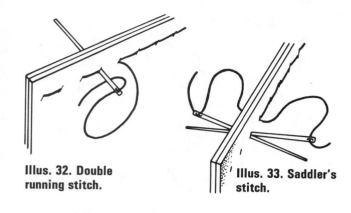

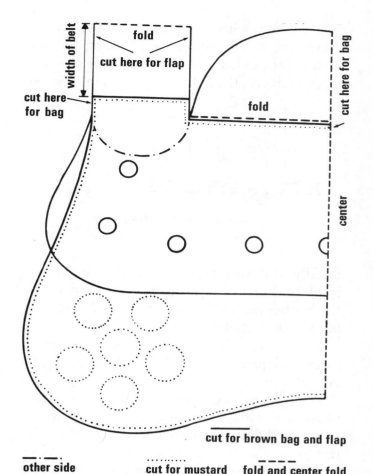

Illus. 32. Double running stitch.

Illus. 33. Saddler's stitch.

putting it in a vice, but use wooden blocks so you do not mar the leather. Saddlers use a special wooden clip.

Your braided belt is ready to wear.

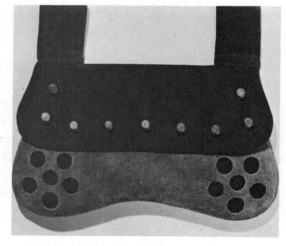

Illus. 34. After you make your belt bag, you can easily make an arm or ankle band to match. Cut two identical strips, cut the motif out of one of them, and then glue the two together.

Belt Bag

Illus. 34 shows a mustard-colored bag, with a brown motif and flap. It is finished off with brass rivets. To make this belt bag with a cut-out pattern, use skin or suede of two colors. Enlarge and trace the patterns for the flap and bag from the diagram onto transparent paper. Note that each pattern piece, almost full-sized, is only one half the actual piece. The straight broken line on each is the center fold. Cut out

cut for brown bag and flap

—·—·— other side .... cut for mustard ---- fold and center fold

Illus. 35. This is the pattern for the belt bag. Note that this is only for half of the bag. The straight broken line is the center fold.

one piece for the flap (or, if the skin is very thin, two identical pieces which you can glue together back to back). You can also sew the two flap pieces, right side to right side, and then turn them out through one side left open. You then have to stitch round the edge.

Put on the brass rivets, either two-piece rivets or split rivets.

If you decide on two-piece rivets (Illus. 36),

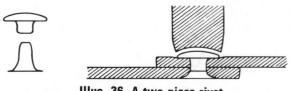

Illus. 36. A two-piece rivet.

drive them in with a rivet setter (which can be home-made). You could use a mallet, but this often ruins the head of the rivet. You can also use split rivets (Illus. 37), even though they are

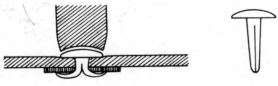

Illus. 37. A split rivet.

usually used to set metal supports or metal discs in place. Force the prongs out to the sides, set the leather on a solid surface and hit the rivet hard with a mallet.

Locks are often riveted on. The exact method depends on the lock, but it is usually very simple.

For the bag itself, you have to cut one piece of leather with straps for the back, and two pieces without straps—one of each color—for the front. Cut the motif out of the front piece which is the color of the bag. Glue the other front piece, the one the color of the flap, to the back of the motif. If necessary, pierce holes with an awl, or use a pointed knife, and then sew the bag together by hand or machine. Sew the flap onto the back of the bag as in Illus. 38. Glue the straps together and sew on as shown in Illus. 39. Attach the bag to your belt, and your project is complete.

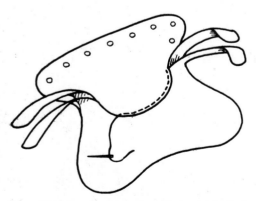

Illus. 38. Sew the flap onto the back of the bag.

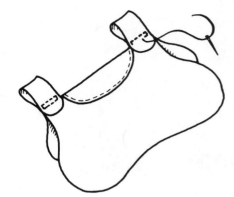

Illus. 39. Glue the straps of your belt bag together and sew as shown.

Belt Pouch

Make a two-color pouch to attach to your belt, using the same motif as for the belt bag. Cut the motif out, leaving as long a strap for the belt as you want. Sew the motif to the pouch with single running stitches. Sew the bag together with small, tight over-cast stitches. First, follow the directions on page 56 for lacing; carefully punch the holes, being sure to correctly adjust the corners.

To estimate how much lacing you need, make a test lacing through 10 holes. Count the total number of holes that require lacing, divide the amount by 10, and multiply the result by the length of the thong you used for the 10 holes. To join leather strips for longer lacing, see page 56. Begin lacing by tucking in the end of the lace under the first lacing stitch. At the end, take a couple of extra stitches in the last hole and glue the end down where it does not show.

You can produce a different lacing effect by making alternately spaced holes, as shown in Illus. 43.

You can achieve another interesting effect by using laces of several different colors.

After you have laced the entire pouch, sew rings onto the upper edge and pull a leather strip or string through the rings (see Illus. 45). You can decorate the ends of the string or leather strip with pearls.

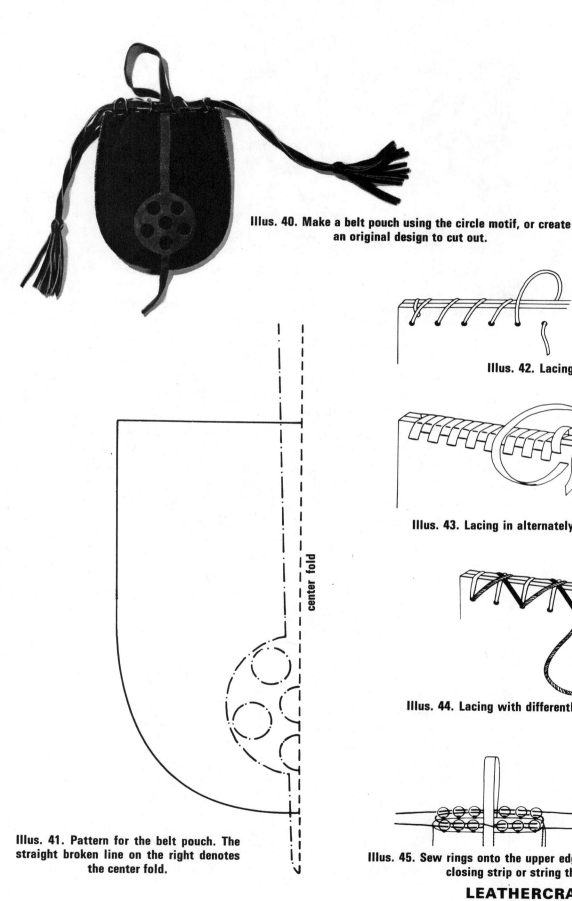

Illus. 40. Make a belt pouch using the circle motif, or create an original design to cut out.

Illus. 41. Pattern for the belt pouch. The straight broken line on the right denotes the center fold.

center fold

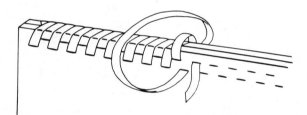

Illus. 42. Lacing.

Illus. 43. Lacing in alternately spaced holes.

Illus. 44. Lacing with differently colored laces.

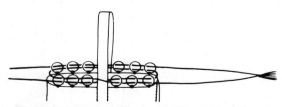

Illus. 45. Sew rings onto the upper edge and pull a leather closing strip or string through.

LEATHERCRAFTING ■ 61

Illus. 46. After you make your leather hat, spray it with silicone, and it will be waterproof.

Illus. 47.

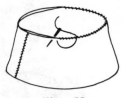

Illus. 48.

Hats

The brim of the hat in Illus. 46 is made of a double thickness of stiff, heavy-duty leather and the crown of a single thickness piece. For a hat the same size as Illus. 46, make pattern following Illus. 49 and 50.

If you want a straight crown, measure your head and cut a rectangle of leather as wide as you want, adding a couple of inches to fold down. For a slanted crown (Illus. 49), make a

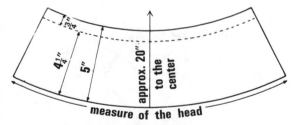

Illus. 49. Pattern for a slanted crown.

circle (use a pencil tied to string and a thumbtack). For the hat in Illus. 46, the radius was about 20″ long. By making the radius shorter, you make the sides of the crown more slanted. On the other hand, if you make the radius longer, the sides will be more steep. Mark off your head measurement on the circle and draw the two lines (sides) into center of circle. Measure off the width of the crown adding enough to bend down, and draw circle for

upper edge. Sew the crown together with small stitches (see page 58). Draw the top part of the crown the size of the upper edge of the side (see Illus. 47). Sew the top and side together from the inside and turn right-side out (see Illus. 48).

For a completely straight brim, make three circles (see Illus. 50), so that the circle in the middle fits quite tightly round your head. Draw the inside circle ¾″ further in, and the outside circle as far out as you want the width of the brim. For a slanted brim, cut out from the pattern as much or as little as you think is right, and re-adjust the measurements. From the inside of the brim, cut small slits at about 1–1½″-intervals, cutting almost to the circle of your head measurement (middle circle), thus making the flaps. Then, punch two holes in each flap. Place the flaps against the edge of the crown and mark the holes onto the crown (see

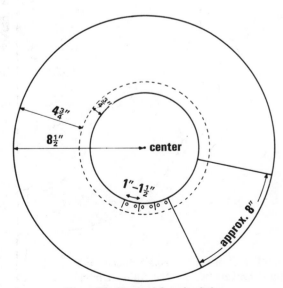

Illus. 50. Pattern for the brim.

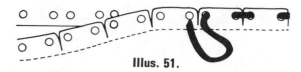

Illus. 51.

Illus. 51). You can clamp the crown and brim together with rings, or lace them together with thongs (see page 56). The hat in Illus. 46 is put together with rings, through which a leather thong was then pulled. Doing it this way makes it possible to adjust the hat a little for a better fit.

Sew the brim together with small stitches. If you wish to make the brim double, sew the two layers separately. When you glue the two layers together, do not glue the flaps together, but place them onto the crown, one layer inside and one layer outside, and attach as above. In this case, cut one layer of the brim slightly larger, and then trim it after the glueing. You may also stitch a double brim together on a sewing machine, and place a light metal wire or something similar between the layers to help stiffen the brim.

Illus. 52. Decorate a hat with lacing.

Illus. 53. Make a hat from one piece of leather. Decorate it with rope.

For easy hats, start out as above. Punch an equal number of holes in the crown and brim and lace them together. You may decorate the outer edge of the brim with lacing (see Illus. 52).

You can also make a hat out of one piece of leather. Cut it out according to the diagram for the crown (see Illus. 50). The crown may be rounded or pointed. Then, wet the brim part and press it out as much as possible. Decorate it with a rope, as in Illus. 53.

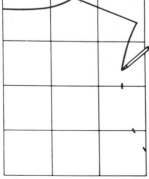

Illus. 54. Even a short leather vest such as this one is warm on a windy day.

Vest with Fringe

Before you make this vest, you should know how to enlarge the size of the diagram. Pick an important measurement—such as the bust measurement. Put this measurement on a line on a piece of paper, and part this line into as many units as on the pattern. Then, draw as many squares on the paper as the pattern has. Transfer the pattern by judging where the pattern cuts the lines of the squares (see Illus. 55). Be sure to adjust the paper pattern before you cut the leather.

Illus. 55. This is how you enlarge a pattern by the square method.

Draw the pattern following the heavy black lines in Illus. 56. If you make each square 2″ by 2″, you get a medium-sized vest, which you can make larger or smaller depending on your own size. Cut out the pattern and the two pieces which go underneath the motif with the holes for tying (Illus. 57). Stitch by hand or machine along the dotted line and round the holes. Decorate with rivets if you wish (Illus. 58).

Put the vest together by stitching the front pieces over the back piece with one or two rows of stitches. Cut the fringe. An easier way to cut these is to measure for four fringes at a time. Then, cut the measured lines. After that, cut each of these into two, and then again into halves.

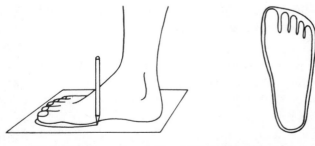

Illus. 59. You can easily make a pair of sandals like these.

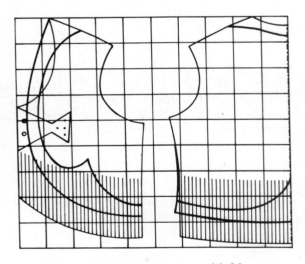

Illus. 56. Pattern for the vest with fringe.

Sandals

For each sandal, you need to cut two soles of cow-hide. For straps, use a good sturdy piece of leather, which you have to cut lengthwise, or it may stretch too much. Sew with heavy-duty saddler's thread and two heavy-duty blunt needles.

Draw a pattern of your feet onto paper (Illus. 60), holding the pencil vertically and following the shape of your foot. Add extra width and length to the toes, so they will not touch the edge when you walk or run.

Cut straps for the sandals shown in Illus. 59 according to Illus. 61. The length of the straps are for medium-sized sandals, so you may have

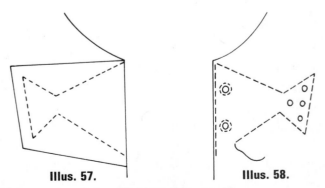

Illus. 57.   **Illus. 58.**   **Illus. 60. Trace your feet onto paper for the soles.**

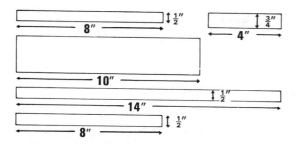

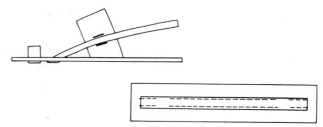

Illus. 61. Pattern for the sandals' straps.

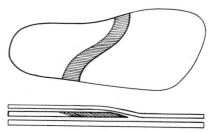

Illus. 63. Sew the narrow strap to the wide one, leaving an opening.

Illus. 62. Cutting and stitching patterns for the toe straps.

Illus. 64. You can place one or more wedges between the soles as an arch support.

to alter the length. You may decorate the straps with lines along the edges. Now, attach the straps to the upper soles. Place the sole right-side-up and measure off for the strap round your big toe. Cut two tight holes, as long and as wide as the strap (Illus. 62). Skive the ends of strap, pierce holes and sew on with the saddler's stitch (see page 58 and Illus. 62). Place a buckle on the heel strap and place the ends about an inch behind the toe strap. Place the heel strap in the sole at an angle, so there is an even pull; attach it the same way as the toe strap. Measure off for the wide instep strap. Before you sew it to the sole, sew on the narrow strap on top of the wide instep strap,

leaving openings on each side of strap; these hold the heel strap in place (Illus. 63).

Glue the two soles together, wrong side against wrong side. Dampen and hammer them into shape if you find it difficult to get them to match. You may place one or several wedges, which you must skive, between the soles. Shape the wedges according to the arch seen in Illus. 64.

Make a slanted cut along the edges in the bottom sole, so the stitches are slightly sunken; this helps to protect them (Illus. 65). An easier way might be to cut a groove, which also protects the stitches (Illus. 66). You may dye the edges of the sandals.

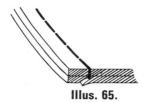

Illus. 65.

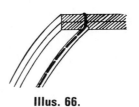

Illus. 66.

TRAPUNTO: DECORATIVE QUILTING

If "quilting" brings to mind only patches or intricately-stitched comforters, this article is certain to change your mind and broaden your craft horizons! Trapunto, sometimes called Italian quilting, is a form of quilting in which you raise only a specially chosen design. You stitch along this design through two layers of fabric and then insert stuffing between the two layers. You may either hand stitch or machine stitch the design, with matching or contrasting thread or yarn, on almost any article of clothing or household item that you have purchased or made.

In either case, you need crisp *woven* "interfacing" (available in fabric and sewing shops) for the backing fabric. If you use a lighter weight fabric than interfacing, the raised effect, which results from stuffing, shows more on the wrong side than on the right side. With interfacing for a backing, however, you force the raised design to the right side. If you choose to stitch your design by hand, you must first decide how prominent you wish your stitching to be before you choose between yarn, embroidery floss (soft cotton thread for embroidery), or sewing thread in a matching or contrasting color. You may use regular sewing thread and straight machine stitching unless you wish the stitching to show. In that case, use special buttonhole twist thread.

The method you use for stuffing depends on your design. You can get some idea of the different methods by following the instructions for the various projects in this article. Generally, use polyester fibre (called 100% polyester fibre), which you can buy in fabric and sewing shops, for stuffing all areas other than narrow strips, such as flower stems or stripes. For such narrow areas, use yarn or cording as stuffing.

Initial Pillow

If your couch or armchair needs an extra something, try personalizing a solid color, cotton suede pillow like the one in Illus. 1. To make an initial pillow, sketch the letter you choose on a piece of paper. When the shape of the letter suits you, draw another set of lines beside the first ones, exactly $\frac{1}{4}''$ away. Use a ruler, measuring at frequent intervals, to be sure of the $\frac{1}{4}''$-spacing. Draw a decorative border round the initials for the edges of the pillow. You may draw a straight border, like the one in Illus. 1, or be creative and make up an interesting one of your own. Again, each pair of lines should be $\frac{1}{4}''$ apart.

When you finish your design, re-trace the lines with a black felt-tip pen. Turn the paper over and trace the design on the wrong side of the paper. Use this wrong side in the next step. Cut a piece of crisp woven interfacing the size you want your finished pillow to be, plus $\frac{5}{8}''$ seam allowances on all sides. Place the interfacing over the wrong side of the design.

Condensed from the book, "Trapunto: Decorative Quilting" by Jo Ippolito Christensen | © 1972 by Sterling Publishing Co., Inc., New York

Illus. 1. An initial pillow is a simple and attractive first Trapunto project. Avoid backtacking (back stitching) and broken threads. As you can see here, they will spoil your creation.

You must use the wrong side of the design or your letter will be backwards on the finished pillow. Using a sharp, soft lead pencil, trace the backwards design onto the interfacing.

Cut a piece of fabric for your pillow front the same size as the interfacing. Place the two pieces—fabric and interfacing—together with the right side of the pillow face down on a table. Put the interfacing on top of the fabric, making sure that the side with the pencilled drawing faces up. (The letter should look backwards.) Carefully pin these two pieces of fabric together. If you wish, you may baste them together, since it is very important that they do not slip.

Fill your sewing machine bobbin with buttonhole twist in a color that contrasts with the pillow fabric. Use regular thread of the same color on top of the machine. On a scrap of fabric, test your machine's tension. It must be properly adjusted, because the bobbin thread appears on the right side of the pillow cover. If the tension is off, follow the directions in the booklet that accompanies your machine to correct it. (If you wish to stitch this by hand, follow the directions on page 70.)

With the interfacing facing you, stitch along all the lines you have drawn, using a long stitch (six stitches per inch). Never cross a line of stitching to finish off. Instead, stop, tie the ends on the wrong side, and then begin stitching again on the other side. *Never* backtack (back

stitch) when machine stitching. You must pull the threads to the wrong side and tie them, because backtacking always shows and looks sloppy. In Illus. 1, you can see where backtacking has spoiled the otherwise professional look of the pillow.

After you have finished stitching, thread a blunt-end, size 18 tapestry needle with yarn or cording. Poke a hole in the interfacing with the

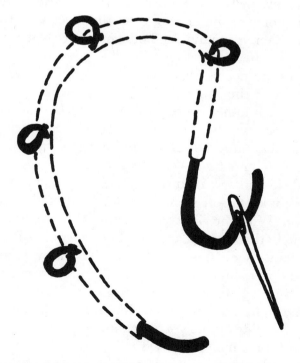

Illus. 2. In turning corners and curves in yarn-stuffed Trapunto, you must leave a small loop of yarn as shown here.

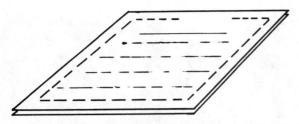

Illus. 3. To assemble a pillow, first place the right sides of the front and back together. Then stitch three sides and all four corners.

needle, taking care not to break the threads of the fabric or interfacing. Carefully work the threaded needle through the stitched area. Turn the corners and curves by bringing the needle out of the interfacing, then by re-inserting it, leaving a small loop of yarn, as shown in Illus. 2. You must leave this loop so that when the pillow, or any other project you make, is cleaned, there is some slack to allow for any possible shrinkage of the yarn. Trim the yarn at the beginning and the end, close to the fabric. Tug gently on the fabric so that the ends of the yarn slip into the holes and lie entirely between the two layers of fabric. With the point of the needle, coax the threads of the interfacing around the hole you poked with the needle back together. Repeat this process as often as necessary to completely fill the area between the stitches.

Cut another piece of fabric for the back of your pillow the same size as the front, either of the same fabric or of a matching or contrasting one. You can make cording from scraps of fabric and sew it to the right side of the pillow or make tassels from yarn for further decoration. With the right sides of the fabric together, stitch three sides and all four corners of the pillow (see Illus. 3). Turn the pillow right side out, making sure that each corner is completely turned. Make an inner pillow, from any light- to medium-weight fabric, $\frac{1}{4}''$ larger on all sides than your Trapunto pillow cover. Stuff the inner pillow with a bought pillow form or with polyester stuffing. Hand sew the fourth side closed.

Afghan

An afghan is a luxurious article with which to decorate any room. Make an afghan from a 60″ square, double thickness of polyester double knit fabric. Sew an original design (Illus. 5) in opposite corners—or, if you wish, in all four corners. In either case, first trace the design onto the interfacing according to the directions on page 66. The interfacing only has to be an inch or two larger than the actual drawn design, because the design only covers a small portion of the afghan, unlike the initial pillow on page 67, where the design is over-all.

Very carefully place the interfacing in the corners of one layer of the wrong side of the fabric. Baste or pin the interfacing in position. Again, remember to check the tension on your machine, because the bobbin thread appears on the right side of your afghan. Using regular thread in a matching color, stitch along the drawn design leaving a 1″ opening (see Illus. 4). Pull the threads to the back and tie. If you wish to stitch this design by hand, follow the instructions on page 70. Stuff the chosen areas with polyester fibre. Use a knitting needle to push the polyester to the ends of each section you are stuffing. Since the double knit fabric stretches easily, you may tend to overstuff. *Do not overstuff.* Remember that your design only needs to be slightly raised to be effective Trapunto. The more you stuff the design, the more likely puckering is to occur. You cannot

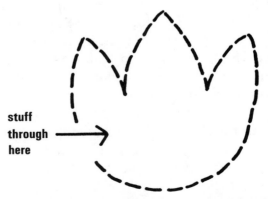

stuff through here →

Illus. 4. Stitch along the design traced onto the interfacing, leaving a one-inch opening.

avoid a certain amount of puckering, which varies with the kind of fabric that you use. The more "give" the fabric has, the less puckering there will be. Sew up the 1" opening.

When you have finished stuffing your design, place another piece of the double knit fabric (the same size—60" × 60") on top of the one with the Trapunto design, right sides together. Stitch, $\frac{1}{2}$" from the edge on three sides and round all four corners, as you did for the pillow (Illus. 3). Turn the afghan right side out and stitch the fourth side by hand. Top stitch all the way round the afghan $\frac{1}{2}$" from the edge. This keeps the two pieces of fabric in place.

Use yarn of a matching or contrasting color for the fringe. Six ounces of yarn makes enough knotted fringe for a 60" × 60" afghan. Cut about 480 strands, each 20" long. With a pencil, place dots 1" apart just over the top stitching on the right side of the afghan. Using a large-sized crochet hook, poke a hole through both thicknesses of the afghan (see Illus. 6). Hook two strands of yarn (in the middle of each strand) onto the hook (Step 1) and pull

through, so that about a 2"-loop appears on the right side of the afghan (Step 2). Pull the ends of the yarn strands through the loop (Step 3). Pull tightly, but not so much that the fabric wrinkles (Step 4). Put three 2"-strand pieces in each corner hole. Follow Illus. 7 for knotting instructions for decorative fringe.

If you use a synthetic yarn (rather than wool), your afghan will be completely machine washable and dryable.

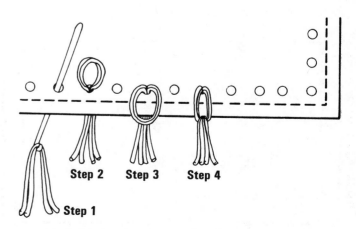

Illus. 6. With a pencil, make dots where you want to place fringe. Follow these four easy steps to attach the fringe.

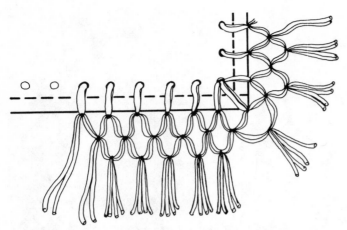

Illus. 7. For a more decorative fringe, follow this knotting pattern.

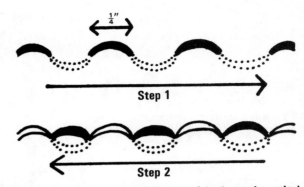

Illus. 9. To hand-stitch a design, take ¼-inch running stitches. Repeat, going under where you went over and vice versa. The dotted lines show the stitches on the wrong side of the fabric.

Table-Top Catch-All

Anyone who does any kind of handiwork is perpetually plagued by small piles of yarn, thread, fabric scraps and other trash. A table-top catch-all like the burlap-covered one in Illus. 10 is the perfect answer to help keep your den or sewing room tidy. Decorate a one-pound tin coffee can with Trapunto.

Burlap is easy to work with and fits into a casual or modern décor, but you can, of course, use any fabric you like. Cut whatever fabric you choose so that it goes round the tin can with a 1″ lap—that is, leave 1″ extra on one end. (Cut

one end on the selvage, if possible.) Allow an extra 1½″ to fold under the bottom of the can. Also, allow an extra 3″ to fold into the top of the can (see Illus. 8).

Draw your design on a piece of paper the same size as the fabric, being sure to mark just where the hems are. You may draw one single motif, an over-all motif, or a border design at the top and bottom. You certainly do not need to be an established artist to create an effective design. See page 543 for inspiration if you are having trouble creating an original design.

Now, transfer your design to the interfacing, which should be the same size as the burlap, as described on page 66. Be sure that your design is well-centered on the burlap. Pin the interfacing securely to the burlap.

Burlap's ruggedness necessitates rugged stitching. Large stitches, hand-sewn with yarn, give this desired look (see Illus. 10). Take ¼″ running stitches, leaving a ½″- to ¾″-opening somewhere between the stitches. Next, go back over the stitches you just made, this time going under where you went over and vice versa (see Illus. 9). This makes the line of stitching so secure that the stuffing cannot ooze out. Stuff each section of your design and then close up the opening with the same stitching before going on to the next section.

When you have finished, cover the tin can by wrapping the fabric round it as tightly as you can. Pin the lapped ends in place so that the

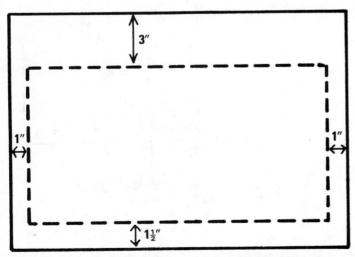

Illus. 8. Cut fabric for a table-top catch-all with these extra allowances on the edges.

selvage end is on top; this eliminates excessive bulk. Blind stitch (take very tiny stitches) the two ends together. Fold under the excess fabric at the bottom and tape it to the tin can with masking tape. Repeat the process at the top, and your catch-all is ready for use. Start immediately by putting in it the left-over yarn scraps, burlap and masking tape.

Toaster and Mixer Covers

Co-ordinated kitchen appliance covers decorated with Trapunto are sanitary and useful as well as attractive. Neither the colors nor the designs have to match. In fact, complementary colors add a special creative effect to your kitchen.

Terry cloth, used for these appliance covers, is another fabric which lends itself well to Trapunto. Note in Illus. 11 and 12 how little puckering there is. Like burlap, terry cloth has a rugged quality and, therefore, you should hand stitch your design with yarn.

Put your design onto the interfacing by the same process described on page 66. If you choose to make covers from a commercial pattern, do the Trapunto before you sew any seams. Stuff with polyester fibre as directed on page 68. Then, assemble the covers according to the pattern directions. If you want to put the

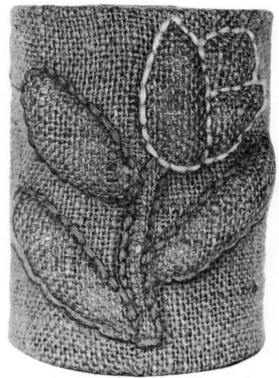

Illus. 10. Close-up of the table-top catch-all.

design on a purchased cover, buy one of a solid color and use your own design on it.

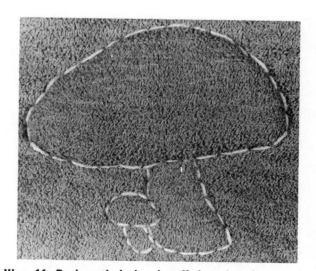

Illus. 11. Design stitched and stuffed on the mixer cover.

Illus. 12. Design stitched and stuffed on the toaster cover.

Illus. 13. You can dress up a plain apron easily by stuffing a Trapunto design on the pocket.

Apron

Add a decorative or even glamorous touch to an apron that you have made or have bought. If the apron already has a pocket on it, like the apron on page E, carefully remove the pocket, put your Trapunto design on it, and then sew the pocket back onto the apron. If your apron does not have a pocket, use a contrasting piece of solid-colored fabric to make one. If you are making your own apron, put the Trapunto design on the pocket before you sew the pocket on the apron.

Transfer a design onto a piece of interfacing that is the same size as the pocket, following the directions on page 66.

Stitch, using a contrasting color, with buttonhole twist thread in the bobbin and the same color regular thread on top of the machine. Ordinarily, it is not attractive for one line of stitching to cross another when you are going

Illus. 14. This is a close-up of the Trapunto design on the orange pot holder shown in Illus. E3 in color.

Illus. 15. Here is the design on the red pot holder shown in Illus. E3 in color.

to stuff both areas. Note that the stem of the mushroom on the left in Illus. 13, however, is not stuffed. In some instances, therefore, stitching can cross other stitching. The tufts of grass in Illus. 13 are hand-embroidered with embroidery floss.

Be careful not to overstuff the apron design. Cotton and cotton blend fabrics especially do not have much "give" and overstuffing would cause excessive and unattractive puckering.

Pot Holders

Utilitarian items, such as pot holders, can also be colorful and imaginative. Choose designs appropriate for the kitchen—draw fruit or even continue the mushroom theme from the apron if you like. Trace your design onto a piece of interfacing the same size as the pot holder. The pot holders in Illus. 14, 15, and E3 are of poplin, which has little or no "give" and, therefore, results in excessive puckering, but any sturdy, washable fabric with a close weave is also suitable.

Stitch, using colored yarn, which emphasizes your design, according to the directions on page 70. Carefully plan your stitching so that you can stuff as you go.

Stuff with polyester fibre. You must stuff the small areas round the orange sections in Illus. 14 by poking a hole in the interfacing as described on page 68. For these small areas, use a blunt-end tapestry needle as described on page 68.

Embroider seeds, as in Illus. 14 and 15, in yarn on top of the pot holder after you finish the Trapunto.

To assemble your pot holder, cut a piece of fabric for the back which is the same size as the front piece. Place the right sides together and stitch three sides and all four corners (see page 68). Turn the pot holder right side out. Insert a piece of cotton batting (a special material made to use in quilts), which is slightly smaller than the pot holder, between the two layers. You could also make a good insulator from an old wash cloth or two. Stitch the

Illus. 16. This is a close-up of the knee-pad fish for a child's crawlers shown in Illus. E2 in color.

fourth side by hand and your handy needlework is ready for use and display.

Crawlers

Make a child adorable knee pads to crawl about in that will be the talk of the baby world. Either buy or make a pair of crawlers, preferably with a snap crotch which enables you to get inside the leg easily to work.

Apply a lively design to interfacing as described on page 66. Try the outfit on the child to mark where his knees are. Center the Trapunto design over this mark and pin it in place. Stitch on the machine, using buttonhole twist thread in the bobbin and the same color regular thread on the top. Set your machine for the longest stitch (six stitches per inch). Remember never to backtack. Leave an opening in the stitching through which to stuff. Embroider any necessary detail (see the eyes in Illus. 16).

Now that you know the basics of Trapunto, see what other projects you can create—for your home, your friends, or even for yourself.

BOTTLE CUTTING

You can transform ordinary bottles of all kinds into vases, drinking glasses, compote jars, or whatever use your imagination dictates—simply by removing the necks.

While there are several methods of removing the necks, the simplest and cleanest method of all is with a bottle cutter that has gained tremendous popularity recently. It consists of a device that comes fully assembled and which makes a scored line around the bottle wherever desired, and then breaks the glass along the score by a tapping from the inside. There is no heat, no water, and no mess. This inexpensive device comes complete with printed directions and is available at hobby shops and craft supply houses. Many hardware dealers also carry it. A new, somewhat more expensive, *electric* cutter is also available.

However, if you like doing things yourself, you can manage very well with nothing more than a length of wool knitting yarn, a bottle of denatured alcohol and a bucket of cold water.

Remove all labels from the bottle, as well as the glue that held them on. Clean the bottle thoroughly on the outside. Watch out you do not get water inside the bottle, and never try to cut the neck off a wet bottle. It will simply not work as well as when the bottle is dry.

First, put on your goggles or shield. Saturate the piece of wool yarn with denatured alcohol, then wrap it round the straight part of the bottle, just below the shoulder. (Do not try to use a cotton string for this. It just will not work.) Before the alcohol has a chance to evaporate, touch a match to the yarn.

When the alcohol is almost burned out, thrust the bottle quickly in water. As a result of the tension induced in the glass by heating and the sudden change of temperature, the neck of the bottle will crack off, precisely at the place where the yarn touched the glass, with a loud cracking sound. It is important to wrap the yarn horizontally round the bottle, not on an angle.

If your first attempt is not successful, try it with another bottle. The first bottle then gets a chance to cool off and dry. You may have to repeat the process several times if the bottle you are using has thick glass.

Generally, the neck seldom springs from the bottle, leaving a precisely square break behind. But, the more bottles you try, the more skill you acquire, and, in time, you will have better results.

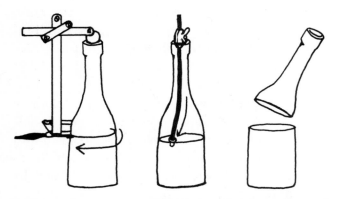

Illus. 1. This is how most commercial bottle cutters work.

Condensed from the book, "Colorful Glasscrafting" by Jos H. Eppens-van Veen | © 1973 by Sterling Publishing Co., Inc., New York

Illus. 2. Wrap alcohol-saturated yarn round the bottle just below the shoulder.

Illus. 3. Set the yarn on fire immediately.

After separation, the edges of the glass will be quite sharp. File them smooth with a fine carborundum stone, and you will have a lovely cylindrical vase. If you cut the top of the bottle off fairly low down, use it as a compote bowl. Clean it on the inside with a good detergent or other strong cleanser, until the glass sparkles.

There is another method of "cutting" the neck off a bottle, which is, however, not as satisfactory, but you should be familiar with it. In this method, fill the bottle with oil to the

Illus. 4. When the alcohol is almost burned away, drop the bottle into a bucket of cold water.

Illus. 5. The quick change in temperature should cause the neck to snap off with a loud noise.

Illus. 6. The break should be exactly on the line where the yarn was wrapped. Be sure to wrap the yarn perfectly horizontally round the bottle.

line where you desire the break to come. Next, thrust a red-hot metal rod through the neck of the bottle, deep into the oil. The oil heats up along the rod, climbs upward, and forms a glowing hot layer on the surface. At this point, dip the bottle in cold water. Theoretically, the neck will snap off with a faultless break. In practice, however, it is not foolproof. Moreover, the oil gives off a terrible smell and you will have a miserable mess of oil spots to clean up afterwards.

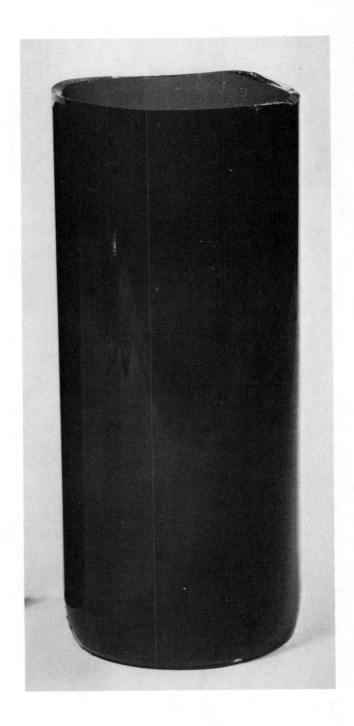

Illus. 7. The edges of the glass along the break will be sharp. Trim them with a carborundum stone until smooth, and you will have a lovely glass vase of your own making.

HORSESHOE-NAIL CRAFT

Crafting with horseshoe nails is an interesting way to make attractive metal jewelry and sculptures. The techniques are surprisingly simple, and the possibilities for intricate and beautiful designs are endless.

Materials

Illus. 1 shows the necessary tools—a pair of universal jaw pliers with an adjustable grip, a pair of cutting nippers, a vice, a spring clamp, a hack saw, and a few ordinary steel pipes of different diameters for bending the nails. For soldering you need: some flat fire-proof tiles, a butane torch or soldering iron (the butane torch is preferable), a nozzle, pin-point burners, solder, and flux. For any finishing-off, you can use a narrow steel-wire brush or steel wool. You can buy all these things at a hardware shop.

The principal materials, of course, are horseshoe nails. Illus. 2 shows some of the different kinds of nails, all available in several sizes. (For these special nails, see Suppliers list on page 560.) You also need ordinary iron wire for making rings and steel pipe for candle-holders. You can purchase glass buttons and beads from craft and hobby shops. (Use a synthetic resin glue or epoxy adhesive for glueing glass to the metal.)

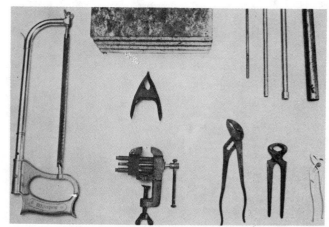

Illus. 1. These simple tools are all you need for crafting with horseshoe nails.

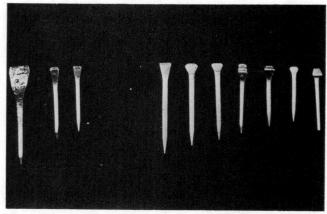

Illus. 2. Horseshoe nails come in a variety of shapes and a wide range of sizes.

Condensed from the book, "Horseshoe-Nail Crafting" by Hans Carlbom | © 1973 by Sterling Publishing Co., Inc., New York

Bending the Horseshoe Nails

Horseshoe nails are made of soft iron and are easy to shape with pliers. The two basic shapes are the circle and the square. To make a circle, fasten a section of steel pipe in a vice and follow the process shown in Illus. 3–17. To make a square, mark off three equal sides, starting from the point of the nail. Hold the pointed end in the pliers (at a right angle to the pliers), and bend down at the first mark. Repeat for each side. The thick end of the nail is the fourth side.

Illus. 6.

Illus. 3.

Illus. 7.

Illus. 3–7. Shape the horseshoe nail over a section of steel pipe.

Illus. 4.

(Many types of horseshoe nails have trade-marks inscribed on the head. Your sculpture will be more attractive if you have all the trade-marks facing in the same direction, either outwards or inwards.)

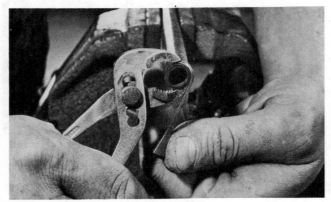

Illus. 5.

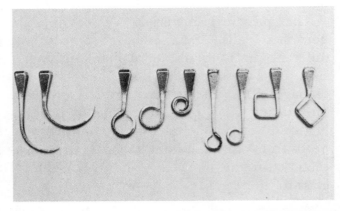

Illus. 8. The basic circle and square shapes can be bent into many different designs.

Joining the Nails

In most cases, soldering gives quite enough strength. However, you should not use ordinary tin solder, which is too soft. You can buy solder containing a little silver in order to strengthen it. Use either acid-core solder or a solid solder with brush-on flux for the iron nails.

For strong joints, try *brazing*. Use a solder containing a large proportion of silver. This kind of solder needs heating up to a temperature of about 1300°F (704°C) and makes a very strong joint, but the great heat gives the nail a blue color which makes quite a lot of subsequent finishing necessary. You only need to braze if you want a very strong joint, or if the product is likely to be subjected to heat exceeding 300°F (149°C).

Remember not to use more solder than necessary. A big lump of solder makes a joint uglier but not stronger. Work with a small flame, and be careful with the acid flux—it is poisonous and corrosive.

After you solder a piece, leave it alone until it has cooled. To remove any flux, rinse the article in hot water, clean gently with a brush, and dry. To prevent rusting, paint your creation with colorless varnish.

If you have no soldering tools, you can still make many types of jewelry and sculpture by joining circles and squares together in the same way that chain links are joined together. You can also use wire to bind and hook nails together.

Projects to Begin

Try making a pendant like that in Illus. 9. The head of the nail in the middle must be reversed, with the two outside nails facing the other way. The wire binding and the position of the nails will then lock them firmly together. Shape the wire rings the same way you did for the nails. (When you form the wire, form a few feet of it at a time, and then cut off the rings as you need them.)

Illus. 9. Try making this pendant. It is easy to put together and requires no soldering.

Illus. 10. Bend the nails and smooth the metal. Then solder the nails to the metal strip and form the strip over a steel pipe.

For your first soldering project, try making a ring. Cut or saw a piece of ordinary sheet iron to the shape shown in the photo. Smooth off the edges of the metal strip and solder on the nails in the middle. Then bend the metal strip over a steel pipe to make the ring (Illus. 10).

Illus. 11–12 show other pendant designs that are easily assembled.

Illus. 11. Horseshoe nails make unique pendants.

Illus. 12.

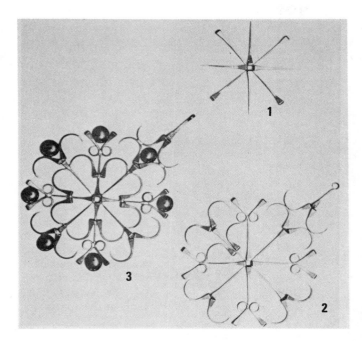

A Window Decoration

Illus. 13 shows how to make the design for a beautiful window decoration. You must do soldering carefully on window decorations, as the fastening surfaces are small. Plan your design before soldering it, or it will not fit together symmetrically.

You can use the bell-shaped window decoration in Illus. 15 as a candleholder if you turn it upside down.

Illus. 15. The window decoration in Illus. 14 is now ready to hang.

Illus. 14. Make the bell shape as shown here. Any round piece of wood will do, as long as it has roughly the same diameter of the bell shape. Or, you can use a tin can (with the diameter of the bell shape) and tape the curved nails to the side to hold them in place. However, you will find the soldering easier if you use a piece of wood like that shown here.

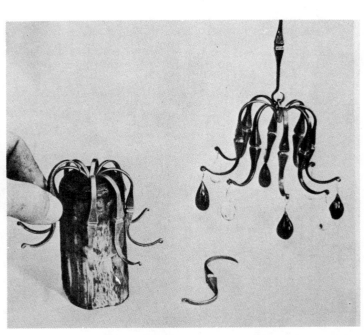

HORSESHOE-NAIL CRAFT ■ 81

A Sconce

Try making a sconce like the one in Illus. 16. A clamp is a useful support when you solder on the candlestick.

A Chandelier

For a final project, make a chandelier like the one in Illus. 17. Patient planning and work are required to balance and construct the

Illus. 16. Careful soldering results in a beautiful sconce that complements any home. Make the candlestick with a section of metal tubing soldered onto a circle of sheet metal.

Illus. 17. Make the center section of this chandelier as you did the window decoration in Illus. 15.

chandelier correctly, and you should measure all the angles before you start to solder. But, the finished creation is well worth it.

Creating Your Own Designs

A few things should be remembered when creating designs with horseshoe nails. A design should not be too complicated, for this may give the viewer the feeling that it is cluttered up or fussy. Do not mix too many shapes in the same design, but have just one or two curves rhythmically recur throughout the pattern. If you are thinking of making a large design, it is best to divide the frame into sections in which the same pattern is repeated. And always remember to distribute the soldering points so that when it is complete the design will be strong enough.

GARDEN IDEAS

Illus. 1.

When you want a room to look lived in and loved, you put pictures on the walls, gay pillows on the sofa, books and plants and flowers on the tables. You are pleased when friends say that your home reflects your personality. They will say the same thing about your garden if you add interesting touches which make it truly yours.

Bring Birds to Your Garden

Spread out a welcome mat for birds and they will be a constant joy to you. They will repay you with song, and will help keep harmful insects away from the plants in your garden. Put up your birdhouses in the fall, so that by the time the birds return in the spring, the houses will be weathered enough to blend into the landscape. Birds are sometimes timid about entering too-new houses.

You can make a birdhouse quite simply from rectangular or square pieces of wood. Use boards that are heavy enough so that they will not warp out of shape after repeatedly being soaked by rain and then dried out by the sun. Wood is the best material to use because it will keep the nest warm on cool nights, and fairly cool when the sun is hot. A metal birdhouse, for instance, would become an oven in the hot sun, but you can use narrow tin strips to seal the cracks between wooden boards and to keep out rain.

For ventilation, drill a couple of small holes in protected spots under the eaves. It is also a good idea to hinge the roof of the birdhouse, so that you can lift it up and clean house after the birds have flown south in the fall.

If you are making a wren house, trace around a coin $\frac{7}{8}$" to 1" in diameter to get the correct size for the opening. A 2" hole will suit martins, and a $1\frac{1}{4}$"- to $1\frac{1}{2}$"-coin makes just the right size doorway for most common species of birds.

Do not build too big a house for your bird tenants. Birds do not like other bird families around. Also, do not paint the house with bright colors, as birds prefer brown or grey.

Condensed from the book, "Herb Magic and Garden Craft" by Louise Evans Doole | © 1972 by Sterling Publishing Co., Inc., New York

There are many different birdhouses that are easily constructed. For example, you can make a square house with a peaked roof and hang it from a tree branch. Use your imagination. A large, dried gourd can even be turned into an admirable birdhouse by cutting a doorway and a few small ventilation holes.

Nail or fasten the birdhouse to a post or tree about 6 feet above the ground. If the post is of wood, nail some tin around the post (to make it slippery) or make a collar of tin, to keep animals, especially cats, from climbing up to pay the birds unwelcome visits.

It is amusing to watch the birds inspect your house before they move in. But in a short time they are at home and building a nest. You can help by leaving bits of yarn, string, straw and cotton nearby.

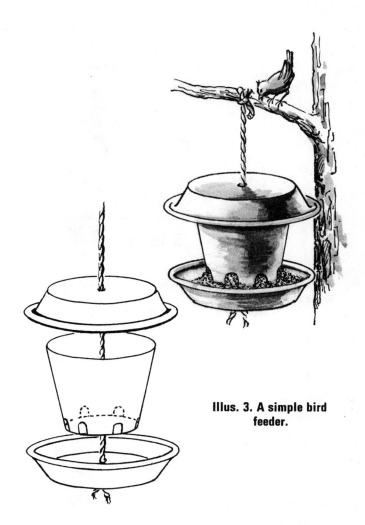

Illus. 3. A simple bird feeder.

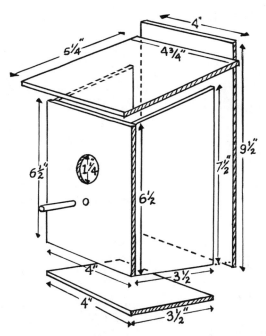

Illus. 2. These are the dimensions for building the birdhouse in Illus. 1.

Bird Feeders

Both you and the birds will get a lot of pleasure from a bird feeder. There are many different ways to make a bird feeder. One simple design is shown in Illus. 3.

To construct the feeder in Illus. 3 you need two old pie-tins—one for the top and one for a base, a plastic ice-cream container, a few feet of wire or strong cord, and a small piece of wood. Punch a series of fairly large holes all around the base of the bin so the feed can spill out onto the pie-tin base. Next punch holes through the two tins and the lid and base of the container, and string wire or strong cord through. Tie a piece of wood or metal to the bottom of the wire to hold the feeder up. You can now fill your bird feeder with food and hang it from a tree branch or overhanging eave or post.

You can construct bird feeders, like birdhouses, in a variety of forms. Put some thought and creativity into the design and placement and you can make a feeder that will attractively complement your yard or garden.

Illus. 4. A tree stump makes a convenient spot for a bird bath. Make sure your basin is heavy enough so that it will not tip over when the birds sit on the edge.

Illus. 5. A cement bath is easy to construct. Simply use a garbage can lid for a mould.

Bird Baths

A bird bath not only attracts birds to drink and splash about in the water, but is an attractive addition to the garden. If your yard has a tree stump in it, that will make a good base. If not, sink a post, but be sure it is large enough and set in firmly enough to support the bath basin without danger of its tipping over.

The easiest way to make a permanent bird bath is with ready-mix cement. Add water, according to the directions on the bag, and pour the mixture into the lid of a garbage can. As soon as the cement begins to harden and hold its shape, scoop it hollow to form the basin. The basin should taper from a depth of $\frac{1}{2}''$ near the rim to $2''$ in the middle. Leave the bottom fairly rough, so that the birds can get a good foothold. If you wish, you can decorate the bath by pushing little pebbles into the cement before it sets. When the cement is completely dry, the bath will come out of the can lid quite easily.

A Garden Pool

Let a small pool be the focal point of your garden. All you need is a plastic or galvanized metal washtub.

Choose a suitable spot and dig a hole deep enough to hold the tub with only $3''$ extending above ground level.

Around the pool you can plant flowers in a careless, informal fashion, or you can use the pool as the central feature of a rock garden. Or, if you have been wondering where to keep your house plants during the summer, you can surround the pool with potted plants.

A Strawberry Barrel

A strawberry bed takes up a lot of space in a garden, but if you really love strawberries, why not make a strawberry barrel? It will only occupy a few square feet.

Get the largest barrel you can find. Drill drainage holes in the bottom of the barrel and

Illus. 6. This charming little garden pool is made from an old washtub!

leave the other end open. Now drill holes, from 2″–4″ in diameter, in the sides of the barrel. They should be about 6″–8″ apart, and the bottom row of holes should be about 9″ from the ground.

Inside the barrel stand an old stovepipe or drainpipe which has been punched full of holes. Fill the pipe with small rocks. It will now stand erect while you fill the barrel. First put 3″ of gravel in the bottom of the barrel, and then fill the barrel all the way up with rich soil.

Your barrel is now ready to be planted. Simply insert a strawberry plant in each hole. To water the plants, run water into the drain pipe with a hose, or pour it in from a bucket.

Illus. 7. A strawberry barrel is an interesting and decorative touch in a garden, particularly a small one.

A Wrought-Iron Garden Bench

It is nice to have a place to sit and admire your garden. It is especially nice to sit on a handsome and unusual bench which you have made yourself.

In a second-hand store or junk yard look for an old treadle sewing machine. You don't need the machine itself, but many of them have very attractive iron supports, and these two pieces of patterned iron-work are just what you need. Simply "plant" them in your garden, about 18″ apart, put a heavy board across them, and you have a bench! Paint the bench white or green or red—whatever looks best in your garden.

Some of the old sewing machines have iron sides which are too tall for a bench. If you find one, you can make a garden table instead. Make a small table by using a short board, or a picnic table if you use a long board.

The Garden Path

Garden paths can do a lot to enhance the appearance of your garden.

Stepping stones are particularly suitable across a grassy lawn leading to a pool. You can

Illus. 8. If you are lucky enough to have an old-fashioned sewing machine, use the base to make a unique garden bench.

Illus. 9. A gravel garden path.

Illus. 10 (right). Make your garden more interesting by having curving and winding paths.

buy flat rocks or slate from a stone quarry, or you may be able to find suitable rocks in a field or along a country road. (Before taking rocks from a field, be sure to ask permission of the owners.) To start such a path, dig slight depressions in which to lay each stone. Measure the distance from one stone to the next by walking and placing a marker at each step.

You can make a garden path of gravel and edge it with low-growing flowers and herbs. Use aluminum stripping to confine the gravel.

In planning your paths, remember that they need not be straight unless you want them that way as part of a design. Curving paths give a casual air to your garden.

However, remember that shrubs and plants will grow and grow! How many times have you been irritated by bushes and even trees planted so close to a walk that you could scarcely pass? Herbs, too, spread. If they are not divided and thinned, they will soon take over more than their allotted space.

Pebbles and Stones

Farmers dig rocks out of their fields and vegetable gardeners sift the pebbles out of their seedbeds. But there is a place for both rocks and pebbles in a flower garden.

A big boulder looks charming surrounded by an irregularly shaped bed of perennial flowers. If your garden has a boulder, build the garden around it, and let some of the flowers snuggle up to the rock.

Use pebbles and small stones to edge a small garden pool. Larger rocks, just big enough to handle, make a fine edging for a garden path. You can whitewash them or leave them natural.

To solve the problem of a difficult corner of the yard or alongside the house where you can't get lawn to grow properly, arrange fairly flat stones over the area, with spaces in between them. Plant flowers in the spaces and you will have a beautiful spot that might otherwise be an eyesore.

Illus. 11. Areas that are in shade or have poor soil can be enhanced by interesting arrangements of flat stones, leaving spaces in between for small plants that thrive in such conditions.

Illus. 12. A garden such as in Illus. 10 would be ideal for adding a special touch right in the middle—a sun dial. Or plan your paths as shown here to lead right up to it, making it the focal point of your garden.

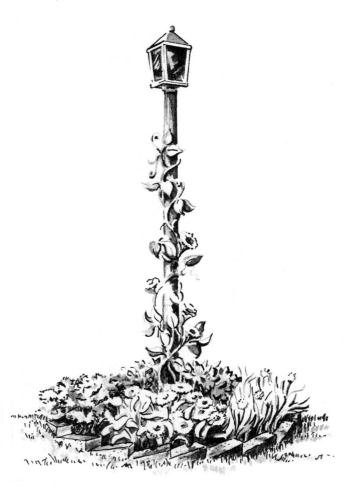

Illus. 13. A lamp post will allow you to enjoy your garden in the evening, too.

Added Touches

If you are short on planting space, or would like to display your plants in an interesting fashion, here are some attractive ideas. An old wheelbarrow will hold quite a few plants, and you can easily move it from sun to shade as the need arises. You may want to wheel it into your basement playroom when winter comes.

If you have a sun dial, a gazing ball or a small statue in your yard, plant a wheel of plants around it, leaving from two to four narrow paths leading up to the central object. This arrangement is particularly attractive with the beds edged with bricks or low fencing.

Do you have a lamp post in your yard? Day or night, it will show off your garden. Plant around the base of the light, then let an attractive climber use the pole.

Do not forget to use fences and walls. A walled garden has great charm. If you are fortunate enough to have one, plant in the crannies or at the base. A fence also provides a wonderful long space which you can line with pots.

Illus. 14. A traditional symbolic design for a formal garden. Other traditional designs are shown in Illus. 15 through Illus. 23.

A Formal Garden

You do not need to wear a 12th-century costume or sing madrigals to plan a formal garden! A simple design will add greatly to the beauty and interest of your plot.

Intricate knot gardens were made hundreds of years ago and became famous in the days of the Renaissance. They are supposed to have gotten their name from the gardeners' habit of taking designs from embroidery patterns. Geometric circles, curves and angles, interlocked rings and diamonds, crosses and ladders were used. Many of the designs were rich in religious or pagan symbolism.

Such elaborate mazes were laid out in the 1600's that on some large grounds, guards were stationed in towers to prevent guests from losing their way among hedges which grew more than head-high.

But do not make the mistake of thinking that "formal" need mean "intricate." A very simple design can be lovely. Here are a few, both formal and less formal, to help set your imagination to work.

Just what to plant in each area is entirely up to you. Look at the plans and choose the one which suits your taste and your space. Then, having bought your packets of seeds and checked as to available plants, decide what is to go where.

If you are planning a knot garden or one with a special design, you may not wish to plant it the first spring that you begin growing. It is a major project, and you will need plenty of time for carrying out your plan.

Illus. 15. Triquetra.

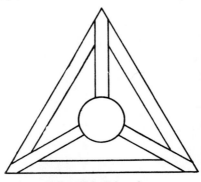

Illus. 16. Triangle.

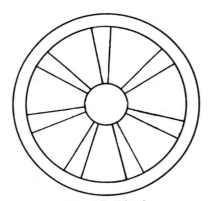

Illus. 17. Wheel.

Illus. 18. Tudor.

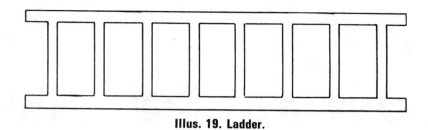

Illus. 19. Ladder.

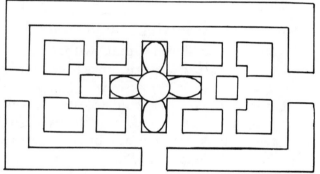

Illus. 20.

Variations of traditional gardens.

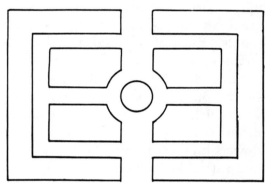

Illus. 21.

Illus. 22. Traditional knot garden.

Illus. 23. Traditional maze.

FLOWER PRESSING

You can preserve nature's plants and flowers by pressing the moisture out of them. Wherever you go in the country—in meadows, woods, along lakes or the banks of streams, by the sea, up hills or a mountain slope—you will find a great variety of flowers, grasses, leaves and plants. Even if you do not live near open country, your local florist can provide you with a large assortment of flowers and greenery. Once you begin selecting plants for pressing, you will notice many different kinds that you never really observed before. To turn your flowers into a permanent memory, use them for decoration in any number of places. The ideas here are just a few suggestions; once you learn the correct way to treat your flowers, you can use them on almost any surface you see!

If you gather the plants yourself, plan to do it in the middle of the morning or in the middle or late afternoon on dry, sunny days. Avoid collecting plants early in the morning when there is still dew on them and in wet weather. Flowers cut at high noon on a hot day wither very quickly.

Most important, select only the most perfect flowers. Choose those which have blossomed very recently so the leaves do not shed. Make sure that the stem, petals and leaves have not been damaged by insects.

Cut the flowers sharply with a knife or a pair of scissors and place them carefully into a plastic bag, then into a large basket, so you do not crush them on your way home. Never tear a plant out by the roots or injure nearby bushes or trees. And be sure to observe local laws and courtesies: never cut flowers in a national park, for example, or on private property.

Pressing and Preserving the Flowers

If you collect flowers that wither quite rapidly, or if you are quite a distance from home, prepare a collector's press so you can begin drying the flowers while you are still in the country. You need two pieces of sturdy cardboard, two lengths of ribbon, and blotting paper, newsprint or a newspaper. The press should be large enough to hold the cut plants, but not so big that it becomes a chore to carry. A popular size is 8″ × 12″.

Make four cuts into the corners of each piece of cardboard with a sharp pointed knife, and pull a ribbon through each set of four (see Illus. 1). Cut a piece of blotting paper the same dimensions as one cardboard and place it between the cardboard layers.

When you put the flowers inside the press, do not place them too close together. Arrange each flower carefully on the blotting paper so that no two flowers touch. The blossoms and leaves should lie flat, without any folds, curls, or creases.

Place flowers that are the same thickness next to each other so that they dry with the same amount of pressure. If flowers of different thicknesses lie side by side, they are not in even

Condensed from the book, "Flower Pressing" by Peter and Susanne Bauzen | © 1968 by Sterling Publishing Co., Inc., New York

contact with the blotting paper and cannot dry completely. If thick flowers prevent thin leaves from being pressed firmly against the blotting paper, the thin leaves will curl and discolor as they dry without pressure.

After you have covered the blotting paper with flowers, place a few sheets of newspaper on them. Then gather more flowers of uniform thickness and arrange them on this layer of newspaper. The important thing is to arrange the thinner, delicate flowers on one layer and the thicker, sturdier ones on another so the flowers dry evenly.

When you have gathered as many flowers as you want, tighten the ribbons of your hand-made flower press with enough pressure to start the drying process right away. At home, immediately add more newspaper between the layers of flowers. Place some heavy books on top of the press to increase the pressure, and after a few days, remove the books and replace the newspaper with fresh sheets. Try not to move any petals or leaves.

The time required to press the flowers varies with the type of flower, the temperature and humidity in the air, and the season of year. It is better to leave the flowers in the press too long, of course, rather than not long enough. Some flowers are sensitive to only a slight

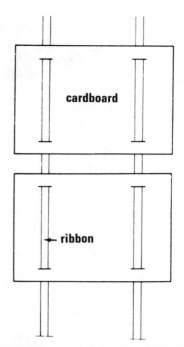

Illus. 1. A collector's press made of cardboard and ribbon should be your first piece of equipment for this craft. Take the press with you when you gather flowers.

touch when they are in a half-dried state, so control your curiosity and leave the flowers in the press as long as possible.

If you are pressing a flower with thin petals but a thick center—like a daisy—you have a problem: how do you apply enough pressure

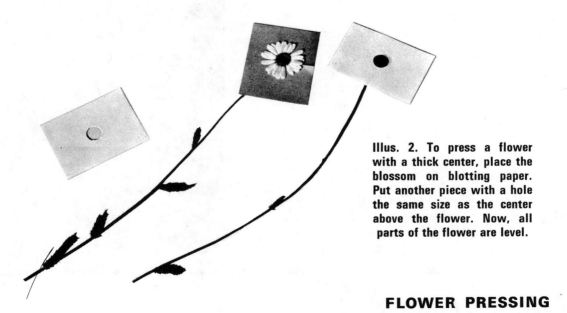

Illus. 2. To press a flower with a thick center, place the blossom on blotting paper. Put another piece with a hole the same size as the center above the flower. Now, all parts of the flower are level.

Illus. 3. To restore lost colors to pressed flowers, paint them with water colors.

to press the flowers as hard and long as possible —at least several days, and at best, several weeks.

After exposure to the air, some dried flowers lose their color and become transparent, or considerably faded compared to their original vibrant hues. The best and surest method to restore faded colors is to paint the plants with water colors after they have dried. On your first try, the water color may run off the dried plants without adhering at all. To avoid this, place a drop of dish detergent on your paint brush and mix the detergent with the water color. Then paint as usual. If a plant is particularly water-repellent, add more detergent so the water color adheres. After painting the natural colors back on the blossoms, stem and leaves, set the pressed flowers aside to dry in the open air. If you pressed them thoroughly,

to the delicate petals without crushing the center? Cut a hole about as big as the center of the daisy out of a piece of blotting paper, and place this holed piece on top of the flower. Add more holed blotting paper until the petal section of the flower is the same height as the center. Cover the entire set-up with a solid piece of blotting paper. When you apply the press and a heavy book, the pressure on all parts of the flower will be uniform.

Keeping the Flowers' Colors

Sometimes, in spite of your precautions, pressed plants turn brown, either during the drying process or after you remove them from the press. Usually these plants did not dry fast enough, and therefore they withered before all the moisture was drawn out of them. Be careful

Illus. 4. For both color and strength, glue pressed flowers to construction paper. Trim close to the flowers.

they will not absorb the paint's moisture, just the pigment.

If thin, fragile petals become transparent when dry, painting them restores their color but does not make them sturdier. So that you can handle fragile petals, glue the blossoms to a sheet of paper which is the same color as the petals. Put some clear all-purpose glue on the paper and gently lay the plant on top of it. Spread the glue under the flower with a pin or toothpick and lightly rub off any excess glue around the petals. After the glue dries, if you do not want any paper around the blossom, cut around it with a pair of sharp scissors, going into every fine line and division of the petals. The paper's color will show through the transparent dried blossom.

Plants under Glass
Plant Flowers on Your Wall

Now that you know how to press flowers, you may be wondering what to do with them. One of the simplest and prettiest projects you can make is a framed arrangement to hang on your wall. You need a piece of cardboard for the backing of the picture, a piece of construction paper the same size in an attractive color that either contrasts or harmonizes with the colors of the flowers, a pane of glass, and a picture frame. You also need the pressed flowers which you have chosen for the composition, and clear all-purpose glue for attaching them to the construction-paper background. If you want to make a realistic hanging, attach real butterfly wings and paper butterfly bodies.

Choose large flowers for a wall decoration so they show up across the room. Large flowers usually have thick, harder stems, however, and you must make these narrower before you glue them to the paper backing so the glass can lie flat on top of them. Carefully remove the back side of the stem with a single-edged razor blade or a sharp knife. When you lay the glass on top of the almost-flat arrangement, it lies evenly on the paper background.

Before you glue anything, place all the flowers on the paper and analyze the arrangement,

Illus. 5. This is a wall decoration made of pressed flowers and butterflies glued to paper, then covered with a sheet of glass.

both from close up and from a distance. Notice the color, size, texture and species of flowers as you arrange them, and add the butterflies to highlight the flowers.

To glue each piece to the paper, first put a few drops of glue behind the fattest part of the flower—most likely the stem or some thick leaves—and then draw some glue to the thinner areas with a pin or toothpick. When the glue has dried, check all pieces of the composition to see that they are firmly attached to the paper background.

There are several types of wire hooks to hold the glass, cardboard and construction paper together. Some grasp the layers at the top and have an extra loop for hanging from the wall, while others are made to hold the layers at the bottom to prevent them from slipping. If you want to frame the entire composition, you do not need these hooks. Take the mounted flowers to a professional framer or buy a picture frame and frame the composition yourself. Hooks for hanging are already on the backs of most frames.

Serving Trays

If you have a few pressed flowers that you want to use on a small project, a round serving tray might be just the thing. The glass surface is easy to clean, and the flowers under the glass

Illus. 6. This round serving tray was made from the lid of a large container.

add a decorative note to an ordinary household item.

There are several kinds of bases you might use for the tray. The lids of large tin containers are ideal, since they already have a "lip" of metal which seals the glass around the sides. If a metal lid is not available, use a round piece of plywood or board and add an extra piece of aluminum around the outside edge.

Attach a piece of heavy paper to the tray's base and glue the flowers to the paper. Remember that leaves, weeds, grasses and even seeds and roots can make just as attractive an arrangement as the colorful petals of a flower do. When the glue under the dried arrangement has set, carefully place the glass on top of the wood or metal circle. If the base already has a lip around the outside, put clear-drying glue which adheres to glass in the small space between the lip and the glass, to protect the flowers from moisture and to keep the glass from falling out. If there is no lip around the base, make one of a flexible metal and glue it to the base and glass.

You might prefer to use clear Plexiglas instead of glass; it is lighter than glass and less likely to break if dropped. Buy Plexiglas from a plastics supplier, who will cut it to the proper size, or cut it yourself with a fret saw after outlining the circle. If there are any ragged or

Illus. 7. Glue cloth over two pieces of cardboard. Then add flowers and plastic film for a book cover.

uneven edges, file them off with fine sandpaper. Use the Plexiglas just as you would glass: remember to add clear-drying glue in the space between the Plexiglas and the metal lip.

Pressed Flowers under Plastic Film

Suppose you have collected, pressed and dried a beautiful arrangement of flowers, but want to use the plants in a project that you can carry around with you? Even if you do not seal your flowers under glass, you can still protect them—just place transparent plastic film over the arrangement. The flowers are permanently fixed, the plastic is as clear as glass, and the project—no matter what it is—can be moved, carried, and used often.

Practice on small projects while you learn to work with plastic film, as it is sometimes tricky to manipulate. There are two kinds: plastic film that is self-adhesive, and plastic film that is not. The self-adhesive kind has two layers to it; one layer is the film itself, and the other layer is a backing which protects the film until it is peeled off. The second type of film requires a special solvent to make it stick, or sometimes a cool iron to melt the invisible backing substance. The craft supply shop where you buy the film will tell you what material you need to make that type of film adhere.

Book Cover

To protect the cover of your book as you carry it with you, make a floral book cover. Before you attach the flowers to the cloth you have chosen for the book cover, glue the cloth to two sheets of cardboard, and attach a narrow elastic strip at the top and bottom of each cardboard, which you will later slip over the book's covers.

Any arrangement of flowers looks attractive on a wide expanse of dark fabric; just be sure to place the flowers carefully. First glue the flowers to the fabric in a few main places. Now you are ready to attach the plastic film.

If you are using self-adhesive film, cut a piece about $\frac{1}{2}''$ larger all round than the book cover.

Carefully peel the backing layer from the film at one side only, and place the film on the cloth exactly where it belongs. Once the flowers touch the film, they are stuck there, so be careful not to touch the film to places it does not belong.

As you peel the backing away, smooth the film (from the middle to the edges) on the cloth with your hand or a rolled-up rag, to get rid of air pockets and to make the film as smooth as possible. Because air pockets are not uncommon even in small areas, avoid using plastic film on very large areas, as sometimes a bumpy, unattractive surface results.

One attractive way to finish your book cover is to punch holes around the outside edges (through the film also, of course) and sew with leather thongs or an attractive thread or yarn, using an overcast stitch. With a plastic film cover for protection, you can carry this book in any weather.

Flowered Stationery

For a gift or for yourself, hand-decorated stationery provides a delightful background for a greeting. And you can make the stationery in

Illus. 8. Neatly print guests' names on cards; then add flowers and cover with film.

any size—small, for note paper, or large, for long letters.

Place cards for a party always add a thoughtful touch that shows how well you planned. First ink in the names on plain white cards—any size is good, but 3″ × 2″ is standard. If you can make fancy lettering, this adds appeal to the cards, but of course even the plainest printing will be appreciated. When the ink is dry, attach the flowers in one corner of the card with clear-drying, all-purpose glue. Spread the glue along the thinner parts of the flower with a toothpick or pin, and set the cards aside to dry.

Since place cards are not handled too much—they are really made only to be admired—you may not want to cover the cards with plastic film. If you think your guests will want to keep their cards, however, attach some film over the front of the card. This project would be a good one to practice on using the second kind of film, the kind that needs either solvent or heat to adhere. Rub the solvent on the film for as long as the manufacturer directs, and then put the cards face down on the film. You can either trim the film along the edges of the card, or fold the film along the edges so it meets in the middle of the wrong side of the card. Press the film together so it sticks; then trim any extra.

Make greeting cards and writing paper in basically the same way: glue the flowers to the paper; then cover just the flowers with film. For a special touch on the front of a card, first attach flowers to a dark piece of paper and cover it all with film. Then glue this paper to a larger piece of white stock, folded in half. Birthday greetings, get-well wishes, or any sort of salutation go well on this card.

For a unique gift, make several sheets of decorated stationery and put them in a flower-covered box. Since the box will probably be used long after the stationery is gone, cover it carefully with heavy plastic film (see Illus. 9).

Illus. 9. Make a stationery assortment with a different flower on each sheet. Decorate the box top too!

Protecting Plants with Lacquer

For wooden objects which could use extra gloss as well as decorative flowers, transparent lacquer does double duty: it protects and fastens the flowers at the same time that it protects and adds shine to the wood. Some lacquers are waterproof when dry; this type would be appropriate for trays, the backs of hairbrushes or anything which might get wet.

When you buy wood for decorating with flowers and lacquer, look at the texture and grain. Try to find an attractive surface, but not so unusual that it detracts from the flowers. Smooth all parts of the wood with fine sandpaper or emery paper, then clean off the fine dust from the surface.

Apply a thin layer of lacquer to the wood with a brush, let it dry, and smooth the surface again with sandpaper. Be sure to keep your brush from hardening by keeping it in a jar of lacquer remover. Now apply a second coat of lacquer. Spread the flowers on the wet surface, and press them gently with the brush so they stay put. When this lacquer layer is dry, cover everything with another coat. If parts of the plant protrude from the wood surface, apply a thick coat of lacquer at those places so the flower does not peel or rub off.

Book Ends

For a pair of book ends for a den or study, cut two pieces of wood into identical shapes. Sand them smooth; then either screw or glue a piece of aluminum bent into a right angle to the bottom for a base (see Illus. 10). Glue some felt or foam rubber to the bottom of the aluminum to protect your furniture from scratches.

Now apply a coat of lacquer to the wood and let it dry. Sand it. Apply a second coat, and while it is still wet, gently place the flowers on top. Add a third coat to protect the flowers. Depending on the thickness of the wood, these book ends can support as much weight as any pair you might buy.

Illus. 10. Buy or make a pair of book ends. Using lacquer as glue, attach pressed flowers to the ends.

Jewelry of Flowers and Wood

Necklaces, pins and fancy hair ornaments are small, easy-to-make gift ideas that will be worn and appreciated for years to come. Buy the most beautifully grained wood you can find for this jewelry, and shape and sand it until it is attractive by itself. Attach small flowers with lacquer, as described above, and then attach jewelry "findings" to the back of the wood. Findings are the pins, clasps, loops, and hooks that turn the wood into a piece of jewelry. You can buy them at a craft or hobby shop.

Printing with Plants

Many plants and especially leaves can be used as stamps for printing. While they are usually not durable enough to print hundreds of copies, with care they can last through a dozen or so prints—enough for a box of

Illus. 11. Make a pendant or pin from a scrap piece of wood. Just attach the appropriate jewelry finding.

stationery or a motif on wrapping paper. Some fragile plants break or curl after only a few uses, but this just makes the successful prints more valuable.

Covering a Photo Album

Albums which hold family pictures are often in need of new covers, since frequent handling makes the old ones fall apart quickly. A simple and inexpensive way to cover an album—or any scrapbook or loosely bound volume—is to attach hand-decorated paper to the top of the old cover. In Illus. 12, the new cover is paper printed with a scattered design of a delicately grained leaf.

Choose a thick, durable paper cut to the proper size. For the album in Illus. 12, only a small amount of paper was needed, since the binding was covered with tape. Make a few test patterns with the leaf you plan to use to find out exactly how much ink or paint you should apply for the best results. Use either India ink or printer's ink. Give one side of the leaf an even coat of ink with a brush, and turn it over so the inked side is against the paper. Cover the leaf with some absorbent paper.

Illus. 12. Ink one side of a leaf and press it on paper. Use the paper for anything—perhaps to cover a photo album.

Using your hand or a rolled handkerchief, rub the paper and leaf with even strokes. Then remove the paper, and finally the leaf carefully.

If some parts of the leaf did not print as darkly as others on the paper, do *not* re-ink the leaf and attempt to place it on top of the first design. At best, you will produce a fuzzy double image, since it is almost impossible to place the leaf in exactly the right spot. To fill in a faint part of the print, dip a thin brush into the ink and carefully and lightly go over the spot on the paper.

When the paper is printed with the design you want, set it aside to dry for a few hours. Fold and trim it to fit around the covers of the album or book you are covering; then glue it in place. For greater protection, cover the paper with durable plastic film.

Now, you are on your own. See what other creative items you can think of to make with pressed flowers.

Illus. 13. With scrap paper as a backing, brush paint or ink on the pressed flowers.

Illus. 14. Quickly and evenly press the painted side of the flower to the paper. Lift it, and the pattern remains.

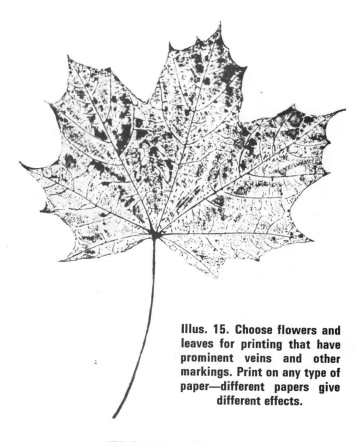

Illus. 15. Choose flowers and leaves for printing that have prominent veins and other markings. Print on any type of paper—different papers give different effects.

FOOD SCULPTURE

Apple Dolls

Faces carved from apples seem to have real personalities and look almost life-like. You can create all sorts of wrinkly-faced characters—Indians, pirates, pioneers, and so on. The special charm of carved-apple figures is that the older they get—that is, the longer you keep them—the more character they take on. The wrinkling process continues for years and years.

Peel the apple as smooth as possible and remove the stem. Use a small spoon to carve the features. Cut deep indentations for the eyes and mouth. The apple tends to shrink as it dries, so make the features slightly larger than the way you want them to look in the finished product. Carve a large nose, round off the forehead and put a few wrinkle lines into it. Carve ears also, if they will show when the doll is in costume.

Dip the apple in vinegar or lemon juice for a few minutes to prevent it from becoming discolored. Then set it in a warm place to dry.

To make the eyes, use beads or carpet tacks or small round-headed nails. Press the nails into the eye openings; as the apple shrinks, the skin forms eyelids round the nails.

Make sure the apple is completely dry before you begin to paint on the doll's features. Use real face make-up or tempera colors. Insert bits of rice or unpopped kernels of corn to form teeth.

Glue on cotton batting, fur or wool to form beards, moustaches, or doll hair.

A bottle can form a doll's body. Carve a hole in the apple so it fits over the top of the bottle. To make the head fit firmly, wrap the neck of the bottle with strips of cloth and then carefully glue the head in place.

Make costumes of doll clothes or crepe paper. Different bottles will suggest various costumes. For instance, a bell-shaped bottle can be dressed as a hoop skirt for a doll.

Cut out arms from cardboard and tape them on to the bottle before putting the clothes on.

Illus. 1. Carve the nose, deep slots for eyes and a mouth, and make cuts in the forehead for wrinkle lines.

Condensed from the book, "Festive Food Decoration" by Sheila Ostrander | © 1969 by Sterling Publishing Co., Inc., New York

Add tissue paper stuffing to fill out the clothes if they do not quite match the contours of the bottle.

Glue wooden legs to the bottom of the bottle if they are necessary to the costume. Make feet or shoes from soap, clay or wood and glue them to the legs or to the front edge of the bottom of the bottle.

And, remember, you can certainly carve all sorts of figurines or animal shapes that do not even need to be dressed!

Illus. 2. Here is another idea for a carved-apple doll you can make.

Nuts

The varied sizes and shapes of nuts suggest numerous appealing creatures and all sorts of animals. An entire nutty menagerie is a perfect decoration for an Autumn party.

Nut Squirrel

Glue a small chestnut on top of a large one. With scissors, cut a tail from a dried fruit, such as a date. Cut bits of dried apricot for ears, eyes, arms and feet, and glue them onto the nuts.

Illus. 3. Nut squirrel.

Peanut-Size Elephant

String together several peanuts to form the elephant's trunk. Attach them to a pecan or Brazil nut head. String together three more large nuts for the elephant's body and attach the head to them. Use a needle threaded with string to put the whole elephant together. Glue on four small peanuts for legs. Glue on round slices of marshmallow for ears. Draw on the eyes and glue on a short string tail.

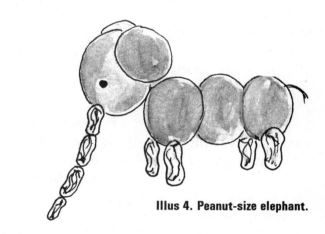

Illus 4. Peanut-size elephant.

Nut Bee

A chestnut in the shell is the bee's body. Two straight pins are its antennae. Glue tiny tomato seeds round the chestnut to create the design on the bee's body. Cut the wings out with scissors from flat slices of marshmallow. Pin or glue sliced marshmallow wings to the side of the nut.

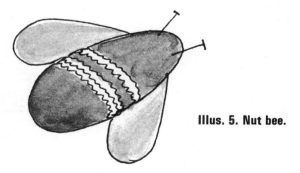

Illus. 5. Nut bee.

Nut Rabbit

Glue a small walnut to form the head on a large walnut. Glue on four pieces of matchsticks as the legs. A bit of peanut shell is the tail. Carve two long ears from a peanut shell and glue them in place. Draw on eyes and a nose. Make the rabbit from either unshelled walnuts or from shells that have been glued back together again.

Illus. 6. Nut rabbit.

Nutty Donkey

Use a long unshelled peanut to form the body of the donkey. His head is a Brazil nut or a large cashew nut. Use a nail to press a hole in both the peanut and the Brazil nut and then insert a part of a toothpick to hold the head to the body. Punch four more holes in the peanut and insert four slightly bent toothpicks as the donkey's legs. Glue on two long grains of rice as the donkey's ears. His eyes can be two caraway seeds.

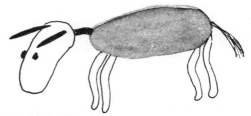

Illus. 7. Nutty donkey.

Nut Star

For a crunchy afternoon or evening snack, arrange 10 narrow stalks of celery of the same size in the shape of a 5-pointed star. Place the star on a platter and toothpick it together. Fill the star with assorted nuts.

Noodles and Spaghetti

Macaroni, spaghetti and noodles are all great for creating flat tableau pictures or unusual designs. For a trombone, for example, use a long piece of soft, cooked spaghetti. Wind it round twice in a long loop to form the tubing of the trombone. Make the bell part of the instrument from one side of a bow-tie-shaped noodle.

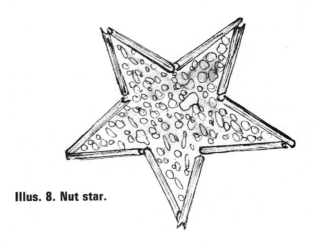

Illus. 8. Nut star.

Illus. 9. Spaghetti trombone.

CREATING WITH NATURE'S MATERIALS

Mother Nature provides an abundance of interesting forms, textures, colors, and lines which, with a bit of imagination, you can break, cut, tear, glue, tie, twist, bend, re-assemble, re-join, re-arrange, and re-unite into exciting compositions which reflect your moods, feelings, and ideas.

Look for interesting sea shells, various colors and grains of sand, unique pebbles, bits of seaweed and driftwood. Search for contrasting colors of bark with smooth and rough, light and dark surfaces. Locate fallen nuts and dried berries, leaves of various sizes, colors, and patterns, as well as pine cones and seeds of various shapes, sizes, and colors. You might incorporate an abandoned bird's nest, or parts of it, into a composition.

Hunt for cattails, smooth stones, fossils, and plant life, such as milk pods, dried Queen Anne's Lace, sand burrs. Investigate barns (with permission!) for wheat, barley, or red, white, and yellow corn. Choose enough examples of one kind of material, color, and texture so that you can repeat the use of it within a single design, thereby establishing continuity and rhythm. Search for light and dark materials for contrast.

Experiment with various kinds of glue such as casein, non-toxic model cement, and liquid cement to determine which adhesive secures the materials most effectively without leaving a messy film.

Various environments, seasons, holidays will suggest numerous avenues for expression as Nature's vast store of materials are found, fondled and re-formed by you.

Make a Sculpture

Just to show you how simply you can create with materials outside your back door, make a crossed-stick sculpture as shown in Illus. 1.

To begin, cross two long twigs and tie them together at the middle. Using different-colored thumb-tacks, tack long, reed-like grasses, such as cattail leaves to the sticks. Cut shorter grasses and attach them over the long pieces onto the sticks. Weave shorter grasses under and

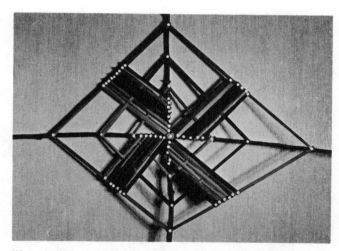

Illus. 1. This decorative wall hanging is made of two twigs and a number of cattail leaves which have been painted with tempera.

Condensed from the book, "Crafting with Nature's Materials" by Chester Jay Alkema | © 1972 by Sterling Publishing Co., Inc., New York

over the long pieces if you wish. Then, you can paint the leaves with tempera colors.

There, you have a unique mobile or wall hanging, all of your own making!

Collage

The French word *collage* literally means a pasting of paper. However, collage has developed way beyond that. A wide variety of materials can be applied to an equally wide variety of backgrounds.

One of the vital elements of a collage is texture, so when planning your collages, try to appeal to both sight and touch.

Illus. 3 is a combination mosaic and collage. Seed tesserae are combined with large pasted objects on a background of corrugated cardboard. This wild bird has a burdock head

Illus. 2. A Nature collage might be composed of white pine needles, beechnut leaves, tulip leaves and burdock to create a new breed of plant. Construction paper and white glue are the only man-made elements here.

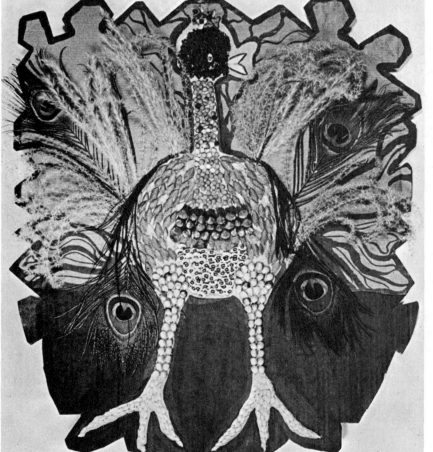

Illus. 3. Try combining a mosaic and a collage to create an unusual specimen such as this.

crowned with bittersweet. Pieces of pine cone, black-eyed peas, and wheat adorn the bird's breast, while Indian corn creates unique legs that end in popcorn feet. Dried weed fronds and peacock feathers fan out in all directions to form the rare creature's plumage. A soft-tip pen creates a heavy line design.

You will find corrugated cardboard excellent for backgrounds because it does not warp easily when objects are glued to its surface. However, as you can see in Illus. 2, plain construction paper is a perfectly adequate background material.

There are certain commercial liquids, such as Mod-Podge and Art Podge, that are ideal for adhering heavy objects, as well as acting as a preservative. These are new latex glazes that are milky white when wet, but dry perfectly clear. One coat, applied with a brush to the background, acts as sealer; the next coat acts as an adhesive to attach the object. Then a final coat, or a dipping of the objects into the liquid, dries to a heavy glaze almost like varnish. Each coat dries in about ten minutes.

These liquids are non-toxic and non-flammable, making them ideal for children to use. Besides, the brushes wash out in plain water, and spills merely disappear with a wipe of a damp cloth. An added advantage is that the liquids can be colored by adding tempera paints before using. Consult your local art supply shop owner for sources, in the event he does not carry them.

Illus. 4 (above). Evergreen twigs, green leaves, and various flowers were dipped into Mod-Podge and applied to wax paper. A piece of white tissue paper, brushed with Mod-Podge, was laid over the collage, sandwiching the materials in between. Natural light emphasizes the opaque natural forms, so if you make this kind of collage, display it in a window, as was done here.

Illus. 5. Plywood, painted with a mixture of India ink and shellac, forms a background for an interesting array of sumac, evergreen twigs, wild berries and foxtail weeds. Cellophane tape and tacks hold the materials to the wood.

Illus. 6. The Lord's Eye is one of the easiest patterns to weave. Here, cattails and branches are used. To add interest, paint the dried leaves with tempera.

Weaving

Nature provides a great variety of materials for weaving. One of the best is cattail leaves. These long, narrow leaves are tough and pliable when green, and can be painted with tempera when dried. Texture and pattern can be added to them with flower, weed, or plant stems. So let's start with a simple "Lord's Eye," as shown in Illus. 6.

The loom consists of two tree branches crossed over each other and tied together with string or cord. Beginning at the middle of the cross, tack the end of a long green cattail leaf to one of the branches.

Going in either a clockwise or a counterclockwise direction, wind the leaf once round the branch. Carry it over to the next branch and wrap it round once, and then go on to the next branch. Continue in this fashion until you are nearing the end of the leaf. Then take a fresh leaf and tack it and the first leaf to the nearest branch. Cut off any ends left over from the first leaf. Then proceed with the second leaf, working your way towards the ends of the branches, tacking and snipping as you go.

When you have reached a point where the design pleases you, stop.

Always be sure to use the freshest leaves possible so you won't be half-way through and have a brittle leaf suddenly break or crack. Set the Lord's Eye aside in a safe spot until the leaves have dried up. Then you can paint it with tempera paints in whatever color pattern you wish.

Illus. 8 shows an imaginative use of cardboard loom weaving. Here, a piece of corrugated cardboard is used as a foundation. (You might want to color it before you begin.) Cut evenly spaced notches along opposite sides of the loom. Notch 1 is on one side at the top. Notch 2 is directly opposite it, and Notch 3 is under Notch 2 on the same side. Then Notch 4 is under Notch 1 and Notch 5 is under Notch 4, and so on.

Now, lace string, cord, or yarn into the notches, moving across the cardboard, from Notch 1 to Notch 2, down to Notch 3 and back to Notch 4 and then 5. Then back across and

Illus. 7. This loom, shown in color in Illus. G2, was constructed from a milk carton.

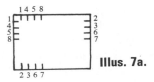

Illus. 7a.

Illus. 8. Nature weaving on a cardboard loom.

back again until you have filled all the notches. Once threaded, you can weave all kinds of materials from Nature in and out. Illus. 8 has pine needles, geraniums, twigs, green leaves, wheat, berries on twigs, all woven round the cord.

If you want to create a three-dimensional woven cube, use a milk carton, preferably half-gallon or gallon, for a loom such as in Illus. 7. Illus. 7a shows the threading procedure. Cut off the top of the carton and make evenly spaced notches along the top rim as shown. Insert cord into Notch 1. Carry it down the outside of the carton, across the bottom, and up the opposite side to Notch 2, back through Notch 3, and down again on the outside to Notch 4, and so on. When these two sides have been completed, start on the other two sides in exactly the same way. Then begin weaving your Nature's materials into the cord.

If you choose a cylindrically shaped carton (Illus. 9) to create a woven article, you thread a little differently, as you can see in Illus. 9a. Here the threading procedure is in a counter-clockwise direction. Illus. 9 has a vertical red-twine warp with leaves from a sugar maple, evergreen branches and twigs from a berry bush woven in.

Illus. 9. Weaving on a cylindrically shaped carton.

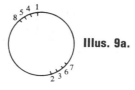

Illus. 9a.

Illus. 10. Here is an unusual Christmas tree you can make. Use the kind of glue sold for laying linoleum, and adhere the cones to a cardboard backing (paint them first, if you wish). Decorate the middle of the tree with sliced cones and add tiny tree ornaments on the tips of the "branches."

Pine-Cone Sculpture

Pine cones, whether used by themselves or with other materials from Nature, are bound to stir your imagination as you explore some possibilities of three-dimensional sculpture. Pine cones can be used whole, or sawed into slices, or broken, or dissected into flakes. No matter what you do with them, they will provide you with innumerable ideas of your own.

Be sure to pick up a great variety of pine cones of various sizes when you are exploring in the woods for material. Look for long, slender ones, fat ones, big and little. You'll be surprised at the range of differences in pine cones—something you may never have noticed before. Let the cones themselves suggest ideas to you.

Wood Sculpture

You can create remarkable sculptures with wood without a single bit of carving. In fact, sculpting from Nature should, whenever possible, be done without artificial means. The secret is to keep your eyes open and really look for all the possibilities in odd pieces of driftwood or dried-out branches of fallen trees. Naturally, once in a while, a piece will require a little carving here and there with a jack-knife to enhance its natural qualities, but if you can, avoid doing so as much as possible. When you find a piece of wood, study it from all angles, and you'll discover it has many suggestions of its own to offer.

Illus. 11. A pine-cone bee with milkweed-pod wings crawls along a branch. Thin florist's wire holds the wings onto the body.

Illus. 12. Here is an example of the beautiful forms that dried wood can take without any help from a carving knife. This is a branch from a Manzanita tree glued onto a walnut wood background, which is painted black. Other materials, including Spanish moss, lupine shells, and "bunny tails," have been added.

Rock Sculpture

You can combine rocks or add other materials onto rocks to form intriguing rock sculptures. The fascinating group in Illus. 14 includes, from left to right, a duck, a beaver, a dog, a man, and a giraffe!

The duck has a tail and body feathers made from pheasant feathers. Enamel highlights his features. The beaver sports a long tail made from a corn-husk, and he has seed eyes. In front of the beaver is a long-bodied dog with a pussy-willow tail and stone legs, head, and ears.

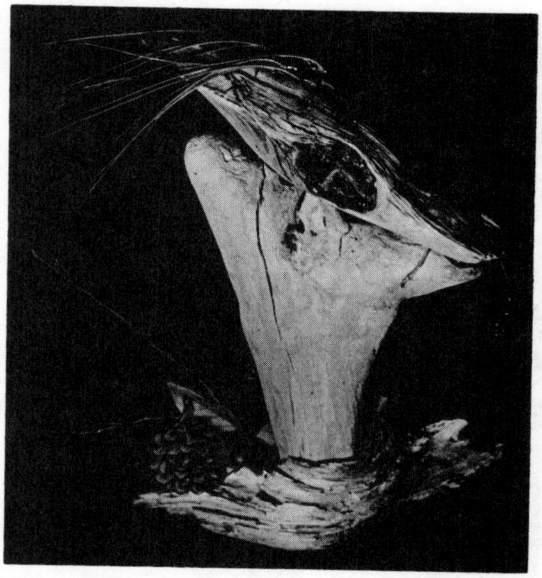

Illus. 13. "A Petrified Woodpecker" is the title of this work. Three different pieces of driftwood of varying forms and texture form the head, body and base. Leaves, berries, and pine needles are attached with epoxy cement.

The stone man has an acorn hat and milkweed-fluff hair. Berry eyes, a corn-kernel nose, pod ears, and a reed mouth are complemented by enamel-painted beard, moustache and eyebrows. His tall companion on the right is composed of three stones with fluffy milkweed decorations.

Illus. 15. A piece of soft driftwood had its outline emphasized with a jack-knife to bring out its owl-like character. Large, round, painted eyes and a triangular beak were the final touches. When the paint was dry, shellac was added for protection.

Illus. 14. You will have hours of enjoyment creating an array of rock-sculptured figures such as this one. Plan to decorate your sculptures with a variety of different materials and paints.

CREATING WITH NATURE'S MATERIALS ■ 111

Illus. 16. Sculptural bouquets might be arranged in a variety of different basic shapes—circular, triangular, square, rectangular, or oval. This composition is decidedly based on an oval, as you can see. You will find that the nature of the plants you collect will very often determine the kind of arrangement you choose. This bouquet includes wheat, milkweed pods, the money tree and berries.

Weed and Plant Sculpture

There is really no end to the possibilities of creating with dried weeds and plants. For any Nature lover, they provide the ideal means of bringing the out-of-doors into the home all year round, but do not require any care such as do house plants and fresh flowers. In addition, if you are fond of having bouquets and plants around you, you can easily simulate fresh flower arrangements, using a variety of materials.

However, bouquets, centerpieces and other flower arrangements are just a few of the many sculptural forms you will be able to create. Why not try making mobiles, large and small, all using a number of the tremendous wealth of materials offered by Nature? You'll not only enjoy creating them to please your own taste and need, but they will provide endless enjoyment wherever you might hang them.

Hang your mobiles from a string or light cord, such as nylon, from the ceiling. From this, you can suspend the top-most horizontal supports of the mobile. Almost any of Nature's light-weight materials can be used in mobiles. The lighter the better, so that every little air current causes a movement. Try to place your mobiles near doors or windows.

Illus. 17. This delicate mobile is hung from a horizontal support made of pussy-willow twigs woven together. Bunches of dried flowers are tied together in cross formations and hung on both ends of the support. In the middle is a central cluster of pussy willows also in the shape of a cross.

Sand-Casting

If you want, you can cast with plaster of Paris. Illus. 19 shows some examples of plaster casting.

First, fill a large tub or pail with beach sand (or from the playbox), and dampen it so it becomes firm. Then press the object of your choice into the sand as shown in Illus. 18.

Remove the object from the sand—the imprint is what you want.

To prepare the plaster of Paris, pour dry plaster into a basin so that the powder forms a mountain. Next, add water until the water level reaches the peak of the "mountain." Stir plaster and water together until smooth and creamy. Pour the liquid plaster into your sand impressions. Allow to dry and you will find your castings have beautifully re-created the natural materials, having every rough spot and nuance of the original.

Illus. 19 shows some attractive examples of plaster casting. Here, in each one, a round bowl-like shape was hollowed out in the sand, and pine cones, sticks, cattails and milkwood pods were pressed into the walls of the valley. Then a small amount of mixed plaster of Paris was poured slowly into the middle of the valley by tipping the pail. The rest of the plaster was poured slowly round the sides and a spoon used

Illus. 18. A pine cone and a mushroom are being pressed into the sand in preparation for the casting process.

to spread the wet plaster along the edges until it set.

The procedure—pouring and spreading—is excellent for creating hollowed-out forms such as a bowl or mask.

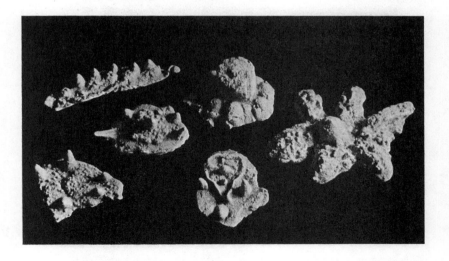

Illus. 19. Rocks, stems, sticks, mushrooms, pine cones, and milkweed pods created these exotic plaster-of-Paris castings.

NATURECRAFT

Naturecraft is a broad field which encompasses a wide variety of subjects and projects. As a naturecrafter, you can plant your own garden—indoors or out—you can observe the beauty of nature and be inspired to duplicate its magnificence, or you can simply enjoy the great outdoors as a huge, exhilarating playground. The projects and games in this section are only a start. See what new ideas you can come up with yourself.

Vegetable House Plants

During the winter, when it is too cold to plant outside, you can raise vegetable plants and have a bit of greenery in your room.

Vegetables that are really tubers or roots are the easiest to raise. Take a sweet potato and put it, narrow end pointing downwards, in a jar of water in a fairly dark place. Soon roots begin to appear. Be sure to add water to the jar because it gets used up.

In about two weeks, little sprouts appear on the upper surface of the potato. Take the jar to a sunny spot. The sprouts grow into vines, and in a short time you have a lovely plant. You can leave the plant in the jar of water or transplant it into a pot with humus and soil.

Carrots and beets are also attractive as house plants. Cut the old leaves off a full-grown carrot and beet. Cut about 2″ off the top of each vegetable. (The top is the part with the leaves.) Set them in a dish or bowl with cut part up. Put pebbles, sand or stones around the vegetables until they are anchored in tightly, but do not cover the tops. Keep your bowl watered. In a short time, leaves will begin to sprout from the carrot and beet. The carrot plant will have fine lacy leaves. The beet plant will have green leaves with deep red veins.

You can plant other vegetables and fruits in the regular fashion, by seeds. Try avocado, orange, lemon, grapefruit and other seeds. Plant them and see what happens!

Illus. 1. Plant a seed in a glass.

See How Seeds Actually Grow

Here is a simple experiment you can perform to watch a seed develop into a little plant.

Take a sheet of clean blotting paper or a small sponge. Put the paper or sponge in a drinking glass so that it is pressing against one side of the glass. Fill the other side of the glass with gravel or sand. This should press the blotting paper or sponge tightly against the glass.

Get some fast-growing seeds like lima beans. Force them between the blotting paper and the glass. They should press tightly against the glass so that you can see them through the glass. If the seeds do not stay in place, you do

Condensed from the books, "Herb Magic and Garden Craft" by Louise Evans Doole | © 1972 by Sterling Publishing Co., Inc., New York, "101 Best Nature Games and Projects" by Lillian and Godfrey Frankel | © 1959 by Sterling Publishing Co., Inc., New York, and "101 Camping-Out Ideas and Activities" by Bruno Knobel | © 1961 by Sterling Publishing Co., Inc., New York

not have enough sand or gravel in your glass, as its purpose is to keep the seeds in place.

Keep the blotting paper or sponge moist. In a few days, the seeds sprout roots. These are called root hairs. They help absorb food for the plant. After the roots become longer, carefully transfer your seeds to a dirt-filled flower-pot or even the garden—if it is warm enough. You have a little bean plant. Just think how well you know this particular plant!

Leafcraft
Autumn Leaf Collection

Often in Autumn, you hike through the woods and see the trees in their fullest glory. The yellow, flaming red, scarlet and orange of the leaves transform the woods and roadside into a blaze of beauty. Soon the wind blows these lovely leaves away. But you can save some, and have them to look at during the winter.

Take an old magazine or large book with you when you look for leaves. As you walk along, collect the leaves you want and put them flat between the pages. Take care not to put all in the center of the page or in the same spot because they make a big bulge and may fall out.

When you get home, pick out the most perfect specimens. Those with the most vivid hues and those that do not have insect holes or webs on them are most desirable.

Arrange the leaves you chose in the pages of the magazine or book so that they are smooth and put a weight of about 15 pounds (about a stone) on top of the book. Keep it there for about five days, and your leaves will get pressed so you can mount them, or frame them, or file them.

Waxed Autumn Leaves

You may want to display your selected and pressed autumn leaves. Waxing them helps preserve the hues and also gives the leaves more body.

Rub some paraffin wax or a candle on the

Illus. 2. Waxed leaves.

ironing surface of a warm (not hot) electric iron. Then carefully press each side of the leaf with the iron. Or, pour some liquid floor wax in a flat dish, dip each leaf into it, and hang it up to dry.

For display, place the waxed leaves on heavy cardboard in an arrangement that seems interesting. Cover them with glass and put the display in a picture frame.

If you prefer, attach the leaves to your window-pane with cellophane tape. As the light comes through the glass, the leaves take on somewhat the same coloration and quality they had when you first saw them on the trees.

Crayon Prints

Collect live (not dried) leaves from different trees and arrange them on a flat table in a pattern that pleases you. Cover the leaves with

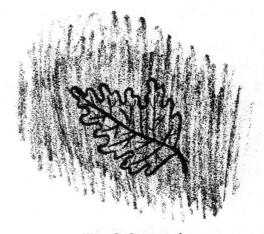

Illus. 3. Crayon print.

a sheet of white paper. Perhaps a piece of typing paper is just the right size.

Hold down the paper over the leaves, and rub with a crayon where you see the outline of a leaf beneath the paper.

The edges and veins of the leaves appear like magic on the paper. These crayon prints have a delicate and lovely effect. Try the same thing with several colors of crayons on different sheets of paper—and perhaps a combination of colors on the same sheet with the same or different leaves. For a hazy-looking pattern, peel the crayon paper off and use the side of the crayon to rub on larger areas.

Use your crayon prints for wrapping paper or drawer linings. Frame your best prints and hang them on the wall, if you like.

Illus. 4. Make a leaf person with leaves, pipe cleaners, and an acorn.

Leaf People

Have you ever tried to make little people out of leaves? All you need are leaves, pipe cleaners and crayons. Use leaves that are not too dry and brittle to handle.

First, make a little pipe-cleaner figure and then paste on some leaves as clothes. Two large leaves make a nice billowy skirt; thin leaves make good trouser legs for a boy. For a cap, break the cap off an acorn and glue it to your little leaf person's head.

If you do not have pipe cleaners handy, you can paste your leaves on a sheet of paper and draw in the rest of the figure with crayons. You'll be surprised at the clever figures you can make once you get started.

Illus. 5. Leaf blue-print.

Blue-Prints of Leaves

An interesting way to keep records of leaves is to make blue-prints of them.

Buy blue-print paper in various sizes in photographic or art supply shops. Keep the blue-print paper in its light-proof envelope until you use it. Get a piece of glass the size of the blue-print paper. If the glass has sharp edges, bind them with masking tape so there is no chance of cutting yourself.

Take the leaves, the blue-print paper and the glass into a darkened room (with dark shades pulled down). Take the paper out. Put the leaf on the coated side of the paper. Cover it with the glass, and carry it over to the window. Raise the shade and let the sunlight fall on the leaf until the paper changes to a grey color. Take the paper out and put it face down in a shallow pan of water. Keep it there for about 10 minutes or until the background turns a light blue. Blot the wet paper between several sheets of clean newspaper.

A white leaf print appears against a blue background. Make a design using blue-prints of different kinds of leaves. After you become expert at making blue-prints, try a montage of many leaves of one type or different types of leaves together in an interesting arrangement.

Spatter Prints

Leaves, or flowers and other plants, make beautiful designs for spatter prints. You need a piece of wire screening about 8 inches square, some water colors, an old toothbrush, paper for your prints, and leaves or other plants.

Cover a table with newspapers. Put about $\frac{1}{2}''$ of each color paint you choose in a pan or small dish in the middle of the table. Arrange your plants or leaves on a clean sheet of paper, white or colored. Pin them down carefully. Dip your toothbrush in the paint, but do not take too much paint. Keep your brush almost dry, because that makes a much finer spatter. Too much paint results in heavy, uneven blobs.

Hold the screen a few inches above the paper and rub the brush back and forth across the screen so the paint spatters your leaf and the paper lightly. If you use several colors, let each color dry before you spatter on the next. Then they won't get mixed together. Let the paper dry before you remove your leaf or plant.

The area the leaf covered has a clean, colorless outline surrounded by the spattered colors.

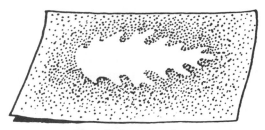

Illus. 6. Spatter print.

You can also make reverse spatter prints in which the object itself is colored and the background white. Place your leaf or flower on a sheet of paper and outline the part you will use. Carefully cut it out with a scissors. Do this with several leaves or flowers.

Take the cut-outs and lay them on some newspaper. Use your spatter paint, covering all the cut-outs. After the paint is dry, pick up the spattered cut-out leaves and mount them on white paper.

With reverse spatter prints, it is interesting to use colored paper for the cut-outs and white paint—or white and black paints—for the spatter.

Illus. 7. Plaster cast of a flower.

Plaster Casts

It is fun to make plaster casts of leaves, twigs, flowers, insects and even animal tracks. For this, you need modelling or potter's clay and some plaster of Paris. You get these at a hardware store; they are not expensive.

First, take your clay and roll it out with your hands into a sheet about $\frac{1}{4}''$ to $\frac{1}{2}''$ thick. Make the sheet of clay big enough for the object you want to cast. Press a flower (or any other object) deeply into the clay with the flat side of a smooth glass and take away the excess clay, leaving a border of about 1". Carefully remove your flower.

Using strips of cardboard, make walls about 2" high all round the clay. Clip or pin the ends of the cardboard walls together, and press the walls into the clay so they stand upright.

Look carefully at your print or impression as it is on the clay, and the border you want to include in the cast. Try to determine how much plaster you will need to cover it for a cast about $\frac{3}{4}''$ thick. It is difficult to judge the amount needed, but you learn with experience.

Fill a dish with what you think will be enough plaster of Paris. Take a wide-mouthed tin can, and a stick to stir your mixture.

Put some water in the tin can first. Slowly shake some of the plaster of Paris from the dish into the water. Let it sink to the bottom. When it doesn't sink any more, you have enough for that amount of water. Stir the mixture with a

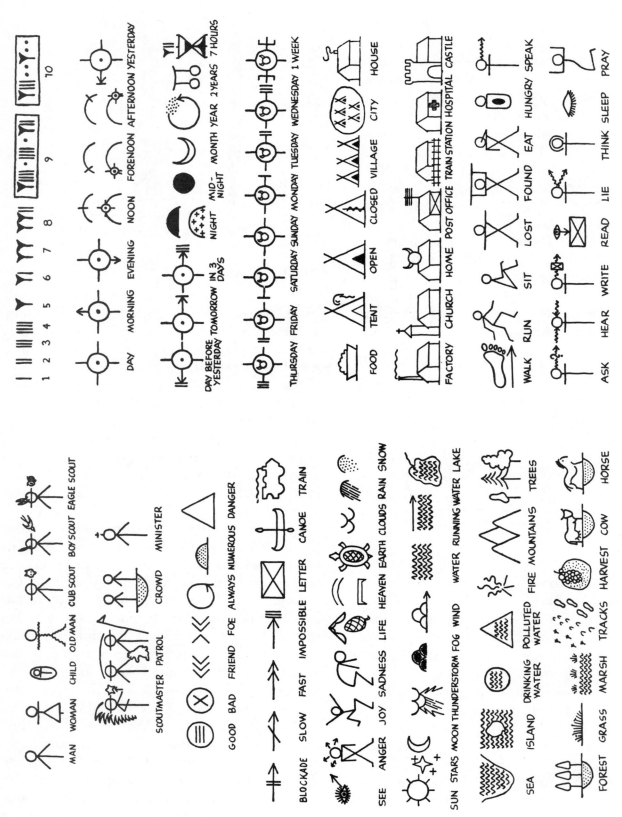

Illus. 8. Examples of picture writing symbols.

clean stick until it is as thick as pancake batter. Keep adding water and plaster until you have enough. Pour the mixture onto the clay impression. If the plaster does not cover, quickly make some more. Leave it alone (once the clay is covered) until it is hard, at least an hour. Remove the wall and the soft clay and you have your cast. The figure will be raised or "in relief."

For an indented cast, start with the relief cast and rub vaseline or grease on it. Build a cardboard wall around it, and pour the wet plaster onto the cast. When it is dry, remove the walls and pry the two casts apart with a table knife or other safe but sharp instrument.

The Message on the Birch-Bark

The Indians, as we know from all the tales about them, drew their messages on strips of birch-bark. There is no need to be that authentic, and it is far better today to leave the birch-bark on the birch trees. Strips of brown wrapping paper serve as well. Carefully singe the edges with a candle, and the paper will look positively ancient. After all, the important thing is the message, not what it is written on.

Birch-Bark Strips

Illus. 9 and 10 show what Indian birch-bark strips looked like. The pictures drawn on them tell stories about the life of an Indian. Since you have not had any practice in reading these picture stories, there is a short text added to each picture.

Picture Writing

Unless you can draw fairly well, this kind of birch-bark picture story is difficult for you. Instead, you and your friends can make up a picture alphabet. Of course, the meaning will be known only to you insiders. Choose signs that are easy to learn, as illustrated by the examples given in Illus. 8.

Invisible Inks

Write clever messages and have a lot of fun using a secret ink only you and your friends know how to make visible.

Use only harmless solutions for your ink. On the trail, always carry your bottles and writing materials with you so they are handy.

Writing with secret ink so that outsiders cannot read your message is not as simple as you might assume. Writing with a sharp penpoint is not as secret as you wish, for the point

Illus. 9.

Illus. 10.

scratches the paper slightly with every stroke. Even if the scratches are not visible to the naked eye, they can be seen with a magnifying glass.

Therefore you should use a smooth, broad penpoint. However, this also has a drawback. The writing fluid leaves a slight shine on the paper. If the strokes are too wide, the writing will be perfectly legible when the sheet is held at an angle to the light.

The most suitable writing tool is a soft stick of wood sharpened to a point. Or, use a toothpick.

Write on light-colored paper that is not too thin, because thin paper wrinkles where it has been moistened. This wrinkling can betray the presence of invisible writing and even make it legible. The best thing is a solid, hard-surface paper. Cautious writers never use blank sheets for their messages. Instead, they write some message with regular ink or pencil which will confuse the outsiders. They write the really important message between the lines with invisible ink. This diverts the attention of anyone not in on the secret from any possible traces of the dried invisible ink.

Combining the invisible ink with the normal writing is really clever. Write a regular message that is confusing or meaningless. Using invisible ink, cross out some letters in the false message or put a dot over or under these letters in a way to make them spell out the important message.

Natural Formulas for Invisible Inks

Make your invisible ink out of any one of the following liquids:

    onion juice
    lemon juice
    salt water
    sugar and water
    milk thinned slightly with water
    water in which egg-shells have been soaked
      for a few days.

After these fluids dry, they are invisible.

To make the writing re-appear, carefully warm the sheet by holding the written side over a flame. Lo and behold!—the writing is visible in a faint brown color.

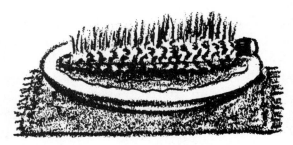

Illus. 11. Growing grass on a corncob.

Growing on a Corncob

Believe it or not, you can grow a patch of grass on a corncob which has been eaten or scraped clean of kernels.

Lay the corncob in a shallow dish and half fill the dish with water. If the cob is dried, fill the dish full and allow a few hours for the water to soak up. Then, sprinkle grass seed generously over the cob. The little pockets which held the kernels will hold the seed. Add water to the dish daily, and in about a week's time the grass will begin to grow. You can let it grow naturally, or trim it smooth or into shapes.

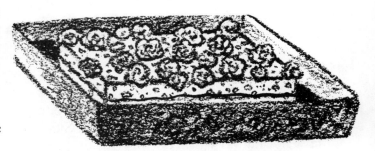

Illus. 12. Growing lettuce on a sponge.

Lettuce on a Sponge

Place a sponge in a shallow dish of water. Any kind of sponge will do—rubber, cellulose or plastic. Sprinkle lettuce seed over the top and pat it down. Put the saucer in a warm place and keep the sponge wet. Soon you will have pretty little rosettes of lettuce growing right out of the sponge!

TOLE PAINTING

Tole painting is a folk art that has been enjoyed by most nationalities for hundreds of years. "Tole" in French means "tin," and the French first applied painted designs to tinware only. Germans used this art on wooden furniture, doors, even floors and walls. Scandinavians preferred to liven up household goods with colorful flowers and called their art "rosemahling." The Japanese lacquered metal heavily before applying designs, and their work is sometimes known as "japanning." American settlers brought their art from the old country and borrowed ideas from settlers of other nationalities. Historians call this work American Folk Art.

Although different techniques and designs developed in various countries, all folk art has one thing in common. The "basic stroke," a simple pressure and release motion, creates all the designs. Today, paintings based upon the basic stroke are usually referred to as "tole painting." But the artist may apply a Scandinavian rose with German style leaves to an Early American tray that has been japanned! The result, of course, is a much more decorative art than that of our forefathers.

Although modern tole painters blend techniques and apply their art to any wood or metal object, tole painting still remains a folk art. You do not need any special talent—just master the basic stroke and invest in a few tole painting supplies. This is what you need:

Artists' Oils. Begin with small tubes of high quality artists' oils in lemon yellow, burnt umber, yellow-green, permanent light green and white. These colors will see you through the first project. You need additional colors for later projects, and you may want to experiment with colors of your choice.

Keep the tubes capped to prevent drying. Loosen stubborn caps by holding a match beneath them.

Water-Color Brushes. The most important tole painting brush is a red sable round-tipped water-color brush, usually a #6. Use it for the basic stroke. A #2 round-tipped brush, called a "liner," makes stems and decorative accents. A third brush, a #5 flat-tipped water-color brush, is handy for wiping off occasional mistakes and creating special effects.

As with artists' oils, high quality brushes are recommended. The bristles of low quality brushes may spread or, worse yet, fall out in the middle of a stroke! Good brushes last for years with proper care. After painting, clean your brushes in turpentine; then rinse them with soap and water. Round-tipped brushes should be shaped into a point while wet. Store with the bristles up.

Turps, Knife and Palette. Use gum spirits turpentine, or "turps," not only to clean the brush when you are finished, but also to clean the brush whenever you change colors.

You need a palette and palette knife to mix the artists' oils. Paper palettes are easy to handle because you can discard each sheet, saving the fuss of clean-up. Palette knives are made with either straight or crooked handles.

Condensed from the book, "Tole Painting" by B. Kay Fraser | © 1971 by Sterling Publishing Co., Inc., New York

Try each style in your hand, and select the one that "feels" best to you.

Odds and Ends. A satin finish interior varnish mixed with artists' oil makes paint flow more easily and dry more quickly. Avoid varnishes containing plastic because they "yellow" the paint in time. Small baby-food and mustard jars are a good size to hold the turps when you tole paint. Use their lids to hold the small amount of varnish you need during each painting session. Paper towels or facial tissues are much easier to use for clean-up than rags.

Transferring a Pattern

With practice, you will be able to paint your designs freehand. However, it may be easier at first to rely on patterns. Draw or copy your design on tracing paper. Use masking tape to place the tracing paper, which you now cover with your pattern, exactly where you want it to be on the object. Then slip a piece of graphite paper—available at art shops—between the pattern and the object. Trace the lines of the pattern with a pencil. And presto, you have transferred the pattern to your object.

Do not bother tracing small flowers and decorative accents. Keep the pattern handy while tole painting and add these smaller items freehand.

A Daisy Project

Because the basic stroke looks just like a perfect flower petal, you can easily make a circle of basic strokes to form a daisy. Indeed, the only problem is deciding what to paint daisies on. For your first project, use something inexpensive, such as a plain pine or fir board, recipe box, tray, watering can or big wooden spoon. Remember that you can use anything made of wood or metal.

Before you paint daisies on the selected item, give the object a base coat. The base coat serves as the background color for your design. Choose an attractive color in a satin finish enamel. You might varnish a wooden

object for a natural look rather than paint it with a color.

It is easiest to paint the basic stroke on a smooth surface. To smooth wood, seal the surface with wood sealer; when dry, sand with steel wool, and then paint on a base coat of varnish or enamel. Smooth metal by sanding or brushing it, then covering with a rust-retardant paint, and finally adding the base coat. Set your chosen object aside to dry while you practice the basic stroke.

The Basic Stroke

Once you learn the basic stroke, you will recognize it on everything from yesterday's painted antiques to today's paper cups. Before you try the stroke, mix the artists' oil and varnish to a "whipped cream" consistency. Squeeze an inch of white oil on the palette. Add an equal amount of varnish, and mash the two together with the palette knife until they are mixed. The mixture should form peaks like whipped cream when you poke them with the tip of the palette knife.

Because varnishes vary in thickness, the one to one ratio of oil and varnish may not always work. If your mixture is too thin, add more oil; if too thick, add varnish.

Now load the #6 round-tipped brush with this mixture. Gently dip and roll the brush in the paint—do not jab it. The bristles should be evenly coated with color.

Hold the brush like a child who is first learning to hold a pencil—low and tight. Using the palette paper for your practice strokes, steady your hand on the paper with your little finger. Begin the stroke by pushing down on the brush (Illus. 1). Pull the brush towards you, gradually decreasing pressure (Illus. 2). As you decrease the pressure, lift upwards, so that the stroke ends itself with a tapered tail (Illus. 3). Note how your little finger acts as a pivot point.

After two or three practice strokes, re-load the brush. If the bristles become too heavily coated with paint, wipe them clean with a tissue paper and re-load. Clean the brush in turps only when you change colors or when you are through painting.

After your strokes begin to take shape and form tiny ridges of paint along the edges, try color blending. Add yellow oil to the palette and mix it with varnish. After loading the brush with white, dip the tip of the brush in yellow. The yellow mingles softly into the white as you make the basic stroke—creating a flower petal as lovely as Nature's own.

Try color blending yellow-green and permanent light green for a realistic leaf.

By now, you will notice that your basic stroke varies, depending upon how much pressure you apply to the brush, and when you apply that pressure. Your pressure on the brush determines whether the stroke will be long, short, wide or thin, and whether the tail will be pointed or blunt. You may pull the brush straight or swing it gently to the right or left. Try duplicating the variety of strokes shown in Illus. 4.

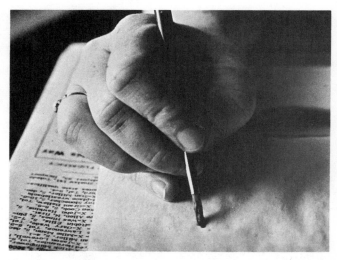

Illus. 1. When you make the basic stroke, hold the brush tightly near the bristles. Push down on the painting surface.

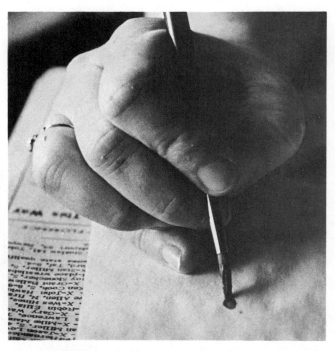

Illus. 2. Pull the brush towards your body as you decrease the pressure on the painting surface.

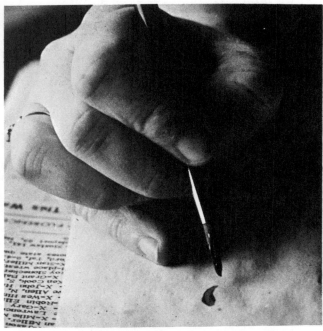

Illus. 3. Quickly lift the brush off the surface while you pull it towards you. This gives the brush stroke a little tail.

Like the practice strokes, daisy petals may be short, fat, long, thin—whatever pleases your eye. The petals may be plain white or tipped with yellow. Turn the object upside-down and sideways to reach a particular petal. If a petal is not satisfactory, simply moisten the flat-tipped brush with turps, wipe off the petal, and start over.

Next, paint the leaves. A basic-stroke leaf of blended yellow-green and permanent light green looks lovely. Or, make a larger leaf by first making a stroke in permanent light green. Then make another stroke right next to the first in yellow-green. Start the yellow-green stroke a bit higher than the first stroke to give the leaf a "tip," as in Illus. 5.

Illus. 6. Thin lines of burnt umber separate the daisy centers from the petals by adding depth.

Illus. 4. Turn the basic stroke in different directions for a variety of effects.

Make daisy centers by placing a little mound of yellow in the middle of the flower. Push this into a round or oblong shape with the brush tip. Finally, poke the paint with the brush tip to create little peaks (Illus. 5).

The last step is to add depth and stems with burnt umber. Using the #2 round-tipped brush, the "liner," make a half-circle of burnt umber dots around the daisy center (Illus. 6). This adds depth. Stems, which are merely squiggles or lines of burnt umber, also require the liner. When making stems, you may wish to thin the paint with more varnish.

Let your daisies dry in a warm, safe spot. When dry (two days to two weeks), protect the surface with two coats of satin finish varnish, sanding between the coats. You may use the same kind of varnish you used to mix with the artists' oils.

Illus. 5. For leaves with highlights, paint light colors next to the first dark basic strokes. Next paint the round daisy centers. Place a drop of yellow paint in the middle of the petals and push the drop until it has little peaks.

Antiquing a Board

The attractive board in Illus. 7 has been "antiqued," simulating the shading which occurs naturally as a result of age and tarnish. Tole painters consider antiquing the crowning touch to their art. By rubbing a mixture of artists' oil and turpentine on a tole-painted object, you achieve a rich, aged look. But antiquing is not easy. In fact, you may spend as much time antiquing as you did painting the design!

Give your board a base coat and then paint it with a pleasing design. Be sure to add two coats of varnish after painting. This protects your work during the antiquing process.

Mix the antiquing formula, which is simply one part burnt umber artists' oil and one part turpentine. Stir the mixture in a saucer or small jar with the palette knife. Use a regular paint brush to apply the antiquing. Cover every nook and cranny with this formula until the board is deep brown and the design is no longer visible (Illus. 8).

When the antiquing loses its gloss, start rubbing the mixture into the wood. To do this, first use a dry paint brush. Stroke up and down, sideways, then up and down again. Wipe the brush clean on tissues or newspaper to get rid of the excess antiquing.

Soon the design will begin to show through. When it does, start rubbing the object with a wadded-up nylon stocking or silk scarf. The silky texture gives the antiquing a feathered look, making it appear a natural part of the object rather than an afterthought. Rub in small circles, rubbing harder where you want less shading (Illus. 9). Again, wipe excess antiquing on tissues or newspaper.

Leave either more or less shading round the design. The contrast focusses attention on the design. Also, leave more shading in crevices, corners, holes—any place where antiquing "ages" the object.

If you want flower petals or leaves to be lighter, remove antiquing from them with a

Illus. 7. This is an antiqued, tole-painted board with a few bright flowers on top of the stain.

Illus. 8. To antique a board, first cover the painted design with two coats of varnish. Then evenly apply a mixture of burnt umber and turpentine to the board.

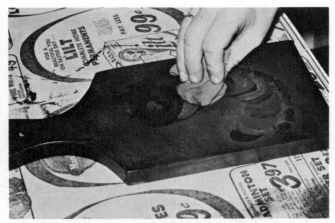

Illus. 9. When the design on the board shows through the antiquing mixture, rub the surface with a nylon stocking. Rub hard for less shading and lightly for dark areas.

cotton swab (Illus. 10), which easily takes off antiquing without disturbing other shading. Or, paint light daisies on top of the antiquing (Illus. 11). Remove as much or as little antiquing as pleases your eye.

When the antiquing is completely dry, protect it with two coats of satin finish varnish. Varnish not only protects but it also enhances the satiny, time-worn appearance of antiquing.

Although the antiquing process described here is a popular method with tole painters, it is by no means the only method. You may antique the object *before* tole painting, to leave

Illus. 10. For small areas where you want the painted design to show, remove the antiquing with a cotton swab.

the colors bright and cheerful rather than aged and mellow. Still another idea is to antique both *before* and *after* tole painting. This gives the richest, most hand-rubbed effect possible.

Or, you may choose not to antique at all—which is especially effective when you use light colors on a dark background. In fact, you may prefer never to antique metalware that has been japanned before it was tole painted.

Have fun experimenting with different

Illus. 11. For very bright details, paint on top of the antiqued surface. The flowers on this board were added after the antiquing had dried.

colors, also. Burnt umber is preferred because it gives the look of hand-rubbed walnut. But burnt sienna resembles maple and can be charming on decorative plaques. By using green in the antiquing mixture, you get a turquoise effect when you apply it over a light blue base coat. If you choose a pink base coat, try antiquing with alizarin crimson mixed with a dab of Payne's grey. Use any color of artists' oil for antiquing as long as it is a darker color than the base coat.

Antiquing with burnt umber is always sure to please. But never be afraid to experiment. You can easily remove mistakes with turpentine. And, after all, your individual ideas are what keep tole painting a folk art!

Daisy Key Holder

This is a simple project that consists entirely of the basic stroke. Not only is a daisy key holder lovely to look at, but it solves the problem of misplaced keys. Or, you might place it near the stove to hold pot holders.

The key holder shown in Illus. 12 was antiqued in burnt umber *before* tole painting. The design was easily painted in an hour, using the same colors as in the first project (page 124). This is also a good design to experiment with. Try color blending the petals in orange and yellow, blue and green, or any other combination that matches your home's décor.

Illus. 13. To break up a large, flat surface on a piece of furniture, tole paint a colorful design.

Illus. 12. This daisy key holder is not only useful, but decorative.

If a board shaped like a key is not available in your hobby shop, cut one out with a coping or jig saw or ask a carpenter to do it for you. Add cup hooks to the bottom edge to hold the keys.

Hearts and Flowers Child's Chair

Chairs, stools, chests, trunks—look carefully at all useful furnishings to see if tole painting will add to their beauty. In the case of a child's chair, the answer is usually "yes."

The child's chair in Illus. 13 is enhanced with a heart, which was a common motif of early French artists. Naturally, a true red artists' oil is beautiful here. Paint the heart first and allow it to dry. Then add flowers, leaves and flourishes with the basic stroke to make this elegant example of tole work.

TOLE PAINTING ■ 127

Illus. 14. Candlesticks, lamp bases, trays, pitchers, cups, boxes, and chests—all become even more attractive when painted with tole designs.

Painting Tinware

"Tole" is French for "tin." If you are tole painting, you may enjoy applying your designs to tin, the original surface that was used for this folk art.

Tinware requires more preparation than wood because you must remove the rust and prevent any new rust. Sanding and scrubbing are sure to get rid of old rust. Rinse the tinware in vinegar and water, then soap and water. Apply a coat of rust-retardant paint. If this paint is the base color of your design, sand it with steel wool and apply a second coat. Some tole painters coat all tinware in off-white rust-retardant paint and then apply a different color enamel for the base coat.

After you carefully prepare the tinware, you may tole paint, varnish and antique it the same as wood.

Folk Art Pitcher and Pail

The tole designs on the back cover are very similar to original tole painting because they are simple and rely heavily upon the basic stroke.

Odd-shaped tinware, like a pitcher or pail, is often difficult to grasp when you paint. Hold the pitcher securely in your lap to paint. Turn it upside-down and paint the cross-hatching on the bottom of the pitcher first with the liner. Then work your way down painting flowers, leaves and stems. Switch between the regular brush and the liner as necessary.

Folk art flowers are particularly gay when they are brightly colored on a white background. Antiquing darkens the white background to yellow. Remove most of the antiquing round the design, but leave edges, crevices and seams heavily antiqued.

Pennsylvania Dutch Canister

Canisters are practical and inexpensive objects to tole paint. Mushroom and flower designs are the usual designs on canisters. But for a change, try painting country figures.

When painting figures, you have the opportunity to use all three brushes. You need the regular brush (#6) for the leaves, baskets and heads. Try the #5 flat brush for clothing —it pulls smoothly to make the pants, jacket, dress and apron. When the figures are dry, use the liner to add facial features, outlines, shoe buttons, and apron trim.

Antique a Pennsylvania Dutch design to add depth, shading, and the age-old look that suggests this design might be an original piece of tole-painted tinware (see Illus. H1 on color page H).

CELLOPHANE CREATIONS

Colorful, see-through cellophane* has many properties that make it an ideal material for unique, artistic, transparent creations. For example:

● It always stays transparent, no matter how many sheets are pasted together. This allows you to create a great variety of different tones and shades other than the basic colors provided by the cellophane itself. It's almost like mixing different-colored paints together.

● If you smear it with cellulose wallpaper paste, which does not discolor it, the cellophane dries as hard as glass but still can be cut into any shape desired.

● If you glue cellophane to glass or some other flat, hard surface, it stays tight and smooth after it is dry.

● If you paste cellophane down over a form made of chicken wire, the material shrinks up tight upon drying.

All these factors make cellophane an easy-to-work-with and inexpensive material. Both young and old can find in it an outlet for their creative energies. It provides an endless play of colors and forms—that you will find fun to experiment with.

Once you have made the simple projects here, you will be able to forge ahead on your own and discover for yourself new ideas and ways of working.

Cellophane can be purchased in rolls in most stationery shops, art supply shops, variety shops, and so on. It may be clear or colored red, yellow, green, blue, orange or purple. You will find out for yourself what colors are available at any given source of supply.

Some packages of colored cellophane sold in America have a note warning you not to use it in direct contact with food. This warning must be heeded, and food which will be in contact with cellophane wrapped in wax paper or aluminum foil first.

All of the projects are to be copied only to learn the technique. Some projects, if made, will be useful, but most have a decorative function. However, those projects which are intended merely for decoration, though "worthless" for any lasting, useful purpose, often provide the most information and the greatest satisfaction to the one who creates them.

A Simple Cellophane Collage

To show you how quickly and easily you can make a remarkable cellophane creation, cut out a variety of simple forms, such as circles, squares, rectangles and triangles. Use just three colors—red, blue, and yellow cellophane on a white paper background. Lay the forms

* Cellophane in England is a trade-mark belonging to British Cellophane Ltd.

Condensed from the book, "Cellophane Creations" by Jo Konijnenberg-De Groot | © 1972 by Sterling Publishing Co., Inc., New York down either adjacent, overlapping, or on top of each other, in random fashion. You will be delighted with the new shapes you have made, the new colors you have created. Watch what happens if you lay several layers of the same color on top of each other. You can paste this collage together permanently later on when you have learned how to use cellulose paste.

Laying out a simple abstract collage will inspire you to try more and more—no two collages will be the same. Using the same geometric kinds of shapes, create a more representational collage—a landscape, seascape, cityscape. No planning is required because the most exciting aspect of working with cellophane is the element of surprise and discovery as new shapes and colors take form. One thing leads to another in cellophane crafting!

Tools and Materials

Scissors will be used for cutting rough forms out of cellophane sheets and for applying finishing touches to a project after pasting and drying. The metallic foils you will be using can also be cut with ordinary sharp scissors.

A pair of *diagonal wire cutters* is useful for cutting wire and poultry netting to size. However, you can get along perfectly well with regular pliers, as the cutting jaws of the pliers will do—or with tin shears, if you have a pair handy.

A *paint brush* can be of any size for applying the cellulose paste and the lacquer thinner. If possible, have one brush for each purpose.

Use *iron wire* to make basic frameworks for such objects as flowers and butterflies, as well as for the wings, antennae and legs of insects made of wire netting. Also use it for making flower stems. In selecting the proper iron wire, you should consider the size and requirements of the parts that are to be made from it, and choose a suitable gauge. The gauge of a wire is its diameter, or thickness. The higher a gauge number the lighter the wire, that is, a 20-gauge wire is lighter than a 12-gauge.

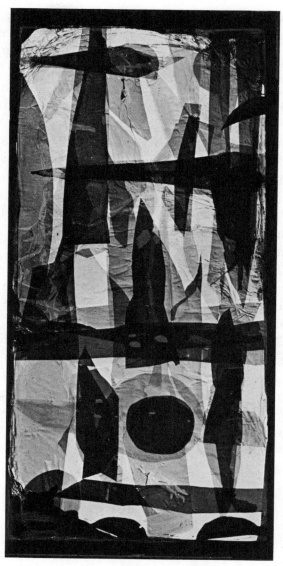

Illus. 1. There is no limit to the exciting effects in both color and design that you can achieve in a cellophane collage. This collage is made on aluminum foil.

What we will call *tie wire* (since it is used for tying forms together) is much thinner and more flexible than iron wire. Use it for binding wings to insect bodies and for making stamens and pistils for flowers and feelers, or antennae, of smaller insects. Again, suit the gauge to the use. For some purposes you might even want to use stovepipe wire, copper wire, or a fine, plated wire available on spools at hardware shops.

You will find *cellulose wallpaper paste* at a

wallpaper shop. Ask for it by that name, as there are other kinds of paste for different purposes and none of these will do. It comes in powder form to be mixed with water for use. This paste is essential in making cellophane collages and for stretching cellophane on wire-netting forms and wire frameworks.

All you have to do is smear the cellophane with a little cellulose wallpaper paste on a paint brush, then stick it to any other kind of material—cardboard, wallpaper, or even glass, tin or other metals. Children tend to smear the paste too heavily on top of the objects to be pasted down, which causes the cellophane to curl up; therefore, it is better for someone to do the pasting for them at the start. The brush used in cellulose paste can be cleaned by a thorough washing in water.

Clear brushing lacquer, being compounded from a base of pyroxylin (cellulose nitrate) or another form of cellulose acetate, has a natural affinity for cellophane and is the perfect medium for sticking sheets of cellophane to glass and metal. While working, the brush used in lacquer can be cleaned and kept flexible by rinsing it in *acetone.* When finished working, clean the brush with acetone, then wash thoroughly with soap and water.

Cellophane on Throw-Away Glass

Now, you can put to good use those endless soft-drink bottles and glass jam jars that you have been forced into throwing away! Take a good look at that jar in your hand the next time you are on your way to the trash container and take note of its shape. There may be a new household function it can fulfill—that of an ornamental or useful vessel.

You can make clever candlesticks out of bottles and jars. Decorated with cellophane motifs and with a fancy, colored candle, you will have a very special candleholder. To prevent wax drip from spoiling your decoration, make a foil "collar" around the top of the jar or bottle. If you have jars that are shallow and wide, you can create unique patio or out-of-doors lights. Candles can be used for lighting in patio jars. Your cellophane decorations should first be pasted down on transparent parchment paper or plastic film which is then pasted to the glass. Or, you can paste the parchment paper to the glass first and then decorate it with your cellophane cut-outs. Whichever way you do it, finish it off by applying a coat of clear brushing lacquer.

Illus. 2 shows a collection of motifs you can use in a variety of different ways. Any motif can be repeated in the same color or in a different color, or you can combine motifs. The little heart shapes in the blossom are formed simply by pasting down cellophane petals over the center-piece. If you wish, you can make your flower even bigger by pasting more petals in between the first ones, about halfway up the hearts.

Give free rein to your imagination and discover what an endless number of forms and variations you can dream up.

Illus. 2.

one wire twisted around the other during the weaving of the mesh. For simplicity's sake, let's call these twisted-wire sides "doubles."

Cylinders of chicken wire are perfect for making "surprise" dolls—hollow dolls containing surprises such as wrapped candy and small gifts at parties, as well as for Chinese lanterns and the bodies of very large "insects." In making cylinders, always be sure that the doubles lie in the lengthwise direction, that is, vertically. A cylinder that turns out a little lopsided can be straightened up by squeezing the doubles a little closer together or spreading them farther apart, as may be needed. Chicken wire is very malleable and you can make many shapes by merely squeezing or pulling.

Illus. 3. Transform a wine bottle and a jam jar into decorative vessels by adding cellophane cut-outs.

"Doubles"

Chicken wire is also called wire netting or poultry netting. The meshes in chicken wire are six-sided but are more lozenge-shaped than hexagonal, which provides both length (in the direction of the roll of netting) and width (across the roll). Both 1″ and 2″ mesh (measured across the width) are generally available, and a smaller mesh is also made, but you may have more difficulty finding it. If you can get hold of some, however, you will find it just right for very small projects.

Two of the six sides of the mesh, you will note (Illus. 4) are composed of two wires each,

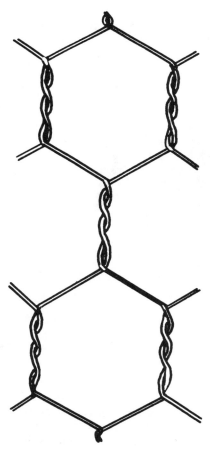

Illus. 4. You can use chicken wire, which comes in various mesh sizes, to make many decorative objects with cellophane. The twisted sides are the "doubles."

CELLOPHANE CREATIONS ■ **133**

Surprise Dolls

Cut a piece of chicken wire 16″ wide (measuring across the width of the mesh) and 14″ long (measuring along the length of the mesh). The doubles must run with the 14″ length. Bend the chicken wire into a cylinder along the 14″ side, allowing the ends to overlap about 1½″ to 2″ (so that the top layer of meshes lines up with those underneath), and "stitch" the two ends together with a length of tie wire.

Now, stand the cylinder up on end. About 5″ down from the top, squeeze a "round" of doubles inward a little, in order to compress the cylinder at that point. The first time around, the wire will be rather stiff—the tension has to be taken out of the meshes. After once around, work over (in the same way) the meshes lying obliquely above and below the meshes of the selected round. Then return to the first round, and you will find that the meshes dent in much more easily. Repeat the procedure as necessary, continuing to work the selected round inward until the "neck" you are forming is about 2″ wide.

The smoothly flowing form of the children's table decoration shown in Illus. 5 is achieved by squeezing each succeeding round of doubles a little less toward each other. The meshes that form the head are, on the other hand, stretched upward and out to leave an opening into which you can stuff goodies. To cover this, the doll in Illus. 5 wears a separate cap. To make a similar cap, cut a circle of chicken wire about 6″ in diameter. Form the skullcap shape by pulling this up in the middle and squeezing it in at the sides until it assumes the desired size.

If you are going to place candies or other edibles inside the head, be sure that you line the head with wax paper or aluminum foil and that the food is paper wrapped. No food should be in direct contact with the cellophane.

Now you are ready to apply your cellophane decorations. For working on chicken-wire

Illus. 5.

Illus. 6. Here are some ideas for your surprise dolls. As you can see, the possibilities are unlimited, even though you are working with one basic chicken-wire frame. The cellophane decorations make the difference. (See also color page I.)

frames, you will use pieces of cellophane dipped in a watery paste. Start with strips, which are easier to handle. After you have a little experience, you can work with larger pieces.

First, mix a thin paste: stir one heaping tablespoonful of cellulose wallpaper paste powder into three pints of water. Pour about a cupful of the mixture into a large jam jar and make a thicker paste out of it by stirring in an extra heaping teaspoonful of the paste powder. This thicker batch of paste you will use to apply small decorative pieces. You will use the larger quantity of watery paste for most of your projects. When not in use, keep it in a small plastic pail covered with a clingy plastic paper to keep dust out.

To paste up a cellophane strip, do it this way: dip the strip with one hand into the watery batch of paste and then draw it through the fingers of the other hand, so that it is soaked but very little excess paste adheres to it. Next, wrap the strip around the chicken-wire form. Continue to wrap strips, slightly overlapping one on the other as you go. Allow the form to dry thoroughly either on newspapers or in a tub, since there will be some drip during the drying process. You will find that when the cellophane has dried, it has shrunk up tightly around the wire.

After it is thoroughly dry, you can make the decorative pieces, such as eyes, nose, and mouth, using the thick batch of paste.

Bowl Flowers

A small bowl without handles serves as a form for these cellophane "flowers," which make charming party table decorations. If you intend to use these bowls as containers for candy, cookies, or other food, first line them with aluminum foil or wax paper, or leave the original bowl form inside the cellophane. These flowers are certainly not one-day bloomers—you can make several and stack them together and store for another party day.

Place a bowl upside-down and measure from

Illus. 7. Use a small bowl as a mould.

Illus. 8. Turn the bowl upside-down, place a dry sheet of cellophane over it, then paste a paste-soaked sheet over that. Allow to dry.

Illus. 9. When dry, remove from mould and cut "petals."

rim to rim over the bottom with a tape measure to ascertain how large a piece of cellophane is needed to cover it. Cut two squares from the cellophane, making every side equal to the measurement you obtained. Place one square over the bowl as shown in Illus. 8. With one hand dip the other square in watery cellulose paste, lift it out, and pull through the fingers and palm of the other hand, stripping off all but a very thin layer of paste.

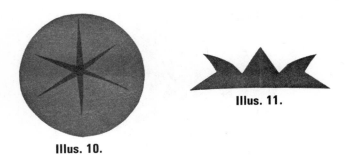

Illus. 10.

Illus. 11.

Cellophane and Wire Blossoms

Cut a circle about 7″ in diameter from a piece of chicken wire. Pull out and press in on the doubles until you have a convex shape. Press in on the meshes around the edges of the circle and pull the middle ones out until you have about a 1½″ or 2″ bulge.

Run a 6′ piece of iron wire through the outside meshes of the bulge so that eight large loops result, each protruding about 3″ or so (Illus. 13). With your pliers, wrap the two wire ends around each other to form the last loop. For a more interesting effect, dent in the outer curve of each loop (Illus. 14).

Cover the chicken-wire flower eye with cellophane dipped in watery paste. Then cut two identical pieces of cellophane, slightly larger than the wire framework of the petals. Dip one sheet in the paste and smooth it out

Illus. 12. You can turn your bowl flowers into egg cups for a festive brunch.

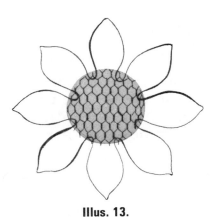

Illus. 13.

Now stretch out the folds and wrinkles that this procedure has left in the cellophane and press it smoothly over the dry sheet covering the bowl. Cut off the points that are left sticking up around the rim. After the cellophane is absolutely dry, carefully remove it from the form and cut the rim into flower petals as shown in Illus. 9.

To transform your cellophane bowls into fancy brunch egg cups, cut a circle from gold-colored heavy paper the size of the bottom of the bowl. Cut slits in star fashion in the middle (Illus. 10) and bend the points up and back to hold the egg in place (Illus. 11).

Illus. 14.

on a level surface. On top of it place the entire flower framework with the bulge side up.

Cut a hole in the second piece of cellophane the size of the eye of the flower. Then dip it in the paste and lay it down over the framework so that it adheres to the underlying sheet of cellophane. Hang the flower up to dry until it is glass-hard; then cut the cellophane around the wire petals.

Now you can glue on whatever decorative pieces of cellophane you want (Illus. 15 and Illus. 16), using thick paste. For instance, you might want to make a frilly ring around the eye as shown in Illus. 16. Make small, fringed rolls of cellophane in contrasting colors and stick these through the holes in the eye, rather than covering the eye in the beginning with a piece of cellophane.

You might make a wire stem for your flower which you can cover with green cellophane and then make small wire leaves also covered with

Illus. 15.

green cellophane. These can be attached to the stem by winding the ends of the wire around it. Make these the same way as the flower petals, that is, cutting out two pieces of cellophane, and pasting under and above the wire frame. Again, hang them up to dry and then cut the shape of the leaves around the wire.

Illus. 16. These wild flowers have blossoms of cellophane and wire with all kinds of decorative touches, such as beads, buttons, and frills.

Illus. 17. Chicken-wire body.

Illus. 18. A huge "beetle-bug" with a chicken-wire body and wing-cases sports fringy, gold-colored paper eyes.

Giant Insects

Make large insects with bodies of chicken wire. Make a cylinder in the same way you did for the surprise doll and form a neck to separate the head from the body (Illus. 17). Snip into the netting at the tail with your wire cutters so that the end can be brought into a sharp point.

To make the legs and feelers of large insects you should use single pieces of wire with a double thickness of cellophane. Cut the strips of cellophane, dip in watery paste, and lay the wire precisely in the middle of the strip. Fold the cellophane over the wire and paste the two sides of the cellophane together. Let dry until glass-hard and then clip to whatever shape you wish.

A Great Beetle-Bug

The "beetle-bug" in Illus. 18 has a chicken-wire body, as well as chicken-wire wing-cases. The wing-cases have black-button decoration.

The delicate wings are made with pieces of wire covered with cellophane. The ruffs around its neck and legs are made of heavy gold-colored paper and its eyes consist of two big black beads cemented to round, fringy pieces of the same gold paper. The body consists of pasted cellophane strips bunched together and wrapped with tie wire.

An Orange Angelfish

This incredible sea creature has a body made of chicken wire. However, this time, instead of forming a cylinder with the netting, fold a large piece over double. Make a paper pattern (Illus. 19) and cut out the shape of the fish in a double thickness. "Sew" the two pieces together with tie wire. Now apply paste-soaked pieces of orange cellophane to the body.

The top and bottom fins are made only from cellophane without any wire to give them stiffness. Rather, several sheets of white and

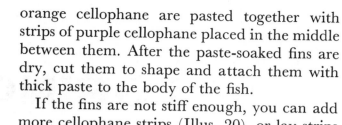

orange cellophane are pasted together with strips of purple cellophane placed in the middle between them. After the paste-soaked fins are dry, cut them to shape and attach them with thick paste to the body of the fish.

If the fins are not stiff enough, you can add more cellophane strips (Illus. 20), or lay strips of dark blue aluminum foil over both the body and fins and paste them down, using thick paste.

Illus. 19. Make a paper pattern for your orange angelfish.

Illus. 20 (right). Add cellophane strips to decorate your angelfish.

COLORING PAPERS

Stationery and department stores offer a wealth of more or less attractive wrapping and writing papers, especially at holiday time. Oddly enough, though, there is a great shortage of beautifully patterned papers for posters, book covers and end papers. The few really lovely, obtainable papers are foreign-made and are so expensive that few people can afford them. So, why not dye your own papers and apply your own designs on them, giving new life to posters, boxes, cartons, books, doll houses, playing cards, toy chests, lanterns, Chinese lanterns and lamp shades?

Fold and Dye

Materials: absorbent paper, highly diluted water colors.

Accordion-pleat the paper vertically in equal-

Illus. 2. Spatter on water color.

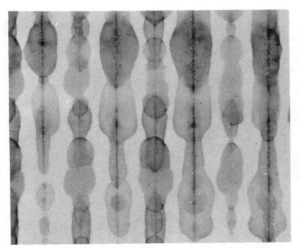

Illus. 1. Fold paper like an accordion and dab the edges with diluted water color.

sized sections. Now, dab the various sections with a brush dipped into diluted water color. Should the paper not quite absorb the color, place the whole sheet, creased like an accordion, into water. Then wipe it dry and press the excessive dampness out. Now dab the creased corners with color. Illus. 1 shows a paper with different nuances of color and fold pattern.

Spray and Spatter

Materials and tools: absorbent white paper, pan of water, sponge, cake water color, window screen grid, spray can, drawing board, paint cup, old toothbrush, thumb-tacks.

Moisten the paper with the sponge and

Condensed from the book, "Coloring Papers" by Susanne Strose | © 1968 by Sterling Publishing Co., Inc., New York

stretch it on your drawing table. Fasten it down with thumb-tacks. When the paper is quite dry, rub the old toothbrush over a damp cake of water color and spatter this color onto the paper by scraping the toothbrush back and forth over the wire netting or window screen. If the color is too wet, the dots will be irregular globs. Therefore it is wise to wipe the brush first on some newspaper.

Instead of the wire screen, you can also use a spray can to spatter the paint. In that case the color has to be extremely diluted before you blow it through the nozzle onto the paper, which must be in a vertical position.

Illus. 2 shows a spattered paper.

Stencil and Spray

Materials and tools: absorbent paper, drawing paper, water colors, sturdy paper for cutting of stencils, paint cup, wire netting or window screen, old toothbrush, scissors, drawing board.

Cut multiple stencils (simple forms) from the sturdy paper and artistically arrange them on the absorbent paper. Next, sprinkle or spray diluted water color over the entire sheet. Following this, place the stencils carefully on other spots and spray the paper again with color. This procedure can be repeated several times. When using large stencils it helps to fasten them with pins, while the smaller ones only have to be laid flat on the paper. Especially attractive is the work whereby colors are changed every time you re-arrange your stencils.

Illus. 3 is an example of a sprayed stencil.

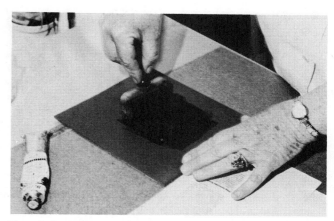

Illus. 4. Spread colored ink on a pane of glass or a linoleum block with a brayer. Be sure the color is evenly distributed.

Roll and Stamp

Materials and tools: two or three lino print rollers (brayers), block-printing colored inks, absorbent paper, a solid support for rolling the ink colors (the most suitable support is glass, Illus. 4).

Squeeze a 1″-long "sausage" of colored ink on the support. Roll it flat until the color is evenly distributed and becomes fibrous in appearance. There are various methods you can use now. One is to apply the color with your brayer on a thoroughly creased sheet of paper as in Illus. 5.

Another method is to cut out a piece of

Illus. 3. Sprinkle water color over cardboard stencils.

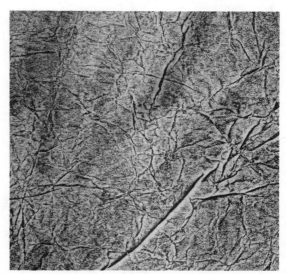

Illus. 5. Roll linoblock color over a sheet of creased paper.

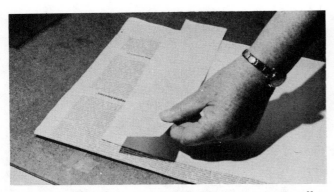

Illus. 6. A strip of paper cardboard will serve as a stencil to cover the areas of the paper you do not want to color.

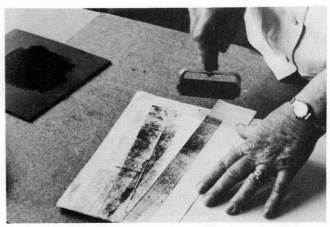

Illus. 7. After inking the brayer by rolling it on the linoleum block, roll the brayer over the area of the paper left uncovered by the stencil. Shift the stencil to another position and color another space until you have printed the entire paper.

cardboard about 1½" wide and place it on your sheet of paper so that only a narrow margin shows on the right. Roll the brayer on this margin. Now shift the stencil slightly to your left and cover the new empty space with the roller. In this way you proceed until the whole sheet has been colored. In Illus. 8, the stencil has not been placed vertically on the paper but at an angle, slanting. This results in "intersections." You can continue to improvise with these patterns by simply shaping the stencil in the forms of waves or jagged corners. Just experiment by yourself.

Papers onto which patterns are rolled by placing the stencils *under* the paper are shown

by Illus. 9. First, cut out several versions of small simple shapes, such as circles, rectangles, trees, houses. Arrange them on a background support and then cover them with a clean sheet of paper. Since you should apply the color here only sparingly, roll your brayer first several times over some newspaper to remove some ink. Use your roller now carefully over the printing sheet. You can repeat this procedure with another color but first reposition the stencils slightly under the paper.

Illus. 8. By slanting the stencil at an angle, you obtain intersections of color.

Illus. 9. You can cut stencils into various shapes and place them *under* the paper.

Cord or Twine Print

Materials : cords or twines in various strengths, pieces of cardboard, absorbent paper, all-purpose glue, linoblock ink, brayer.

Illus. 10. Ink cord with brayer rolled in linoblock color and print.

Glue the pieces of cord in shapes such as curlicues, serpentine lines, circles, etc., on small areas of cardboard. Cut them out roughly and the result is blocks for printing. When you apply your colored roller over them, they are ready to be impressed on paper. Avoid double layers of cord or twine when glueing them on the cardboard. Simply cut the piece off where it touches cord or twine that has been fastened on the cardboard.

Material Print

Materials : cork scraps, bottle caps, toothpaste caps, crumpled paper, brushes, chains, necklaces, braided borders, basketwork, absorbent paper, poster color or water color.

You can use any materials, but try to find articles that have interesting shapes and textures. In many cases you can dip the actual material into the color and make prints directly from them. If you find only one item with a pleasing design effect, use it in such a way that the repeat or composite pattern is not boring. Find a pattern to stimulate the imagination.

Illus. 11. Make blocks for printing by glueing cord to cardboard in a design.

Illus. 12. You can use various objects, such as small bottle caps, as stencils.

CRAFTING WITH PAPER

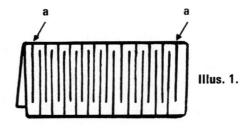

Illus. 1.

Illus. 2.

Paper is one of the most versatile, inexpensive, and easy-to-work-with materials available. This section contains some projects simple enough for a young child and other more complicated projects that will interest adults. Imagination and creativity are the only limits to the unusual and decorative items anyone can make from paper.

You can use any kind of paper—construction paper, wrapping paper, cardboard, tissue paper, writing paper, and even wax paper. Besides paper, you need only a few more supplies—a pair of scissors (safety scissors for a child), glue, tape, paints, crayons, and imagination.

Magic Tricks from Paper

Crawling through a Playing Card

Can you crawl through a playing card? It seems impossible, but it is very easy. Take an old playing card that is no longer used. Fold it lengthwise (see Illus. 1). Make a series of cuts on the open side as shown in Illus. 1. Now cut the folded side from *a* to *a*. Unfold the card. If the cuts are close enough together, the card becomes a large ring you can easily step through (Illus. 2).

Crawling through the Hoop

Crawl through the paper hoop without tearing it!

The exact size for the paper strip from which you make the hoop depends on your age and

your own size. A strip about 24″ long should be enough for 8- to 12-year-olds. The approximate diameter of the hoop would then be about 7″ or 8″.

Does it sound impossible to crawl through such a small hoop? It would be, except that this is a trick. Only you will be able to do it, to the amazement of your friends. Before you

Illus. 3.

Illus. 4.

Condensed from the books, "Creative Paper Crafts" by Chester Jay Alkema | © 1967 by Sterling Publishing Co., Inc., New York, and "How to Make Things Out of Paper" by Walter Sperling | © 1961 by Sterling Publishing Co., Inc., New York

paste the hoop together, give the paper strip a half twist. Illus. 3 is a simply pasted hoop; Illus. 4 is the prepared strip. You can see very plainly that the strip has a half twist. A mathematician once discovered that such a strip does not fall into two parts if cut apart lengthwise, but results in a hoop of twice the size. Try this amazing thing. Now the hoop is large enough for you to crawl through easily without breaking it.

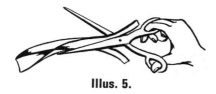

Illus. 5.

The Magic Envelope

Have you ever seen a magic envelope? With it, you can make a coin disappear and re-appear, so that people will wonder at your magic powers!

First, make a simple envelope from a piece of paper cut into the form of a cross. With a ruler and pencil, mark a cross consisting of five connected squares of equal size on a piece of paper (see Illus. 6). Draw the squares neatly and cut them out carefully, or you will have difficulty later when you fold the sides together.

Cut out the cross, fold the four legs inward towards the center, and lay them over at an angle as the arrows show (see Illus. 6). (Two legs are already folded down in Illus. 6.)

Fold the four triangle points in, as you see in *a*, *b* and *c* in Illus. 7. Put the point *d* into the slit between *c* and *a* so that the envelope holds together and cannot come open. Press the folds in place firmly with the base of your thumb.

You have made an ordinary envelope which can be very useful to you—even at this stage, before it becomes magic. Suppose you want to send little greeting cards or to enclose

flowers. Such an envelope is just the thing to put them in. If you use decorative paper or even gold paper, the results are especially attractive.

Now we come to the magic. Fold two more envelopes, using black or dark paper to conceal the trick. Draw squares of 2 to 3 inches. Be sure that both envelopes are exactly the same size. Paste them together back to back. Paste neatly, right to the edge. Put a book on top of them while they are drying.

To fool your friends, open the envelope on one side and place a dime in it. They do not know what is on the other side! Then close the envelope and lay it on the table. Turn it in your hands so the back faces upward. Let your audience touch the envelope and confirm the fact that the coin is still there. But, you show them it is no longer there: you open the flap slowly, the coin is no longer visible to your audience. It lies hidden in the back part of the envelope. You can make the coin re-appear after closing the envelope and turning it again.

Be very careful that your audience doesn't discover your trick. Don't ever show them the back of the envelope! And now, have a good time and much success with your first magic demonstration of this secret double envelope.

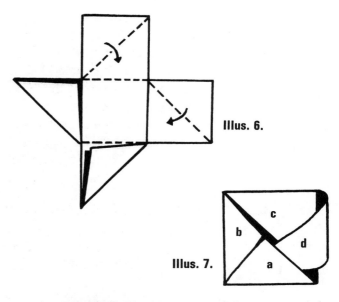

Illus. 6.

Illus. 7.

The Swan Family

Make a whole swan family from white paper —Father Swan, Mother Swan and a flock of babies. Illus. 19 shows an example.

For the big swans, use pieces of paper about 8″ square. Make the youngsters from pieces 4″ square. If you use other sizes, the relative proportions between the big and little swans should be about the same. Use good stiff writing paper.

First fold the square along both diagonals (see Illus. 8) and then open it up *after* each fold. Turn the paper over.

Fold the paper in half in both directions (see Illus. 9). Open it up once more after each fold.

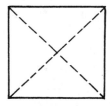

Illus. 8.   **Illus. 9.**

It is easy to fold Illus. 10. Take two diagonally opposite corners and bring them in to meet at the center. Push in the other two corners. The previous folds make this form possible. As usual, crease the folds sharply.

Open the paper and lay it flat on the table as shown in Illus. 11. Place a finger at *a* and lift the edge at *b*, laying this edge exactly along the diagonal *c*. You now have the sheet as shown in Illus. 12. Press down the round spot at *a*, creasing it from the corner to the middle

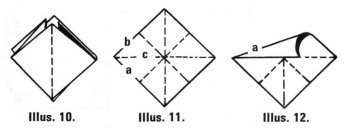

Illus. 10.   **Illus. 11.**   **Illus. 12.**

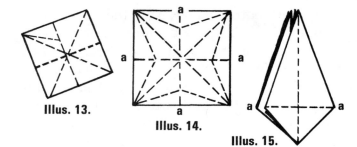

Illus. 13.   **Illus. 14.**   **Illus. 15.**

fold. Open the sheet and you have the result shown in Illus. 13. Repeat this procedure at every corner until the sheet has all the folds shown in Illus. 14.

Make Illus. 15 by pressing the sides of the square up and in at the points marked *a* in Illus. 14. It almost forms itself; just help it a bit with your fingers. Crease all the edges neatly so that the figure will keep its form.

Turn down the long tongues of Illus. 15 at *a-a*, both in front and in back. The result looks like Illus. 16. Hold the paper at *b* as shown in Illus. 16 and turn the upper flap at *a* onto *b*.

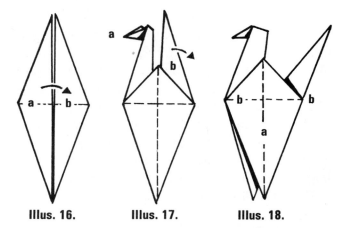

Illus. 16.   **Illus. 17.**   **Illus. 18.**

Turn the paper around so that it looks like Illus. 17. You only have to add a few details to finish the swan. Hold the left point at *a* and push the tip down and in, forming the swan's beak. Bend out *b*, the right point, to make the tail. Press down all the folds.

Illus. 19.

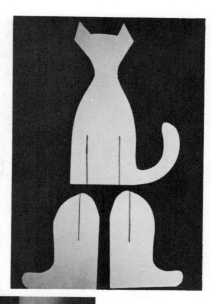

Take the flap under *b* and pull it in the opposite direction.

In Illus. 18, the profile of the swan is complete; only the wings are missing. Fold the long tongues, *a*, up along the dotted line *b-b*. To eliminate a stiff appearance, make a few creases in the wings so that they fan out from the front to the rear.

Now admire your work. Once you have done it a few times, the procedure will become automatic and you will be able to make as many swans as you like without referring to the directions.

Illus. 21.

Slit and Slide Technique

Make three-dimensional objects with flat sheets of paper by using the "slit and slide" technique. Cut slits into two flat shapes and slide them together perpendicular to each other.

The simple cat, seen in Illus. 20–22, shows clearly the steps of the slit and slide technique. In Illus. 20 are the parts of the cat before it is put together. Cut two vertical slits into the body, beginning from its lower edge. Each of the two legs is also cut with a vertical slit, starting from the top edge. Illus. 21 shows how legs are fitted to the body—they are slid in perpendicular to it. Illus. 22 is the standing cat, looking quite happy with its accomplishment!

Illus. 22.

Illus. 23. The wax-paper technique creates a light and airy abstract design on this paper-window transparency. Yarn and colored tissue paper are all that you need.

Wax-Paper Technique

A simple method of making paper-window transparencies is the "wax-paper technique." Make a design of yarn and colored tissue and place it between two sheets of wax paper. Apply a hot iron to the surfaces of your wax-paper window. Do not use a back-and-forth movement because the iron tends to tear the wax paper when it glides over the raised strands of yarn between the two wax-paper surfaces. Place the iron down, lift it, and place down in another area. Continue until you have completely covered the surface.

String or yarn can play an important rôle in paper transparencies. They serve as tracings either to outline shapes or add accents where there are vague areas of color.

Repeated opaque shapes add interest to a window design when juxtaposed with transparent areas of tissue paper, cellophane paper or clear wax paper. Or use opaque materials to block out certain areas. You can use black construction paper to fill shapes formed by string or other lines. Or, India ink or a mixture of black tempera paint and hand soap might cover the resisting wax-paper surfaces when painted over certain areas.

The window in Illus. 23 reveals one approach to abstract design. The yarn does not entirely serve as a definition of shape, but unifies the various elements of the design. Place the yarn on the wax-paper surfaces *after* the tissue paper and construction papers are arranged.

Paper Pillow Figures

Another method for making three-dimensional figures is to stuff paper into the figures just the way you stuff a pillow with down. You can make a really plump turkey, a substantial Santa Claus, or a sleek, fat cat!

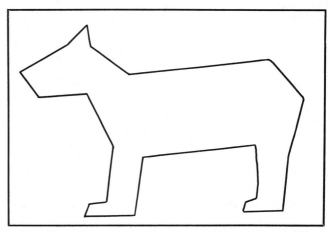

Illus. 24. This is the first step in making a pillow figure, using six sheets of newspaper.

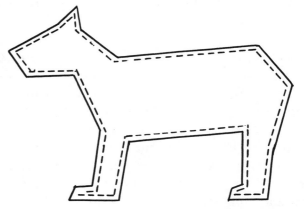

Illus. 25. "Sew" the sheets of paper with staples along the dotted lines shown here.

Place six unfolded sheets of newspaper on top of one another. Using pencil, crayon, chalk, or paint, draw an outline of your figure on the top sheet. Try to make the figure almost as large as the newspaper (Illus. 24). Cut through the top three sheets first. Using your top cut-out shape as a guide, cut the three remaining sheets. Now, pile all six together again.

The dotted lines in Illus. 25 indicate where, with a staple, you sew the papers together. However, you can, if you prefer, paste little paper strips around the papers so that they lap over on the two sides and the edge of the pillow as in Illus. 26. Keep these strips rather small and narrow if possible.

When approximately three fourths of the figure is sewn up, start stuffing. Bathroom tissue, facial tissue, napkins, crushed newspaper, or even foam rubber are fine stuffing materials. Be sure to stuff the thinnest parts of the figure first, such as tails, arms, legs, etc.. It is important, when first planning your figure, that its parts are not too narrow to allow for stuffing.

Decorate your pillow next. Although you will probably want to paint all or part of the figures, you can also apply scrap materials, such as yarn, string, cotton batting, drinking straws, broom straws, and so on. Add jewelry in the form of real earrings, bracelets, buttons, brooches.

Also try fashioning old pieces of clothing into stockings, trousers, shirts, skirts, hats. Experiment with textured surfaces such as glued-on macaroni, beads, dry cereal, buttons, sequins, rice, split peas, watermelon seeds, colored popcorn, pebbles, sea shells.

Make three-dimensional protrusions in the surface of a pillow. An X shape, such as that in Illus. 27, can be repeated all over the figure. Make incisions in the form of the X through the top sheet of newspaper and pull the tabs back as in Illus. 28. Paint the underlying layer in a contrasting color to the folded-back tabs, making an interesting pattern.

Illus. 26. Instead of staples, you might glue small strips of paper over the layers to hold the shape together.

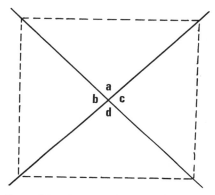

Illus. 27. To make an unusual three-dimensional pattern, draw X shapes all over the pillow. Carefully cut along the solid lines shown here.

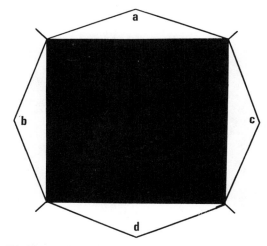

Illus. 28. Then pull the resulting "tabs" back so that you have a window like this. Paint the underlying layer in a contrasting color.

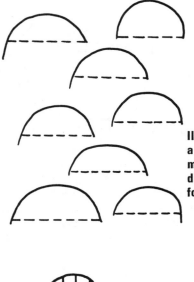

Illus. 29. If you are making a fish pillow, you could make fin-like, three-dimensional protrusions by following this pattern.

Illus. 30. If your animal pillow has "fur," try this pattern.

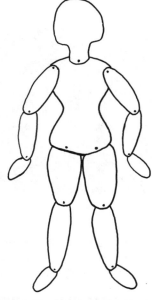

Fold arch-shaped incisions, such as in Illus. 29, along the dotted line indicated to make fin-like protrusions, or make a fur-like effect by following the pattern in Illus. 30. Here, you can fold a number of parallel slits cut into a fin-like protrusion forward and curl or twist them any which way.

A colorful turtle is shown in Illus. J1. This busy swimmer was painted all over with orange tempera, and black tempera lines formed the typical shell divisions. Then circular tissue-paper shapes were placed within the divisions and spattered with glitter mixed with glue. A black rick-rack border outlines the shell and its scalloped pattern is repeated with a black tempera design along the outermost edge of the shell, Strips of construction paper were curled and glued in place for a realistic turtle tail. A red construction-paper tongue and glitter eyes complete the figure.

It is not, of course, necessary that you use newspaper for the outer layer of your pillow. You could even use a piece of cloth.

Paper pillow people are great fun. Make a life-size replica of yourself, someone you know, or a character from fiction.

To make a self-portrait, use long brown wrapping paper instead of newspaper. Lie down on the top sheet and have someone draw your silhouette around you.

When making human figures, it is a good idea to observe the body parts in action since you may want to make a figure running, sitting, kneeling, or even dancing.

Assemble a number of paper pillows to make one large figure. One big body pillow, a head pillow, and three pillows each for the arms and legs make the man in Illus. 31. Join the pillow parts with brass paper fasteners.

Illus. 31. A large paper-pillow person is easy to make from many small pillows. Hold the pillow parts together with brass paper fasteners, which serve as hinges to allow the various parts to move, and your figure can assume a variety of poses.

PAPIER MÂCHÉ

Papier mâché has probably been known for as long as the art of paper-making has existed—for at least 3,000 years.

Now various synthetic glues and such finishing materials as epoxy resins make it possible to create—from ordinary paper—objects that will be almost indestructible. Epoxy makes papier mâché objects virtually unbreakable, waterproof, flameproof, burnproof, alcohol- and acidproof, stainproof and soilproof. Wiping with a damp cloth is all that is needed to keep epoxy-coated objects clean. Of course, you can protect papier mâché with a coating of the traditional materials—lacquer, shellac, paint or varnish finishes. But epoxy coatings do more than finish papier mâché articles—epoxy enters *into* the papier mâché and strengthens it.

Materials

Paper. The basic papier mâché raw material is paper, and newspapers are the chief source of materials. However, you should not hesitate to experiment with other types of paper.

As you work with newspapers, you may find that the paper used in them (called "newsprint" in the trade) varies from newspaper to newspaper.

Grain. During the paper-making processes that transform the various vegetable fibres into what we know as "paper," the finished product acquires a certain pattern of fibre—called "grain." The easiest way to determine the grain is to tear it. Take an ordinary sheet of any newspaper. Tear it in the direction in which the columns of type run. Notice how it shreds, whether raggedly or evenly, and whether it tears easily. Now tear it in the other direction—across the columns. Notice how it shreds in this direction and compare the ease or difficulty of tearing. In general, you will find from your own experience that paper strips torn with the grain are stronger than the same-sized strips torn against the grain.

Pastes and Glues. Although you can mould objects from strips or lumps of moistened newspaper (and such objects would be reasonably firm), the addition of even a small amount of paste or glue will give the things you make added strength and permanence. In preparation for each papier mâché project, it is a good idea to make a fresh batch of paste-glue mixture as follows:

Take 1 quart of water and 1 cup of flour. Mix, and then cook in the top of a double boiler. Stir occasionally (with whisk shown in Illus. 1) and cook until clear; then add $\frac{1}{2}$ teaspoon oil of wintergreen. This prevents mould and fungus and keeps the paste sweet-smelling. Keep the paste in your refrigerator prior to use.

If you are making trays or any product where warping must be averted, add $\frac{1}{4}$ cup powdered waterproof glue to the recipe after cooking.

The most satisfactory glue for dried papier mâché is a white casein glue which dries clear. ("Sobo" is the trade name of the preferred product.) In the same way that a carpenter uses glue to join pieces of wood, use casein glue to join pieces or parts of dried papier mâché.

Condensed from the books, "Original Creations with Papier Mâché" by Mildred Anderson | © 1967 by Sterling Publishing Co., Inc., New York, and "Papier Mâché and How to Use It" by Mildred Anderson | © 1965 by Sterling Publishing Co., Inc., New York

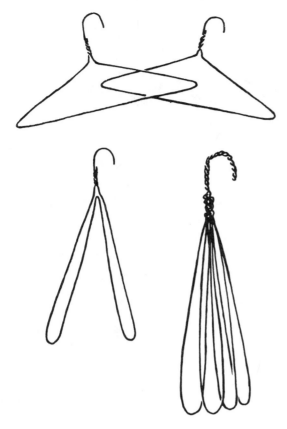

Illus. 1. Make a whisk for mixing paste and casein glue. Take two light-weight coat hangers, bend each in half, and then tightly press together at the hooked end. Spread bottom ends to 3" wide. Twist one hook tightly around the other to hold them together.

Methods

In making objects of papier mâché, you can use two basic methods: First, you can build up objects around a mould, using paste-coated strips of paper. Second, you can make objects from the pulpy mass of boiled paper called "mash."

One word of advice before you begin: Be sure that you have all your materials before you start.

Because of the nature of paper and in particular because of the relatively large quantity of water used during the papier mâché making, objects of papier mâché have a strong tendency to warp—often differentially. A mould, therefore, is a "must"—particularly for beginning projects. After you have learned

how to handle papier mâché and to know its qualities, you can dispense with moulds and create papier-mâché objects without them. The things that you make then may even seem twisted and crooked, but this will only add to their charm.

The moulds that you use depend upon the article that you are making. All kinds of wooden and cardboard boxes may be used; dishes make excellent moulds for rounded objects. Anything with sides sloping in towards the bottom is good—there will be no problem in removing the object you have made.

A few layers of dry newspaper should cover the mould before you build up the papier mâché.

Beads

Here is an easy way to make small beads for necklaces; when finished, the beads will be $\frac{1}{2}$" in size. They can be smaller or even as large as an egg—depending on the size of the pieces of paper you start with. Beaded curtains are again popular, and an unusual beaded curtain can be made with large papier-mâché beads.
Materials:
   stack of newspapers
   flour and powdered resin glue mixture
   very heavy thread or dental floss
   No. OO crochet hook (a heavy piece of wire from a wire coat hanger may be substituted)
   clear lacquer and lacquer thinner
Tear quarter sheets of paste-coated newspaper into four strips. Combine them and tear each four-layered strip in half. Using one half of each of these strips at a time, fold it on itself (like rolling) so that you have a strip measuring about $\frac{1}{2}$" across and 5" long.

Press this with your fingers from the middle outwards to flatten it and to remove excess water, paste, and air.

Remove about three quarters of the thickness of each end of these strips so that the ends are not as thick as the rest of the strip. This thinning of the material at the ends makes it

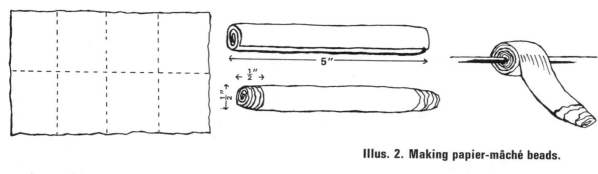

Illus. 2. Making papier-mâché beads.

easier to blend the ends in when you make the beads (Illus. 2).

Using a No. OO crochet hook, wrap the strip round the shank, holding the strip firmly on the crochet hook as you wrap it round. Smooth it firmly with the fingers and blend the end of the strip in smoothly.

Slip the bead off the hook and smooth it lightly with your fingers. Be careful not to change its shape or to close the hole while it is soft.

Make as many beads as you want for a necklace. You should be able to make enough for a 3-foot string in less than half an hour.

Bake your beads in the oven on a baking sheet or sheet of heavy aluminum foil. When dry, you can sand them lightly with emery paper and finish as follows.

Buy small cans of clear lacquer and lacquer thinner. (For small numbers of beads, you can use clear nail polish, and use polish remover in place of lacquer thinner.)

Place a small amount, say, one half cup, of clear lacquer in a paper cup. Add an equal quantity of lacquer thinner.

String your papier-mâché beads loosely on a thin thread and dip them in the lacquer mixture. Lift out and let dry. (Lacquer dries rapidly.) Dip the beads twice a day until ten coats have been applied. Use thinned lacquer for the first two coats; after that, use the lacquer full strength. Remember that lacquer is highly inflammable and do your bead-dipping away from a fire or flame. Out-of-doors is best.

String your finished beads on bead-stringing thread or dental floss. For beaded curtains, raffia makes an exciting contrast of texture with the roughly shaped beads. Knot the raffia between each bead to hold the beads in place. Alternate large and small beads for variety.

Illus. 3. You can make your necklaces as long as you like. You can double over a very long one to look like two strands when you wear it.

Buttons

Materials:

    stack of newspapers
    flour and powdered resin glue mixture
    { button shanks or
     6″ square of plywood and two or four
       1″ nails.

There are two ways to make buttons: One is to use a shank in each button; the other kind has two or four holes through each button for sewing the button to the fabric.

For buttons with a shank, get one or two dozen shanks from a dressmaker or from a dress-

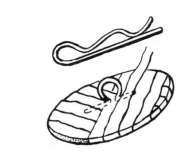

Illus. 4. Two different ways of making papier-mâché buttons: (Top) Making a shank button. (Middle) Making a button with holes. (Bottom) Finished buttons.

makers' supplier. These will be more than you need, so make some extra buttons as gifts. Shape the buttons, making them flat, rounded, or sculpted as flowers, insects, animals, or non-representational shapes. Bake them (page 159) and sand them. Finish with one of the finishes described on page 160. Cement the papier-mâché button to the shank with some casein glue.

Buttons with holes for sewing are made in a different way:

Nail two or four nails through a 6″ square of plywood. Make the nails about $\frac{1}{4}$″ apart. Build each button round the nails, using strips or bits of paste-coated newspaper (Illus. 4). If the buttons are all to be more or less the same shape, draw this shape directly on the plywood. If it is circular, inscribe it with a compass. When the button has been built up to the shape and thickness that you want, slide it off the nail and make another.

Bake your buttons on a baking sheet or on a sheet of heavy aluminum foil. Sand, decorate, and finish. The texture of papier-mâché buttons is particularly suitable for use with woollens and heavy cotton materials. They look just right on knitted dresses, sweaters, coats and most casual or sports clothes.

Blinds

These blinds will be similar to split bamboo blinds, yet will retain a texture peculiar to papier mâché.

Materials:

    stack of newspapers
    flour and powdered resin glue mixture

First measure the window for which the blinds are intended. The blinds can either fit inside the window or lap over the frame by about 2″.

Start with a thick section of newspaper. Open this at the middle and tear at the fold. Tear each sheet in half again lengthwise. Make a stack of these half sheets, which should measure about 7″ × 22″.

Dip sheets in water to wet them. Remove the sheets and apply paste with your hand. Smooth off excess paste. Fold this in half lengthwise. Apply more paste, remove excess and fold again. Keep folding in half, pressing and smoothing until you have a strip about an inch wide. Your blinds will be even more attractive if you vary the width of the strips—these can be from $\frac{1}{2}''$ to $1\frac{1}{2}''$ in width.

Make enough strips for the length of your window. Smooth each strip lightly with emery paper. Tint the slats for the blinds with dye or finish with several thin coats of clear lacquer. Using two pieces of colored raffia or dyed hemp, lace up the blinds as shown in Illus. 5. The end lacing should be about 3″ from each end. An extra lacing of raffia or hemp in the middle of long blinds will keep them more even.

Woven Wastepaper Baskets

Woven baskets look easy to make, but are tricky in the larger sizes unless you know the technique. Make some smaller woven baskets before attempting larger ones.
Materials:
    stack of newspapers
    flour and powdered resin glue mixture
    wastepaper basket or bucket (to serve as a
        mould)
First turn the mould upside-down. Measure from one rim up one side, across the bottom, and down the opposite side to the rim. This distance determines the length of the longest strips you will need.

Make the strips in exactly the same way as the strips described for making blinds. For smaller baskets, make the strips narrow, about $\frac{1}{2}''$ wide. Strips 1″ or more in width are appropriate in larger baskets. Strive for variety rather than uniformity in the width of your strips; it will make your finished woven wastepaper basket more interesting.

Lay strips across the mould in a parallel pattern. Tear one strip in half and insert one of the halves among the other strips, pasting

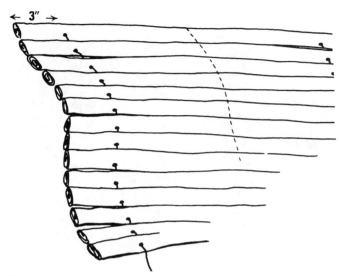

Illus. 5. Papier-mâché window blinds are similar to bamboo blinds, but they have their own special texture.

it at the middle (Illus. 6). There must be an odd number of splines (uprights) in your basket or you will not be able to weave the sides.

Start weaving the strips from the inside at the middle. Splice ends of strips together to give a continuous effect. Be sure that each strip ends inside the basket before splicing— you may have to tear off a piece at the end of the strip to achieve this.

Dry the woven basket on the mould until it is absolutely dry. Do not remove it from the mould while it is still wet, or it will collapse in a heap. After it has dried, take it from the mould and check for sturdiness. Note the adhesion between vertical and horizontal strips where they cross. If there is poor adhesion,

Illus. 6. Steps in making the woven wastepaper basket.

Illus. 7. A woven papier-mâché wastepaper basket will be enhanced by a liberal application of colored lacquer.

apply some paste mixture to the joint and squeeze it tightly together. (A weight on the joint will help to hold it while it is drying.) Allow the basket to dry, and check it again. Repeat the reinforcing until the basket is sturdy. Apply linseed oil all over the basket, inside and out, and let dry. Finish the woven basket with several coats of thinned colored lacquer, then with un-thinned.

Mash

One of the advantages of working with mash is the fact that it can be made in advance and kept. Mash improves in texture and consistency with age.

Materials:

1 or more large galvanized or enamel buckets
stack of newspapers
flour
oil of wintergreen
2 asbestos stove mats
strainer or colander
whisk (see Illus. 1)

Tear newspapers (not tabloids) into quarter sheets. Then, tear narrow strips $\frac{1}{4}''$ to $\frac{1}{2}''$ wide *with* the grain of the paper. Bunch these together in your hand.

Next, tear the strips crosswise into pieces about 1″ to $1\frac{1}{2}''$ long. Fill the bucket with water and bring it to a boil. Sprinkle the pieces of newspaper into the boiling water as if you were cooking noodles. Stir the pieces of paper to separate them well.

Cook the paper until the fibres are broken down and the paper has disintegrated. Add water from time to time if necessary to keep the bucket full. Add one-half teaspoon of oil of wintergreen. This keeps the mash smelling sweet.

Using a whisk (Illus. 1) or an electric beater, if you have one, beat until the mixture is smooth. Any small pieces that happen to escape the beating process may be left in the mash, except when it is to be used in fine casting—in which case the pieces can be taken out as they are found. Drain in the strainer or colander until there is no water standing in the mixture. The mash will be moist and will still contain much water.

Measure four measuring cups of flour and add these to each gallon of mash that you have made. Mix well. Now, place the bucket back on the stove with an asbestos mat under the bucket. Cook at the lowest heat. Remember that flour scorches easily. Cover the bucket for the first hour until the mash has heated throughout. Remove the cover from the bucket and continue cooking (adding no water) until the mash is stiff enough to stand in piles by itself.

Dump the mash out upon about a dozen thicknesses of newspaper to cool. Use the mash as soon as it is cool enough to handle or store it in the refrigerator. In hot weather, cool mash is pleasant to work with. In the winter, let it reach room temperature before trying to work with it.

Papier Mâché Pulp

This is an improvement over boiled mash, and we call it pulp to distinguish it.

1. Fill an electric blender with 3 cups of water.
2. Tear two sheets of newspaper into $\frac{1}{4}$ sheets, then to strips about $\frac{3}{4}'' \times 2''$, and add them to the water.
3. Blend until smooth, making $1\frac{3}{4}$ cups.
4. Drain in wire strainer.
5. Make enough to fill the top of your double boiler.
6. Add 1 cup flour to 1 quart pulp.
7. Place water in bottom of double boiler.
8. Cover until hot. Remove lid.
9. Cook until excess water has evaporated, then until stiff and darker colored. Cooking time for $4\frac{1}{2}$ quarts is about 3 hours, depending on boiler and heat.
10. Add $\frac{1}{2}$ teaspoon oil of wintergreen.
11. Store in plastic bag in refrigerator until time to use. If you want to use immediately, dump it on a pad of newspaper and spread to cool.

Another kind of papier-mâché pulp starts with a whole roll of toilet paper. If you are not inclined to tear up newspaper, and if you need fine pulp that is particularly suitable for small things, this is the mash for you, because it is very finely textured.

Unroll the toilet paper (as much as will fit) into the top of a double boiler. Add enough water to cover. Cook until disintegrated. Add 1 cup of flour to each quart of pulp, and cook until thick enough to work with.

(There are bags of cellulose and adhesive available which you have only to mix with water to get a form of pulp. However, this is an expensive way of making a very finely textured pulp.)

Child's Stool and Toy Box

Materials:

heavy cardboard carton at least 12" square
mash

Cover the cardboard carton with about half a dozen layers of dry newspaper. Applying mash liberally, coat the mould to a thickness of about $\frac{3}{4}''$ all around. If your mould is not too large, bake the stool and toy box in the oven while it is still on its mould (page 159). Otherwise, let it dry naturally—this may take a week or more.

Remove from the mould when dry and coat the inside with a $\frac{1}{4}''$-thick layer of mash. Build up the corners thicker on the inside to reinforce the box. Remember that in a child's room it is likely to receive some rough treatment.

Color each side a separate shade by dyeing (see page 160) and paint a large (8") letter of the alphabet on each of the five sides. If you make several of these combination stools and toy boxes, children will love to use them as giant building blocks.

This makes an excellent project for finishing with epoxy coatings. (See page 160.)

Rectangular Boxes with Lids and Lips

Here is a simple method for making boxes with lids that match.

Materials:

stack of newspapers
flour and powdered resin glue mixture
mash

With a pencil, draw tearing-and-folding lines on one quarter-sheet of newspaper.

Illus. 8. If you paint large letters on the papier-mâché stool, it will look like an over-sized child's building block.

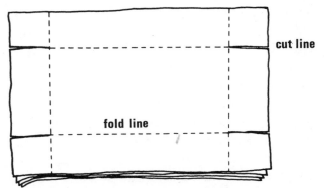

Illus. 9. Start your box by drawing tearing-and-folding lines like this.

cut line

fold line

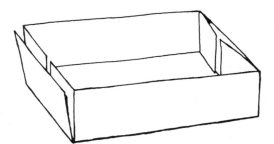

Illus. 10. Then fold into a deep tray shape.

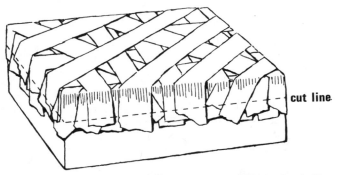

cut line

Illus. 11. Mark a line in the mash with the back of a knife blade as a guide for later cutting.

Cover the top and outside of the box with a $\frac{1}{8}''$-thick layer of mash. While this is still relatively soft, cut a line at the midpoint round the sides into the mash layer with the back of a knife blade. This line will be used as a guide-line for cutting later (Illus. 11).

Bake the box in the oven until the mash is dry. Cut the lid from the box with a sharp knife, following the guide-line incised in the mash (Illus. 12). Now add four thicknesses of $2\frac{1}{2}''$-wide paper to the inside of the box to form the lip (Illus. 13). Bake the box once again.

Line the inside of the box with $\frac{1}{8}''$-thick layer

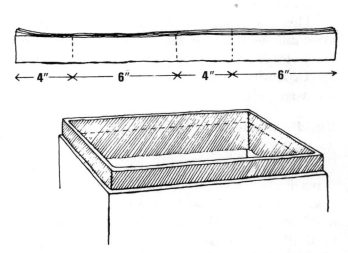

cut

Illus. 12. After baking, cut the lid from the box with a sharp knife along the guide lines you made in Illus. 11.

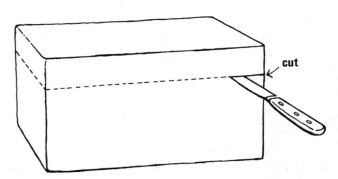

←— 4" —×—— 6" ——×— 4" —×—— 6" —→

Illus. 13. Add a lip to the inside of the box and bake again.

(Illus. 9). Now paste four quarter sheets of newspaper together, making the marked sheet the top one. Cut the paper with a pair of scissors along the cutting lines. Fold into a deep tray shape (Illus. 10). Bake at 200°F. Trim the top edge with scissors so that it is even. Cover the top with paste-coated strips; build these up to a thickness of four layers. Bake again. Smooth off any rough edges.

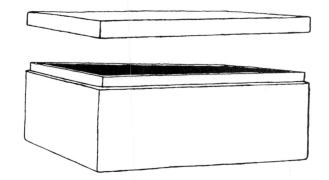

Illus. 14. Here is the box ready to be decorated or left plain.

of mash. Place the lid on the box and bake again. (Baking with the lid on makes it less likely that the lid will warp out of shape.)

If the box is to have a surface decoration, add more mash to the outside and make designs in the mash while it is still soft. Bake again and your box is finished. If you prefer a plainer box, leave it as it comes from the oven and finish according to the directions on pages 160 to 161.

Baking

If a piece can be baked in the oven, drying will be quicker. However, if it is too large, the sun will dry anything. Use an aluminum sun reflector or an aluminum-painted roof top to intensify the temperature. Leave the papier mâché drying in the sun long after it is dry. For baking in the oven, 200°F is the ideal heat. It makes a better, harder product.

For large pieces or large quantities of papier mâché, convert a closet or a small room to a dryer. Line the room completely with aluminum foil. (This intensifies the heat for the drying of your papier mâché.) Anything will dry naturally in an ordinary room with ordinary heat, but the air can get a bit damp if you are making several pieces and the damper the air gets, the slower they will dry.

There may be some warping each time you bake a piece. Provide for it in your design.

Some papers and glues will warp more than others, but it is the nature of papier mâché to warp, so take advantage of this to give your work individuality. Warping will not happen if your piece is dried on the mould. Give it a finish coat immediately after it is dry.

Decorating

Many of the pieces you make will look just right with a minimum of decoration, even though the texture of papier mâché is often decorative enough in itself. Part of the charm of papier mâché lies in the fact that you can achieve textures that cannot be obtained with other materials.

There may be times, however, when you will want to add something to the natural texture. One technique is collage, which is nothing more than the application of cut-out or torn designs, forms, or materials to an object. Simply paste them on the object.

Mash lends itself well to the punching or incising of designs into the surface of the semi-solid mash. Use pencils, pieces of dowelling, buttons, hairpins, etc., as tools.

Lay the mash on thickly so you can draw lines deep enough to make a dark, sharp shadow. Lay the mash on evenly too—a $\frac{1}{4}''$ depth works well. If the tool sticks to the

Illus. 15. As you can see, the texture of papier mâché is really decorative itself; however, there are several ways you can enhance it if you like.

mash when you press it in, and draws some of the mash back out with it, dip the tool in water and press the mash into the space again. The whole surface must be incised within a few hours, before a skin begins to form on the surface.

Dyes and water colors are excellent for coloring mash-coated objects— either as the ground color for over-all decoration or for the background color upon which other designs will be laid on. Use batik, fabric, leather, furniture or food dyes. Some of these may be available in alcohol-soluble or water-soluble types. The water-soluble dyes are simpler and more easy to use.

Finishes

Many objects should be coated or soaked with raw linseed oil and baked. Papier-mâché articles that have been given the linseed-oil treatment before baking are impervious to water. They tend, too, to be harder and stronger than articles that have not received such treatment. Where strength and durability are considerations, always treat your papier-mâché articles with linseed oil before baking them.

Opaque Finishes

Lacquer: Colored brushing lacquers are widely available and are easy to handle. (*Note:* Brushing lacquers are preferable to the spraying type of lacquer.) As with many finishes, lacquer is best applied in thin coats that are allowed to dry between coats. (Lacquer dries quickly by the evaporation of the vehicle, which is highly volatile.) For an extremely high-gloss finish, the surface can be smoothed with fine emery paper between coats.

Paint: Ordinary oil-base and water-base paints can be used on papier mâché, but their use should be limited to emergencies when other materials like lacquer are not available. Tempera (water) colors can also be used, but because the real enemy of papier mâché is moisture, the best finishes are those that repel moisture.

Transparent Finishes

Lacquer: Clear brushing lacquer is as widely available as the pigmented, opaque kind. As you may already have discovered when you made the papier-mâché beads, it is simple to work with. Small objects can be dipped repeatedly in thinned clear lacquer to give a quickly applied and attractive finish. Objects like large bowls and wastepaper baskets require that the finish be applied by brushing. Unlike paint and varnish, which seem to lie on the surface, succeeding coats of lacquer blend into under-coats. If you find that one coat has left brush marks, cover them up by blending them in on the next coat. (*Tip:* The thinner the lacquer, the easier it is to blend. Use lacquer thinner to dilute it, adding more thinner at intervals to make up for the solvent lost by evaporation.)

Shellac: Here is another relatively quick-drying finish that you can use to advantage on certain pieces. On papier mâché, shellac has a soft "feel" and, like lacquer, it is taken up in part by the papier mâché instead of lying on the surface. Shellac comes in clear (white) and orange types; use the white shellac for most finishes, but experiment with orange shellac if you want some interesting antique effects. Always thin shellac to a water-like consistency with denatured alcohol.

Unfortunately, shellac does not make a good finish on objects that are to be exposed to alcohol or water. A shellac-coated papier-mâché surface would soon be marred if glasses were set on it; shellac would be an inappropriate finish for coasters of papier mâché or for a table covered in papier mâché. Water causes a whitish "bloom" to appear on shellac-covered surfaces; this bloom seems to persist even after the surface is dry.

Liquid Epoxy: Various liquid epoxy finishes are available in clear and colored (pigmented) form. These are marketed in two containers, one containing the epoxy resin and the other the hardener.

An object coated with epoxy can be bent

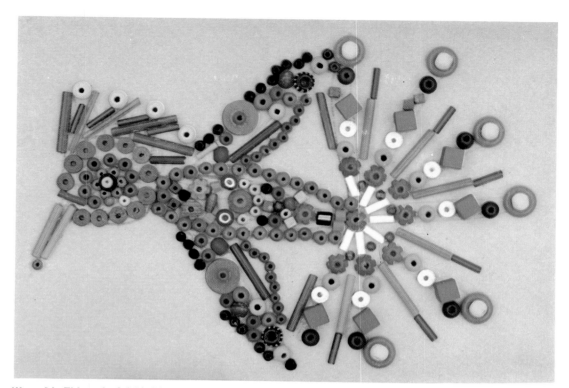

Illus. A1. This colorful bird looks so lively that he seems about to fly off the page! All these beads are attached with glue to a paper background.

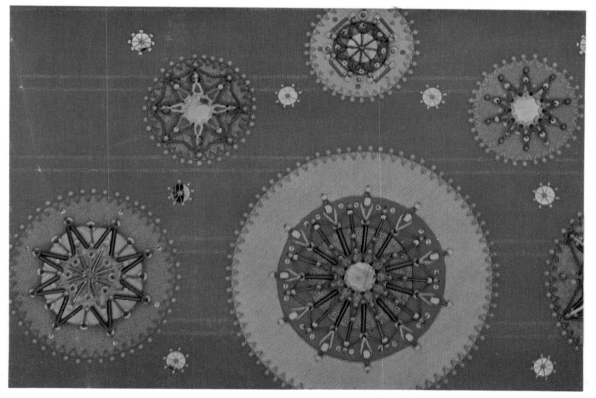

Illus. A2. This colorful assortment of geometric motifs was embroidered randomly on a piece of fabric. Sequins and beads between the circles add sparkle to the wall hanging.

Illus. B1. This crayon-etched collage was made by cutting interesting shapes from single-color crayon etchings and pasting them onto a background of a contrasting color.

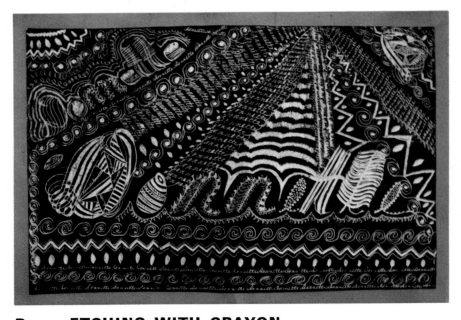

Illus. B2. Donnette used her name as her dominant motif in this crayon etching. She embellished the name with a variety of intricate line designs, and surrounded these delicately etched patterns with bold waves and stripes.

Illus. C1. You do not need to place a crayon-etched design on tagboard around a container. Instead, you can finish it as described on page 30 and make a stabile.

Illus. C2. Make functional vases and other containers by placing a crayon-etched design around tin cans and cardboard cartons. (Left to right) A coffee can, an oatmeal carton, and a gallon-sized milk carton covered with etched crayon designs.

ETCHING WITH CRAYON ■ C

Illus. D1. You can repeat a batik design as many as four times without redrawing it, merely by folding the cloth. This cotton voile scarf was folded in half twice.

Illus. D2. Where you must draw a batik design carefully in wax, as in this wall hanging, you use a special tool called a "tjanting."

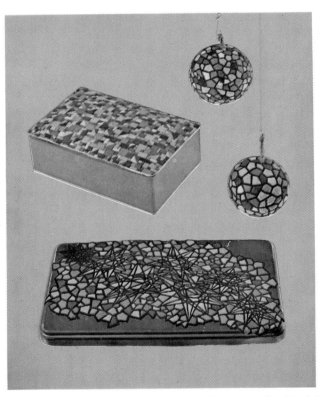

Illus. D3. These colorful items are all decorated with felt mosaic. The technique is simple, the results intricate-looking and attractive.

D ■ BATIK—FELT CRAFTING

Illus. E1. Serve a delicious home-made dinner in this handsome apron decorated with Trapunto.

Illus. E2 (right). Make knee-padded Trapunto crawlers for any active little crawler! Instructions are on page 73.

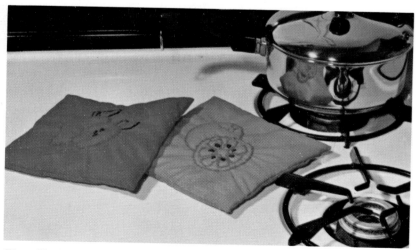

Illus. E3. Colorful Trapunto pot holders help you "keep cool" in the kitchen.

Illus. F1. You can use a naturally-colored assortment of pressed flowers to decorate innumer-able projects. See the article *Flower Pressing* for some ideas.

F ■ FLOWER PRESSING

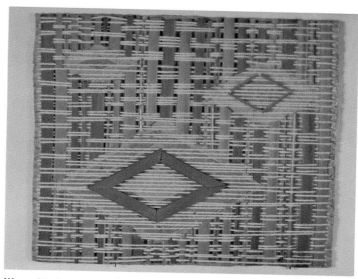

Illus. G1. In cardboard loom weaving, corrugated cardboard is the foundation for woven patterns. Here, four-ply yarn provides the warp and spray-painted cattail leaves, small twigs and plant stems make up the woof.

Illus. G2. A large milk carton forms the loom for this unusual container. Strands of straw, yellow chrysanthemums, poppies, tree twigs, and Mexican fire-bush twigs are woven into the vertical warp. See page 109 for instructions.

Illus. G3. This uncarved piece of wood immediately suggested a wild duck to the observer. When the feathers and spots were painted in, there was no doubt left as to what it was. A protective coat of shellac adds a fine sheen to this bird's body.

Illus. G4. Rock painting, using enamels, transforms a group of rocks into totally different forms. Note how each rock suggests its own decoration—a round one demanded a geometric design, a rough one, an abstract design, and so on.

CREATING WITH NATURE'S MATERIALS ■ G

Illus. H1. You can tole paint on tin using the same techniques that you use on wood. This canister has been painted with three sizes of brushes, and then antiqued for an aged look. Use a canister like this to hold flowers or, filled with sand, as a doorstop. Instructions are on page 129.

Illus. H2. Decorated with hearts and flowers, a smooth and shiny child's chair is not hard to paint, but it adds just the right touch to a simple room.

Illus. H3. A metal chrysanthemum plaque uses just the basic tole painting stroke to make fat "mums" and realistic leaves.

H ■ TOLE PAINTING

Illus. I1. You can make many brilliant cellophane creations using chicken wire. See if you can make a vibrant fish like this one.

Illus. I2. A surprise doll made of cellophane is a novel idea for a party gift. Instructions for surprise dolls are on page 134.

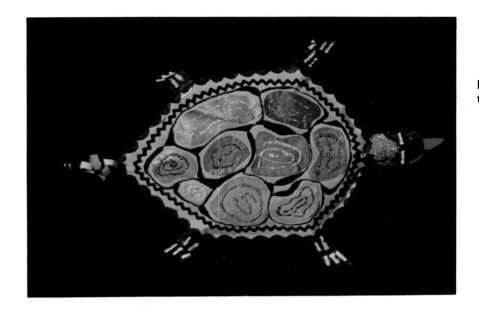

Illus. J1. This richly colored paper turtle pillow is decorated with temperas, glitter, rick-rack, and tissue paper.

Illus. J2. Vibrant, symmetrical string creations, not difficult to create, make unusual wall decorations.

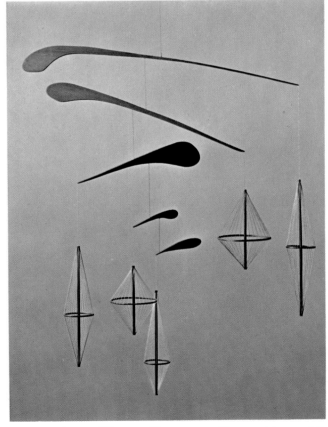

Illus. J3. For a different effect, try making a string mobile such as this one. Instructions are on page 180.

J ■ CRAFTING WITH PAPER—STRING THINGS

Illus. K1. Easy to make, light-weight balsa-wood boomerangs can be painted or decorated with decals.

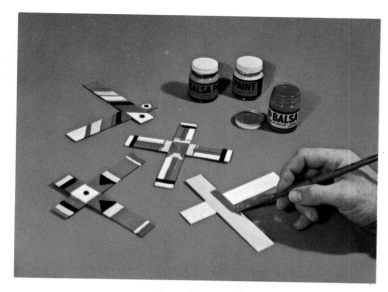

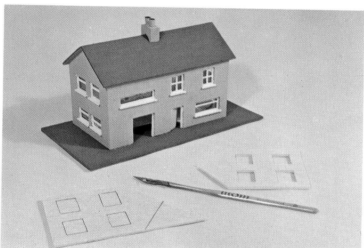

Illus. K2. It is best to make buildings with cut-outs for windows by using templates or patterns.

Illus. K3. Box kites are very efficient flyers, and can be all balsa or balsa-and-tissue constructions.

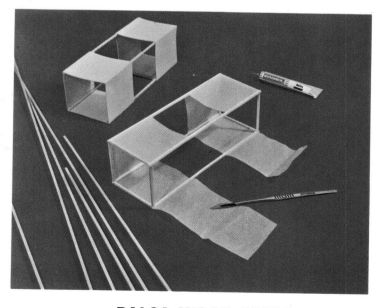

BALSA WOOD MODELS ■ K

Illus. L1. Cover up that bare spot on your wall with a rustic-looking Hairpin Lace wall hanging which is sure to catch the eye—and admiration—of all your guests.

Illus. L2. Once you learn the Hairpin Lace technique, you will surely want to make longer and longer strips. Join the strips together into a lovely afghan such as this one.

L ■ CROCHETED HAIRPIN LACE

Illus. M1 (right) and M2 (below). Searching for an idea for your needlepoint? Have a youngster color a pleasing scene. Plan your stitches and colors according to this picture and then stitch! Follow the irregular lines of the original drawing for an interesting design.

Illus. M3. This pillow's design is a Bargello line pattern stitched in pairs. This means that you make two stitches instead of one next to each other before the next step in the pattern.

Illus. M4 (left). Buy a large, uncovered button and cover it with needlepoint. Cut Mono 14 canvas according to the pattern accompanying the uncovered button and then plot and stitch—with one strand of Persian yarn—a Cross stitch design. (For Mono canvas, you must cross each stitch as you go.) Also try using Penelope 10 and stitch with tapestry yarn and embroidery floss.

Illus. N1. You can stitch an elegant purse like this one simply using the Cross stitch, or you can choose any other of the decorative stitches described in the article *Needlepoint*.

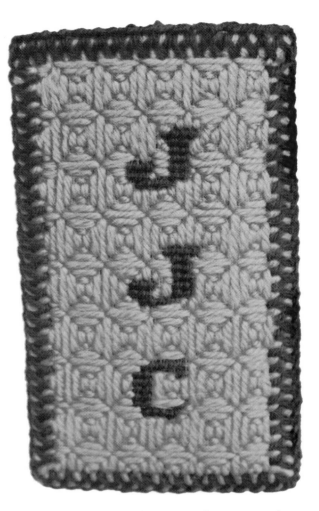

Illus. N2. You can make an eyeglass case using small scraps of canvas left over from other projects. For an inexpensive, yet thoughtful gift, personalize a case with the recipient's initials.

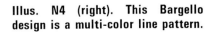

Illus. N3 (above). There are several types of Bargello belts you can make. This one is a zig-zag line pattern.

Illus. N4 (right). This Bargello design is a multi-color line pattern.

N ■ NEEDLEPOINT

Illus. 01. The variety and combination of color, pattern and stitch in this patchwork doll make it a totally unique needlepoint item. Stitch any of the needlepoint stitches that you wish and your result is bound to be as imaginative as this.

Illus. 02. A triangular framework pattern is another possibility for a Bargello belt.

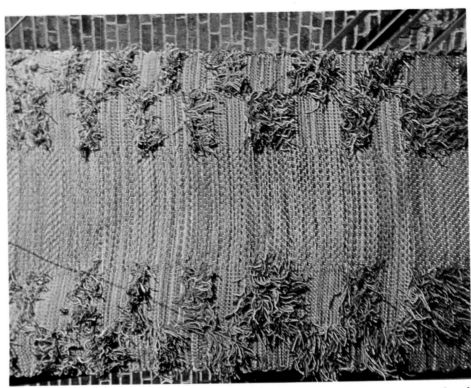

Illus. P1. This multi-colored rug was not even woven on a loom! To make it, use the pile technique described on page 255.

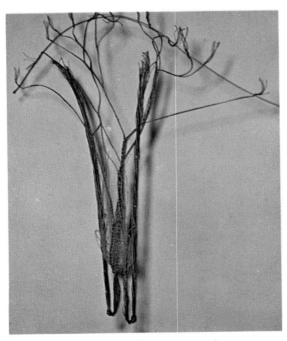

Illus. P2. A mobile using tabby weave and warp wrapping softly moves when the slightest breeze blows. See pages 259 to 260 for instructions.

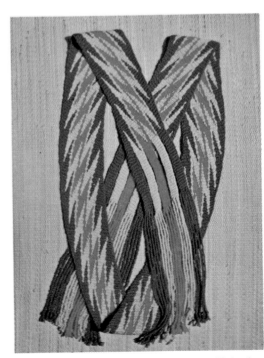

Illus. P3. Vibrant colors and the striking lightning design combine to create this outstanding finger-woven belt.

P ■ OFF-LOOM WEAVING—FINGER WEAVING

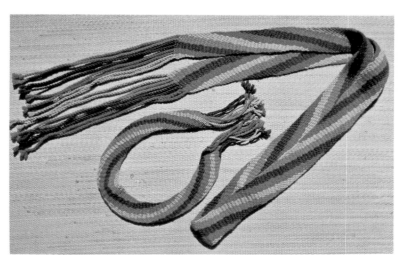

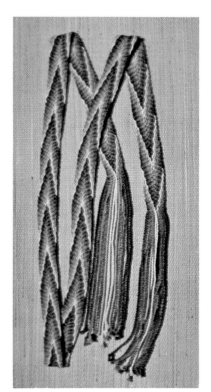

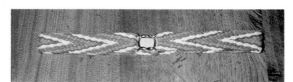

Illus. Q1 (left). This is the diamond pattern which will result if you finger weave following the directions on pages 267 to 268.

Illus. Q2 (above). For an unusual gift, make a diagonal design belt and matching collar. Strikingly colored yarns emphasize the diagonal patterns.

Illus. Q3. Not all belts need to have a fringe. This chevron belt was handsomely completed with a buckle instead.

Illus. Q4. Weaving the chevron design is like weaving the diagonal design from the center in both directions—first to the right and then to the left.

Illus. Q5. This splendid Peruvian rep braid was masterfully woven in vibrant colors.

Illus. R1. Fabric cut-outs add depth to this collage of magazine cut-outs and hand-colored papers.

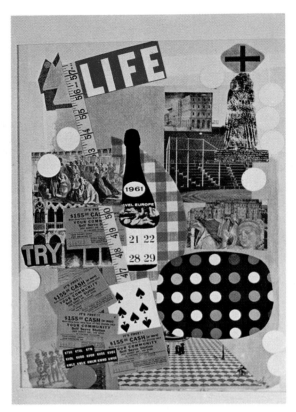

Illus. R2. Raffle tickets, a tape measure, magazine cut-outs, playing cards, and calendar numbers are pasted on a rice-paper background to make this attractive collage.

Illus. R3. This is a charming greeting card of colored tissue paper. The light areas are made by brushing on a design of liquid bleach.

R ■ COLLAGE

Illus. S1. Angora yarn covers the kittens searching for missing mittens in this diorama. Real leaves decorate the stage, and a cylinder wishing well is on the far right.

Illus. S2. Green velvet curtains attached to pipe cleaners give this diorama a theatrical touch.

Illus. S3. This gruesome mask was made with melted crayon. See the article *Decorative Masks* for instructions.

DECORATIVE MASKS—DIORAMAS ■ **S**

Illus. T1. Stories and poems can be exciting sources of inspiration, as is shown in this marvelous diorama of ''Jack and the Beanstalk.''

Illus. U1. The folded form of a paper square has been shaped into a belladonna lily.

Illus. U2. Cup shells dyed natural pansy colors make a particularly lovely and true-to-life arrangement.

Illus. U3 (right). You can arrange gar scale zinnias of various sizes and colors in many striking and artistic ways.

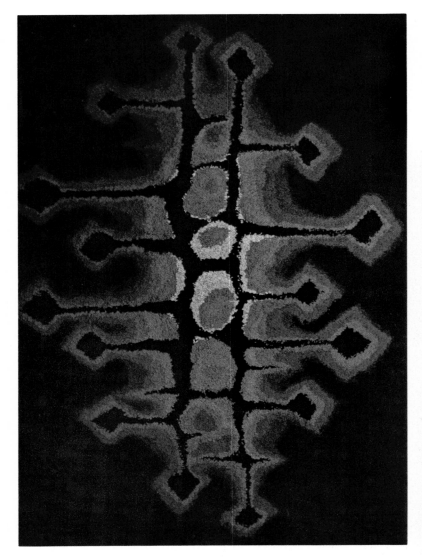

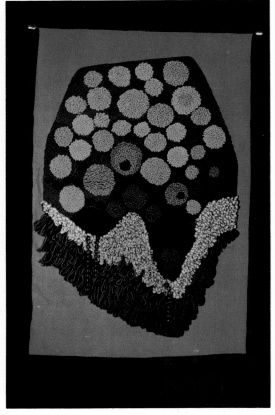

Illus. V1. A harmony of color and shape blend attractively in this wool hooked rug made with short, un-clipped loops.

Illus. V2. When you have learned the hooking and knotting techniques on pages 335 to 343, try combining them for a truly original rug or wall hanging. This is basically a hooked wall hanging with a triple row of fringe at the bottom made of long, unclipped knotted loops.

Illus. V3 (left). This colorful knotted rug is very compact, with $2\frac{1}{2}''$ clipped pile of 4-ply worsted yarn.

V ■ HOOKED AND KNOTTED RUGS

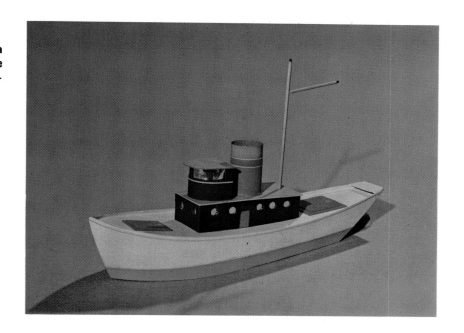

Illus. W1 (right). Model boat building is a fun pastime. After you have read the article *Model Boats*, see if you can construct a tugboat such as this one.

Illus. W2 (below). To make a submarine, follow the instructions on pages 366 to 371.

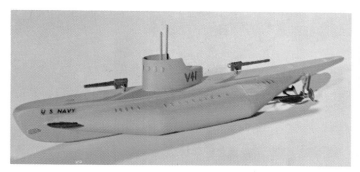

Illus. W3. The tesserae in this crayon mosaic are cut in varying shapes from paper that has been rubbed with crayon. Contrast in color values is the key to a pleasing crayon mosaic.

MODEL BOATS—MOSAICS ■ **W**

Illus. X1. The head and neck of this proud peacock mosaic are made from rice, sunflower seeds, and pussy willows. Bird seeds and chicken feathers adorn the splendid tail.

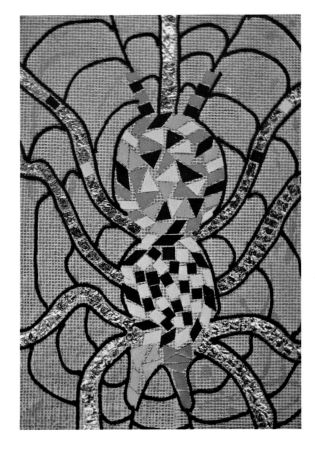

Illus. X2. A sheet of Japanese Shibui rice paper, placed over green construction paper, makes an appropriate web-like background for this spider mosaic. The dullness of the background serves to emphasize the richness of the body and the brilliance of the tin-foil legs. Black yarn outlines the insect's body and emphasizes the web-like character of the rice paper.

Illus. Y1. A wallpaper sample book provided this rooster with a wonderful variety of color and texture.

Illus. Z1. This junk sculpture was made from 21 thread spools, 7 ice cream sticks, 100" of string, a wooden trophy base, 3 sections of a ¼" dowel, 4 short, rectangular wood scraps, a perfume bottle top, and 9 wooden pegs. The entire sculpture was painted with tempera paint.

Illus. Z2. This is a tempera-painted fruit tray on a poster-board backing.

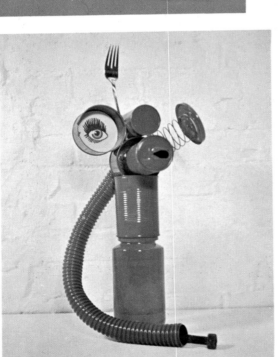

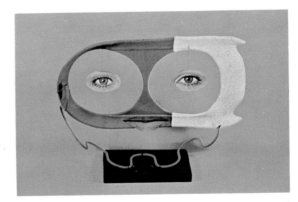

Illus. Z3. An unbelievable mass of junk was compiled to create this masterful sculpture: a pickle jar with colored water, vegetable can, tuna can, juice can, hair-roller spring, plastic coffee lid, metal fork, vacuum-cleaner hose, large nut and bolt, and magazine cut-outs. The entire ensemble was sprayed with red enamel paint.

Illus. Z4. This bizarre sculpture was based around an automobile headlight bezel (faceplate), and incorporates an automobile seat spring, string, magazine cut-outs, and a pine baseboard. The sculpture was painted with latex.

Z ■ JUNK SCULPTURES

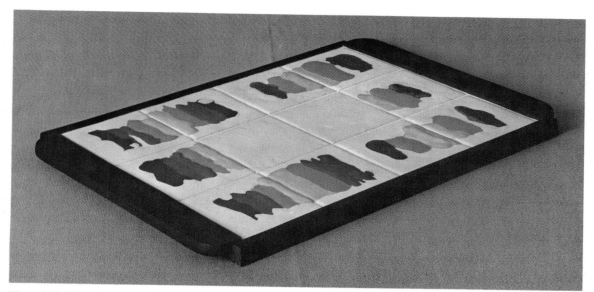

Illus. AA1. The abstract enamelled design on this cheeseboard does have a regular pattern; the colors blend pleasingly from red to yellow to red on one half, and from blue to yellow to blue on the other.

Illus. AA2. Bright colors and lively patterns make an extraordinary menagerie of enamelled plastic foam animals.

Illus. BB1. This bright "sail" adds definite character to this table setting.

Illus. BB2. The name of this style of folded napkin, the "Princess," illustrates the elegance and dignity it brings to your table.

Illus. BB3. An attractive buffet table is charming as well as fun to decorate.

BB ■ **NAPKIN FOLDING**

Illus. CC1. For a wilt-proof bouquet, make flowers such as these using the curling and quilling techniques.

Illus. DD1. These are tumble-polished Oregon beach agates.

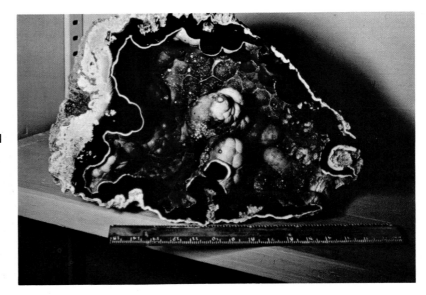

Illus. DD2. This is chalcedony after coral from Tampa Bay, Florida.

Illus. DD3. You can easily mount your polished pebbles on silver wire which you wind around pebbles as shown here.

DD ▪ PEBBLE POLISHING

Illus. EE1. Potatoes are an easily accessible medium. This delicate design was potato printed.

Illus. FF2. This bell was made by pressing clay around a glass jar. Strips of clay and pressed designs add interest. A tin can and a bolt head placed inside the pot make the bell ring.

Illus. FF1. A brightly glazed vase was made by first pressing clay inside a cardboard box, and then peeling away the box.

Illus. FF3. These weed pots were made by forming clay over smooth rocks.

Illus. FF4. Make coasters by pressing circles of clay over a shallow glass bowl. These designs were pressed with texture tools. Bright oil colors were added to clear sealer glaze to achieve a uniform color.

FF ■ SLAB CERAMICS

repeatedly until it breaks, yet the coating will not chip, crack or break. When you make an object where strength is a requisite, coat it with a liquid epoxy product and you will find that you have created something practically indestructible. Be certain to use epoxy to coat wastepaper baskets, furniture and architectural panels.

Fibre-Glass Resin: This coating has a higher gloss finish than epoxy, dries just as hard, and withstands heat just as well. Keep in refrigerator to lengthen shelf life before use. Follow the manufacturer's directions. Fibre-glass resin comes in a large can containing the material itself and a small bottle of catalyst to add just before use. You must use all the mixture within $\frac{1}{2}$ hour of mixing. Use rubber gloves and follow all other precautions and directions on the can to the letter.

Fibre-glass resin is recommended for those objects which can be placed in an automatic dishwasher with water and cleaning agents.

Chess Table and Chessmen

Materials:
    stack of newspapers
    flour and powdered resin glue mixture
    38-inch circle of $\frac{1}{4}$-inch plywood
    32 small lead weights
    mash (approximately 1 gallon needed)

CHESS TABLE: For the table, cover the surface of the circle of plywood with a $\frac{3}{8}$"-layer of mash. Mark off the squares, 8 each way, $2\frac{3}{4}$" for each square. Set the plywood up at an angle so it will be easier to see and work on. Punch the surface, almost to the wood, in a pattern in each square. The alternate squares that are to be black make one pattern; the squares to be red, another. A border round the edge with flowers and leaves to fill in the curved space completes the pattern.

In working on such a large piece, finish the punching before the mash gets so dry as to form a skin on the top. If it begins to form, blot it with tapping motions with a damp cloth. This will cause trouble only on dry, hot days. Ordinarily you will have several hours—much more than the few it will take you to punch-decorate the surface.

When the table top is thoroughly dry, paste a four-layer thickness of paste-coated paper around the edge, its top edge $\frac{1}{16}$" below the level of the top of the mash-covered top. Let the edge dry with the table standing on its edge, leaning against the wall. Cover the surface of the edge of the table with a $\frac{3}{4}$"-thickness of mash and punch in a decorative border. Let dry. Sand. Use water color or dye to color the alternate squares red and black, the border and edge black.

plywood table top

Illus. 16. Steps in making a chess-table top. A papier-mâché chess table will complement your set of papier-mâché chessmen.

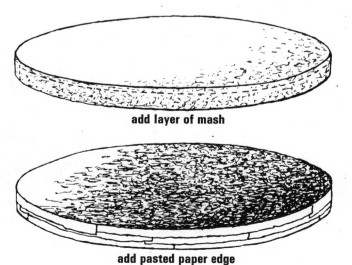

add layer of mash

add pasted paper edge

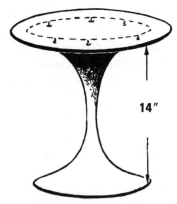

Illus. 17. Table base.

Illus. 18. Here are the six chess pieces from left to right: pawn, knight, queen, king, bishop, and rook (or castle).

Make a pedestal-shaped base of $\frac{1}{2}$"-screening, covered inside and out with a $\frac{1}{2}$"-layer of mash. Attach it to the table with six screws (see Illus. 17). The base of this table is 14" high, to serve also as a coffee table. You may wish to play chess at standard table height, 28".

CHESSMEN: Paste four quarter sheets of paper. Tear in 1" strips, and make little rolled sticks for armatures as follows:

   2 Kings—2, 5-inch sticks
   2 Queens—2, 4$\frac{1}{2}$-inch sticks
   4 Bishops—4, 4-inch sticks
   4 Knights—4, 4$\frac{1}{2}$-inch sticks
   4 Rooks or Castles—4, 3-inch strips
   16 Pawns—16, 1$\frac{1}{2}$-inch strips

The pieces will be of different heights and thicknesses, but will be built in exactly the same way except for the head which identifies the piece. The horse's head of the knight is made by bending down one inch of the stick and fastening it in place with a one-thickness strip of paper to hold it till it is dry.

Dry the sticks on a baking sheet or aluminum foil. Sort out the sticks in rows in this and all the following procedures. This will save you time in sorting later. Work with the baking sheet in front of you and place each piece back on the sheet in the same place after you have worked on it. Build the base on each piece with mash, punching a border around the

Illus. 19. A complete chess set and table top. Dye half of the pieces black, and the other half red, using fabric dye, and you are ready for a tournament.

lower $\frac{3}{4}$ inch. Press a lead weight into the bottom of each and make sure that the bottom is concave, so the chess piece will not rock.

Bake the pieces on the baking sheet, standing them up in a normal position. Build the heads on all the pawns: Make a little round ball, roll it in the palms of your hands and stick onto the head of the stick.

Build the tops of all the major pieces, then bake them all in the oven. Cover the shank of the pieces between the top and the base with mash. Bake again. The reason for baking between steps is a good one: The pieces are much easier to handle if you can hold them firmly without damaging a part you have already completed.

Dye half of your pieces black (16 in all, half of each type), and half Chinese red. Apply one coat of clear lacquer and give the table one coat of lacquer. Mix a package of cerise fabric dye and dip all the chess pieces, standing them on layers of paper to drain. Apply the cerise dye to the chess table with a brush and wipe off any excess with a cloth.

Apply ten coats of clear lacquer to the finished chess table on which succeeding generations of your family can learn to play the Royal Game.

Illus. 20. A set of papier-mâché candle holders is simple to make and will add a festive touch to any table.

FLEXIBLE PLASTIC FOAM

Flexible foam is a plastic called *polyurethane,* and it has many practical uses: mattresses, cushions, and insulating and packing materials are a few examples. It also lends itself to bending, cutting, fluffing and shaping. All the projects in this article are made from remnants of medium-weight foam picked up at a mattress factory. Factories are all too often glad to give the stuff away. The scraps from a factory are usually available in straight bars that are often more than a yard long. If you do not have a mattress factory nearby, try department stores and upholstering shops. Look in the telephone book for wholesale dealers and manufacturers of the material under the category "Plastics"; even if you cannot find it free, it is not expensive to buy.

Be forewarned that flexible foam changes color. It comes either white or pale cream, but eventually turns a dull yellow. You can slow down the change in color by keeping the material out of direct sunlight, but it will change eventually anyway. If you find this objectionable, you can paint your project with poster colors, gouache, or acrylic paints. You will be more satisfied, however, if you just accept the color as a property of the material, instead of trying to camouflage the eventual change.

The main tool you need is a pair of *sharp* scissors that cuts right up to the point. A knife cannot make straight, even cuts in foam the way a scissors can. A paper cutter works well on foam, but it is not necessary since a scissors is satisfactory.

You also need a tube or squeeze-bottle of glue. The kind of glue you use with flexible foam is very important. Ordinary glues for wood or paper dry out and become hard and brittle, cracking the foam. Art and craft shops sell all-purpose glues that remain flexible when dry, and you should buy one of these for your hobby.

To bend the bars of foam permanently, you must insert wire right down the center of the bars. For foam bars which are $1\frac{1}{2}''$ square, 18-gauge iron wire is thick enough. If a bar is thicker, however, this wire is too light and the bar will spring back to its original position. Use a heavier wire (16-, 14- or even 12-gauge) for thicker pieces of foam. Instructions for straightening and inserting the wire are on page 165.

To cut the wire, use a pair of 6″ long-nosed pliers with side cutters. These cut any gauge wire you use, and you can bend loops in the ends of the wire with the long pointed nose.

Not necessary but sometimes fun to use are scraps and trinkets to highlight the flexible foam figures. Pins with plastic or glass heads, twine, cloth and paper are only a few of the odds and ends available to you. Do not rely on these additions to define your figure, though; use them only to accent it. Flexible foam is easy to work with, and you can cut an identifiable shape that needs very few additions!

Condensed from the book, "Creating with Flexible Foam" by Ab de Brouwer | © 1971 by Sterling Publishing Co., Inc., New York

Illus. 1. A small puppy is a good first project: you can make him as plain or as intricate as you like. Snips into the foam bars make fluffy fur, and scraps of colored paper become eyes and a nose. Try bending this pup's limbs into amusing positions.

Illus. 2. These four bars, with wire inserted down the middle, are the parts of the dog in Illus. 1. If the wire accidentally comes out one side when you insert the wire into the foam, pull it back and re-direct it. The hole will not show.

Modelled Animals

Dog

For your first project, try modelling a little dog like the one in Illus. 1. (After you learn the techniques, create your own original design!) Cut two bars of flexible foam about 1½" square by 16" long, another bar 1½" square by 20", and another ⅜" square by 4" long. Set these aside while you prepare the wire:

If the wire is bent or curved, you must straighten it before you insert it into the foam. Take a wire a couple of yards long and grip one end in a vice or twist it around an object firmly fastened to a base. Grip the free end of the wire with the pliers and pull as hard as you can. Pulling stretches the wire slightly, thus straightening it. Cut it to the proper lengths— a few inches longer than the flexible foam bars —or it will curl again.

Take one of the wires and insert its end into the end of a foam bar. Thrust the wire down the center of the bar along its entire length and out the other end. By pinching the foam, you can feel how the wire is travelling and thus guide its progress. If the wire is angled wrong and comes out through the side of the bar, pull it back a bit and continue. Leave some wire sticking out at both ends of the bar.

Insert wire in the other two bars of foam, Now you can bend the bars any way you please. and they will stay put. If the bars unbend to their original position, the wire is too thin for the bar. Remove the wire and insert one of a heavier gauge.

For the dog in Illus. 1, use the 20"-bar for the head, neck, body and tail. Before you bend this bar for these sections, place a 16"-bar on top of it in the center and bend the shorter bar downward on both sides to make the front legs. Keep the body rather short by setting the hind legs about two thirds of the distance from the

Illus. 3. When you first assemble the four foam bars, this creature does not look like much of anything. In the view on the left, he could be a horse, goat, or a dog. But when you move his limbs and make a few quick snips with the scissors, he becomes a personality all his own.

front legs to the end. The tail section is short —bend it up so it wags!

Bend the neck and head portion up also, and decide how long a head you want. Place the shortest bar under the head and bend up it while you bend the head down. The ends of the short bar become, of course, ears on your little foam dog. Shape them with your fingers so they cup outward.

Now you can snip off those little ends of wire that stick out of the foam bars. Do this to every end except the feet: strip the foam back a little way from the end of the wire, as if you were pulling up a pants leg. Cut the wire close to the foam, and then push the foam back to its original position. The wire is now invisible.

In Illus. 3, another little dog is clowning around by striking a humorous pose. His left front and back paws are raised and bent (and the wire ends snipped off as well), while the wires on the right paws were pounded into a board so the dog could stand. To do this, cut off the protruding wire except for a length

equal to the thickness of the board. Pull the foam back a little so you can see what you are doing: bend the wire into a 90° angle and tap it into the board with a hammer.

This method of attaching foam to a board works for small figures, but if your piece is large, secure it this way: leave the end of the wire long enough so it is twice as thick as the board. Pass the wire through a small hole pierced in the board. On the underside, loop the end of the wire back towards the board so it is shaped like a hook. Hammer the point into the bottom of the board.

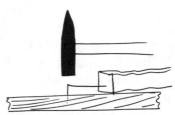

Illus. 4. To attach a foam figure to a board, pull the foam away from the wire a little—as if you were pulling up a pants leg—and hammer the wire gently.

Now, how about a realistic head for this playful fellow? Run a wire from the end of the head into the upper jaw as far as the nose—about 2½″ to 3″. Give the foam a couple of snips with the scissors to open the mouth, and then bend the upper jaw away from the lower one. This makes an indentation for the eyes. Make two cuts along the side of the nose to lift it, and two more cuts for the nostrils. Almost without realizing it, you have started to sculpture the form.

The eyes, tongue and nose of the little dog add to his perky appearance—but they are only paper, cut, curled and glued to look astonishingly real. A large orange or brown circle serves as the eye, and upon this is a smaller black circle, the pupil of the eye. Glue these two pieces together carefully—and highlight this rather ordinary eye with a narrow, white paper triangle, the sharp end pointing towards the middle of the eye. Close up, the eye looks unrealistic. But when you stand back and see the piece from another point of view, the little eye sparkles with life.

The pup's paper tongue is made of red con- struction paper which was curled before it was glued into place. There are several ways to form the nose. You could, of course, cut a plain black circle and glue it just the way it is. But for more depth, take a black circle and fold it so the center of the circle is the apex of a cone or a three-dimensional triangle. Glue this to the foam for a realistic nose.

A coat of fur adds life to a flexible foam animal! Make the fur by snipping the foam at an angle, with the cuts pointing towards the body. On the head, the snips should angle towards the nose. The completed pup is all fluffed up and eager for a romp!

But do not let this pup be the end of your animal models. You now have the know-how, so you can go on to create an entire menagerie. Horses, cats, camels, donkeys—even whimsical creatures that have no relation to reality!

Dragon

A flexible foam dragon is built basically the same way that a dog is, but there are some fine points. Take a foam strip about 32″ long and snip it with scissors so it tapers from head to

Illus. 5. Narrow foam bars with wire through the middle curve and bend in different directions for an eerie dragon. The sharp features—pointed tongue, bulging eyes and bizarre wings which seem to take off— help to emphasize the spiny, uneven texture which the artist has purposely created.

Illus. 6. These paper features—the sharp points and crisp folds—contribute to the fiery appearance of the dragon in Illus. 5.

tail. Then work a wire through the bar and make jagged cuts to indicate spines. Instead of just clipping the foam as you did for the dog, snip little wedges completely out of the foam to make the spines stand out more strongly on the back.

Because the body is so long, the legs must be strong: place them under the body, perpendicular to it, and bend them *upward*. Wrap them completely around the body and bend them downward on the sides. Without this complete turn around the body, the legs would slide off and would not support the body.

The features and wings of the dragon are pieces of other materials attached to the foam. The dragon's wings are made of paper that was pleated several times like a paper fan. The pleats radiate from one point which you cut off (Illus. 6). Form the spikes by trimming each pleat to a point. Remember to make the right one the opposite of the left. Each dragon claw is a long narrow paper triangle, folded in half the long way and then bent in the middle. For a comb, that spiky row along the back of the dragon's head, cut a curved piece of red paper and trim it with points. The flames

spewing from the dragon's jaws are also bright red construction paper. His eyes are rolled paper tubes.

When you add features to your flexible foam creatures—whether they are paint, paper, pipe cleaners or plastic—remember that the most interesting chap is not the one who has been taken over by his ornaments, but the one who has been accented and individualized by them. Do not go overboard when you decorate.

Modelled Human Figure

You can create a whole gang of little men from flexible foam with the same principles used for making animals. Observe human figures carefully and note their proportions:

The legs are usually as long as the body, head and neck together, while the knees fall in the middle of the legs. When the arms hang loosely, the finger-tips are about a hand's length above the knee. The elbow lies in the middle of an arm with a clenched fist. The head measures about one seventh or one eighth the height of the entire figure. The width of the shoulders is equal to twice the height of the head. Pay close attention to these proportions so you understand them, but then forget them as quickly as possible. Only uninteresting figures correspond to an exact formula!

An upright human figure without a head is shown in Illus. 7. It is made of two bars of foam, each one wider than it is thick. The legs are bent from a bar 14″ long. The body and arms are from one bar which is slightly thinner than that used for the legs, but 21″ long. (The exact lengths do not matter, of course, but keep the bars in the ratio of 2 to 3.)

Bisect the long bar with the short one, in the middle of each, so the short bar is on top. Bend the legs downward around the long bar. Now bend the long bar *up*, and find a point on the torso where the shoulders should be. Cross the two ends at this point, and bend them downward for the arms.

For a simple foam head, first insert a wire into the shoulders. Stick a round (or oval) piece of foam on the other end of the wire by holding the wire coming from the body firmly with two fingers around the torso.

Showing Movement

The running figure in Illus. 7 is a first cousin of the headless man next to him. Notice that even without any additions of beads, trinkets and colorful ornaments, it is still possible to make a lively figure showing a lot of motion. The main addition here is a scarf, actually a long thin piece of foam. No wire is necessary for the scarf. Instead, place the middle of the scarf against the back of the neck; bring the ends forward and down over the shoulders. Then cross them over each other in front and turn them to the back again. Tie the ends together in a half-knot. The material is stiff enough to stay there without any other fastening.

Make a cap from a piece of foam the same thickness as the scarf. Wrap it around the head and attach it with a few drops of glue. Small pieces of foam stuck on the ends of the wire make very satisfactory hands and feet. Leave enough wire protruding through the feet to insert in a block of foam or a board for support. Bend the fellow's legs, arms and torso—and there he goes, running to catch a bus!

Flexible Foam Heads

In the human figure you just made, there was not enough room on the face to add features. Nor was there a need to—the feeling of movement was conveyed without small details. But to use up small bits of foam—and also just for fun—try making a weird face with protruding lips, bulbous eyes, and a bizarre nose. Do not try to copy nature—it is difficult with flexible foam anyway, and not very creative. Instead, use your imagination and exaggerate the normal features of a face.

Illus. 7. At the left is the basic form of a human figure, still without a head. At the right is a crouching figure who looks as if he is running. Notice his separated, slightly bent legs, and the bent arms which help propel him forward.

Illus. 8. If the piece of foam to which you are attaching a bead is thick enough, use wire instead of thread as a fastener. String the bead on the wire and bend the wire in half. Insert the wire through the foam and out the back. Wrap the ends of the wire around each other to secure the bead, and fasten this eye to the rest of the face with glue.

For a large head, use a rectangular foam block. Cut just enough off the corners to establish a shape. Glue odd pieces that you have cut—blocks for ears, long narrow scraps for eyebrows, triangles for a nose. There are as many ways to create a face as there are people's faces. But keep the following points in mind as you work:

Exaggerate the features and keep them as three-dimensional as possible. You are not painting, you are modelling! Let the features jut out, even to outlandish proportions, but be sure your sculpture is still recognizable as a face. Avoid painting any part of the head until you have attached all the pieces. Painting is too often an attempt to camouflage a bad form.

In constructing an imaginary head, beads often serve as eyes. To press a bead deeply into the foam, use a strong thread (waxed button-hole or nylon thread) or wire. Insert the needle or wire into the foam *behind* the eye and bring it out in front. String the bead on it, and stick the needle or wire back into the foam. If you use thread, pull both ends tightly and tie them together to hold the bead in place.

If you pull tightly as you tie the bead, you create a hollow that is like the actual hollow around a real eye. For even greater realism, create a fuzzy foam eyebrow and glue it along the upper rim of the hollow. Add upper and lower eyelashes, and you might find yourself winking back at your life-like creation.

Besides the ordinary features, add a beard of twine, a moustache, pipe and a pair of wire-rimmed glasses. A flexible foam head is not too realistic—but who cares?

Sculptured Figures

Now create something different—sculpt, or carve, a large piece of foam. When you sculpt, you must take a large piece of material within which the imagined form is already contained, and simply carve away the excess substance surrounding it. Sounds easy, right? The hard part is remembering what are the form's proportions, and where its outlines lie.

In Illus. 9, there is a block of flexible foam with the front and side views of a human figure represented on two sides by black paper cut-outs. The easiest way to carve a figure from a solid block is to place these cut-outs on the block and then cut around them, first the side view (it has less detail), and then the front. Cut side A first, then, all the way through to the opposite side. You now have a narrow bar with the same cross-section as A. Next, snip around the figure on side B. If you had started with B, you would have had a lot more work. Look for and cut the simplest form first.

If sculpting does not go as quickly as you had hoped, do not be disappointed. Carving in flexible foam is good practice for carving in other substances—soap, wood, or even stone. Even if there is no cut-out or drawing to guide you, you have a mental image of your finished project that serves the same purpose. Keep that image constantly in mind while you work, for if you lose it, you might easily carve away an important arm or leg!

Illus. 9. Before you even pick up your scissors, closely observe the figure you are going to carve. Cut a silhouette out of black paper or draw the outline on two sides of the foam block. Then cut around those lines for a three-dimensional figure. Follow this procedure for carving in any substance.

Illus. 10. Two cute mice nibbling on cheese are really carved out of flexible foam. Beady little eyes (actually beads on the end of pins) and whiskers (strands of twine that have been separated) make this sculpture a frightfully realistic one.

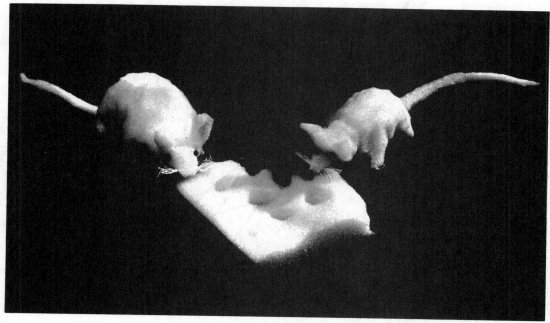

STRING THINGS

With filament of any kind—thread, wire, yarn, crochet cotton, fishing line, string, or any other—you can create colorful, effective, and very appealing designs and sculptures. Creating a filament design is as simple as drawing a straight line.

This article will familiarize you with the two basic forms—the straight line and the circle—utilized independently or in combina-tion in designs and dimensional structures. After learning these two basic techniques, the number of designs and types of projects you will be able to create is limited only by your imagination.

Whereas originally string-craft creations were often symmographs—artworks in which string was wound attractively and symmet-rically round nails in a board—this article

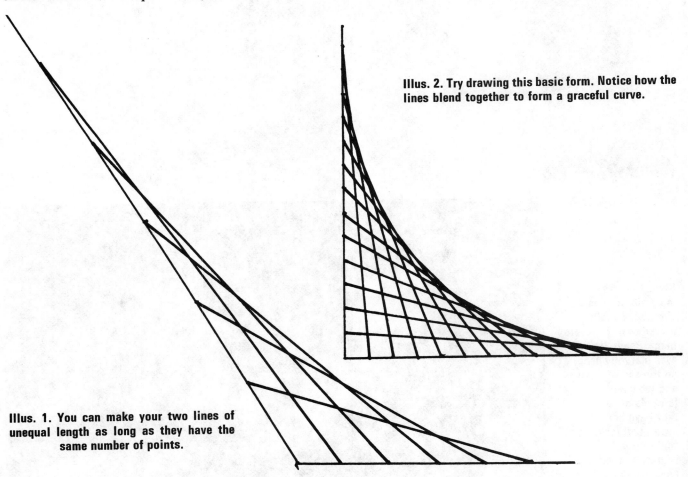

Illus. 2. Try drawing this basic form. Notice how the lines blend together to form a graceful curve.

Illus. 1. You can make your two lines of unequal length as long as they have the same number of points.

Condensed from the book, "String Things You Can Create" by Glen D. Saeger | © 1973 by Glen D. Saeger, published by Sterling Publishing Co., Inc., New York

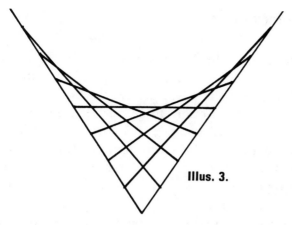

Illus. 3.

deals with string in other artistic forms as well. Your nature and your creative impulses will determine the character and appearance of your string things, whether you want to make a traditional symmograph, or a mobile to hang, or a stabile to display, or a wall hanging to frame. Also, do not feel restricted by the potential designs and projects presented here. See how many strings thing *you* can create.

Tools

Because the entire principle of this art is the creation of curves from straight lines, you need a *ruler*. All straight lines are measured with specific units; the basic unit of measure for string things is the inch and fractions of the inch—half inch, quarter inch, and eighth inch. Because you also work with circles, you need a *protractor*, which measures the units of a circle in degrees. For this craft your concern is with three basic units of degree: 5°, 10°, and 15°. This does not mean, however, that you cannot use other measures once you have gained some skill in this technique.

In addition to the ruler and protractor, you need: a *pencil* or *pen*, a *hole punch*, and a *compass* (for drawing circles).

Two-Dimensional Designs

From Straight Lines

You can create two-dimensional designs from two straight lines which are either connected or disconnected (see Illus. 1 to 3).

Notice four things about these drawings before you draw your own. First, each pair of lines has the *same number* of points measured off. Second, the *distance* (space) between each point is the same on any one line. Third, you can make one line longer than the other (as, for example, in Illus. 1), provided you have the same number of points on each line. And last, you begin drawing connecting lines from point to point of each line from opposite ends (see Illus. 4 and 5). You can start drawing connecting lines from either of the opposite ends.

Experiment with various line lengths and arrangements until you have a good idea of the different perspectives and "curves" you can achieve.

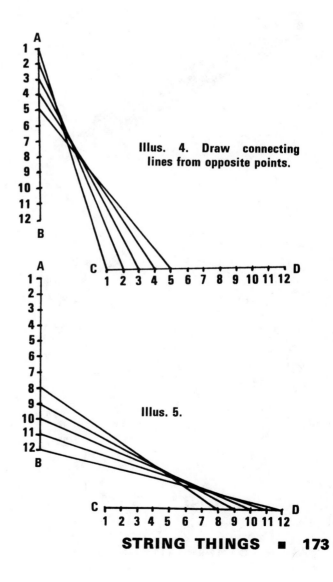

Illus. 4. Draw connecting lines from opposite points.

Illus. 5.

From a Circle

You can also create two-dimensional designs from a circle. With a compass, draw a circle that measures approximately 2″ through the center. With your protractor, mark off the circle with measurements of 15°, as shown in Illus. 6. With your ruler going directly through the center of the circle, extend the 15°-points to the curved arc of the circle (Illus. 7) until your drawing looks like Illus. 8. Number each point, beginning with 1, through 24.

Determine the number of spaces you want between each line—say eight. Place your ruler at point 1 and point 9 (9 minus 1=8) and draw a straight line connecting the two points. Continue your numbering sequence: 2–10, 3–11, 4–12, 5–13, and so on until you have connected all the points, as in Illus. 10.

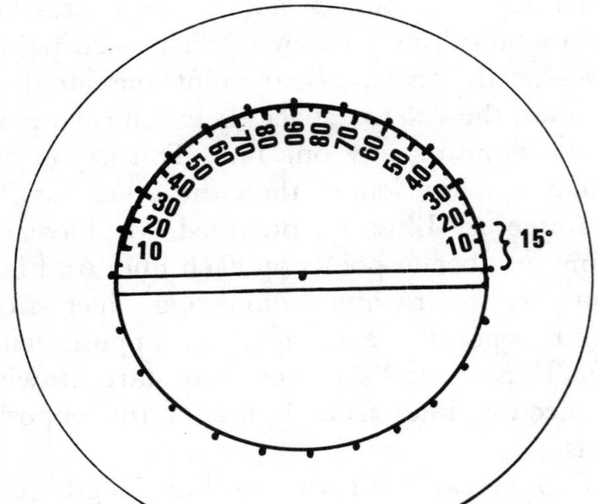

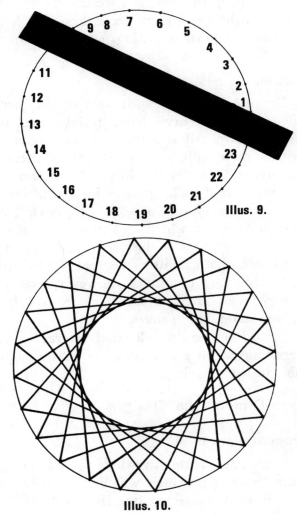

Illus. 6.

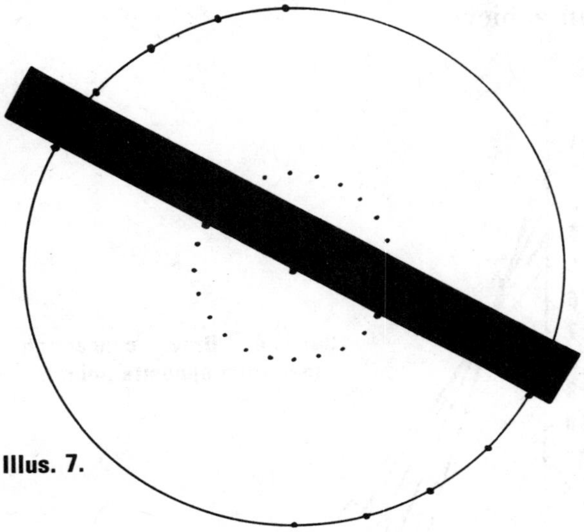

Illus. 7.

Illus. 8.

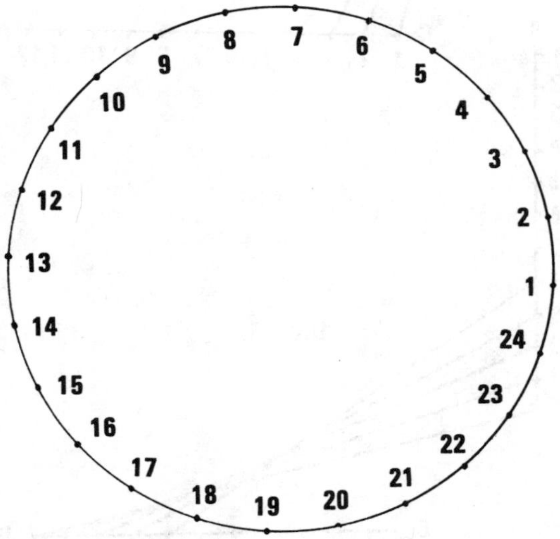

Illus. 9.

Illus. 10.

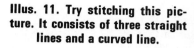
Illus. 11. Try stitching this picture. It consists of three straight lines and a curved line.

Notice two things about your completed circle: The spacing between each point is equal and the space between each connecting line is the same, forming a circle within a circle.

Practice on your own various angles, pairs of lines, different line lengths, and circles, to get the idea of what is happening. Use colored pen or pencil in drawing your lines for more effect!

Notice two things about the designs: Both connecting pieces, whether they are a line and curve, line and circle, or line and line combination, have the same number of points. Also, the distance between the spaces of each individual circle, line, or curve is the same.

Create a String Thing

By now, you should be familiar with plotting patterns on paper using the two basic shapes described. Now, instead of drawing on paper with pen or pencil, you are ready to "draw" (stitch) the lines with a needle and thread or string. For pictures that are small (6″ × 8″, for

example) and fine, use thread or thin string as the filament. The larger the picture, the heavier your filament should be. Some other filaments you might experiment with and use are: crochet cotton, thin wire, yarn, fishing line, metallic thread, and if you are making a very large picture, you can also use cording.

The procedure for stitching the designs is the same as drawing them. For your first project, stitch the picture in Illus. 11.

Materials: a piece of cardboard (8″ × 10″), fabric (Illus. 11 was done on dark gold corduroy, but you can use any suitable dark color), glue (any white glue), hole punch, pins, needle, and thread (any dark color to go with your color of fabric).

Step 1: Plot points on your cardboard with a ruler and pencil, following Illus. 12. This will be the *front* of your picture.

Step 2: Because you are using cardboard, you must punch out the points on your lines and/or curves with a pin or hole punch. Place the cardboard on a padded surface. Using the hole punch, punch through the cardboard at each

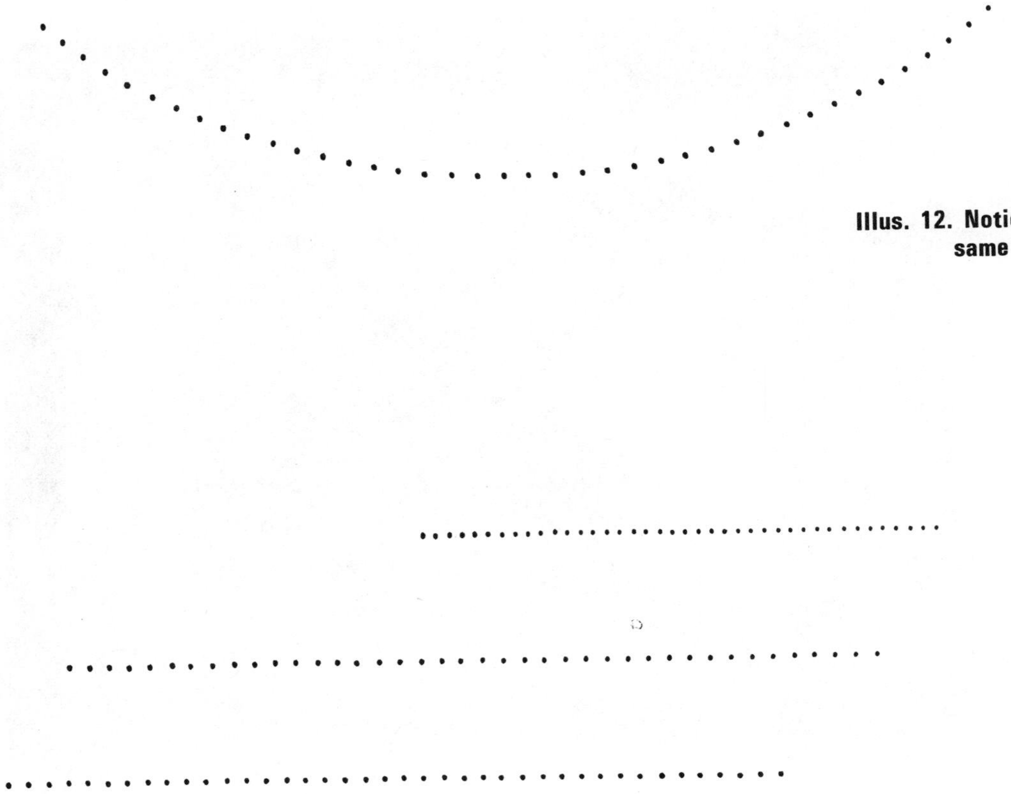

point you have made on each of the lines.
Make sure you punch *on* the line for good
symmetry.

Step 3: Center your cardboard, *front side
down,* on top of the fabric. The right side of
the fabric should also be facing *down* (see Illus.
13). Glue one edge at a time. Put a thin line
of glue on one edge of the cardboard and
smooth it out with your finger (Illus. 14A).
Beginning from the middle, bring the edge of
the fabric up and over the glued edge of the
cardboard and pin it in place (Illus. 14B).
Work out towards each side from the middle
to the edges (Illus. 14C).

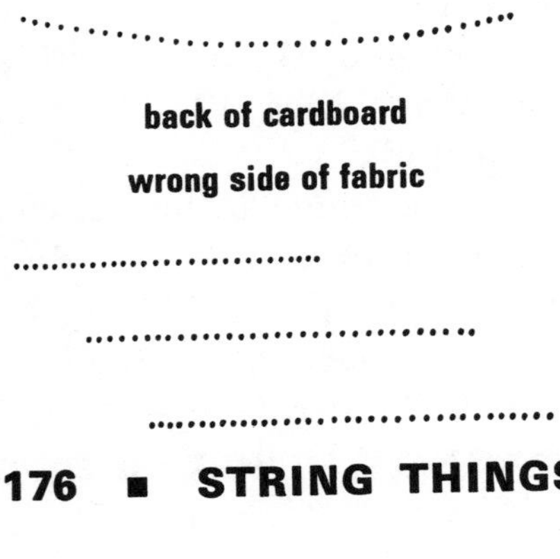

back of cardboard

wrong side of fabric

Illus. 13.

Step 4: Now you are ready to stitch your
design. Thread your needle with approximately 3 feet (about an arm's length) of
thread. Sew this project with only a single
strand of thread, although, depending on other

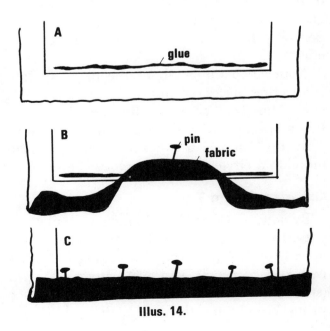

Illus. 14.

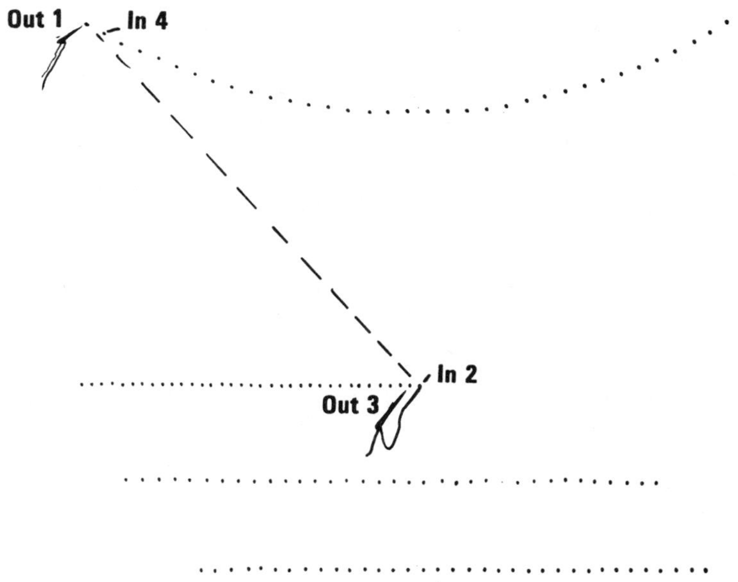

Out 1   In 4

In 2

Out 3

Illus. 15. Anchor the thread in the edge of the fabric. Then begin stitching to opposite ends. The stitching is the same for each of the three straight lines.

pictures' designs, you may want to use a double strand. Make a double knot at the end of the thread. Sew the first stitch through a fabric edge on the back (see Illus. 15).

These four steps are the basic ones you will use in your string pictures. As the procedure is the same in every instance, these steps are not repeated in the following patterns. It is understood that you will choose an attractive fabric and an appropriate weight and color or colors of string or thread or some other filament, and that you will always follow these four steps before you begin each project, unless it is a three-dimensional piece or a mobile. In these instances, specific instructions are given.

Remembering that you are "drawing" the lines with the thread, begin sewing from point to point (connecting opposite ends), until you have connected all points. Notice in Illus. 11 that the three bottom lines are connected to the top curved line. Begin connecting the closest line to the top curved line first; otherwise, you will sew over and through the other threads as you progress. See Illus. 15.

Always stitch through the holes you have punched as they are directly on the line of symmetry. To locate a hole to sew through from the front, punch a pin through from the

back. It is important that you stitch through only those holes you have punched so you can achieve near-perfect symmetry in your design.

After you have sewn as much as you can with your strand of thread, add a new strand. Simply tie the two threads together in the back with a double knot. Be sure to tie the knot as close to the hole as you can. Continue until you have connected all the points on the curve with all the points on the three lines. Frame your project, and you have your first string thing.

Circle Designs

Two-Dimensional Circle

The color picture in Illus. J2 is a circle with 24 points. To begin, draw a circle with your compass, making the diameter the size you want. To mark the 24 points on the arc of the circle, measure every 15° using your protractor and following Illus. 6 and 7. Punch holes and attach the cardboard to the fabric as you did on page 176. You may want to number your points on the side of the cardboard which faces up. You can stitch with one color thread, or vary the pattern by using either different shades of the same color, or a rainbow of colors. Work your numbering pattern out from the middle of the picture. You will be creating 12 circles, the first of which has 12 units between lines. Each following circle has one less unit between the lines, as you can see from the pattern below. Notice the number sequence.

See the pattern in Illus. 16 for the curves in the corners above and below the circle.

Circle 1

1 to 13	15 to 3
14 to 2	4 to 16
3 to 15	17 to 5
16 to 4	6 to 18
5 to 17	19 to 7
18 to 6	8 to 20
7 to 19	21 to 9
20 to 8	10 to 22
9 to 21	23 to 11
22 to 10	12 to 24
11 to 23	
24 to 12	
13 to 1	
2 to 14	

Circle 2

1	12	19	6
13	2	7	20
3	14	21	8
15	4	9	22
5	16	23	10
17	6	11	24
7	18		
19	8		
9	20		
21	10		
11	22		
23	12		
13	24		
1	14		
15	2		
3	16		
17	4		
5	18		

Circle 3

1 to 11
12 to 2
3 to 13
14 to 4
5 to 15
16 to 6
etc.

Circle 4

1 to 10
11 to 2
3 to 12
13 to 4
5 to 14
15 to 6
etc.

Circle 5

1 to 9
10 to 2
3 to 11
12 to 4
5 to 13
14 to 6
etc.

Circle 6

1 to 8
9 to 2
3 to 10
11 to 4
5 to 12
etc.

Circle 7

1 to 7
8 to 2
3 to 9
10 to 4
5 to 11
etc.

Circle 8

1 to 6
7 to 2
3 to 8
9 to 4
5 to 10
etc.

Circle 9

1 to 5
6 to 2
3 to 7
etc.

Circle 10

1 to 4
5 to 2
3 to 6
etc.

Illus. 16.

Circle 11	Circle 12
1 to 3	1 to 2
4 to 2	3 to 2
3 to 5	3 to 4
etc.	etc.

Three-Dimensional Circle

To make a three-dimensional circle, you gradually raise the circle from a wooden base, giving it a three-dimensional effect. Do this with 2″ panel-finishing nails. Draw a circle on a piece of wood which you have stained dark. Plot 36 points on the arc of the circle, each point 10° apart. Drive nails in at each point about ½″ into the wood. In this project you connect every other point (see Illus. 17).

The numbering sequence for each circle is started for you below:

Circle 1	Circle 2	Circle 3	Circle 4
1 to 18	1 to 16	1 to 14	1 to 12
19 to 2	17 to 2	15 to 2	13 to 2
3 to 20	3 to 18	3 to 16	3 to 14

Circle 5	Circle 6	Circle 7	Circle 8
1 to 10	1 to 8	1 to 6	1 to 4
11 to 2	9 to 2	7 to 2	5 to 2
3 to 12	3 to 10	3 to 8	3 to 6

Circle 9

1 to 2
3 to 2
3 to 4

You can use any filament to create a very nice effect. Start Circle 1 at the bottom of the nails and start each succeeding circle approximately two filament thicknesses above the circle below it. Each circle is actually one continuous thread which you wind around the nails. For Circle 1, for example, begin at point 1, wind the thread around point 18 towards and around point 19 and then to point 2, continue on around point 3 and go on to point 20, and so on. Try using alternating colors for an unusual design.

Angle Design Treble Clef

The next project illustrates a simple but effective design utilizing the angle in various

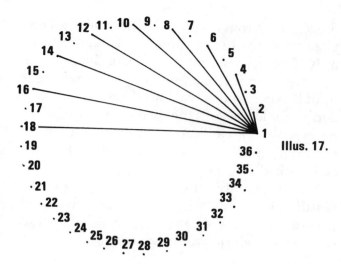

Illus. 17.

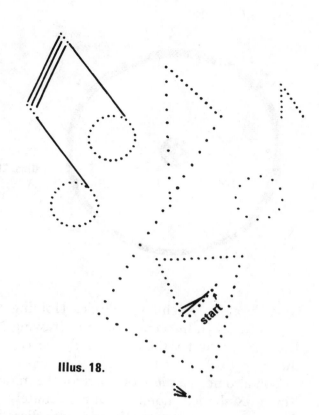

Illus. 18.

ways. Before any further explanations on how to execute the design, an apparent contradiction needs to be clarified. Earlier in this article, it was pointed out that in connecting two lines, you need an equal number of points. However, when you are working with a series of angles, you need to *increase* the number of points on one line in order to achieve the effect you want.

The treble clef with notes, shown in Illus. 19 is another example of how to connect an unequal number of points. The pattern is shown in Illus. 18 with some starting sequences to help you complete it on your own. The size of the picture in Illus. 19 is 6″ × 8″ but you can enlarge it to any size you desire. Keep in mind that if you enlarge it a great deal, you need additional points between the points already given. The circles for the musical notes ($\frac{3}{4}$″ diameter in Illus. 19) consist of 12 points (30° spacing) and are made up of two stitched circles. Again note the pattern that is developed in the stitching sequence that follows for each circle:

Circle 1		Circle 2	
out	in	out	in
1 to	7	1 to	5
8 to	2	6 to	2
3 to	9	3 to	7
10 to	4 etc.	8 to	4 etc.

As the design progresses, it should become apparent to you that a new dimension is always being added.

Tree Decoration

Make a tree decoration, a dimensional sculpture, using a length of $\frac{1}{4}$″ dowelling and a plastic ring. Mark and notch the ring, with a coping saw, just enough to hold a double strand of thread. To mark the points on the ring, draw a circle with the same diameter as the ring. Mark with your compass the number of points you wish to make, following the same

Illus. 19.

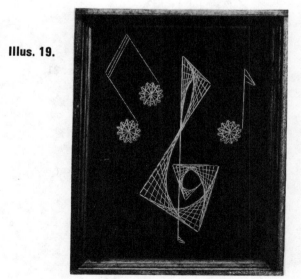

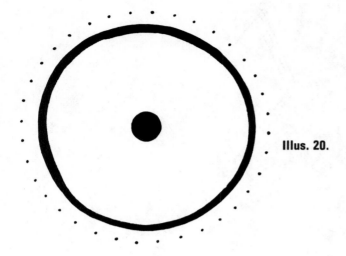

Illus. 20.

dowelling through the ring and make a complete wind with your thread, dividing the ring in half with your first round. Continue in this manner, moving one notch over each time round. After you have completely wound the entire circle, tie off the string at the end. If necessary, you can easily center or straighten the ring. In fact, you may even push it to one end instead of centering it.

For a sparkly effect, you may cover a plastic foam ball with glitter or any other decoration and slide it onto the wooden stick *before* you begin to wind the string.

Mobile

The mobile shown on page J is an elaboration of the tree decoration on page 179, utilizing various sized rings. Use thread or string of various colors and vary the lengths of the center dowelling. Suspend each component with a length of thread and fasten to contoured pieces of painted wood or heavy-duty cardboard (the pieces shown in the photograph are balsa wood), balancing each part as you fasten. Build from the bottom of the mobile.

procedure for stitching a circle. Holding the ring securely in the center of your drawing (see Illus. 20), transfer these points to the edge of the ring.

You also need a piece of wood for the middle. Make X-shaped notches, approximately $\frac{1}{8}''$ deep, with a coping saw, in the same direction at both ends of the stick (see Illus. 21).

Using a double strand of string or thread, tie a heavy knot at the ends and fasten it in one of the notches in the dowelling. Place the

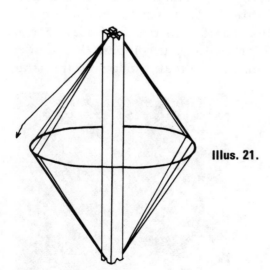

Illus. 21.

Illus. 22. Try making this flower design.

BALSA WOOD MODELS

Balsa is a natural wood, and being very light and soft, it is much easier to cut and shape than other woods. It also has the advantage that it can be glued very easily with *balsa cement*. Joints, properly made, are as strong as the wood—and unlike many other glues, balsa cement sets hard in a matter of minutes. This can speed your assembly work. You will find good use for a supply of long, round-headed pins for holding joints while the cement hardens.

Yet another advantage of balsa wood is that it is readily available from most hobby shops in standard sizes of SHEET, STRIP and BLOCK—all free from defects and knots. The standard length to which balsa is cut is 36 inches. Sheet balsa is available in 2″, 3″ and 4″ widths, and in thicknesses from $\frac{1}{32}$″ up. Strip sizes range from $\frac{1}{16}$″ square, upwards. Block sizes start with 1″ square, and go up to about 3″ × 4″.

You must, therefore, design models and other projects in balsa wood with these standard sizes in mind. It is much easier to work from standard sizes, as this avoids a lot of cutting work, and also unnecessary joints to build up larger sizes.

You also need a special technique for working with balsa. Ordinary woodworking tools are not suitable. Balsa has to be cut with a very sharp knife, or a fine toothed saw. You will find the type of tissue paper for model aircrafts useful, along with the PVA glue or tissue paste made especially for this purpose.

This article starts right off with basic technique. But instead of showing you how to get

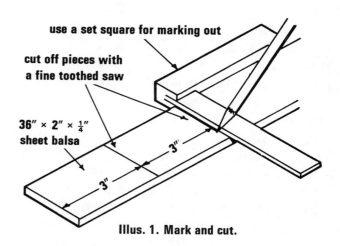

use a set square for marking out

cut off pieces with a fine toothed saw

36″ × 2″ × ¼″ sheet balsa

3″

3″

Illus. 1. Mark and cut.

the technique correct on practice pieces, it starts with *making* simple projects, right from the first cut! As learning the technique progresses, the projects get more ambitious until, after working through them all, you could call yourself a master-craftsman in balsa.

There is no need to stop with the individual models and projects described, either. Each project, whether you are working with sheet balsa, making frames, or using any other technique, opens up further scope for building other models on similar lines—to your own creative ideas and designs. It is quite easy once you have got started on the right lines.

Working with Sheet Balsa

Thick sheet balsa is best cut with a fine toothed saw, preferably a razor saw which fits into a modelling knife handle. For accurate marking out of square shapes, use a metal set

Condensed from the book, "Balsa Wood Modelling" by Ron Warring | © 1973 by Sterling Publishing Co., Inc., New York

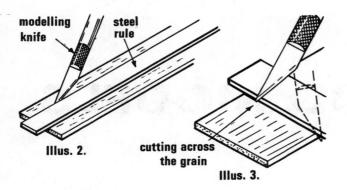

modelling knife

steel rule

Illus. 2.

cutting across the grain

Illus. 3.

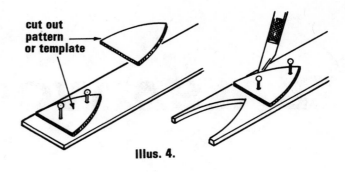

cut out pattern or template

Illus. 4.

square or try square and a pencil or ballpoint pen. You can also use the set square as a guide for the saw when making the cut. Keep the saw upright so that the cut is vertical, not slanting.

You can easily cut thin sheet balsa wood with a modelling or X-acto knife. When making straight cuts, use a steel rule to guide the knife blade (Illus. 2). You can also make cuts across the grain in the same manner. This time, however, do not cut right across the sheet from edge to edge in one go. Stop before reaching the second edge. Then reverse the knife and cut in from the edge to join up with the first cut (Illus. 3). This will prevent the edge of the sheet from splitting, which is very likely to happen if you make the cut right across from edge to edge.

You can also use a "professional" trick for cutting out a number of identical shapes. First, draw out the shape required, actual size, onto a piece of stiff cardboard or thin plywood. Then cut it out accurately and sand edges quite smooth.

This shape then serves as a pattern or TEMPLATE to be used as a guide for the knife when cutting out a number of these shapes from a balsa sheet (see Illus. 4). Simply pin the template to the sheet balsa, and then guide the knife around the outline. For the next cut-out, unpin the template and move it along to the next whole piece of sheet—and so on.

Making Boomerangs

Select a piece of heavy $\frac{1}{16}$" balsa sheet and cut off a 6" length. From this, cut two 1" wide strips (if you start with a 2" wide sheet, this means that you cut the 6" strip down the middle). Bind the two 6" × 1" pieces together with an elastic band, as shown in Illus. 5.

You have made a simple boomerang, suitable for flying indoors—or outdoors in very calm weather. Hold it by the end of one strip and throw it forwards, at the same time giving the boomerang a spinning motion. With a little practice you should be able to make the boomerang fly a complete circle and return to your hand.

The size of circle such a boomerang will fly depends on the lengths of the two arms. Try strapping the two pieces together with equal arm lengths, to form a true cross (Illus. 6). Then try with the two pieces joined to form long and short arms (Illus. 7). We will not tell you which will give you the largest flight circle —it is easy enough to find out for yourself. Try it first out of doors.

You can adjust the boomerang to suit the size of your room (be sure you remove everything breakable) for indoor flying in this way. Once you have found the best set-up, cement the arms, using pins to hold until the joint is secure (Illus. 8). Round off the edges of the boomerang with sandpaper. This will improve the performance.

Try making other sizes of boomerangs on the same principle. You can decorate the boomerangs by painting, or by using decals. Remember, the larger the boomerang you make, the heavier it needs to be to fly properly: use thicker sheet balsa of heavy grade. Painting also helps to add weight.

Painting and Decorating Balsa

Balsa is a soft wood and even a smoothly finished balsa surface, if painted with ordinary paints or model airplane dopes, will become quite rough as the paint dries. This is due to the grain being pulled up by the paint. Painting balsa to get a smooth finish demands special attention.

For a *quick* finish, there are two methods you can use:

1. Paint with *poster paints* or *emulsion paints*. These are thick paints which will not raise the grain of the balsa to any great extent. Also, they will cover well even with a single coat, applied generously. The finish with these paints will be dull (matt), not shiny, however.

2. Cover with one of the special iron-on covering materials sold for model airplanes. These will give a really smooth, colorful gloss finish, which will be as perfect as the balsa surface underneath. Be sure that this surface is first sanded really smooth and quite clean. Any traces of balsa dust on the surface will show up as lumps through this high gloss covering.

If you are prepared to spend more time, however, then this is the finishing method to use:

1. Smooth the balsa surface as much as possible by sanding, using garnet paper for the final finishing. Then paint the surface all over with *balsa grain filler*. Leave until quite dry. The surface will be rough and the appearance patchy.

2. Sand down the wood quite smooth again and coat again with grain filler. Leave to dry. Then smooth down again with garnet paper.

3. Repeat this as many times as necessary until the final sanding with garnet paper gives you a perfectly smooth, glass-like surface over all, with no blemishes.

You can then paint the surface with a gloss finish, such as model airplane dope, to the color of your choice.

Instead of using balsa grain filler, you can use *polyurethane sealer* and follow the same

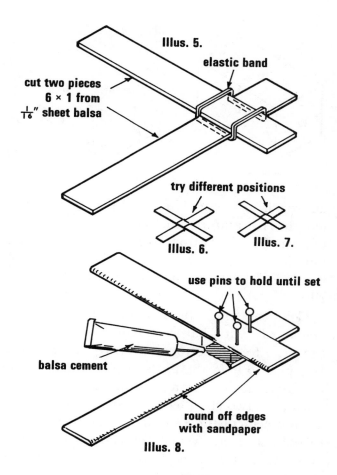

Illus. 5.

cut two pieces 6 × 1 from $\frac{1}{16}$" sheet balsa

elastic band

try different positions

Illus. 6.   Illus. 7.

use pins to hold until set

balsa cement

round off edges with sandpaper

Illus. 8.

method. The finish coat in this case should be polyurethane high gloss color. Do not try to stain balsa to imitate the colors of other woods, such as mahogany, etc. The use of wood stains on balsa will always produce a blotchy, uneven result and excessively dark coloration.

Making Boxes

Having mastered the art of cutting out rectangular shapes accurately from sheet balsa, making boxes is easy. Balsa boxes are very useful, as you can make them in almost any size or shape you want. The larger the box, the thicker the balsa sheet needs to be to provide a strong, rigid assembly.

First decide on the box you want (see page 184), its length (L), width (W) and depth (D). These dimensions determine the sizes of the various pieces you need to cut for the sides, bottom and ends.

The set of diagrams here show the easiest

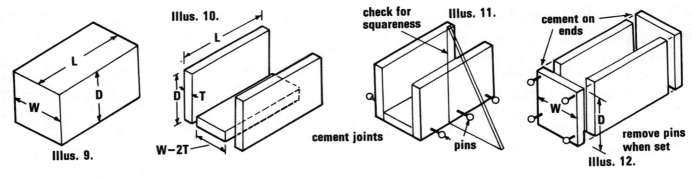

Illus. 10.

Illus. 9.

Illus. 11.

check for squareness

cement joints

pins

cement on ends

remove pins when set

Illus. 12.

approach to box-making. Cut two sides to the length (L) and depth (D) of the box you require. Cut the bottom to the same length (L), but to a width of W, less twice the thickness of the balsa sheet you are using (W—2T) (see Illus. 9 and 10).

Coat the long edges of the bottom pieces generously with balsa cement, and then join the sides to the bottom as shown in Illus. 11. Use pins to hold the parts in place, and check for squareness, using a set-square.

Cut the two end pieces to dimensions W and D, and cement these in place, again using pins to hold securely. When the cement has set—allow at least an hour to be on the safe side—the pins can be removed.

Another way of making a box is shown in Illus. 13 to 16. This time the base is made smaller than the box dimensions, so that the joints between bottom and sides are hidden. Cut the base panel first, then the ends. Join with balsa cement, as shown. If you cut the ends true and square, these will ensure that the final box is square when you cement on the sides to complete the assembly.

Completed balsa boxes can be sanded down all over to a smooth finish, and any irregularities in the joint line can be removed at this

stage. You can leave the corners square, or round them off with sandpaper, if preferred.

You can easily add lids, cut to matching dimensions from another piece of balsa sheet. Also, you can cut interior compartments from thinner sheets. For hinged lids, use ordinary thin metal hinges, which can be recessed and cemented in place with epoxy adhesive (this sticks metal to balsa very well).

Making a Periscope

The basis of a periscope is a long box containing a mirror at each end, and with openings to see in and out. All balsa parts should be cut from $\frac{3}{16}$" sheet to the dimensions given:

two parts 24" × 3"
two parts 21" × 3"
two parts 3" square

Using one 24" × 3" piece as a base, cement on the two ends and one side (Illus. 17). Note that on the side there will be an opening left at one end. Then cement the second side in place, leaving an opening at the other end (Illus. 18). Use pins to hold the assembly until set, as when making boxes.

You are now ready to install the mirrors. First cut two 2½" squares of balsa, and then saw each across diagonally to make four triangular

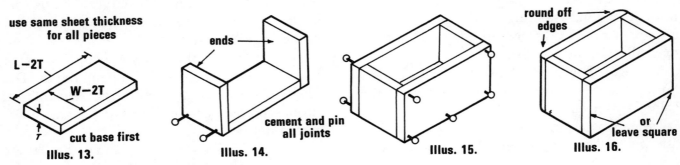

use same sheet thickness for all pieces

L—2T

W—2T

cut base first

Illus. 13.

ends

cement and pin all joints

Illus. 14.

Illus. 15.

round off edges

or leave square

Illus. 16.

pieces in all. Two of these pieces need to be cemented at each end to support the mirrors (Illus. 19 and 20). The best mirror is a 3″ square handbag mirror or something similar about that size. Mount the mirrors in the periscope by glueing them to the triangular pieces with epoxy adhesive or contact adhesive. Make sure that they are accurately lined up, then cement on the final 24″ × 3″ facing piece (Illus. 20). Your periscope is now ready to allow you to see over fences and other people's heads.

Making Balsa Buildings

Model buildings are easily designed as balsa boxes with cut-outs for windows and doors in the sides and ends. If the size of your building is small you can avoid cut-outs by painting the window areas black and indicating doors by outline markings with a ballpoint pen, but the effect is not so good.

Apart from cut-outs, the main difference between buildings and the basic balsa box is that you use a thinner sheet for buildings. A sheet $\frac{1}{16}$″ thick is suitable for all small buildings, say up to 4 to 8 inches long. For larger buildings, work with $\frac{3}{32}$″ sheet up to $\frac{3}{16}$″ sheet, according to the amount of rigidity required. You can easily test by cutting a typical side piece out of the sheet and judging whether this will be stiff enough.

The use of patterns or templates for cutting out duplicate parts has already been described (see page 182). You can use this technique for model buildings, as the ends are usually the same shape, and so also are the front and back pieces. By marking only one front and one end you can use these parts for patterns for cutting the other pieces. This will ensure an accurate match and a speedy way of cutting a number of parts for several buildings of the same size and shape.

Illus. 21 to 23 show a basic design for a building. The two ends and the front and back can be assembled to form an open box with cemented joints. Cut out windows and doors before assembling. Because the sheet is thin,

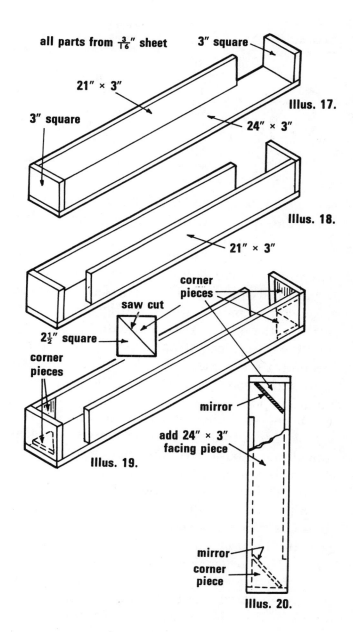

Illus. 17.

Illus. 18.

Illus. 19.

Illus. 20.

cement corner braces in to strengthen the joints and add rigidity to the assembly. Cut these from a square section balsa strip. A suitable size is at least twice the thickness of the

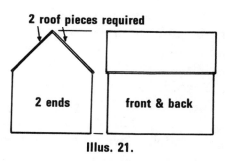

Illus. 21.

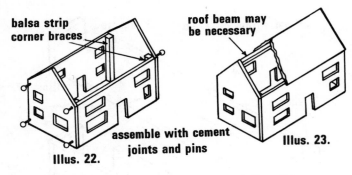

balsa strip
corner braces

roof beam may
be necessary

assemble with cement
joints and pins

Illus. 22.

Illus. 23.

sheet being used. For example, if the sides are cut from $\frac{1}{16}$" sheet, use two $\frac{1}{8}$" square corner braces.

The two roof pieces will require a little trimming to fit neatly. The top edge of each panel needs angling off, or chamfering, so that the two roof pieces form a neat joint line when fitted to the model. You can do this chamfering easily with a piece of fine sandpaper wrapped around a scrap piece of balsa sheet. You can also add a roof beam inside if the roof needs some support.

Of course, buildings vary a lot in size and shape. Most shapes, however, can be broken down into a basic box construction, or a number of boxes joined together.

Model houses, of course, need finishing in detail to add realism. On the *inside*, window cut-outs can be covered by a piece of clear acetate sheet, carefully cemented in position—Illus. 24. Use cement sparingly so that when you press the acetate in place, surplus cement is not squeezed out to leave a smear on the edges of the window area. Other detail work to be done on the inside consists of hinging the doors which open inwards. A small strip of cellulose tape, or better still a piece of gauze cemented in place, will make an effective working hinge. You can, of course, add a lot more interior detail—a ceiling and partitions dividing the interior up into separate rooms, for instance. But this is really only suitable for large models.

On the *outside*, you can add window frame detail. The smallest standard size of balsa strip is $\frac{1}{16}$" square. This may look out of place on a small model, in which case you will have

to cut thinner strips carefully from $\frac{1}{32}$" sheet. You will probably find it best to hold such small pieces with tweezers rather than your fingers when cementing them in place.

Hinging doors to open outwards can be a bit of a problem. One of the best ways is to use a tape hinge as shown in Illus. 25. Keep the tapes quite narrow. Doors which open upwards like garage doors can readily be hinged on pins pushed through the side of the building. Cement a piece of strip balsa behind the top edge of the balsa door to take the pins.

Large buildings may need end or side panels bigger than the standard width of balsa sheet available. In this case you must cement two (or more) pieces of sheet together edge-to-edge to build up the width required. To strengthen the joint, and give the panel more rigidity, add bracing strips as shown in Illus. 26. Position the strips so that they are clear of any door or window cut-outs required.

Finishing model buildings can be done in various ways. Straightforward painting is usually easiest, using non-glossy paints (e.g.,

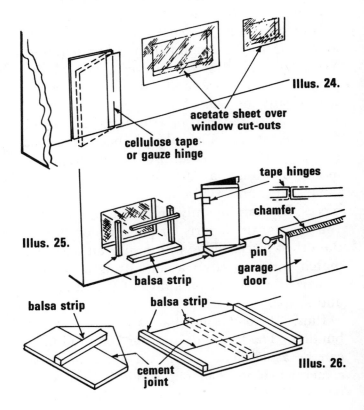

acetate sheet over
window cut-outs

Illus. 24.

cellulose tape
or gauze hinge

Illus. 25.

balsa strip

tape hinges

chamfer

pin

garage
door

balsa strip

balsa strip

cement
joint

Illus. 26.

emulsion paints). Scale brickwork is best represented by printed "brick paper," cut to matching shapes and stuck on with PVA glue. These model building shapes are also available in other finishes—slates, shingles, etc.—and in different scales.

The following scale equivalents will be useful in deciding suitable balsa sizes for detail work (and as a general guide).

Every $\frac{1}{16}'' = 2''$ (approx.) in 1/36 scale
$= 3''$ in 1/48 scale
$= 4\frac{1}{2}''$ in 1/72 scale
$= 6''$ in 1/96 scale
$= 9''$ in 1/144 scale

For instance, if you were trying to make 1/48 scale window-frame members equivalent to a full-size dimension of $1\frac{1}{2}''$ square, then

every $\frac{1}{16}'' = 3''$ in 1/48 scale
so $\frac{1}{32}'' = 1\frac{1}{2}''$ in 1/48 scale

Thus the scale window frame sizes will be $\frac{1}{32}''$ square.

Making Kites

A box kite is a very efficient flyer, and you can readily make small box kites from thin balsa sheet. For a rigid kite of this type, cut the following pieces:

8 pieces 3" square, from light $\frac{1}{32}''$ balsa sheet.
4 pieces 9" long, cut from $\frac{1}{8}''$ square balsa strip.

Lay two of the 3" squares 3" apart and cement two of the $\frac{1}{8}''$ strips along each edge, as shown in Illus. 27 (left). Make a second assembly in the same manner. Then join them to form a square box, using the remaining four pieces of 3" squares (Illus. 27, right). Use a set square to check that the assembly is true and square, attach a cotton line and fly your kite!

A lighter type of box kite can be made step by step (see Illus. 28 and 29). Instead of using balsa sheet panels, cover the frame with model aircraft tissue. Cut two strips of tissue, each equal in length to four times the frame size. For example, if you are making the same size of kite as before (3" square), the tissue panels to

wrap around need to be 3" wide and four times 3" or 12" long.

Cement the balsa strips to the tissue as shown in Illus. 29—use four long strips with four short strips, one at each end, to produce a rigid frame. Then fold the kite up, 90 degrees at a time, with two further short strips added, until the square frame is complete. Then, cement the final lengths of tissue in place. Use a cotton line for small kites, attached at the same point as shown in Illus. 27.

If you make the balsa-and-tissue kite the same size as the all-balsa kite you can test which flies best.

For pictures of completed balsa wood projects, see color page K.

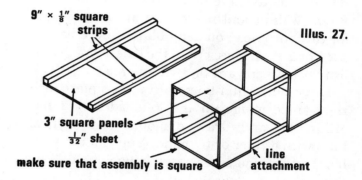

9" × $\frac{1}{8}''$ square strips

Illus. 27.

3" square panels $\frac{1}{32}''$ sheet

make sure that assembly is square

line attachment

balsa strip

model airplane tissue strips

strip

Illus. 28.

strip

make sure that assembly is square

strip

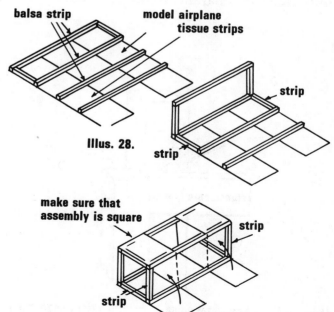

strip

Illus. 29.

WOOD CARVING

Staff Carving

In many parts of the world, shepherds adorn their staffs by cutting rings of bark from freshly cut branches. This is probably the oldest form of wood carving as a folk art. All you need is the short, well-sharpened blade of a pocketknife to carve into a square bar of wood. Birch, walnut and mahogany are good woods for this purpose. You can obtain square bars of 1×1 or 2×2 inches, cut to the length you want, from a lumber yard or a cabinetmaker.

Draw horizontal lines with a try square or a right-angle gauge on the four sides of a bar (Illus. 1), and draw diagonal and vertical lines with a ruler or by hand. You can use your hand and pencil as a scratch gauge if you draw lines which run parallel to the vertical edges.

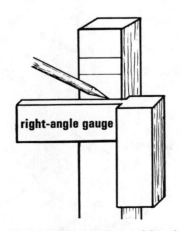

Illus. 1. Draw horizontal guide-lines with a right-angle gauge.

Make horizontal cuts by dividing the desired width in half and cutting along the dividing line with the pocketknife perpendicular to the wood. Then, holding the knife at an angle, cut towards the bottom of the dividing line from both sides of it. If the wood is hard, cut small notches at the edges of the bar.

When planning a design, be sure to leave bars of wood between the horizontal cuts; otherwise, the corners can easily crack off.

A Chess Set

Make a unique set of chess pieces with this simple technique (Illus. 2). You should choose a heavy wood, as the pieces must be stable. If necessary, however, you can drill a hole in the bases and tap some lead into them. For the dark pieces, use mahogany or walnut, and for the light ones, use birch or maple. After the whole bar has been carved, saw off the individual pieces in a mitre box (Illus. 3), and then add all the details you want.

Chip Carving

Ornaments such as friezes, mouldings, and rosettes are executed with this ancient technique, which is based on geometric figures—triangles, squares, circles, and so on.

Carving knives for chip carving have a short blade as they are held with one hand only. You only need three knives for your work (Illus. 4). You can purchase these in most hardware shops or in special handicraft shops. You can also use the short blade of your pocketknife,

Condensed from the book, "Whittling & Wood Carving" by H. Hoppe | © 1969 by Sterling Publishing Co., Inc., New York

Illus. 2. Create chess pieces by carving the bar, dividing it into sections and adding details. At the left are three castles; at the right are three views of a knight piece.

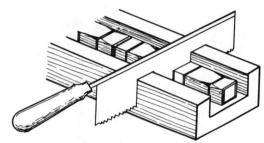

Illus. 3. Divide the carved bar into sections with a mitre box and saw.

which you should have ground to a point by an expert. Have the back of the blade ground half-round. Wrap the connection between blade and handle with insulating tape to protect your index finger.

For chip carving, you cut mainly with the point of your knife, which therefore must be kept very sharp. The best woods for chip carving are those without a strong grain

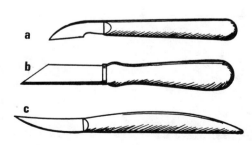

Illus. 4. Chip-carving knives: (a) regular; (b) for deeper, larger cuts; (c) for straight and curved lines.

effect, as the grain detracts too much from the design. For use with knives, only soft woods are suitable, but you can use the same technique on medium-hard woods if you use a mallet and chisel.

Using a try square, a compass and a ruler, draw a design on the wood. If you cannot do this, trace the design with graphite paper on light woods and with carbon paper on darker woods. You can erase remnants of graphite lines after carving; remove lines of carbon with fine sandpaper.

For safety, clamp the board to a work table and keep both hands behind the cutting tool. When it is necessary to turn the work in another direction, either shift your position, or re-clamp the board. By turning the board, you can cut with the grain or across it, instead of against it (Illus. 5). Never cut towards your body.

Illus. 5. Carve with the grain.

First draw two horizontal lines with your try square to form a space $\frac{3}{16}''$ in width, and then divide the horizontal space vertically in distances of $\frac{3}{8}''$ (Illus. 6). Also draw the diagonal

WOOD CARVING ■ 189

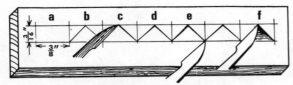

Illus. 6. Draw your design first.

Illus. 9. Grip knife firmly.

Illus. 10. Use dagger grip for hard wood.

lines shown in rectangle *b*. Now carve the diagonal lines on the left and right sides with your knife "a." Hold your knife vertically. Carve the tops of the triangles deeply.

With the third cut, shown in rectangles *e* and *f*, hold your knife rather flat and carve out the little triangle from the right to the left. This last cut is more difficult than the diagonal ones. After some trying, you will succeed in making the cuts in a "clean" way. Your knife must be so sharp that the freshly cut surface of the wood has a gloss. For the diagonal cuts you can also hold your knife as a fountain pen; the index finger then exerts pressure from above (Illus. 9).

Illus. 7 shows a finished row of triangles.

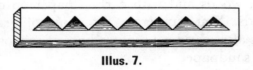

Illus. 7.

Deep Cuts

For deeper and larger cuts, work with the knives "a" and "b." Start again by drawing the horizontal lines and dividing them vertically, but increase the measures (Illus. 8). Draw the triangles and divide as shown by the lines in *b*. Place your knife in the middle of the triangle and cut along the three dividing lines to the corners.

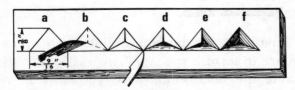

Illus. 8. For larger and deeper cuts, divide triangle.

Hold the knife in a pen grip if you are using very soft wood; for harder wood, hold the knife in your fist (Illus. 10). Cut out the triangles as shown in Illus. 8, *c* to *f*, slicing out each of the three chips by cutting along the perimeter. Make diamond-shaped cut-outs the same way, but divide the diamond into fourths instead of thirds (Illus. 11).

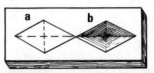

Illus. 11. Divide diamond shape into quarters (a); then carve as usual (b).

Straight Lines

Cut straight lines with your knife "c" or with your pocketknife. You must hold the knife so the blade penetrates the wood for its maximum length; that is, instead of having the blade perpendicular to the wood, hold it at an angle (Illus. 12). This makes it easier to cut straight lines. The width and depth of the cuts depend on the desired effect. Deep cuts cause deep shadows.

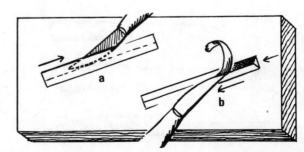

Illus. 12. For straight lines, make two oblique cuts (a and b) that meet in the middle of the desired width.

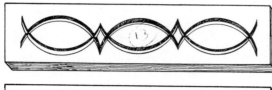

Illus. 13. Curved lines.

Illus. 14. A very pointed knife cuts curved lines best.

Curved Lines

Cut curved lines with a knife that is as narrow and as pointed as possible. Hold the knife more upright than for straight lines. Curved lines are often carved wider and deeper in the middle, with both ends narrow.

Illus. 15. Chip carving can ornament useful objects such as book ends, but keep designs of natural forms simple.

Veneer Carving

You can attain a lovely contrasting color effect by applying a veneer—a thin layer of high-grade wood—to a board and carving it. Veneer carving is very effective and easy to do.

Glue a dark veneer on a light-colored underground, or vice versa, with wood cement or

Illus. 16. Glue veneer (thin wood) to a dark board and carve parts away in a design. You also need other tools.

light veneer   dark board

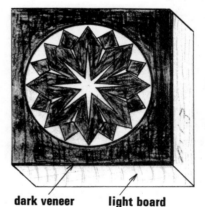

Illus. 17. You can also glue veneer to a light board and then carve.

dark veneer   light board

special veneering glue. Then you draw and carve as before. Take into consideration that light lines on a dark background seem thinner than dark lines on a light background, so if your design consists mainly of lines, dark on light is preferable.

For large pieces, you can use furniture veneer (mahogany, walnut, etc.), but this is too thick for small objects. You can still use furniture veneer, which is $\frac{1}{16}''$ thick, if you carefully plane and polish it after cementing it onto the wood. Clean your knives after polishing to prevent them from becoming dull.

WOOD CARVING ■ 191

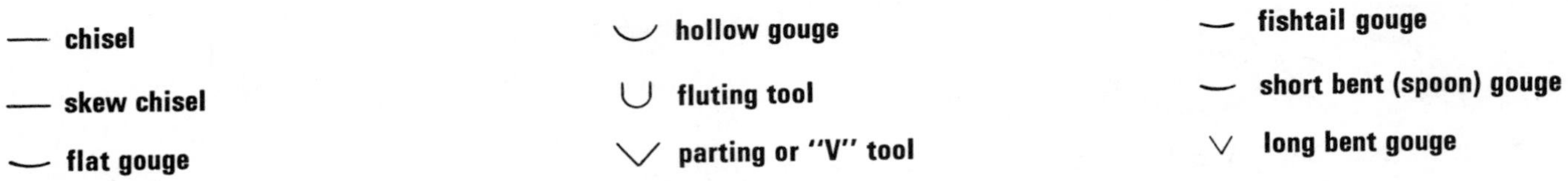

— chisel	⌣ hollow gouge	⌣ fishtail gouge
— skew chisel	⊔ fluting tool	⌣ short bent (spoon) gouge
⌣ flat gouge	⌄ parting or "V" tool	⌄ long bent gouge

Illus. 18. You need various chisels and gouges for cutting deeply into the wood and carving out forms.

For small pieces, you use a type of wall-covering which consists of very thin wood veneer glued on paper. After soaking this material for about one hour with a wet cloth, separate the veneer from the paper. Some plywood companies also manufacture paper-thin veneer, 1/85″ thick, which has been reinforced by paper or cloth on its back. You cannot separate the veneer, as it is too thin. This veneer, glued on, is sometimes used for small work and for display material, but requires expert handling.

Large, solid boards warp. Therefore, you should use plywood if you make large objects, cementing one or two layers of veneer onto it, depending on whether or not you can use the surface of your plywood board as a background for the design. You cannot use the plywood surface if it is of low-grade and blemished.

In typical chip carving, the effect is a result of the shadows cast by the cuts and lines. In veneer carving, the effect is obtained by the contrasting colors of the woods. The results are similar to prints made from linoblocks and woodcuts.

Bowls and Candlesticks

For chip carving, you did not need more than three knives. To carve bowls and boards, you will need some cutting tools called chisels, which are flat, and gouges, which are curved. These are available in widths from $\frac{1}{8}$″ to 2″. If you intend to make various types of objects, you should purchase a set of tools composed by experts.

The lines in Illus. 18 indicate the cut each tool makes. A gouge with a deep curvature is called a fluting tool. Shanks may be straight or bent.

Chisels have straight cutting edges and function in two ways: the straight cutting edge cuts into and separates the wood along a specific path, while the bevel and thickness of the chisel serve as wedges and force the wood apart. The cutting and splitting may occur simultaneously or one may rapidly follow the other. The smaller the wedge-angle or bevel on the chisel, the easier will be the carving.

Gouges are tools with curved cutting edges. There are many varieties of them. Gouges with bent shanks are used for deep cutting. You will

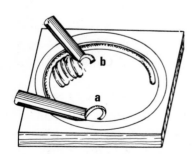

Illus. 19. Carve trench (a) and hollow out bowl (b).

Illus. 20. Saw hollowed form from block.

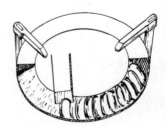

Illus. 21. Clamp upside-down and shape bottom.

Illus. 23. If you make this bowl shallower, it could be a tray.

Illus. 24. You can ornament the inside of the bowl.

Illus. 22. This old-fashioned candlestick has a bowl shape with a handle.

find out which tools to use through experience.

Keep your tools clean and as sharp as razors. When not in use, protect them by lightly oiling them and keeping them in a dry place. Never keep more tools on your work table than those you need for the work in progress. Hang the others on a wall rack. Too many tools on your work table is confusing. If you have to carry your tools somewhere, use a large piece of soft, clean cloth, with partitions for the different tools, which you can roll up and carry with you and which will protect the cutting edges when you are not using the instruments.

For carving wooden utensils, use woods without much grain effect—like maple, birch, oak or American walnut—or, if you prefer, you can stress the shape of a bowl by using prominently grained wood.

Draw the contours of the bowl on the surface of the wood and then clamp the piece to a work table with two screw clamps or C clamps, using cardboard between the top of the clamp and the board to protect the wood surface. For blocking out the bowl area roughly, use a large gouge driven by a mallet. Work as much with the grain as possible. To prevent damaging the inner rim of the bowl,

first cautiously carve a trench with your gouge (Illus. 19, *a*). Then carve the inner edge with a rather flat gouge (Illus. 19, *b*), and from top to bottom block out the hollow form of the bowl. The finishing cuts should produce an artful, smooth effect and polishing should be done only if required by the use of the bowl, for instance for a fruit bowl.

After you have made the hollow form, the round shape should be sawed out of the board with a coping saw or a jigsaw (Illus. 20). Then fasten the board with the hollow side down and carve off the mass of the wood from the bottom with a large gouge and the mallet (Illus. 21). Thereafter, finish with chisel and flat gouge.

There are only a few basic forms for bowls and plates. Base your work on these and—in

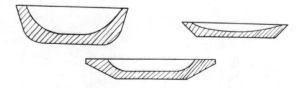

any case—do not imitate turnery. Carved and turned bowls each have their own characteristics.

Carving bowls is an excellent exercise to prepare for sculpting in wood. You learn to make larger objects and to carve deeper into the wood.

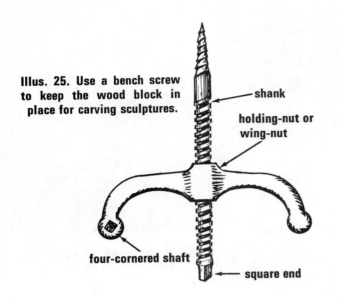

Illus. 25. Use a bench screw to keep the wood block in place for carving sculptures.

shank

holding-nut or wing-nut

four-cornered shaft

square end

Sculpture in the Round

So far, your work has required a plank only an inch or two in thickness. Sculpture in the round is meant to be viewed from all sides and requires a large block of wood. This means you must hold the block securely while you work on it with gouges and mallet. One effective method is to use a bench screw (Illus. 53).

First, with a hand drill, drill a hole in the base of the block. Screw the pointed end of the bench screw into the hole, which should be

the diameter of the screw's shank and not of the threads. Then the free part of the screw (with the wing-nut removed) is pushed from above through a hole either in the work table or in a horizontal block of wood clamped to the work table (Illus. 26). If you use the work table itself, add a drilled block of wood beneath it. Then secure the bench screw tightly with the wing-nut.

You cannot use the long bench screw with some pieces. In those cases, fix a larger board to the bottom of the carving block with wood screws and attach this board to the work table with clamps.

Other aids, such as a wood worker's vice and a swivel vice are available.

Animals

For your first try at carving in the round, choose a simple animal shape such as a fish or an owl.

After you have decided on the size, draw the main view on the block of wood. If you are using a small block of wood, you can now saw out the contour with a coping saw or fret saw. (For larger pieces, rough out the form with a crosscut saw and a ripsaw.) You will have an animal figure similar to a toy (Illus. 27). By

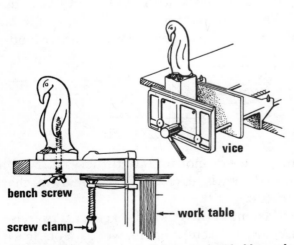

vice

bench screw

screw clamp

work table

Illus. 26. Bench screw in position, or vice, holds work.

Illus. 27. Saw the contour of a horse from a block of wood.

filing and sandpapering its edges, you have already produced a simple animal sculpture. Now, if you want to have a more finished looking piece, carve out more of the wood with chisel and gouge (Illus. 28).

For blocking out initial masses, start by using a fairly large gouge, which you drive with a wooden mallet. As carving progresses, use flat chisels and smaller gouges. The tools become finer and, if you use a mallet, your stroke becomes lighter. For this type of work, you will often use bent gouges, as there are more deep-lying parts. Finish the surface with a flat gouge and the diagonal chisel. Whether you finish with large or small carving cuts on the surface is a matter of taste.

Certain small forms allow you to saw the block from all four sides instead of sawing one contour as in the previous project. Draw the front and side views on the block (Illus. 30).

Illus. 28. Some work with gouges and chisels transforms the cut-out.

Illus. 29. Leaving out details, as in this fox, can add power to the form.

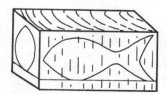 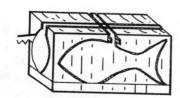 

Illus. 30. Draw front and side views on block, saw along contours to pedestal, cut away excess wood, and then carve.

Illus. 31. Both the cat and the seal pictured here are simplified forms, with the wood smoothed to a fine finish. The grain on the seal is appropriate to the animal's pose, while the cat's stance requires no special grain pattern.

Illus. 32. A good finish, like the matt sheen on this fox, enriches the artistic effect of the sculpture.

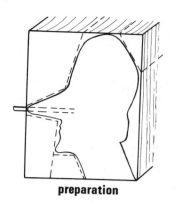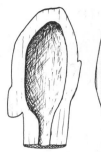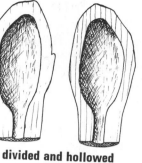

preparation   **carved**   **divided and hollowed**   **rejoined and detailed**

Illus. 33. Draw profile on block, insert peg, saw out form. Carve face; split and hollow carve; cement carving back.

Then saw along the drawn lines with the coping saw, but do not saw farther than the pedestal. This is done to leave a firm base. At the top, place a small peg in the saw cut. Carve off the superfluous wood at the bottom after the four sawings have been completed.

Often you can complete this type of work with a sharp pocketknife only. Hold the workpiece in your left hand and turn it, while you carve with your right.

Puppet Heads

Making puppet heads is good preparation for sculpting portrait busts in wood. Start by making some sketches of the size and expression of various faces.

Draw the profile on the block, fixing the position of the point of the nose. At this point drill a hole and insert a thin peg or dowel to prevent a long nose from chipping off. The dotted lines in Illus. 33 show the peg and the saw cuts. Now start carving, going deeply into the block but leaving the nose sticking out. Indicate the forehead, eye sockets, mouth and chin. Then carve the sides with ears, and conclude with the back of the head.

Before carving the finished details, first make the head hollow. This makes it lighter to handle when in use. Separate the head in two parts behind the ears. With most woods, this can be done by splitting: take a large chisel or a hatchet and drive it with a sharp blow of a wooden mallet. You can also saw the head in half. As an alternative, start with two separate blocks and join them with wood cement before carving. If you do that, place a sheet of paper between both halves when cementing them together, so you will know exactly where to split open the cement seams after your initial carving.

After hollowing out both halves, cement them back together again and finish your carving with details. Be sure to hollow out a hole in the neck for the finger of the puppeteer.

Coloring

You can often greatly enhance the effect of wood carving by applying a stain or oil. A wide variety of wood-colored stains are available from paint shops and are easy to apply. Linseed oil has a light, pleasing color and you can use it on wood to great effect. Rub it well into the wood, and darken it by additional coats. You can also use furniture polish. However, for bowls or kitchen utensils, or anything that holds food, use olive oil, or melted beeswax mixed with mineral oil. Or you can leave the utensil as is. Long use and handling provides the best finish for these functional items.

You can also use paint to accentuate carved-out lines or for contrast. It is usually preferable for puppets. But applying paint means that the natural beauty of the wood is lost, so be sparing.

CROCHETED HAIRPIN LACE

Laces are open, airy products which can be created by several techniques. Each technique produces certain effects and correspondingly appropriate uses. Basically there are five different methods of producing lace: the needle-point method, using net, tapes, cords, with thread and needle to fasten them together; the bobbin method, weaving by numerous threaded bobbins, twisted and whirled in a pattern on a pillow; the knitted method; the tatted method; and the crocheted method. Each of these techniques involves an individual set of instructions, stitches, patterns and equipment.

The word "lace," derived from the Latin word *laqueus*, means noose or snare. Noose, in turn, is "a loop with a running knot that binds closer the more it is drawn." This is certainly true of the crochet loop which makes one kind of lace—Hairpin Lace. This article deals with Hairpin Lace, usually made on a hairpin-shaped frame. This is crocheted lace with variations limited only by your own imagination. You can create useful and attractive lacy products with a relatively small investment in equipment and materials, and with a modest amount of time, effort and skill. All you have to do is master the few basic rules and stitches.

The basic stitches, called loop (lp), yarn over (yo), chain (ch), single crochet (sc), double crochet (dc), and half double crochet (hdc), are the stitches most used in this type of lace-making. (The instructions will refer to the stitches by their letter abbreviations. The *

means repeat from that point.) The projects you create can be large or small, fine or coarse —from afghans, stoles and shawls, to wall hangings, curtains and floral decorations. Even a wedding dress, made 50 years ago and handed down as an heirloom, is the product of the Hairpin Lace process. Use any combinations of the basic stitches that you know, such as the Popcorn, Star, Shell and Cluster stitches, to further enhance your Hairpin Lace projects. You may even, hopefully, develop patterns of your own for unique and individual, one-of-a-kind Hairpin Lace creations.

Materials

Almost any kind and size of yarn, worsted, twine, string, cord, rope, or thread, made of cotton, linen, wool, silk, metal, nylon, or artificial fibres, is suitable for making Hairpin Lace. However, you need a few precautions. Select a material whose shape, in cross-section, is round. Because most ribbons and other flat, lifeless materials usually do not work up well, use materials that have some firmness and body to them. Raffia and other straw-like materials, which have some stiffness, are an exception, and the twist which develops during the Hairpin Lace process actually seems to enhance them. Other slippery, limp materials are not as easy for the beginner to use. With patience, practice, and experience, though, you will be able to produce a luscious fabric using chenille and velvety yarns even though they have less body.

Condensed from the book, "Creative Lace-Making" by Harriet U. Fish | © 1972 by Sterling Publishing Co., Inc., New York

For small projects, use left-overs and odds and ends.

If you are going to buy crochet cottons, remember that the higher the number, the smaller the thread diameter. Size 30, then, is thicker than size 80. Wools are usually measured by plys (the number of strands of wool). The more plys, the larger the diameter of the yarn. So, 4-ply wool is thicker than 2-ply.

Equipment

Crochet Hook

NOTE: Crochet hook sizes in this book are American. Convert to English and Continental metric sizes as shown in Table I.

Although crochet hooks are available almost universally, sizing methods vary. In metal hooks, the smaller the number, the larger the hook end. A high number such as 14 would be very small and fine. In plastic hooks, the sizing is from D to J, and D is smaller than J; in aluminum hooks, the sizing is from B to K, and B is smaller than K. The smallest aluminum hooks are comparable to the largest of the metal hooks.

Hairpin Lace Frames

The Hairpin Lace equipment is known by several terms—frame, fork, loom. All of these are looms in the sense that fabric is made on them. The three words are, however, used interchangeably by lace-makers and equipment manufacturers.

Hairpin frames are available in knit and weaving shops where you would buy crochet hooks and yarn-type materials. There are several styles with different width settings. The

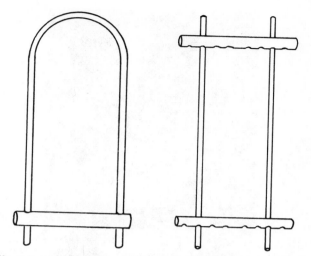

Illus. 1. Hairpin fork (left) and Hairpin crochet frame or fork (right).

diameter of the material you use has a definite relationship to the size of the crochet hook and the width of the Hairpin Lace frame. The crochet hook and the frame can be too large for the size of the material, or the frame can be too narrow for the size of the hook and material. For smaller diameter yarn, you must use a small hook and narrow setting on the frame.

In the Victorian period, when Hairpin Lace-making was at its peak, the ladies actually used their large bone hairpins for frames. Today, you can use any of several different types of frames.

The Hairpin fork in Illus. 1, the older style loom, is shaped like a hairpin and has two points like a fork. Open at one end and rounded at the other, the Hairpin fork has a spacer bar which slides up and down to keep the distance between the prongs even. Remove

TABLE I

American		K/10¼	J/10	I/9	H/8	H/8	G/6	F/5	E/4	D/3	C/2	B/1
English			2	3	4	5	6	7	8	9	10	11	12	13	14
Continental metric	7½	7	6½	6	5½	5	4½	4	3½	3¼	3/2¾	2½	2¼	2

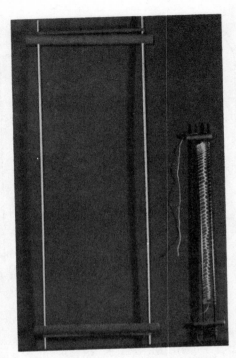

Illus. 2. Home-made Hairpin Lace frames of any width are simple to construct.

cally, so the rods will be parallel. Do the same thing with the second pair of needles, but space the holes differently, so that you have two Hairpin Lace frames for fine work.

If you wish to have a longer and larger frame for afghan and stole work, buy welding rod or aluminum rod $\frac{1}{8}''$ or $\frac{3}{16}''$ in diameter and do the same thing as for the smaller frame, using dowelling large enough to accommodate the evenly spaced holes.

If, for any reason, the rods or prongs slip out of the holes in either the handmade or commercial frames, wind an elastic band round the metal ends outside of the dowelling or bar (see Illus. 2). Also, be sure the ends of the prongs and rods are smooth, so they do not scratch or catch your yarn or thread.

The rule for success in scale in making Hairpin Lace is to set the frame *wide* for coarse or heavy materials, and *close* together for fine materials. You will notice that the wider the fork, the more awkward is the rotating motion you use and the more room is necessary for the lace-making process.

Basic Stitches for Hairpin Lace

NOTE: Crochet terms and instructions given in this book are American. Substitute English terms as follows:

American	*English*
yarn over (yo)	wool round hook
chain (ch)	chain
slip stitch (sl st)	single crochet
single crochet (sc)	double crochet
half double crochet (hdc)	half treble crochet
double crochet (dc)	treble crochet

You must be familiar with the basic crochet stitches before you can make crocheted Hairpin Lace. Start with a medium-sized hook (F or G) and at least a 2-ply or, preferably, a 4-ply worsted or yarn. Of course, large-sized hooks work with fine thread, but the result is unattractive and flimsy. Using a small hook with large yarn is not as easy to do, but is equally as unattractive and bunchy. Gauge

this bar when you complete your work. This type of loom is a fixed size, so you must have several of varying widths if you are interested in more than one size lace.

Although the Hairpin crochet frame or fork in Illus. 1 does not actually have prongs as a fork does, the points are still called prongs. This frame is composed of two metal side rails and two plastic or wooden bars which slide up and down and equalize the spacing as you work. The Hairpin crochet frame is adjustable, and on it you can make lace in eight different widths from $\frac{1}{2}''$ to 4″ in $\frac{1}{2}''$ intervals.

You can also make your own Hairpin Lace frame, in any size you wish, which will look and work like any commercial frame. To make a frame for very fine lace—using small diameter thread and a tiny crochet hook—purchase a set of small-sized, metal double-ended sock needles for knitting (they come four in a set). Decide the width you wish to use, and drill holes the size of the needles in two pieces of $\frac{1}{4}''$ dowelling, making sure that both pieces are drilled identi-

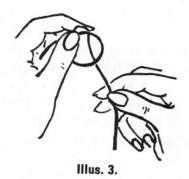

Illus. 3.

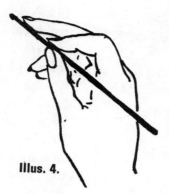

Illus. 4.

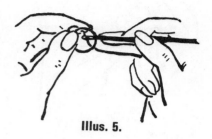

Illus. 5.

your thread and crochet hook compatibly. After a few stitches, you can tell which change should be made, if any, for the result to be useful, attractive and worth your time to make.

Make the loop first.

Step 1: Grasp the thread near the end between the thumb and forefinger of your left hand. Lap the long thread over the short thread (supply thread over end) and hold the loop in place between your thumb and forefinger (Illus. 3).

Step 2: With your right hand, take hold of the flat bar of the hook as you would a pencil. Then, bring your middle finger forward to rest near the tip of the hook (Illus. 4). Holding the hook this way enables you to control the position of the hook end.

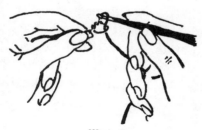

Illus. 6.

Step 3: Put your hook through the loop, catch the long end of the supply thread (attached to the ball of yarn), and draw it through (Illus. 5).

Step 4: Do not remove the hook from the thread loop. Pull the short end and supply thread in opposite directions to bring the loop close, but not too tight, round the end of the hook (Illus. 6).

Hold the thread with your left hand.

Step 5: Measure with your eye about 4″ of the supply thread from the loop on the hook. At about this point, insert the thread between your ring and little fingers with the palm of your hand facing up (Illus. 7).

Step 6: Bring the thread towards the back, under your little and ring fingers, over the middle finger, and under the forefinger towards the thumb (Illus. 8).

Illus. 7.

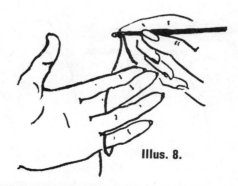

Illus. 8.

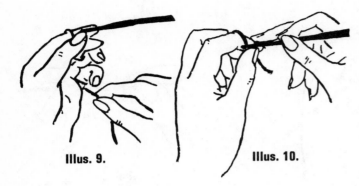

Illus. 9.   Illus. 10.

Step 7: Grasp the hook and loop between the thumb and forefinger of your left hand. Gently pull the supply thread so that it lies around your fingers firmly but not tightly (Illus. 9). This gives you control.

Step 8: Catch the knot of the loop between your thumb and forefinger. Bend your middle finger in such a way as to regulate the tension of the thread and regulate the ring and little fingers to prevent the thread from moving too freely (Illus. 10). As you practice you will become familiar with the correct position for you. Keep in mind that the motion of the hook in the right hand and the thread in the left hand should be easy and smooth. One of the most common faults of beginners is to crochet either too tightly or too loosely.

Chain Stitch (ch)

You already have one loop on your hook.

Step 1: Pass your hook under the thread and catch the supply thread with the hook (Illus. 11). This is called "thread over" or "yarn over." Draw the thread through the loop on the hook. This makes one chain (ch). If the hook does not slide easily, the thread is too tight.

Step 2: Repeat Step 1 until you have as many chain stitches as you need. One loop always remains on the hook (Illus. 12). Always keep the thumb and forefinger of your left hand near the stitch on which you are working. Practice making chains until they are even in size and lie flat, all in the same direction. If too much light shows through each loop and it looks loose, the hook is too large for the diameter of the yarn.

Single Crochet (sc)

Step 1: Make a foundation chain of 20 stitches to use for practice (ch 20). To begin the row, insert the hook from the front, under the two top threads (front and back) of the second chain (ch) from the hook (Illus. 13).

Step 2: Catch the thread with the hook (yarn over) (Illus. 14) and draw through the stitch (st). There are now two loops on the hook (Illus. 15).

Step 3: Yarn over and draw it through both loops. One loop remains on the hook. You have now completed one single crochet (sc) (Illus. 16).

Step 4: For the next single crochet (sc), insert the hook under two top threads of the next stitch (st) and proceed as before (repeat Steps 2 and 3). Repeat until you have made a single crochet in every stitch (20 sc). At the end of the row of single crochets, chain 1 (ch 1) (Illus. 17). Turn your work so that the reverse side is facing you (Illus. 18).

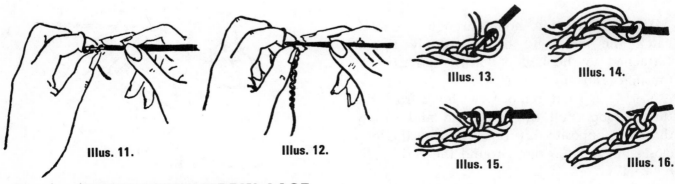

Illus. 11.   Illus. 12.   Illus. 13.   Illus. 14.

Illus. 15.   Illus. 16.

Illus. 17.

Illus. 18.

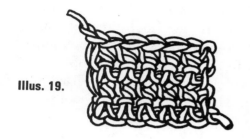

Illus. 19.

Double Crochet (dc)

Step 1: Make a foundation chain of 20 stitches (ch 20) for a practice piece. To begin the row, yarn over (yo) and insert the hook from the front under the two top threads of the fourth chain (ch) from hook (Illus. 20). Yarn over (yo) and draw the thread through the stitch (st). There are now three loops on the hook.

Step 2: Yarn over (Illus. 21) and draw through two loops. Two loops remain on the hook (Illus. 22).

Step 3: Thread over again and draw through the two remaining loops (one loop remains on the hook). You have now completed one double crochet (Illus. 23). For the next double crochet (dc), yarn over, insert the hook from the front under the two top threads of the next stitch and proceed as above. Repeat until you have made a double crochet in every chain.

Step 4: At the end of the row, chain three (ch 3) (Illus. 24) and turn. The three chain stitches count as the first double crochet (dc) of the next row.

For the second, third and however many remaining rows you wish to crochet, insert the hook from the front under the two top threads (front and back) of the second stitch from the hook (first stitch on the previous row). Then, repeat Steps 2, 3 and 4 in the directions for the first row.

At the end of the last row, do not make a turning chain. Clip the thread about 3″ from your work, bring the loose end through the one loop remaining on the hook and pull tightly (Illus. 19). Now you have completed a practice piece of single crochet.

NOTE: In crochet, it is customary to pick up both of the two top threads (front and back) of every stitch unless otherwise directed. When you only pick up the back stitch, the result is called rib stitch.

In crochet, you must add a certain number of chain stitches at the end of every row. Then, turn the work so that the reverse side is facing you. You have noticed that in the single crochet, you use only one chain for turning. The number of turning chains depends upon the stitch with which you intend to begin the next row. The exact number will usually be given in the directions. The turning chain always counts as the first stitch, except in single crochet where ch 1 only raises the work to position, but does not count as the first stitch.

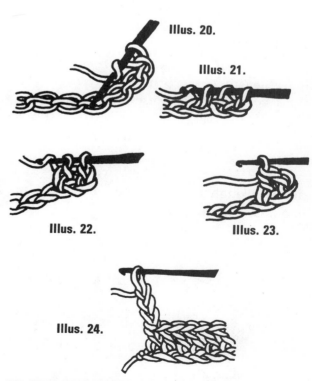

Illus. 20.

Illus. 21.

Illus. 22.

Illus. 23.

Illus. 24.

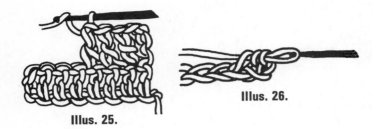

Illus. 25.   Illus. 26.

To begin the second, third and remaining rows, yarn over, insert the hook from the front under the two top threads of the fifth stitch from the hook (second stitch on the previous row). Proceed as above (Illus. 25).

Finish off at the end of your desired length by cutting the thread 3″ from the last double crochet. Bring the end through the loop and pull tightly.

Half Double Crochet (hdc)

Make the stitch known as half double crochet (hdc) by first repeating Step 1 of double crochet. At that point, there are three loops on the hook. Then, yarn over and draw through all three loops at once (Illus. 26). In half double crochet, chain 2 (ch 2) to turn.

Slip Stitch (sl st)

Use slip stitch only for joining or when an invisible stitch is required. When the directions say join, always use a slip stitch.

Step 1: Insert the hook from the front through the two top threads of the stitch (Illus. 27).

Step 2: Yarn over and with one motion, draw through the stitch and the loop on the hook. One loop remains on the hook (Illus. 28).

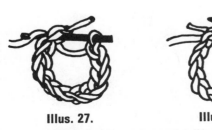

Illus. 27.    Illus. 28.

Increase

If you are instructed to increase, make two stitches in one stitch. Each time you do this, you make an extra stitch on that row.

Decrease in Single Crochet

Step 1: Complete the single crochet to the point where two loops remain on the hook. Keep the two loops on the hook and insert the hook from under the two top threads of the next stitch. Yarn over and draw through the stitch. There are now three loops on the hook (Illus. 29).

Step 2: Yarn over and draw through the three loops at once. One loop remains on the hook. You have now worked two single crochets together and there is one stitch less on the row (Illus. 30).

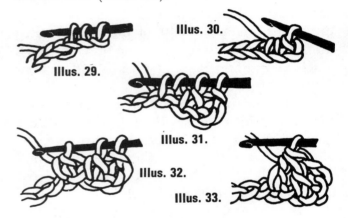

Illus. 30.

Illus. 29.

Illus. 31.

Illus. 32.

Illus. 33.

Decrease in Double Crochet

Step 1: Make a double crochet to the point where there are two loops on the hook. Keep the two loops on the hook, yarn over, and insert the hook from the front under the two top threads of the next stitch. Yarn over and draw through the stitch. There are now four loops on the hook (Illus. 31).

Step 2: Yarn over again and draw through two loops. Three loops remain on the hook (Illus. 32).

Step 3: Yarn over and draw through the three loops. One loop remains on the hook (Illus. 33). You have now worked two double crochets together and there is one less stitch on the row.

Edge on Handkerchief

Now that you have mastered the basic crochet stitches and understand the size relationship of material to hook to patterns, apply it to the Hairpin Lace technique. The first Hairpin Lace was edging on dainty handkerchiefs as in Illus. 35.

Materials: One hemstitched handkerchief (hemstitching is a method of hemming that involves drawing threads from the handkerchief at the hemline and then uniformly stitching several of the loose perpendicular stitches together); one ball of white or colored cotton tatting thread, #30 or finer; size 8 metal crochet hook; Hairpin Lace frame, set at $\frac{1}{2}''$.

Work sc around all four edges of the handkerchief, having about 12 sc to the inch, and remembering to do 3 sc in each corner stitch. End off. Count sc stitches. Hopefully, you have an even number.

Make enough Hairpin Lace loops on the frame to match the number of sc along the edges of the handkerchief. If this is an even number, the pattern following will work out evenly without adjustments.

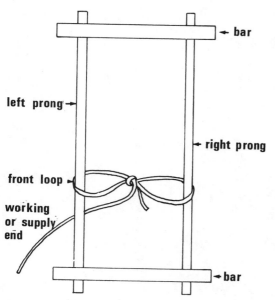

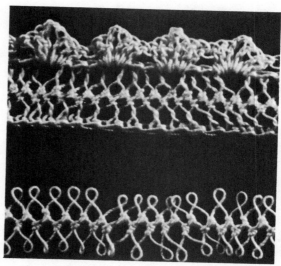

Illus. 35. Attach the plain Hairpin Lace (shown on the bottom) to a handkerchief and then add the dainty shell edging (pictured on the top).

Hold the frame in your left hand; loop yarn round the frame and tie a secure knot in the center, leaving a 3″ end for use later if necessary. Always keep the supply or working end of the yarn at the rear of the work and hold it in your left hand as you would for crocheting (see page 201).

The lace edging shown in Illus. 35 has a single crochet center.

Step 1: Insert the hook under the front strand of the left-of-center loop and pull a thread through (one loop on the hook). Chain 1 stitch (still 1 loop on hook).

Step 2: Rotate the frame one-half turn from right to left towards you, winding a loop from the supply around the left prong of the frame, which now becomes the right prong (Illus. 36). To do this, either remove the hook from the loop and replace it back in the loop from the opposite side, after the loom is rotated, or pass the shank of the hook through the middle of the loom, to the other side as it is rotated. If you are using a hairpin without any bar, you can throw the hook from side to side without removing it from the loop. Simply pass it through the open end of the hairpin. With the hook in the remaining stitch, pass the hook

Illus. 34. Parts of an adjustable Hairpin crochet loom or frame.

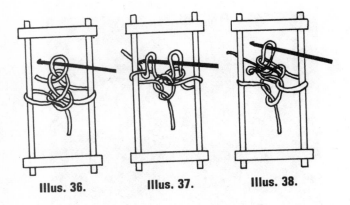

under the front of the loop on the left-hand side. Pick up the thread with the hook (yo) and bring it through the loop (two loops on hook) (Illus. 37).

Step 3: Pick up thread (yo) and pull through both loops (Illus. 38).

Repeat Steps 2 and 3 until you have made as many loops as sc stitches on the handkerchief. Remember that when a pattern calls for a certain number of loops, you must have the designated number of loops on *each* side of the loom. 20 loops means 20 right and 20 left.

If the frame fills up and you still need a longer strip, slip the bar from the bottom of the loom and take off all but three or four loops on each side of the loom. Replace the bar and roll up the loops that have been removed and fasten them with a stitch holder to keep them from twisting and stretching.

To fasten off, always leave an 8″ strand of thread at the end of each strip. Pull it through the last loop of the single crochet to keep the strip from unravelling.

Now, remove the lace from the frame, being careful to keep the twist in the loops.

Step 4: Keeping the twist in all the loops, join the thread to the first sc in one corner of the handkerchief and sc each loop of lace to each sc on the edges of the handkerchief, remembering to fasten three loops at each corner so it will lie flat. Fasten off.

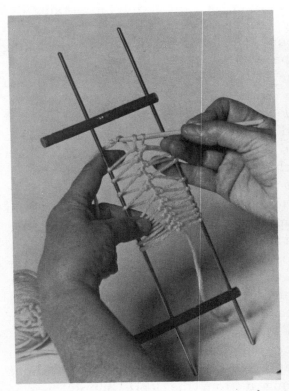

Illus. 39. For Hairpin Lace with a sc center, insert the hook under only the front loop on the left-hand side.

Illus. 40. Even your first attempts at Hairpin Lace should look like this. Hairpin Lace is not at all difficult to make.

Step 5: Join the thread to the outside of the Hairpin Lace loops and, again, keeping the twist in all the loops, do one row of sc all round.

Step 6: For the second row, do a shell stitch along this sc edge of lace. Make the shell stitch as follows: * 3 dc in first space between loops, ch 3, 3 dc all in same space. This is a shell. Skip 3 spaces between loops and repeat from * around the handkerchief. Remember to make two shells at each corner.

Try other crocheted edgings with this fine thread to use on blouses, slips, baby clothes and table linen. This is true Hairpin Lace.

Wall Decorations

Bell Cord

Materials: one adjustable Hairpin Lace frame, set at 2″, or a 2″-wide fork; size H or larger crochet hook; two balls of contrasting sisal cord; two yards of contrasting ½″ grosgrain ribbon (or 1″ doubled for extra rigidity); felt of a blending color: one piece for the top, $2\frac{1}{4}$″ × 1″, and two pieces for the bottom, $2\frac{1}{4}$″ × $1\frac{1}{4}$″, trimmed so that the bottom edge is ½″ narrower than the top edge (Illus. 41); one 1″ metal rung for top hanging; one 2″ bell for the bottom.

Step 1: To make a bell cord, you first single crochet one strip of Hairpin Lace (make a strip with a single crochet center) with 40 loops on each side, working the two colors

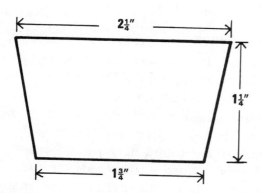

Illus. 41. Trim the felt for the bottom edge like this.

together simultaneously. Leave at least 4″ ends at the beginning and end.

Step 2: Remove the strip from the frame and place it on a flat surface. Without keeping the twist in the loops, thread the grosgrain ribbon through the loops, using one yard for each side.

Step 3: Hand stitch the top piece of felt, folding it lengthwise at the top to catch the center sc of the lace and the ends of the ribbon. Tack the metal ring to the center top. To shape the bottom pieces of felt, hand stitch them one on each side of the lace, widest side up towards the sc and the ribbon. Tack the bell to the center of the bottom of the felt.

The bell cord is an unusual gift or addition to your own home.

Wall Hanging

Materials: two balls of hemp rope in two contrasting colors; Hairpin Lace frame, set at 3″; size H crochet hook; 12 pieces of 1″ veneer of cedar, birch, redwood or other wood; large, strong stapler; 12 ceramic beads (optional).

Sand the edges of the veneer and set the pieces aside.

Step 1: To make the smart-looking wall hanging in Illus. L1 on page L, work five lace strips—two of one color and three of the other —with 34 loops on each side.

Step 2: Cable the strips together in a one to one joining (cabling or weaving are other terms for joining) from bottom to top, alternating the colors. To do this, place two strips side by side on a flat surface, making sure each strip has the beginning knot end at the bottom, and the last loop end at the top. In this way, you can make adjustments to the number of loops fairly easily. Work on the right side of the lace. Working from bottom to top, insert the crochet hook into the first loop on the left-hand strip, reach with the hook for the first loop on the right-hand strip and pull it through the left one on the hook (see Illus. 42).

Step 3: Proceed, alternating sides, pulling loops through, in the manner shown in Illus.

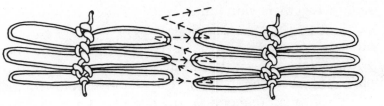

Illus. 42. One to one joining or cabling.

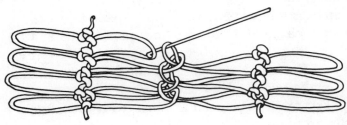

43. This one to one joining pattern may be varied by using two or three loops at a time, especially if you are fastening a longer strip to a shorter one. Continually check on the back side to be sure you have not skipped any loops.

Step 4: When you reach the end, work the tail end of yarn (left when you fastened off the sc center) through the last loop to prevent it from unlooping backwards.

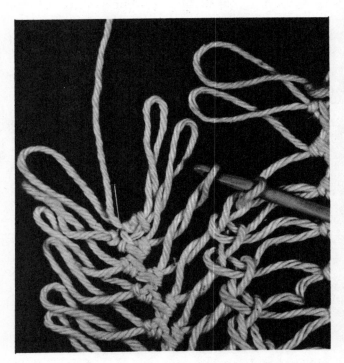

Illus. 43. These two strips are joined by one to one cabling. Notice that you can maintain the twist as you work.

Step 5: Following the same procedure, join all five strips together. You may notice a twist in the loops as they rest on a flat surface. You add additional charm to the lace by encouraging and maintaining this twist as you join the strips.

Step 6: Pass six of the pieces of veneer vertically through the rows of loops on both sides of the two outside and center strips.

Step 7: Finish off by latticing the additional strips of wood at the top and bottom.

Step 8: Staple the latticed veneer strips together and use a piece of rawhide for a hanger at the top.

Step 9: You may hang ceramic beads strung on lengths of hemp from the bottom.

Use this same technique on a larger scale for decorative and unusual room dividers, screens or window curtains. If you do not insert the veneer strips, the five Hairpin Lace strips cabled together make wonderful place mats for your patio.

Flower Plaque

Hairpin Lace flowers are so lovely that you will undoubtedly think of many ways in which to display them—in decorations, corsages, trimmings and a wall plaque. You can even make Christmas tree ornaments of metallic threads in the round flower-like form.

Materials: straw materials; raffia; sisal; metallic cordings; other firm or stiff materials.

Large flowers result from wide-set frames and

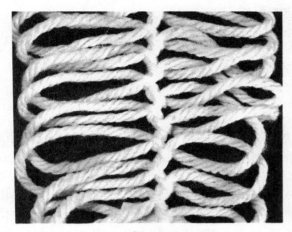

Illus. 44. Hairpin Lace with a chain center.

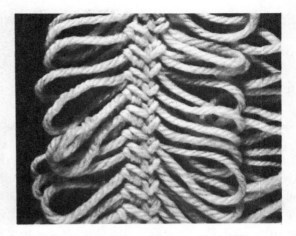

Illus. 45. Hairpin Lace with a double braid center.

small ones from narrow-set frames. Be sure to use crochet hooks of the proper size for the diameter of the yarn or thread you choose.

Add further originality by making other center stitches for the strips than the single crochet center (see page 206). One possibility is the simple chain center, pictured in Illus. 44. Begin as you did for the sc center with a loop round the frame and a knot in the center. Instead of inserting the hook under the loop, however, simply do a chain stitch. Rotate the frame and form a new loop, the same as in Step 2 on page 205. Again, do a chain stitch, using the supply thread. Always make your stitches in front of the prong left of the center knot.

Another possible center stitch is the double braid stitch in Illus. 45. This is a simple variation of the sc center, for which you pick up both sides—front and back—of the left loop when you pick up the thread with the hook (see Illus. 46). For a sc center, remember, you only pick up the front strand on the left loop. Continue with Steps 2 and 3 of the sc center, always picking up both loops instead of only one (see pages 205 to 206).

Flat Flowers

Step 1: Set the frame at $1\frac{1}{2}''$ to make a 3″ flower. Work 20 loops, both sides, with a single crochet center. More than 20 loops at this frame setting results in a rippled flower.

Step 2: Before removing the loops from the frame, run a sturdy thread up through the loops on one side only. Use this to pull up the center after removing the lace from the frame. Tie the thread in a square knot to make a circle. Use the end threads to close the gap where sc meets sc. Fasten off with a hook or needle.

Cone-Shaped Flowers

Raffia is not very long, so if you use it here, tie several strands together first.

Illus. 46. For the double braid center, pick up both the front and back of the left-of-center loop.

Step 1: Set the frame at 4″. Make 24 loops of single raffia, both sides.

Step 2: Run a piece of yarn through the loops on one side only. Remove the lace from the frame and pull the yarn up tightly, fastening as you did for the flat flower.

Step 3: For the center, make one 15-loop strip of double yarn or raffia (two colors) on a frame set at 2″. Set the frame at 1″ and make a 12-loop strip. Pull a strong thread through one side of the loops of both of these strips to shape them into cones. You may cut the outside loops of the smaller strip, after pulling it into a cone, to make a fuzzy center.

Step 4: Superimpose the three sizes of flowers and, using the end threads, fasten them together at the center.

Stems

Use an 18-gauge uncovered floral wire to make stems. Make a small hook at one end of the wire and pass the wire down from the flower center (through the tie hole) to form a stem. You can wrap the wire stem with green floral tape. Wire flat corsage flowers in this same manner.

You can also make stems simply from a row of chain stitches.

Leaves

To make leaves, sc 8-, 12-, and 14-loop green strips, on frame settings of less width than the flowers. Pass a piece of yarn through one side of the strip before removing it from the frame. Pull the yarn only until you form an oblong shape, round at one end and flat at the other. After you have made as many leaves as you want, assemble the plaque. Use a casein-type (white) glue to fasten the flowers to the background. Then glue the stems in place with the leaves.

Ribbon Belt

Follow this simple pattern for an unusual belt. The materials and instructions here are for a 34″ belt. Be sure to make adjustments for larger or smaller sizes.

Materials: one ball of ornamental crochet cotton thread with a metallic twist, any color; Hairpin Lace frame set at 1″; two yards of ¼″ grosgrain ribbon and a long-eye needle; one pearl or metal buckle with a 1″ slot; felt or soft leather of a shade related to the thread and ribbon for the buckle end and tip.

Step 1: Work a strip of 130 loops, both sides, using the sc center stitch. This piece of lace has some stretch.

Step 2: Before removing the lace from the frame, thread the ¼″ grosgrain ribbon onto the needle and pass it down one side, through the loops and up the other side through those loops. Remove the whole thing from the frame and adjust the ribbon evenly.

Step 3: Cut two pieces of felt in an elongated diamond shape for the belt tip (Illus. 47). Be sure to cut the felt the width of the belt.

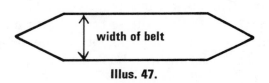

width of belt

Illus. 47.

Step 4: Stitch, preferably on a sewing machine, but by hand if a machine is unavailable, one piece of felt on the inside and one on the outside of the belt, covering the ends of the ribbon and catching the first loop of the Hairpin Lace. Trim even if necessary.

Step 5: Cut two pieces of felt the width of the belt and 2″ long. Stitch the felt pieces together, again preferably by machine, over the buckle end of the belt, catching the last loop inside. Pass this felt end through the buckle and hand tack it securely in place.

Necklace of Metallic Thread

Materials: Hairpin Lace frame, set at 2″; size G crochet hook; three sizes of gold or silver cording—heavy, medium and fine; 34 gold or silver beads with holes large enough to carry the fine cording; one gold or silver button.

The gauge for the length of the cording is: one yard of cord equals four loops, both sides, at a 2″ frame setting.

Step 1: Work 33 loops, both sides, with the double braid center stitch (see page 209), leaving 6″ ends of cord on both ends.

Step 2: With the medium cording, sc loops together (see page 208) on one edge, which then becomes the neck edge.

Step 3: On the opposite edge—now the outside edge—do one sc in the first loop with heavy cording, * ch 1, sc in next loop. Repeat from * across the lower edge, thus increasing the width.

Step 4: String the 34 beads on the fine cording which is still connected to the ball. On the outside edge * sc in the first sc of the previous row, move up one bead on the thread, sc in ch on the previous row. Repeat from * to the end of the necklace, using all the beads. Work the ends of the fine cording back into the crocheted edge. The beads lie flat on the outside of each Hairpin loop.

Step 5: You now have a semi-circular necklace with three long cord ends protruding from each end. Work these into the center of the Hairpin Lace so that all the ends are bunched in the middle and stick straight out at each end (see Illus. 48). These will form the fastening part of the necklace.

Step 6: Using this bundle as a core, fasten the medium-weight cord to the body of the necklace and sc tightly around these bunched ends, covering them from the neck edge outward. After each end measures about 4″, ch a loop for buttoning at one end and a flat area on which to sew the button at the other.

Illus. 50. Close-up of the Hairpin Lace afghan shown in color on page L. Choose joining and center stitch patterns according to your own creative taste.

Step 7: In order to make this closing more graceful, join the medium-weight cord at the base of each end and chain from corner A to the covered core center and back to corner B (see Illus. 49). This makes a triangle fastening the ends of the necklace together.

Step 8: Work any loose ends in with the hook and glue flat with white glue/paste called "Tacky White Glue" or with Elmer's Glue.

Sew on a decorative button to complete this original necklace, pictured in the top right-hand corner on the front cover.

Shawls, Stoles and Afghans

If you want to make a shawl or stole or an afghan like the one in Illus. L2, first make yourself an extra long—but not longer than 18″—Hairpin Lace frame.

To make a long frame, use a long set of metal knitting needles about size 8 (English size 5), or use welding rods of about this same diameter. Cut the heads off the knitting needles and smooth the ends. Cut two pieces of ½″ dowelling 4½″ long, and two pieces 3½″ long.

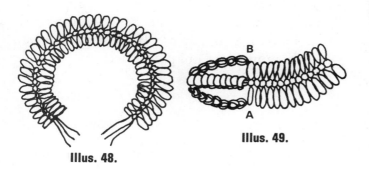

Illus. 48.

Illus. 49.

Drill holes the diameter of the needles 4″ apart and 3″ apart respectively on the two sets of dowelling. This provides two separate Hairpin Lace frames for long strips of lace.

Make Hairpin Lace as you have learned, of a length you select and with a center stitch of your choice. A time-saving tip for this project— as well as for any projects with long strips—is to mark each 25 stitches with a safety-pin to facilitate counting. Also, mark your frame on the front side with a soft-tip marker, so you know when the front is towards you. Then, you know that both sides have the same number of loops on them.

When removing already-made lace from a frame to continue longer lengths, use a knitting holder, as long as you can find. By placing the loops of one side on the holder, you protect the lace from twisting and taking extra time to straighten when you cable the strips together.

Always cable the long strips together from the bottom (beginning) to the top (ending) to allow for adjustment of the numbers of loops. It is sometimes hard to work the proper number of loops when it is in the hundreds.

The charm of an unusual stole or shawl is in the method of cabling the Hairpin strips together. One to one is usual, but grouping the

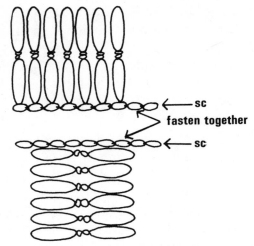

Illus. 52. Use an end-to-side joining to create an unusual patterned look for your Hairpin Lace.

loops in threes and fours makes a lacier finished product.

In addition, a crocheted edging on each side of the Hairpin Lace loops is most attractive and has a charm all its own. One such possible pattern is a shell edging like the one for the handkerchief on page 205. Another type of joining is an end-to-side joining, pictured in Illus. 52. For this, sc the loops of one end of the strip together and sc the loops along the side of the other strip. Then, sc the two rows of sc to each other.

An attractive way to finish the edge of a shawl or afghan is to make fringe of Hairpin Lace. Work a strip of the length necessary for the fringe. Cable the strip onto the body of the afghan or stole. Either leave the second side of the fringe in loops or cut it, as in Illus. 51, for open fringe.

Try making a bedspread as you would an afghan, using a contrasting bright lining and a lacy joining. As you can see, with a little imagination, you can use Hairpin Lace in an endless number of unique projects.

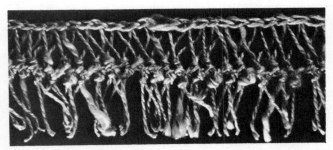

Illus. 51. Hairpin Lace fringe is really easy to make. Simply cut open the loops on the outside edge of your project.

KNITTING

Even if you do not know how to knit, you have undoubtedly seen someone else do it. The process may look difficult, but the basics really are not. The instructions here are only the most elementary steps you need to learn to knit. Practice these simple projects until your knitting is smooth and even. Then, you will be ready to tackle larger, more complicated items, whose patterns you may find in knitting books and magazine articles.

Place Mat or Doily

For your first project, make a small place mat or doily to protect a table top. Use 4-ply knitting worsted. When you are a proficient knitter, you will be able to experiment with different weights and types of yarn, such as cotton, silk or metallic threads, but it is easiest to learn with standard knitting worsted.

Knitting needles, used in pairs, are available in many sizes—from very thin to very thick. For the doily, choose medium-sized needles, about size 9 (size 4 English). (See below for a conversion chart of knitting needle sizes.)

Cast On

Casting-on is the process of putting the foundation row of stitches on your needle. There are several different ways to cast on, but you will learn only one way here. This method may be a different one than you see your

friends using, but it is an easy-to-learn, fast way of casting-on.

Step 1: Leaving a 4"- to 6"-length of yarn at the end, make a slip knot or loop and slip the left needle through it as shown in Illus. 1. Tighten the knot round the needle by pulling the yarn (Illus. 2).

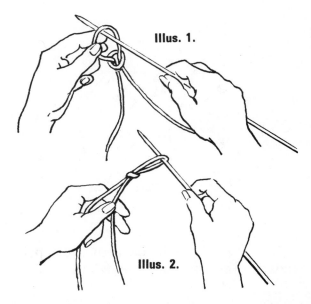

Illus. 1.

Illus. 2.

Step 2: Take the other needle into your right hand and insert it into the slip loop, placing the right-hand needle in *back* of the left-hand one. Pull the yarn, which should also be in back of the left needle, so the loop is fairly taut.

Step 3: Arrange the yarn round the fingers of your left hand as shown in Illus. 3.

Knitting Needle Conversion Chart

American	15	13	12	11	10½	10	9	8	7	6	5	4	3	2	1	0	00
English	000	00	0	1	2	3	4	5	6	7	8	9	10	11	12	13	14

Written especially for this volume by Louisa Hellegers ; drawings by Minn

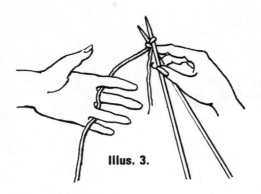

Illus. 3.

Step 4: Holding your hands as shown in Illus. 4, move the right-hand needle under and behind the yarn, thus forming a loop around the right-hand needle.

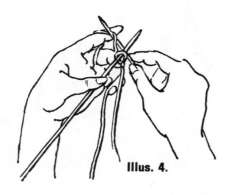

Illus. 4.

Step 5: Pull the loop through the slip loop already on the left-hand needle (Illus. 5).

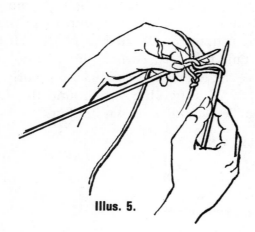

Illus. 5.

Step 6: Twist the loop on the right-hand needle and slip it onto the left-hand needle (see Illus. 6). You have completed one cast-on stitch. Your right needle should still be inserted in the second stitch.

Continue casting-on in this manner, repeating Steps 4, 5, and 6 until you have the proper number of cast-on stitches. For this first project, cast on 35 stitches.

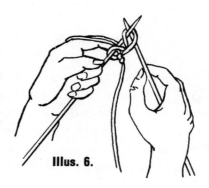

Illus. 6.

Knit (K)

Knitting itself is similar to the casting-on method you have learned. You hold the needles and yarn in the same way. (This method of knitting is sometimes called Continental Knitting.)

Step 1: Insert the right-hand needle into the top cast-on stitch on the left needle. The right needle should be behind the left one.

Step 2: Move the right needle under and behind the yarn, as you did for casting-on, forming a loop.

Step 3: Pull the loop through the top stitch. You now have a complete loop on the right needle (see Illus. 7).

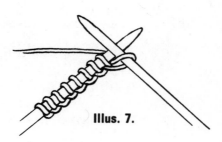

Illus. 7.

Step 4: Carefully slip the top stitch *only* off the left needle. You have knit one stitch (K1).

Repeat Steps 1 to 4 for each cast-on stitch. As you proceed, use your left hand to slide the stitches on the left needle to the top. This motion will become automatic as you gain experience.

As you knit, you must try to keep the tension—the tightness of the yarn—even. Try not to pull the yarn too tightly, or your knitting will be stiff and lumpy. If, on the other hand, the yarn seems too loose, pull it slightly to tighten it. Otherwise, your finished piece will be limp and unattractive.

When you have knit all the cast-on stitches, you have completed a *row*. The number of rows you knit determines the length of your finished project (the number of cast-on stitches determines the width). Knit as many rows as you want.

Illus. 8. Knit two together (K2 tog) to bind off.

Bind Off

When your doily is the length you want it to be, you have to *bind off* or *cast off*—that is, end your piece with a finished edge which will not ravel. As for casting-on, there are several different ways of binding-off. Here, you will learn one way, which, if you take care not to make the stitches too tight, will be useful in binding-off any knit piece you make.

Step 1: Knit two stitches together (K2 tog). You now have one stitch on the right needle.

Step 2: Slip that one stitch, keeping it loose, back onto the left-hand needle.

Be very careful, as you bind off, not to pull the yarn too tight, because your knitted piece

will not lie flat and will not be uniform if you do. Continue in this manner, always knitting the first two stitches on the left-hand needle together, until you have bound off all the stitches. When there are only two stitches left on the left needle, knit them together. You should now have one loop on the right needle. Cut the yarn from the skein and pull the end through the loop. Do not make a knot because it will show as an unsightly lump.

Weave the end pieces of yarn into the knitted fabric. You have finished your doily. Put it on a table with a vase of flowers on top.

Scarf

You are now familiar with the basics of how to do a knit stitch. If your stitches are not yet even and smooth, do some practice squares before you attempt a larger project.

To make a scarf, cast on as many stitches as you wish, remembering that the number of cast-on stitches determines the width of your scarf.

Purl (P)

The purl stitch is the only other basic stitch besides the knit stitch in knitting.

Step 1: Hold the needles and yarn the same way you did in Steps 3 and 4 for casting-on, but place the yarn from the skein or ball in *front* of the left needle. Insert the right-hand needle into the top stitch on the left needle (Illus. 9).

Step 2: Move the right needle over and around the yarn, thus forming a loop (Illus. 10).

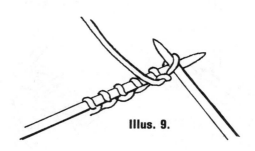

Illus. 9.

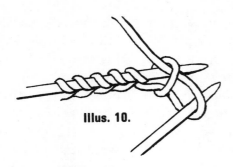

Illus. 10.

Step 3: Pull this loop through the top stitch on the left needle. You now have one loop on the right needle.

Step 4: Carefully slip the top stitch off the left needle.

You have now completed one purl stitch. Continue in this manner to the end of the row.

Continue to do the purl rows until your scarf is the length you want it to be. Cast off the same way you did for knitting (see page 215). Add fringe, if you want, to complete the scarf.

Knit and Purl Combinations

Stockinette Stitch

You may, if you want, purl one row and knit one row and then continue to alternate purl and knit rows (*K1 row, P1 row, repeat between *'s for pattern). (In knitting, the * means to repeat from that point.)

When you knit one row, purl one row, the resulting stitch is called the *stockinette stitch.* The side with the knit rows is the right side; the side with the purl rows is the wrong side.

Sometimes, you will have to leave your work in the middle, and you will then have to decide whether to begin with a knit row or with a purl row. Try not to stop knitting in

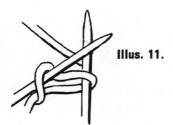

Illus. 11.

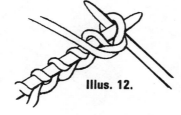

Illus. 12.

the middle of a row, because it is easy to either get mixed up direction-wise or to lose stitches.

If the last row you knitted was a purl row, your work will look like Illus. 11, with the right side facing you. The yarn will come from behind the left needle, and you should insert the right-hand needle for each stitch of that row into the back loop (otherwise, your stitches will be twisted and unattractive). In fact, whenever the stitch you are picking up from the previous row is a purl stitch, you *must* insert the right needle into the back loop.

If the last row was a knit row, your work will look like Illus. 12, with the wrong side facing you. The yarn will come in front of the left needle and you should insert the right needle into this front loop. Whenever the stitch you are picking up from the previous row is a knit stitch, you *must* insert the right-hand needle into the front loop.

Ribbing

If you look at the cuffs or bottom edge of a sweater, you will notice that the knitting is tighter and has more "give" than the rest of the sweater and also that the pattern is in rows. This is called *ribbing.* Ribbing is easy to knit. You simply knit one stitch and purl one stitch across the row (*K1, P1, repeat from * to end of row). You could also, for wider ribs, K2, P2 or K3, P3.

If you cast on an even number of stitches, simply begin each row with a knit stitch, since the last stitch will always be a purl stitch. If, however, you cast on an uneven number of stitches, you must alternate. Begin the first row with a knit stitch, the second with a purl, the third with a knit, and so on. In this way, you will be beginning each row with the opposite stitch with which you ended the previous row. Use the instructions above to determine whether your last stitch was a knit or a purl.

If you lose count of your knits and purls within a row, you can easily determine which stitch should be next by the position of the yarn. If the loop comes from behind the left needle, as in Illus. 13, the stitch in the previous row was a purl and you should do a knit. Also, if the previous stitch you just did (on the right needle) was a purl, the yarn comes from the front of the stitch on the right needle.

If, on the other hand, the top loop on the left needle comes from in front of the needle, the stitch in the previous row was a knit and you should purl. Also, if the last stitch on the right needle was a knit, the yarn comes from behind the stitch on the right needle (Illus. 14).

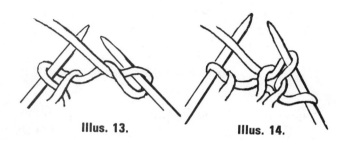

Illus. 13.   Illus. 14.

Patterns

With these few instructions and stitches, you should now be able to knit numerous square, rectangular, or oblong projects—such as blankets, afghans, and scarves—for which there are many patterns available for you to buy.

At the beginning of every pattern, there will be a listing of the size needles you need, the number of skeins of yarn and the *gauge*. The gauge is the number of stitches per inch that you should achieve following that pattern with the specified needles and yarn. It is helpful if you make a practice piece before you begin your project to determine if your knitting is the same gauge as the pattern calls for. If it is not, your finished item will not be the proper size.

You can, of course, compensate if your natural knitting tension produces either too tight or too loose a gauge. If your gauge is more than that required (if you have too many —smaller—stitches per inch), use larger needles. If your gauge is less than that required

(if you have too few—larger—stitches per inch), use smaller needles.

All knitters make mistakes as they are learning and even after they are experts. The most common mistake is to drop a stitch. If a stitch slips off your needle, quickly, but carefully, catch it with your needle and replace it onto the needle. If you have dropped a stitch several rows back, or cannot pick up a stitch you just dropped, there will be a loose stitch or loop in your knitted piece. Use a crochet hook to pick up this loop and then draw the yarn above the loop through the loop. Continue in this manner until you have caught up to the row you are working. See Illus. 15 for how to pick up a knit stitch and Illus. 16 for how to pick up a purl stitch.

The only other thing you should know before you make large projects is how to join a new skein of yarn when you run out. Never tie a knot in the yarn, because it will inevitably show. If possible, you should try to join new yarn at the end of a row, but sometimes you may have to do it in the middle of a row. There are several methods of joining yarns. One of the simplest is to overlap the ends of the yarn about 3″ of 4″ before the end of old yarn. Knit or purl your stitches with the double yarn until the old runs out and you are using exclusively the new skein. In the next row, work the double thickness as one stitch.

This section is an introduction to knitting. There are many combination stitches that you can learn after you are familiar and comfortable with the basics presented here.

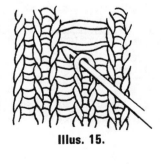

Illus. 15.

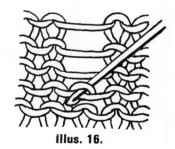

illus. 16.

NEEDLEPOINT

Needlepoint is embroidery on a canvas background. There are three basic kinds of stitches—horizontal, vertical, and diagonal. By combining these component parts, you can create about 150 needlepoint stitches with which you can cover canvas. Some stitches are better suited to certain designs than others, and the designs that you can make by combining different stitches and colors are virtually endless.

The canvas you choose for the background largely determines the appearance of your finished needlepoint—rugged, on a canvas with few mesh per inch, or dainty, on a tightly woven canvas. Most needlepoint is done on Penelope 10 (10 mesh to the inch), but for stitches which cover canvas densely, use a looser canvas, and for stitches which do not cover well, use a tighter canvas. Canvas comes in two styles, Penelope and Mono. Mono is woven with a single thread, while

Illus. 2. One method of threading the needle.

Penelope is woven in pairs of threads. Generally, do vertical stitches on Mono, and diagonal ones on Penelope, for best coverage.

You can buy canvas by the yard the same way you buy fabric, and then plan and stitch an original design.

You stitch all needlepoint with a blunt-end tapestry needle, which should be small enough to drop through the holes in the canvas. To thread a needle easily, flatten the yarn between your thumb and index finger. Then push the needle between your fingers and the needle threads itself. Never wet the yarn, as this weakens it. Another way to thread a needle is to cut a rectangle of paper narrow enough to fit the eye of the needle. Fold the paper over the yarn, push it through the eye, and your needle is threaded (see Illus. 2).

As a general rule, use tapestry or Persian yarn in stitching needlepoint pieces. It is mothproof and it comes in long, strong fibres. You should not have trouble in matching colors when you run out, for it comes in matched dye lots. It is *essential* that you use either tapestry

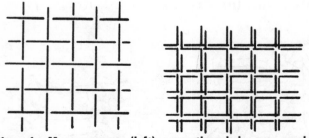

Illus. 1. Mono canvas (left): one thread is one mesh. Penelope canvas (right): each pair of threads is one mesh.

Condensed from the books, "Bargello Stitchery" by Jo Ippolito Christensen and Sonie Shapiro Ashner | © 1972 by Sterling Publishing Co., Inc., New York, "Cross Stitchery" by Jo Ippolito Christensen and Sonie Shapiro Ashner | © 1973 by Sterling Publishing Co., Inc., New York, and "Needlepoint Simplified" by Jo Ippolito Christensen and Sonie Shapiro Ashner | © 1971 by Sterling Publishing Co., Inc., New York

or Persian yarn for items which will receive lots of wear. Decorative items, on the other hand, may have sections of various yarns for unusual effects (see the doll on page 234). Remember, however, that these yarns do *not* have the strength of tapestry and Persian yarns.

Unfortunately, all needlepointers make mistakes every now and then and must rip. To do so, carefully clip the wrong stitches on the right side of the canvas. Turn the canvas over and, using tweezers, pull out the loose threads. Work in any loose ends with a crochet hook. *Never* re-use yarn. The rough canvas wears each strand thin, and re-use just wears it thinner—past the point of beauty. For this reason, you should never stitch with a strand any longer than 18″. If you use weaker, novelty yarns, your strand should be even shorter.

If you inadvertently cut your canvas, simply place another piece of canvas under the hole. Match the holes exactly and baste the new piece in place; then, do needlepoint through both thicknesses.

Personalize your work by placing your initials and the date in a corner. If they do not work into the design, use the *Continental stitch* (Illus. 4) to form your initials in one corner of the canvas.

Spray your finished pieces with a water-proofing product to protect them from dirt. When they need a thorough cleaning, send them to a reputable dry cleaner. Tell him that the fibre content is wool and he will treat your pieces properly.

Express yourself in needlepoint the way an artist expresses himself in painting, with colors and textures to complement your design. Needlepoint is not difficult, and it should not become a chore. Pick colors and patterns that please you, relax with everything you need nearby, and enjoy your stitching!

Doorstop

You can buy a needlepoint canvas with the design already worked, on which you fill in just the background. These canvases are

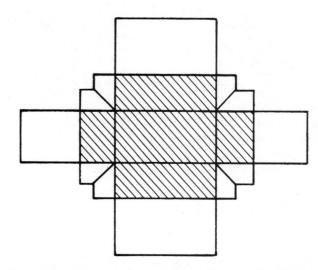

Illus. 3. The shape to stitch for a brick doorstop. The shaded area represents the brick. Stitch an extra ½″ all around the marked area, as the canvas will shrink as you work on it.

designed by skilled craftsmen who are familiar with the suitability of a pattern for needlepoint, and who can determine the most pleasing designs and colors. When you are more skilled with needlepoint, design your own pattern— but while you are practicing the stitches, a canvas that is already stamped or partially stitched is a great learning aid!

Cover a brick with needlepoint canvas to make an attractive doorstop. The canvas for one project was purchased with an owl and mushroom motif already completed and just the background to be filled in with any color and stitch. You may, of course, design your own doorstop (see page 222). But whether you are stitching a bought or hand-drawn design, it is important that you plan the shape of the area you will stitch before you begin. A covered brick uses only a certain area of a square canvas. Fold the sides of the canvas up around the brick and, with a waterproof marker, draw a line on the canvas where it touches the edges of the brick. Lay the canvas flat again and strengthen those lines, which are the boundaries of your stitching. The shape you stitch should be like that in Illus. 3.

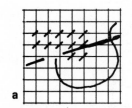 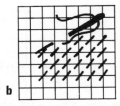 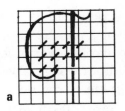 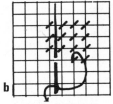

Illus. 4. Continental stitch. Always work it from right to left (a). Turn the canvas upside-down on even rows (b).

Illus. 5. Half Cross stitch. In a, a row is stitched from left to right. In b, the row is stitched from right to left.

After you have planned the background, you can fill it. The following are some background stitches most commonly used:

Continental stitch: Also called the *Tent stitch,* this is the most common of background possibilities. Bring the needle, threaded with an 18″-piece of yarn, from the wrong side to the right side through one hole about 2″ from the edge of the canvas, and pull the yarn until about 1″ remains on the wrong side. As you stitch, work over this end to hold it in place. This is the way to start all new threads in needlepoint.

Insert the needle to the wrong side through the hole above and to the right of the first one, then to the right side through the hole to the left of the first one. Pull the yarn evenly but not tightly. Work an entire row; then turn the canvas so you work in the same direction for the second row. To end a thread, run it through several stitches on the wrong side of the piece. There should be no knots in needlepoint. The *Continental stitch* uses a lot of yarn for a small area, because it covers both the front and back of the canvas. A piece done with this stitch can therefore take much wear.

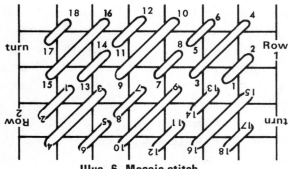

Illus. 6. Mosaic stitch.

Half Cross stitch: This stitch looks like the *Continental* on the right side, but it is made differently and does not cover the back of the canvas well. Use it on articles that receive little wear—pictures or wall hangings, for example.

Begin stitching in a hole at the upper left corner of the canvas. Insert the needle to the wrong side of the canvas in the hole diagonally above and to the right of the first one and come to the right side again directly under the second hole; continue across the row this way. When you work a row from right to left, the needle points up rather than down (see Illus. 5).

Creative craftsmen like to personalize a piece that they buy with the design already worked. Most all of the designs you buy are worked in the *Continental stitch* and *Petit Point,* its smaller version. To make this doorstop a bit extraordinary, stitch the background of the owl and mushroom design in the *Mosaic stitch.* This is a set of three diagonal stitches: short, long, and short, each set covering a 2 × 2 mesh box (that is, 2 vertical and 2 horizontal mesh). Follow Illus. 6 for this stitch. Work from the right to the left for continuous motion. Where the *Mosaic stitch* meets the design, just do as much of each set of three stitches as there is room for.

Blocking

The shape of your canvas will inevitably be slightly distorted once you have filled in the background, but you can restore the piece to its original shape by blocking it. Even if the

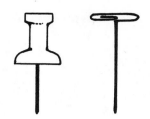

Illus. 7. Secure your needle-point on a blocking board with push pins, left, or T pins, right.

piece is not out of shape, however, you must block it in order to re-set the starch. Find a piece of scrap wood or insulation board a little larger than your needlepoint. (Insulation board is better because it allows a free circulation of air, so your needlepoint can dry quickly.) You also need a piece of paper the same size as the board to protect the canvas from stains and either a staple gun or a large supply of push pins or T pins for a border of blank canvas (see Illus. 7) or tacks for a finished edge.

Draw a 1"-grid—that is, criss-crossed, horizontal and vertical lines one inch apart—on the paper with a *waterproof* pen or marker and tape the paper to the board. (Do not trust the manufacturer when he says his marker is waterproof. Test it yourself.) Wet the needlepoint with a sponge dampened with cold water. (Hot water shrinks wool.) You should block needlepoint that is not textured face *down*, and needlepoint which is textured face

up. Place the doorstop right side down on the board. Tugging gently, staple or tack one side of the margin *in a straight line*. Make sure that the corner is 90° and staple or tack the next side. Gently but firmly pull the other two sides into place, stapling as you proceed. The staples or tacks should be about $\frac{1}{2}''$ to $\frac{3}{4}''$ apart. Allow the needlepoint to dry thoroughly for two or three days. If the piece is still drastically out of shape after blocking, apply rabbit skin glue, which you can buy in art supply shops, to the back.

Assembling

Find a solid brick with no chips or weak points which may crack. Pad the brick by wrapping a piece of foam rubber sheeting around it and glueing it in place. Place the canvas face down on a table with the brick centered on top of it. Cut away the excess canvas in each corner, but not too closely to the stitching, since canvas ravels.

Fold sides A and B around the brick and whip them (with an over-and-over stitch) together with yarn. Turn up sides C and D, and stitch along the corners. Then whip the edges of sides C and D to each other. To cover the whipped stitches, glue a piece of felt to the bottom of the brick.

Illus. 8. A close-up view of the butterfly (page 222). The background here is the Hungarian stitch.

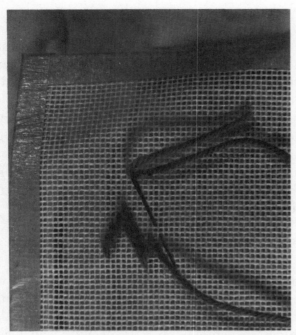

Illus. 9. Always use a short strand of yarn—about 18″ long—since the roughness of the canvas wears a longer one thin.

Butterfly Picture

If you have searched the needlepoint shops for a challenging design but none seems quite right, you are probably ready to design your own pattern. Ideas for a design are endless: Children's coloring books are a good source for bold, simple shapes which you can fill in with fancy stitches. There are books on needlepoint at your library, and many of these have patterns that you can trace. A geometric pattern stitched in bold colors makes a striking accent, particularly in a contemporary home.

Sketch the subject on paper in the size you want the needlepoint piece to be. When you are satisfied with the lines of your drawing, go over them with a black soft-tip pen. Place the proper canvas (see page 218) over the design. The canvas should be the size of the area to be stitched plus 2″ or 3″. Trace the design on the canvas with a *waterproof* soft-tip pen. If you plan to use white or light yarn, do not use black ink, as it shows through the yarn. Write the colors of each section on the original sketch and keep it nearby for reference.

Before you start stitching, bind the edges of the canvas with masking tape to prevent ravelling (see Illus. 9). Keep the selvages—the closely woven sides of the canvas—on the sides of the needlepoint, not on the top and bottom.

The butterfly in Illus. 8 is a freehand design. Most of the stitches are vertical, so Mono 14 canvas was chosen (that is, canvas woven with one strand, 14 mesh per inch). White is a better choice than ecru (beige), because the bright yellow could be dulled by the darker color.

The black body of the butterfly is filled in with the *Brick stitch*, a simple vertical stitch over two mesh (see Illus. 10). Work in horizontal rows and skip every other mesh. When you stitch the second row, each stitch goes in the vertical row of mesh you skipped in the first row. Begin each stitch in the second row just one mesh below the line of mesh where the first row begins.

The black lines separating the colors on the wings are done in the *Continental stitch*. The *Parisian stitch* forms the larger sections of the wings (see Illus. 11), and the rest of the wings are completed with vertical *Filling stitches*. Simply cover the canvas with one long vertical stitch to fill in the area between the black *Continental stitches*.

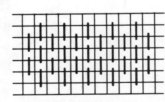

Illus. 10. Brick stitch.

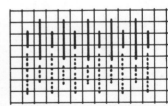

Illus. 11. Parisian stitch.

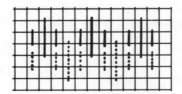

Illus. 12. Hungarian stitch.

For a natural subject like a butterfly, a green background is a logical choice. The *Hungarian stitch*, a vertical stitch which looks like a diamond pattern, was used. It is based on three vertical stitches: work one stitch over two mesh, one over four, one over two, and skip a space. In the second row, place a short stitch under a short stitch, a long one in the space, and skip a space under the long stitch. The vertical columns are thus either all long or all short stitches.

Framing

When you have finished the stitching on your original design, block the piece as instructed on page 220. What you do with the needlepoint is as much up to you as the stitches and colors you use, but you might want to frame the piece by surrounding it with soft cork. Buy a piece of Masonite (pressed board) or plywood the size you want both needlepoint and frame to be. Use white glue to attach the blocked needlepoint to the Masonite. Cut out the middle of a piece of heavy, dark brown cork, or cut four separate strips to surround the stitchery. The cork must be even with both the edges of the Masonite and the edges of the stitching so no blank canvas shows.

Eyeglass Case

Needlepoint items are not limited to home decorations. Anyone will enjoy showing off a handmade needlepoint eyeglass case with his initials on it. Even if he does not wear prescription lenses, he still needs a case for sunglasses!

With all the new shapes in lenses and frames, standard measurements no longer apply. Measure the particular glasses that the case is to fit to determine the area of canvas you need. For the case on page N, Penelope 10 canvas was chosen. Allow five mesh ($\frac{1}{2}$" of canvas) on all sides for a hem, and one mesh at the fold line. There are two ways of constructing the eyeglass case, shown in Illus. 13. The

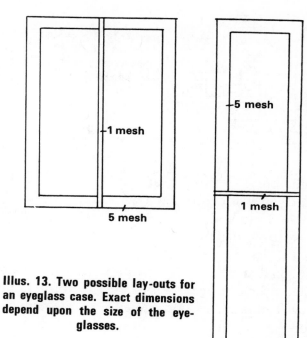

Illus. 13. Two possible lay-outs for an eyeglass case. Exact dimensions depend upon the size of the eyeglasses.

width of scraps you have determines which layout you should use.

The first stitches you make should be the initials. Decide where they are to be and work them in the *Continental stitch*.

Fold the five-mesh hem to the wrong side. Line up the holes and baste the hem in place with heavy carpet thread. When you stitch over this hem, work as if it were one thickness. The edge will be one mesh of canvas, and you cover it with the *Binding stitch* (see Illus. 16).

Work the border next in the *Two-Color Herringbone stitch*. Stitch from the left to the

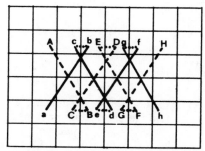

Illus. 14. Two-Color Herringbone stitch requires two trips across the canvas.

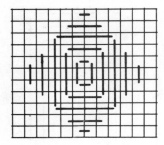

Illus. 15. The Jo-Jo stitch creates a textured background as the stitches change direction.

right only. Beginning in the upper left mesh that you want to cover, take a diagonal stitch down 3 mesh and to the right 2 mesh (that is, 3 × 2). Bring the needle out again one mesh to the left in the same row. Take a 3 × 2 diagonal stitch up and to the right, and bring the needle out one mesh to the left in the same row. Continue around the edge of the canvas. For the second color, begin three mesh directly below the start of the first stitch. Take a 3 × 2 stitch up and to the right. Continue as for first color.

The background is worked in the *Jo-Jo stitch* (Illus. 15), which creates a diamond effect but is made with horizontal and vertical stitches. Start at one side of the case and when you meet an initial, do only as much of the stitch as you have room to stitch. Continue on the other side of the initial as if you had used the *Jo-Jo stitch* straight across. Continue with

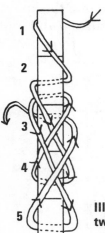

Illus. 16. Use the binding stitch to sew two pieces together or to neatly finish off an edge.

the *Jo-Jo stitch* on the back of the case, or use another stitch in this article.

When there is no margin of blank canvas on the edge of the stitching, as is the case here, use copper tacks instead of staples to hold the needlepoint while you block it. Staples cut the wool, but tacks do not leave marks.

To protect the lenses of the eyeglasses, line the canvas with a soft fabric. Instead of sewing it to the canvas, use one of the new products that allows you to bond the fabric to the canvas by ironing (Stitch Witchery by Dritz, for example). Follow the directions that accompany the product.

To put the eyeglass case together, use the *Binding stitch*. Begin stitching along the fold and move to the right, following Illus. 16 as you read these instructions. Secure the thread by taking one stitch in each of the first two holes from the back to the front. Skip one hole and go into the fourth hole from the back to the front. Go into the second hole from the back; then go into the fifth hole from the back. From the fifth, go into the third, then sixth, fourth, etc. Notice that you are skipping one space when you travel backward, and going into the next empty space when travelling forward. Always bring the wool over the edge and always go into the back of the canvas. The stitch looks like a neat braid along all the sides of the eyeglass case.

When you are finished assembling the case, spray it with a waterproofing product to protect it from dirt, dust, and stains. In spite of the precautions you take to keep the piece clean, it will someday need a thorough cleaning. Send it to a professional dry cleaner.

Bargello

The *Bargello stitch*—a vertical stitch (that is, made up and down on the canvas, rather than diagonally or horizontally)—has several variations and is very suitable for stitching a pillow. In its original meaning, *Bargello* is the *Flame stitch*—that is, a vertical stitch made over the same number of mesh in steps to resemble a flame. Through the centuries, *Bargello* has come to mean any vertical stitch over a reasonable number of mesh, in any step.

For the best coverage of the canvas, do *Bargello* and the other vertical stitches on Mono 14. On projects which will not receive too much wear, use Mono 12 or even Mono 10 with a double strand of yarn. The larger canvas does make the stitching go much faster, but remember that the project cannot stand as much wear as a project made on Mono 14.

Since *Bargello* does not use complicated stitches, it is color and pattern, rather than texture, that give *Bargello* its majesty. There are two kinds of patterns: *Line patterns* are most effective in monochromatic color schemes—that is, several shades of one color ranging from dark to light (see Illus. 17). *Framework patterns* look most attractive in complementary or monochromatic colors that can be reversed in each adjacent frame (see Illus. 19).

Line Pattern Pillow

Needlepoint adapts itself to many projects, but none is so popular as the pillow. The close-up in Illus. 17 is part of a pillow a ten-year-old girl designed, based on her initial M, in a line pattern. Once the pattern line is established across the canvas, you just repeat it above and below the original line in different shades.

Illus. 17. The M line pattern is one variation of the basic Bargello zig-zag line pattern.

Cut your canvas so it has at least a 2″-margin all the way round the design. Bind the edges with masking tape to prevent the canvas from ravelling.

Always start stitching in the middle of the canvas so the design is even on both sides. Fold the canvas in half, and then in half again. Where the two fold lines meet is the middle of the canvas.

Each stitch in the pattern of the pillow is over four mesh, with a two-mesh step. (From

Illus. 18. To vary a line pattern, sew more stitches on the upswing than on the downswing, or vice versa.

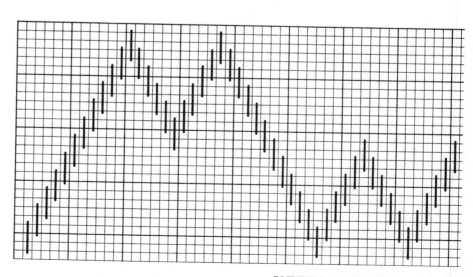

now on, this description of a pattern will be referred to as a 4:2 line pattern.) This type of pattern looks attractive in a monochromatic color scheme—that is, several shades of one color.

To stitch, thread the needle as described on page 218. Insert the needle from the wrong side to the right side of the canvas, and pull it until only a 1″ tail is left on the wrong side. Cover this tail with your stitches as you proceed.

Stitch across the canvas in the line pattern you have chosen. Change colors as your pattern requires. You will find that the *Bargello stitch* goes quickly, particularly with a line pattern, and your canvas will be covered in no time at all.

When you have finished the piece, you will be pleased to see that the *Bargello stitch* does not pull your canvas out of shape the way many other stitches do. Still, the piece needs to be blocked to re-set the starch on the canvas. See page 220 for blocking instructions.

To finish your pillow, choose a fabric for the reverse side that complements the needlepoint design. Corduroy, velvet, velveteen and cotton suede make excellent backings. Pre-shrink the fabric by machine washing and drying it, or by dry cleaning. Cut the fabric to the same size as the needlepoint canvas.

Make cording from scraps of fabric and sew it to the right side of the needlepoint piece by machine. Put the right sides of the needlepoint and fabric together and stitch them by machine on three sides and around the four corners. (See Illus. 3 on page 68). Be sure to place your machine stitching two rows inside the worked canvas, for durability and strength.

Turn the pillow right side out, making sure to completely turn the corners. Stuff with a purchased pillow form or an inner pillow of 100% polyester stuffing. For a plump pillow, the inner pillow should be $\frac{1}{4}$″ larger on all sides than the needlepoint cover. Insert the inner pillow into the completed pillow cover and stitch the fourth side closed by hand.

You may add tassels on the corners as you stitch the pillow together by machine.

Framework Pattern Pillow

A different type of repeat design you can stitch is a framework pattern. This design (see Illus. 19) can be described as a 4:2 framework pattern. It is easiest to stitch the outline of the framework and then fill in each motif. By making one pillow in a line pattern and one in a framework pattern, you can make more than one pillow for the same room without duplicating the pattern.

Follow the pattern in Illus. 19, or design your own on graph paper. Stitch the outline of the motif first, and then fill in the pattern with different color yarns until you reach the middle.

NOTE: When you reach the end of the area of canvas to be stitched, stop. Do not go on with the full length of the stitch.

Block the stitched canvas as instructed on page 220, and then assemble it the same way you did for the Line Pattern Pillow. If you made these pillows in similar colors, they will look dazzling decorating a sofa or chair.

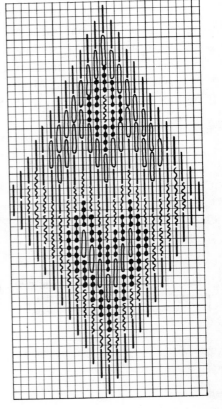

Illus. 19. The easiest way to make a framework pattern is first to make a line pattern. Then, turn your canvas upside-down and repeat the pattern below the first line.

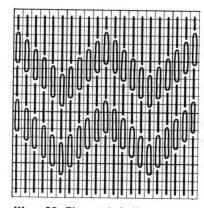

Illus. 20. Zig-zag belt line pattern.

Line Pattern Belt in Two Colors

Bargello does not have to be a pillow, of course. You can make an unusual accessory that anyone in your family can wear—even you!

With the revival of the belt, needlepoint adds interest to the newly discovered waist- and hip-line. The belt pattern in Illus. 20 is an attractive yet simple 4:1 line pattern in two shades of blue. The red background of the belt is made with *Filling stitches*—just long stitches that fill in as much canvas as necessary. Of course, this is not a very durable stitch, since each thread may travel over several mesh. Still, it covers quickly and looks dramatic.

You can make this belt as wide or as narrow as you want—but remember that to go through belt loops on a pair of pants, it cannot be too wide.

First plan your design on graph paper. Then cut the canvas the proper number of mesh wide, plus 1″ on each side. Stitch the design you have chosen.

To finish the belt, turn the margin of canvas under so no blank canvas shows. Stitch the blank canvas to the back by hand. Attach a lining to the back of the belt—perhaps gros-grain ribbon, or any lining fabric. Fasten a purchased belt buckle to the front—and your belt is ready to ornament any outfit. Line pattern belts are shown in color on page N.

Triangular Framework Pattern Belt

A framework pattern can also make an attractive belt, like the one in Illus. O2. The framework pattern for this belt is 2:2 for the triangular outlines, and 2:0 for the solid lines. *Filling stitches* complete the triangles and add more color to the belt.

This belt was finished in a different way, which you can use to finish the other belts as well. When you cut the canvas for this belt, leave a six-mesh margin on each side. Turn four mesh under as a hem on each side. Baste this hem in place with carpet thread. Treat this area as one thickness and stitch right up to two mesh from the edge with the pattern you have chosen.

Cover the two-mesh edge with the *Binding stitch* (see Illus. 16). Stitch along the fold, holding the belt with the right side toward you. Always stitch to the right and always bring your needle from the wrong side of the canvas to the right. Take two stitches in each of the first two holes to secure the yarn. Now follow the directions on page 224.

To block this piece of needlepoint that has no margin of blank canvas, use rust-proof copper tacks or T pins, not staples, which cut the wool and leave marks. Line the belt and attach a purchased buckle as described before.

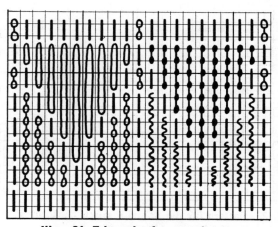

Illus. 21. Triangular framework pattern.

Illus. 22. Detail of the bolero shown in color on the front cover. The Bargello stitch makes this wavy pattern.

Bolero

The bolero on the front cover was also done in the versatile *Bargello stitch*.

Choose a prepared pattern for a vest. Press the tissue paper pattern pieces with a cool iron and lay them flat on a table. Tape the side seams of the front and back together. Trace the pattern on Mono 14 canvas, turning the pattern at the center of the back to draw the other half of the bolero. Draw in the stitching lines (dotted lines) and the darts with a *waterproof* marker.

Work the *Bargello stitch* according to the sketch in Illus. 23. Start in the center of the back and work to the front to balance the pattern. To work the center of a large canvas, roll the excess. Stitch into two mesh on the canvas you allowed for the seam allowance at the shoulders, and into two mesh on the center of the darts. Block the canvas before you assemble it.

With your sewing machine, make zig-zag stitching around all the edges where the stitching ends to prevent ravelling. Cut off any excess canvas, leaving a $\frac{1}{4}''$-seam. Sew the darts and shoulder seams on the sewing machine. Cut the lining from a light-weight lining fabric, according to the same pattern. Sew the darts, shoulder and side seams of the lining on the sewing machine.

With the wrong sides together, baste the lining and the needlepoint around the outside edges. Bind these edges by stitching a braided edging to the needlepoint on the sewing machine. Finish the bolero by attaching a button-and-chain closing.

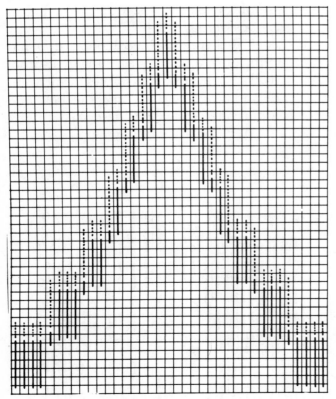

Illus. 23. Pattern for the Bargello stitch background of the bolero.

Cross Stitchery

When you place the basic horizontal, vertical, or diagonal needlepoint stitches one on top of another, they become *Cross stitches*.

Although *Cross stitches* work up better on Penelope canvas, it is possible to do them on Mono 14. To do so, you must cross each stitch as you go (see Illus. 25).

Tote Bag

Show off your handiwork in the form of a needlepoint purse or tote bag. The one in Illus. N1 is worked on plastic sheets that resemble Mono canvas and which are available at yarn shops. You need three sheets: one for the front, one for the back, and one for the gussets and the bottom. Cut the third sheet in thirds lengthwise. Plastic sheets are ideal for a tote bag because they have more body than canvas, and, thus, the bag maintains its shape. Also, stitches never distort plastic sheets, as they do canvas. Blocking, then, is not necessary.

It is color, rather than stitches, that gives this purse its stunning design. Using colored pencils or markers, chart any design you wish on graph paper. Be sure the graph paper has the same number of squares per inch as your plastic sheet, which has 10. Otherwise the size of your design will be wrong.

Work your design by placing a *Cross stitch* for every square on the graph paper. Begin your first row in the upper left-hand corner of the plastic sheet. Start the first stitch just below the second mesh at the top of the sheet. Bring the needle from the wrong side to the right side through the first hole on the left side of the plastic sheet. Pull the yarn through until 1″ remains on the wrong side. As you stitch, work over this end to hold it in place. Next, insert the needle to the wrong side from the right side of the plastic sheet in the hole diagonally above and to the right of the first one. Come through to the right side in one continuous motion directly under the second hole (Illus. 5). This is the *Half Cross stitch*.

Illus. 24. **Complete the Cross stitch.**

Illus. 25. **Cross stitch; cross as you go.**

To complete the rest of the *Cross stitch*, simply reverse the direction of your needle, and work directly over the stitches that you have already worked. This produces a stitch that looks like Illus. 24.

NOTE: You may cross each *Half Cross stitch* as you go if you like (Illus. 25). When you run out of yarn and need to end it, simply run the end under the back of stitches that you have already worked. To begin the next thread, run it under stitches that you have already worked.

Stitch the back and gussets of your purse in the same design. Then use this stitch or another stitch from this article to put your initials on the other side (see Illus. 26).

Assemble the purse by stitching the seams with the *Binding stitch*. Hold the pieces so that the same side is towards you throughout the stitching of that seam. Call it the front, and the other side the back. Also work the *Binding stitch* over the top edges to give your purse a finished look.

Attach two sets of chain handles—one end in each corner. Line the purse with sturdy fabric.

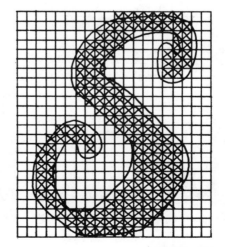

Illus. 26. **Sketch your initials on graph paper and then "X" in the squares.**

Suspender Trim

Illus. 27 shows a charming trim for suspenders. First, work out the design completely on graph paper with colored pencils. Transfer the design to canvas by working with the *Cross stitch* (see Illus. 24) on Penelope 10 canvas in tapestry or Persian yarn.

When cutting the canvas for your suspender trim, allow a hem of five mesh all the way round. Finish the edge with the *Binding stitch.* Block this piece face down as described on page 221.

Attach the suspender trim to leather, fabric, or needlepoint suspenders. Remove the needlepoint for cleaning when necessary.

Sewing Box

Decorate a wooden box in which to keep your sewing supplies. Cover the top with needlepoint and make it a pin cushion. The first step is to decide what sort of a design you want on the top of your box. One idea is to show a sewing box with scissors, tape measure, needle, and thread on the top. The tape measure is particularly useful, if you make it in full-sized inches. No longer will you have to search far

and wide for a tape measure just to measure a few inches.

Sketch each item that you wish to include on paper. Cut them out. (Hint: *trace* around the scissors.) Place the cut-out pieces on another sheet of paper which is exactly the same size as the top of your box. Move them until you are pleased with the composition. When your design is completely finished, re-trace the lines with a black soft-tip marker.

Penelope 8 is a very useful canvas for doing the *Cross stitch.* On the more widely used Penelope 10 canvas, you must split a strand of tapestry yarn to do the *Cross stitch.* Since Penelope 8 is larger, however, you may use a full strand of tapestry yarn to do the *Cross stitch.* Also, since Penelope 8 is larger, your work goes faster. In addition, Penelope 8 is available with a blue thread which counts off every 5 mesh. This is very handy when you have to count mesh for the *Cross stitch.* However, if you are using light-colored yarn, the blue line may show through. It is for this reason that this canvas is *not* recommended for use with light colors.

Whether you choose ecru or white canvas

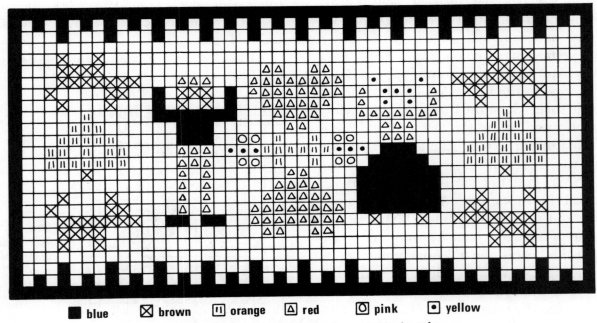

■ blue   ⊠ brown   Ⅲ orange   △ red   Ⓞ pink   • yellow

Illus. 27. Pattern of the design for a suspender trim.

depends on the colors you intend to use on your needlepoint piece. If you are planning to use white or pastel colors, choose the white canvas; however, if your colors are darker, ecru canvas suits your needs perfectly. Cut your canvas 1″ larger on all sides than the top of your box. Bind the edges with masking tape to prevent ravelling.

To transfer your design onto the canvas, place the canvas on top of your drawing. The black lines show through. Trace the design with a grey *waterproof* marker. Grey is best because it does not show through pastel colors and white as black does.

Work the design in *Cross stitch* (Illus. 24). To emphasize your design items (scissors, tape measure, needle and thread), use the *Outline stitch* (Illus. 28). Then, work the background to within ½″ of the edge on all sides. Always personalize your piece by putting your initials and the date in one corner, using the *Cross stitch*. Block your piece.

To attach the needlepoint to the top of the box, fold under the raw edge of the canvas and tack it to the edge of the box along one side with *small* nails or a staple gun. Tack down two more sides. There should be extra fullness since the needlepoint is larger than the top of the box. Stuff the area between the needlepoint and the top of the box with steel wool, which keeps your pins and needles sharp. Tack the fourth side in place. Crochet a chain of matching or contrasting yarn, or buy an attractive trim to use. Place it, wrong side up, along the edge of the canvas. Glue it in place to cover the nails or staples. Pile in your sewing supplies and admire your practical handiwork.

Illus. 29. Close-up of the tape measure on the sewing box.

Key Case

This key case is just the perfect thing as a gift item. It is also good for yourself for that quick trip to the grocery store, for inside the key case is a place for your driver's licence and your money.

Illus. 30 and 31 show ideas for decorating the front and back of a key case, which is actually two pieces of canvas—even just scraps—which you sew together with the *Binding stitch* (see page 224) on three sides. Cut two pieces of canvas 4″ × 5″. This includes five mesh on all sides for hems. Turn them under as you have before—four mesh for the hem and one for the edge. Cut the canvas if necessary. Put

Illus. 28. Use the Outline stitch to emphasize your design.

Illus. 30. Pattern for the winter side of the key case. Stitches that resemble snowflakes are: Diamond Eyelet stitch, Double Cross stitch, Double Leviathan stitch, Triple Leviathan stitch, and Upright Cross stitch.

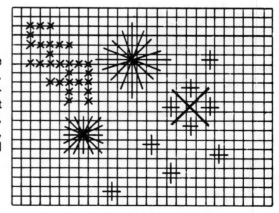

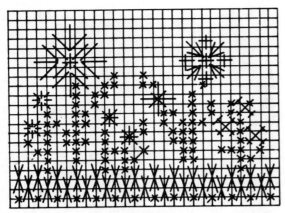

Illus. 31. Pattern for the summer side of the key case. Stitches are:

    Grass: Alternating Oblong Cross stitch
    Leaves and background: Cross stitch
    Flowers: Double Straight Cross stitch, Medallion stitch, Rice stitch, Smyrna Cross stitch, Star stitch

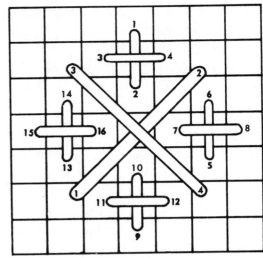

Illus. 35. Double Cross stitch.

your initials on one side and add snowflakes—placed at random—for winter. To stitch your intials, first sketch them on a piece of graph paper and then "X" in the appropriate squares as shown in Illus. 26. The following stitches suggest snowflakes:

Diamond Eyelet (see Illus. 32). This stitch covers a diamond-shaped area on 8 × 8 mesh—that is, it covers an area of 8 × 8 mesh (hereafter every cross stitch will be referred to as 2×2, 3×4, 4×4, and so on)—and is made up of 16 completely separate stitches, each of

which go *into* the center. It is easier to make the four longest stitches that form the upright cross first. Each of these stitches is over four mesh.

Double Cross (see Illus. 35), for which you use a double strand of tapestry yarn to work a 4 × 4 *Cross stitch* on both sides. At the top and bottom, add an *Upright Cross*.

Double Leviathan (see Illus. 33), made up of eight stitches which cover a 4 × 4 square. Do the X first and do the *Upright Cross* last.

Triple Leviathan (see Illus. 34), which covers a square 6 × 6 mesh. The *Upright Crosses* are 2 × 2 and they touch.

Upright Cross, made from two perpendicular

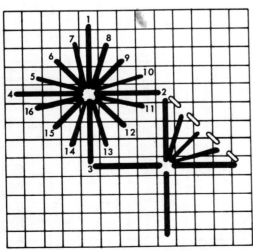

Illus. 32. Diamond Eyelet stitch.

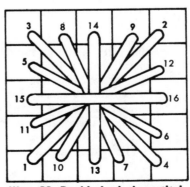

Illus. 33. Double Leviathan stitch.

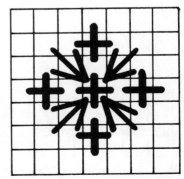

Illus. 34. Triple Leviathan stitch.

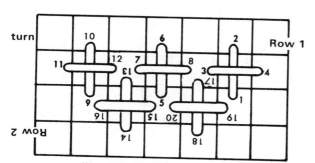

Illus. 36. Upright Cross stitch.

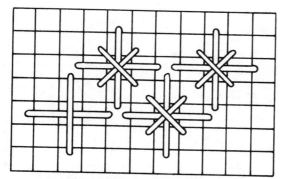

Illus. 37. Double Straight Cross stitch.

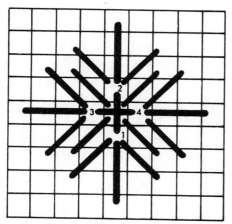

Illus. 38. Medallion stitch.

stitches, each two mesh high and two mesh wide (see Illus. 36).

Flowers are suggested by the following stitches:

Double Straight Cross stitch (see Illus. 37), which is composed of a 2 × 2 diagonal cross superimposed on a 4 × 4 *Upright Cross*.

Medallion stitch, best done by following Illus. 38. Hint: make the small *Upright Cross* in the center last. This stitch covers a square 8 × 8 mesh.

Rice stitch (see Illus. 39), a 2 × 2 *Cross* with each of its arms tied down by a 1 × 1 *Half Cross* which slants in the opposite direction from the arm which it ties down.

Smyrna Cross (see Illus. 40), which adds a great deal of texture. A hint in making the *Smyrna Cross* is to work the X (numbered 1 to 4 in Illus. 40) first.

Star stitch (see Illus. 41), which covers a 4 × 4 square made up of eight stitches, all going *into* the center of the star. It is easier to work if you do the four stitches that form the *Upright Cross* first.

Work the grass in the *Alternating Oblong Cross* (see Illus. 42). Work the leaves and the background in the *Cross stitch*.

Block each of the pieces. When dry, sew three sides together with the *Binding stitch*. Go across the tops of both fourth sides separately with the *Binding stitch* to give a finished look. When going round the corners, treat each corner as

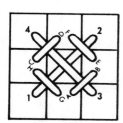

Illus. 39. Rice stitch.

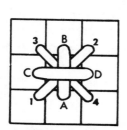

Illus. 40. Smyrna Cross stitch.

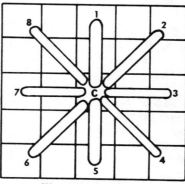

Illus. 41. Star stitch.

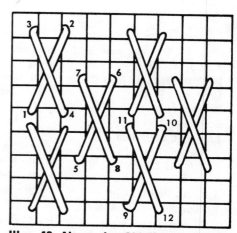

Illus. 42. Alternating Oblong Cross stitch.

NEEDLEPOINT ■ **233**

if it were two holes. Attach the key ring to one corner with the *Binding stitch*.

If you wish to line your key case, use a long-wearing fabric of a matching or contrasting color. Make it ¼" smaller on all sides than the needlepoint. Stitch three sides together. Insert it into the key chain with the wrong sides together. Turn under the raw edge at the top and hand stitch in place. Hand sew velcro—a material which sticks to itself and is, therefore, often used in closings—across the top for a closing. Put the velcro as close to one corner as you can get it. Leave room for your finger to get in at the other corner, otherwise you will not be able to open the case very easily.

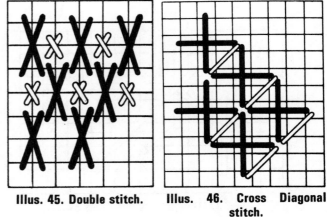

Row 2

Row 1

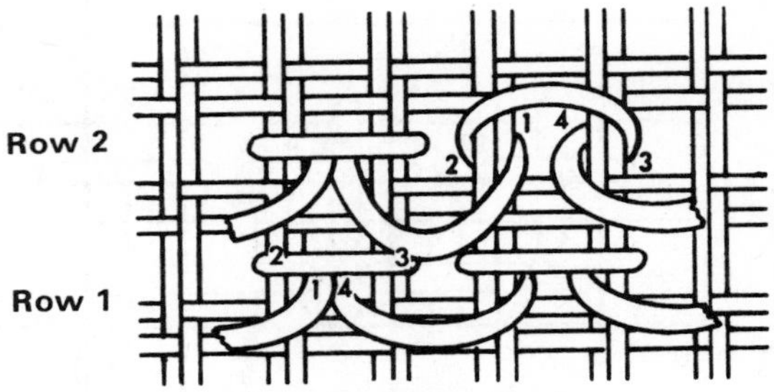

Illus. 44. Turkey Work.

Illus. 45. Double stitch.

Illus. 46. Cross Diagonal stitch.

Doll Pillow

A needlepoint doll, like the one in Illus. O1, will be a family heirloom for many generations to come. The crazy-quilt skirt gives you a chance to make many different stitches.

Transfer your design onto Penelope 8 canvas as described on page 222. Illus. 43 shows the stitches that were used for this doll.

To achieve the alert expression in the eyes, work them in *Petit Point Cross stitch* (see Illus. 47).

Here, *Turkey Work* is worked three different ways to create three different looks. Work this stitch only from *left* to *right* and from *bottom* to *top*. Start your yarn on the *right* side of the canvas at 1. Come out at 2. Go in again at 3 and out at 4. Place the next stitch in the next hole. Pull the second stitch tightly, and every

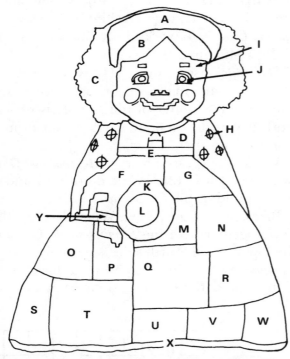

Illus. 43. Stitches used in the doll shown in Illus. O1:

A: Upright Cross	M: Star
B: Alternating Oblong Cross	N: Cross Diagonal
C: Turkey Work	O: Double Straight Cross
D: Fern	P: Crossed Scotch
E: Greek	Q: Brick Cross
F: Triple Leviathan	R: Rice
G: Double Star	S: Outlined Star
H: Wound Cross	T: Patterned Cross
I: Cross	U: Double
J: Petit Point Cross	V: Double Cross
K: Spaced Cross Double Tramé	W: Outlined Cross
	X: Turkey Work
L: Turkey Work	Y: Oblong Cross

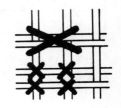

Illus. 47. Petit Point Cross stitch.

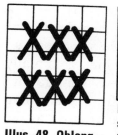

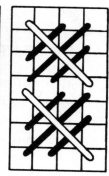

Illus. 48. Oblong Cross stitch.

Illus. 49. Scotch stitch.

Illus. 50 (right). Crossed Scotch stitch.

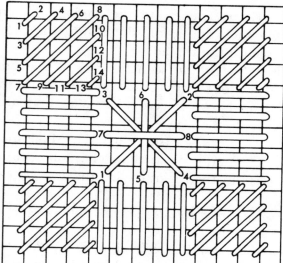

Illus. 51. Patterned Crosses with Scotch stitch.

next row in all one color. Then work another two-color row.

New stitches include:

Double stitch (see Illus. 45), a combination of a 3×1 *Oblong Cross stitch* and a 1×1 *Cross stitch*.

Cross Diagonal stitch (see Illus. 46). Make a series of *Upright Crosses* which are 4×4. Place a diagonal *Outline stitch* between them.

Oblong Cross stitch (see Illus. 48).

Crossed Scotch stitch. This stitch is very similar to the *Scotch stitch* in Illus. 49. Compare Illus. 49 and 50 and note that the two smallest stitches have been omitted and that a diagonal stitch crosses the three center stitches. Use a second color for the cross stitch.

Patterned Crosses with *Scotch stitch.* Work a checkerboard pattern of three components: *Smyrna Cross stitch*, *Scotch stitch* (see Illus. 49), and *Straight Gobelin stitch*. In Row 1, work one *Scotch stitch*, one block of five *Straight Gobelin stitches* (over four mesh), one *Scotch stitch*, one block of vertical *Straight Gobelin stitches*, and so on. Compose Row 2 of one block of horizontal *Straight Gobelin stitches*, one *Smyrna Cross*, one block of horizontal *Straight Gobelin stitches*, one *Smyrna Cross*, and so on. Repeat Rows 1 and 2 until you have covered the area to be worked (see Illus. 51 for the pattern).

Patterned Crosses Variation. This stitch is worked just like Illus. 51 except that you do not use any *Scotch stitches*. Replace them with *Smyrna Crosses*.

Outlined Crosses. Work a 2×2 *Cross stitch* and then place the *Outline stitch* round it. Vary the colors of the *Outline stitch* if you wish.

other one thereafter. Loop the yarn downwards after you pull the stitch tightly. Loop it upwards for the next stitch. Loops may be of variable length, cut or uncut. The doll's hair is worked with long loops that have been left uncut. To create depth of color in the hair, work each stitch with two plies of tapestry yarn in one shade of brown. Twist to those two plies one strand of Mohair yarn in another shade of brown. The center of the flower, also *Turkey Work*, is worked in a short, cut loop. A lace petticoat, created by making *only* three rows of uncut medium-length loops, peeks out of the bottom of the skirt. If you use Persian yarn, the strands separate for a lacier look after being worked.

The *Upright Cross* (headband) is worked in two colors to give a polka-dot look. In the first row, skip every other stitch or dangle two needles threaded with both colors. Work the

Illus. 52. Straight Gobelin stitch.

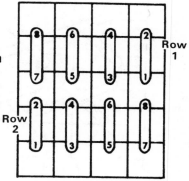

Illus. 53. Wound Cross stitch.

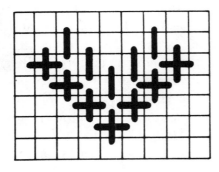

Illus. 54. Brick Cross stitch.

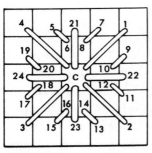

Illus. 55. Double Star stitch.

Illus. 56. Spaced Cross Double Tramé.

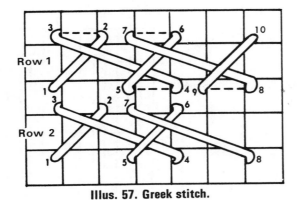

Illus. 57. Greek stitch.

Wound Cross stitch (see Illus. 53). Lay a ground of *Cross stitches.* Then place the *Wound Cross stitch* on top of it. (This is *surface embroidery*.) Make a 4 × 4 *Upright Cross* which is actually four stitches (each over two mesh) that go into the center. Bring the needle from the wrong side of the canvas to the right as close to the center as you can get without actually coming up in the center. Then run the needle under the arms of the *Upright Cross* in a circular pattern. Do *not* penetrate the canvas. To end, simply stick the needle down into the canvas and secure the thread.

Brick Cross stitch (see Illus. 54). Work a diagonal row of *Upright Crosses* and alternate with a diagonal row of vertical stitches that are 2 mesh high.

Double Star stitch (see Illus. 55). Make the X first. Then add the small stitches following the numbers in the diagram. Do the *Upright Cross* last.

Spaced Cross Double Tramé. Follow Illus. 56 to make this stitch.

Greek stitch (Illus. 57). This is another *Cross stitch* with arms of unequal length. Actually, it has one short arm and one long arm. Each *Greek stitch* is intertwined with the next one, and you must work it only from the left to the right, using a double strand of tapestry yarn. The short arm is a 2 × 2 diagonal upwards and to the right. Next, bring the needle up in the same row, two mesh to the left. Make a 4 × 2 diagonal downwards and to the right. Bring up the needle two mesh to the left in the same row. Repeat these moves to the end of the row. To start the second row, come back to the beginning of the first row and start directly below it.

Fern stitch (Illus. 58). This is a stitch which takes its form in vertical rows. You must work it only from top to bottom. Take a 2 × 2 diagonal stitch downwards and to the right. Bring the needle up one mesh to the left in the same row. Take a 2 × 2 diagonal stitch upwards and to the right. Begin the second stitch one mesh below the hole where you began the

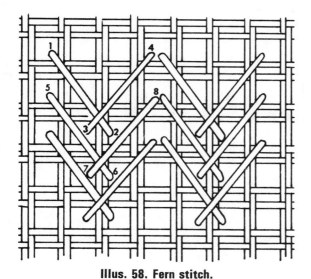

Illus. 58. Fern stitch.

first stitch. To begin a new vertical column, go back up to the top and work down again.

Place your initial on the bodice of the doll's dress; work it in metallic thread for emphasis. Then work two rows of the *Continental stitch* all the way round the doll. Block face up.

To make the pillow, cut a piece of sturdy backing fabric the same size and shape as the doll. Add a $\frac{5}{8}$"-seam allowance when you cut. To sew, place the right sides of the fabric and needlepoint together. Stitch on a machine with the needlepoint towards you. Leave a 5" to 6" opening, through which you turn and stuff the pillow. Trim the excess canvas so that it is even with the fabric seam allowance. Stuff the pillow with 100 per cent polyester fibre.

Illus. 59. You can easily design attractive and useful coasters to resemble playing cards. Use a piece of cork $\frac{1}{4}$" thick as an absorbent backing for the coasters.

WEAVING

Weaving is one of the most natural and enjoyable crafts. People of all ages, both men and women, can create woven fabrics or articles with only a few instructions. If you have ever braided a pigtail, sewn the running stitch, darned a sock or even played checkers, then you already know how easy weaving is, because you have already woven.

Although the terms "weaving" and "clothing" are related in the minds of most people, apparel is not the only thing made by weaving. You can make dolls and handbags, lamp shades and hammocks, pillow covers and muffs by weaving. And you do not always need cumbersome, expensive looms to make them.

You can choose the equipment you need depending on the type of weaving you want to learn—from large floor looms to table looms to ice cream sticks to a small, soft pillow! The following three articles introduce you to three totally different methods of weaving. The first is handweaving on looms, complete with instructions for constructing your own inkle loom. Next is off-loom weaving, if you do not have, or do not want to invest in, a standard loom. Third is finger weaving, also known as Indian braiding, a craft for which you only need some yarn, a dowel, a small pillow, and your fingers!

HANDWEAVING

Handweaving is a gratifying way to increase your understanding of the different yarns which feature so prominently in the textile craft of today. Twines, twists, and textures will become an obsession to such an extent that you will examine even machine-spun fabrics with new eyes, and analyze them for threading, pattern, and color combinations.

More advanced weaving than is discussed here requires larger looms with more shafts and pedals for the wider range of pattern work. Correspondingly, the larger the loom, the greater the financial outlay. True, it is wise, if you are purchasing a loom, to acquire an all-purpose large 4-shaft with 6, 8, or 10 pedals and one that will take a 48″ material, but not every modern home would have the space to house it.

Still, there is much creative work that you can accomplish on smaller, less expensive looms involving *tabby* weave only. (A tabby-woven piece of material should show 50 per cent of warp and 50 per cent weft. The *warp* is the measured lengths of threads that are attached from end to end of any loom. The *weft* is the thread used to fill in—to interlace like darning across the width of the loom.) For this reason, this section is confined to plain weaving and what can be accomplished on handmade inkle looms, 2-shaft table looms and rug-making looms, all of which are easy to thread up and which all offer wide scope for design, color, and texture.

Inkle Looms

The easiest loom of all to make and operate is a small inkle loom, an adaptation of the Scottish inkle loom used originally for braids. You can hold the small model on your knee and operate it while you watch television. A larger model can stand on the floor and be high enough for you to sit at comfortably on a low chair.

The materials required for an inkle loom are:
5-ply wood, 24″ by 12″;
2 pieces of scrap wood for the stand;
6 old camera film spools or pieces of dowelling;
cotton to make *heddles* (sets of cords which make up the harness to guide the warp threads)—Anchor Pearl No. 8 or an equivalent cotton yarn;
5 screws and washers, one wing nut.

Cut the 5-ply to the exact dimensions given on the plan in Illus. 1. Smooth the edges with a wood rasp to prevent threads from catching on any rough edges. Cut a slot for peg D, as this peg must be adjustable to tighten the warp ready for weaving. For a standing floor model, make the slot at peg D run vertically, to accommodate a longer length of weaving. Screw the camera spools to the inkle loom at positions A, B, C, E, and X, as shown in the diagram. Attach peg D with washer and wing nut. Nail or screw the loom to a stand. The height recommended for the floor model is 2′ 6″ from peg B to the floor.

Condensed from the book, "Spin, Dye and Weave Your Own Wool" by Molly Duncan | © 1973 by Sterling Publishing Co., Inc., New York published in New Zealand by A. H. & A. W. Reed Ltd.

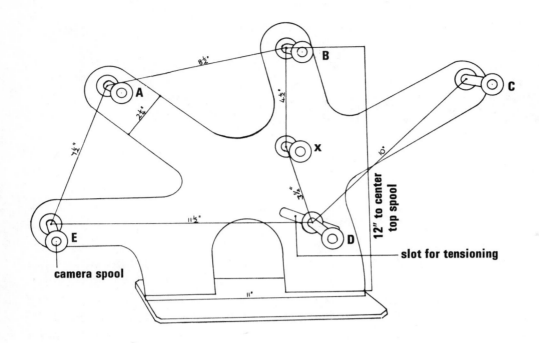

Illus. 1. Pattern for a home-made inkle loom. You may increase the height of the loom by extending the length of the legs and by changing the tension slot at D so that it runs vertically.

slot for tensioning

12" to center top spool

camera spool

How to Make the String Heddles

Cut four dozen pieces of cotton 10–12″ long. To find the correct size to knot these heddles, stretch a string very taut between pegs A and C. Loop a heddle string over this and knot it below peg X. The function of peg X is to hold these heddles. Knot with a square knot (right over left and under, left over right and under) the four dozen pieces of cotton exactly the same size, loop them over the taut string between A and C, and slip them onto peg X.

How to Mount the Warp

Begin the winding of the warp at peg A. As the warp threads show up more than the weft, place color in the warp. Always tie any new thread, before you begin a new round, at peg A onto the previous thread, so that no unsightly knots spoil your weaving. The warp colors need to be balanced evenly—the center strip should have the same number of color changes on either side of it. Temporarily fix the beginning of the warp thread on spool A with cellophane tape. Take your thread across the loom from left to right, passing between the pegs B and X, then around C, D, and E and back to A. This forms a continuous circle.

On the second round, take the thread through the first of the cotton heddles, up and over the top of peg B and then around the rest of the pegs, C, D, E, and back to A.

Take the third thread straight across (not through a heddle) between pegs B and X, as in the first round.

The fourth round goes through the next cotton heddle and over peg B like the second.

Carry on thus until the warp is completed—that is, until you have the number of threads you calculate for the width. Note that all the warp threads that pass through a heddle must go over the top of peg B, and the alternate threads that go straight across must pass under peg B.

How to Weave in the Weft

First, wind the weft threads around a ruler or any flat, thin stick. It is advisable to make the weft color the same as the outer edge of the warp, the reason being that it is easier to make a neat edge with the same color.

Weaving in the weft consists of lifting and lowering the warp threads to form a *shed* or division through which you pass the weft. On

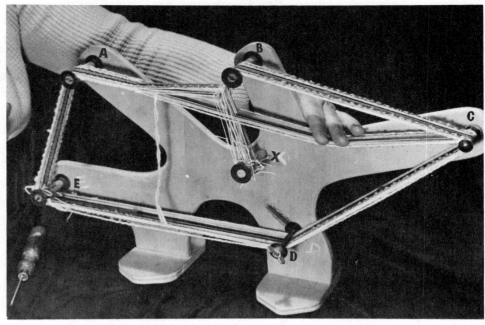

Illus. 2. Press the lower threads down with your hand to form a shed.

the lower threads between pegs B and X press *down* with your hand. This makes the first shed. Insert your weft thread across. Place your hand *under* the lower threads and raise them up above the level of the cotton heddle loops to form the second shed. Pass your weft thread back.

Now, beat the weft threads back towards peg A with the ruler or stick on which you wound the weft yarn. Change back to the first shed and continue weaving in the same way.

As the strip grows, you will have to shift the warp round the loom back towards peg A by loosening the bottom peg D and then re-tightening it afterwards.

On an inkle loom, you can make strips from

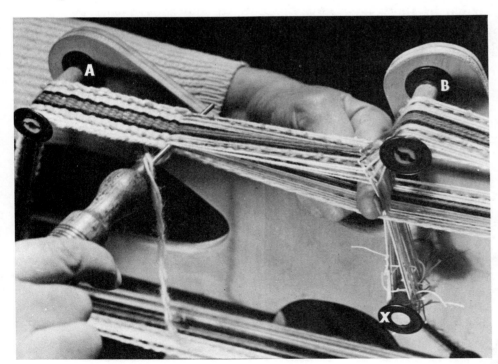

Illus. 3. Beating the weft threads back.

42″ long (on the small model here) up to 6–7′ (on a floor model), depending on how large the frame is and the extension of the outer adjustable pegs. The position of peg X is not altered, since it holds the cotton heddles. If you want wider strips, use wider pegs and not camera spools which can only take up to 2″ in width.

A few suggestions for weaves on these looms are handles for shoulder bags, colored linen or cotton braids to add individuality to a dress, a matching belt and hair band, a wider strip for cuffs on a blouse, a man's tie in either home-spun wool or machine-spun wool, bookmarkers in colored weaves, and edgings of all kinds.

The character of the yarn you use makes the texture and the design—for example, use a thick warp with a thin weft, and this weft scarcely shows at all. Very tight beating of the weft gives a different effect from that obtained when you beat the weft loosely. A wool tie in home-spun yarn needs to be beaten loosely so that when tied in a knot it is not too bulky.

A Shaft Loom and its Parts

The type of 2-shaft loom shown in Illus. 4 is a table model with two heddle frames. The same principles of construction and manipula-tion apply to a 4-shaft and to a pedal loom, but a greater variety of weaves are possible on the 4-shaft. The width of the 2-shaft can range from 8–30″, the smaller width being ideal for weaving experimental samples before mounting a long warp on a large foot loom. You can work out color combinations on a small warp before buying or making the quantity of thread necessary for a large piece of weaving.

In addition to the increased width and length, the more advanced features in the 2-shaft in comparison with the inkle loom involve the heddles being more firmly supported on heddle frames or shafts, which are raised and lowered by means of a *lever*. This changes the shed through which the weft passes much quicker than changing it by hand. Also, a *beater* with its comb-like *reed* is incorporated in the construction to allow for the increased number of threads. *Rollers*, too, are added to carry a longer length of warp.

Raising the Heddle Frames with the Lever on Top

Two *heddle frames* made of strips of wood (a top and a bottom for each frame) are spaced to hold the cotton heddles in position. The top shaft of each frame is attached by means of tapes or cords to the *harness roller* at the top of the loom. The tapes are strong calico, $\frac{1}{2}″–\frac{3}{4}″$ wide. The cords, $\frac{1}{8}″$ wide, can be set in a

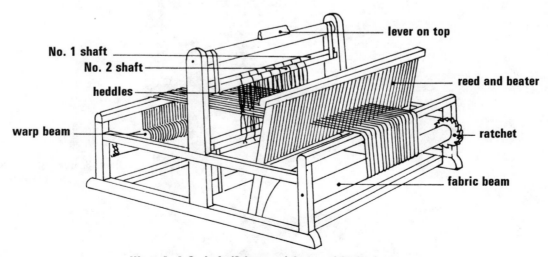

Illus. 4. A 2-shaft (2-harness) loom with the lever on top.

groove to prevent slipping, or tied to screw eyes set in the shafts.

The harness roller holds the lever. To be sure of making a good wide shed, attach the bottom shafts to a harness roller also. These shafts are removable and must be about $\frac{1}{4}''-\frac{1}{2}''$ shorter than the space between the center posts to allow them to be raised or lowered easily. By pulling the lever forwards or backwards, the heddle frames may be raised or lowered as needed.

Both the warp and the fabric beams are locked in place with a *ratchet*.

The beater pivots on two upright side legs from the lower side beams of the loom frame. These legs can be either on the inside or the outside of the frame. Whichever position you choose, make sure that the beater is adjustable so that it can swing from two or more grooves. This allows a wider beating area and saves shifting the warp too frequently.

The top of the beater lifts off so that you may insert reeds of different sizes when you wish. The purpose of the reed is to keep the warp threads evenly spaced. The teeth of the reed are set at certain spacing to the inch. For an all-purpose reed choose a 12-dent (a reed with 12 dents or notches per inch); its width depends on the width of your loom. You can purchase reeds in standard sizes or have them made to order.

Apron bars (once made of cloth and hence the name) can still be made of cloth, but are more often thin, flat pieces of smooth wood tied at an even distance from the warp and fabric beams. They are used for tying on the warp threads in small bundles and to hold an even tension across the width of the warp.

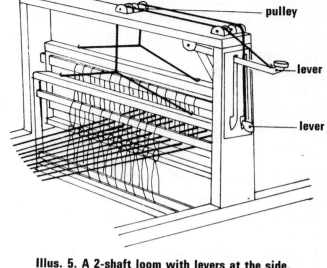

Illus. 5. A 2-shaft loom with levers at the side.

Raising and Lowering the Heddle Frames with Levers at the Side

Notice in Illus. 5 how the cord is attached to the top of the heddle frame and how it runs over a pulley at the middle of the frame to connect with hand levers. The lever locks in position, and when released automatically falls back into its original position. The heddle shafts can swing loosely or slide up and down in grooves cut in the inside edge of the two upright pillars.

How to Tie Your Own Heddles

A heddle is a threading device made of either thin light-weight metal or of string. It is advantageous to know how to make a string heddle in case you need to add more to your shafts at any time. Each heddle string has an eye or loop in its center through which you should be sure to thread the warp ends to the exact

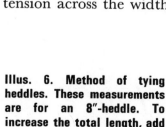

Illus. 6. Method of tying heddles. These measurements are for an 8"-heddle. To increase the total length, add to either end of the heddle.

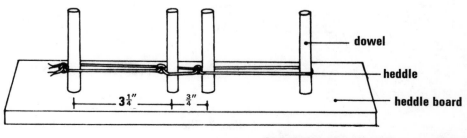

level of the other heddles. The eye opening is usually $\frac{3}{4}''$ wide. To make a heddle board with four dowels or four 6″ nails, the standard spacing is as follows:

For a 6″ heddle	2″	$2\frac{1}{4}''$	$\frac{3}{4}''$	$2\frac{5}{8}''$	2″
For a 8″ ,,	2″	$3\frac{1}{4}''$	$\frac{3}{4}''$	$3\frac{5}{8}''$	2″
For a 9″ ,,	2″	$3\frac{3}{4}''$	$\frac{3}{4}''$	$4\frac{1}{8}''$	2″
For a 10″ ,,	2″	$4\frac{1}{4}''$	$\frac{3}{4}''$	$4\frac{5}{8}''$	2″
For a 12″ ,,	2″	$5\frac{1}{4}''$	$\frac{3}{4}''$	$5\frac{5}{8}''$	2″

Estimating the Amount of Yarn for the Warp

This depends on three factors. First is the number of warp *ends* (individual warp threads) per inch, which is called the *sett*. The sett determines the density of the fabric; 12 ends in a 12-dent reed would mean that you thread one warp end through each dent in 1 inch. Sometimes, you may require finer texture and so you thread two warp ends to every dent, and your number for calculation is then 24.

The second factor is the width of the warp, to which you add approximately 3 per cent to each side for shrinkage and selvage. Thus, to a finished width of, say 28″, add another 2″=30″. Now you can have some idea of how many warp threads to wind on the warping board—30″ × 12″ or, for the finer texture, 30″ × 24″.

The third factor is the length of the warp. Add an extra yard to your desired total length. This extra allows not only for shrinkage and contraction in weaving and finishings, but also for wastage in tying up and in the unwoven end of the warp.

Now, assess the amount of yarn for the warp.

For a woven length of warp of 10 yards (a finished length of 9 yards) and a woven width of 30″ (a finished width of 28″) with 12 ends per inch, the amount of yarn is 30″ × 12 × 10 =3,600 yards. For the finer cloth, it would be 30″ × 24 × 10=7,200 yards. The weft generally takes a little less yardage than the warp. It is a helpful practice to weigh every warp and record it before mounting it on the loom.

Winding a Short Warp

Once you have determined how much warp you need, use a *warping board* to measure and wind your desired yarn lengths. The threads made on a warping board lie on the loom in exactly the same order as they are threaded into the heddles and reed. Illus. 7 shows a warping board set for a length of 2 yards. By adding more pegs at the two ends, you can make a warp of up to 7 yards. Always test the length with a piece of string measured to the warp length you require.

Make two crosses on the warping board— one between B and C, and one between E and D. Tie the first thread at A and guide it over B, and under C, around X and Y, over D and under E. This makes one warp end. The return trip makes the second warp end. Continue around E and under D, back around X and Y, over C, under B, to A again. Repeat this cycle until your required number of ends are on the warping board. If you have a large number of ends, it is helpful to keep count of them as you go along. Simply tie a string round every 20 or 25 threads.

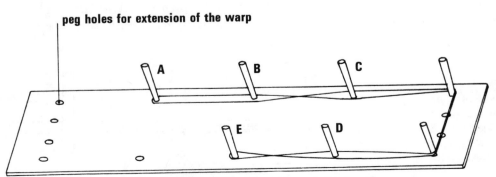

peg holes for extension of the warp

Illus. 7. The first thread on the warping board.

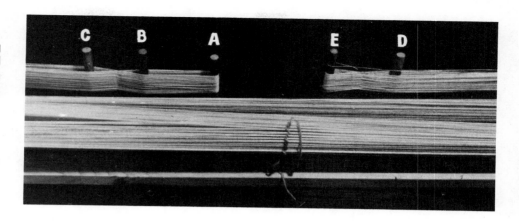

Illus. 8. Threads on the warping board. Notice the strings tied around groups of threads to help keep count of the number of ends.

Securing the Crosses

While the warp is secure on the board three ties are essential (see Illus. 10). First, tie the cross between D and E. The loop over E is the end that goes on the warp beam. The loop at A is the beginning of the warp. Tie threads here to mark where to cut to thread them through the heddles and reed. Then, tie the cross between B and C. This one shows the order of the threads for entering into the heddles.

Winding a Long Warp

Warps of more than 7 yards are made more quickly on a *warping mill* (see Illus. 9) which revolves on a base. The uprights on the mill are spaced one yard across, and the lower bar holding pegs D and E is adjustable. The crosses are made in the same position as described for the short warp—between B and C and between D and E (see Illus. 9). Secure the crosses with string ties as shown in (Illus. 10).

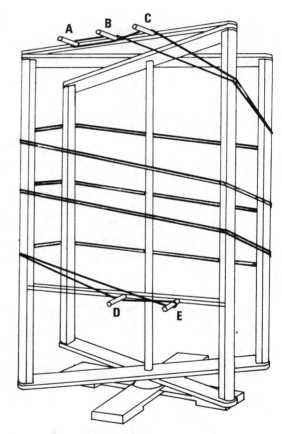

Illus. 9. Revolving warping mill.

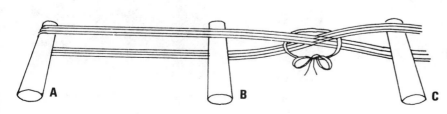

Illus. 10. Securing the cross between B and C.

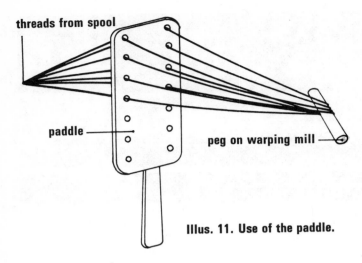

Illus. 11. Use of the paddle.

For further speed, it is usual to warp with several spools placed on a spool rack, the end threads of the spools being threaded through a *paddle* (Illus. 11).

Tie yarns to the first upper peg on warping mill at A. To make the first cross, hold the paddle in your right hand; with the forefinger of your left hand, hook the back threads on the paddle to the front, passing over the first front thread, pick up the first back thread, over the second front, pick up the second back, over the third front, pick up the third back, and so on. Thus the group of threads forming the first cross are all on your left forefinger. Slip your left thumb up between those threads and the paddle. The cross lies between your forefinger and thumb. Slip this group of crosses onto pegs B and C (see Illus. 12).

Now your left hand is free to rotate the warping mill round and round clockwise. When you reach pegs D and E, wind the group of threads under D, over E, around E and back over D. This forms the D and E crosses.

Change the paddle to your left hand and rotate the warping mill counter-clockwise with your right hand, grouping the bundle of threads directly over the previous line of threads. Make the crosses between B and C in

Illus. 12. Making the first cross.

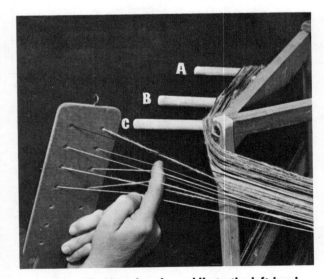

Illus. 13. Changing the paddle to the left hand.

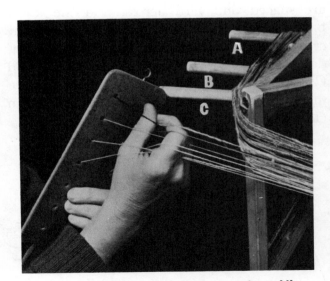

Illus. 14. Slipping right thumb up to the paddle.

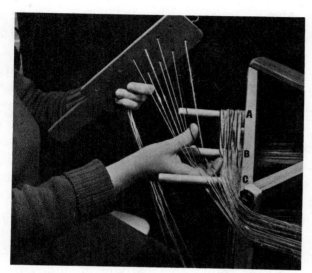

Illus. 15. Transferring the cross to pegs B and C.

Illus. 16. A chained warp with shed sticks placed between the B and C cross.

the same manner but reversing the position of your hands (Illus. 13)—with the paddle in your left hand and using the forefinger of your right hand, pick up the back threads, slip your right thumb up near the paddle, and transfer the cross from your fingers to pegs B and C (see Illus. 14 and 15).

Pass the paddle with the group of threads around peg A, turn the paddle down and under so that the threads are counter-clockwise and change the paddle to your right hand. Make the cross at pegs B and C as described above and continue warping until the required number of threads is on the mill. Secure the crosses with string ties as shown in Illus. 10.

Chaining the Warp

Starting at the bottom of the warp board or mill—that is, at pegs D and E—release the bundle of threads, grip them firmly in your left hand, wind the entire warp round and

round the closed fist of your left hand in an over-and-under motion. Tuck in the looped end from peg A and slide out your left fist.

An alternate method of chaining, instead of winding round your left fist, is to make a series of small chains—make a loop and pull a few inches of warp part way through this, repeating every 12" or so.

Threading and Dressing the Loom

Dressing the loom means preparing it for weaving. First, take the apron bar from the back warp beam and slide it through the loop of threads you made at peg E. Tie the two ends of the string which secured the D and E cross to the ends of this apron bar (Illus. 17).

The warp threads must now be spaced on a special pegged frame called a *raddle*. If your warp was designed for 12 threads per inch, place groups of 6 threads in each raddle space. Have the middle of the raddle clearly

Illus. 17. The end threads securely on the apron bar.

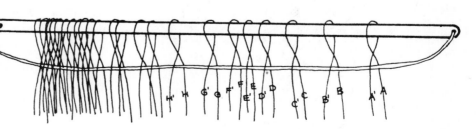

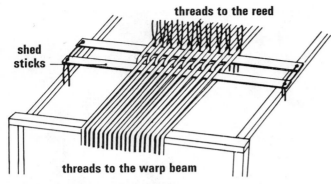

Illus. 18. Shed sticks holding the B and C cross.

Illus. 19. These shed sticks remain in position while threading.

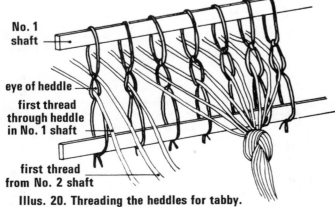

Illus. 20. Threading the heddles for tabby.

marked and place the middle of your warp there. Tie the raddle securely at both ends. Immediately the warp is spaced on it.

Now transfer all (the warp, the apron bar, the securely-tied raddle) to the loom. Tie the apron bar back in position on the warp beam. Clamp the raddle on the loom or rest it on long poles placed on the loom for this purpose. Take the other end of the warp very firmly in both hands, pull tightly and shake the warp. This is where a helper is invaluable because the warp must be rolled on with firm and even tension. Remove the stop pin from the ratchet, place strong brown paper or several sheets of newspaper round the warp beam, and wind on the warp.

Now place in position and securely tie the shed sticks as shown in Illus. 18. Release the string you originally used to secure the cross at B and C. On no account must you ease or alter the order of the threads in the cross. The warp threads come over and under the shed sticks in the correct order for threading and you can move them in pairs along the shed sticks. Cut the warp threads at A where the string was tied. Using a threading hook or fine crochet hook and, beginning at the right-hand side, enter the warp ends alternately through the eye of the first heddle on the No. 1 heddle shaft, and then through the first heddle on the No. 2 heddle shaft (see Illus. 20). (This is for tabby only.)

Loosely tie the ends in groups of four to avoid slipping back. Place the reed in the beater. Starting again from the right side, untie the first bundle of four threads, and enter each one into the dents of the reed in exact order. A skipped dent will leave an open space in your weaving.

As before, tie small bundles of threads together in loose knots as you go along the reed. Release the ratchet of the fabric beam and allow the apron bar to pass over the front of the loom. Tie the warp ends in bundles on this apron bar, making the tension even.

Remove the shed sticks; re-check the tension on the warp. Now you can begin weaving.

The insertion of the weft consists of three operations: making the shed, passing the shuttle through, and beating the weft threads in place.

Even weaving follows when these movements become rhythmical.

A few practical facts for consideration:

Start a new shuttle by overlapping two ends for about $\frac{1}{2}''$ in the same shed.

Very thick yarn should be mitered or cut at a slant.

If you are weaving narrow stripes, you can carry the weft up the side selvage edge.

For even weaving, make sure the beater is at right angles to the warp threads; otherwise, the finished work will be crooked.

Most looms allow for about 5" of weaving before shifting the warp, but you can move the beater forwards or backwards on its grooves.

The strength of the beating depends on what type of weaving you are doing—a wool rug requires firm, heavy beating; tapestry weaving demands that the warp be beaten out to make the weft predominate; soft material needs very little hand pressure on the beater because the swing of the beater is sufficient.

Always pass the shuttle from the right when the front shaft is down; thus, the position of the shuttle will indicate which shed comes next.

Pin a tape measure along the selvage edge to check the measurement of your weaving.

Rug Weaving

You can make very interesting and effective floor rugs on 2-shaft looms using the same weaving techniques as already described. The looms can be either horizontal or upright, but must be very strong to take the heavy beating. The upright takes less space in a room, and most rug looms have only two pedals. Another advantage of the upright model is that when you are using several colors simultaneously, as is done in tapestry weaving, the small bundles of colors can hang downwards, out of the way, whereas in a horizontal warp, these need to be continually shifted to avoid tangling.

It is possible to make a rug in sections on a

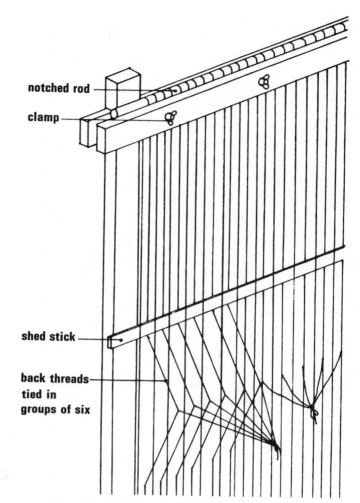

Illus. 21. Section of a tapestry rug frame loom.

rug frame loom made from a large picture frame, which you can mount on legs, if necessary. The proportions for the rugs are better rectangular rather than square: for example, $2' 6'' \times 4'$, $3' \times 5'$, $4' \times 7'$. Plot the design for tapestry woven rugs on graph paper first, but for tufted rugs, simpler in design, you can sketch with less detail. (Illus. 21 is a tapestry rug frame loom.)

For the warp, use a strong 8/4 (size 8, 4-ply) cotton, commonly used in rug weaving, or 2-ply flax twine and/or rug wool and about 6 ends per inch—this depends on the size of the frame on which you are experimenting. A notched rod at both ends helps to keep the warp threads straight, and two wooden clamps at top and bottom hold the warp taut.

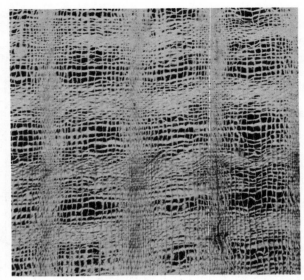

Illus. 22. Pattern resulting from irregular denting of single-ply home-spun wool.

Make a shed by lifting each alternate string with a shed stick and then by turning the stick on its side. The reverse shed is made by threads tied in groups of six which you pull forward by hand.

Pattern Work

Any weaver on a multiple-shaft loom will acknowledge that after tying up the 6, 8, or 10 pedals, the two that are tied for tabby are used the most. Pattern work followed from a book becomes repetitive, it is someone else's design, and somehow the joy of invention and ingenuity is lost. Plain weaving, well executed and with a correct balance of threads, has charm in its very simplicity. Most pattern weaves need the contrasting plain to highlight the pattern for good design. Nor does plain weaving need to look like a machine-made product if you select raw materials and yarns imaginatively.

Plain weaving is often referred to as tabby weaving but there is actually a distinction between the two in the texture, though not in the threading and the pedalling. Plain weaving does not necessarily show 50 per cent warp and 50 per cent weft as tabby does. Both are, however, like darning—a simple over one and under one interlacing of threads.

Let us consider the potential of 2-shaft weaving under the headings of color, irregular denting, and yarn combinations. Inlays, tufting, pick-up leno, and brocades are too complex for our purpose here.

Color offers the widest range of variations in weaving. Be bold with it. Use bright colors in the warp whenever possible, remembering that when woven the color loses some of its strength and gives different tones and half-tones. If you use a striped warp and a plain weft, the stripes on the material will be vertical. If you use a plain-colored warp with different colored weft stripes, the stripes in this fabric will be horizontal. These become even more interesting if you use a thicker weft yarn such as *gimps*, *slubs*, and other fancy twists. Evenly spaced stripes in both warp and weft produce checks. You can weave a light warp background with a dark thread for the tabby weft to give a deeper tone to the original threads, and vice versa—a dark warp becomes lighter if you use a light shade for the weft.

To help in the selection of colors, try winding the yarns round a ruler or notched stick in either broad or narrow bands until you achieve a pleasing sequence. With a blunt wool needle, darn a few rows across to get a better idea of the tone effects.

Also, try to make certain warp colors predominate by using a pick-up stick. Raise one shaft and pick up every other thread on this shed, thus passing over three and under one thread. Or, leave the shed down and pick up every two threads along the weaving.

Irregular denting. You can make meshes or open weaves by missing dents across the reed and weaving with weft spaces to match. It is a safe rule to weave a small sample first, then wash and iron it to see if the chosen yarns are suitable. Smooth plied yarns are not suitable in tabby meshes as the groupings slip and disappear after laundering. Home-spun wool lends itself very well to this form of texture work.

Yarn combinations. Here, you are recommended to start a collection of fabric samples

6–8″ square because it is only by seeing and feeling different woven yarns that experimentation begins to yield its rewards. Many yarn combinations are available for this—thick and thin yarns, lustrous and dull, fancy and plain, varying twists, hand-spun and machine-spun. Choose all wisely, remembering always that the resultant fabric must wear well and be suitable for the purpose for which it is intended.

There are a few do's and don'ts worth mentioning. When combining coarse and fine yarns in the same material, which undoubtedly adds effect and character, watch particularly for any distortion of the fabric. To prevent this, increase the number of fine threads in relation to the number of coarse ones. A harmonious balance of threads is necessary to avoid puckering. Measure your sample square exactly.

A finished fabric is nearly always more pleasing if a correct balance of the same kind of yarn is selected for both warp and weft; for example, a woollen material looks and feels right if you use wool for the warp also, rather than a cotton warp with a wool weft.

Concerning rug making, there are three types of rugs to try out on a rug frame. The first is the tapestry rug, which is a reversible rug. The weave is plain tabby with the weft beaten down to cover the warp entirely—all the design is in the weft.

Put the weft through in loose loops in a bow effect, comb it in place with your fingers first, push it firmly in with a strong comb or a kitchen fork. Beat it with a strong metal comb. (This applies to the picture frame when you do not have a proper beater.) The purpose of looping the weft is to prevent the selvage sides from pulling in.

Thick home-spun wool makes an interesting texture for these rugs. The patterns you make by breaking the line of weft into small color areas of dark and light contrasts must be looped to avoid slits, which are permissible in tapestry pictures but not in floor rugs. Illus. 23 shows the correct and incorrect way of doing this.

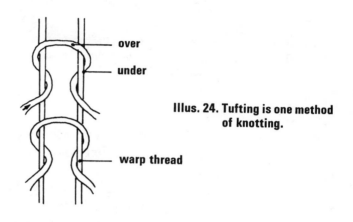

Illus. 23. How to break into the line of weft and loop to keep a flat surface and to avoid slits.

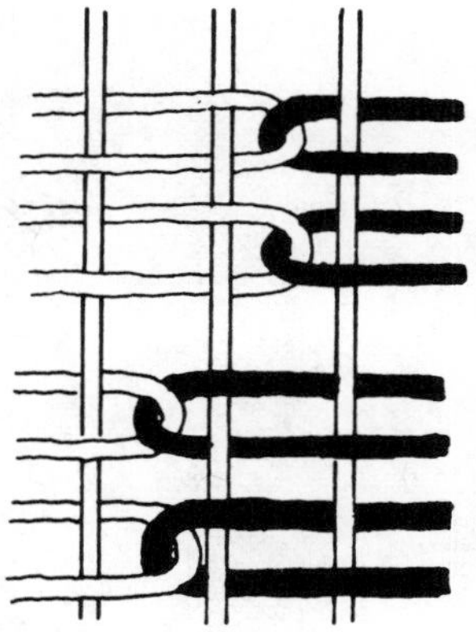

incorrect

correct

incorrect

correct

over

under

Illus. 24. Tufting is one method of knotting.

warp thread

The rule is: link so that each loop passes over its fellow if it passed over its last warp end, and under its fellow if it passed under its last warp end. By looping correctly, the joins are less bulky. If slits do occur, hand-sew them afterwards.

The second type of rug, the tufted or Rya rug, derives its name from the village of Rya in Sweden. Knotted rugs are not really exclusive to this area, a similar tuft or pile effect having been developed for many years in Asia Minor, Caucasia, Persia, and other countries. All these rugs have a shaggy look and because of this need a simple design with delightfully blended colors.

There are several ways of knotting. Illus. 24 shows a standard method which certainly is an ideal way to use odd ends of wool imaginatively. Knots are tied on each pair of warp strings across the loom, on the flat warp without any shed. A strand of wool that is

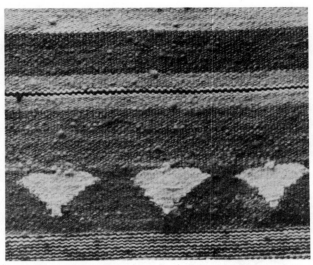

Illus. 25. Texture of home-spun wool tightly beaten in a tapestry rug.

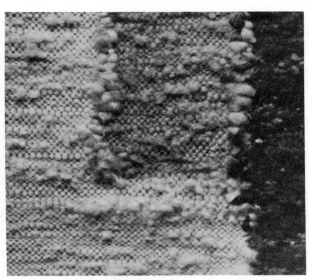

Illus. 26. Texture of an unspun finger-twisted wool rug.

going to make the loops is put over the two threads, one end passed to the left and taken under the left warp thread, brought back to the middle, looped over the right-hand warp thread, then under it, bringing it back to the middle again. The two ends are pulled tight to make the knot. Weave several rows of tabby before tying on the next row of knots. Beat firmly to keep the knots in place.

Tufting is not confined to Rya rugs—you can use it as decoration for edgings, bags, pillow covers, curtains, and so on.

The last type of rug is the finger-twisted fleece wool rug. You can use second-grade wool—scour it well, tease and card it into long rolags (cigar-shaped rolls). Twist these rolags a little as you place them in the shed. If you beat them very hard, they keep in place with-

out tabby weave in between, though sometimes the tabby adds to the design. Fine rolags, of course, make a different texture than thick ones. Whatever the size, make sure the beating is so firm that the rolags cannot be shifted with your fingers, otherwise your rug will not wear well. You can weave very attractive color combinations with naturally-dyed fleece wool, blending with natural grey and brown fleeces. Or, you can simply use a white warp for a white rug.

Try, also, in your rug making, a combination of finger-twisting and Rya, using the Rya knots to accent the design; the finger-twisting gives a textured background.

Finish your rugs either with knotted fringes or bind with soft leather concealing the reef knots holding the warp ends.

OFF-LOOM WEAVING

If you are interested in weaving but not in the expense or space that a loom involves, try off-loom weaving. Off-loom weaving eliminates equipment that requires a whole room and a month's budget, and substitutes small, available equipment such as picture frames, ice cream sticks, or your own body. The weaving strands, like everything else in off-loom weaving, do not have to be expensive for good results. Wool left over from knitting, cloth scraps cut into strips, colored telephone cables, reeds from a pond, or a willow tree's young branches are some examples of materials to weave.

The thrill of making something from "scratch" can never be equalled. And the unique, hand-woven articles that you make with your own striking designs are sure to be valued by whoever owns them—yourself or the one who receives your thoughtful gift.

Collar

A woven collar is like jewelry: it perks up your clothing by adding new colors and textures to a plain neckline. Collars are good beginning projects, as they are easy and quick to weave.

With a tape measure, loosely measure the circumference of your neck. Draw a circle of the same circumference on a double thickness of newspaper, and draw a second circle with the same midpoint as the first, but with a radius at least 5″ larger. You can sketch this by measuring and marking 5″ from every point on the outer edge of the first circle, or use a compass for greater accuracy.

The first circle represents the edge of the collar that lies against your neck, while the outer circle is the bottom edge of the collar. Connect the neckline and bottom edge by drawing two diagonal lines that start at the same point on the neckline, but reach the bottom edge 4″ apart.

Cut the collar pattern out of the newspaper and try it on in front of a mirror, adjusting it if necessary by pinning and cutting. Trace this fitted newspaper pattern on a piece of stiff cardboard, and make small pencil marks along the neckline edge on the cardboard every $\frac{1}{8}$″. Place a ruler from the midpoint of the circles through one of the marks on the neckline edge. Then make a mark on the bottom edge of the collar when the ruler crosses it. Continue to mark the entire outer edge by placing the ruler through the midpoint and every neckline mark to find points on the bottom edge corresponding to those on the neckline.

Trace lightly around both circles of the collar with a single-edged razor blade or knife in a holder.

Go over this outline with the blade several times, scoring deeper and deeper each time until you have cut through the cardboard's entire thickness. Then use the blade to make notches $\frac{1}{4}$″ long on every point which you just marked on both collar edges.

Now that you have prepared the pattern, you are ready to fasten the warp threads around it. Tie a knot at the end of a piece of yarn and catch it on the underside in the first notch of the neckline edge. Bring the yarn

Condensed from the book, "Off-Loom Weaving" by Marion H. Bernstein | © 1971 by Sterling Publishing Co., Inc., New York

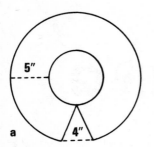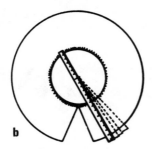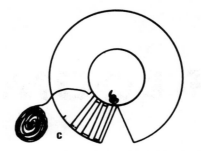

Illus. 1. In *a*, pattern to cut from cardboard for a woven collar. In *b*, ruler helps mark notches along outside edge of pattern. In *c*, warp is wrapped along top of pattern. In *d*, fill goes over and under warp threads.

across the top of the cardboard to the first notch on the bottom edge and slide the yarn into this notch. Carry the yarn along the back of the collar to the second notch of the bottom edge; then bring the yarn back up to the top side in this second notch. Take the yarn across the top of the cardboard to the second notch of the neckline edge, slide it in the notch, and carry it along the back side to the third notch of the neckline edge. Continue wrapping the yarn back and forth between the notches of both edges *on the top of the cardboard*. If you wrap the cardboard up in the yarn by simply winding the warp threads around and around the pattern, you will not be able to remove the cardboard when you are finished weaving.

After you have attached the warp threads so they are uniformly taut, begin weaving the fill, or *weft* threads. Using a needle or safety-pin, thread or knot a different yarn and begin to weave it over and under every other warp thread—that is, over one thread and under the next. This basic weave is called the *tabby* weave. Leave several inches of the fill thread hanging at the starting point. When you have woven one row of fill, use a comb or fork to *beat* the yarn into place close to the neckline edge.

Weave five rows with this simple tabby weave. As you reach the end of one row, turn the thread around the end warp thread, so that if you went under that thread in the previous row, you go over it in the next row. If you run out of yarn in the middle of a row, overlap a new piece of yarn on top of the old. When you beat that row to the edge, be careful to treat

the ends together so they do not separate. Never knot the yarn in weaving. If you run out of weft at the end of a row (called a *selvage*), weave a new piece of weft into the warp the same way you began the first row, leaving a tail a few inches long. When you finish your weaving, thread these tails in the body of the weaving with a needle.

Once the weaving has a firm foundation, use other kinds of "yarns." Weave the next few rows by alternating one row of ribbon with one row of yarn, for example. You might put the ribbon in carefully so that it lies flat, or purposely crinkle and bend it. Weave right up to the notches on the bottom edge with any sort of material—yarn, cord, ribbon, twine, or leather.

Remove the collar from its cardboard pattern by sliding the warp threads off the notches. Weave the hanging tails into the wrong side of the piece with a needle, and trim them close after several stitches. Then sew three pieces of yarn 15″ long to each end of the neckline edge. Braid these ends and tie them together to fasten the collar round your neck.

Make your next collar more involved by using other materials. For example, string large beads on the weft thread as you weave it into the warp. When you beat the rows into place toward the neckline edge, the beads will distribute themselves between each warp thread.

You might make the collar 8″ deep, instead of the 5″ you just used. Stop weaving 3″ or 4″ before you reach the bottom edge, and cut the warp threads open on that edge. Then slide a bead on each warp thread, and tie a knot to hold it in place. Your collar begins like a woven piece of fabric, but ends like a necklace.

Fluffy Muff

Oriental carpets are made with a looping technique of *half hitches* that creates a fluffy surface. While you probably do not feel ready to tackle as large a project as a carpet, you can use the same technique to make a small but warm winter muff.

To make an improvised frame, cut two branches 21″ long. Cross them at the center so that the open ends of this "X" are 12″ wide, and lash the sticks together where they meet. Cut two more branches 12″ long and lash these to the open ends of the 21″-branches. With a pen-knife, make notches in the 12″-sticks, 12 notches to the inch.

Wrap a strong cotton or linen warp around the 12″-sticks, placing one thread in each notch as you wind. The warp threads for a muff must surround the frame, not lie on top of it as for the preceding collar. Since the muff is hollow, weave the warp threads on the front and back separately, and then slide the muff off the frame.

Collect heavy yarn in several shades of one color (for example, pink, red and maroon, which are all in the red family). For contrast, add a related shade that has a lot of another color in it (perhaps purple, which contains red, the original color, as well as a new color, blue).

To begin, weave four rows of purple in the tabby weave (over and under consecutive warp threads) on the front face of the frame. As soon as you weave a row, beat it to one end of the frame. Then with the next darkest color, maroon, make a row of loops:

First lay a ruler or other stick on top of the warp. With the weft thread, make *half hitches* in pairs facing each other, as shown in Illus. 3. Pull loops towards you as you make them up. Finish the entire row and remove the ruler. For thicker pile, make two or three rows of

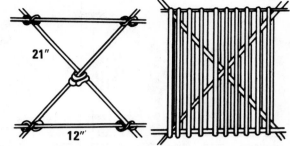

Illus. 2. (Left) Four branches crossed and lashed to make a frame. (Right) Wrap warp around frame like this.

loops together, without separating them by any rows of tabby weaving. Begin the loops around the second warp in even rows to avoid weaving holes into the fabric. When you have completed the muff, decide whether or not to cut these loops open to have an even fluffier, more raised surface.

Weave three more rows of purple and loop another row of half hitches in red, the next darkest color. Weave another three rows of purple and again loop half hitches, in pink this time. Repeat this pattern. The gradations of color, from dark to light, make the pile appear deeper and richer than it actually is.

When you have woven across the front face of the frame, carefully pull a section of the unwoven warp around the end of the frame, so that it lies on top, and complete the weaving on this portion of the muff. Slide the woven muff off the frame.

For extra warmth, you should line the muff. Take a piece of lining fabric 1½″ wider and 1½″ longer than the muff itself and sew the ends

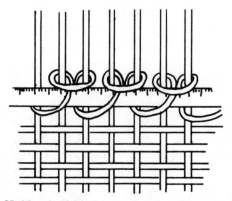

Illus. 3. Making half hitches by looping fill around a ruler.

Illus. 4. To make a Persian Garden carpet with a design in half hitches, weave several squares, each with a portion of the design. Sew the squares together to complete the carpet.

together for a cylinder. Turn the lining so that its right side is out, and turn the muff so its wrong side is out. Slide the lining fabric over the wrong side of the muff. Sew the two pieces together by hand on the edges, turning the lining edge under at both selvages. Then turn the muff right side out and, with a combination of several of the yarns used for weaving, make a braid that is long enough to slip through the muff, hang around your neck, and balance the muff at about your waist. Thread this braid through the muff and tie the ends together in a square knot. Put your hands inside the muff and try it out on a brisk winter day!

To make a fluffy pillow, weave a muff as described above, but do not line it. Sew one end together and either stuff the pouch with scraps or insert a ready-made pillow. Toss pillows are decorative, as well as soft and cuddly, when they are covered with pile.

You can even make a rug by sewing together small rectangles of woven pile. This would be a simple way to make a Persian Garden Carpet, composed of boxes filled with flowering plants. Pile of different colors alternated with flat areas of tabby weaving gives the impression of growing plants. The pile areas are the plants, and the flat background represents the surrounding earth.

Scarf

From Peru to Pakistan, weaving on a *back strap* is an ancient method to hold the warp tight. The equipment is always available: you use your body to stretch the weaving as taut as it should be.

Place two nails in the floor or two pegs in the ground, 45″ apart, and wrap 40 warp threads around them, counting each 45″-length as one thread. Use soft yarns which are comfortable against your skin for the weft threads. You also need a needle with a large eye, a comb or fork to beat the weft, and a pair of scissors. Place a long wood dowel or stick through each end of the warp and remove the warp threads from the nails or pegs. Spread the warp threads evenly across the dowels and lay the dowels on a flat surface. Tape the threads to the dowels. With a belt or a piece of cord, tie one dowel to a stable object like a tree and the other dowel to your waist.

You can either sit or stand as you work, but stay far enough away from the solid support so that the warp is tense. Thread the needle with weft yarn and work it over and under alternate warp threads. Comb each row of weft towards you. Beat some weft strands tightly, others loosely, so that in one section warp dominates, in another weft does, and in another, there is a balance.

For more variety, make a pattern in the weaving by changing the number of warp threads the needle passes over and under. See Illus. 6 for some diagrams of different designs.

If you want to speed up your weaving, make a *harness* to raise and lower several warp threads at one time. This saves you the time-consuming task of separating the warp threads individually. Collect or buy four flat sticks 10″ long and 20 ice cream sticks. Drill a hole in the middle of each ice cream stick and place the sticks next to each other, $\frac{1}{8}$″ apart, so that each end of every ice cream stick lies on top of a 10″-stick. Glue the ice cream sticks in place there, and then glue the other two 10″-sticks on top of each end of the ice cream sticks. The ends of the ice cream sticks are thus sandwiched between the 10″-sticks.

If you use a harness, you must wrap the warp threads differently than before. Place two nails in the floor or pegs in the ground 45″ apart, another peg 4″ from one of them, and another 3″ from the third. Wind a warp of 39 threads 50″ long over the four pegs, so that the yarn crosses itself between the third and fourth pegs. With another strand of yarn, tie the warp threads securely at the cross. Place a dowel

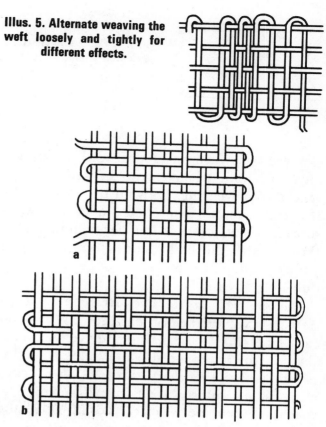

Illus. 5. Alternate weaving the weft loosely and tightly for different effects.

Illus. 6a and b. Some variations of tabby.

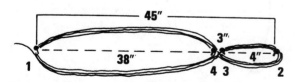

Illus. 7. If you are using a harness, wrap the warp around four pegs according to the dimensions shown here.

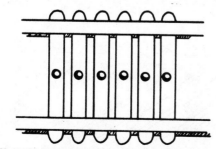

Illus. 8. Harness made of ice cream sticks.

at the far end from the cross and tie the end of the warp thread to this dowel. Insert another dowel where the second peg is. Remove the yarn from the pegs and cut the warp open at the end where the second peg was.

Now you are ready to *thread the harness*—that is, string the warp through the ice cream sticks. Untie the warp threads at the cross. Start with the first warp thread and insert it through the hole on the first stick. Put the second thread in the space between the first and second sticks. Continue in this manner, threading the odd threads through the holes and the even ones through the spaces between the sticks. Then tie pairs of warp together in square knots behind the heddle, and tape the warp threads evenly to the dowels. You have constructed a simple loom—but with no expense, no carpentry, and no special skills. Now you are ready to weave.

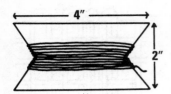

Illus. 9. Cardboard shuttle with weft wound on it.

Wind weft yarn on a cardboard or wooden *shuttle*, a bobbin which carries the weft yarn and speeds your weaving. Unwind the yarn as you insert the shuttle over and under the warp threads. Using a shuttle is easier than the single thread: with the bulky shuttle wrapped with yarn, you can throw it through the warp quickly and easily.

Tie yourself into the back strap with a cord or belt, as you did before (page 256). When you raise one end of the harness above the warp threads, the other end drops. While one end is raised, every other warp thread is also raised, and the alternate threads are lowered. The space between the warp threads is called the *shed*, and by opening a shed you can pass the weft, wrapped round the shuttle, through all the warp threads in a single motion. Leave a few inches of the weft thread hanging at the beginning corner of your scarf.

Beat the first row of weft towards you. Now change the position of the warp threads by reversing the harness: lower the end that was raised, and raise the end that was lowered. You have created a new shed, and the warp threads are opposite to the position they were just in. Weave the complete warp, changing the position of the harness after every row, and re-winding the shuttle when it runs out of weft. In almost no time at all, you can complete a hand-woven piece of cloth—in a color and design that you have chosen.

Weaving patterns more complicated than tabby is not necessarily more difficult: re-thread the harness so that you skip either some holes or spaces. When you raise one end, then, several adjacent threads will be raised. You can also raise warp threads by hand with a pointed stick.

Poncho

You can make ponchos, tunics or dresses without a loom if you make your garment of separately woven pieces. You will need a frame on which to weave, about 21″ × 31″. To make notches for the warp threads, hammer nails $\frac{1}{8}$″ apart on the frame's 21″-sides, or else saw $\frac{1}{4}$″-deep slits $\frac{1}{8}$″ apart on the shorter sides. You can also use the frame without any notches, but you must then position the warp carefully as you wind.

Choose a warp which is stronger than the weft. To make a rich color and texture, combine several different threads for the warp or weft. One attractive method is to use several related colors and one unrelated, for contrast. The color wheel in Illus. 10 should help you make your color choices. Because adjacent colors are related to each other they blend harmoniously. Colors opposite each other are strong contrasts and form striking combinations.

Tie one end of the warp yarn to the corner of the frame, or around a corner nail or slit. If you

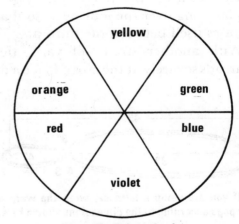

Illus. 10. Color wheel.

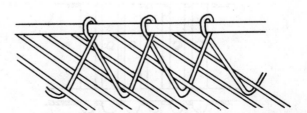

Illus. 11. String heddle bar attached to every other warp thread.

hammered nails or sawed slits as instructed above, they are $\frac{1}{8}''$ apart, and the warp threads you wrap around the frame are also $\frac{1}{8}''$ apart. If you are not using nails or slits, wrap and tape warp threads $\frac{1}{8}''$ apart. Surround the frame with warp and then end the warp the same way you began it.

For the poncho, a string heddle bar raises threads while allowing a greater flexibility of design. Find a smooth stick or dowel 23″ long, or slightly longer than the narrow edge of the frame. Loop a strong string in half hitches (see page 255) alternately between the dowel and every other warp thread. (You weave the warp threads together which are wound on the front and back of the frame, so you might attach those threads on the back to the string heddle bar.) You can use other arrangements for different weaves, of course. Place this bar towards the top of the frame. When you lift the string heddle bar, the warp threads which are connected to it also rise.

Find a flat, smooth stick approximately $2'' \times \frac{1}{4}'' \times 23''$ to slide over every warp thread connected to the string heddle bar, and under every one not connected. When you turn the stick so its $\frac{1}{4}''$-side is against the warp, the threads that it lies under are raised, while the threads below it are lowered. Position this *sword* towards the back of the frame, at the opposite end from the string heddle bar. By alternately raising the string heddle bar and the sword, you make opposite sheds to weave into.

Make a simple cardboard shuttle (see page 258) and wrap the weft around it. Raise the string heddle bar and throw the shuttle through the shed. Beat this first row of weft to the end of the frame with a comb. Then turn the sword on its side so it raises those warp threads which were lowered in the first shed, and pass the shuttle through this shed. Repeat this pattern, changing sheds and throwing weft. Change the weft yarn—either randomly or regularly—to vary the color and texture of your work.

When you are weaving the second shed (that

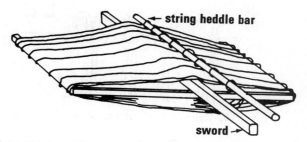

Illus. 12. Weave by alternately turning the sword and pulling the string heddle bar.

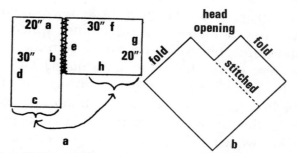

Illus. 13. Sew the poncho together as shown in view *a*. View *b* shows the completed poncho.

is, when the sword is turned so it raises some threads), release the heddle bar so it does not raise the other threads—but do not release it so much that the thread connecting it to the warp becomes woven into your cloth.

Weave right up to the ends of the frame, and then cut the front and back warp threads apart so you can remove the cloth. Knot the warp threads together in small groups of two or three threads and finish off these ends by threading them back into the weaving.

To construct the poncho, weave another piece of cloth the same size and color as the first. Sew the two pieces together with yarn by curving and stitching them as shown in Illus. 13. A poncho of this size fits an average woman.

Mobile Using Warp Wrapping

A mobile makes a decorative ornament to spruce up a bare wall or hang above a baby's crib. A woven mobile is particularly good for babies, as it is soft and safe. The technique of *warp wrapping* is used for the mobile shown in Illus. P2.

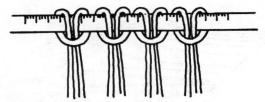

Illus. 14. Make 50 half hitches on a ruler.

Loop about 50 half hitches on a ruler or other rigid stick, for 50 cords that are each 1 yard long. Tape the ruler to a solid support like a window ledge—something which is immovable, but which protrudes from the wall so there is working space all around. Tie the ends of the strands in pairs through curtain weights (found in a sewing notions shop). Weighting the warp threads with heavy objects makes weaving easier, because you can work with the free hanging warp without worrying about knotting at the ends of the threads.

Divide the warp into eight or ten groups with the same number of threads in each group. Use a needle to weave two rows of tabby in one group of warp, so the weft is caught in it. Tightly holding that group of warp towards you, simply wrap the weft thread round and round the warp threads. If you do not twist the warp yarns, the wrapped weft threads will not undo when you release the tension of the warp.

After working on one group of warp for a distance, weave a temporary row of tabby to hold your weaving in place and move on to another warp section. Repeat the procedure with the groups of warp across the ruler. Re-group the warp threads and wrap them also, so that every part of the mobile is connected to

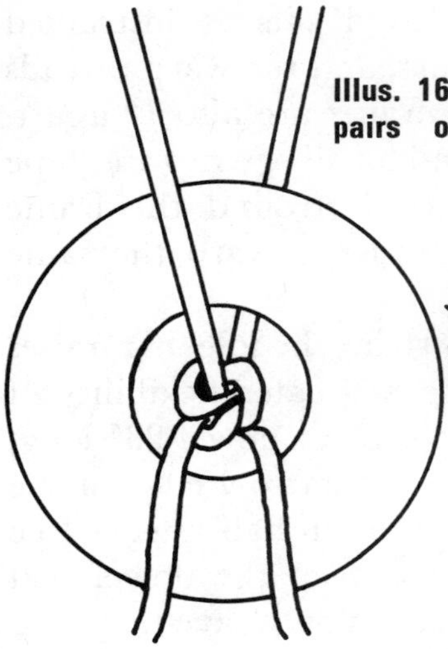

Illus. 16. To weight the cords, tie pairs of warp through curtain weights.

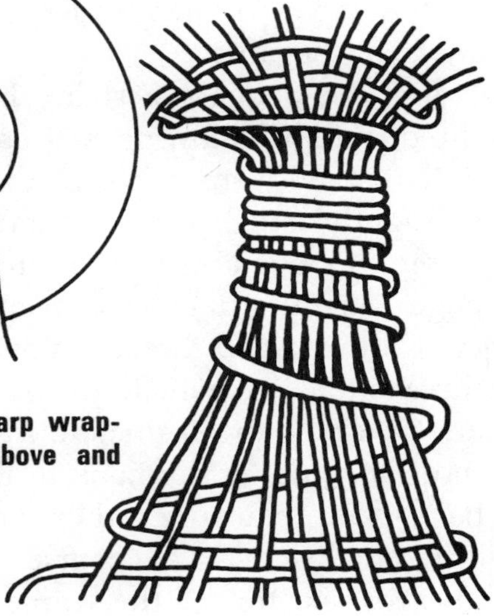

Illus. 17. Secure warp wrapping with tabby above and below.

every other part. The wrapped groups should come together and separate throughout the piece to hold it together.

As the weaving takes shape, plan how you would like the rest of the mobile to fall. Join the strips of warp wrapping so that the air catches and blows them at random. The mobile pictured here combines the tabby weave with warp wrapping, but you may use any weaving technique you wish.

When all the warp has been wrapped and woven, you may leave it on the stick from which it hung, or substitute a flexible reed. You may suspend the mobile from hooks on the ceiling, or you may fasten it to the wall. Whichever you choose, secure the wrapped sections away from each other, so they do not just hang limply.

Now that you are familiar with some of the basic off-loom weaving techniques, see what other projects you can create.

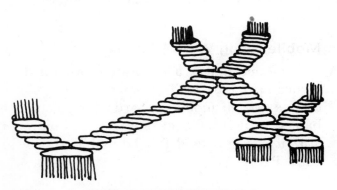

Illus. 15. Group wrapped warp threads together and wrap a few times. Then separate again.

FINGER WEAVING (INDIAN BRAIDING)

Finger weaving, also defined as flat braiding, is a very old method of thread interlacement, surely predating the use of looms in most parts of the world. It is referred to as finger weaving because you use your fingers to pick up the vertical warp threads through which you pass the horizontal weft.

There are not many references available with directions for decorative braiding, so it has been necessary to study certain braiding techniques from the actual bands and sashes which can be seen in museum collections. Some of these bands date from A.D. 300. Over the centuries, a number of different methods have been developed for achieving these designs. There are different ways for securing the warps, different ways for drawing the tension and different ways to do the actual weaving. In fact, although the term "finger weaving" has been applied to work practiced for centuries by primitive tribes using two sets of elements— namely separate vertical warps and separate horizontal wefts—this article concerns a type of finger weaving for which you use only one set of threads or yarns. The warp and weft are not separate elements as they always are in loom weaving.

People in many parts of the world have worked out techniques for weaving one set of threads with the fingers.

The directions here, however, are limited to several designs made by North American Indians and to some of the designs made by ancient Peruvians. You will learn to weave belts, hair ties, collars, neck-ties and dress or skirt trimming bands. Most instructions are for long narrow bands, but as you progress, the technical knowledge and experience you gain should lead you to create new designs or combinations of designs.

To finger weave, you begin with a definite number of warp threads which you also use, in a definite order, as the weft threads. When you pick up a warp thread to use it as a weft, you should always be aware of its function as a weft. Then, just as you used the warp as a weft, you drop the weft back, in a definite order, into the warp to use it again as a warp. If you unwove the weaving, the result would be, of course, only a single set of parallel vertical threads.

The opening through which you pass the weft is called the shed. The name "finger weaving" also applies here because you use your fingers instead of a shuttle—as in loom weaving—to draw the weft through the shed.

Except for a $\frac{1}{4}$"-wide, 6"-long dowel and a safety-pin, there is no intervening, expensive equipment in finger weaving to come between you, the craftsman, and your medium. The absence of cumbersome tools makes finger weaving a mobile craft which you can pursue even while travelling. A few strands of colorful yarns and some degree of concentration are all

Condensed from the book, "Finger Weaving: Indian Braiding" by Alta R. Turner | © 1973 by Sterling Publishing Co., Inc., New York

you need to provide hours of pleasure and satisfaction.

Four-ply wool knitting yarn, readily available in yarn shops and department stores, is suitable for finger weaving the designs explained in this article. As you become proficient in the craft, you will be able to experiment with yarns of various sizes and spins, as well as with original designs and projects. As you discover numerous ways to arrange your colors, keep in mind that light and dark contrasts accentuate the pattern and that closely related colors result in a more subdued, blended design.

Diagonal Stripe Pattern for Belt

Select three contrasting colors of four-ply knitting yarn. Cut 10 2½-yard lengths of each selected color: A, B and C. Arrange each color in a solid stripe on a ¼″ dowel 6″ long in the following order: 10A 10B 10C, looping the middle of each length of yarn round the dowel (see Illus. 1). Dividing the length of yarn in the middle makes it possible for you to work with a shorter length when weaving and eliminates the thread entanglement which would occur if you started the weaving at one end instead of in the middle.

Tie a piece of yarn round the 30 threads at a

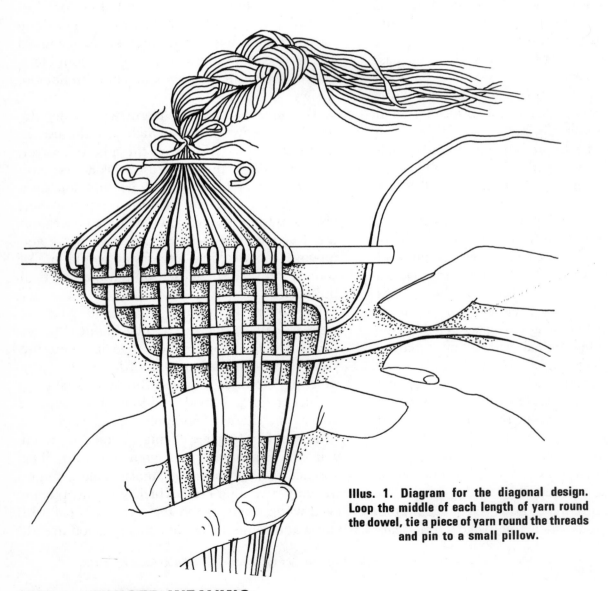

Illus. 1. Diagram for the diagonal design. Loop the middle of each length of yarn round the dowel, tie a piece of yarn round the threads and pin to a small pillow.

point just above the dowel and, with a safety-pin placed at this tie, secure the warp to a small pillow (see Illus. 1). The lengths above the dowel will be the second half of the belt.

Step 1: In front of the dowel, start with the left outside thread, placing it under the second thread and then over and under succeeding threads to the right. Place this first weft up under the dowel on the right as you must weave it with the second weft to start the right selvage.

NOTE: It is very important to keep the order of the threads in parallel lines. Do not allow the warp threads to cross out of position.

Alternate strands always go up for each shed or division; the strands which are up in the first shed are down in the second shed. Make a shed by picking up the old warp threads on your left forefinger, and draw the weft through this shed to the right. Then pull the separated threads in opposite directions to pack the preceding wefts into place.

Step 2: When the second thread is woven to the right, pull the first thread, which you previously put under the dowel, down around the second thread and into the warp to form the selvage. The first weft thread now becomes the right thread of the warp. As the weft threads return to the warp on the right, pull them free from the remaining warp threads to avoid large entanglements. Continue to weave from left to right.

As the work progresses, advance the safety-pin in the weaving to maintain good tension. Examine the belt critically and adjust any looseness in the work. To make a firm belt, you must place the wefts rather close to each other. They should be *well covered* by the warp threads.

Keep the left selvage a bit loose and weave each weft securely into the right selvage, pulling it into a straight line. Otherwise, the weaving will curve.

When the weft thread no longer reaches to the right of the dowel, you may hook it round the end of the safety-pin.

Step 3: Continue weaving in the same way, always weaving from left to right, with each succeeding outside left thread going under the adjacent thread and then over and under the remaining threads to the right, continuing to the desired length (see Illus. 2).

Step 4: In order to continue the diagonal stripes in the same direction when weaving the second half of the belt, re-pin the belt to the pillow at a point near the dowel and then remove the dowel. Take a firm hold of the loose half of the threads and pull the loops straight. Turn the belt around. Be sure you are turning the work *around*, not over.

Step 5: Weave with the left outside thread to the right selvage. Repeat with each following left thread, straightening the selvages at intervals to avoid curves in the belt. Continue until the second half is the same length as the first half.

Making Fringe

The Indians often braid these belts to the exact waist measurement and then make a long fringe for tying.

Step 6: You can make fringes in different ways: you can braid three or four strands or ply two or four ends.

FINGER WEAVING ■ 263

Illus. 3. Make a diagonal pattern collar as you did the belt except that you must pull the left selvage securely to form a curve. Keep the right selvage loose.

To ply two ends, take the first one between your thumb and forefinger and twist tightly (until it kinks) to the right. Place a clip clothespin on the end of the twisted strand and then place it where it will not unwind—under the edge of the pillow will do. Now, twist the second thread tightly to the right. Then pull both ends firmly together, at the same time removing the clothespin. Start the two ends twisting to the left. The two easily ply. You may ply each pair of ends in the same way. Tie a knot at the end of each plied pair of threads and cut the fringe to an even line at the bottom.

Press the belt with a damp cloth with the iron gauge set at "wool." Your first woven creation is completed.

To Make a Collar

Cut 30 threads, 10 each in the same three colors you used for the belt, each 1½ yards long. Arrange the threads on the dowel—10A 10B 10C.

Step 1: Start the weaving by proceeding in the same manner as for the belt (see page 262) *except that* you should pull the left selvage tightly into a curve and keep the right selvage loose.

Step 2: To weave the second half of the collar, turn the work *over* (not *around* as for the belt) and start from the left again. The diagonal lines then converge at the center, making the curve of the collar run in one circular direction (see Illus. 3).

Step 3: Ply each pair of warp ends for a short fringe. Tie the collar in front or back.

Once you have become an expert in weaving the diagonal design, you can experiment. Try, for instance, reversing the direction of the diagonal at the end of the pattern.

Chevron Design

For this design, you need 2½-yard lengths of yarn in four colors.

Step 1: Cut four lengths of the lightest color D, six lengths of the next lightest color C, four lengths of a darker color B, and six lengths of the darkest color A.

Arrange the lengths on the dowel as you did on page 262, with the lightest color in the middle and the other three colors in a progression of light to dark with the darkest color on the outside, as follows: 3A 2B 3C 4D 3C 2B 3A.

Step 2: Tie a piece of yarn round the 20 threads above the dowel and secure with a safety-pin to a pillow.

Step 3: Locate the middle of the group of threads in front of the dowel—it is in the middle of the center color. The first thread you weave is the D thread left of center. With your left forefinger, starting in the center and moving towards the right, pick up a shed of the odd numbered threads 1, 3, 5, and so on. With your right hand, pull the D thread left of the center through the shed to the right and place it under the dowel (see Illus. 4). Later, you use this thread to start the selvage with the second weft thread.

Step 4: Pick up a shed from the center towards the left edge, odd threads up, and draw the D thread right of center through the shed to the left. Place this first weft on the left side up under the dowel so that you can use it with the second weft to start the left selvage.

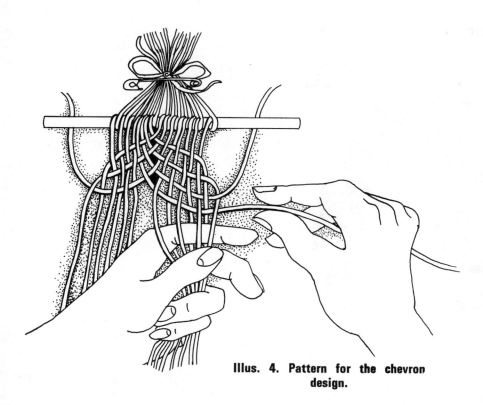

Illus. 4. Pattern for the chevron design.

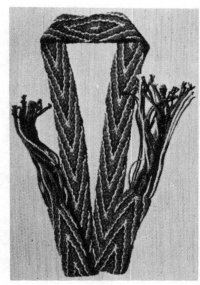

Illus. 5. For a more subdued belt, use subtler colors, such as the grey, black, and white which were used for this chevron pattern.

NOTE: The left-of-center thread always crosses to the right and the right-of-center thread always crosses to the left.

Be sure to keep the warp threads in the proper order.

Step 5: Now, weave the next thread left of center, an up thread, under the adjacent right thread and through the shed, with the odd numbered warps up, to the right edge. Pull the first weft, which is under the dowel, down round the second weft to start the selvage, and place the second weft up under the dowel.

Step 6: Pack each weft into place by pulling the upper and lower separated warps of the shed in opposite directions.

Weave the thread right of center, an up thread, under the adjacent left thread and through the shed, with the odd numbered warps up, towards the left edge. Pull the first weft which is under the dowel down round the second weft to start the selvage and place the second weft up under the dowel.

Step 7: Pull each weft firmly in a horizontal direction to the right or to the left. This helps cover the wefts by the threads in the warp position. You should hardly have to pull the threads in the vertical position except to straighten selvages and to remove a possible loop.

Step 8: Continue weaving first with the up left-of-center thread moving to the right and then with the up right-of-center thread moving to the left (see Illus. 6).

Advance the safety-pin as you weave in order to have proper tension on the warps as you work.

When the work progresses to the point where it is difficult to reach the dowel with the selvage threads, you may be able to place them under the end of the safety-pin. If not, add two extra safety-pins—one on each side of the safety-pin that secures the work to the pillow—and catch the selvage threads round these pins. In this way, you can easily see where the selvage threads are at all times.

If or when you find you have made a mistake in your work, such as not weaving in a selvage thread, not keeping the alternating sheds in order, or picking up the wrong weft, you need to go back *at once* to make corrections. Finger

Illus. 6. Here, the up left-of-center thread moves to the right through the shed. The selvage threads are shown on each side of the dowel.

weaving calls for precise work and you cannot proceed with a design until you have corrected any errors.

Step 9: Weave to the desired length and make fringe as on pages 263-264.

Step 10: Adjust the safety-pin back to a near-center position and remove the tie round the remaining half of the warp. Remove the dowel, straighten the loops and weave from the left of center to the right edge, and then from the right of center to the left edge. The chevrons now reverse to form a diamond in the middle of the belt. Finish the belt and press.

As you can see, the general directions which you must use for all finger-weaving patterns—that is, removing the dowel and pulling out the loops at the half-way point, making the fringe, pressing the weaving when finished—are fairly routine. As a result, from here on, these general directions will not always be repeated.

Chevron Design for Neck-Tie

After you learn to do the chevron design neatly and with an even tension, you are ready to weave a neck-tie.

Step 1: Cut 24 threads 2¼ yards long, using two colors. On the dowel arrange 12 threads of color A followed by 12 threads of color B.

Step 2: Weaving the narrow end of the tie first, make about four patterns or chevrons

exactly as you did on pages 264–265. Find the center of the warp threads and weave the A thread left of center through the shed made of color B to the right edge. Then, picking up the B thread right of center, weave to the left edge through a shed of color A.

The design, because of the color arrangement, is one of alternating rhomboid shapes.

Step 3: After you have woven four patterns, or about eight inches from the center for the neckband, measure a length of yarn of each color twice as long as the remaining unwoven threads.

Step 4: Place the middle of the matching length of yarn over and under the two right outside warp threads—the selvage threads (see Illus. 7).

Step 5: Add the matching double length of warp on the left side, looping it over and under the two selvage threads. In this way, you increase the width of the neck-tie by two warp threads at a time on each side.

Step 6: Keeping these added warps pushed up to the other warps as closely and neatly as possible, continue to weave another chevron pattern.

Step 7: Increase again, in the same way, at the end of this pattern by adding a double warp at each selvage.

Continue increasing at the end of each

pattern until you reach the desired length—which is about 24 inches from the middle. You should have increased the number of warps from 12 to 18 or 20 on each side of the lower end of the tie.

Step 8: Now, turn the work around and weave one pattern only towards the front with the original 24 warps.

Step 9: In order to make the front of the tie wider than the back, weave only one chevron pattern before starting to increase the width with two warps on each side. Then, increase in the same way at the end of each pattern and also at the middle of each pattern. You need to increase seven or eight times to end up with 26 or 28 warp ends of each color.

Step 10: Ply each two ends of warp for a short fringe at each end and trim to a V. Then, knot each ply and press.

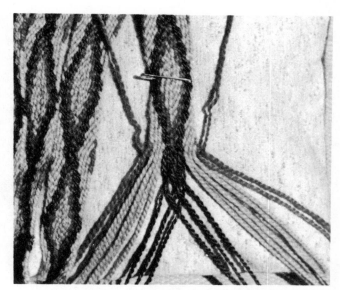

Illus. 8. This close-up of the basic diamond braid shown in color Illus. Q1 shows the crossing of the six center threads before reversing the pattern.

Diamond Design

You make the diamond design by weaving the chevron and then reversing the process by weaving from the outside to the middle.

Arrange on your dowel 24 threads 2½ yards long in three colors, using the following order: 3A 3B 12C 3B 3A. Secure to pillow.

Step 1: Find the center of the warp threads and pick up a shed of the threads to the right of the center, odd threads up. Draw the thread left of the center through the shed towards the right edge. Place it under the dowel.

Step 2: Pick up a shed from the center to the left, odd threads up, and draw the thread right of center through the shed towards the left edge. Place it under the dowel.

Step 3: Continue the chevron technique, as on pages 264–266, until the 3A warps originally on the right and the 3A warps originally on the left have reached the center. Then weave the first A thread located to the right of the center over, under and over the 3A threads to the left of the center. Then weave the next right A under, over and under the left 3A, and finally weave the last right A as you did the first. The 3A right-of-center warps should cross to the left. Without this

Illus. 7. To increase for the neck-tie shape, add a length of yarn to the outside warp threads.

crossing of the center threads, there would be a slit in the center of the work where you begin to reverse the chevron for the diamond (see Illus. 38).

Step 4: Now start to weave, using the same general procedure, but with the outside right B warp, weaving towards the center. Then weave with the outside left B warp, weaving towards the center. Continue to weave, alternating from the right and left sides towards the center, always crossing the two center threads in the same over and under pattern.

When the 12C warps are in the center again, as they were at the beginning, begin to weave from the center to the outside as for the chevron on pages 264–266.

Step 5: Alternate weaving the chevron design and the reverse to the desired length. Then turn the work around, remove the dowel and weave the second half of the belt in the same way.

NOTE: It may be more difficult to gain an even tension when weaving the reverse of the chevron—that is, when you are weaving from the outside towards the center. As with all of the other techniques, you must, therefore, examine your work frequently for necessary straightening of selvages and to tighten loose threads.

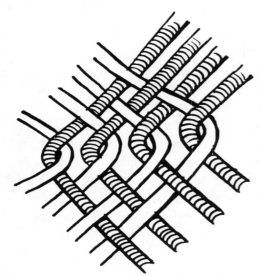

Illus. 9. Diagram of interlocking which you use in the lightning design.

Lightning Design

This design makes use of an interlocking technique. The work progresses from left to right with three colors—A, B, C—as for the diagonal design on page 262. In each row of weaving from left to right, one A thread interlocks with one B thread and this B thread interlocks with a C thread.

Step 1: Arrange on a dowel eight ends, each $2\frac{1}{2}$ yards long, of three colors in the following order: 8A 8B 8C. Place the lightest or brightest color between the two darker colors or place the darkest or brightest color between the two lighter colors.

Step 2: You create this pattern by moving the wefts from left to right. Begin with the left thread of color A. Carry it under the second left thread and then over and under succeeding threads as far as the fourth thread of color B, counting from the left. Interlock the A weft with this fourth B thread as shown in Illus. 9, returning the A color to the warp in place of the fourth B.

Step 3: Continue to weave under and over with the B thread as far as the fourth thread of color C, counting from the left. In the same way as before, interlock the B weft with the fourth thread of color C. Return the B thread to the warp to take the place of the fourth C warp thread.

Step 4: Weave with the C thread to the right selvage and you have completed one row of the pattern. After you see what is required to interlock the threads, you should learn to pick up the shed on your forefinger, interlocking the two colors as you draw the weft through the shed.

Step 5: Now, with the left A thread, weave as far as the third B thread (counting from the left), interlock and continue with the third B thread as far as the third C. Interlock these two colors—the third B and the third C—and continue with the third C thread to the right selvage.

As you weave this second row of the pattern, you must be careful to weave the first interlocked A and B warps in the proper position. That first A warp, which was interlocked in the fourth B warp position, tends to fall out of line, as does the interlocked B thread from its place where you interlocked the fourth C. Be sure to pull them into place.

Step 6: With the left A warp thread, weave as far as the second B thread, interlock and continue with the second B thread, weaving in the third and fourth A already there and on as far as the second C. Interlock the second B with the second C and continue with the second C to the right selvage.

Step 7: With the left A warp, weave as far as the first B thread, interlock and continue with the first B to the first C, weaving to the right selvage with the first C. Illus. 10 shows color A interlocked completely with color B.

Step 8: All of the colors are now in solid stripes again as they were at the beginning. Stop here to examine your work and to adjust any looseness in the weave. The warps should cover the wefts. The tension is difficult at first, but becomes more firm as you proceed. You have to adjust the interlocked threads especially to tighten the tension.

Step 9: Now repeat the interlocking of the left A with the fourth B and the fourth B with the fourth C. Next interlock the left A with the third B and the third B with the third C. As before, proceed by interlocking the left A with the second B and the second B with the second C. Then, to complete the pattern, interlock the left A with the first B and the first B with the first C. Examine and adjust the warp threads to cover the wefts.

Step 10: Weave to the desired length, leaving enough yarn at the end for a fringe.

Step 11: To make the second half, remove the dowel, turn the work around (*not over*). As you weave, the points of the design should all run in one direction.

Peruvian Rep Braid

(Multiple Wefts, Single Warps)

In this pattern, for which you learn one

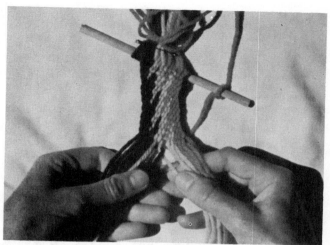

Illus. 10. This close-up shows the interlocking of the left A with the fourth B thread from the left.

Peruvian method of braiding, you will see that half of the warp threads are never used as wefts and are never covered by wefts. The result is a zig-zag design along the full length of the belt. Illus. 11 shows the ancient Peruvian technique in which the zig-zag is evident.

Illus. 11. A dramatic zig-zag design evolves when you weave a Peruvian rep braid.

Illus. 12. Draw the upper right dark weft group to the left through a shed of the remaining 8 dark and 12 light threads.

This design calls for an equal number of dark and light threads and the number must be divisible by four.

Step 1: Arrange on a dowel 24 threads 2⅓ yards long from left to right as follows: 4 dark B, 4 dark C, 4 dark B, 12 light A.

Using the left group of 4 dark B threads as one weft, weave from left to right through a shed of 8 dark single warps and the 12 light single ones. Place the weft group on the pillow parallel to the dowel on the right.

Step 2: With the 4 threads of color C at the left, weave to the right through a shed of 4 dark B threads and the 12 light A ones. Place the second weft group below and parallel to the first weft group.

Step 3: With the last left group of 4 dark color B, weave to the right through a shed of the light A warp and place this weft group below and parallel to the others on the right.

Step 4: The next step is to weave with the top B group that is on the right and next to the dowel. Pick up the shed on your left fore-finger beginning with the left light A thread, continuing through the 12 light A threads and on through 8 of the dark threads: 4 dark B, 4 dark C. Draw the top dark B group through this shed to the left (see Illus. 12). With the separated warps, pack the wefts into position.

Step 5: Next, pick up the shed beginning with the left light A thread, continuing to the right through the 12 light A threads and the 4 dark B threads. Draw the dark C group at the upper right through the shed towards the left.

Step 6: Pick up the shed beginning with the left light A thread through the 12 light A threads only. Draw the last group of dark B threads through the shed from right to left. Pack the wefts into place and adjust any loose threads.

Now all of the dark threads are on the left as they were in the beginning.

Step 7: Weave following directions in Steps 1, 2 and 3 as you did the first time through.

Continue weaving with the three dark groups from left to right. When the three dark groups are on the right again, weave from right to left as you did in Steps 4, 5 and 6.

Step 8: When you have finished the first half of the belt, remove the dowel and the string round the upper half of the warp. Pull out the loops and follow the same pattern for weaving the second half.

After you learn this technique you may wish to arrange a belt with wider light and dark bands. You could also arrange to have the dark warps zig-zag through the center of the design.

Peruvian Cross Rep Braid
(Multiple Wefts, Single Warps)

You observed for the Peruvian rep braid that you can easily cover a group of wefts woven together as one by weaving them over and under single warps. This fact is useful in making original designs. In this design, you first cross groups of threads in the middle of the braid, instead of moving them directly from one selvage to the other.

For the simplest design to weave to learn this technique, try 8 dark threads and 8 light threads—each 1⅔ yards long.

Step 1: Arrange the threads in the following order on the dowel: 4 dark threads, 8 light threads, 4 dark threads. Tie a piece of thread round the upper warp and secure it to a pillow with a safety-pin.

Step 2: Pick up the 4 left dark threads and weave under and over the left 4 light threads, placing the 4 dark threads on the left side of the center between the light threads.

Step 3: Pick up the 4 right dark threads and weave through the 4 right light threads and on through the 4 dark threads you already placed at left center. You have now made the first center cross of dark threads.

Step 4: To make the center cross of light threads, first make a shed of the 4 left light threads. You have 2 threads above and 2 threads below your left forefinger. Draw the left group of 4 dark threads through this shed to the left, leaving 4 light threads left of center.

Step 5: Do the same with the right group, making a shed with the 4 right light threads and drawing the 4 dark threads through the shed to the right.

Step 6: Now make a shed of the 4 light threads left of center and draw the 4 right light threads to the left through the shed to make a cross (see Illus. 13).

The light threads are the covering threads in this pattern and the dark groups show only at the selvage and where they cross each other in the center.

Step 7: Continue making the alternate light and dark center crosses in this manner, making the shed always with the light groups of 4 threads, except where the two dark groups cross each other in the center.

This procedure makes a narrow band suitable for trimming the neckline of a dress or blouse.

Peruvian Cross Rep with Three Colors

(Multiple Wefts, Single Warps)

For the design in Illus. 14, use 16 threads of one color and 8 threads each of two other colors. The dominant color (the one with 16 threads) is the covering color in this design. Use each thread of the dominant color singly, except when the color crosses with itself in the center.

Step 1: Arrange on a dowel 2½-yard lengths of colors A, B, C, as follows: 8A 4B 8C 4B 8A.

Illus. 13. In a two-color Peruvian cross rep braid with multiple wefts and single warps, each color crosses in the center.

Pick up a shed from the left to the center using 8A 4B 4C. Draw the right 4C threads through the shed to the left.

Step 2: Pick up a shed from the right using 8A 4B and draw the remaining 4C threads through the shed to the right. This crosses the C threads.

Step 3: Pick up a shed with the left 4C 8A

Illus. 14. This step in weaving the three-color Peruvian cross rep with multiple wefts and single warps shows the crossing of the lower small diamond (B) threads. Next, cross the A threads in the center to complete the large lozenge.

and 4B and draw the right 4B threads through the shed to the upper left.

Step 4: Pick up a shed with the right 4C 8A threads and draw the remaining 4B threads through the shed to the upper right. This makes the cross of color B.

Step 5: Pick up a shed with the 8 left color A and draw the 4 near right color A group through the shed to the left.

Step 6: Pick up the reverse shed with the same 8 left color A threads and draw the 4 right remaining color A threads through this shed to the left. You have now made the cross of 16A threads.

Step 7: Pick up a shed with the left 4C and 8A threads and weave the 4 upper left B threads through this shed to left center.

Step 8: Pick up a shed with these left 4B threads, the right 8A and 4C threads and weave the 4 upper right B threads through this shed to left center. This makes the second cross of 8B threads.

Step 9: Now there is a group of 4C threads on the upper left and the upper right sides.

Weave each C group through the respective sheds to cross in the middle. This cross of the C color makes a dot in the middle of the diamond of colors A and B.

Step 10: Before you can cross the B groups to complete the B diamond, you must weave each group of 4C threads through sheds made up of 4 color B and 8 color A threads first to the left and then to the right selvage.

Step 11: Now you can cross the B groups and weave them through the 8A groups on each side and on through the upper 4C groups (see Illus. 14).

Step 12: Cross the two right groups of 4A threads each through respective sheds of the left 8A threads, as you did above, and you have completed the lozenge. Continue this pattern to your desired length.

Study the design to learn to judge what step you are required to make to bring the succeeding color crosses to the center. You will also discover that you can create other designs using the crossing technique.

the
THING
is
the thing

**The Use of
Different Media to
Make Specific Things**

CANDLES

You can make beautiful and professional-looking candles right in your own kitchen or home work area. The techniques are easy *if* you know them, and here is your opportunity to learn.

Scenting Your Candle

You can scent your candle by stirring in a small amount (1 teaspoon of scent for every pound of wax) of candle scent to the molten wax. Many varieties are available from hobby or craft shops.

Block Candles

Block candles are any large candles made with a mould. They are fast and easy to make, and you can vary them to suit your taste. Any materials you might not have on hand are available at your hobby or craft shop where you purchase the wax and mould.

Illus. 1. Make a block candle in a mould.

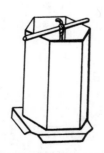

Illus. 2. A six-sided metal mould for making a block candle.

For the basic block candle you will need: a metal mould; one yard of medium-size braided cotton or wire core wicking; 5 pounds of 145°F (63°C) melting-point wax (wax is usually designated by its melting point); various colors of candle dye (solid or liquid); a candy, candle, or deep fat thermometer; a few large tin cans; a few ounces of stearic acid; a pot to hold water for heating; a large plastic or metal container a few inches higher than the candle will be; and an oven mitt.

Add 3″ of water to the pot and place it on a burner to heat. Break up a few pounds of wax and place them in the tin cans. Set the wax-filled cans in the water for melting. (With the double-boiler method, the wax will never overheat, but do watch that the water does not boil dry.)

String the wick through the bottom hole of the mould, sealing it with the small screw included in the package. Pull the wick fairly taut and wrap it around the dowel provided with the mould. Lay the dowel across the top of the mould. To further ensure that the wick is sealed at the bottom of the mould, stick a small piece of florist putty or mould sealer around the screw and wick hole.

Spray a small amount of mould release into the mould, taking care not to use too much. Test the temperature of the melted wax, and as soon as it registers 185°F (85°C), add enough dye to color the wax (about 1 cube solid dye or 1 drop liquid per pound, or more or less for special effects) and stir until the dye is dis-

Condensed from the book, "Tall Book of Candle Crafting" by Gary V. Guy | © 1973 by Sterling Publishing Co., Inc., New York

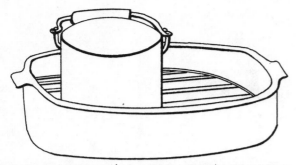

Illus. 3. You will need a large pot for holding the candles and a large container, made of either metal or plastic, to hold hot water for melting the wax.

solved. Now add 3 tablespoons of stearic acid for each pound of wax, and stir until it is dissolved.

Fill the large plastic or metal container with water, making sure there is enough water to come up to the level of the wax once the mould has been placed in the water to cool.

When the melted wax has reached a temperature of 195°F (91°C), pour it into the mould to within ½″ of the top. Pour slowly or air bubbles will be trapped in the wax. Let the mould stand for 30 seconds or so before placing it in the water bath. Take care that no water runs into the mould and if it tends to float, place a weight across the top of the mould.

As soon as the wax forms a thin film across the top, remove the mould from the water bath and place it on a level table. After an hour has passed, take a knife and puncture the wax so as to open the air pocket resulting from the shrinkage of wax within the center of the candle. Once the wax has cooled to the touch, heat more wax to 195°F (91°C). Use this wax to fill up the cavity that is caused by the wax shrinking.

Cut the wick just below the level of wax in the mould and fill the cavity with the molten wax, making sure that you do not run over the sides. Let the candle cool for six to eight hours, depending on its size. Then, remove the wick sealing screw and wick sealer (if used). Pull the wick straight so it will slide through the wick hole when you remove the candle.

Now, gently squeeze the sides of the mould. Turn the mould over and gently tap the bottom of the mould with your hand. The candle should slide out. If the candle sticks in the mould, allow it to cool for a longer period and try again. If that does not work, place the mould in the refrigerator for a half hour and you should have no trouble.

If you still have trouble, scrape the small film of wax away from the top of the mould, around the candle. Use your finger nail or a blunt object, taking care not to scratch the sides of the mould. If the candle still sticks, run hot water over the sides and bottom of the mould until the candle slides free. You should only do this when all other things fail as it mars the finish of the candle.

Trim the bottom of the candle with a knife if it is not level. Cut the wick so it is about ½″ long and, if you wish your candle to be shinier, polish the wax with an old nylon stocking.

The metal mould is made specifically for block candle-making, and is usually preferable. However, you can use milk cartons, glasses, and other suitable containers. Just make sure that the material will not be affected by the hot wax. Follow the directions for the metal mould, except for the wick. If you use a container without a hole in the bottom, use a wire core wick or attach a small bolt or metal washer to the bottom of the wick. Otherwise the wick will not be straight. Just remove the bolt after the candle is out of the mould. And remember, the wax at the bottom of the mould will be the bottom of the candle, whereas the bottom of the metal mould is the top of the candle.

Illus. 4. Block candles composed of different layers of color are very easy to make.

Layered Candles

Making layered candles is also very simple. Heat up several containers of wax, following the procedure described earlier, and color them. Then pour the first color into the mould to the desired thickness. Let this layer cool (but not completely) and then add the next color. Continue until you reach the desired size, cool, and then remove the candle.

You can achieve a variation of the layered candle by tilting the mould for each layer. Let the last layer cool in a level position so the candle will stand straight.

Glow-Through Candles

You can also make glow-through candles of solid colors. Just pour a regular candle in any shape mould, using clear wax. When you have removed the candle from the mould, hold it by the wick and dip into a colored wax heated to 190°F (88°C). Swirl the candle around to melt off any scale and rough edges. Let the candle cool a minute and dip again. Do not leave the candle in the hot wax longer than a few seconds. Repeat this process until the color coating has formed on the outside of the candle.

Sand-Cast Candles

Sand-cast candles can be symmetrical or free-form with the sand left on or removed. You can use different colors and sizes of sand to achieve a variety of effects and textures.

To make a sand-cast candle, you will need: a large container to hold the sand (if you use cardboard, line it with plastic); a quantity of sand of the desired color and size; a seamless pot (with a top) to heat the wax in; 145°F (63°C) melting-point wax; wire core wick; and stearic acid, scent, and dye.

Put the sand in the box and moisten it with water. Add enough to turn the sand dark, but not so much that it is muddy and sticky. The sand should be damp, but quite firm.

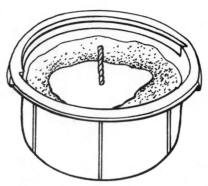

Illus. 5. Making a sand-cast candle. Moisten the sand so that it is firm enough to allow you to make a hollow in the middle into which you will pour the hot wax.

Make an impression in the sand by either digging a hole with your hands, or setting a form in the sand and packing the sand around it. Be sure to leave several inches of sand all round the form.

Now, heat the wax. Do not use the double-boiler method, however. Just put the pot itself on the stove. Let the wax heat to between 225°F (107°C) and 250°F (121°C). Wax at this temperature is very dangerous, so be very careful. Stir in the stearic acid, dye, and scent. You are now ready to pour the wax.

Hold a long spoon or knife in the middle of the hole and pour the wax over it. This prevents the wax from eroding a hole in the sand as you pour it. Fill the hole almost to the top.

Let the wax cool until it has a thick film across the surface. Take an ice pick, coat hanger, or nail and poke a wick hole into the middle of the candle. Try not to force it all the way through and out the bottom. Place the wick into this hole and make sure it is long enough to extend well above the surface of the candle. Fill the wick hole and the shrinkage with more wax.

Let the candle cool overnight before removing it from the sand. Then brush off the loose sand.

If you wish to make the sand crust thinner, simply heat the wax to a lower temperature.

Illus. 6. You can make wide, thick tapers with moulds or by hand dipping as shown in Illus. 7.

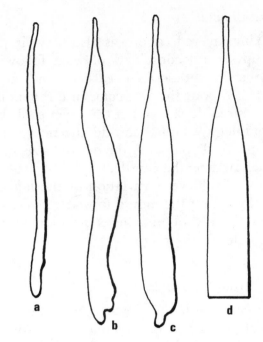

Illus. 7. Candle dipping: (*a*) the wick after it has been dipped only once in wax; (*b*) a wick dipped several times, but the candle is still soft and shapeless; (*c*) the candle has been straightened; (*d*) it has been cut into shape at the bottom with a heated knife.

Taper Candles

You can make tapers—either fat and short or long and thin—with moulds or by hand dipping. For most tapers use either 135°F (58°C) or 145°F (63°C) melting-point wax. You will also need stearic acid, and dye and scent if desired. Use cotton or braided wicks.

Dipping tapers is a slow, but rewarding, process. The container size you use for the dip tank depends on how many tapers you wish to dip at once. You can start by making two at a time, using a long wick held in the middle.

The secret of dipping tapers is keeping the temperature of the wax about 10°F (6°C) over the melting point of the wax used as a dip. Each time you dip the wick into the wax, you want the maximum amount of wax to build up on them. If the wax is too cool, it will scum over and the taper will have bubbles on it. If it is too hot, no wax will build up on the wick.

Each layer of the taper must cool before you dip the next layer. To cool the tapers, either let the tapers air-cool or dip them in water after each dip in the wax. If you dip the tapers in water, wipe any excess water away between dips.

Make sure your wax container is deep enough to accommodate the length of the wick. If you use the water-cooling method, place the bucket close by, and if you use the air-cooling method, have something handy that you can hang the wick over between dips.

Test the temperature of the wax to see that it is right. Use a clear wax to make the bulk of the dip and make the last four or five coats the color of your choice. Trim the end of the taper with a heated knife if you want to shorten it or make it even.

Painting Your Candle

The simplest way to paint candles is with melted wax. Use 135°F (58°C) melting-point wax and double or triple the amount of dye that you melt into the wax. Heat the wax using the double-boiler method. It does not need to be very hot. Then simply brush on the wax.

Illus. 8. If you want to decorate your candles, "paint" them with melted wax of different colors.

COLLAGES

If you have ever made a valentine of paper hearts and lace, pasted mementos in a scrapbook, or decorated furniture with flowers cut from magazines, you have made a collage. There is nothing really new about collage. It is a pasting medium as old as folk art and as modern as the 20th century. It can be as simple as the valentine you made or as complex as the most intricate work of art. In fact, collage can be just about anything you care to make it.

One of the many attractions of collage is the lack of expensive materials involved. Basically, all you need for collage are paste, any object that can be pasted, and an appropriate backing material, which can be anything from a cardboard shirt backing to a lamp shade.

Look around you for your materials. They are everywhere—in your wastebasket, in a used-book shop, and in your storeroom, basement, or attic. The Christmas wrapping paper you might have thrown away, an old piece of lace from your grandmother's trunk, old shoelaces, the ticket stubs from last night's movie, an outdated calendar—you can use all of these in a new way.

You can make your own collage materials or use the discarded fragments of your world to create a collage of purely abstract beauty, a collage that tells a story, or with your own photos, a bit of personal history. With cutouts from newspapers, you can re-create a chapter of world history. With old letters,

scraps of ribbon and old lace, you can evoke a mood of Victorian nostalgia. You can "paint" a still-life collage, a landscape, or a modern geometric design with paper or fabrics.

The only problems you may ever have in making a collage are how to start and when to stop.

Making Paper Collages

Paper is the classic collage material and, possibly, the one you will use most often. There are so many papers available to the collagist, ranging from discarded grocery bags to elegant Japanese rice papers, that it is sometimes a dizzying prospect to make a selection.

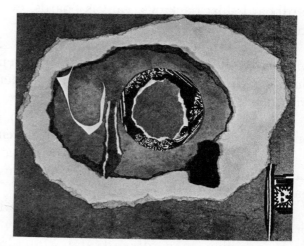

Illus. 1. A white illustration board is the backing for this simple collage of torn, mottled (see page 287) paper shapes. Small pieces of wallpaper cut-outs provide interest.

Condensed from the book, "Ideas for Collage" by Joan B. Priolo | © *1972 by Sterling Publishing Co., Inc., New York*

Make a simple paper collage as an experiment.

The first thing to consider when starting is size. It is best to start small—probably no larger than 9″ × 12″—until you become more familiar with the technique.

Next, choose a backing. There are many suitable backings on which to paste your collage. Almost any fairly stiff cardboard will do. You can use the cardboard backs of drawing pads, illustration boards, mat boards, cardboard shirt backings, canvas boards, even stretched canvases.

One of the most satisfactory backings is Masonite. It is heavy enough to prevent buckling which sometimes occurs with lighter-weight boards.

If you want a white background, which is only necessary if you are using transparent paper or plan to leave white areas showing, you can brush several coats of white vinyl house paint on the front of the board.

Gesso boards are Masonite boards already prepared with a white gesso ground.

(In addition to cardboard and Masonite, after you have made a few experimental collages, try lamp shades, boxes, furniture— even walls—for your collages.)

Then choose your basic background paper— newspaper, wallpaper, tissue paper, gift paper, rice paper, etc. Start experimenting, without pasting down, by working with cut or torn pieces of construction paper* which approximate the size, shape and color of your final elements. You need not select the final paper materials until you are satisfied with the arrangement. The pieces of construction paper will undoubtedly suggest many items when you see them in place—flowers, bottle labels, letters, photos—anything that comes into your mind.

It is not a good idea to use construction paper in a final collage because of the fading-color problem.

A word here about tearing, since you will be doing a lot of it. Depending upon the kind of paper that you choose to work with, you will find that the paper tears more easily in one direction. All paper—even cellophane—has a grain just as does wood.

In most papers it is very difficult to detect the grain by eye, so you should practice on various papers to determine which way the grain runs. Take a sheet of newspaper and try

*Cut or torn pieces of colored tissue paper may be used as well as construction paper.

Illus. 3. A background of mottled paper is divided into two areas by a torn paper of darker color, suggesting a landscape. Notice the white linear edge made by tearing the paper after it was colored.

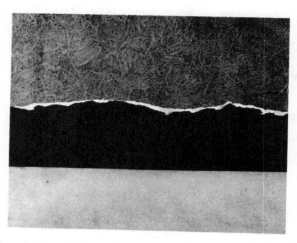

Illus. 4. The addition of a cut strip of light-colored paper to the divided background of Illus. 6 suggests a seascape.

tearing it, first up and down, and then across. You will find one direction tears in a straight line—this is the direction of the grain. Tear in the other direction and you find the paper tears any which way.

On many occasions, you will find torn papers produce more exciting results than cut papers. After practicing, you will also discover you can control the tearing process to create the kinds of shapes you want. Experimental tearing against the grain might result in fascinating forms you could never achieve by careful planning and cutting.

Unless you have a clear idea in mind, it sometimes helps to get started by dividing your selected background into two or more areas. Try placing a torn or cut paper over one third of the background, either vertically or horizontally (Illus. 3). This will give you the beginning of a structure on which to build and may suggest a landscape or other images to you.

Now, using your pieces of construction paper which you can either tear at random before you begin or as you go along, start shifting them around on the background paper. Keep it

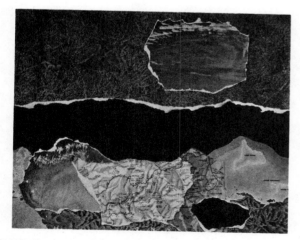

Illus. 5. If you paste torn pieces of maps on the background of Illus. 3, you can carry out the landscape idea in a semi-abstract manner.

Illus. 6. The seascape theme in Illus. 4 is made more realistic by adding cut-outs of sea vegetation from a nature book and pieces of bleach-spotted tissue paper.

Illus. 7. Diluted white glue is brushed on the back of a photograph of roses, cut from a magazine.

simple, and shift and shuffle until you are satisfied.

From here on, it is simply a matter of building by addition and subtraction. Don't overlook subtraction! It is an important factor in the making of a collage. Take away shapes and colors that aren't working and try something different. Since you don't have to paste anything down until you are satisfied, you are free to try anything.

Sometimes, you may find that when placing and shifting the papers, they do not lie flat and cause shadows and other distractions. A few straight pins or coins will temporarily hold down unruly edges so you can see what you are doing.

Once you are happy with the composition, make a rough cartoon of it. Number your pieces of construction paper and place corresponding numbers on your cartoon. Assemble your final paper elements and you can paste if you want.

The most popular pasting medium is white glue, or casein glue, commercially called Elmer's glue. It will paste down plastic, paper, board, foil—almost anything.

When pasting paper, white glue should be diluted with water to the consistency of milk. If it is too thick, it tends to dry too fast and make positioning your paper difficult. Simply brush

the diluted glue (using an inexpensive brush) on the back of the paper to be pasted down and also on the surface to which the paper is to be pasted.

When you have positioned your paper, smooth it with your hands from top to bottom and side to side to eliminate air bubbles and prevent wrinkling. Often, when using very large pieces of paper, some wrinkling is unavoidable. If this occurs, you can weight your collage when it is finished. In most cases, this will flatten out any wrinkles or air bubbles.

However, if you are planning to paste additional paper over the wrinkled paper, it is a good idea to weight the wrinkled areas of the collage for between half an hour and an hour before proceeding with more pasting. If you choose to weight as you go along, simply leave the collage face up, place waxed paper over the surface and then place cardboard, with weights, on top. *Don't forget the waxed paper* because, at this stage, there is the chance that there are some spots of still-tacky glue that will need the protection of waxed paper. You could wind up with an unexpected and permanent addition to your collage—a second cardboard!

Glue that comes in a spray can is more expensive than white glue, but it is less messy and cuts pasting time in half because you need to spray only one surface with glue. It also

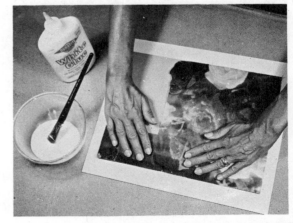

Illus. 8. The paper is pasted down and smoothed from side to side with both hands to prevent wrinkling.

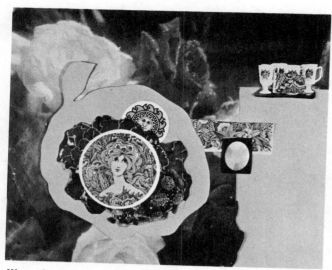

Illus. 9. Other pieces of paper, cut from magazines, are pasted over the background of roses to complete the collage.

eliminates most wrinkle problems, even with large pieces of paper.

To help prevent buckling of the lighter-weight background boards, especially when using diluted white glue, saturate the back of the board with water before you start pasting. This will help to stabilize the stress on the board. This step is seldom necessary when using spray-can glue because this glue does not soak the board enough to cause much stress.

Another type of glue often used in collage work is an acrylic painting medium which is used primarily to thin acrylic paints. However, it makes a satisfactory glue and is used in the same manner as white glue. The advantage of this glue is that, as you paste, you can brush the glue over the surface of the papers and in this way build up layers of a waxy varnish, giving depth and protection to your finished collage.

While in most cases (except when working with tissue paper) you will probably not paste the collage down until the final stage in planning, there are times when it is beneficial to work quickly and paste as you go. It is a good way to force decisions when artistic paralysis has set in. This condition is caused by too much indecisive staring. When this happens, pasting something down sometimes gets you

and the collage moving again. Although you can't remove the pasted paper, you can usually paste other papers on top to block out unsuccessful areas.

Collage is a flexible craft, and very few decisions are irrevocable. There is almost always something that can be done to rescue a collage.

When is a collage completed? Only you will know when to stop. You may experience the feeling of elation that comes when everything seems to fall magically into place and you know you have finished a good piece of work. However, you may reach a point just short of completion where something seems amiss, but you don't know why or what to do about it. If you aren't sure what is needed, put the collage away. A few days' time will give you a new perspective and you may be able to spot just what is needed to bring the collage to completion, or you may even decide to give up the whole thing. In any case, give yourself and the collage a trial separation before you decide.

Wallpaper Collages

Wallpaper is one of the most decorative of collage papers. For this reason, it should be

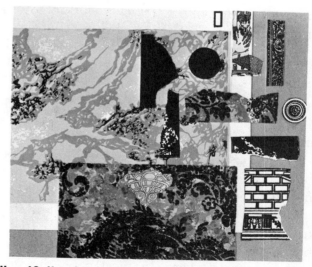

Illus. 10. Here is a variety of pieces cut from patterned wallpapers. For one idea of putting them together, see Illus. 11.

Illus. 11. This is a possible arrangement of the materials in Illus. 10 to create a wallpaper collage of patterned papers.

used with some restraint or your creation may end up looking like an attractive wall! Generally, it is a good idea to use wallpaper in combination with other papers. Areas of colored tissue paper, bottle labels, hand-colored papers or newspaper can help keep the wallpaper under control.

Collages with a Victorian aura can be made by combining old-fashioned flowered wallpaper with paper lace, old photos and bits of ribbon. Textured wallpaper can add areas of interest, while bolder elements can be cut out from modern wallpaper for striking contrasts.

However, there are no hard-and-fast rules in collage and it could be a real challenge to make a collage entirely from wallpaper. Moreover, it is a good visual exercise to see how well you can arrange decorative, patterned papers into a unified collage.

When pasting wallpaper, white glue is good, but, with some of the heavier papers, you may find the spray-can glue more satisfactory.

You should have no difficulty in obtaining, free of charge, enough wallpaper to paper a house if you go to your local wallpaper store and ask for leftovers. In most cases the store will be happy to get rid of remnants or discontinued pieces and rolls of wallpaper.

Collage with Books and Magazines

The literary world is one of the richest sources of collage material. Browse around in used-book shops whenever you have a chance. You will come across wonderful old prints of birds, mechanical diagrams, old books with odd, old-fashioned illustrations and, often, beautiful lettering. Nature books and old encyclopedias are full of drawings and photos of birds, fish, shells, plants and flowers. You will also find many, many, old, fully illustrated children's books. If you are very lucky, you may come across old sheet music—both the covers and the music itself would make rare additions to a collage. Thrift shops and junk shops are other treasure troves of old paper materials.

If you have a worn-out atlas, look at the maps with their complex traceries. Historical maps are particularly interesting with their colored-in areas. You might also save your old road maps and combine them with pictures from travel brochures to create a collage of vacation memories.

Scientific magazines hold a world of surprises. Intricate diagrams, graphs, arrows and precise drawings can be used to make collages of pristine elegance.

Illus. 12. Here is the beginning of a collage using illustrations and diagrams from a nature book. First, three diagrams are pasted onto a background of mottled paper (page 287).

Illus. 13. Then, a large piece of torn black paper simulating a mountain and a small black rectangle are added.

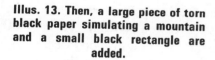

Illus. 14. A global illustration is pasted over the black area. For the finished collage, see Illus. 15.

Illus. 15. The finished collage shows the addition of two more diagrams and a torn, circular shape. Notice the arrows which add interest and movement.

The contemporary slick magazines with their sophisticated illustrations and advertisements contain endless collage elements. Here you will also find interesting lettering. Letters can be as effective as abstract patterns or as words to convey a message.

Do not forget seed catalogues as a source of flower photos, as well as mail-order house catalogues, which are also very colorful.

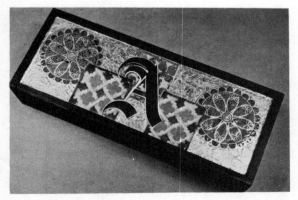

Illus. 16. The top of this jewelry box "for Ann" is collaged with a background of crumpled gold paper over which are pasted gift paper cut-outs and a large letter A.

Make Your Own Collage Papers

Once you have worked with a variety of ready-made papers, you will, on occasion, want to obtain special effects by making your own collage papers.

Colored tissue paper, because of its bleeding properties, lends itself perfectly to special effects. One way to obtain an interesting result is to drop water with an eyedropper or brush on the tissue paper. The water will take off some of the color, leaving soft areas of lighter color. If you substitute liquid bleach for water, the areas will be white. You can leave the bleached areas white or tint them with water colors or acrylic colors.

Almost any white paper can be used for coloring purposes: drawing paper, charcoal paper, water-color paper. It depends on the weight you require. For small areas, light-weight paper is satisfactory, but for very large areas, it is best to use heavier paper. Large pieces of thin, light-weight paper are difficult to paste down. They tend to exhibit a contrariness of spirit and flap about doing their own thing. Tissue paper is an exception since you can anchor it immediately by brushing white glue directly onto the surface.

To color your collage papers you can use water colors, acrylic colors, oil pastels, wax crayons, and even tea, coffee, frozen orange juice concentrate, or grape juice.

Probably one of the simplest coloring methods, and one that works well for backgrounds, is to give your paper a wash of color. Wet the paper thoroughly with a sponge or brush. While the paper is still wet, load a brush with water color or acrylic color and paint into the wet paper. If your paper is well saturated with water, the paint will spread into uneven, feathered areas. Be sure to put enough color on your brush since the water will dissipate the color somewhat. This is effective as a background for further collage or as a means of coloring small pieces of paper. Colored pastel or charcoal paper makes a good background

Illus. 18. The first step in mottling paper is to brush on a wash of color. Here, acrylic color is being used.

when treated with a wash of a contrasting color.

For a mottled paper, paint the entire paper surface with a color, let it dry a few seconds, and then blot the paper gently and evenly with a facial tissue. You can take this a step further and use two colors to obtain a luminous effect. For example, if a violet color is desired, mottle

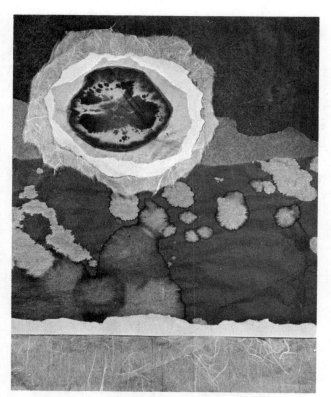

Illus. 17. An ethereal collage made with water-spotted blue tissue paper. The roundish shape at the top is torn from translucent, white rice paper with an inner circle of white pastel paper and an accidentally stained piece of blue tissue. The bottom strips are torn from rice paper and pastel paper.

Illus. 19. After the color has dried for a few seconds, gently blot it with a facial tissue to produce the mottled effect.

the paper with a blue color. When the mottled blue has completely dried, go over it with a wash of crimson and you should have a luminous violet color. To darken or tone down a color, use black as the first color, blot it, let it dry and wash a clear color over it. Do some experimenting with this technique. By combining color with color or black with color you will discover a new range of colors. It is possible to "paint" a collage by using mottled papers without other collage elements.

Torn edges give still another dimension to this technique because, by tearing the paper before mottling, the color sinks into the torn edge and gives an almost linear dark edge to the shape. If you tear the paper after coloring, you will have a white linear edge. (See Illus. 3.)

Another way to texture paper is to crumple a piece of white paper, smooth it out and wash a color over it. The color will sink into the creases, leaving a pattern of fine lines. For a softer texture, saturate the paper with water before coloring.

Keep your eyes open for paper that has been accidentally textured or colored. Take a

Illus. 21. To make smoked and burned areas, saturate a piece of paper with water. Then hold it over a candle flame. It is safest to do this in a sink.

Illus. 22. Small pieces are cut from smoked paper and from a magazine to be used in the collage in Illus. 23.

Illus. 23. The materials in this collage are arranged and pasted on a background of creased paper to create a "cityscape."

second look at the paper with a coffee or tea stain on it. A used sheet from a paper palette often has fascinating areas of dried color that can be incorporated into a collage. A piece of black tissue paper that landed, wet, on blue tissue paper can leave a stain to delight the heart of any collagist.

Wax crayons or oil pastels can give your paper a patchy, cross hatched texture. It is best to use at least two colors with this method. Scribble over the entire paper with one color. Then scribble in the opposite direction with a

second color. Since some of the paper will show through, try scribbling on colored construction or pastel paper for a three-color effect.

You can make interesting collage paper by smoking or burning the paper. Saturate the paper with water and pass it over a candle flame, but not too close. This will create smoked areas, or, if you hold the paper closer to the flame, burned holes. Be sure to do this in or near a sink or you may create some startling and undesired effects!

Finishing Your Paper Collage

If, when you have finished your paper collage, you find that it has buckled, as is sometimes the case with light-weight backings, you can weight it.

Place the completed collage face down on clean newspaper, making sure that the glue is dry. As an added precaution against sticking, place waxed paper between the surface of the collage and the newspapers. Then place more newspapers on the back of the collage. Wet the newspapers with water, using a sponge or brush. On top of the wet newspapers place a piece of cardboard, Masonite or even an unsuccessful collage (it does happen) the same size or larger than your collage. Then pile anything heavy, such as large books, on top of the board. Leave the weighted collage at least overnight.

Illus. 24. Cut and torn pieces of gift paper and black paper are pasted on a background of colored pastel paper cross-hatched with oil paste.

Illus. 25. "Misery, Charlie C." by Katy Meigs. In this delicate collage, an old letter, sealing wax, and a piece of tulle are combined with hand-colored tissue paper and water-color paper.

By morning you should have a nice, flat collage. The weighting should also take care of any wrinkles or air bubbles that might have occurred while pasting.

You undoubtedly will want a protective finish for your collage. Glass is, of course, an obvious solution. If the collage is fairly small it can be glassed with no problem. With very large collages (30″ or more), some expense is involved along with a weight problem. In these cases, try some of the acrylic varnishes available at your art shop. They are easy to brush on and will give your collage a glossy or matt finish. If you have used an acrylic painting medium as your glue, you probably have built up enough layers of a protective varnish already. There are also lacquer sprays available that will protect your collage.

Illus. 26. Velvet, calico, flowered fabric, lace flowers, and ribbon are some of the many fabrics that you can use in a collage. For one idea, see Illus. 27.

Illus. 27. A simple, but elegant collage is created with the fabrics in Illus. 26. Cut-out paper flowers and a paper butterfly are added to the velvet circle for a change of texture.

Illus. 28. Gauze bandaging material gives an interesting texture to this collage of small pieces of hand-colored papers pasted on a wash background.

Every kind of paper, as you will find out for yourself by trial-and-error, must be handled according to its own characteristics. For instance, yellowing of paper is caused by acid in the fibres. Some papers are more highly acid and will yellow more quickly than others. Some papers are affected by skin oil and will eventually discolor where overhandled. Take care of your paper productions by avoiding overexposure to heat, moisture or sunlight.

Collage with Fabrics

You will find cloth fabrics a fascinating source of color and texture for collage. Cloth has a distinctive and personal quality quite unlike paper, perhaps due to the fact that we use cloth in such a personal way in our clothes and homes.

Each cloth fabric conjures up an image.

Velvet becomes elegance, old lace evokes nostalgia, torn burlap or sackcloth is a sad story, flowered chintz becomes a sunny morning—each fabric has its own character.

Every type of fabric can be used for collage, from old paint rags to a child's hair ribbon. Look in your closets, sewing drawers, and go to thrift shops for odds and ends of fabric. Make a collage entirely from scraps of cloth or cut-out elements from a patterned fabric and combine them with paper. You will find that the addition of cloth elements gives another dimension to a paper collage. You can cut cloth, tear it, crumple it, paint it or drape it.

Because fabrics are not as stiff as paper, you will find it easier to paste them with spray-can glue rather than white glue. Masonite is probably the most satisfactory backing for fabric collages.

CREATIVE GIFTS

Home-made gifts are great fun to make and a pleasure to receive. You show your thoughtfulness by spending time and effort to make something with your own hands. The following gift items use simple and inexpensive materials, can be made by a child, and would please any adult.

For example, for your mother, a friend, or anyone who has jewelry that she likes to organize and display, any of the jewelry organizers would make a perfect gift.

Jewel Nest

Pick out a ring or pin to wear with a flick of this jewel twirler. Cut a short length from a waxed-paper tube. Glue a covering of velvet firmly round the tube. Cut slits through the velvet and the tube lengthwise at $\frac{1}{2}''$ intervals. Glue circles of cardboard at each end of the tube, and place it in a box. Insert a nail through each end of the box into the ends of the tube so that it can turn. Cuff links, rings, earrings and pins can be inserted by the lucky recipient.

Illus. 2. Bracelet bar.

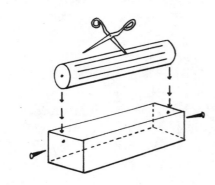

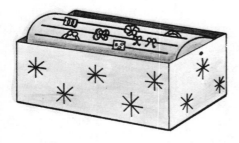

Illus. 1. Jewel nest.

Bracelet Bar

Make this lovely bracelet bar which displays an armful of jewelry and keeps it from being misplaced. This gift is especially good for someone who can never find her watch. Simply glue a velvet-sheathed cardboard tube to a square of wood painted brightly and sprinkled with gold dust or colored glitter.

Condensed from the books, "Creating from Scrap" by Lillian and Godfrey Frankel | © 1962 by Sterling Publishing Co., Inc., New York, "Gadgets and Gifts for Girls to Make" by Sheila Ostrander | © 1962 by Sterling Publishing Co., Inc., New York, and "Nick-Nacks for Neatness" by Sheila Ostrander | © 1963 by Sterling Publishing Co., Inc., New York

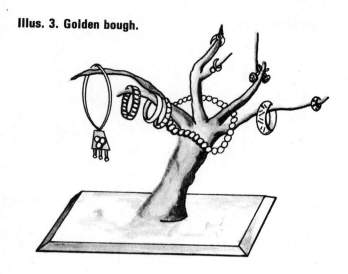

Golden Bough

This golden bough, an elegant and distinctive gift, is a lovely setting for all types of jewelry. Gild (paint gold) a small branch of driftwood. Use household cement to glue the branch to a mirror or tray base. Cover the bottom of the mirror with felt to prevent scratching. Show off necklaces, rings, beads and pendants on this glittering gadget.

Sweater Dryer

Does a friend have trouble drying sweaters on the floor because pets step on them or they get in the way of family activities? This gift may make everyone's life a little easier.

Cover a large piece of cardboard with oilcloth or plastic. Place two extra long lengths of string diagonally across the cardboard and staple them firmly to each corner. Attach a hook and sweaters can be hung up to dry on a clothes-line or shower rod.

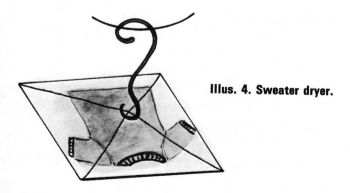

Illus. 4. Sweater dryer.

Sweater Link

Like to throw your sweater over your shoulders, but worry about its slipping off? Make this charming sweater link for yourself or a friend. Glue two small safety clasps or safety-pins to the back of two shiny new coins. Attach one coin to each end of a discarded locket or key chain and link up a sweater.

Illus. 5. Sweater link.

Pencil Sharpener

With this pencil-shaving-holder, you can save a busy person the time and trouble of running to a wastebasket everytime he or she sharpens a pencil. Remove the lid from a glass jar and punch a hole in it large enough for a pencil to go through. With household cement, carefully glue your pencil sharpener over the hole in the lid so that it will be on the inside of the jar. Screw the lid on the jar and it's ready for sharpening.

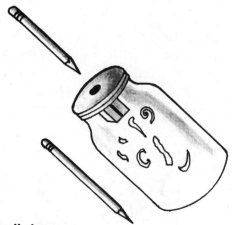

Illus. 6. Pencil sharpener.

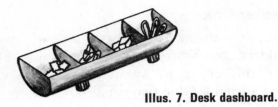

Illus. 7. Desk dashboard.

Desk Dashboard

Help your friends organize their messy desks. Everytime they open their drawer and find their supplies neatly laid out, they'll thank you. Halve a waxed-paper tube, divide it into compartments, glue toothpaste tube caps to the bottom to prevent rolling. Paint, and then slide in supplies—stamps, clips, erasers, elastic bands, etc.

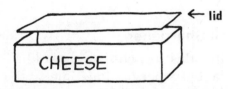

Illus. 8. Turn a cheese box into a periscope!

Periscope

You can make a working periscope that will give you or a friend many hours of pleasure from these simple materials: a long wooden cheese box or cardboard box (with the lid attached), two small mirrors from old pocketbooks or compacts, and a block of wood about $2'' \times 2'' \times 2''$.

Remove the cover of the box, but save it. Saw the block of wood in half diagonally (see Illus. 9). Glue one half of the block into one corner of the box and glue the mirror to it so the mirror rests at a 45-degree angle (see Illus. 10).

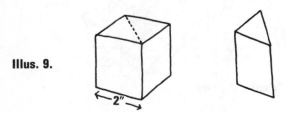

Illus. 9.

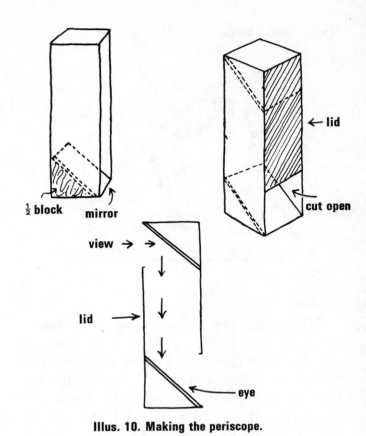

Illus. 10. Making the periscope.

Now cut 2″ off one end of the lid and put it back on. Glue it if necessary to keep it in place.

Turn the box around and cut away a 2″ section of the bottom of the box at the opposite end from the mirror. Now glue the other half of the block into place and glue the second mirror to it. This mirror faces in the opposite direction from the first mirror.

Your periscope is now ready to use.

Sponge Painting

Save those worn-out kitchen sponges! Their texture makes them interesting to paint with. Clean and dry a sponge and then soak it lightly in water colors or enamel paint. Squeeze out the excess paint.

Press the sponge lightly on paper to make imprints in an over-all design. You may want to plan your design first and mark it in pencil. If you have several sponges, use one for each color. You can overlap the sponge prints or leave space in between.

Paint familiar objects such as animals, houses or boats to hang on the wall. Or, paint free abstract forms and designs and use the paper to line your desk drawer after the paint dries. Sponge paintings also make unique gifts.

Illus. 11. A sponge painting.

Illus. 12. A real cracker barrel.

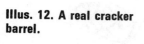

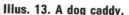
Illus. 13. A dog caddy.

Cracker Barrel

Make a gift with an edible theme. A clever conversation piece for parties or gatherings is a genuine cracker barrel made from a circular cardboard carton. Arrange several crackers, cookies or potato chips in the form of flowers and glue them on the outside of the container. Paint on stems and leaves and then varnish the holder.

Dog Caddy

Surprise the family dog by making him his own dog caddy for a wall or closet door. Cut a fairly large rectangle of cardboard and tack onto it pockets of heavy cloth for your dog's collar, leash, comb and other belongings. Personalize it with your dog's signature by dipping his paw in ink and pressing it onto the cardboard. Be sure you wash the remaining ink off his paw.

Garden Apron

For the gardening hobbyist, cut out the front of an old pair of slacks or blue jeans and lop off the legs just below the knees. Thread an apron tie through the loops at the waistband and stitch a plastic bag containing a sponge to each knee to make kneeling easier. Attach roomy patch-pockets for garden tools. Now make one of the following garden gifts to accompany the garden apron.

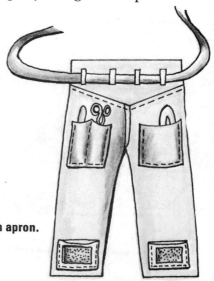

Illus. 14. Garden apron.

Illus. 15. Eggshell planter.

Easy Eggshell Planter

Get a head start on gardening this year. Start your seedlings indoors in eggshells, while it is still cold outside. By the time it is warm enough for outdoor planting, your plants will be a good size.

Save up a dozen empty eggshells in an egg carton. Just save the larger part of the shells. Fill the shells with dirt, place a seed in each shell and cover with more dirt. Water daily.

After a few days, depending on the seed you planted, a little shoot will emerge. When your plant is several inches tall, either give the seedlings to a friend who loves flowers, or prepare to transfer them. The weather should be warm enough to plant your seedlings in the ground outside. Just poke a few holes in the bottom of the shells and plant them, eggshells and all! This is a quick and easy way to transplant seedlings without disturbing them. Try it!

Illus. 16. Landscape in a box.

Landscape in a Box

For this garden project, all you need are some scraps: a cigar box, some wallpaper and a color picture. Also, have some soil, stones, twigs, plants, paste, string, and toothpicks on hand.

Select a real-looking landscape painting from a magazine and paste it to the inside lid of a cigar box and along the upper part of the inside back of the box itself. Hold the lid open until the paper hinge sticks.

Cut wallpaper pieces to fit the outside of the box, sides and front, and paste them down smoothly. Place some tiny potted plants in the box. Fill the rest of the box with earth, interesting stones and small twigs. Plant a little grass seed in the earth. You can add sea shells if you have any. Make a trellis or fence of string and toothpicks. This is your miniature garden landscape!

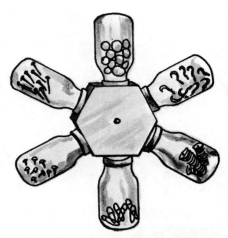

Illus. 17. Make a tidy-up pinwheel to keep track of all your gift-making materials.

Tidy-Up Pinwheel

This pinwheel will help anyone tidy up. Cut a piece of one-inch board into a hexagon, with each of the six sides about two inches long. To each side nail a jar lid. Nail this pinwheel to a bulletin board or a closet door with a large nail. Fill the jars with odds and ends such as safety-pins, tacks, string and sewing supplies. When you want a particular item, spin the wheel.

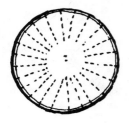

Illus. 18. Cut slits in a pot-pie tin to make aluminum flowers.

Aluminum Flowers

You can make a silvery flower garden from aluminum plates and dishes. Small pot-pie tins are especially easy to work with, since they are already round and easy to cut and shape. To make a flower head, cut slits from the edge almost to the center, leaving about a 1½″-circle. Curl each strip to give the flower a fringed effect. Make stems from the outer reinforced rims of larger pans. Cut the flat parts of these larger pans into leaf shapes.

Make two little holes in the head of the flower and poke one end of a stem in one hole and out the other to attach the flower. Twist one end of a leaf round the stem and you have a complete flower.

Make many different kinds of flowers. You can double some of them by using two pie plates. You can twist the petals into different shapes, and cut them in different sizes. When you have enough flowers, cover a small can with foil. Fill it with sand and place your flowers in it for a silvery bouquet—and a sparkling gift item.

Crystal Garden

Believe it or not, you can grow a pretty crystal garden on a piece of brick! All you need is a piece of brick (an old chipped one will do), common table salt, liquid blueing, household ammonia, and ink or food coloring.

First put the brick in a low dish. Now mix 6 tablespoons each of salt, liquid blueing, and household ammonia. Pour this mixture over the brick and put a few drops of blue or red ink or food coloring into the dish. This adds color to the crystals when they begin to form.

In 15 or 20 minutes you will notice little

Illus. 19. Crystal garden.

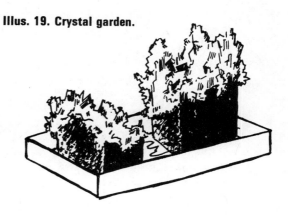

crystals forming all over the brick and around the rim of the dish. To keep your crystal garden blooming, just add a teaspoon of ammonia every week. See how long you can keep your garden growing.

Some of the ideas you have been given in this section should open your eyes and stimulate your mind to create other thoughtful gifts from ready-to-be discarded scraps and other simple household goods. From here, you are on your own—you may never buy a gift again!

DECORATIVE MASKS

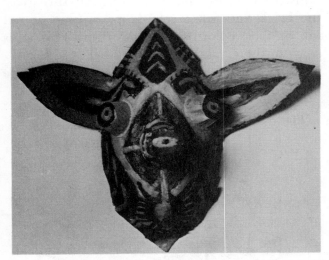

Illus. 1. A melted-crayon mask made over a papier-maché base (see page 151).

Masks can be traced back to the prehistoric cave men who had very little defence against wild beasts, storms, fire and thunder. These natural enemies were thought to be governed by evil spirits, so men made frightening masks to resist the spirits and guarantee them freedom from danger and success in hunting. The more shocking the mask, the stronger was their power to resist.

For centuries, all over the world, masks have been made of all kinds of materials. The Greeks and the ancient Peruvian Indians even used terra cotta. The Chinese and Tibetans preferred papier mâché, cloth, and copper, while the Japanese specialized in heavy metal masks. Today, in the southwest United States, Indians make masks from leather. And wood has always been a popular material throughout most of the world.

We all know it is fun to wear masks, but do you know how much fun it is to *make* them and use them for decorative purposes? Most of the masks that are available in variety shops are the old, cut-and-dried stand-bys that children wear at Halloween parties or adults wear at masquerade parties, and masks intended for decoration, such as those from Africa, Mexico or the Far East, tend to be expensive. It is surprisingly easy to make your own interesting and original masks, and far more satisfying than buying one.

Before we begin our discussion of the techniques of mask-making, however, a word of caution is in order. These masks are all intended for decoration only. None of the masks have holes for breathing. Also, be especially careful in the construction and handling of masks made from sheet metal and pie-tins, for the cut edges are quite sharp and jagged.

Illus. 2. The papier-maché mask is painted with melted crayons.

Condensed from the book, "Monster Masks" by Chester Jay Alkema | © 1973 by Sterling Publishing Co., Inc., New York

Melted-Crayon Masks

The gruesome beast in Illus. 1 is composed of scrap crayons. All those little butts and stumps that are usually thrown away can be put to good use in your mask-making. Painting with melted wax is an ancient practice and creates stunning effects. You can melt your wax crayons in an electric palette made just for that purpose (Illus. 2), or place crayons of the same colors in small juice cans and set them in a pan of boiling water until the wax is melted. Then, while you are working, place the cans in an electric frying pan turned to a low temperature.

The completed monster in Illus. 1 was painted in black and red with a $\frac{1}{2}$-inch wide bristle brush on a papier mâché mask which was constructed over a bowl. This method requires pasting four layers of newspaper together and moulding them over a bowl. Set the bowl with the paste-soaked paper aside to dry overnight. When completely hard, you can start decorating it. Don't attempt to wear this kind of mask—it's strictly for decoration.

Illus. 3. Making a tin-foil bas-relief mask.

Tin-Foil Bas-Relief Masks

A three-dimensional tin-foil mask can easily be constructed on a tagboard base. Although you can use a variety of materials to form the bas-relief effect, pieces of cut clothesline were used in Illus. 3. Glue the pieces of cord on the

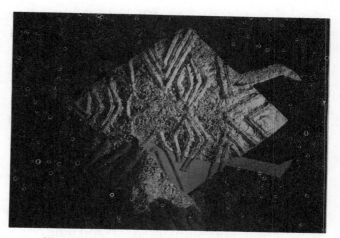

Illus. 4. Pressing foil into low areas of design.

tagboard upon which you have sketched a design.

Since the effect of the tin-foil will be striking in itself, choose a simple shape such as the diamond in Illus. 3. Cut a piece of tin-foil somewhat larger than the piece of tagboard. Then crumple it up carefully and smooth it

Illus. 5. An application of India ink creates an eerie effect.

out again. Using white (Elmer's) glue, smear the areas between the pieces of clothesline, and then lay the foil on top. Very gently, using your finger-tips, press the foil into the low areas of the design (Illus. 4).

If you find it too difficult to work with one piece of foil, tear or cut the foil into several pieces. The finished uneven surface will cover the telltale joined edges.

In Illus. 5, the finished mask has had an application of black India ink painted into the low areas of the foil. By leaving the raised areas shiny and unpainted, a splendid eerie effect is achieved. If you do this, make sure you lay the foil on the base with the dull side up, as the ink will cover more effectively if you do. If necessary, rub the foil lightly with steel wool before applying the ink.

Illus. 7. A tooled aluminum mask.

Illus. 6. A variety of aluminum containers went into the making of this fellow.

Aluminum Masks

Aluminum is so abundant we take it for granted and, without thinking, toss out all of those empty pot-pie plates, TV dinner trays, and so on, never realizing how useful they can be. Easily cut with heavy shears, available in all shapes and sizes, they are ideal for decorative mask creations.

The deceptively innocent little fiend in Illus. 6 has a coffee-cake-container face with four pie-rim whiskers attached with brass paper fasteners. The flat parts of pie plates were cut to form the out-sized ears and pointed horns, while a piece of aluminum inserted into slits in the face serves as a nose. Black yarn, glued on, emphasizes the outlandish shape of this monstrous menace.

Aluminum can also be tooled very effectively using nothing more than tongue depressors, ice cream sticks, bone or plastic knitting needles, and so on, as tools. For directions on tooling, see the next section on "Tooled Copper Masks." You can do the same with aluminum

—with one important exception. When antiquing aluminum, do not use liver of sulphur as it will not oxidize. Instead, bathe the tooled aluminum with a solution of ammonia and water to remove all fingerprints.

When dry, lightly rub with steel wool to dull the surface. Next, paint India ink over the tooled areas. When almost dry, wipe the mask with a cloth, removing the ink from the raised areas, but leaving it in the recessed areas. An exciting, light and dark sparkle results as you can see in the hair-raiser shown in Illus. 7.

Tooled Copper Masks

Sheets of copper, thin enough to be tooled, provide one of the most fascinating materials for mask-making. When you are finished making one of these grotesques, your friends will think it is an example of native handcraft-

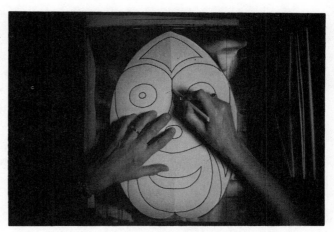

Illus. 9. Place your copper sheet on a thick pad of newspapers and trace your design onto it.

ing from a foreign country such as Mexico. Tooled copper masks are ideal for wall hangings. You might mount one on a piece of beautifully finished wood.

To begin, draw your design on a large sheet of paper. Keep the general outline and features as simple as possible, since the textures and patterns of tooling add a great deal of detail and variety.

When you are satisfied with your plan, tape it down on a sheet of copper foil under which you have placed a good solid pad of newspapers (Illus. 9). With a pencil or wooden modelling stick, lightly trace over the pencilled lines—just hard enough to leave an imprint of the entire design on the underlying copper.

Remove the paper and study the design to

Illus. 8. A tooled copper mask is ideal as a spectacular wall hanging.

Illus. 10. Successful tooling requires a constant, even pressure on the tool, working on both sides of the metal alternately.

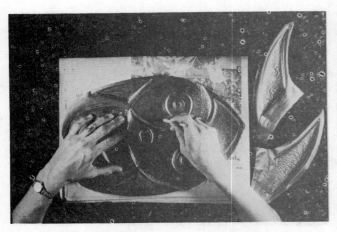

Illus. 11. You can make all kinds of tooled effects. Here, the mask is being stippled. Never use a metallic tool for such effects.

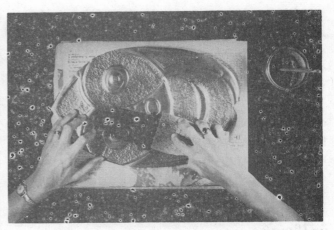

Illus. 12. For antiquing on copper, apply liver of sulphur with a sponge.

decide which shapes you would like to have raised and which recessed. Copper modelling tools are available at a very low cost, but you might use the blunt end of a spoon handle if you wish. Keeping a constant and regular pressure on the tool, move it back and forth in the areas you wish to have *recessed* (Illus. 10). When you are finished, turn the copper sheet over and your design will be reversed. Now, rub the areas that appear to be recessed on this side—they will actually be the raised areas on the "right" side of the mask. Continue this on both sides until you are pleased with the effect.

If you want to add texture as shown in

Illus. 11, use the sharp point of a modelling tool or other non-metallic instrument. You can stipple, make parallel lines, checkerboard patterns, tiny star shapes, circles, triangles or any other special effects that suit you.

Now you are ready for antiquing, or oxidizing, the copper. The agent, liver of sulphur (potassium sulfide), is available wherever you can buy aspirin. Dissolve the liver of sulphur in water, and then apply it to the copper with a sponge. When dry, rub the blackened copper with steel wool to bring out the highlights. To prevent the darker areas from eventually becoming grey or chalky, you can give the mask a coat of shellac, varnish or clear lacquer.

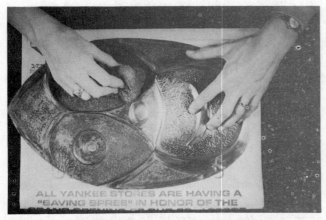

Illus. 13. When the liver of sulphur has dried, rub the copper with steel wool.

Illus. 14. You can achieve an open, lacy effect by removing shapes from the copper with either a safety-edge razor blade or an X-Acto knife.

Illus. 15. A fibreboard wall mask is effective whether left plain, as here, or painted, as in Illus. 17.

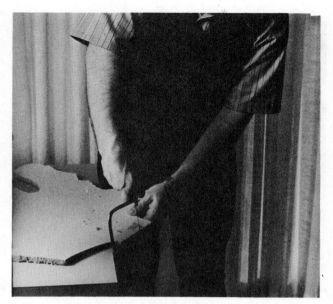

Illus. 16. Although fibreboard is thick, it is easy to cut with a small saw.

Fibreboard Wall Masks

Fibreboard is an excellent material for making wall masks—it is inexpensive, thick, and easy to saw. With it you can create spectacular three-dimensional masks. *Never wear a fibreboard mask*, unless, of course, you provide adequate ventilation. However, there are so many other materials you can wear, why not just use fibreboard for decorative purposes?

The easiest way to construct a fibreboard Frankenstein such as in Illus. 15 is to sketch out a design for the parts first. Then cut them out when you are sure you have every piece you need. You can then proceed to build up a three-dimensional mask by glueing the pieces together with Elmer's glue.

Fibreboard takes tempera paint very well, so you can give some color to your creation unless you really prefer the ghastly quality shown in Illus. 15.

Illus. 17. Tempera is the most satisfactory paint to use on fibreboard.

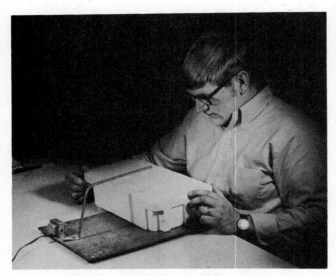

Illus. 18. You will need a hot-wire cutter to make your plastic foam mask.

Plastic Foam Wall Masks

As with fibreboard, do not use plastic foam for face masks unless you provide plenty of breathing spaces. It makes an ideal base for

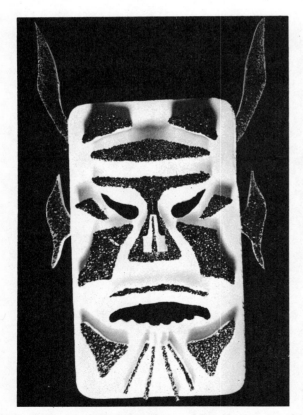

Illus. 19. Plastic foam is weather-proof, so you can hang your mask out-of-doors if you wish.

hangings, indoors and out, and is readily available in parcels you might receive containing breakable articles. You can also find scrap pieces free of charge at a lumber-yard where it is sold for insulation in building.

You will, however, need a hot-wire cutter for mask-making with plastic foam. These are specially made for working with foam and cut it like butter, leaving a fine smooth surface. The mask in Illus. 19 has foam features glued onto a foam base. Red Christmas glitter adorns the small pieces.

Illus. 20. A clay mask such as this looks as though it came from an ancient civilization.

Clay Masks

The haunting mask in Illus. 20 is enough to make anyone's hair stand on end. The three-dimensional qualities of clay provide ample room for expression of all kinds of evil powers.

If you have a large piece of oil-cloth, lay

Illus. 21. Roll out your clay between two boards so it will be even on the edges.

Illus. 22. Hollowing out a depression in the moistened sand is the first step in making your sand-cast mask.

it, canvas-side-up, on a table. On top of this, spread out a piece of cheese-cloth.

Place a large ball of clay on the cheese-cloth and set two pieces of wood, each approximately ¼-inch thick, on either side of the clay (Illus. 21). These help you roll the clay out evenly. Use a rolling pin (preferably one you will never use in the kitchen again!) to roll the clay into the shape of a flat oval.

Crumple up a double sheet of newspaper into a football shape. Lay the clay oval, with the cheese-cloth under it, over the newspaper (Illus. 21) which you should tape down onto the table top so it won't shift in the modelling process. (Be sure the cheese-cloth is in place for easy removal of the clay.)

Using your fingers, or a fork or spoon, mould the basic features of the mask as shown. You can use small pieces of clay to exaggerate and add to the features. You could make a drawing to work from, but it's often more exciting to see the face take form without a definite plan in mind. You can punch holes on either side for insertion of a leather thong for hanging.

When the mask is leather-hard, remove it from the newspaper backing, and allow it to dry thoroughly before bisque firing. If you wish, you might glaze it before firing.

In case you cannot finish the moulding process in one sitting, store the mask in a tightly closed plastic bag so it won't dry out.

Sand-Cast Masks

Fill a tub with sand to within an inch of the top and level it off. Then moisten it with water so it will hold its shape. In Illus. 22, a shallow oval is being formed with the finger-tips.

You can use a piece of tagboard, shaped into a cone, to make features and decorative effects (Illus. 23). Various objects such as stones, beads, shells, twigs, can be used to cast whatever impressions you want to make.

Place dry plaster of Paris into a bowl or basin in such a way that it forms a peak in the middle (Illus. 24). Then slowly pour water

Illus. 23. A cone-shaped piece of tagboard is used here to make the features of the mask.

Illus. 24. Pour water round the edges of the "mountain" of plaster of Paris until it reaches the top. Then mix it.

into the basin along the edges, until it reaches the level of the peak. Mix the plaster of Paris until it has the consistency of thick cream.

Next, use a small jar or cup to pour the plaster of Paris into the sand impression, and do it slowly so as not to disturb the delicate hills and valleys of the cast (Illus. 25). Continue the pouring procedure until the plaster of Paris reaches the very top of the sand hollow (Illus. 26). You must now let the plaster set until it is solid. It will not be completely dry, however.

When you are sure it is set, loosen the plaster of Paris with a knife drawn along the edge and remove the cast mask. Then, very carefully brush away the excess sand with the finger-tips (Illus. 27). A rinsing under a running faucet will remove the last particles of sand. The plaster of Paris casting retains the rough texture of the sand and gives the impression of being an ancient artifact (Illus. 28).

All the innocent face in Illus. 28 needs is a little color here and there to point up his unsavory character. Plaster of Paris, being absorbent, will take tempera paints beautifully. In Illus. 29, an unearthly blue is being used to cover his entire face, while his spiky protrusions and mis-shapen mouth are painted lilac.

His evil spirit is completely unveiled by delicate touches of lilac on his cheeks and eyes and spidery triangular forms all over his face (Illus. 30). An ancient oracle come to life!

Illus. 25. Slowly pour the plaster of Paris into the sand.

Illus. 26. After the plaster of Paris reaches the top, allow the plaster to set.

Illus. 27. After removing the cast, carefully brush the sand "crumbs" off.

Illus. 28. Rinse the cast under running water to remove all the loose sand you can. The plaster cast will now have the texture of sand.

Illus. 29. Use tempera paint on your sand-cast mask if you decide to color it.

Illus. 30. This awesome wall hanging has lilac cheeks on a blue face. Lilac also covers his eyes and spiky protrusions.

DIORAMAS

You can get great pleasure and satisfaction by creating a three-dimensional diorama. A diorama is a painting seen through an opening —by placing figures within something, you are actually making a theatrical scene upon a stage. You can make up your own scenes, or use familiar ones from plays and stories. A dramatic moment from a fairy tale might inspire you, for example, or a lovely setting from a movie, opera or operetta.

To begin your diorama, carefully select the cardboard box in which you will place the figures. The size of your box is important, because you want to have the correct size ratio between your figures and the objects which will surround them—trees, houses, mountains, etc. —as well as the ratio of all the objects to the surrounding enclosure. Therefore, if your box is small, your figures have to be very tiny, and they will be harder to construct and see. If your box is an enormous one, your paper objects should also be large and reinforced with cardboard to stand up. A box which is just a few inches larger than a shoebox provides a good, medium-sized stage.

Place your box on a side, so that its bottom serves as the back of the stage. In order to make sure there is enough lighting on the stage, you can cut out the side which forms the ceiling. If you want the stage to have a top, however, to hang such things as a chandelier or tree foliage, you can cut a rectangle in the ceiling near the back.

You can add a backdrop, also made of cardboard, to your stage. This decreases the size of your stage area. By making two vertical folds in the backdrop, you can have diagonal walls between the back and sides of the stage. This enables anyone to see the whole stage from the extreme right or left—diagonal walls are in a legitimate theatre for this purpose. When making the vertical folds, measure the backdrop against the back of the box and score the lines so that you can place the folds exactly.

To score, use the point of a scissors, knife, letter opener or other sharp instrument. Often, even a blunt, fine edge, such as a nail file, will do. Press a line gently onto the surface of the paper. You will then be able to fold more easily.

Your backdrop can also be a semicircular one—tagboard is a good material to use in this case (see Illus. 28).

By placing the backdrop a few inches in front of the back of the box, you create an illusion of great depth. You can, for example, cut windows and doors in your backdrop, and paint mountains or meadows and rolling hills on the inside of the extreme back of the stage. The viewer's eye is then drawn through the openings in the backdrop to the distant scenery behind it, and the effect is that of a great deal of space. Cover the windows with cellophane to give them a realistic touch. To throw light on the distant scene, cut a rectangle out of the ceiling between the backdrop and back. If you want light on your backdrop also, you can cut a rectangle in front of this as well. Experiment yourself with different lighting techniques. Perhaps you could get a bulb into a lower corner of the stage, or a whole row of them

Condensed from the books, "Alkema's Complete Guide to Creative Art for Young People" by Chester Jay Alkema, published by Sterling Publishing Co., Inc., New York, and "Creative Paper Crafts" by Chester Jay Alkema / © 1967 by Sterling Publishing Co., Inc., New York

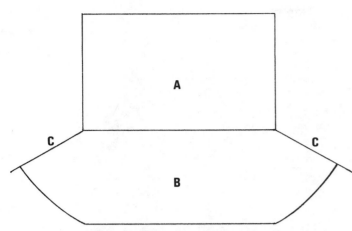

Illus. 1. To make an extra floor piece for your stage, cut a piece of cardboard in this shape. Place section A over the regular floor, and section B will form the new front. Tape the side flaps to the extra piece at lines C.

If you keep the flaps of the carton on it, you can bend the top flap upward and use it to announce the subject of your theme. Either draw right on the flap with crayon or tempera, or paste on letters cut out from paper. By bringing all four flaps forward so that each one extends a side, you can, of course, increase the depth of the stage. Or you can just increase the floor by cutting off the upper flap and bending the two side flaps outward.

You might wish to create a floor section out of cardboard which will extend even farther out towards the audience, and also will reach sideways to the flaps when they are bent diagonally outward. You can then tape the sides to the extra piece. Illus. 1 shows the floor section before it is added to the stage.

Add curtains to give a touch of authenticity. Attach cloth or crepe paper to florists' wire, baling wire or pipe cleaners to run across the top front of the stage. Fold the top inch of the

across the front of the stage as footlights. If you do have footlights, you might want to put a strip of cardboard across the opening to cover them.

Illus. 2. Here is Little Red Riding Hood on her way to her grandmother's house. Cardboard boxes are ideal for making dioramas. Notice how effective the little cloth curtains are in heightening the stage-like quality of the setting. Real twigs and leaves add a touch of reality.

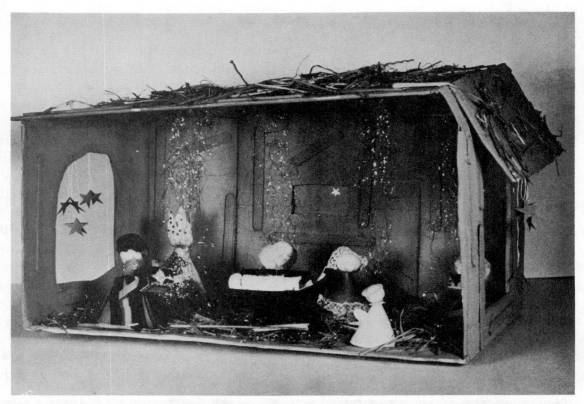

Illus. 3. A shoebox is the base for this nativity scene. The top of the shoebox has been replaced with a slanting roof—popsicle sticks represent the beams. The roof is covered with construction paper and straw. Cellophane strips add a celestial touch as do the arched windows looking out on gold stars hung on the outside. The construction-paper cradle is filled with straw. All the figures are made from cones (see page 312).

cloth or crepe paper over the wire and hem it with straight pins, thread or glue. You can insert the wire or pipe cleaners through holes in the upper two front corners of the box, and knot them on the outside so they stay. The diorama in the lower right-hand corner on the front cover shows a stage with a curtain.

After you get your stage assembled, you are ready to add the figures, buildings and scenery. The three-dimensional figures and objects can be monofold forms, cone figures or cylindrical ones. All of the figures in Illus. 3 were made from cones (see page 312). You could combine techniques, having both round figures and flat ones on-stage.

Use such things as crayon, paint, cotton batting dabbed with paint, fabric and pipe cleaners to accent your figures.

Monofold Animals

Because of their body symmetry, both animals and people are ideally suited as subjects for three-dimensional, single-folded forms. However, animals are constructed on a horizontal fold and people on a vertical fold—that is, the animal shapes are mirror images from side to side, and the people shapes from front to back.

Start by making an animal from two pieces of paper. Take a large sheet of construction paper and fold in two in the direction shown in Illus. 4. Using a soft-tip pen, outline the body of your animal and cut it out with the paper still folded, as shown in Illus. 5. Since this animal is a llama, it has a nice straight back that corresponds to the folded edge.

Next, cut a 2-inch slit, starting from the right edge, along the fold. This slit serves to accom-

Illus. 4.

modate the long neck and head piece. Now, in the same way, draw and cut out the neck and head. Place the neck in the slit and glue it between the two layers, pressing together until dry (Illus. 6).

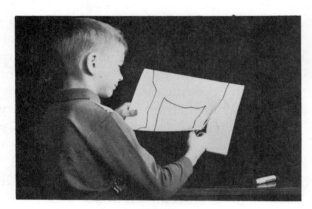

Illus. 5.

Paint or decorate the animal. Most animals have distinctive markings or features that make them ideal subjects for decorated monofold projects and dioramas.

Illus. 6.

Illus. 7. The completed llama, made from a single fold of paper.

Illus. 8. Here is a single-fold construction that is done somewhat differently. The fold was made on the diagonal, rather than on the horizontal, and the giraffe outline was drawn on the resulting triangular shape. The original fold runs along the highest part of the back to the head.

Illus. 9. This representative of the Law has three-dimensional legs and a two-dimensional torso and head.

Illus. 11. People from countries that have national costumes are easy to make with a single fold. It is not difficult to guess where these two come from.

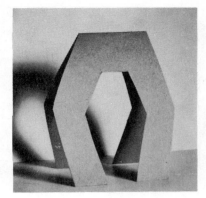

Illus. 10. The sheriff's monofold legs.

Monofold People

Three-dimensional paper people offer an opportunity to exercise a great deal of imagination. Here, in addition to portraying people from various professions, occupations, stories, or from history, you can add a very important touch—character. Although most of your characterizations will be in the form of decorative techniques, remember that the way people stand or hold their heads and their bodies very often is a key to their character or personality.

The lanky sheriff in Illus. 9 is made up of two main parts. From the waist down, he is three-dimensional, that is, made up of a folded piece of paper (Illus. 10). From the waist up, he is two-dimensional—made from a single piece of paper which was pasted to the lower section.

Hair, eyebrows, eyes and mouth are all made of pieces of colored construction paper, as well as the boots, belt, and holsters.

Cone Creations

The cone shape forms a perfect basis for creating three-dimensional people. The Spanish dancer in Illus. 15, believe it or not, is—underneath it all—a cone. The designs on her outfit were accomplished by the crayon-relief technique.

Place thin sheets of newsprint paper over three different-patterned and different-sized plastic doilies. Using the side of a peeled crayon, rub each doily until the patterns show through (Illus. 12). Now cut out each pattern,

Illus. 12

Illus. 13.

Illus. 14.

and cut a circle through the middle of each. The largest piece of paper should have the largest central circle, etc. (Illus. 13). Fit the circles over the cone and place tape against the top side of each circle and against the side of the cone to hold them in place. Slightly crease to make them fluff out and down (Illus. 14).

See what other ideas you can come up with for making cone figures (see Illus. 17, 18 and 23).

The base of the owl in Illus. 16, for example, is a very fat shallow cone. To make the head, fold a sheet of paper and cut out the head, using the fold line as the top of the skull. Then drape the folded head over the cone body and glue it to the front and back sides. The wings can also be made from a mono-folded piece of paper, or make each wing separately and join them to the body with brass fasteners. If you make them from a single sheet, attach them to the front of the cone before glueing the head on.

This owl has a three-dimensional feather pattern achieved by cutting slits and pushing them through. Make monofold ears and glue them on each side of the head. Colored pipe cleaners make excellent bird legs and feet as you can see, as well as owlish spectacles.

Illus. 15.

Illus. 16.

Illus. 17. This little chorus is made up of cone shapes. The angel at left has a tin-foil halo. Her body is made of a white paper cone with a Christmas-glitter border. Construction paper forms the middle songster completely and the legs, head and hat of the chorister on the right, whose torso and arms are made of wallpaper.

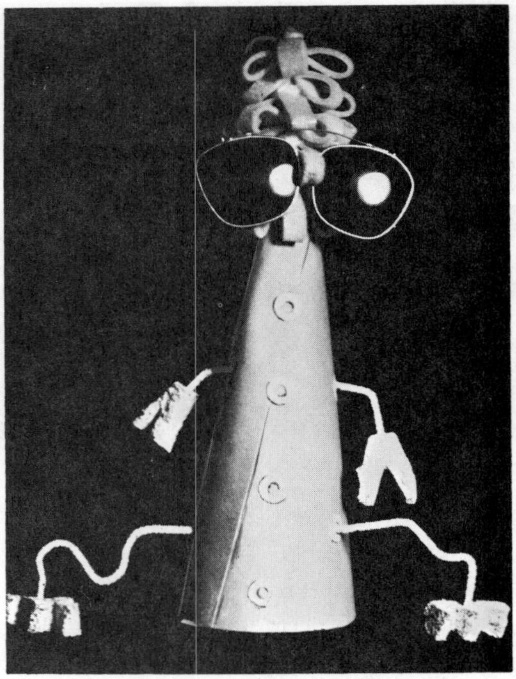

Cylindrical Creations

Have you ever stopped to think of how many of nature's forms are shaped like the cylinder in Illus. 19? Tree trunks, caterpillars, animal and human legs and arms, torsos. Try to think of as many cylindrical shapes as possible to use for your dioramas.

Illus. 18. This cone creature has bent pipe-cleaner arms and legs and sponge hands and feet. His head is made of insulating foam.

Illus. 19.

Illus. 21. Tagboard cylinders covered with tin-foil make a realistic robot. Notice that even his ears, hands, and feet are cylinders.

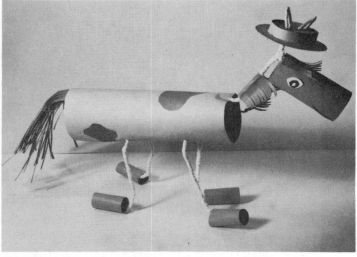

Illus. 20 (left). This old Dobbin is made completely of cylinders!

Illus. 22. Cylinders all by themselves are ideal for most of the body parts.

Illus. 23 (right). Goldilocks is trying out Baby Bear's chair sitting on her large cone body to which are attached two cylindrical legs. Her foam head wears a cone bonnet.

Ideas for Dioramas

Illus. 24 portrays several people surrounding a mulberry bush as they act out the different verses of the song. By putting the box within its cover, you enlarge the floor space of the stage.

You may recognize the tale that is being portrayed on the front cover. In case you do not, it is a scene from "The Pied Piper of Hamlin." The sense of depth in this stage is shown in many ways. The bottom flap is extended forward, a backdrop of paper has had buildings painted on it, and a paper picket fence has been placed a few inches in front of the backdrop. The construction-paper house also has depth with its open windows, door, and green paper steps. Brown construction paper covers the floor, with cobblestones of black crayon drawn on it. In the foreground, the figure on the left is dressed in cloth while the one on the right is clothed chiefly in tissue paper. You can see that either cloth or tissue paper do nicely for costumes. Both of these figures are cone-shaped with pipe-cleaner arms. Materials that were used to decorate them include nylon stockings, corduroy, cotton

Illus. 24. Fairy tales, children's books, poems, nursery rhymes—all are rich sources for diorama ideas. Here is a depiction of "All Around the Mulberry Bush."

balls, toothpicks, embroidery floss, human hair, pearls and velveteen. In the background at the extreme left is a monofold little girl who is leaning against the fence in front of a monofold tree.

Illus. 25 is a scene from the days of King Arthur. Materials rich in color and texture decorate the scene. Green velvet, trimmed with golden ribbon, makes the tapestry on the wall and the contrasting background to the red throne. The throne itself is a complex structure—the high back is made of tagboard covered with red tissue paper. Its lower half is composed of a thread spool surrounded by red rug filler. Construction paper covered with a light water-color wash and pencil outline suggests the stone wall in back.

The fair damsel has a cone body, her knight-errant a cylinder one. Both have small cotton balls for heads with hair of unravelled binder twine.

In Illus. 26, Cinderella is being put upon the stage. Her helpful fairy godmother is in the background—a two-dimensional figure cut out of white construction paper and suspended from the ceiling by a pipe cleaner. Cinderella

has a pipe-cleaner body, and is clothed in paper towelling. Her head is made of a ball of tissue paper which has been covered with starch-soaked strips of tissue.

The background of Illus. 28 is a semicircular one of white paper, washed with transparent water color to suggest the ocean. Aquarium gravel, shells and stones are glued to the floor of the diorama, and a mesh vegetable bag hangs over the front left side to suggest a fisherman's net. Each fish is supported by a pipe cleaner which has been poked into the floor.

Now you are on your own to utilize these instructions and techniques to create original dioramas.

Illus. 26. Real grass and weeds are used in the background of this scene from "Cinderella." On the far right a paper-cylinder tree trunk is topped with crumpled green tissue-paper foliage.

Illus. 27. Betsy Ross, warm and comfortable in a cozy room, is making the first American flag. Paper stars, red felt and blue cotton strips on white satin compose the flag. Betsy's body is made of pipe cleaners covered with tissue paper. A cone forms her skirt and bonnet, and cylinders make up the blouse and its sleeves. The fireplace was made by crumpling tissue paper and pasting it against the wall, then painting bricks on it. Cardboard forms the chest, and braided rag strips the rug.

Illus. 28. An under-water scene makes a fascinating diorama.

PAPER FLOWERS

Roses, tulips, carnations—all flowers are charming and attractive creations of nature. And because all blossoms begin to fade and die within a short while, people all over the world have used various means to capture the natural beauty of flowers in order to decorate rooms and also to create festive garlands as presents.

Making paper flowers is a cheerful activity for children, teen-agers, and adults alike. It stimulates the imagination, induces an appreciation of colors, and develops a feeling for forms and shapes. It leads to dexterity and to boldness in exploring; at the same time it gives great pleasure, because you can obtain attractive results with comparative ease.

The major aim in making paper flowers is *not* to obtain an exact copy of the blossom. A paper flower should always be recognized for what it is—an imitation. However, you will copy the general appearance of the blossom from nature. The colors you select for your paper flowers can either follow natural coloring or differ from it, depending on the color range of the available papers. You can depart completely from nature and make a green or scarlet peony with navy-blue leaves if this color scheme will fit better in your surroundings. Finally, the shape of the flower can differ from Nature's model if you decide to make entirely imaginary flowers.

The projects that follow give you elementary guide-lines that enable you to create a wide variety of flowers. But these are just a few possibilities. As soon as you acquire some skill, you will want to follow your own inclinations.

Illus. 1. A crepe-paper flower.

Crepe Paper Flowers

Crepe has a grain—a series of tiny lines running along its width. A strip of crepe paper cut across the grain "stands up" (Illus. 2A); cut with the grain, it "falls" (Illus. 2B). The paper

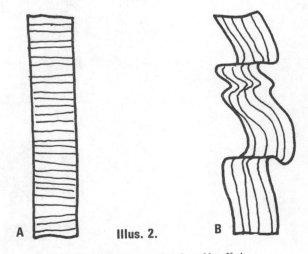

A   Illus. 2.   B

Condensed from the book, "Making Paper Flowers" by Susanne Strose | © 1970 by Sterling Publishing Co., Inc., New York

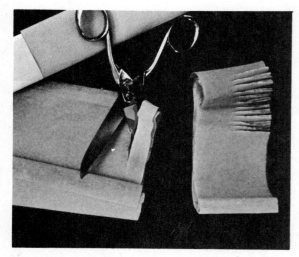

Illus. 3. You must always cut crepe paper across the grain.

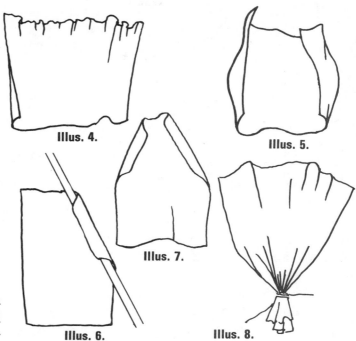

Illus. 4.

Illus. 5.

Illus. 7.

Illus. 6.

Illus. 8.

comes folded up in flattened rolls, from which you cut strips by unfolding part of the roll until you have a thickness of layers that your scissors can penetrate (Illus. 3). Then · you cut the strip out with your scissors going *across* the grain. Always cut petals out of such strips and never out of circular pieces.

Crepe paper offers many advantages for making paper flowers. The range of colors available is great. The grain of the paper (which runs the *length* of the petal) offers additional advantages—you can crimp the paper (Illus. 4) by pinching the width between your fingers; you can stretch it (Illus. 5); you can curl its corners over a knitting needle (Illus. 6) or roll them (Illus. 7) and they will stay in place; and you can easily gather the paper (Illus. 8).

Roses

Make five to seven petals with rolled-in, pointed tips (Illus. 9) and stretch them a bit

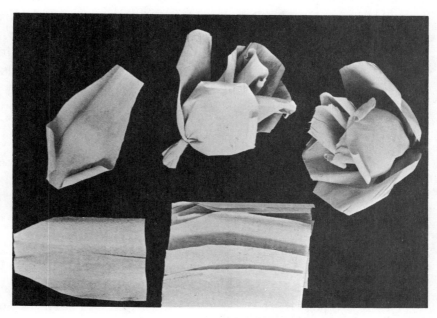

Illus. 9. Curl individual petals and fasten them at the base with wire for crepe-paper roses.

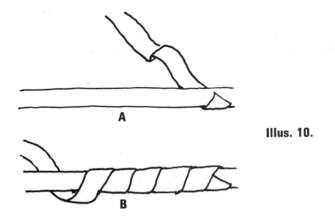

Illus. 10.

Illus. 13.

at the top. Arrange them in the shape of a blossom, and hold them together with a piece of wire wrapped tightly around the bottom of the form. Leave the wire long enough to form a flower stem. Then roll a narrow strip of green crepe paper round the bottom of the blossom to form the receptacle and glue it in place.

Now the wire stem has to be wrapped to make it more attractive. Take a ribbon of silk or crepe paper, $\frac{1}{4}$ to $\frac{5}{8}$ of an inch wide, and glue it at an oblique angle to the stem under the blossom (Illus. 10A). (If two wires form the stem, twist them together first.) Then roll the ribbon spirally round the wire in a close, even manner (Illus. 10B).

For the leaves, use double layers of crepe paper cut into the desired shape (Illus. 11A to C). Insert a piece of wire between the two layers to form the main vein of the leaf and the leaf's stem; then glue the two layers together. In larger, serrated leaves (Illus. 11C), several veins can be inserted. Pinnate leaves are made of several small leaves fastened together (Illus. 12).

A different method of making leaves is shown in Illus. 13. Cut a piece of crepe paper as indicated in A and gather it at the bottom. Then wind a piece of wire round the gathered part and spread the points on top (B). This method of making leaves is particularly useful if you want to make bouquets or wreaths.

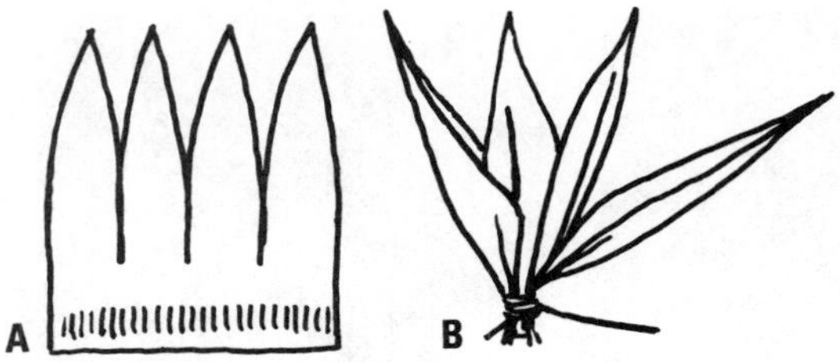

Folded Flat Blossoms Made from a Square

Folded flowers can be used to decorate invitations, letterheads, place-cards, or as a pattern in the composition of posters. When you use folded flowers to make up bouquets, you have to add stems and leaves to the blooms.

Materials

Square sheets of paper suitable for folding can be obtained in toy shops, craft and hobby shops. At one time, the paper was always dyed throughout, but now folding paper comes with bright colors on one side only, the opposite side being white. When you use this kind of paper, you have to be very careful to start folding with the right side out, otherwise the end result will be a white flower. When you use dyed-through paper this does not matter. In the diagrams, the white side of the paper is indicated by shading so that you will always know which side of the paper should be white and which side colored.

Code for Diagrams

The diagrams shown throughout the text have various lines. Here is what the lines mean:

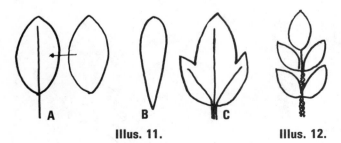

Illus. 11.

Illus. 12.

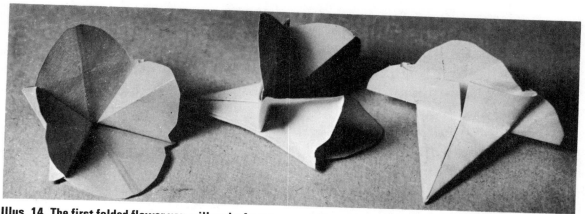

Illus. 14. The first folded flower you will make from a square sheet of paper is the lilac. See Illus. 15 for folding procedure.

Solid lines = Outline of the folded form.

Dashed lines = Sharp ridges of the fold on the surface of the paper facing you.

Dot-dash lines = Sharp ridges of the fold on the opposite side of the paper.

Dotted lines = Guide-lines for folding paper or for cutting paper.

Shaded surfaces = White surface of the paper.

White surfaces = Colored side of the paper.

Lilac (Illus. 15)

(A) Take a small sheet of paper between 2 and 4 inches square with the white side up and make the three separate folds shown in Illus. 15A. Note that you must open the sheet up again to make each succeeding fold.

(B) Fold the square in half as shown.

(C) Hold the paper firmly at the ends of fold 3–3 and push the two diagonal folds (each labelled 1) towards each other so they meet. The paper will almost automatically fold into a diamond form that, when flattened, is actually a small square one-quarter the size of the original. (Note that the forward corner 2 will meet the left corner 3 and the rear corner 2 will meet the right corner 3.)

(D) When the diamond formed in step C is held loosely, it will look like this. The front is marked x; the rear is y. The two front flaps are labelled t and the two rear ones are labelled u.

(E) Fold the two front flaps at the corners marked t over towards each other, as shown by the arrows, along the dotted lines until the corners meet on the vertical line of the diamond (drawn here as a guide). The resulting form is diagram F.

(F) The two triangular forms (the two t's)

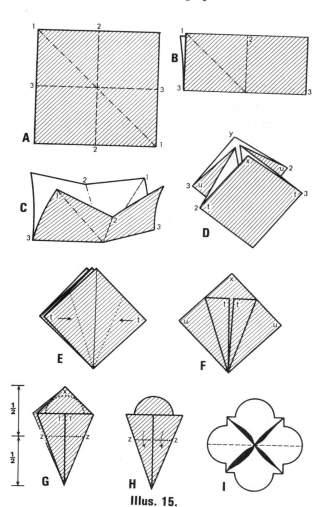

Illus. 15.

within the square leave the two rear flaps (*u* and *u*) protruding. Turn the entire paper form over and fold the two corners marked *u* in the same way as you did for the two corners marked *t*. You should have the kite-shaped form shown in diagram G. Turn the form over again so that the triangles marked *t* are face up.

(G) Draw a guide-line for folding the paper form in half (line *z–z*). Draw a semicircle in the top triangle marked *x* and cut through all the layers of paper, removing all excess paper outside the semicircle.

(H) Fold the entire top of the paper form along the line *z–z*, bending it down towards the bottom of the kite.

(I) Unfold the blossom carefully by keeping the front petal bent down along the fold and flattening out the side petals, which leaves the rear petal at a slight upward angle. (See flower at left in Illus. 14.) This diagram is the top view. You can make many small blossoms in this way and use them for attractive arrangements.

Other Flat Blossoms—Marguerite, Arnica, Ox-Eye Daisy, Pink (Illus. 17)

This folding pattern is very similar to the Lilac. Follow the steps described for Illus. 15A through F to obtain the basic kite form. Then proceed as follows:

(A) Hold the kite-shaped form at the bottom. You see that there are two pointed flaps (1) inside the kite. Draw one of these inside points out of the kite so that the central fold (starred) of the original flap is reversed, forming a new outward-pointing flap (B).

(B) This is a three-quarter view of the kite with one inside point pulled out and the central fold (starred) of the original flap reversed to form a new flap that protrudes.

(C) The top edge of the new flap is shown open. Close it and align it so that it extends the side of the top triangle. Flatten the form out. Repeat steps A, B, and C for the other point labelled 1, pulling in the direction shown by the arrow.

(D) Draw a semicircle as shown by the dotted lines, and cut away the excess paper, cutting through all the layers of folded paper.

(E) Open the top of the form, bending the front semicircle forward but leaving the rear semicircle flat.

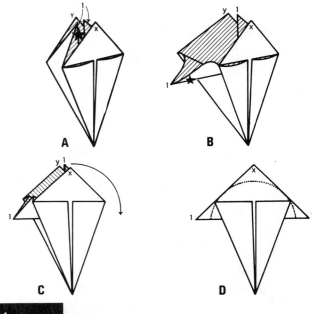

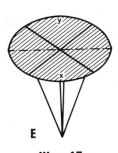

Illus. 17.

Illus. 16. By adding fringed petals, you can create pinks or daisies. See Illus. 17 for folding procedure.

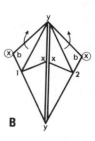
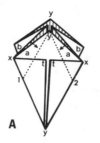

A　　　　　　**B**

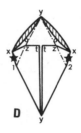
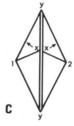
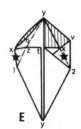

C　　　　**D**　　　　**E**

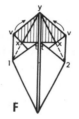

F　　　　**G**　　　　**H**

Illus. 19.

Illus. 16 shows several variations that can be obtained by cutting the edges differently or by pasting other pieces of paper over the circle of petals.

Chinese Lantern Plant (Illus. 19)

(A) Start with a square of paper and again follow the steps given for Illus. 15 A through F, but keep the *colored side up* from beginning to end. When you have obtained the resulting kite shape (the front is labelled a–a; the back, b–b in this semi-opened view), bend the double top left and top right edges (arrows) of flap a–a down along dotted lines y–1 and y–2, so that the edges lie vertically, extending from top point y to where corners x meet along the central lines formed by flaps t and bottom point y. The new flaps partially cover flaps t and, the resulting shape is diagram B.

(B) Repeat the shape on the other side of the form by folding the exposed parts of flap b–b to the rear along top lines y–1 and y–2. (Circled x's are corners of flap b–b.) Now you have diagram C.

(C) After having obtained this shape, insert an index finger at the point where the two x's meet and lift the top flaps again on one side of the paper so the flaps are perpendicular to the surface of flaps t. (See diagram D.)

(D) Insert an index finger between the sides of the top right flap (shaded portion y–x and line y–2) at point x. With your thumb at the star on the flap's outside fold (x–2), push down until that outward fold coincides with the flap's inward fold along the diagonal z–2. The

circled part of the flap will be reversed to the white side. Press the paper down to sharpen the new folds. The results will look like diagram E.

(E) Now repeat the procedure in D on the left flap to obtain diagram F.

(F) When this shape has been obtained, fold triangle y–v–2 backward along line y–2 so it is directly behind triangle y–2–t. Fold triangle y–v–1 behind triangle y–1–t. Repeat procedures C through F on the rear side of the paper form.

(G) Now fold the top flap x–y–x down toward you.

(H) Diagram H shows the first flap turned down. Turn down the other three flaps and expand the bag which has been formed by blowing into it. Illus. 18 shows some views of the finished flower.

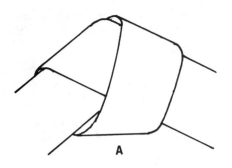
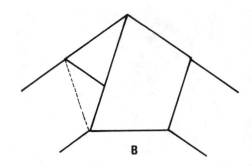
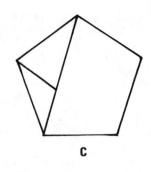

Illus. 20.

Blossoms Made from a Pentagon

Since you cannot buy pentagonal sheets of paper, you will have to make a pentagonal pattern to use in cutting out the sheets. Here are two methods:

1. Take a long rectangular strip of paper (its length should be about seven times its width) and tie it into a simple knot as shown in Illus. 20A. Tighten and flatten the knot as shown in Illus. 20B. Illus. 20C shows the finished pentagon after the superfluous ends of paper have been cut off. (Be sure the sides of the finished pentagon are equidistant. If not, cut them so they are.)

2. On a sheet of heavy drawing paper or cardboard, draw a straight line to represent the base of the pentagon (Illus. 21). At each end of this line, use a protractor to mark off angles of 72°. Holding a ruler at those angles, from each end of the base line, draw an extending line the same length as the base line. Set your compass to the length of the base line. Starting at each unconnected end of the lines extending from the base line, swing two arcs towards each other. Connect each of the two extending lines to the point where the two arcs intersect.

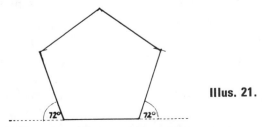

Illus. 21.

Azalea Blossom (Illus. 23a and 23b)

(A) Make the folds of this pentagon simply by using each of the five sides as a base line to divide the form in half from five different positions. The white side of the paper is face up for each fold, which you open up after having made it. For instance, with the white side of the paper up, fold corner *a* over to cover corner *b* and corner *e* over to cover *c* to form the central fold from point *d* to base line *a–b*. Open the halved form and turn it so line *b–c* is the base. Fold corner *b* over corner *c*, and corner *a* over *d*. Open the form and repeat this procedure with the remaining three base lines. You will then have all of the folds shown in the pentagon in diagram A. Then close the form along fold *e–v* placing edge *d–c* over base line *a–b*.

(B) This diagram shows the final results of step A. The colored side of the paper will be on the outside. Hold the form at the point marked with a circle. At the point marked with a star, press the folded edge *e–x* down and insert it between the paper figure's two sides by reversing it so it is enclosed by outward fold *x–y* in front and corresponding fold *x–y* in back (hidden here—see diagram C).

(C) This is a partially open view of the resulting form.

(D) Flatten the form and hold it in your left hand between your thumb and index finger with your thumb at the point marked with a circle. Take only the top sheet of the paper at the point marked with a star and move the

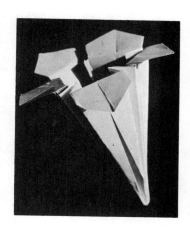

Illus. 22. Two views of an azalea (top at left and side at right) made from a folded pentagon. See Illus. 23a and Illus. 23b for folding procedure.

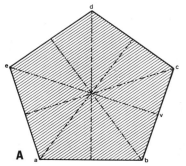

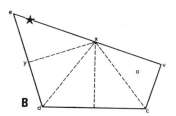

Illus. 23a.

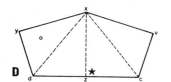

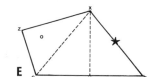

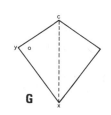

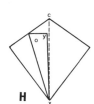

outward fold *x–z* to the left until you can place it along the edge *x–y*. When this is done, the outward fold along line *x–d* will be reversed inside the flap just created and the figure will change shape.

(E) Now hold the paper between your thumb and index finger with your thumb at the point marked with a circle. Push the folded edge *x–b* inward with your finger at the point marked with a star. Keep pushing until you reverse the fold inward and it is enclosed by the outward fold *x–v* in front and the fold corresponding to *x–v* in back.

(F) Turn the figure over and hold it as shown in diagram F.

(G) Fold corner *y* of circled front flap *y–c–x* over towards the middle so that the edge

y–x lies along the midline *c–x*. (The letter *y* here has no relationship to those in previous diagrams.)

(H) The front flap has been folded over. Return it to its original position.

(I) With the flap in its original position, insert your finger at the point indicated by the arrow and reverse the direction of the crease just made along the line *x–x* from inward to outward. At the same time, pull the flap edge

PAPER FLOWERS ■ 325

y–x over to the right so it lies on top of midline c–x.

(J) When you flatten it, the figure will look like this.

(K) This shape is obtained as follows: On each of the three remaining sides shaped like G, repeat the procedures outlined under steps G through J. The fourth remaining side is shaped like the form x–x–o–c in diagram I; that is, x–x is now a solid line and triangle x–y–x has disappeared. Therefore, you use corner o instead of corner y to make the flap, return it to its original position and spread it open by pushing to the left instead of to the right. Diagram K is the final result.

(L) There are five flaps shaped like diagram K. On two of them, fold one half over the other, to the right or left as necessary, so that the front and rear faces of the figure are as shown in this diagram.

(M) A three-dimensional view of diagram L. Inserted between the front and rear diamonds are three others (dotted flaps within shaded area), as well as five flaps shaped like diagram K (dotted flaps below shaded area and opened flap at right).

(N) Fold corner w of the diamond-shaped flap in diagram L over towards the middle so that the edges w–x lie along the midline c–x. (Circled w's belong to flap behind folded one.)

(O) Repeat this folding over of flaps for each diamond corresponding to the one in diagram L. (You have to open the form to expose the inner diamonds.) When the final form looks

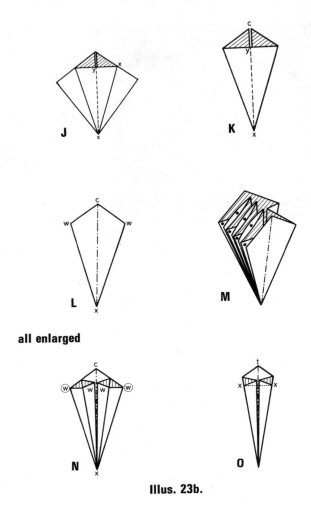

all enlarged

Illus. 23b.

like this, pull down each of the five top points (t), fold along dotted line x–x, and spread the petals apart. The main body of this flower will be colored and the small petals will be white, unless you use paper colored on both sides.

Illus. 22 shows a finished flower of this type.

SHELL FLOWERS

Do delicate and colorful sea shells fascinate you? Then you are in good company, for they fascinate scientists, artists, and shellcrafters too. By following the instructions for the projects in this article, and then creating your own designs, you can make beautiful, permanent flower arrangements to use as centerpieces, or as paperweights, or for ornaments on other objects.

Sea shells that you have gathered on your vacation or a few that you buy from your hobby or shellcraft shop are all you need to start with. There are many shops that stock all the shells needed to make the flowers here. See page 560 for a list of shops that can help you. The larger shops usually have a catalogue available, and make prompt shipment on mail orders.

The majority of the flowers here are made from tiny bivalves, which are hinged shells with two halves, like a clam shell. Each half is used for a petal, and the instructions tell you exactly which way to use the shell—with the hinge (the narrow end) in the center, or the cup side (the concave side) lying face up or face down. Be sure that all shells you use for your flowers are perfect—do not use any that are chipped, stained, or pitted. Sort your shells according to their sizes and species, making sure that they are clean and free of sand.

You probably already have most of the tools and supplies that you need, but so you can gather everything beforehand, here is a complete list of the materials mentioned in this article:

- shell bond glue
- sheet of poly plastic (6″ × 8″) for a worksheet
- cloth-covered wire of all weights for stems
- needle-nosed pliers
- wire cutters
- manicure scissors
- curved-point tweezers
- absorbent cotton
- green and brown floral tape
- fixative spray
- plastic foam (Styrofoam) block, 6″ × 12″ × 2″
- clear plastic discs in assorted sizes
- toothpicks
- shell lacquer
- plastic foliage

If you prefer, use a sheet of glass in place of the plastic for a worksheet. To remove the dried flowers from the glass, you need a single-edge razor blade, but the flowers come off the plastic sheet easily when you peel it away.

Experiment until you learn how to work with the clear-drying glue. It is fast-drying, so it is important to know just how much you need. Too little does not hold the flowers firmly, and too much shows on the finished flower. Flowers made flat on the worksheet can be trimmed when dry with manicure scissors. Before you trim, be sure that the flower is thoroughly dry, and cut away only the excess glue from the back of the flower before you attach the stem.

To the unique floral arrangements you make,

Condensed from the book, "Making Shell Flowers" by Norma M. Conroy | © 1972 by Sterling Publishing Co., Inc., New York

add other natural accessories, such as driftwood, coral, sea fans, dried sea life, and other marine trinkets. While shell flowers sometimes look remarkably like real flowers, the true source almost always shows through their disguise. But there is nothing wrong with that! Both shells and flowers are natural, and whatever your arrangement looks like—shell-like flowers or flower-like shells—it is sure to be attractive.

Roses

Make roses of White Chula (also known as Strombus canarium) shells. These are tiny univalves, or shells that are formed in a spiral. In the bottom of each shell there must be a small hole so the stem can be inserted. If you buy the shells, they will be drilled and ready to use. If you have a Chula shell and want to make the hole yourself, drill the shell with a very fine bit.

The first step in assembling your shell roses is to attach the stems to the shells.

Stems

The stems you use on your sea-shell flowers are made from various weights of cloth-covered wire. The gauge of wire you use depends, of course, on the size and weight of the sea shells the stems are meant for.

For sea-shell roses, use medium-gauge wire for the stems. Cut the wire with your wire cutters to the length you want each stem, plus about 1". Wrap one end of the stem with a small piece of cotton which has been saturated with glue, and push this end of the wire into the hole of the shell. Do not insert the stem so far into the shell that you can see it in the center.

Painting the Shells

When the glue on the cotton has dried, the shell is ready to be painted. Give the shells two coats, making sure that the lacquer covers the entire shell—both inside and out. Do not apply the second coat until the first one is completely dry.

To hold the shells while they dry, insert the ends of their stems into a block of plastic foam. Be sure that the shells do not touch each other. The shiny color makes the shells look like real rose buds—but the roses seem naked! To remedy this, add leaves.

Leaves for Finishing

When the paint has dried completely, put a dab of glue on the bottom of the shell. Slip a plastic calyx, which you buy in a craft shop, on the stem. A calyx is the group of small leaves which surrounds a bud at the base of a flower. Hold the plastic calyx tightly to the bottom of the rose until the glue begins to hold.

When the calyx is dry, cover the wire stem with green floral tape. Start at the top and wrap around and around, inserting the stems of plastic leaves wherever they should go. When you finish, you have an attractive bouquet of permanent, non-wilting roses.

To make an arrangement with your roses, insert the flower stems in green plastic foam cut to fit and placed in an attractive bowl or vase. Place the tallest roses in the middle and the shorter ones to the outside, so that the rose bowl is attractive from all sides. Use florist's moss to cover the plastic foam.

Daisies

Make daisies of large and small Rice shells, some in their natural white color and others dyed yellow. Rice shells are tiny univalves. There are three kinds of daisies you can make: large double daisies, semi-double daisies, and single daisies.

Large Double Daisy

Place a circle of glue about $\frac{3}{4}$" to 1" in diameter on your glass or plastic worksheet. Cover the glue with a small piece of cotton and add a little more glue so the cotton is saturated, adding substance to the glue. The first shells you lay down form the outside row of petals. Place large Rice shells at the outside edge of the glue-soaked cotton, making sure that all the openings of the shells face in the same direction. This gives the effect of curled petals.

With a tube of glue with a fine tip, place another circle of glue along the inside edge of the shells. Place a second row of large Rice shells on top of the glue and cotton, using a tweezers or toothpick to raise them slightly. The flower then has a three-dimensional appearance.

Using small Rice shells, glue a third layer of petals, raising them also so that they form a cup for the center of the daisy.

The center of the yellow large double daisy in Illus. 7 is the dried brown center of a real daisy. You could also make a center of tiny Whelk shells dyed yellow. You can use the Whelk shells with their points either up or down. Attach each center with a drop of glue and let it dry completely before you remove the flower from the worksheet.

NOTE: When you add glue during the construction of a flower, always use the fine-point tube. This way, there is less chance of getting excess glue on the flower petals.

When all the shells have completely dried, peel the plastic away from them, or lift the glue holding the flower together from the glass.

Illus. 1. To make a daisy, first glue a single Rice shell to a piece of absorbent cotton which has been saturated with glue.

Illus. 2 (left) and 3 (right). Continue to glue a circle of large Rice shells, thus forming the outside row of daisy petals.

Illus. 4. To form the inside row of petals, place glue along the edge of the outside shells.

Illus. 5. Then, add another row of large Rice shells on top of the glue and cotton, making sure to raise them slightly.

Illus. 6. Glue a third row of Rice shells— small ones this time—inside the second row, also raising them to form a cup for the daisy's center.

Illus. 7. For the center of the daisy, you can either use dried brown centers of real daisies or tiny Whelk shells.

Semi-Double Daisy

This daisy is made exactly like the large double daisy, except that you do not add the third row of small Rice shells. Just glue two rows of large Rice shells, leaving a small circle for the flower's center.

The center of this semi-double daisy is tiny Whelk shells dyed yellow.

Single Daisy

The small single daisies consist only of one row of small Rice shells. Place them on a small piece of cotton as you did the larger shells.

The center of the single yellow daisy in Illus. 10 is composed of small brown seeds (any kind small enough). Again, you may use tiny Whelk shells dyed yellow for the center of a single white daisy.

Daisy Stems

When the flowers are completely dry, add a *coiled stem* to each one. Cut a piece of wire to the desired length, plus about 2″. Using the needle-nosed pliers, make a double coil at one end. Bend the long end of the wire back under the coil, so the stem drops down from the center, not the side. Mix a few wisps of cotton with glue and cover the top of the coil. Place the daisy on top of the coil, and insert the stems in plastic foam to dry.

When they are dry, put a dot of glue underneath the coil of each stem and slip a flat calyx up the stem to the bottom of the flower. Let this dry also, and wrap the stems with green floral tape, adding other plastic foliage to make the daisies look even more realistic.

Daisy Buds

Make buds from the largest Rice shells. First make the stem: cut a short length of fine wire. Dip the end of the wire in some glue, and place this on the large end of the shell. Set this stem aside to dry. Add four Tear shells dyed green to the bottom of the bud, pointed ends up, covering the place where the stem was glued

Illus. 8 (left). A semi-double daisy has only two rows of Rice shells, with a cluster of tiny dyed yellow Whelk shells as its center.

Illus. 9 (right). A row of small Rice shells glued to a piece of cotton forms a single daisy.

Illus. 10. After the center of your single daisy— brown seeds are shown here—or any other daisy is dry, add a coiled wire stem (below) to complete your creation.

Illus. 11. Buds, made from large Rice shells surrounded on the bottom by four Tear shells dyed green, are an attractive final touch to your bouquet of daisies.

to the shell. With the fine-point tube of glue, add a tiny bit of glue in the open end of the bud and insert a center: use Whelk shells dyed brown (pointing downward) or brown seeds in the yellow buds, and Whelk shells dyed yellow or yellow seeds in the white buds. This gives the effect of the flower's center peeking through the petals.

Assemble the small single daisies and the buds in a spray. Cut a length of medium wire and, starting at the top, wrap two or three buds together. Then include a few single daisies to make a flower spray. Add the larger flowers as you wrap with more wire. When the flower arrangement is complete, spray it lightly with fixative spray.

Zinnias

The zinnias shown in color on page U are made with natural white and dyed Gar scales of several sizes. A Gar is a type of long-bodied fish. The large scales are from Mississippi Gars, and the medium and small ones from Florida Gars. Your craft or shell supply shop probably has these scales.

Place a circle of glue with a diameter about 1¼″ to 1½″ on the worksheet. Cover this with cotton, and add a little more glue so the cotton is saturated. Starting with the outside petals, place a circle of large Gar scales pointing outward on the outside edge of the gluey cotton. Using the fine-point tube of glue, add a circle

Illus. 12. Coiled stem.

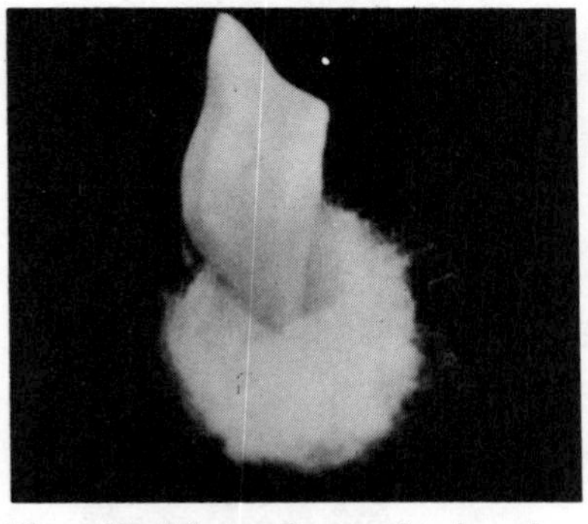

Illus. 13. A large Gar scale placed on a glue-saturated piece of cotton is the beginning of a zinnia.

Illus. 14. Continue glueing a circle of large Gar scales along the outside edge of the cotton.

Illus. 15. Begin an inner row of petals, staggering the points of the Gar scales between those of the outside row.

Illus. 16. Be sure to raise the outside edges of the Gar scales as you place them into position.

Illus. 17. Add a third row of large Gar scales in the same way as the first two.

of glue along the inside edge of the petals. Add another row of large Gar scales, staggering the petals so that the points of the scales on one row come between the points on the row underneath it. Use tweezers or a toothpick to raise the scales slightly on the outside edge. If you do not do this, the flower will be flat instead of raised. Add a circle of glue as before and another row of large scales.

After glueing these three rows of scales, use small scales to fill in the middle of the flower. Raise these slightly, the same way you did the large scales. Leave a small circle in the middle for the flower's center.

You can make these flowers smaller or larger, depending upon the number of rows of petals that you glue. If you make smaller flowers, start with a circle of gluey cotton only about $\frac{3}{4}''$ in diameter. Follow the same instructions for building up the flower regardless of its size.

Pile the center shells (the list of those used in the color picture on page U follows) so that the center is somewhat rounded, and let the center extend a little over the tips of the inside row of petals. Real zinnias have large centers, but make the center in proportion to the size of the flower.

The zinnia centers used in color Illus. U3 are the following:

Illus. 18. For a larger zinnia, simply add more rows of large Gar scales.

Lower right flower: Lilac shells, dyed lavender

Upper right flower: Natural white tiny
Whelk shells (points down)

Upper left flower: Crushed shell, dyed
yellow

Lower left flower: Tiny Whelk shells, dyed
yellow (points down)

When the petals are dry, attach a coiled stem
(see page 331) of medium-gauge wire. Stand
the flower stems in plastic foam until the stems
and petals dry. Add a little glue and cotton to
the bottom of the coil of stem, and slip a plastic
calyx up over the stem. Be sure that the gluey
cotton is covered by the calyx cup, and that the
calyx is large enough to cover the cotton base
on the underside of the flower. You may have
to hold the calyx firmly for a minute until the
glue sets a little.

When everything is dry, wrap the stems with
green floral tape, adding foliage to the stem.
Spray the flowers lightly with a fixative spray,
and arrange them in a vase.

Pansies

Make pansies with #2 Cup shells (these are
tiny bivalves), in white and dyed colors. Use
any color combinations which you would find
in a natural pansy. The pansy is a five-petal
flower, so you need five shells for each pansy.
Sort the shells by size, using the same size
shells for each flower.

Place a little glue on the worksheet in a "T"
shape. Attach two shells, with their cups facing
up, to the top of the cross of the T. Place two
more shells right below these in the same
position, slightly resting on the bottoms of the
first two shells. Add the fifth shell in the center,
with its cup facing up and the hinge to the
outside. Let the shells dry thoroughly.

Always use darker shells for the two top
petals and lighter colors for the three bottom

Illus. 19. You can make zinnia centers of crushed shell or tiny whole Whelk shells.

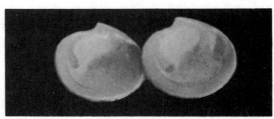

Illus. 20. The #2 Cup shells you use to make a pansy should be uniformly sized.

Illus. 21. The bottom shells must be lighter in color than the top ones.

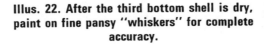

Illus. 22. After the third bottom shell is dry, paint on fine pansy "whiskers" for complete accuracy.

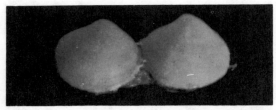

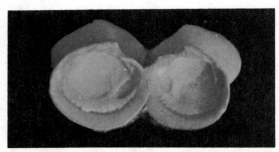

Illus. 24. Place the second two #2 Cup shells for violets up, right in front of the first two.

Illus. 25. Place the last shell face down. When all five shells have dried, add a yellow center seed and fine, violet "whiskers."

ones when you make a flower of two colors. This is the way real flowers are usually shaded.

When the pansies are dry and still attached to the worksheet, paint in the "whiskers"—those fine lines of color found on real pansy petals. Use thinned oil paint or colored ink in a purple or mauve shade. With a fine-point brush, draw very thin lines on the bottom three petals. Put a dot of bright yellow paint or ink on the hinge of the bottom shell, where the

bottom shell joins the two center shells. These "whisker" lines take some time to dry, so leave the pansy alone for a while, so that you do not smudge the lines.

When the paint is dry, add a coiled stem to the flower. Slip a flat calyx up over the stem and glue it to the back of the flower. Wrap the stems with green floral tape, adding plastic foliage as you go, and spray the flower lightly with fixative spray.

Violets

Make violets of tiny dyed #2 Cup shells, the same kind that you made the pansies with (page 333). Dye your shells lavender, lilac, or any shade in the violet family. Sort the shells by size, and use the same size for each flower.

Place a little glue on the worksheet in a "T" shape. Place two shells, their cups *down* and hinges up (away from the glue) side by side at the top of the glue. Then place two shells, cups *up* and hinges to the top, directly in front of the first two shells. Now place one more shell, cup *down* and hinge to the top, in the center. This shell should touch the two center shells. Using the fine-line tube of glue, dab a tiny dot of glue at the top of the bottom shell, and put a yellow seed in the center of the violet.

Before you remove the flower from the worksheet, paint some "whiskers" on the bottom shell. Use purple or mauve oil paint or colored ink. If you use oil paint, thin it so that the lines are not too thick or heavy. Paint very thin lines, using a fine-point brush.

When the flowers are completely dry, add a coiled stem. Slip a flat calyx up over the stem and glue it to the back of the flower. When this has dried, wrap the stem with green floral tape and add plastic foliage. Keep the leaves tiny, or you will hide the shell petals. Spray the finished flowers with fixative spray before you arrange them.

All shades of blue, violet, lavender, white and purple can be used for the different varieties of violets. A bunch of violets looks especially natural and fresh in a small container—for example, a decorative cup and saucer.

HOOKED AND KNOTTED RUGS

Originally, craftsmen hooked and knotted primarily floor rugs, but today they also use these processes for making beautiful wall hangings. For generations, commercial stamped patterns for making hooked rugs have been available on the market, but very little encouragement has been given to individuals to express their own imagination and to create works of art. This situation has certainly improved; in fact, most craftspeople prefer to design their own projects altogether. This article attempts to inspire you to design and then to make your own hooked and knotted rugs.

Hooking

The term "hooking" is actually a misnomer as far as most of today's hooking is concerned. The early rugs were literally hooked with a large crochet-type hook which was inserted into a woven foundation fabric and which brought the pile material to the surface in the form of a loop. The entire surface was covered with loops to make a compact, durable surface for a rug. In the early designs, the loops were usually made from old woollen garments which were cut into strips narrow enough to be pulled through the background fabric to form loops on the surface. Rug-hookers still use this method today, but, unless they hold or pull the loop underneath with their fingers, they do the majority of hooking with a punch-type needle which is adjustable to several different lengths of loops, varying from $\frac{1}{4}''$ to $1''$. Instead of old woollen garments, they use yarns because of the wide variety of weights and colors now available on the market, and also because of the ease of manipulating the punch-type needle.

In this article, the craft is referred to as "hooking" whether you use a punch needle or a hook. Commercial rugs with a similar pile are usually referred to as "tufted."

For your first project, make a small rug, perhaps $2' \times 2'$, which you can hang on a wall to brighten an empty corner.

Frames

To hook a rug, you first need a solid, well built adjustable, non-adjustable or easel-type

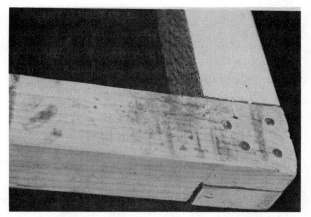

Illus. 1. Fit four pieces of 2″ × 2″ wood with notched ends into each other for a large rug frame.

Condensed from the book, "Hooked and Knotted Rugs" by Ethel Jane Beitler | © 1973 by Ethel Jane Beitler, published by Sterling Publishing Co., Inc., New York

Illus. 2. You can make another type of rug frame if you nail four pieces of $\frac{3}{4}'' \times 2''$ wood together in a butt joint as shown. Then reinforce with flat, prong-type braces.

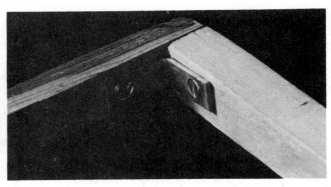

Illus. 3. For a smaller rug frame, nail four pieces of $1'' \times 1''$ wood together in a butt joint and reinforce with metal corner braces as shown.

frame, depending on the size of your project. Pieces of wood $2'' \times 2''$ from which you may cut areas out of the ends to interlock the pieces at right angles (see Illus. 1), make a sturdy frame, especially for a large hooked piece. The $2''$-wood is rather heavy to handle, however, when you turn the frame back and forth to look at the hooked area when you are using a punch needle. Instead, you can cut and nail together a $\frac{3}{4}'' \times 2''$ or $3''$ piece of wood (see Illus. 2) like a box frame (no mitering at the

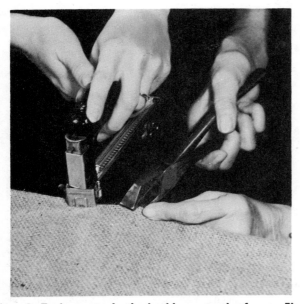

Illus. 4. Tack or staple the backing onto the frame. First, staple two adjoining sides; second, the remaining corner; next the middle of the last two sides, then the rest of the fabric.

corners is necessary). While you hook, suspend either of these types of frame between saw horses or between two card tables.

For this small rug, construct a frame from wood $1'' \times 1''$, which you nail together in a butt joint and reinforce with metal corner braces as shown in Illus. 3.

You may sometimes use an adjustable frame similar to a quilting frame if you plan to make a very large hooked piece, because you will not be able to reach the middle of a box frame if it is wider than $30''$ to $36''$. If your rug is on a quilting frame, you can roll it so you are able to reach all parts.

Background Fabric

You are now ready to choose the background fabric for your first rug. Good quality burlap (hessian), firmly woven 2-ply monk's cloth, coarse linen, or upholstery fabric which has no rubberized backing, all make satisfactory background fabrics. Use burlap for this project. Buy enough so that you can make a $2' \times 2'$ rug with enough extra fabric to turn under about an inch before you attach the fabric to your frame and to leave another few inches unhooked for a hem. Stitch the edge of the material along the edge with a zig-zag stitch on the machine so the fabric will not ravel.

Now, stretch your backing securely on the frame and hold it in place with short, broad-headed tacks or staples (see Illus. 4). Before you staple, be sure the backing is taut enough to feel firm, but not so tight that the threads of the fabric will break when you push the hooking needle through it. Turn under at least 1″ of fabric to make a double thickness when you tack or staple it. Also, be certain that the fabric on the frame is straight with the weave. Staple two adjoining sides first. Next, staple the remaining corner, and then the middle of the last two sides before stapling the rest of the fabric.

If you plan to hook the entire surface (except a few inches of border to turn under for a hem), the fabric may be natural and undyed. However, if you want to have some of the background fabric show and wish to choose a color to harmonize with your yarns, remember that most burlap is not color fast. It is fine to use burlap to learn the process of hooking, but if you become a professional and are filling commissions which involve large amounts of money, your client will want a fabric which will not fade.

Sketch and Transfer a Design

The next step before you begin to hook is to choose a design. Start with a simple pattern—perhaps a circle, a triangle, a square, or even a small abstract motif.

The abstract pattern in Illus. 5 is a selection of simple cut-out paper shapes, traced round onto burlap (see Illus. 6). For this first rug, you could hook only one cut-out to fit your 2′ × 2′ piece of burlap.

Whatever design you choose, sketch it directly on the burlap with chalk, crayon, grease pencil, or soft-tip pen. If the fabric is dark enough for white chalk lines to show, sketch the design freehand. If you make mistakes, you can easily erase the chalk with nylon net. Repeat the chalk lines occasionally as they gradually rub off as your hand rubs over them while you are hooking. If you wish, you can go over the lines with crayon or soft-tip pen to make them more permanent.

In transferring your design to the burlap, keep in mind that most rug needles today are

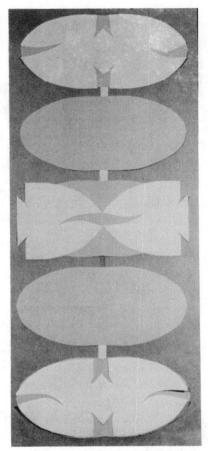

Illus. 5. Cut abstract shapes and arrange them artistically on your backing.

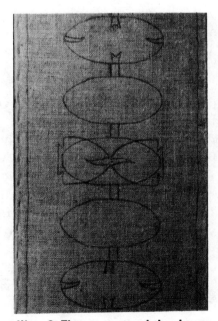

Illus. 6. Then trace round the shapes onto the burlap.

HOOKED AND KNOTTED RUGS ■ **337**

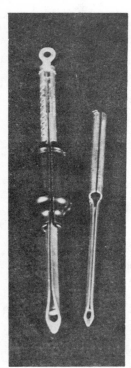

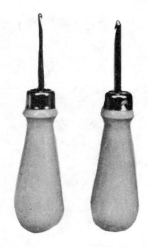

Illus. 7. Two sizes of Susan Bates Rug Hooks.

Illus. 8 (left). The Columbia Minerva Deluxe Rug Needle has two sizes of needle and adjusts to 10 lengths of loops.

designed to punch the yarn through from the *back*, so the loops for the right side of the rug are underneath while you are working on the rug. This means that the design will be in reverse when you have completed it. Most geometric, abstract and non-objective designs are quite satisfactory in reverse, but you must reverse a design which should be seen from a particular angle *before* you put it on the burlap. If it does not really matter, as for the abstract design in Illus. 5, then draw the design directly on the burlap.

In addition, there are various types of hooking needles available, and the one you decide to use also influences how you should draw the design. One type is the Columbia Minerva Deluxe Rug Needle, with two sizes of point for different sized yarns, which is adjustable to 10 different lengths of loops (see Illus. 8). You may purchase less expensive needles, but they only make one length of loop. The Susan Bates Rug Hook is more like a large crochet hook. You use it mainly with fabric strips hooked from the right side of the fabric, using your eye as a gauge in determining the length or height of loops (see Illus. 7).

If you plan to use a true hook, like the crochet hook, you should draw the design on the right side of the backing. If, on the other hand, you plan to use a punch-type needle, draw the design on the reverse or wrong side of the fabric. For this first rug, use a punch-type needle, and trace your design onto the back of your burlap.

Instead of drawing the design directly on the burlap, you may draw it on wrapping or tracing paper with a grease pencil or marking pencil (*not* wax crayon). Then turn over the paper, pin or tape it to the burlap and press with a hot iron to transfer the design to the burlap. It is generally easier to do this before you staple the fabric to the frame. The design must be straight with the weave of the fabric.

Winding the Yarn

Before you begin to hook your rug, you should choose and prepare your yarn. Today, most hooked rugs are made with 4-ply yarns, heavy rug yarns, or strips of woollen materials. For a wall hanging, you may use a variety of textures and weights of yarns, such as "thick and thin" (one yarn), Angora, eider-down, cow hair, goat hair, rayons and blends.

If you purchase the yarns in skeins, you should

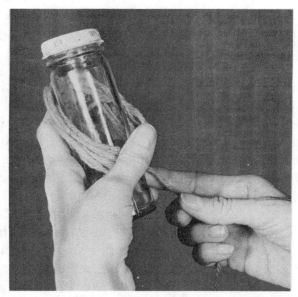

Illus. 9. Start winding the yarn in a diagonal direction.

wind them into balls. There are commercial yarn winders which you can buy, but you can make your own neat balls by winding the yarn, as your grandmother used to do, over your thumb, over a long, slender bottle (see Illus. 9), a thick dowel, or a cardboard paper-towel tube.

Whatever you use, keep a loose hold on the yarn so the ball will not be hard when completely wound. A hard ball indicates that you have stretched the yarn. Start the winding by holding the beginning end so the yarn pulls from the middle. Sometimes you may want to have two strands of the same color in the needle. You can pull them from the same ball—from the inside and the outside.

You also have the choice of cutting the fabrics for hooking into strips with scissors or, more evenly, with a strip cutter which you can fasten to the edge of a work table and adjust to several widths of strips. Single-edged razor blades, the cutting tools, are inexpensive, easily replaceable cutters.

How to Hook

In Illus. 10, a punch-type needle has been threaded with two strands of 4-ply yarn. Note in Illus. 11 that the two strands threaded into the needle come from two balls of yarn. They *could* extend instead from the middle and the outside of just one ball. When you wish to have a gradation of hue or of dark and light, use two strands of yarn in the needle. You can then change one strand each time you wish to change the hue or tone. For instance, if you have three different color gradations of yarn, use two strands of, for example, color A, then a strand of color A and color B, then two strands of color B, then a strand of color B and color C, then two strands of color C. In this way, the change from color A to color C will not be too much of a sudden contrast.

After you decide on yarn colors, choose your desired loop length and lock the needle in place. (The needle in Illus. 10 was adjusted

Illus. 10. This needle is adjusted to the longest loop. The open side of the needle must face the direction of the hooking.

to the #1—longest—length of loop and was then locked in place.) Thread the yarn through the hole at the top and through the eye of the needle and pull it taut through the needle.

Illus. 11. A side view of the burlap on the frame shows the needle in the same position as in Illus. 10.

Illus. 12. Push the needle all the way through the fabric to the handle of the needle.

You may follow the straight weave of the fabric or the curves of your design (if, for instance, you are hooking the abstract in Illus. 5)—this depends upon the effect and the lines of the design you desire. You need to hook short loops more closely together than long loops. In Illus. 15, several loops have already been made.

It is quite important that you have sufficient yarn unwound from the ball when inserting the needle. If you only unwind a small amount, there will be tension on the loops and they will either be shorter than desired, or they will pull out entirely.

This first rug is actually a trial piece. Experiment to determine the effect of different

Illus. 13. A side view of Illus. 12. Push the needle all the way through to the handle. Hold the ends of the yarn as you pull the needle back to the surface.

Place the open side of the needle so it faces the direction in which you plan to hook. Push the needle all the way through the fabric to the handle (see Illus. 12). Be sure to place the point of the needle *between* two threads in the weave of the burlap. Do not split threads.

In Illus. 13, the ends of yarn extend below the needle. Hold onto them as you pull the needle back up to the top surface of the fabric. Continue to hold them in place as you punch the needle into the fabric further along the lines of the design. (You can trim the ends even with the loops when the rug is all hooked.) Note that you must push the needle all the way down to the handle for each loop. Pull the needle out of the burlap just enough so the point of the needle clears the burlap and insert it in the next space desired.

For especially long loops, hold the loop underneath as you pull the needle back to the surface for the next loop. For thick and thin yarns, hold the yarn underneath for each loop as you pull the needle back to the surface of the burlap. Skip one, two, or three threads (see Illus. 14).

Illus. 14. For the second insert, push the needle through the burlap skipping one, two or three threads. Push the needle all the way to the handle for each loop.

lengths of loops, clipped or unclipped, one, two or three strands in the needle.

When you come to the end of the yarn, or to the end of a desired color area, allow the end to extend through to the right side of the rug before you cut it off. When you re-thread the needle, insert it in the same hole that it came out of for the last loop. This means that the two ends come out of the same hole and give more even thickness of pile with no empty or thin spaces.

The beauty of a hooked rug depends not only upon the design, but also upon the way it is hooked, the length and evenness of the loops, whether the loops are clipped or unclipped, and the materials or combinations of materials you use. A beautiful texture is more important than a definite design. The basic design is important, of course, but you can enhance any design by the colors you use and the technique of hooking you apply. For this reason, especially, you should consider your first practice rug as an experiment in design, color and hooking techniques. Do not worry if it is not perfect.

Finishing the Rug or Wall Hanging

Finishing a rug or wall hanging after you have taken it off the frame is very important, just as is the finishing of seams on the inside of a garment: It is the mark of a good craftsman.

As you work, leave an unhooked border about 2″ wide all the way round your rug. You will turn this under for a hem after you take the rug off the frame. Before you turn the hem, however, cover the back of the loops with a liquid rubber (latex) backing, which you can purchase in shops or departments where floor coverings are sold, even though it is later difficult to sew through the rubber backing.

It is easier to apply the latex backing if you do it before you take your project off the frame. To apply the liquid to the back of a hooked piece which you have completely covered with loops, pour the latex on the back over an area about 12″ square and smooth it

Illus. 15. Several loops have been made. Try to keep the loops even.

out with the edge of a piece of cardboard, a putty knife, or a plastic scraper.

Anchor the loops even if you are not planning to use the piece as a rug on the floor because you may wish to use a vacuum cleaner or a soft brush to clean a wall piece, and you could easily pull out the loops, especially clipped ones. In fact, in hooking the design, if you are not satisfied with a particular part, you can easily pull it out and fill the area in again in a different color, or with different length loops. Do not feel that once you have hooked an area that you must leave it.

After the backing is dry, remove the rug from the frame, and turn under and stitch the unhooked border for a hem.

Now, find an empty wall space and hang up your first rug. If you are pleased with the section of the abstract or geometric design you hooked, you could go on to make a larger rug using the whole design.

You are now familiar with the basic rug-hooking techniques. Continue experimenting with different backing fabrics, different yarns and yarn combinations, and different loop lengths. Search for unusual, original ideas for designs.

Remember only that a rug is usually viewed from all sides and should, therefore, have no top or bottom. If you plan to hang your rug on the wall, however, the design may or may not have a top and bottom.

Knotting

Knotted rugs are similar in appearance to hooked rugs, but instead of looping the yarn through the backing and anchoring it with latex, you tie the yarn to the backing in a series of knots. Plan, sketch and transfer your design for knotting in the same way as you did for hooking (see pages 336 to 338), either by tracing or by drawing freehand.

You can make knotted rugs on a frame like those on which you hooked rugs, but it is not necessary and *may* be quite inconvenient for a large rug. It is difficult to reach the middle if the rug is more than 32″ to 36″ wide. In most contemporary hooked rugs, you hook the design from the wrong side (or under side). You make a knotted rug, however, from the right (or top) side, so you can enjoy its beauty while you are working on it. After all, the joy you derive from the actual working time is just as important—in fact, more so—than the pleasure you derive from the completed article.

The backing for knotting may be a coarse mesh called Smyrna rug canvas, burlap in which you have pulled filling threads at regular intervals of $\frac{1}{4}$″ to $\frac{1}{2}$″, or a special, closely woven Swedish rug backing which has an open area every $\frac{1}{2}$″ which allows you to insert the needle for tying in the knots. The Smyrna rug canvas is available in more shops than is this Swedish rug backing, which, in most instances, is imported from Sweden. You may make the knots with a Dritz latch hook or with an ordinary darning or tapestry needle, but this article is only concerned with needle knotting.

Needle Knotting Method

In needle knotting, you thread the needle with one, two or more strands of yarn, depending upon the compactness you desire and the weight of the yarn you are threading into the needle. You may knot on burlap in which you have removed every fourth, sixth or eighth filling thread to allow space to tie the Rya knot (see Illus. 16). You may also sew knots into the Smyrna rug canvas as in Illus. 17. (The knot is sometimes referred to as a Turkish or Giordes knot.)

To determine the length of the loop for the knot, hold the yarn over your finger, a ruler, a heavy piece of cardboard, or over a narrow strip of wood which has a groove cut into one edge. Sand the wood well so it does not snag the yarn. Vary the depth of the cardboard or wooden strips (1″, 1½″, 2″) in order to make different lengths of pile. For a cut pile, cut along the top edge of the cardboard or use scissors, a sharp knife, or a razor blade along the groove of the wood.

Most people who do needle knotting in the Rya manner use one of two kinds of rug backing instead of burlap. You do not need to tack the coarse mesh of the Smyrna rug canvas onto a frame. Therefore, you can take your work with you more easily wherever you go. With the heavy canvas, you can use two or

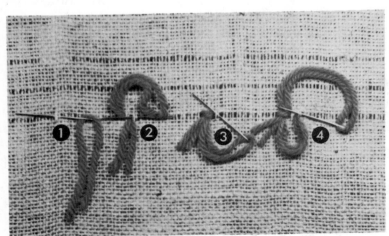

Illus. 16. To make the Rya knot on burlap, remove every fourth, sixth or eighth filling thread and "sew" loops in the space from which you removed thread. Use a blunt-end tapestry needle with a large eye and thread it with one or two strands of yarn. 1: Insert needle under two warp threads. 2: Pull yarn through while holding ends of yarn down. Flip yarn on needle upwards. Hold ends taut while you insert needle under next two warp threads. As you pull needle through, knot forms. 3: Repeat these two steps, but hold your finger or thumb over yarn while you pull needle through for the first step. 4: Flip yarn upwards again before you repeat the second step. Try to keep the loops even. You may clip them later, if you wish.

Illus. 17. You may make the Rya knot on Smyrna rug canvas. Note that the ends or loops extend upwards instead of downwards as in Illus. 16. Thread one or two strands of yarn into needle. 1: Insert needle under left one of a pair of warp threads. 2: Pull yarn through, holding ends of yarn upwards. Flip yarn on needle downwards. Hold ends taut while you insert needle under next warp thread of pair. As you pull needle through, knot forms. 3: Repeat these two steps, but hold your finger or thumb over yarn while you pull needle through for first step. 4: Flip yarn downwards again before repeating second step. Try to keep loops even. You may clip them, if you wish. For a very thick pile, thread three strands into needle and skip pair of warp threads between each knot. Make second row of knots on row below first, but in between knots above.

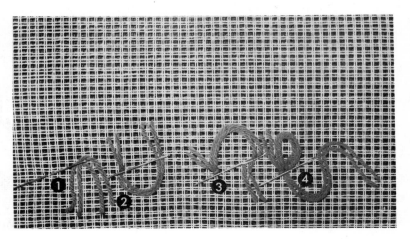

three strands of yarn in the needle and put a knot around each pair of threads in the canvas, or use two or three strands of yarn in the needle and skip a pair of warp threads and still get a compact pile. This makes fewer stitches to the inch, but it is also a bit harder on your fingers when you pull the needle through. Note that the loops in Illus. 16 hang downwards and you fill the space upwards as you work. In Illus. 17 and 18, the pile extends upwards and after you have completed one row across, you fill the space downwards as you work. Either method makes the same type of knot, but if you are making a fairly large rug or wall hanging, you may find the latter method easier because you can keep the extra weight of the project on a work table in front of you rather than on your lap. A piece that is about 40″ × 72″ can get a bit heavy as you near the end of the project.

You can also use Swedish rug backing (see page 342) for needle knotting.

You do most needle knotting in straight, horizontal rows, although you may change needles to use different colors or different lengths of loops, all within the same row.

Practice needle knotting a small rug or hanging before you attempt a large project. When you feel confident that you know the technique, you are ready to create a large rug.

You may leave all the pile in a knotted rug unclipped, or you may clip it all. You may also leave a combination of clipped and unclipped loops to produce a variation in texture.

Needless to say, you can change colors more easily and do more complicated designs in a hooked rug than in a knotted one. But, you can work a greater variety of textures of yarns in a knotted rug. Metallic and rough yarns are easier to use with a large darning or tapestry needle than with a hooking needle. For a hooked project, rough yarns or ones with small, fuzzy projecting ends, such as Angora, have a tendency to pull out of the burlap as you pull the hooking needle out for the next loop. In the knotted rug, the knot holds them in place.

See color page V for examples of finished rugs.

Illus. 18. This sample of Swedish woven backing for Rya knotting shows the space left for tying in the knots. Wind the yarn round a wooden ruler-type stick that has a groove in the top edge to give the right height of pile. Cut the loops with scissors or a razor blade along this groove in the edge.

JUNK SCULPTURES

This article is designed to show you all the essentials of junk sculpture, starting you off with simple projects and advancing you to more complicated works. The whole point of junk sculpture is to make use of whatever is at hand, so if you do not have the specific material suggested here, just improvise. The important thing to remember is to look for possibilities in the junk objects you see about you. You may need to train your eyes, but you will soon be recognizing potential faces or beautiful designs in even the humblest junk.

Materials

First, you need junk. Look for pieces that can be easily bolted or attached together. Try to find something large and solid, with a level bottom, for the base of your sculpture. You will also need a variety of nuts, bolts, screws, nails, and washers, as well as glue, string, wire, and solder. Tools required depend on the materials you work with. Have a can opener, saw, hammer, screwdriver, pliers, wire cutter, knife, and scissors at hand.

Use tempera or poster paints for paper or cardboard surfaces. Spray paints are good for wooden, metal, and most plastic surfaces (they dissolve plastic foam). Latex and acrylic paints, and household paints and enamels, can also be used. However, latex does not cover rust well.

Egg-Carton Sculpture

Start out with a simple sculpture involving easily accessible materials, such as the egg-carton sculpture in Illus. 1.

To build this sculpture you will need a small cardboard box, several cardboard egg cartons, two unwaxed paper cups, and a flat piece of corrugated cardboard, 8″ × 15″. You also need a dozen 1″ paper fasteners (or glue), some masking tape or packaging tape, and a scissors.

First cut four 2″ × 15″ strips of cardboard. Then carefully fold over 2″ at the base of each strip so that it makes a right angle.

Next, lay two of these strips next to one another so that they touch lengthwise. Then

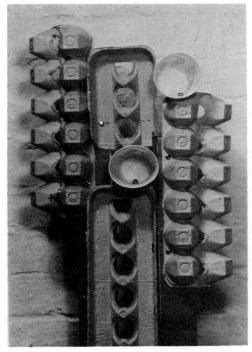

Illus. 1.

Condensed from the book, "Junk Sculpture" by Gregg LeFevre / © 1973 by Sterling Publishing Co., Inc., New York

interesting shapes. Experiment—try making an egg-carton mobile from brightly painted pieces of an egg carton. Or combine the egg carton with different materials.

Wood Sculpture

The triangular scraps of wood composing the sculpture in Illus. 3 were salvaged from the trash at a wood-working shop.

This sculpture was constructed by threading the pieces on a metal rod anchored in the round log and then glueing them together when a suitable arrangement was found. However, if you know the exact shape you want, you can simply glue the wood without threading it on a rod. A large log, or anything similar, makes a perfect base.

run a piece of tape down the unfolded part of the seam where the two pieces touch, joining them together. In the same fashion, tape together the other two cardboard strips. Fold each pair of strips along this taped seam to make a right angle.

Now, tape both strips to the base box (Illus. 2). They should be positioned about 3″ apart, with one side of each parallel to the front of the box. Then lay the 2″ flaps which were flat against the surface of the base box, and tape down securely.

Before you attach the cartons, cut them into sections which form the various elements of your design. Here, the lid of each of the two cartons has been removed, and the bottom halves folded lengthwise down the middle.

Attach the cartons to the cardboard supports by first positioning them, then cutting a hole through the carton and the supports and pushing a paper fastener through and spreading its prongs. (Use glue if you do not have paper fasteners handy.) Finally, place and attach the paper cups.

Egg cartons can be cut into a variety of

Illus. 3. "Stack II," 11″ × 11″ × 43″.

A fairy-tale castle is easy to make from a number of different types of wood. Start with a small baseboard. The one in Illus. 4 measures 10″ × 7″. Then glue spools together to form columns, using either large spools, or some other suitable wooden shapes. Two spool columns connected at the top by glued ice cream sticks make an interesting gate or arch. You can make other towers by glueing together small wooden blocks or dowels.

Make the turrets from decorative bottle tops or by either filing plastic foam scraps into pointed forms or by glueing together some wooden wedges. Yarn running from one of the tower tops to holes drilled in the base-board adds a drawbridge effect.

Illus. 4. "Camelot," 10″ × 7″ × 13″. This sculpture was constructed with thread spools, ice cream sticks, wooden dowels, assorted wood scraps, a perfume bottle top, and yarn; and painted with tempera paint. (See color Illus. Z1 on page Z.)

Found Objects

A single piece of junk can sometimes make an interesting sculpture. "Found Objects" is the title often given to such sculptures. Both of the pieces in Illus. 5 and Illus. 6 were "found"

Illus. 5. "Mother and Child," 6″ x 6″ x 14″.

Illus. 6. Untitled, 8″ x 4″ x 23″.

just as they appear and mounted on a base block. The stove burner in "Mother and Child" was painted and then bolted onto the base block. The shaft of the cast-iron section in Illus. 6 was inserted into a broken cinder block and wooden wedges were hammered in to secure it.

TV Dinner Tray Sculpture

TV dinner trays can be used to make a junk wall sculpture. For best results, carefully remove the dinners from the trays before

Illus. 7. Untitled, 23" x 20". Instead of throwing out your used TV dinner trays, put them to good use as interesting pieces of junk sculpture.

eating, because utensils will dent the aluminum (unless you want a dented effect). After cleaning four trays, paint them with enamel or spray paint. The bottoms were painted for the sculpture in Illus. 7, but painting the insides works just as well. Next, nail holes in the corners and attach the trays to a poster-board or cardboard backing with paper fasteners. You can tie a hanging wire or string between these on the back.

Metal Strip Sculpture

While a chrome strip from the side of an automobile was used for the sculpture in Illus. 8, you can use any form of long metal strip for the same purpose. Aluminum siding, counter siding, or metal framing strip can all be used. Or, bolt shorter pieces together to make strip designs.

Begin by applying masking tape in several lines along the entire length of both sides of the metal strip. Spray-paint the strip. Remove the tape and you should have stripes of color alternating with the metal finish.

Next, use a piece of wire the same length as your strip to experiment with different designs. When you have worked out a suitable design, bend the strip into the same configuration.

Illus. 8. Untitled, 19" × 14" × 35". Long, gleaming strips of chrome make interesting junk sculptures and are easy to obtain from automobile junk-yards.

Then bend over a short portion of the bottom end of your strip, make several nail holes in it, and screw it down to your base block. A redwood 4 × 4 mounted on top of a pine-wood square was used for the base block in Illus. 8.

To add motion to your piece, bolt together two tin cans with the tops and bottoms removed, and suspend them on a string or wire from the strip design.

Metal and Mixed Media Sculpture

All the different pieces of junk in Illus. 9 were used in constructing "Clown with Hat" (Illus. 11). Most of the pieces were chosen either because they already had holes or brackets and could be easily attached, or because they were made out of a material light enough to be easily pierced.

You will not find, naturally, the exact objects used in this clown, but you can follow the same general procedures for assembling a figure of your own.

The first operation involves driving holes into the hub-cap base so that the central support for the rest of the sculpture, in this case a large T-hinge, can be bolted in place. To do this, first mark where the holes are to go, and then hammer the holes using either a heavy nail (like a masonry nail or spike) or a nail punch. The safest way to do this is to hold the nail with a pair of pliers.

Then bolt the square end of the T-hinge onto the hub, holding the nut from one side with a pliers and turning on the bolt on the other side with a screwdriver. Because the other end of the hinge is still free to move, use thin wire to secure it in place.

On top of the vertical hinge, bolt on the pulley. This was a well chosen piece of junk because it contained a number of different-sized holes and four side sprockets to which things could be attached.

You can then paint the piece. Next, drive a hole through the ham can. Insert a bolt through this hole and through the middle

Illus. 9. "Clown with Hat" was constructed with the following materials (left to right, top to bottom): desk-lamp arm base, T-hinge, hub cap, wheel ring, small metal spring, carburetor section, anchovy tin can, pulley, light socket, film reel, heavy spring, and a ham tin can.

Illus. 10. Solder the anchovy tin can onto the carburetor section.

hole in the film reel, and then attach both to the hole, half-way up, in the vertical hinge.

Following this, bolt the triple light socket onto the face of the pulley. Break off the lower socket leaving the two remaining sockets to serve as eyes, and the metal lamp-shade brace between them to serve as a nose.

Now solder an oval-shaped anchovy can onto the carburetor section (Illus. 10). Use either a soldering gun or soldering iron. (When soldering, first clean the surface and heat the pieces at the jointing point before applying solder. For iron, use acid-core solder and rosin flux; for other metals, use any solder other than acid-core; for aluminum, use special aluminum solder.) Then bolt the carburetor section with the anchovy can soldered to it to the face of the pulley below the sockets. The oval can forms a mouth and the carburetor section forms the cheek, jaws, and lower face.

Next, on either side of the clown's face (the pulley), attach the "earrings"—on one side the spring is hooked in place, and on the other, the desk-lamp base.

At this point, squeeze a short section of

tubing (aluminum, plastic, or rubber will do) onto the top sprocket of the pulley. Use wire to tie the wheel ring (the white painted circular "hat" in Illus. 11) to a hole made in the top of this tubing. The tubing simply elevates the wheel ring so that it encircles the face.

Finally, paint the entire piece.

After the paint dries, you can add several finishing touches. Twist on a wound-wire necklace, paste on a magazine cut-out flower, screw in two light-bulb eyes, and cut paper eyelashes for them. Pin a scrap cloth round a coat hanger hung from the back of the pulley to give the clown a cape.

Illus. 11. "Clown with Hat." Try to construct this bizarre and comic clown (or a semblance of him, since you probably will not find the exact materials used here). This clown is made of various ordinary pieces of junk, and painted with latex and enamel.

KNICK-KNACKS FOR NEATNESS

Everyone likes to have a tidy room—but not everyone likes to make it tidy. Here are some fun ideas which will make cleaning-up a creative, pleasurable activity. All you need are a few inexpensive, common household items and some imagination. Who knows—you may even come to enjoy being neat!

Belt Valet

Saw off the handle of a discarded (preferably bamboo) rake. After painting the fan-like part of the rake, nail it on your wall. Hang up belts, ribbons, and odds and ends on the teeth of the rake.

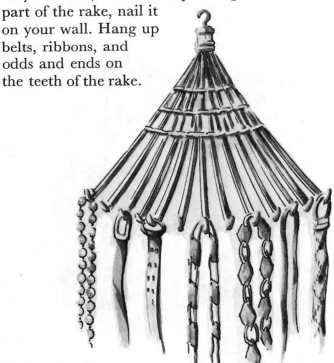

Illus. 2. Wall apron.

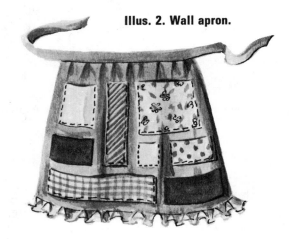

Illus. 1. Belt valet.

Wall Apron

Stitch pockets all over a large apron. Tape or tack the apron by its ties to a bulletin board, desk or door as a convenient resting place for room overflow.

Knife Holder

The safest and most convenient place to keep sharp knives is in a knife holder. You can make one out of a cigar box. Open the box and glue small pieces of base moulding as deep as the box in each corner to reinforce the box.

At one end of the box, cut three or four slots 1½″ apart for the knives. Now glue down the lid. Select a decorative piece of wallpaper from your scrap collection and paste it neatly round the box.

To hang the knife holder, place screw eyes at the top corners and hang it on the wall.

Condensed from the books, "Creating from Scrap" by Lillian and Godfrey Frankel | © 1962 by Sterling Publishing Co., Inc., New York, and "Nick-Nacks for Neatness" by Sheila Ostrander | © 1963 by Sterling Publishing Co., Inc., New York

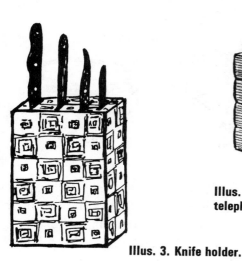

Illus. 3. Knife holder.

Illus. 4. Glue and then tape old telephone books together for a foot stool.

Illus. 5. Add decorative tassels to your completed stool.

Pattern Caddy

To sort and index all your patterns, construct a caddy from cut-down cereal boxes. Cut several of the boxes from a top corner to the middle of the opposite side. Then glue the boxes together side by side. Decorate the holder and label the front of each compartment with a picture of the type of pattern it is holding—that is, skirts, dresses, blouses, or whatever.

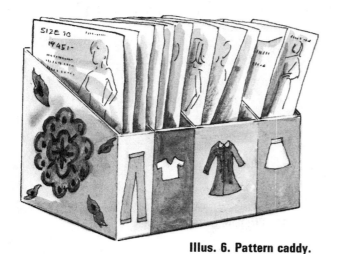

Illus. 6. Pattern caddy.

Scent Tray

You'll never have to remove scratches or perfume stains from your dresser top if you have this sleek perfume tray. Paint or decorate a picture frame and place a mirror in it instead of the glass. Cover the whole back of the frame with felt to scratch-proof it. Perfume bottles show off their elegant reflections in the mirror.

Foot Stool

You can speedily put together a clever foot stool or hassock from a pile of old telephone directories or catalogues. Glue the books together and tape them firmly with adhesive tape (Illus. 4). Cover them over with heavy paper and then wrap them in a piece of burlap or attractive, sturdy cloth. Stitch a cushion which you have bought or made to the top to make the stool comfortable. Add decorative tassels to each corner (Illus. 5).

Nail-Keg Stool

For this stool, you need an empty nail keg, a burlap bag, $\frac{1}{2}$ yard of oilcloth, a box crate and old pillow or foam rubber scraps. Also, you need 100 upholsterer's nails and 100 tacks.

When you finish putting these scraps together

Illus. 7. Scent tray.

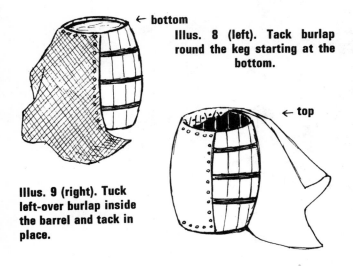

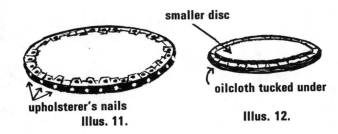

← bottom

Illus. 8 (left). Tack burlap round the keg starting at the bottom.

← top

smaller disc

oilcloth tucked under

Illus. 12.

upholsterer's nails
Illus. 11.

Illus. 9 (right). Tuck left-over burlap inside the barrel and tack in place.

you will have quite a nice piece of furniture. Stand the keg bottom side up, and wrap the burlap bag around it so that the burlap just reaches the bottom (closed end) of the keg. Tack the burlap to the keg around the top and bottom, and nail or sew the side seam. Turn the keg right side up and tuck the left-over burlap inside the barrel. Use a few tacks to hold it in place.

Cut strips of oilcloth long enough to go around the two ends of the barrel. Tack them down with upholsterer's nails and add more nails to form a design on the barrel. Illus. 10 may give you an idea.

You now need a seat for your stool. Take the two sturdy ends of an apple or orange crate and draw an $11\frac{1}{2}$" circle on one and a 9" circle on

the other. Carefully saw out these circles. Use an old pillow, pieces of quilt or foam rubber to pad the $11\frac{1}{2}$" circle and cover it with a circle of oilcloth 18" in diameter. Place the oilcloth over the padding and nail the overlap to the underside of the wooden circle. You have to make little pleats as you work because the oilcloth is larger than the seat (see Illus. 11). Now nail or screw the smaller circle to the bottom of the seat (see Illus. 12) to keep the seat from slipping off the barrel. Your last step is to trim around the edge of the seat with upholsterer's nails.

Your nail-keg stool is now finished and ready for use. You can store some of your belongings inside the stool as a secret hiding place.

Wrapping Station

To keep your gift wrapping paper, ribbon and bow supplies, scissors and tape organized,

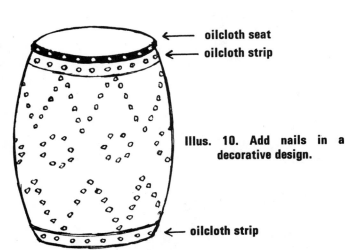

← oilcloth seat
← oilcloth strip

Illus. 10. Add nails in a decorative design.

← oilcloth strip

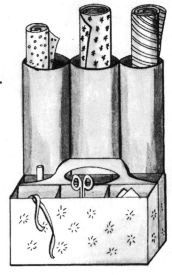

Illus. 13. Wrapping station.

try constructing a Wrapping Station. Put tape over one end of each of three wax paper or paper towel tubes and glue them to one side of a soft drink carton. Paint the holder and sparkle it with glitter. Roll the wrapping paper and store it in the tubes. This allows you to save bits of attractive paper to use again. Sort ribbons, cards, stickers, and so on, into the front compartments.

Spare-Time Neatness

Do you want to make better use of your leisure time? Try these knick-knacks to help you find supplies quickly and cut down the time you spend tidying up afterwards.

Protect blouses and shirts from stains and splotches with plastic pull-overs. To have pull-overs up your sleeves, find two long plastic bags, slit the ends and stitch a seam lengthwise to make them narrow enough to fit comfortably round your arms. Cut off the excess from the seam. Turn up a narrow hem at the elbow end of the pull-overs and put an elastic round it to hold the sleeves on. Instead of wrinkling your blouse or sweater sleeves by rolling them up, simply pull on your "pull-overs" (Illus. 14).

Time and again it is easy to pick up the right brush or pencil when they are arranged in this stylish hobby accessory, a paint brush "spray." You can make it in minutes by inserting the end of one funnel inside the end of another. Then, paint them a glistening gold. The smaller funnel on the bottom forms the stand and the top funnel holds the pencils in easy-to-pick-out order (Illus. 16).

Illus. 14 (above). Slip these easy-to-make pull-overs over your blouse or shirt to protect it.

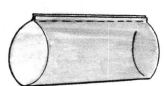

Illus. 15 (above). Stitch slit plastic bags as shown.

Illus. 17. Cut a piece of thick sponge and then cut a hole in it for the thermos.

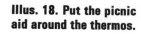

Illus. 18. Put the picnic aid around the thermos.

Illus. 16. Pencil or paint-brush "spray."

Picnic Aid

Collar a thermos bottle so there is no danger of its rolling off a desk, lunch table or picnic table and breaking its glass lining. Cut a square or triangle of thick sponge about $4\frac{1}{2}'' \times 4\frac{1}{2}''$ and cut out from the middle of this a circle as big as the diameter of your thermos bottle. Slide the collar over the top of the bottle and tape or glue it in place. This hardy collar also helps prevent drips as well as falls.

Think of Your Pet

Dog or Cat Nest

A dog or cat couch made from a worn-out automobile tire is a comfortable place for your pet to bed down. Either cover the tire with burlap or place it inside a burlap bag and stitch the bag closed. The hollow middle of the tire forms a perfect nest for the animal.

Cat Fish

Protect your walls, furniture and clothes from cat scratches with this special "cat" fish for your puss to scrape his paws on. Cut off a discarded cotton or nylon stocking about 8″ above the foot. (Use the foot section later as part of the fish's stuffing.) Fold the cut-off edge of the stocking section into a point to form the fish's head and stitch it closed (Illus. 25). Stuff the stocking with rags, bits of catnip and discarded nylons. Tie the wide end of the stocking 2½″ from the top to form the fish's tail (Illus. 26). Paint on fish scales and embroider on the fish's eyes and mouth. Attach a string to the fish and hang it indoors or outdoors (Illus. 22).

Bird's Flight Deck

Have a close-up view of birds dining on this flight deck in your window. Two frozen TV dinner trays make a convenient place to put food for birds. Tape the trays together side by side with adhesive tape. Fasten them securely to your window ledge or a branch in a nearby tree. Fill the various compartments of the trays with bread crumbs, water and suet.

Illus. 19. Use an old tire for your pet's couch.

sack

Illus. 20. Cover the tire with a sack.

Illus. 21. The completed pet nest.

Illus. 22. Cat Fish.

stuffing

Illus. 25.

Illus. 26.

tie

cut

Illus. 24.

fold and stitch

Illus. 24, 25, and 26. Making a cat fish.

Illus. 23. Flight deck.

MOBILES

Materials

There is practically no limit to the materials that you can use in making mobiles. Probably the only limiting factor is weight! In addition to cardboard, paper, plastic, and glass, there are miscellaneous materials such as nuts and fruit, table-tennis balls, driftwood bits, wood shavings, and drinking straws, both natural and plastic tubing types—in fact anything that you may want to use. The only limitations are whether the supporting materials you choose are strong enough to hold the materials you select, adapt or create.

Hanging

The best way to display an indoor mobile is to suspend it from the ceiling or from a light fixture affixed to the ceiling.

You can insert lead, fibre, or plastic plugs into holes drilled in the ceiling. (Be sure the hole is only as deep as the plug is long.) When you screw a screw into the plug, the screw expands to grip the plaster sides of the hole. Or, better still, you can use a flange-type fastening device. (It has several names but is basically a bolt with wings that fold down when going through the hole and expand in the hollow space behind the plaster.) You can suspend outdoor mobiles, of course, from posts, poles, or tree branches.

Nylon thread or nylon fishing line are best for suspending mobile parts, but you can also use heavy sewing thread.

Galvanized iron wire, most frequently used

as fencing, is the most easily obtainable wire and can be bought at most hardware suppliers'. Wire thicknesses are measured and described in gauges. The most useful gauges for the maker of mobiles will be Nos. 18, 16, 14, and 12. (The wire gets thicker as the gauge number decreases.)

If you use wire, your pliers should be the long-nosed type, with jaws about 4″ long. Get the kind with side cutters in the jaws. You will use the pliers to cut wires and to bend loops in the wires with which your mobiles will be hung.

Construction

Generally speaking, mobiles are made "from the bottom up." Start by assembling the lowermost arm or arms and add others above them. You can usually change a mobile consisting of, say, three parts to one of five, ten, or any greater number, simply by adding additional parts at the top. You can *design* a mobile and—having its design fixed in mind or on paper—proceed to construct your mobile from the top down. But in your early, experimental mobiles you will certainly want to start at the lower level and work upwards, adding the higher levels as you proceed.

You can attach cardboard mobile parts to wires or thread through punched holes and by looping or tying the wires and threads. Or, they may be joined with glue. Metal mobile pieces can be soldered to wire arms; if suspended from them, the pieces can be punched to receive threads or fine wires or the loops of the wire

Condensed from the book, "Make Your Own Mobiles" by T. M. Schegger | © 1965 by Sterling Publishing Co., Inc., New York

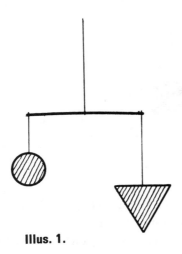

Illus. 1.

arms. Use a long-nosed pliers to form loops in wire arms.

The important rule to remember about mobiles is that there are no rules. There are no fixed dimensions for objects or designated lengths of support arms, lengths of suspension threads, etc. Whether you wish your assemblages to hang in symmetrical horizontal balance or to be balanced in asymmetrical equilibrium, or whether your wire support arms will be straight or will curve in gentle arcs is up to you.

Once having created, adapted or selected the objects for inclusion in a mobile, your only problem will be the arrangement or balance of the particular objects. While the balance point of two objects of equal weight is obviously at the exact middle of the supporting arm (Illus. 1), that of unequal objects can only be determined by trial and error.

Of course, the parts of a mobile do not always have to be in perfect balance. If you fasten two coins at one end of a ruler and one at the other end and balance the ruler at about

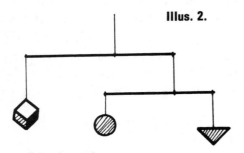

Illus. 2.

6 inches, you will notice that the ruler will incline itself at an angle and eventually come to rest and hold the inclined position. The whole system of coins and ruler is in equilibrium, even though it is not horizontally and symmetrically balanced.

So it is with a mobile, too. Two objects on one arm of a mobile may be asymmetrically balanced in equilibrium by a single object if you vary their position slightly or alter the position of the balance point. To achieve perfect balance, if, for example, you were using a cardboard cut-out mobile, you could make the single side heavier by using a larger piece of cardboard or by using two smaller pieces of cardboard glued together (double-thickness), thus equalling in weight the two pieces on the opposite side. (See Illus. 2.) Instead, you could balance two cardboard objects with one of a heavier material, such as metal.

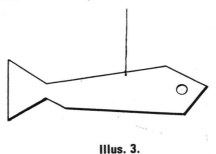

Illus. 3.

Flat Fish

Anyone who can use a pair of scissors can make a whole school of these flat fish in a few minutes' time. Cut a series of simple, angular forms as shown in Illus. 3. They don't have to be all of the same size or shape—in fact, they will look better when assembled in a mobile if they display a wide variety of sizes and shapes. Use cardboard, heavy metal foil or patterned gift-wrapping paper. For an unusual effect, cover the cardboard "fish" with paper-thin adhesive-backed wood veneers, alternating the grain direction from fish to fish (Illus. 4). Or paint the cardboard shapes in gay colors.

For something different, try this unusual material: Paste cut-open plastic straws on a

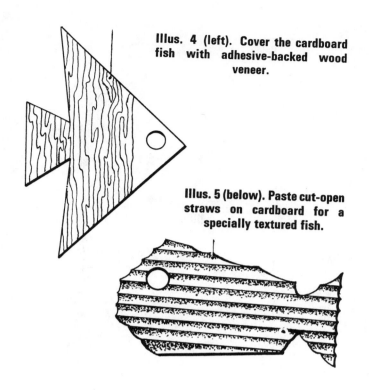

Illus. 4 (left). Cover the cardboard fish with adhesive-backed wood veneer.

Illus. 5 (below). Paste cut-open straws on cardboard for a specially textured fish.

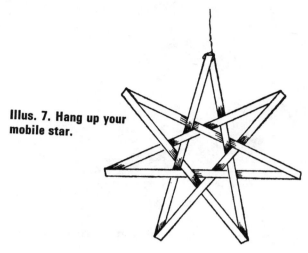

Illus. 7. Hang up your mobile star.

piece of cardboard and cut out fish with a rugged, corduroy-textured surface (Illus. 5).

When your fish are completed, punch the single hole for the eye using a small hand punch.

Straw Stars

Flatten drinking straws with a knife or the bowl of a spoon for making stars.

To make a seven-pointed star you will need seven flattened straws. Glue the end of these together as shown in Illus. 6, using all-purpose glue—but first scrape the wax from the end of each straw so as to make a better joint.

Pin the straws to a board with a pin through the middle of each straw and you will find that they are easier to glue in the shape you want them. Another pin lightly through each joint will help to hold the parts being glued while the glue is drying.

Illus. 8.

Cork Birds

A mobile of cork birds, darting and dancing about, is fun to watch.

The body of each bird is a colored or undyed cork (Illus. 8). Cut the beak from glazed paper. A table-tennis ball will do nicely for the bird's head. Impale both the beak and the head of the bird on a long pin and press its pointed end into the cork until the head meets the body.

Next, stick some dyed feathers to simulate wings and tail into the cork. Drill holes for these beforehand with a thick needle and fasten the feathers in the holes with drops of glue.

Fasten the suspension thread at the balance

Illus. 6.

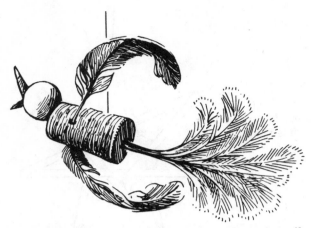

Illus. 9. Add dyed feathers to simulate wings and a tail.

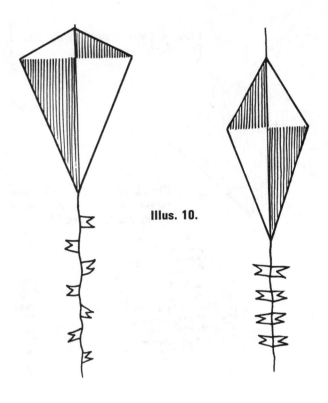

Illus. 10.

point by means of a small tack or pin stuck into the cork body of the bird.

Miniature Kites

Full-size kites need a windy day to perform well; a miniature kite mobile will delight everyone in even the whisper of a wind.

Cut a variety of kite-shaped mobiles from heavy drawing paper or colored, glazed paper following Illus. 10. Fix a piece of cord to the bottom part of the kite as a tail. Glue some colorful paper streamers on this tail as shown.

You can vary the shapes of your kites by making some of them multi-sided. With the use of fine wire and tissue paper, you can even turn out some box kites that look like the real thing.

Hang them so that some float near the ceiling.

Nutshell Sailboats

When you have enjoyed nutmeats, don't discard the shells. Save them for use in your next mobile.

Fill one half of an empty nutshell (walnut shells are the best for this purpose) with

Illus. 11. Nutshell sailboats.

Illus. 12. Devise stylized cats and mice for an unusual mobile.

modelling clay. Insert a toothpick or long thin stick into this clay, and fasten a galleon-type sail to it by impaling it on the mast. (Pricking all the holes beforehand with a sharp knife will help to get them started.) Examine the boats in Illus. 11 for hints on the various kinds of sails that you can hoist on your nutshell sailboats.

Cat and Mouse

Cut a flat, highly stylized cat body out of light-weight cardboard or glazed paper. Cut the tail separately from paper and "kink" it slightly, curling it by running it between your thumb and the cutting edge of the scissors. Or you can make the tail from Christmas gift-wrapping ribbon, curled in the same way. Make the mice in the same fashion.

You can also make the cats and mice out of metal foil strips. Table-tennis balls can also be transformed into cats (Illus. 12, right) and many different animal heads. Use hat pins with glass heads for eyes. Snip off the long ends of the pins and glue the eyes to the table-tennis balls with a dab of colorless cement. Yarn or twine, shredded slightly, will provide the whiskers.

Balloons

You can recapture the days of early aeronautics with a mobile full of dancing balloons.

Tiny figures in the baskets will complete the picture.

Make the balloons from table-tennis balls. Clean smudged balls—and take off manufacturers' imprints—with fine emery paper. If you want a mobile of many colored balloons, paint the individual table-tennis balls with

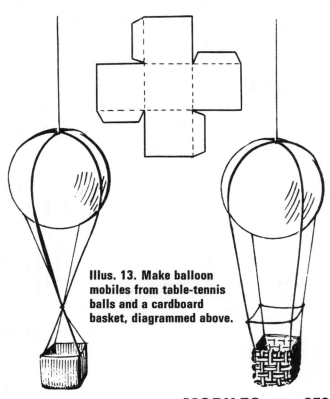

Illus. 13. Make balloon mobiles from table-tennis balls and a cardboard basket, diagrammed above.

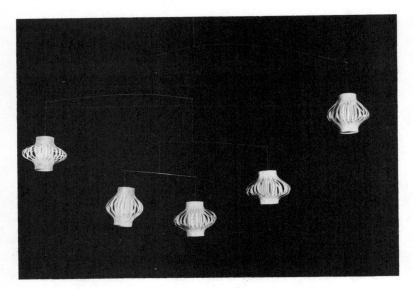

poster colors. Let them dry. Now brush the middle of two pieces of wool yarn 10″ long with glue (a distance of about 1″). Stretch these "cables" over the ball, crossing them at right angles. Let these dry.

Make a small basket out of light-weight cardboard (following Illus. 13) and cover it with a scrap of coarse cloth. Hang from the mid-point by puncturing the ball and stuffing your knotted thread through the hole. If you hang one balloon low over a table and others high, it will give the impression that the balloons are ascending.

Japanese Lanterns

Fold a 12″-square piece of light-weight cardboard in half. Make a number of evenly spaced cuts along the folded edge to within 1″

of the open edges (Illus. 15). Glue the two uncut sides together with a small overlap so that a tube results. Set this tube upright on a table and press down with your hand; you will see that it is very flexible and springy.

Make another (uncut) tube, of the same diameter about 8″ long, of light-weight cardboard and insert it inside the cut tube. Now push the top and bottom parts of the outer (cut) tube together so that it expands in an outward direction. Hold this and glue the top and bottom edges of the outside tube to the inside tube. A fine wire across the top of the lantern will serve as the hanger for attaching the suspension thread. A completed Japanese lantern mobile is shown in Illus. 14. Of course, you should not try to illuminate these "lanterns" with candles.

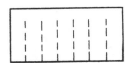

Illus. 15. Cutting the folded
piece of cardboard.

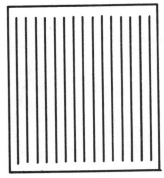

Illus. 16. Open the folded, cut
cardboard.

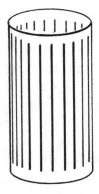

Illus. 17. You should
have formed a tube with
the glued, cut cardboard.

MODEL BOATS

Imagine the excitement of putting together your own model ship—making a vessel of simple paper, wood, a tin can or cardboard that duplicates an ocean-going liner or a swift sailboat. Not only will these models look authentic, they will actually sail in water. Most important of all, you can build these models from inexpensive materials and with tools found at home or at school. Sheets of cardboard, for example, are easy to obtain.

Building a model ship is much more rewarding than merely assembling ready-made kits. As you cut out the parts and fit them together, you will learn the various components of a real ship.

Besides building the model as it is presented in this section, you create your own variations by moving the different parts around—repositioning cabins, masts, and hatches. You make your models any size you wish, and you paint them according to your own taste. From this basic work, you can go on to build other ship models—larger, more detailed or entirely different. You should, however, never try to make a model, or parts of a model, without reading all of the instructions first. Make sure you understand what to do before you start.

Parts of Ships

It is simpler to put ship models together if you know the nautical names of some parts of ships.

The most important part of a ship is its hull. This is the shell-like framework that supports all the other parts of the ship, and it is this structure that actually floats in the water. It has a bottom, a back (stern), and two sides that meet in front (the bow). The keel of the ship is its backbone that runs vertically from bow to stern along the bottom of the hull.

The top of the hull is the deck, which supports one or more cabins, depending upon the ship.

The deck has various openings giving access to storage spaces below. The openings are covered in a manner similar to trap doors in floors. Openings and their covers are called hatches.

All ships have rudders, used for steering. Rudders are placed at the rear of the ship's hull and they go down into the water.

Masts are the tall, round sticks that stand up above the deck and carry sails on sailing craft or radio antennas on many ocean liners. Sometimes they only carry flags or are used as hoists to take cargo on board. The spars are the sticks or poles rigged (set up) parallel to or at an angle to a mast and they are used to hold the sails. The ropes that hold the masts and spars are called the ship's rigging.

The portholes are a boat's windows. They can be in the hull or in the cabins.

The load water line is the level the water comes up to on the hull when the ship is fully loaded. A large vessel has lines at its bow to indicate its various loads.

Anything located above the main deck is usually said to be topside.

You never call the right or left side of a ship

Condensed from the books, "How to Make Things Out of Paper" by Walter Sperling | © 1961 by Sterling Publishing Co., Inc., New York, "Model Boat Building" by Herb Lozier | © 1970 by Sterling Publishing Co., Inc., New York, and "101 Toys Children Can Make" by Robert and Katharine Kunz | © 1959 by Sterling Publishing Co., Inc., New York

right or left. The right side of a ship is always starboard and the left side is always port. Starboard is to your right as you face the bow; port is to your left.

Tools and Materials

The only tools you will actually need are ones you have available: a pair of scissors, a ruler, and a soft-leaded pencil. You also need some quick-drying clear, waterproof cement to glue pieces together. Never use cellophane tape to hold cardboard or paper parts together. Each time you take the tape off, it takes most of the paper or cardboard with it, and spoils the part and the model.

If you use pins to hold the parts together while the cement is drying, push them in just far enough for them to hold, and no farther.

Other tools that are handy, but not necessary, are a modelmaker's knife, like the X-Acto with a pointed blade, or a utility knife, both especially good for cutting straight lines through cardboard. You can use a metal ruler as a guide, moving the knife along the ruler's edge, which you hold firmly next to the line.

Always use your tools so that you work away from your fingers. Keep your fingers away from the knife's blade. In addition, always cut away from your body. This is a good rule when you are cutting with scissors, too. Also remember, when you push pins through cardboard, to keep your fingers clear of the points on the other side.

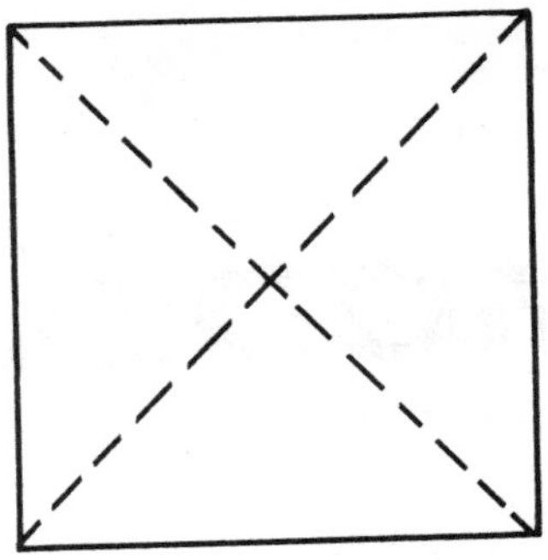

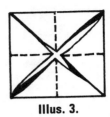

Illus. 2.

Illus. 3.

A compass is a valuable aid whenever you have to draw circles. A tweezer will help you pick up and move pieces which are too small to hold with your fingers.

At times you will want to smooth off the edges of the cut cardboard. Some very fine sandpaper wrapped around a sandpaper block is an ideal tool for this.

Besides these tools, you also need some tracing paper and some carbon paper for tracing and transferring the patterns from the book to your cardboard. Straight pins and cellophane tape also come in handy for tracing.

A work table provides you with a flat surface for drawing the patterns and assembling the models. Be sure to protect the work table with a thick, smooth layer of newspaper or an extra board when you cut.

You will have to buy things like the wooden sticks that are used for the masts and spars, and the propeller shafts. But these sticks, called iodine dowels, are easy to get at the drugstore or pharmacy. They are about 6″ long and about $\frac{1}{16}$″ in diameter. You can judge from the modelling instructions how many you will need.

Paper

Steamboat

One of the first things you learned to make was probably a little paper boat. Here is a way to fold a steamer with a funnel.

Take a sheet of stiff writing paper about

Illus. 1. Steamboat.

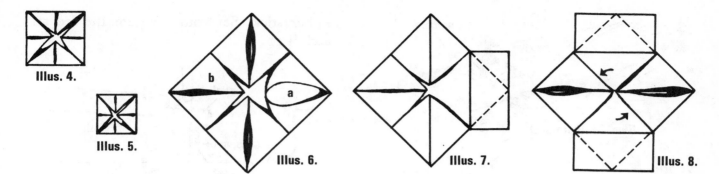

Illus. 4.

Illus. 5.

Illus. 6.

Illus. 7.

Illus. 8.

6″ × 6″. Each time you make a fold, be sure to crease the edges sharply.

Illus. 2: Fold the paper along each diagonal, and open it again.

Illus. 3: Turn the four corners in towards the middle.

Illus. 4: Turn the whole thing over, and again turn the four corners inward.

Illus. 5: Turn again and turn in the corners once more. Your sheet of paper has become much smaller by this time.

Illus. 6: After the last folding, turn it over and compare it to the picture. With your index finger, reach into the pocket (a) and spread the sides out. Press down the whole flap as shown in Illus. 7. Do the same with the opposite pocket to get the shape shown in Illus. 8. Lay this on the table, and press the folded edges firmly with the base of your hand so that everything stays in place.

Illus. 8: Slide your left and right index fingers under the flaps at the places shown by the arrows. Push them in right to the peaks.

Next, push both corners all the way out to form the ship's hull. The shape shown in Illus. 9 will be the result.

Illus. 9: You have now completed the hull of your steamer. Reinforce bow and stern by

turning down the points at a. Let the hull of the ship open slightly, then on the side facing you, turn down the edge at b to the base line c. Crease the fold, and repeat the procedure on the side of the hull facing away from you. Make the same folds at the other end of the ship. Illus. 10 shows the result.

Illus. 10: Make the middle structure shorter by half. Fold both parts forward and back and paste the edges behind the hull of the ship. Fold down c in the direction of the arrow and place it behind the ship's hull. The result is shown in Illus. 11.

Illus. 12: From a strip of paper, build a little platform with a hole in the middle. Slip this into the two folds at the top of the middle structure. Make a funnel by rolling up a strip of paper and pasting it together. Place it firmly in the hole of the platform. All that is missing is the smoke. Blacken a bit of cotton with cigar or cigarette ashes or paint, and stick a wad of it into the funnel. You can add two masts made of toothpicks to the hull and put paper flags on them.

Paint the steamer with water colors. Paint the funnel black with a red ring and the hull light blue. Don't forget the portholes. Let the deck remain white.

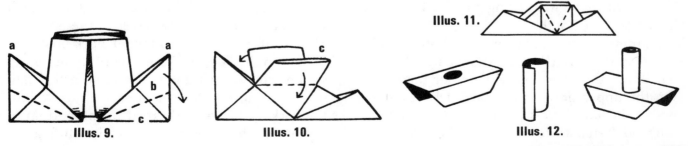

Illus. 9.

Illus. 10.

Illus. 11.

Illus. 12.

MODEL BOATS ■ **363**

Illus. 13. Motorboat.

Wood

Motorboat

Make a motorboat that races through water. You need only two pieces of wood and an elastic band.

Your boat can be any size you want. Cut it to the shape in Illus. 13 and make notches in the back, as shown. Cut another small piece of wood and make notches in the middle of that too. Your boat lasts longer if you put a coat of varnish or paint on it.

Put the elastic band round the small piece of wood so that it rests in the notches. Faster it to the back of the boat, stretching the elastic band so it fits in the other set of notches. Turn it to wind it up, put the boat in the water and let it go. As the elastic band unwinds, the boat will be pushed through the water.

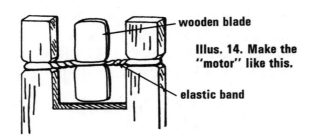

Illus. 14. Make the "motor" like this.

Ice Boat

You will have fun sailing this ice boat on a frozen lake or pond.

Hammer three nails on the bottom of a board and bend them as shown in Illus. 15. These are the skates on which your boat runs. On the upper side of the board, fasten a spool with thin nails. Press a stick into the hole on top and fasten to it a sail made of cloth and

another stick. Set your boat on the ice and watch it go.

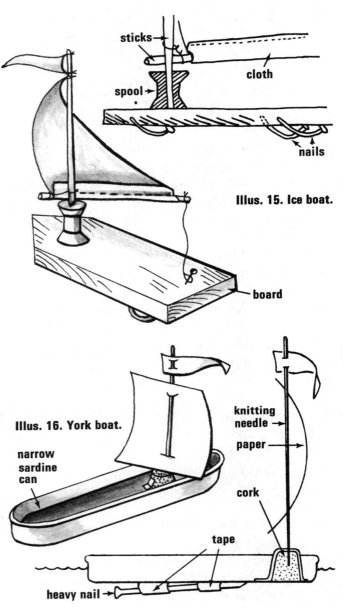

Illus. 15. Ice boat.

Illus. 16. York boat.

Tin-Can York Boat

Long ago York boats were used in North Canada and on the Red River in the northern United States. Making a model York boat that floats is quite simple. Tape a cork in an empty sardine tin. Attach a paper sail and a tiny flag to a knitting needle and press the needle into the cork. A heavy nail taped to the bottom of the tin can balances the boat so it can float.

Cardboard

Before you start your model ship, it is a good idea to learn a little about cardboard and the way to cut things out of it. Before you do any tracing of patterns do some practice first.

Take a sheet of cardboard of the kind found packaged with commercially-laundered shirts or found on the back of unbound writing tablets. Or buy cardboard (show card) at an art supply or office supply shop. Remember to buy grey or white sheets. Colored board is hard to use because the lines you draw are difficult to see. Different kinds of cardboard vary in flexibility, so never use two different kinds. Make sure that the cardboard is clean and not bent or cracked.

Take a ruler and draw several squares on the cardboard with a soft pencil. Cut out these practice squares to get the feel of the cardboard.

Try something different. Draw a strip ¾″ wide and 8″ long on your cardboard sheet with your pencil and your ruler. Make sure that the cardboard's grain runs up and down the strip. You see grain in wood, but perhaps without identifying it. Look at a wooden table top and you see definite lines—either vertical or arranged in patterns. This is the fibrous structure or grain of the wood and it runs in one direction only. Cardboard also has a grain with the fibres going in one direction, but it is not easy to see this grain. Therefore, there is a simple test to show which way the grain is going—up and down the sheet, or across it.

Finding the direction of the grain is easy; merely flex the cardboard sheet gently in both directions. If you flex it against the grain, you feel a stiff resistance. If you flex it with the grain, the board feels springy. This knowledge is important because folding or bending a piece of cardboard against the grain causes the board to crack. However, if you fold or bend cardboard with the grain, the results are smooth and neat, which is essential to your boat.

Measure out and draw on your cardboard sheet a rectangular piece that is 2″ wide and 3″ long. Make sure that the 3″-length has the cardboard's grain running from top to bottom.

Cut this piece out. Find something cylindrical to wrap the cardboard piece over, keeping the grain vertical. You can use a broom handle or anything round and small enough for the piece to fit over.

If nothing else is handy, you have to form the cardboard piece into a tubular shape with your hands. Do this by rolling a round pencil lengthwise along the cardboard, going back and forth between the two sides of the 2″-width. The rectangle takes a curved shape. The rest of the shaping is easy to do with your fingers.

If you place the cardboard rectangle over a round object to curl it, make sure that you put a piece of wax paper between the cardboard and the object. The wax paper prevents any glue from holding the cardboard to the round handle.

Whichever method of curling you use, you glue the cardboard into the tubular shape. Put cement on the two edges that are to meet. Slip

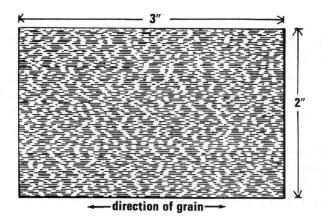

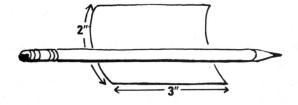

Illus. 17. Forming a cardboard tube with the aid of a pencil.

or tie an elastic band round the cardboard to hold the edges together until the glue is dry. Be careful not to tighten the elastic band too much or it will crush the tube. Remember that you must always form curved or hollow parts gently or they crack and break.

When you remove the elastic band, you have a hollow tube 3″ long. The tube is the basic shape of a smokestack. Save it to use on your model boat.

Now that you have a good idea of the tools and other materials for building the cardboard ship models, the next important thing to know about is how to put the patterns onto your cardboard. Certain parts of cardboard ships *must* have the grain of the cardboard run in a certain way. This is very important, because if the grain does not run correctly, the fold or bend that you make will not work correctly. Instead of folds and bends you will have cracks and breaks!

Therefore, see that when you transfer the patterns onto your cardboard sheet the parts marked with arrows have the grain running in the direction of the arrows! Refer to instructions on page 10 for tracing and enlarging the following submarine pattern.

Submarine

All the previous boats move above the water. This one is actually designed to move both above the water and beneath it! This model cannot submerge itself, but it looks like a real submarine and floats in water.

To enlarge these patterns to the size of the original model, note that ¾″ in the diagrams equals 1″ on the original; 1″ equals 1¼″. All the measurements that are in this section are those for the original model. If you use a different scale, adjust these measurements to fit.

You make the hull of the submarine of three main parts, to which you attach two ballast tanks, one for each side. These tanks each have three parts: a front, a middle, and a rear.

To complete your submarine you need the deck, the keel, the rudders, the propellers, their shafts and brace, and the guns, conning tower and periscopes (see Illus. 18 and 19).

First trace the parts. Keep the tracing paper flat, use a soft pencil without pressing down too hard, and use a ruler whenever you draw a straight line.

Before you do any enlarging or transferring of the pattern shapes, make sure to trace *everything*. The dashed lines indicate folds or

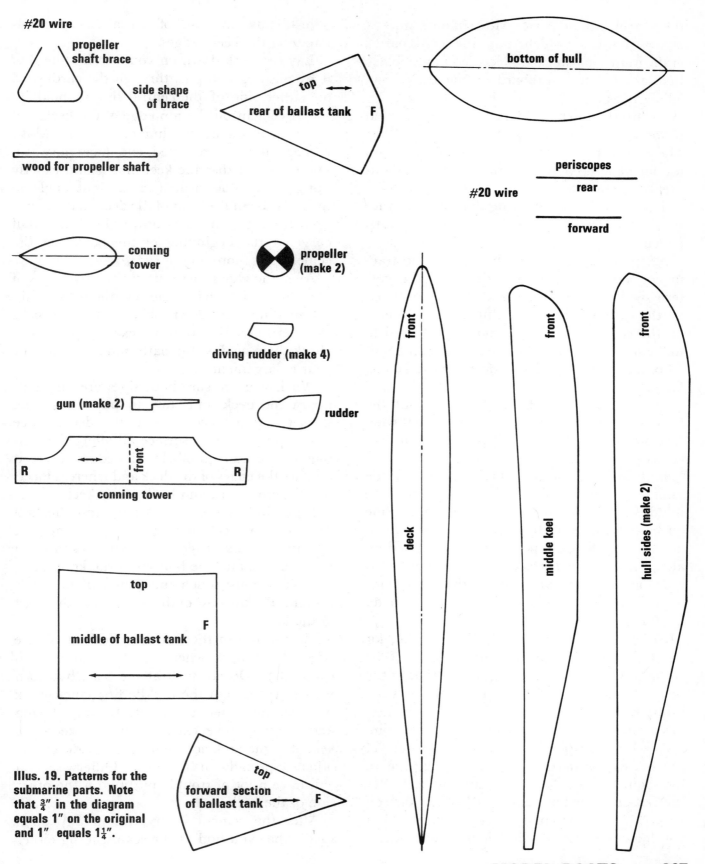

#20 wire

propeller shaft brace

side shape of brace

wood for propeller shaft

top

rear of ballast tank   F

bottom of hull

periscopes

#20 wire

rear

forward

conning tower

propeller (make 2)

diving rudder (make 4)

gun (make 2)

rudder

R   front   R

conning tower

front

front

front

deck

middle keel

hull sides (make 2)

top

F

middle of ballast tank

Illus. 19. Patterns for the submarine parts. Note that $\frac{3}{4}''$ in the diagram equals 1″ on the original and 1″ equals $1\frac{1}{4}''$.

top

forward section of ballast tank   F

MODEL BOATS ■ 367

the placement of parts. Most important, the arrows indicate which way the cardboard's grain must run on each piece. You must place the parts on the cardboard so that the arrows follow the grain. You cut the pattern tracings away from the sheet in order to place them properly on the cardboard, so be aware of this. Make sure that any sheet of cardboard you use for your models is clean, flat and without breaks or ripples.

Take your carbon copying sheet and transfer the patterns with your ruler and a soft, sharp pencil.

After finishing, remove the carbon and tracing papers. If you worked carefully, the patterns will now be clearly and sharply outlined on the cardboard sheet. Compare the patterns on the cardboard with the ones you traced to make sure that you did not leave anything out. Also, *label the parts*, so you do not mistake one for the other.

Start construction by first cutting out the submarine deck. The grain runs lengthwise. Cut outside the lines on all pieces so you can correct errors.

Both sides of the deck must be exactly the same, so draw a line lengthwise down the middle. The submarine needs the central line on both surfaces of the deck. The keel (which acts as a brace to support the deck) is lined up along it on one surface, and the guns and conning tower are lined up on the top surface of it. Draw your central lines before you do anything else.

Next, cut out the keel. Be very careful, for the top edge and the bottom edge must be straight. Cut both of the edges, and that of the rear of the keel with a model-maker's or utility knife and a ruler. Note, too, that the keel has a curved front from the top to the bottom.

The keel is important, for the entire shape of the submarine depends upon its being cut to the right shape. Place the cut-out keel over the pattern you have used, either the one on page 367 or your enlargement of it. See that you have followed all directions closely. Make

adjustments, in case of mistakes, by sandpapering the keel's edges.

Lay the deck down on your work table. Pin it by pushing two pins through the cardboard on either side of the central line to hold it.

Put cement on the top edge of the keel, and lay it along the central line of the deck. Make certain that the rounded end faces forward. Do not forget that the keel must stand exactly upright—in other words, at a right angle to the deck. Bend the front of the deck that extends from the top of the keel down along the small curve at the beginning of the bow. Let the cement dry thoroughly.

After the glue is dry, cut out the two sides of the hull sides, with the cardboard's grain running up and down. Place the hull sides together to see that they are exactly alike. Also check them against the pattern on page 367 or your enlargement.

When you are sure both sides are all right, unpin the deck and start to put one of the sides on to the keel and to the deck. Place cement on the inner surface all along the contour of the hull, just below its edges where it touches the edges of the deck and where it meets the bottom, front, and back of the keel.

Beginning at the rear (stern), pin the hull sides to the keel, letting the top edge rest against the deck's edge. Push your pins through the hull side and the bottom of the keel; these two pieces must touch and match all along the bottom. Pin the bow of the hull side to the front of the keel.

Pin the top of the hull side flush along the edge of the deck where the two parts touch each other. Do not start at the rear, but push your pins through the middle first; then work the rear and then the front. During glueing and pinning, take extreme care to keep the keel straight and not bent to one side or the other, especially at the bow. Otherwise you will have a lot of trouble putting on the other side of the hull.

After the cement is dry, fill in any open spaces that you find at the seams, using either

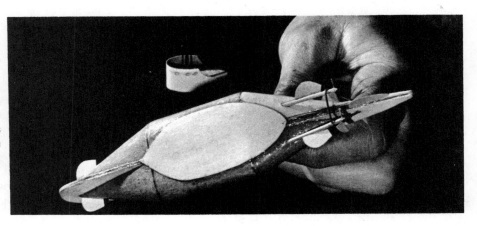

Illus. 20. Here is the bottom of the submarine and its position on the hull. You can see the four diving rudders, two attached to the propeller shafts, and two attached to the hull's sides at the front. A close look will show how the wire brace for the propeller shaft is glued. The finished conning tower with its two periscopes is in the background.

glue or model putty. Put the other side of the hull in place. Do this exactly as you did the first one, but take care to see that everything "lines up" in the bottom, the rear, the bow, and the deck. Push your pins carefully through the cardboard, so that the cardboard is not torn. If this does happen, do not try to repair anything now, just put the pin in another spot, and re-glue and sandpaper the tear later.

Take out your pins, and very lightly sandpaper the edges and the pin bumps down, until everything is smooth. Rub the waterproof cement into the cardboard wherever any fuzz or small opening may appear. Fill in all pinholes with the cement or model putty.

The two sides of the hull form a "V" shape. Along both sides of this "V" hull go the two ballast tanks, made up of three pieces each. You may have to trim them to fit.

Cut the pieces from your patterns, first marking the top and front of each one. Because there is a right and left to each of the tank's pieces, you must mark them left and right, as well as front and top. The cardboard's grain must run the long way, front to back, on all the ballast tank pieces.

Cut out the middle for each ballast tank. Round each middle piece to a "U" shape, as it is shown in Illus. 18. (The piece for the right side is pictured here, lying in front of the right side of the hull.) Remember you can curve the cardboard over a broomstick handle.

Take the middle of the ballast tank and cement the top edge against the hull about $\frac{1}{16}$" below the deck line, and about $2\frac{3}{4}$" back from the bow. Let the cement dry. Glue the bottom edge of the tank to the hull so it is flush with the bottom of the keel. Pin it so that it will hold until the cement dries.

Put the middle part of the left-side tank in position, doing it in the same manner. Check and see that the front edge of both the right and left tank sections are lined up. Look from the top, as well as the bottom. Keep your pins in both sides until the glue has dried.

Give the right rear piece of the ballast tank the same "U" shape as the middle section. Put it against the hull and the back of the middle section of the tank. Hold the "U" shape as best you can with your hand. See that the front edge of the rear section matches the back of the middle piece. It does not have to fit perfectly, but it should come close. If it does, fine. If not, check and make certain that you used the correct piece, or that you have not curved the "U" in the wrong direction.

Cement the top edge and point of the rear ballast section against the hull, in the position you fitted it for. Let the glue dry thoroughly. Pin it if it is necessary.

Put cement along the front edge and the bottom of the rear ballast section, and fasten it to the back of the middle section and to the hull. A side view of where the ballast tank pieces go can be seen in Illus. 21.

Remember that both the top and bottom edges of the rear tank piece should be on line with those edges of the middle section. Make sure, too, that all edges are tight against the hull.

Glue the left-side rear tank to the hull in the same manner. Do this with care, and be certain that the points of both rear sections are the same height up from the keel's bottom when you look at them from the back of the hull.

Put the front sections of the right and left ballast tanks in place just as you did the rear sections. Try to get the points of the front tank pieces set so they go about $\frac{3}{8}$" down from the deck. This is where you cement them to the hull.

Remove all your pins from the ballast tanks, fill any holes with cement or model putty, and sandpaper away any pin bumps. If the model is to float, rub the hull with your waterproof quick-drying cement. When the cement is dry, lightly sandpaper it smooth. Fill in any openings between seams.

Cut out the bottom piece of the hull and cement it to the bottom formed by the ballast tanks, keel and hull sides. The point goes forward and lines up with the central line of the keel. (See Illus. 20.) As you put the bottom piece in place, try to get all its edges to fit tightly against the hull. Use plenty of cement, and pin everything down.

Remove the pins, after the glue is dry, fill in the holes and any spaces in the seams. Sandpaper as usual. Rub some cement all over the bottom piece to make it waterproof. Of course, if you just want a shelf model, you do not have to rub in cement except where it is necessary to smooth down any sandpaper fuzzing.

The hull is now ready for you to attach two propellers and their shafts to it. The propeller shafts are $\frac{1}{16}$"-diameter iodine dowels. Cut these off to a length of $1\frac{3}{4}$". Sandpaper them smooth and point the ends.

Make a hole in the bottom of the rear of each ballast tank. These holes are $2\frac{5}{8}$" in front of the hull's stern and they come down about $\frac{5}{8}$" from the deck line. Make the holes by drilling through the cardboard, or pushing through with a sharp nail the same diameter as the wooden propeller shafts. Glue the wooden propeller shafts into these holes, pushing the shafts in about $\frac{1}{2}$".

The original model has a wire brace, made of #20 iron wire, bent so that it fits over the shafts. The ends of the wire are long enough to stick into small holes made in the hull. (See Illus. 20 and 21.)

The outline for the brace is given in Illus. 19, but, if it is too difficult to make, you may

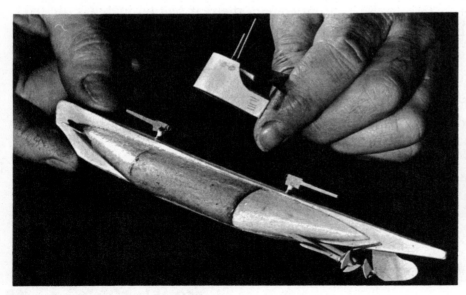

Illus. 21. The completed submarine is ready to have the conning tower mounted on the deck. Study the position of the ballast tank, the rear main rudder, the two guns, the propeller blades, and the propeller shaft's wire brace. Compare the submarine's size with the builder's hands.

make a simple one out of three pieces of wire. Glue one wire to the top or the outside of each shaft and to the hull above it. Glue the third wire between the shafts at the bottom.

Remember that both ends of the propeller shafts must come out of the hull at the same distance, which should be $1\frac{3}{8}''$ or close to it.

The two propellers are easy to make. Cut out a disc as the patterns and pictures show, for each propeller. Cut the two blades from the disc. Cement the pointed end of each blade to the propeller shaft about $\frac{1}{8}''$ back from the end. Glue them to the shaft so they appear twisted, like a model aircraft's propeller. Do the same for the other propeller. Be sure that the right propeller is twisted in the opposite direction from the left propeller. This is done because each of the shafts in a real submarine revolves in a different direction.

Cut out the main rudder. Cement this to the middle of the keel, so that the front of the rudder goes $1\frac{1}{4}''$ forward from the stern's end. Use plenty of glue here and make sure that the rudder faces directly forward and extends straight down. (See Illus. 21.)

There are four diving rudders on our model. Cut them out and then check to see that they are all alike. Do this by putting them all together and matching their outlines. Sandpaper all their edges before you glue them in place.

Glue one of the diving rudders to the outside of *each* propeller shaft, halfway between the propeller and the hull. One forward-diving rudder goes on to *each* ballast tank, just at the point. See Illus. 21 for a clear picture of the positions. Glue all diving rudders so that they are secure and run straight, looking at them from the side.

Make the conning tower of three pieces: the conning-tower sides, the bottom, and the deck. The bottom and the deck are the same, so one pattern serves for both. Cut them from the pattern given to you on page 367, and check that they are identical.

Cut out the conning tower itself. Pinch the back ends (marked R) together so that the front of the conning tower becomes curved. Check the edges and see that they match up and that they are even. Next put some cement between the back ends of the conning tower and pin them together.

Push the bottom between the conning tower's sides after the glue is dry. Keep the bottom even all along. If you are careful, the bottom will stay in place without pins, and you can glue it in position. Put the deck inside the conning tower. The deck should be flush with the rear, cut-down part of the tower, as it can be seen in Illus. 20. Cement this in place.

When the glue has dried, everything may be sandpapered smooth, and if necessary rubbed in with cement.

Two periscopes go into the deck of the conning tower. These are simply two lengths of #20 wire, cut off with a small wire cutter so that one is $1\frac{1}{2}''$ long and the other $1\frac{1}{4}''$. Push them into holes made in the deck with nails, and glue them securely. They should be about $\frac{1}{8}''$ apart, and the shortest one should go forward, $\frac{1}{4}''$ back from the front of the conning tower.

Line up the conning tower assembly along the deck's central line. Cement it to the top of the deck with its front about $2\frac{3}{4}''$ back from the bow.

There are two guns mounted on the deck. Cut them out of cardboard, and cement them to the central line of the deck. One gun faces forward; the other aft. Mount them on short bits of $\frac{1}{16}''$-dowel sticks if you wish. The forward position on the deck is generally $1\frac{1}{2}''$ from the front of the gun to the bow; the tip of the rear gun is $2\frac{1}{8}''$ back from the stern. Complete the construction of your submarine by mounting the guns. You need only to waterproof and paint it.

You may paint it any colors you wish, but for one idea, see Illus. W2 on color page W.

MOSAICS

A mosaic is a picture or design made by attaching bits of colored material, called *tesserae*, onto a suitable background. You may use crayons, bits of colored paper, seeds, pebbles, wood, tiles, or almost anything that suggests itself to your imagination to make beautiful mosaics.

The first step, no matter what material you use, is to pick a background. You can use paper, wallboard, plywood, cardboard, or some similar material. The background can add a great deal to your mosaic, and you should use care in selecting it. Choose colors and materials that complement the design. The background must not in any way "fight" the design or compete for the attention of the viewer. If the design has weak colors, a strong-colored background might overpower it. In the

same way, a vibrantly colored mosaic might appear to pour over the edges of a weak-colored background.

Next, plan your mosaic design. Lightly draw a general outline on your background. Create shapes which you can easily fill with small pieces of tesserae and keep the shapes as simple as possible.

In choosing colors, consider ways to achieve contrasts. Juxtapose cool blues and greens with warm reds, browns, oranges, and yellows. Use light areas of color next to dark so that all of the mosaic's shapes will show up vividly, even from a distance.

Contrast may also result from varying the sizes of the tesserae. The total pattern takes on added interest when you juxtapose areas of small tesserae with areas of large tesserae.

Illus. 1. Notice how, in this crayon-rubbed mosaic, the tesserae which are different in color are also different in size, weight, and value. All were cut from crayoned sheets and pasted onto a designed background of black paper.

Condensed from the books, "The Complete Crayon Book" by Chester Jay Alkema | © 1969 by Sterling Publishing Co., Inc., New York, "Crafting with Nature's Materials" by Chester Jay Alkema | © 1972 by Sterling Publishing Co., Inc., New York, and "Creative Paper Crafts" | © 1967 by Sterling Publishing Co., Inc., New York

Illus. 2. Here the crayon has been applied heavily to the various sheets of paper so that the tesserae are waxy. Variety in the tesserae lends interest to the over-all design.

Crayon Mosaics

Preparing Rubbed-On Tesserae

You can use crayon in a variety of ways to construct interesting, colorful designs. For the first method, rub a solid color of crayon on one sheet of paper. Cover a second sheet with another crayon, and so on. For interesting variety, color some sheets lightly and other sheets heavily. When you have rubbed all your chosen colors on separate sheets of paper, cut the crayoned sheets into various-sized tesserae. You are now ready to paste the crayoned shapes onto your designed background.

The mosaic in Illus. 1, created from crayoned sheets of paper, represents an aerial view of a country scene. Fields, crops, a road, trees, and a small red barn are represented by clusters of tesserae on black construction paper. Observe the placement of the various tesserae: some shapes run in a horizontal direction, others in a vertical direction, while some run diagonally.

The proud, lanky, stylish bird pictured in Illus. 2 was likewise created from tesserae cut from crayon-rubbed paper, but the total effect is quite different from Illus. 1. Observe all the tiny tesserae applied to the bird. His tail, back feathers, breast feathers, legs, and head-tuft all display different tesserae patterns.

Illus. 3. This mosaic is composed of melted wax crayons which were poured onto tin-foil to harden. The solidified, broken layers are glued to paper. India ink and pen were used for the lines that further define the basic shapes.

MOSAICS ■ 373

Illus. 4. This bird upon a treetop also makes use of the wax-layer approach. This kind of mosaic, with its large, raised wax pieces, provides a texture that appeals to the sense of touch.

In Illus. W3, a sailboat on the evening waters, a single color for the waters would have been monotonous. The artist has realized this and has, therefore, used many shades of blue and blue-green. These subtle color variations are likewise in the design's other areas. The sails are orange and yellow-orange, the boat is green and chartreuse. The moon and distant sailboat repeat and balance the dominant orange colors of the large sailboat. The sky is a mixture of blue, blue-grey, and white tesserae, with the white representing flying sea gulls.

Mosaic designs become intensely alive when subtle color variations are contained in a single shape. Try not to fill a shape with a single color. Instead, use a family of colors which are close in hue and value. For instance, use green with chartreuse, use light, dark, bright, and dull shades of blue together, and let red, maroon, and dark pink occupy another area.

Tesserae of Melted Wax Crayon Painted on Paper

A second method for preparing your tesserae involves the use of melted crayon. Place cast-off crayons in empty cans of suitable size, taking care not to mix colors. Place the crayon-filled cans in a pan with just enough water to prevent the cans from floating. Bring the water to a boil and heat until all of the crayons have melted within the separate cans. Remove the pan from the stove and place it on pads of newspaper on your work table. The hot water will keep the crayons in a molten stage for quite some time.

Using a stiff bristle brush, paint the melted wax on sheets of drawing paper, one color per sheet. The wax will quickly harden. Then you can cut the paper into the desired shapes, and apply as tesserae onto your background design. The melted-wax approach allows you to use thick, waxy, vibrant colors. The final design may be gently rubbed with a cloth or paper towel, causing the wax to shine and glow.

Tesserae of Melted Crayon Layers

A third approach in the execution of a crayon mosaic involves the use of melted crayon without the paper backing. Heat your crayons in the same manner. Pour the melted wax onto a sheet of tin-foil or tagboard, allowing the build-up of a layer $\frac{1}{8}$-inch thick or less. (Take caution during the pouring process, as the wax is extremely hot and can cause severe burns to the hands. Use a pot holder to grip the cans.) When the wax layer has hardened, bend the tin-foil so that the layer breaks into small pieces of hard, colored wax. The tin-foil may be re-used. With rubber cement or white liquid glue, paste the wax tesserae to a stiff background.

A word of caution: the wax-layer method is not recommended for young children. The handling and pouring of hot, molten wax is dangerous and a drop of molten wax upon the skin can be most painful.

Tesserae of Sliced Crayon

A fourth approach to mosaics is with chopped or sliced wax crayons. Peel the crayons and chop them into small pieces with a knife. Heat your metal knife blade over a lighted candle to facilitate the cutting process. Press the heated knife on the peeled crayon and rock the crayon back and forth to establish a groove completely around the crayon. Then, press down until the crayon breaks on the slice where the groove is located.

Create pieces which are even in size, and make certain that the ends are flat and smooth. Apply glue to the end of each circular piece and arrange them into a colored mosaic. Plywood or stiff cardboard provides an effective backing.

Illus. 5 shows a finished mosaic created in this manner. A border of yellow crayon slices

Illus. 6. In creating this transfer design, the artist observed that her white tesserae did not show up nearly so well when transferred. White wax against a blue background in the original on the left was quite vivid, but contrast was lost when the white wax was transferred to the white background. To remedy the problem, she used a ballpoint pen to outline some of the white shapes.

ties in the edges, and the contrasting texture of white broken crayon pieces fills the background area.

Making a Mosaic Transfer Design

If your mosaic has been created by the tesserae of melted wax crayons on paper, it is fun next to create a transfer design from the finished product. Place a thin sheet of paper, such as newsprint, over the mosaic design. Run a warm iron over the newsprint, so that the wax will melt slightly. Each of the tesserae shapes of the original mosaic design will be clearly

Illus. 5. With white glue, colorful crayon slices are here adhered to a wallboard backing.

imprinted upon the second sheet of paper. There will be plenty of colored wax on the original tesserae which can easily be transferred to the print design. The other mosaic techniques do not always supply enough wax for a transfer design, and the tesserae may be separated from the backing.

It should be evident by now that the crayon is truly a remarkable tool for creating a mosaic. Experimentation will lead to other exciting discoveries as you use the crayon to explore the mosaic technique.

Paper Mosaics

An infinite variety of papers are well suited to mosaics—construction paper, poster paper, metallic foil, colored tissue, Japanese papers, tagboard, magazine paper, cellophane, gift

Illus. 8. This paper mosaic is made of pieces of colored construction paper which were pasted onto a large sheet of grey construction paper. Notice how the large plain areas surrounding the Madonna and the simplicity of her face provide a pleasing and restful contrast to the busy patterns of the paper tesserae. The strips radiating from the Mother and Child are made of tin-foil.

Illus. 7. A jack-in-the-box composed of a variety of paper tesserae—construction paper, cardboard, magazine paper, and the corrugated paper used as dividers in cookie boxes. Notice how the less-defined area of the spiral is emphasized by black yarn outlines.

wrapping paper, newsprint, paper towels and napkins, cardboard, stationery, sandpaper, and wallpaper.

The first step is to draw your design on the background. Then cut the paper you have decided to use into the desired shapes. You can also achieve interesting effects by freely tearing papers into bits. You might use both cut and torn shapes in a single mosaic. The paper bits can either overlap or you can leave evenly spaced open areas.

Feel no hesitation about using different types

Illus. 9. This paper mosaic shows a multitude of patterns. In spite of this, the ship stands out immediately. Long, narrow paper strips suggest a calm sea under a threatening sky of squares and rectangles. Notice how well balanced the lights and darks are in the whole composition.

Illus. 10. Three calico cats, made of construction-paper tesserae placed on a black construction-paper background, peer out of tin-foil eyes.

of paper in your mosaic. While it is sometimes better to use only one type of paper in your composition, you can use different textures to great effect. For instance, in Illus. 7, construction paper, cardboard, magazine paper, and the corrugated paper used as dividers in cookie boxes were all combined to heighten the contrasts and give an interesting texture to the jack-in-the-box. You can also add materials such as yarn, tin-foil, cloth, and so on, to enliven a design. Illus. X2 shows a beautiful spider made with tin-foil, yarn, construction paper, and Japanese Shibui rice paper. The rice paper was placed over a background of green construction paper and yarn added to outline the body and emphasize the web-like background. The dullness of the background serves to heighten the richness of the body and the brilliance of the tin-foil legs.

Make another type of paper mosaic by pasting bits of newspaper or magazine to the background. Illus. 9 shows an ocean liner with its lower decks composed of newspaper, giving a feeling of life and activity to the ship that it would otherwise lack.

These examples are just hints of the types of paper mosaics you can make. Devote some thought to your compositions, and you will be rewarded by lovely and striking works of art.

Illus. 11. This rooster would probably enjoy eating himself up if he had the chance! Everything he likes best went into his portrait—corn, beans, peas, wheat, and sunflower and watermelon seeds. All of these materials are glued onto plywood.

Mosaics from Nature

You will find Nature one of the richest sources of ideas for mosaics imaginable. All around you, you will find ideas for materials for your own mosaic-making. Use seeds and grains of all kinds, including rice, bird seed, and flower seeds. Make a habit of saving all the seeds and pits from various fruits you might eat, such as oranges, grapefruits, melons, prunes, etc. There are also certain vegetables that provide interesting tesserae—squash or pumpkin seeds, corn kernels, dried peas, and beans.

In addition to grains and seeds, there are pebbles, shells, pods, and many other natural materials. Even eggshells, when crushed, are a marvelous addition to a mosaic. Wood chips cut from logs or branches are still another

source. The important thing is to let the material suggest the mosaic to you.

You can use the same techniques of construction you learned for crayon and paper mosaics for mosaics from nature. Although the colors of natural materials are subdued in comparison to those of crayon and paper, you achieve much greater contrasts of texture with natural materials. For example, in Illus. 11 several varieties of beans, seeds, and grains were used to give the rooster a rich, visually complex texture. Similarly, in Illus. X1, seeds and rice have been combined with pussy willows and feathers to form the splendid peacock. It is a good example of what you can do with greatly dissimilar materials.

Enamels, stains, dyes, and food coloring are valuable tools to have when making your mosaic. In Illus. 12 food colorings were used to brighten up the composition. As this picture shows, your mosaics can be functional as well as attractive.

The abstract design in Illus. 13 was made with wood stains. When making a wood mosaic, remember that different types of wood have different grains and textures, and you can combine them for a very interesting effect. Wood stain or linseed oil are ideal for accen-

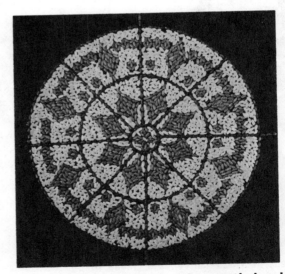

Illus. 12. A dyed-rice mosaic on a glue-coated glass background makes a unique serving tray.

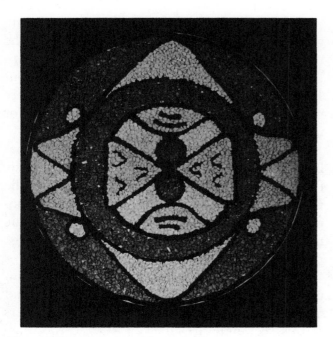

Illus. 13. Aquarium gravel is available in a variety of colors, and you can make a stunning mosaic with it. Black yarn is used here to define lights and darks and to create a pattern. Epoxy cement holds the gravel to a ceramic-plate background.

tuating the knots and lines in the wood. You might also try making a mosaic entirely from driftwood, which you can also stain or rub with oil. However, avoid sawing driftwood, or conceal the saw-cuts, because this detracts from the natural beauty of the wood.

Do not limit yourself to the suggestions for natural mosaics outlined here. Just let your fancy run free, and you will never be short of projects for your spare time.

Mounting Your Mosaic

In most cases, simply paste your mosaics over one or more sheets of construction paper which serve as the frames. Illus. Y1 is a nice example of this. Or you can mount them in the same way on a thin sheet of plywood, cut slightly larger than the design. Using wood stain, or shoe polish, you can give the plywood a finished look. Another simple material is Masonite (pressed board), which you can paint with enamel or acrylics. Sheets of cork are available from many arts and crafts shops and you can use them in conjunction with other materials to make a double frame. For a small composition that requires support, tagboard, being stiff, is a suitable framing material.

For a more professional-looking frame, you can use a 14-ply mat board, available in white, black, grey, as well as warmer colors, and easily cut to shape.

Place your design against the reverse side of the mat board and lightly sketch its outline. Then remove it and make a ruled outline at least $\frac{1}{4}''$ *smaller* than the sketch. Now cut a window through the mat board, carefully following your outline. Place your composition against the reverse of the board so that it shows through. Using gummed paper tape, secure it to the back side of the board. In order to avoid future warpage, run the tape on each side so that it ends a short distance from the corners.

Illus. 14. This wood mosaic is made up of various-sized squares sawed from pine and redwood branches. Walnut and maple stains are used on some pieces, while others are left bare.

To give the finished mat board extra stability, glue a piece of corrugated cardboard to the reverse. Cut the cardboard slightly smaller than the board. Place a narrow band of glue about 1″ from the outer edges of the board. Be sure not to touch the composition with the glue or it will wrinkle up.

You can construct a three-dimensional frame, simple to make and very inexpensive, from corrugated cardboard. Illus. 16 shows the procedure for making this frame. The inner rectangle marked "A" is the exact area of the mosaic. Outline this area in pencil on a large piece of cardboard.

Since your cardboard must be larger than this, allow, let us say, 2″ for the frame, and make another outline 2″ larger. The corners of this rectangle are marked "C" in the illustration. Select a point a short distance from the first "C" corner and mark it "B." Measure exactly the same distance in the other direction and mark that "B." Do this for all four corners. The distance should be exactly equal in each place. Draw a light pencil line from these "B" points to the corners of the rectangle "A," as shown in the drawing. The length of the "B"–"C" line will determine whether your frame is shallow or deep. The closer to "C" that "B" is, the shallower—and the farther away, the wider—your frame will be.

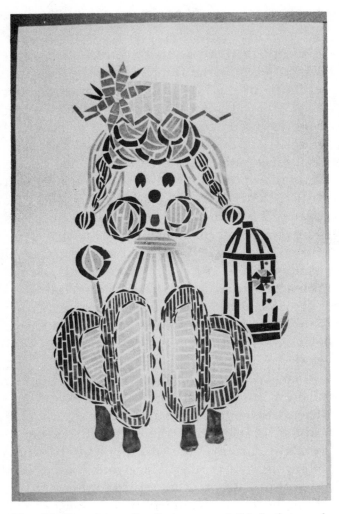

Illus. 15. Many interesting features are visible in the mosaic poodle. A limited range of colors was effectively repeated and balanced. Throughout the composition, a variety of tesserae of different sizes and shapes were artistically placed.

Illus. 16. Here is a simple three-dimensional cardboard frame you can make to mount your mosaics. From one large piece of cardboard you can—by making the few incisions indicated by the dotted lines, folding the resulting edges over, and cutting out the large rectangle "A" which is the outline of your composition—have a recessed frame. Decorate it with tissue paper, burlap, or paint.

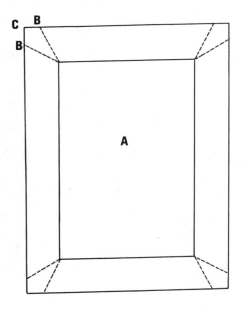

With a sharp knife, cut along the drawn "B" lines to the corners of "A." Remove these triangular pieces. Now with the knife, score (mark the lines so that you create a groove, not a cut) along the four sides of rectangle "A." This will allow the cardboard to bend so that the edges marked "B" can touch one another. Using gummed paper tape, join the "B" edges together from the rear side, along all four corners. You now have a three-dimensional frame.

Before pasting your composition into place, you will undoubtedly want to decorate the cardboard frame. Crumpled tissue paper is an unusual covering.

Cut four strips of white tissue paper to dimensions which are slightly wider and longer than each of the four borders of your three-dimensional cardboard frame. Crinkle them up in your hands. Then slightly smooth out the many creases and paste the tissue strips over the four borders, using white paste.

Bend the tissue over the outside edges of the frame.

Choose a suitable color tempera and paint the tissue. Be sure you brush color into all the recesses and raised areas. When dry, paint over the tissue with a slightly deeper shade of the same color. Use light brush strokes when applying the second coat so that the color touches only the raised areas of the crumpled paper.

Natural or colored burlap also makes a nice covering for this kind of frame. Cut the burlap about 2″ larger along all four sides than the frame. Soak the burlap in diluted white (Elmer's) glue and leave it there long enough for it to become slightly tacky. During the tacky stage, place the burlap over the frame and press it against the cardboard surface. The soaked burlap will easily adhere to the frame, whereas it will not if dry and simply pasted on.

There are innumerable ways you might want to decorate the cardboard frame. Try to think of what materials or designs would be most effective with the composition.

You can either paste your design over the rectangle "A" or you might make a window so that it will show through. The nature of your work will probably determine the best means of showing it off.

If you are really proud of your creation, you can put it on the mat board described earlier, and either buy a wooden frame or turn to the article *Picture Frames*.

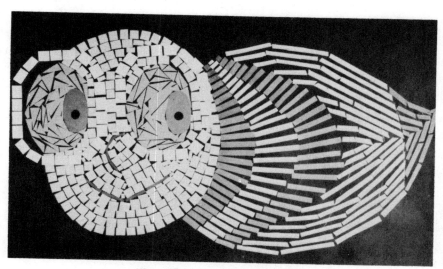

Illus. 17. A mosaic bumblebee.

MUSICAL INSTRUMENTS

As you create your own musical instruments and play them, you not only have fun, but you also add to your understanding of music. In a sense, these instruments are a call to your own imagination and inventiveness and are really only examples of the kinds of things you can make up yourself. Create your own instruments by varying the materials, sizes, and so on. Many musical instruments came into being because the country in which they developed had a ready supply of a material—bamboo, gourds, silk, and metals. Look around you. You can unearth raw materials for musical treasures from the kitchen and bathroom, the butcher and baker, the garage and the junkyard, the woods and the seashore.

When you have created enough instruments to give yourself variety, form a band with your friends and use the instruments to accompany dancing or singing, or the phonograph, radio or television.

Minstrel Bones

Have short ribs of beef for supper and rescue two of the bones. Cut off all the meat. Wash them clean with plenty of hot water and soap and a brush. Dry the bones well, preferably in the sun.

Play them by cupping one in your hand and hitting it across the top with the other bone. Or, grasp two bones between the index and middle finger of one hand and tap out a rhythm by shaking your hand. The wonderful resonance will surprise you.

Sandpaper Sticks

Wrap rough sandpaper around 12″-lengths of dowel (one inch wide). Tack or glue them in place. Scrape the dowels back and forth across each other.

Bone Rattle

The Indians made dance rattles from buffalo and deer claws and hoofs. The round bones of lamb chops make just as effective a bone rattle and you can put it together with few tools.

Each shoulder chop has one bone; you need four to six. Clean off the meat thoroughly and dig out the marrow from the center. Soak the bones in hot water and detergent to get rid of all the grease. Dry them out in the sun.

Usually the bones have a handsome ivory look and need no further decoration. If they are discolored or if you prefer a highly colored rattle, paint each bone a different bright color.

With their ready-made center holes, the

Illus. 1. Minstrel bones.

Illus. 2. Bone rattle.

Condensed from the book, "Make Your Own Musical Instruments" by Muriel Mandell and Robert E. Wood | © 1957 by Sterling Publishing Co., Inc., New York

Illus. 3. Coconut halves.

Illus. 4. Coconut rattles.

bones are easy to attach to a ring made from a wire hanger. Unwind the ends of the hanger so that you have a long length of wire. Break off a 10″- or 12″-piece by bending the wire back and forth at the same spot until it snaps. Don't touch the broken ends for a few seconds—they are hot from the friction. Thread the bones on.

Wind the ends of the wire around each other, with the help of pliers if necessary, and make a short handle (see Illus. 2). Wrap any sharp points with colorful tape.

Hold the rattle by its taped ends and shake away. Try shaking it slowly side to side for a "change of pace."

Make the rattle louder by mounting it on a wooden base. Sand down and shellac a slab of scrap wood. Wedge a nail through the two wire bound ends and hammer it to the wood.

Coconut Halves

Using a sharp saw, cut a coconut in half. Drain out the milk, pry out the meat and clean the inside thoroughly. Sand the edges smooth. Paint or shellac both inside and outside.

Tap the two halves lightly together in rhythm. Does it sound like galloping over ice?

Place a sheet of paper between the two coconut halves and rub in time to music. Does it sound like walking through snow?

See how many different sounds you can make besides just clapping the halves together.

Coconut Rattles

Transform a coconut into an excellent rattle that sounds and looks just right for rhythm—Latin, Hopi or jazz.

Drill a hole at one end of the coconut and let the juice run into a glass. Bore a good-sized hole (no more than one inch in diameter) on the other end of the coconut. Saw the coconut in half between the two holes you have bored.

Pry the coconut meat out of the shell with a knife until the hard, brown inside is completely exposed. After the coconut shell is thoroughly cleaned, dry it in the sun. Keep the edges of the shell clean as you are going to glue the halves together again.

Prepare a handle of one-inch dowelling or a section of a broom handle at least 12 inches long. Part of it will run through the length of the shell. Whittle the handle down a bit to fit into the smaller hole on top of the shell. Sandpaper it smooth. About an inch down from the smaller end (top) of the handle, bore a small hole from side to side.

Put a handful of rice or split peas or dry cereal into the coconut shell. Fit in the handle so that the hole you bored is exposed at the top. Carefully glue the two halves together around the handle. The shell takes the glue well, but let it stand at least overnight.

Make a one-inch peg of a piece of pencil or scrap wood. Ease it into the hole you bored through the dowel.

The rattle will have an interesting rustic appearance and you can leave it as is. However, if you prefer, shellac the shell or rub it lightly with linseed oil or paint it in bright colors. Shellac or paint the handle and peg.

Of course, don't shake it until the glue and paint are thoroughly dry.

Gourd Rattle

In the world of music, gourds have many uses. They make fine drums, banjos, and scraping instruments. It was from the gourd that the Indian made his rain rattle. The gourd rattle you make is a Latin American version which has found its way into the music of many composers. It is surprisingly easy to make, too.

Select a large well-shaped gourd, preferably

Illus. 5. Gourd rattle.

one with a narrow neck handle of its own. Make sure the shell is hard and firm.

Saw off a small section of the narrow neck, but do not throw it away. Pull out the seeds and scrape out the melon meat until the rind is smooth and hard. Dry the rind in the sun and shellac it. Fill the gourd with its own seeds if they sound interesting. Otherwise, use pumpkin or watermelon seeds (or, if necessary, corn, bean, rice, sand or pebbles).

Either glue the small piece of gourd back on or make a handle to fit in the neck of a length of broomstick or 1″-dowelling.

Secure the handle by hammering a heavy nail through the top of the gourd into the top of the wood handle.

String necklaces of pumpkin or watermelon seeds round the outside of the gourd, too.

Shake out those Samba rhythms.

Balloon Babbler

Stuff three or four paper clips into a balloon. Blow up the balloon and tie it with an elastic band or string. Shake energetically (you'll be surprised at the *deep* rumble). Stay away from friends with pins.

Bottle Prattle

Soak off the label from an empty ketchup bottle and wash out the inside. Put into the bottle half a dozen nails, screws, and bolts, but keep them small or you will break the bottle. Replace the cap. Use the neck of the bottle as a handle, and hold the bottle upside down to shake. The tone will be high and pleasing.

Use tempera paints to decorate the bottle. Try red and black stripes.

Bell Stick

Decorate a 6″-length of dowelling ($\frac{1}{2}$″ to 1″ in diameter) with colorful paint. When it is dry, staple on a tiny bell or two at each end of the stick. Play by shaking.

Illus. 6. Bell stick.

Cardboard Bell Tambourine

The tambourine is really a shallow drum with loose jingling discs or small bells inserted in its narrow hoop frame. Beat it with the bare hand, shake it, or throw it up in the air and catch it again.

With half a dozen tiny bells (the variety shop carries them), your tambourine sounds melodic for the time that it lasts.

Illus. 7. Tambourine.

Use two paper plates—or, from laundry shirt cardboard, cut out two circles the size of a dinner plate (trace the outline of a plate). Place one on top of the other and pin the bells around the edges with safety-pins. Better yet, sew through the two layers of cardboard with heavy cotton or elastic thread and attach 5 or 6 bells loosely on the rim, evenly spaced around the cardboard. Crayon or finger paint a design on the face.

If you have a *round* cereal box top, cut 5 or 6 slits evenly around the edges. Fasten the bells at those places with safety pins or by sewing with elastic thread. Paint or paste over the cover.

Illus. 8. Prattles.

Salt Box Drum

A barrel-type salt box makes a good drum even if the box is not quite empty. Tap the top with the rubber end of a pencil. Pound the box against the table with your left hand and the salt inside adds a rattle.

Make the drum sturdier by pasting a double layer of wrapping paper on the top. Decorate and shellac.

Shoe-Box Strummer

A cardboard cigar or shoe box supplies a ready-made frame. Remove the cover and use only the open box.

Half an inch from both ends of the shorter sides, cut small grooves with an ordinary kitchen knife. Place your box so that the longer sides face you. Select a thin, short elastic band. String it around the box and fit it into the pair of grooves nearest you. Into the grooves on the far side, put your widest, longest band.

Measure off two more pairs of grooves an equal distance between the two end grooves. String on two more elastic bands grading them as to size.

Pluck the strummer with your fingers or a used kitchen match stick.

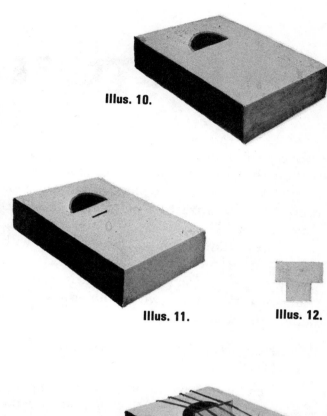

Illus. 10.

Illus. 11.

Illus. 12.

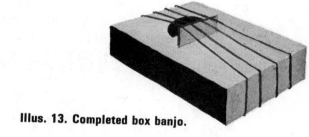

Illus. 13. Completed box banjo.

Illus. 9. Shoe-box strummer.

Box Banjo

Raid the kitchen for the main ingredient for a box banjo. You can make it in a matter of minutes, but it sounds surprisingly like the real instrument.

Search for a sturdy, small carton—from cereal or dry milk or whipped butter, for instance. It may be square or round but should not be more than 2″ deep. Use cellophane (Scotch) tape or gummed paper to anchor the cover on or to seal the spout.

Lay the box flat on its widest surface and carve away. One inch from the left edge, cut out a semi-circular sound hole. (See Illus. 10.) Another inch down to the right, cut a 1″-slit (Illus. 11).

To make a bridge, cut a 2″-square of heavy cardboard. From two corners remove half-inch squares. Your bridge will have a one-inch tab (Illus. 12).

Fit the bridge into the slit, and string your banjo with four elastic bands of different sizes. The smaller ones stretch more and play higher notes. Pluck them gently with your fingers or with a used kitchen match.

Try to think of other instruments you can make.

PICTURE FRAMES

Everyone knows a frame can "make" a picture, but did you know *you* can make a frame? You *can* make a picture frame that is every bit as attractive, a good deal less expensive, and a great deal more satisfying than those sold commercially. Starting with the picture-frame mouldings described here, you will get a good start towards creating your own mouldings with your router and radial arm or bench saw.

Calculating the Amount of Moulding You Need

The length and width of the frame opening must be at least ½" less than the length and width of the picture or mat to be framed.

(Example: The opening for an 8″ × 10″ picture would be 7½″ × 9½″.) To each frame side thus derived, add twice the width of the frame members (this takes care of the length added by the mitre cut at each end). Now add the four sides together to get the actual, outside perimeter of the frame. Add 2″ or 3″ for saw cuts and waste.

Tools

In addition to your power saw and router, a few more items are shown in Illus. 1.

Moulding Profiles

In Illus. 2, Profiles 1 and 2 require only the power saw for making them. In Profile 1,

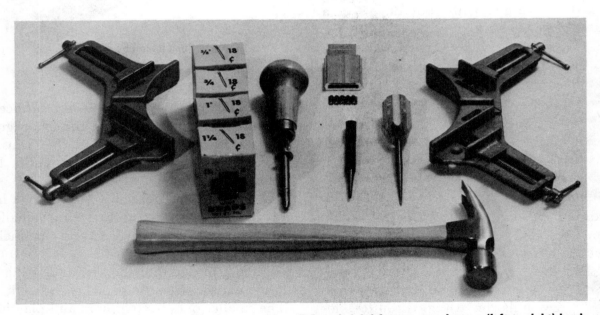

Illus. 1. Some tools that you need for frame-making: (left and right) four corner clamps; (left to right) brads, brad pusher, nail set, brad awl; (top) corrugated nail set; (bottom) light-weight hammer.

Written especially for this volume by Manly Banister

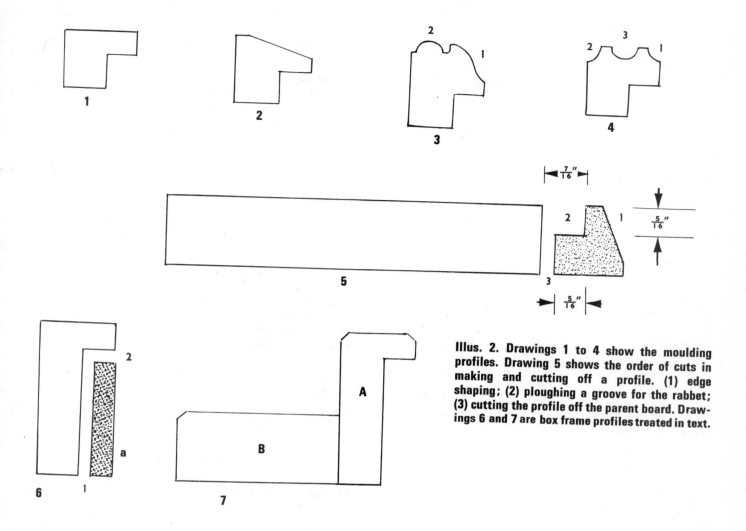

Illus. 2. Drawings 1 to 4 show the moulding profiles. Drawing 5 shows the order of cuts in making and cutting off a profile. (1) edge shaping; (2) ploughing a groove for the rabbet; (3) cutting the profile off the parent board. Drawings 6 and 7 are box frame profiles treated in text.

the edge is left untouched; in Profile 2, the edge is bevelled at a 20° angle, leaving about $\frac{1}{8}''$ flat. Use a hollow-ground, combination blade on the saw, as it leaves a smooth surface.

Drawing 5, Illus. 2, shows graphically how the profile is first shaped and then cut free of the parent board. The rabbet (the ledge that retains the glass and the picture within the frame) is cut with the dado head and measures $\frac{5}{16}'' \times \frac{5}{16}''$ when the profile is cut off. As you subtract only $\frac{1}{2}''$ from the length and width of the picture to determine the size of the opening, the $\frac{5}{16}''$ rabbet gives an extra $\frac{1}{16}''$ clearance all round for easy fitting of glass and picture.

Note the small numbers accompanying Profiles 3 and 4. These indicate both the number of cuts and the order in which they

are made (Illus. 3). Profile 4 is made with the $\frac{1}{4}''$ veining bit only, using the edge guide on the router, or the router table, to position the cuts. Setting the edge guide or fence to the center-line of the veiner allows only one half the width of the cutter to be shaped, resulting in the little cove at each corner. Then re-set the fence to position the cutter between the two previous cuts. You should, in making these cuts, run the board through on edge. It is a good idea, therefore, to clamp a guide board to the table to keep the work piece from drifting away from the cutter (Illus. 3, Drawing 3).

The entire procedure of making the moulding profile is shown in Illus. 4 through Illus. 7. Now cut the moulding into lengths required

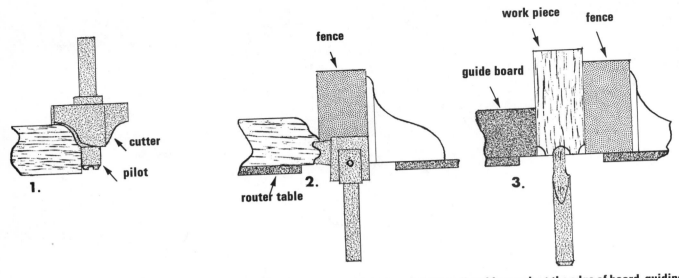

Illus. 3. Drawing 1 : $\frac{5}{32}$" Roman Ogee bit in position to shape the edge of the work. The pilot rides against the edge of board, guiding the cutter. Drawing 2: The router attached under the router table with surface beading bit, which has no pilot. The router table fence guides the work into the revolving cutter. Drawing 3: The router table set-up with a $\frac{1}{4}$" veining bit in the router. The work piece is fed on edge between the fence and a guide board clamped to the table.

for the frame members. Cut them about $\frac{1}{16}$" to $\frac{1}{8}$" over-length. Illus. 8 and 9 show how to make the mitre cuts using a mitre vice bolted to the saw-table fence and a hollow-ground, combination blade for smooth cutting. If you prefer, you could make a jig for mitering, instead of the mitre vice. The design in Illus. 10 combines both mitre angles in one. Placed as shown, you cut the right-hand mitre; then give the jig a quarter-turn to the

left to make the left-hand mitres. Butt the jig firmly against the saw fence and clamp it to the table. With a mitre vice or jig, always use a stop block (Illus. 9) to ensure that each pair of opposite frame members are the same length.

The Box Frame

Drawing 6 of Illus. 2 shows the basic profile of the box frame. It is cut from stock 1" × 2". You can shape the edge as described

Illus. 4. You may handle the router freely for cuts like this one, which has just shaped a Roman Ogee on the edge of a Philippine mahogany board.

Illus. 5. Attach the router to the bottom-side of the router table to make this cut with the surface beading bit. It is important to hold the work firmly in against the fence and to feed at an even rate.

Illus. 6. The third step in creating the moulding profile is to plough a $\frac{7}{16}$"-wide groove $\frac{5}{16}$" deep, the length of the board. Note dado head and the wood springs holding the work firmly against the fence to ensure a straight cut.

Illus. 7. This set-up is the same as in Illus. 6, except that the dado head has been replaced with a combination saw blade. As smoothness of cut is not important, use the type of blade shown and save your mitre blade for precision cuts. This step cuts the profile free of the parent board.

Illus. 8. After cutting the frame members slightly over-length, make the first mitre cut on each piece to the right of the saw blade. The mitre vice shown is a handy accessory for mitering light frame elements like these.

Illus. 9. Make the second mitre cut of each piece to the left of the saw blade. Measure and mark the first piece, clamp it up as shown, then clamp a stop block to the table, bearing against the mitered end. Make the cut, pulling the hollow-ground mitre saw only as far forward as shown. When you place the second piece with the mitered end against the stop block, it will automatically be cut to the same length as the first one.

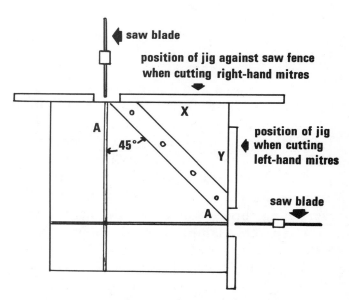

Illus. 10. Make your own mitering jig from a perfect square of ¾"- plywood with a piece of straight 1×2 nailed and glued across one corner as shown. Lines A-A indicate saw kerfs. Clamp jig to table for use.

in the section on moulding. The deep rabbet allows you to frame paintings on stretched canvas (for which the stretchers are ¾" thick), as well as pictures that require a glass. The box frame is deep enough so that you can install the screw eyes for the hanging wire inside the frame. When hung, the frame rests flat against the wall instead of leaning forward from it.

Illus. 11. With one frame member in the corner clamp, apply glue to the end of the adjacent member, fit the mitre joint accurately in the clamp and tighten up. Glue and clamp all four corners.

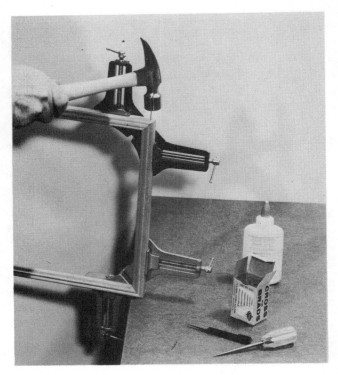

Illus. 12. Drive two 1″-brads into one side only of each corner. A small frame may have the opposite corner braced against the table as shown. If it is necessary to drive nails in a large frame lying flat, always buck the frame up against a solid top to assure clean, accurate nailing.

Drawing 7 in Illus. 2) shows how to nail and glue a 1″ × 2″ flange to the basic profile (see Illus. 20, middle).

Assembling the Frame

Take two adjacent frame members (a long side and a short one) and fit them into a corner clamp until the mitres match perfectly. Tighten the clamp on one piece; then remove the other and apply white glue to the mitered end (Illus. 11). Re-fit the mitre and tighten the clamp. Glue up and clamp the remaining three corners, holding each corner in a separate clamp. Illus. 12 shows how to nail the corners with 1″ brads. Take care not to hit too hard and mar the corner—that is why a light-weight hammer is recommended.

After you have nailed the four corners, set the brad heads below the surface with a nail set having a $\frac{1}{16}$″ tip (Illus. 13). If you have a number of frames to assemble, you can remove the frame from the clamps, and lay it on a *flat* table with a piece of plywood on top to hold it flat. In this way you can stack a number of frames crosswise to each other. If you are making only one frame, leave it in clamps until the glue sets.

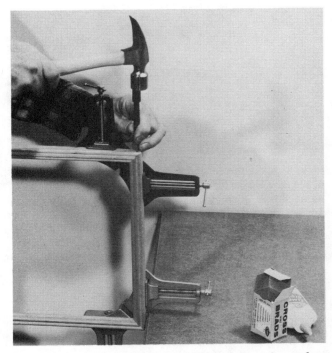

Illus. 13. Finish driving the brad heads below the surface with a nail set.

Illus. 14. Fill the nail holes with filler, let dry, then sand smooth. Apply stain generously to the frame with a brush or rag, let stand a few minutes, then wipe down to an even tone. Let stain dry before finishing with several coats of clear, quick-drying finish.

Finishing

For the best results with a frame made of such wood as Philippine mahogany (the wood used in the illustrations), redwood, red cedar, walnut, chestnut, maple, and so on, use a stain and natural finish. First, fill the nail holes with a wood filler of the proper color and, when dry, sand smooth. Then stain, preferably with a water stain, though an oil stain will do (Illus. 14). After staining, apply several coats of a clear, quick-drying finish. For woods such as pine, fir, and gum, which do not look attractive with a clear finish, use an opaque paint such as satin or matt black or some other dark color as a finish.

Sand all finishes lightly between coats to facilitate adhesion of the following coat. When using a clear finish, rub down the final coat with #000 steel wool, then wax with a quality paste floor wax (except open-grain woods like Philippine mahogany where the wax gets in the grain and shows up white).

Cutting the Mat

You should mat an etching, lithograph, drawing, or other picture before framing. Colored mat boards as well as Museum Board (an all-rag mat board for prints of fine quality) are available at art supply shops.

A mat is composed of two parts, hinged together: the mat board with the opening cut in it for the picture, and the backing of illustration board. The opening may overlap the picture if that has ragged edges—such as water colors, some drawings, etc.—or, it may allow a margin of $\frac{1}{4}''$ or so all around the picture, as when matting etchings, colored reproductions of paintings, and so on. Center the opening horizontally in the mat, so that the side margins are equal in width. The top margin, however, is generally a little narrower than the bottom one to produce a better optical balance.

First mark the opening on the back of the mat board, which you should already have cut to size (Illus. 15), and then cut it out,

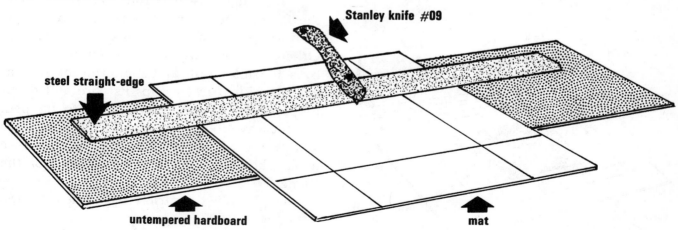

steel straight-edge

Stanley knife #09

untempered hardboard

mat

Illus. 15. Hold the straight-edge firmly and draw the knife point along the lines marking the cut-out. Hardboard under the mat protects the table top.

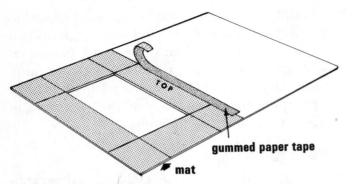

Illus. 16. Lay the mat face down on the table, with the top edge contacting the edge of the backing. Hinge the mount together with 1″ gummed paper tape.

using a metal straight-edge and a sharp-pointed mat knife as indicated. Do not try to cut through the entire board at one stroke—make three or four strokes. Illus. 16 shows how to hinge the mat to the backing board with 1″-wide gummed paper tape. Illus. 17 shows how to attach the picture to the mat backing with masking tape or gummed paper tape after you accurately center it behind the opening. Never attach the picture to the back of the mat with the opening and never fasten it down except along the top edge, or it will buckle in the frame and look unsightly.

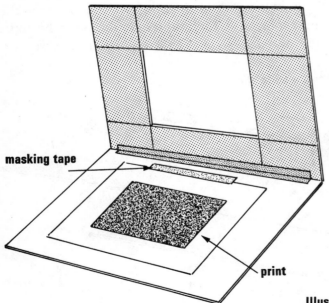

Illus. 17. Attach the picture to the backing along the top edge only, as shown, with the masking tape overlapping the paper only $\frac{1}{8}$″.

Framing the Picture

You can buy glass for the frame, cut to size, at a hardware dealer's, or, you can buy glass in quantity from a glass-supply house and cut your own (in which case you will need an inexpensive glass cutter). Clean the glass thoroughly on both sides and lay it in the frame, which you have placed face down on the table. Next, put the matted picture on top of the glass and on top of this place a piece of corrugated cardboard to fill the remaining space. Using a brad pusher (Illus. 18), drive $\frac{5}{8}$″ or $\frac{3}{4}$″ brads at about 2″ intervals around the frame. If you push a brad through the frame member, or otherwise do it badly, pull out the offending brad with pliers.

To protect the picture from dust seeping in at the back of the frame, you can seal it off with brown wrapping paper (Kraft). Cut the paper about $\frac{1}{8}$″ shorter and narrower than the outside of the frame and dampen it a little with a moist sponge. Spread a string of glue along the back of the wood frame members, lay the dampened paper in place, rub down the edges into the glue, and then leave until dry. As it dries, the paper stretches so that it fits tightly across the back (Illus. 19).

Install screw eyes about one quarter of the way across the frame as shown in Illus. 19. Pass the picture wire through the eye from the inside, pass it *twice* round the shank under the eye, and then twist it round itself as shown at the far end of the wire in the photo. *Always* wrap the wire round the shank before twisting. Otherwise, you may be awakened in the night by a horrible crash and shattering of glass as your cherished frame slips its wire and drops to the floor. It has been known to happen. Do not leave too much slack in the wire, since neither the wire nor the wall hanger (picture hook) should be visible over the top of the frame.

Illus. 20 shows a variety of finished frames.

Illus. 18. The picture has been inserted and backed with a piece of corrugated cardboard from a carton. Drive $\frac{5}{8}''$ or $\frac{3}{4}''$ brads all round with a brad pusher. Use pliers to pull any badly driven brads.

Illus. 19. Note Kraft paper glued to the back of the frame. In wiring, pass the wire through the eye, then twice around the shank of the eye before twisting it back upon itself as shown at the far end of the wire.

Illus. 20. The 11×14 frame demonstrated here is shown framing the etching at the lower left. The remaining are (top to bottom): 8×10 box frame, stretched canvas oil painting; 12×16 flanged box frame, oil painting on stretched canvas; 14×17 box frame, oil painting on panel of braced hardboard.

PUPPETS

Just as in live theatre, puppet theatre requires many talents. Script writers, costume designers and actors are all necessary for a good puppet production, as they are in any performance. But unique in puppetry is the puppet-maker—the craftsman who actually makes and decorates the puppet as he should appear to the audience.

You do not need fancy materials to create a cast of puppet characters. In most cases, everything you need is probably already in your home. An assortment of paper bags, construction paper, tagboard, newspaper, ice cream sticks and cardboard tubes, gives you a good start on basic construction materials. For decoration and costumes, use anything and everything: paper doilies, buttons, ribbon, glitter, paper cups, rick-rack, fabric, cotton, toothpicks, broom straws, foil, construction paper, tissue paper, crepe paper, jewelry, artificial flowers, yarn, scouring pads, fake fur, netting, twigs, gummed paper stars, wood shavings, twine, feathers—anything! And to fasten the parts together, use waterproof glue, brass paper fasteners, paper clips, staples, wheat or flour paste, library paste, and elastic bands.

Paper Puppets

Paper-Bag Puppets

The paper bag is the easiest of all materials to use to make a puppet. The flap on the bottom allows a puppet's head to move—all you need to do is draw features on the face. You can decorate the bottom flap in two ways, as

Illus. 1. Make a paper-bag puppet.

Condensed from the books, "Puppet and Pantomime Plays" by Vernon Howard | © 1962 by Sterling Publishing Co., Inc., New York, and "Puppet-Making" by Chester Jay Alkema | © 1971 by Sterling Publishing Co., Inc., New York

shown in Illus. 1: paint the top lip of your character on the flap and the bottom lip on the bag itself, so that as your puppet moves, his lips also move and his voice is heard. Or, for a flirtatious puppet, paint the eyes on the flap.

After you design the puppet's face, add a body. The winsome miss on the left in Illus. 2 has become a whole being with cut-out curves, drawn with soft-tip markers. Her friend has a slight paunch, made by stuffing his paper-bag body with newspaper. Soft-tip markers detail his shirt and tie. Use tempera paint or crayon if you prefer.

For a large paper puppet with legs, as shown in Illus. 3, fasten two small paper bags to a stuffed paper-bag body. Add construction paper feet and hands, and decorate the body and head in any way you can imagine. The creature in Illus. 3 has painted tagboard ears, yarn hair, and foil eyelashes and nose. Paint, gift wrap, pipe cleaners, and buttons accent other features on his body. There is a slit big enough for a hand in the back of the head.

Illus. 2. Paper bodies cut from large paper bags are not necessary, but they add to the realism of your puppets.

Paper-Bag Fist Puppets

Small paper bags without folds on the bottom are just big enough for your fist to fit into, and they make simple puppets. Bags this size vary greatly in texture, color and pattern—from brown paper for candy to shiny foil for ice cream. Look for the right kind of bag for the puppet you have in mind.

To give your puppet support, make a tagboard tube big enough for your index finger to fit in, and long enough to extend from below the puppet's neck to the top of his head. Put this tube inside the bag and fill the head area with crushed paper. Gather the bag at the neck

Illus. 3. A puppet as big as a boy! Because it is made of paper, such a large puppet is easy to handle.

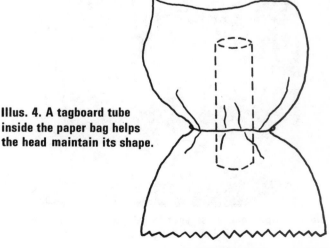

Illus. 4. A tagboard tube inside the paper bag helps the head maintain its shape.

Illus. 5. This perky little mouse, with a head crammed full of newspaper, stands ready to frighten an innocent passer-by.

and tie it with yarn, string or ribbon. The little mouse in Illus. 5 has construction paper and buttons of felt glued on his body, while yarn forms the features of his face.

To manipulate a paper-bag fist puppet, insert your index finger in the tagboard tube, and put your thumb and middle finger through holes in the front of the bag.

Illus. 6. Open and close your fingers to make your puppet speak his piece.

Folded Paper Puppets

For a three-dimensional paper face, folded construction paper is ideal: it is soft enough to bend, sturdy enough to last, and colorful enough for an interesting background.

First, cut a piece of construction paper into a 12″ × 3″ rectangle. Fold the paper in half, 3″ sides together, and fold each edge back towards the fold (see Illus. 6). The fold becomes a mouth which you can open and close. The paper in Illus. 6 was stapled along the folds so the fingers had "pockets" to hold on to.

Complete your folded paper puppets by surrounding the mouth with a face: paint or paste a paper tongue on the inside of the mouth. The large eyes in the owl on the left (Illus. 7) make him quite realistic, while the creature on the right has eyebrows of glitter and a fringed V-shaped beard.

Paper-Plate Puppets

One fold turns a paper plate into a puppet face. The puppet in Illus. 8 is almost all mouth. Glue a piece of cloth to the top of a plate to provide a hiding place for your fingers (your thumb goes under the chin), so you can open and close the mouth. Add paper circles for eyes, a red tongue, white fangs, and a cloth sleeve for a body (it hides your **arm** at the same time).

Illus. 7. Whenever your puppet character talks onstage, be sure to move his mouth so the audience knows who is speaking.

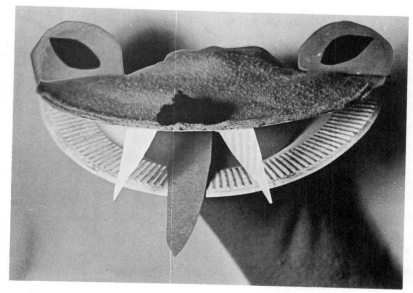

Illus. 8. The head of a snake with a sly smile smirks at the audience.

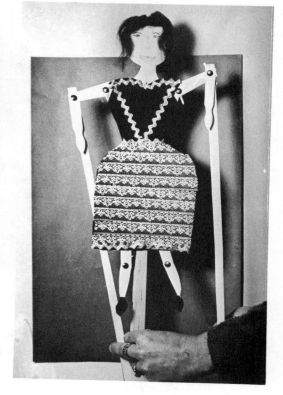

Illus. 9. Brass paper fasteners make movable joints, allowing rod puppets to dance round the stage.

Stick and Rod Puppets

The most essential equipment for a stick puppet is, of course, a stick—either an ice cream stick, ruler, branch or thin wooden dowel. Cut shapes from paper. Staple or glue them to the stick. Then decorate them—be realistic, unusual, or downright fantastic.

To manipulate a stick puppet, hold the stick at the end. Raise it, lower it, wave it from side to side as the character in your puppet play speaks. If you crouch behind a table or hold your puppets inside a cardboard box, the audience sees only the puppets and not your hands.

A rod puppet also allows more movement and more realism. A wooden dowel glued to a tagboard body forms the main support, while you manipulate strips of tagboard up and down to move the puppet's arms and legs. Brass paper fasteners at the joints let each limb move independently of any other.

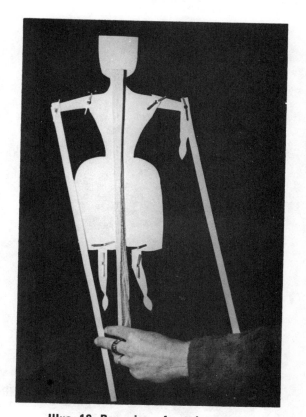

Illus. 10. Rear view of a rod puppet.

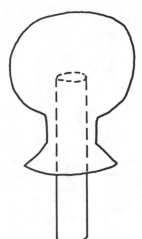

Illus. 11. The finished papier mâché head, shaped over a tagboard tube.

Papier Mâché Puppets

Papier mâché uses newspaper and flour-and-water paste. When dry, papier mâché is almost as hard as any wooden object. The puppets here have papier mâché heads built over various objects.

Tear newspaper from top to bottom into strips ½″ wide, or even narrower if you are making delicate features. Soak the paper strips in flour-and-water paste which you have blended to the consistency of light cream, or use library paste instead. Apply at least four layers of saturated strips in four different directions—horizontal, vertical, and two ways diagonally—and allow the head to dry *completely* before you paint and decorate it. To be sure the head is dry through and through, bake it in a 250°F oven.

No matter what base you form the papier mâché over, model the head in the shape drawn in Illus. 11. First roll and tape a tagboard tube large enough to surround your index finger. Build the head around this tube, modelling the neck so it expands outward at the bottom to provide a "shelf" for a piece of clothing.

Over Crushed Newspaper

Inexpensive, light-weight and always available, crushed newspaper is an ideal base for papier mâché. First make a tagboard tube about 4″ long to fit over your index finger. Poke this tube into a ball of crushed newspaper—just one large sheet makes a good-sized ball—and wind string or tape around the ball to keep it tightly packed.

Illus. 12. The finished head before decoration.

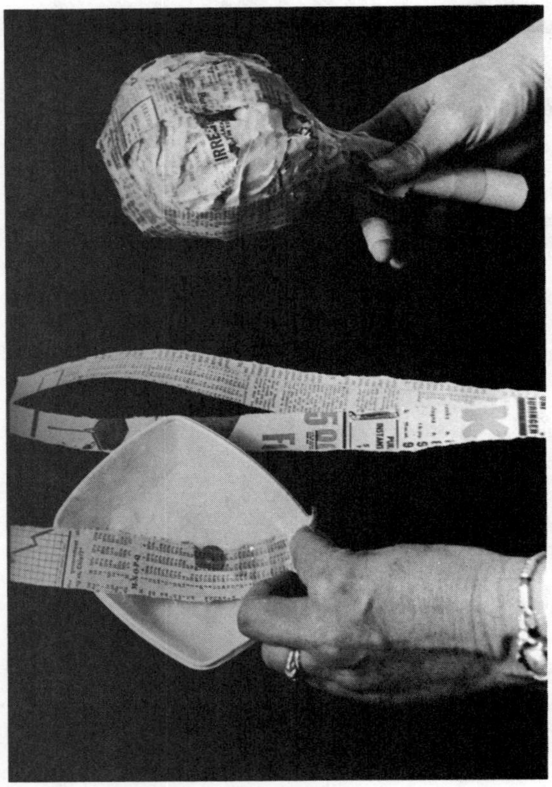

Illus. 13. Slide newspaper strips through flour-and-water paste; then wrap the base with the strips.

Pour some flour-and-water paste into a large shallow pan and slide one strip at a time through the paste, making sure the strip is thoroughly saturated. Lay the first layer of strips in one direction across the newspaper base, squeezing the excess moisture and air out of each strip by smoothing it firmly with your fingers from the middle to the ends. While the newspaper is still wet, mould the head with your hands to shape features.

Apply the second layer of strips right away, without waiting for the first to dry. Place these strips at right angles to the first layer, again pressing firmly to get rid of excess water and air bubbles. For a sturdy, rock-hard head, apply the third and fourth layers diagonally across the others.

Your finished head probably looks something like the one in Illus. 12. Note the "collar" at the base of the neck, moulded as the newspaper strips were added, which will hold a dress or shirt. For curves and bumps on the face—the eyebrow ridge or lips, perhaps—use saturated tissue paper instead of newspaper. It is thinner and therefore easier to mould.

In decorating your puppet head, paint is probably the first thing you think of. But you can add other features even before the head is dry. Press trinkets into the wet papier mâché—marbles and buttons for eyes, beads for freckles or moles, or a jewel in the forehead. Be careful if you plan to bake the head in order to dry it that the doo-dads you attach can also be baked (plastic beads melt, for example.)

Over a Newspaper Tube

A papier mâché head over a rolled newspaper tube is as easy to make as a head over crushed newspaper. The strips are layered here just as they were before (page 398), but the base is a bit trickier to make.

Roll a folded sheet of newspaper into a tube, narrowing it at one end to fit comfortably round your index finger. Fasten the tube with masking tape to hold it together. Roll the wide end of the tube toward the narrow end until the roll is about 4″ from the end, and wrap

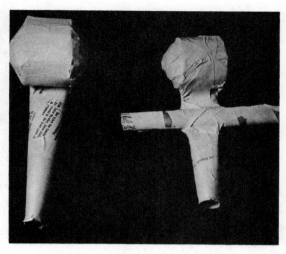

Illus. 14. Two versions of a rolled newspaper tube. The finished puppet built on the base on the right will have arms.

Illus. 15. This dapper fellow has a matching hat and suit.

masking tape around the roll to hold it in place. Apply saturated newspaper strips as you did for the papier mâché head over crushed newspaper.

The little man in Illus. 15 has a head made of papier mâché over a newspaper tube.

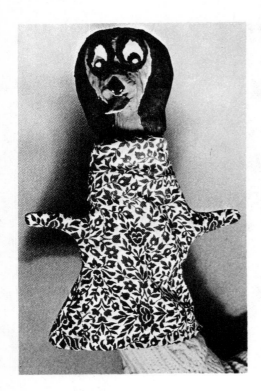

Illus. 16. Follow the curves of the light bulb exactly as you apply the newspaper strips.

Illus. 17. Light-weight and perfectly shaped, a light bulb covered with papier mâché makes an outstanding puppet head.

Over Light Bulbs

A light bulb offers a perfect shape for a head: round at the top and narrow toward the neck. Glue a tagboard tube to the bottom metal section of the bulb for your index finger. Layer saturated newspaper strips over the bulb, first one way, then another. Allow the four layers of strips to cover the tagboard tube as well as the bulb so the tube stays securely fastened. When the layers of papier mâché have dried, the rock-hard covering on the bulb protects the glass inside. There is no danger if the head is dropped and the bulb shatters, as the broken glass remains inside the shell.

Sawdust and Paste Puppets

Sawdust is available at no charge from a carpenter and is an easy-to-work-with material for a puppet head. Mix half a cup of sawdust, half a cup of plaster of Paris and a quarter cup of wheat or flour-and-water paste with one cup of water. Stir the mixture thoroughly to blend all the ingredients and then model the stuff into shape as you would model clay. Form the head round a tagboard tube so you can turn the head by moving your index finger.

Illus. 18. Although the texture of the dried sawdust is rough and bumpy, this can be an advantage—to imitate fur, for example.

If you just place a lump of the sawdust mixture on the end of the tube, however, it may crack as it dries. To prevent this, put just a small portion on the tube and let it dry. Add more layers as the first ones dry, and make facial features with the last layers. Modelling the head layer by layer allows the paste to dry from the inside out, making a very durable head.

Stuffed-Sock Puppets

Similar to a paper-bag fist puppet (page 395) is a stuffed-sock puppet, easily made by stuffing a sock with newspaper or some other material. The Christmas character in Illus. 20 has a firm head, formed by a plastic foam ball placed in the heel of the sock. The toe of the sock swings around over the head and is stitched on, for a hat. Bells jingle when the puppet moves, which he should do whenever he speaks onstage.

Manipulating a stuffed-sock puppet is quite simple, but it depends on what material you use to stuff the head. If newspaper rounds out the puppet's face, a tagboard tube is easy to insert into the crushed ball. Wrap string round the paper to hold it together. If you use a plastic foam ball to form the head, you do not need a tube. Just hollow out a hole in the ball large enough for your index finger.

Glove Puppets (upright position)

Gloves and mittens keep your hands warm, but they make very different puppets. While a mitten puppet might not have differentiated parts—that is, separate arms and head—the cloth you cut for a glove puppet does, and your fingers control the parts. Your thumb and middle finger control the puppet's arms, and your index finger works his head (see Illus. 21). When you cut the pieces for a glove puppet, make the head section wider and taller than the arms.

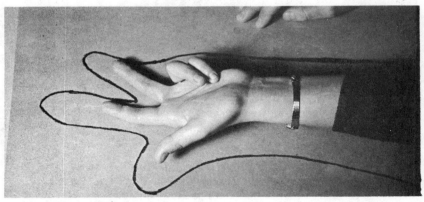

Illus. 21. Let your index finger support the head, and your middle finger and thumb wiggle the arms of your glove puppet.

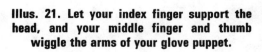

Illus. 22. Made from a pink knitted dishcloth, this bunny has wire in his ears to keep them upright.

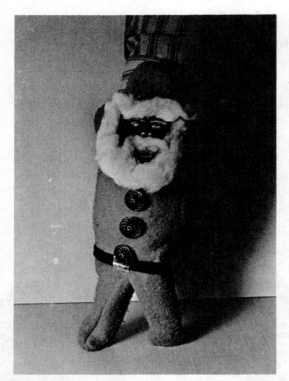

Illus. 23. That old stand-by, fluffy cotton, surrounds the face on this bright red glove puppet.

Illus. 24 (right). Smiling broadly because they have on new outfits, these two are ready to go into their act.

The bunny in Illus. 22 is a glove puppet cut from a textured dish towel. His head is stuffed with cloth scraps, and pink felt emphasizes his ears. His black button eyes twinkle and his wire whiskers shimmy as he waves at us with a delicate pink paw.

Glove Puppets (downward position)

A five-fingered glove is a ready-made base for a puppet. Just slip the glove on your hand, fold your thumb, ring and little fingers toward your palm, and "let your fingers do the walking." The fellow in Illus. 23 began his life as an old red felt glove, and blossomed into the Christmas character shown here. Fluffy cotton for a beard and hair, aluminum foil for facial features and black cord for a belt—all he needs now are his reindeer!

Painted-Hand Puppets

Your hands are the most convenient bases to decorate. Draw features on the back of your hand with lipstick, crayon or make-up. Color the tips of your first two fingers also, so your character is not barefoot. Clothing is never a problem for small folks: paper, attached to your hand with double-sided sticky tape, is always at hand. Cloth is usually just as available and looks a bit more realistic. The figure on the right in Illus. 24 has fluted cupcake liners for a full skirt.

Cloth-Monofold Puppets

Make a cloth puppet with a hard head, with nothing to mix or measure! Cut a strip of tagboard 2½″ × 6″, and a piece of cloth about 10″ × 36″. Bring the short edges of the tagboard together and tape them to make a ring. With the ring in the center of the cloth, bring the short ends of the cloth together over the ring. Wrap an elastic band or string round the cloth at the base of the tagboard ring. Decorate the cloth which covers the tagboard with buttons and other trinkets for features.

The cloth which hangs down from the neck becomes both the body and costume of the puppet. Follow the stitching diagram in Illus. 27b to make a boy puppet and the one in Illus. 27c for a girl puppet. No matter which sex your puppet is, leave the ends of the arms and bottom of the garment unstitched. Insert felt hands and feet into these openings and sew them to the cloth.

Manipulating the puppet is easy, once your hand is inside him. Cut a slit about 4″ long through the back layer only. Insert a finger in each arm, and in the head. As you curl and bend your fingers, your puppet acts out his part!

Illus. 25. Simple to make and attach, small finger puppets require an audience that sits close to the stage.

Finger Puppets

To represent a large number of puppets onstage, attach a finger puppet to each finger. The five puppets on one hand might be a choir, band, flock of sheep or a group of "extras"—characters necessary to the performance because of their numbers, but not because of any individual traits. If one of the puppets speaks,

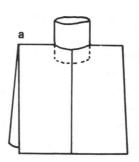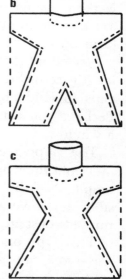

Illus. 26 (left). You can make a floppy clown less floppy by stuffing him with scraps of cloth.

Illus. 27. In "a," the unstitched cloth surrounds a tagboard head. In "b," the stitching diagram for a boy puppet. In "c," the stitching diagram for a girl puppet.

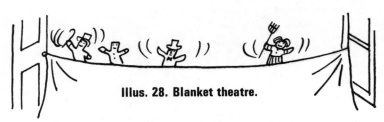

Illus. 28. Blanket theatre.

Illus. 29.
Table theatre.

move him forward and from side to side slightly so the audience knows which character is talking.

The two puppets in Illus. 25 are made of construction paper. Since these puppets are small, they cannot support too many ornaments, so the details in their faces are drawn on with ink. To hold a finger puppet, glue a narrow strip of paper to the back of the legs and curl it to form a ring that fits over your fingers. Keep your fingers straight while the characters are onstage.

Making a Puppet Theatre

Your puppet theatre can be as simple or as fancy as you like. The important idea is to make the theatre and its stage suitable for the kind of show you are going to present. A show having several puppets needs a stage larger than one used for a one-man show.

Here are several ways to build a puppet theatre:

BLANKET THEATRE: A blanket theatre is excellent for presenting plays with a large cast. Make the stage as wide as necessary. As many as six or seven puppets, or even more, can perform onstage at the same time.

Stretch a blanket or sheet out to any desired length across the room or yard. Fasten the ends to solid objects to hold the blanket up. Perhaps you can fasten the ends to a door or a window.

The puppeteers stand behind the blanket and hold their puppets above its top edge. The ample room behind the blanket makes it possible for several puppeteers to have their puppets onstage at the same time.

This type of theatre is perfect for outdoor use—you can suspend the blanket between posts or trees.

TABLE THEATRE: Here the top of a table serves as your stage. Fasten a blanket or sheet over one side of a table and let it hang down as far as the floor. The purpose of the blanket is to hide you from the audience. Sit or kneel behind the table and hold your puppet up to perform on the table top.

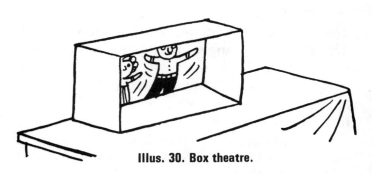

Illus. 30. Box theatre.

BOX THEATRE: This is a small theatre which is good for one or two puppets. First, follow the instructions given above for making a table theatre. Next, find an oblong box, and remove two of its sides. This leaves you with a frame consisting of the other two sides and the two ends. Place a blanket on top of the table (to prevent the box from scratching it); then set the box on its side on top of the blanket. Stand or sit in back of the table and let your puppets act inside the box.

DOORWAY THEATRE: Your stage will be as wide as the doorway you use. Fasten a blanket or sheet across a doorway so that its lower half is covered. Stand behind the blanket and hold your puppet above it.

WINDOW THEATRE: Find a first-floor window that offers room on one side for your audience and space on the other side for the puppeteers. A porch window is often just right. Open the window, stay below the sill, and hold your puppets up.

Illus. 31. Doorway theatre.

Illus. 32. Window theatre.

Ideas for Shows

In most cases, puppeteers remain hidden behind the stage. However, a single puppeteer can perform in full view of the audience and without any stage at all. He can do this by holding the puppet away from him and turning his head away from the audience when the puppet is supposed to be speaking. He speaks to the puppet with one voice and answers with another. The puppet should wiggle around a bit when it is speaking. Also, the puppeteer can sit on a chair with the puppet on his knee.

If your stage has no curtain, the play can begin as the puppets come onstage for the first time. The puppets can end their act simply by bowing and leaving the stage. Another idea is for an assistant to flash a card reading THE END.

The director can introduce an act with a few words, including a welcome to the theatre and a brief description of the background of the act. For instance, "The play which you are about to see takes place at the seashore. Let's see what happens down among the sands and waves." A single performer can introduce his own act, or he can let the puppet speak!

You need very little scenery and stage properties for a puppet show. In many cases you can do without them altogether. However, it often adds to the showmanship of the play to set the stage with toy furniture and such.

Sound effects always add extra punch to a performance. Appoint someone to make the sounds that go with the onstage action. With very little equipment you can create sounds like storms and explosions and galloping horses. The sound effect should be timed correctly so that it is heard at exactly the same moment that the onstage action occurs.

In the language of the theatre, the *right wing* means the wing to the right of the puppet as he stands onstage and faces the audience, while *left wing* is to the puppet's left. *Upstage* is to the rear of the stage, while *downstage* is towards the audience.

Tug-of-War

Here is a picnic stunt that you can perform onstage with entertaining results. You can present the act using four puppets, or only two, so long as you have an equal number on both sides.

Before the puppets appear onstage, fasten a length of cord to them with small safety-pins so it appears that the puppets are grasping the rope. This prevents the rope from slipping off during the tugging.

Use your imagination to think of clever actions for the puppet-athletes, such as:

1. Let them tug back and forth as if one side is winning, then the other.

2. Let one side pull so hard that they move backward into the wing and off the stage completely, then have their opponents struggle back to do the same in the opposite wing.

3. Let them tug in rhythm to offstage music.

4. Let one side pull its opponents offstage so swiftly that all of them shoot into the wing with a loud crash.

"Puppet" Puppets

This stunt is always good for a few minutes of fun at a puppet show. The announcer tells the audience that some of the puppets have been trained to obey any orders that anyone cares to give them. He invites members of the audience to command the puppets to perform.

The announcer stands aside as two or three puppets bounce onstage and bow. The audience then commands them to perform whatever stunts come to mind. They ask them to run in a circle, to bump into each other, or sing a song. Half the fun of this stunt is that the audience will ask the puppets to do difficult or strange things. When the puppets get all mixed up, the fun begins!

Rhyming Puppets

Start by writing down pairs of words that rhyme, such as *gate* and *late; pig* and *fig; song* and *long*.

Next, build a two-line poem from each pair of rhyming words. Here are examples of how they might come out:

> *Why are you late?*
> *I was stuck in the gate.*
> *I see a pig.*
> *Go feed it a fig.*
> *Sing me a song.*
> *A short one or long?*

A pair of puppeteers can write six or seven of these rhymes and speak them one after another. One puppet speaks the first line and his partner the second.

To help remember the lines, write them down on a sheet of paper and pin it to the back of the stage.

The Wrestlers

1. One of the wrestlers appears onstage from right wing. The other appears at left.

2. They eye each other, growl, and stir their feet around as they get ready to rush at each other.

3. They yell, rush at each other, miss completely, pass by each other and crash offstage.

4. They re-appear, sway groggily about for a few seconds, again growl at each other.

5. Again they yell and speed towards each other. They hit head-on, bounce back violently and fly offstage with another crash.

6. They re-appear, rush at each other, and wrestle.

7. One wrestler throws the other offstage. The other returns and throws his opponent offstage.

8. They wrestle furiously, shrieking and groaning.

9. With swift movements they repeat the action of rushing at each other, missing, and ending up in an offstage crash.

10. They rush at each other several times, knocking each other in various directions.

11. They wrestle some more, but both grow slow and tired. They fall together to the floor where they lie in silence for a moment or two.

12. They rise together. One says, "Let's be friends." The other replies, "It's much better to be friends." Arm in arm they exit happily.

SILVER JEWELRY

WIRE
Round

B & S Gauge	
9	●
12	●
16	●
18	·
20	·
24	·

Flat

— 18 B & S

(10 gauges hard)

SHEET

B & S Gauge
12
14
16
18
20
22
24
26

Illus. 1. Thicknesses shown are actual size.

You can produce stunning, individual jewelry—*without any difficult techniques*, such as sawing, drilling, or soldering. With your own two hands and a minimum of materials and tools, you can turn out in combination with beads the most intricate, finely wrought silver jewelry imaginable.

Silver is one of the most attractive, one of the most malleable, or softest, of all metals, natural or man-made, and in addition, it is far less expensive than, say, gold.

Before you begin any project, read the instructions carefully, so you have a clear idea of what you are going to do. Assemble *all* of your materials and tools so you won't be left hanging in mid-air, both hands occupied, and minus a vital piece of wire.

Do not be deceived by the elaborate appearance of some of the projects. Every piece is as simple as the few techniques you will learn right in the beginning!

Materials and Tools

The first thing you will need of course, is silver wire and sheet silver. There are many different sizes and shapes available which you can purchase from a metal supply house, as well as through specialized hobby shops. You will find round, flat rectangular, square, beaded, half-round, etc. However, for your beginning work, you will use only round and flat.

Wire thickness is expressed in terms of gauge: 1 gauge is equivalent to 7.341 mm. or 0.289 in. The higher the gauge number, the finer the wire; that is, a 10-gauge wire is heavier, or thicker, than a 20-gauge wire. Round wire (see Illus. 1) is difficult to work with in the heavier gauges, so keep to the 16- to 24-gauge area. Silver flat wire comes in various widths, but you will find the $\frac{1}{8}$"-width suitable for your jewelry. A piece of 18-gauge flat wire can be hammered out to make it wider if so desired (see Illus. 1).

You will generally want to use the higher gauge (light-weight) wires which, incidentally, are the least expensive. Silver is sold by weight and therefore the lower gauge, or thicker, wires are heavier and cost more. Also, the thinner the silver, the more malleable it is.

The same holds true for *sheet silver*. This you will find available in a variety of sizes and shapes—strips, circles, squares, and so on, in gauges from 10 to 28. You will, of course, as with the wire, want to use the lighter-weight pieces, say from 18 gauge up. As you can see from Illus. 1, 12 gauge would be entirely too thick for your purposes. It is advisable to use

Condensed from the book, "Creating Silver Jewelry with Beads" by Marianne Seitz / © 1971 by Sterling Publishing Co., Inc., New York

Illus. 2. You are sure to have odds and ends of beads tucked away that are just right for combining with your silver jewelry.

none heavier than 24 gauge, and preferably 28 gauge.

Beads: You no doubt already have a collection of broken or unused necklaces, bracelets, earrings, even bead-like buttons around the house. If not, you can easily find glass, plastic, wooden, or enamel beads at variety shops. Do be sure to get an assortment that have varying sizes of "eyes" to adjust to the width of the wires you will be using.

Findings are ready-made devices to use as backings for many of your finished pieces. However, in much of your silverwork you are going to make your own clasps and such, but for earrings, you will probably want ready-made findings.

Round-nose pliers (see Illus. 3a) are used to bend and shape both round and flat wire, as well as for gripping, in the same way a tweezers is used. They have two round jaws that taper to points. Generally, you will use the round-nose pliers for making rounded forms.

Flat-nose pliers have flat jaws and are used for squeezing materials together and for shaping

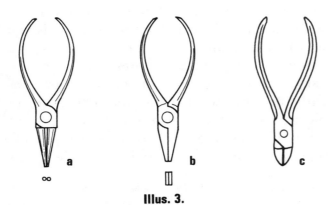

a   b   c

∞   ▯

Illus. 3.

such things as square or angled windings, as well as for straightening out warped pieces. Avoid the pliers that have serrated jaws, or if they do, file them down smooth to keep them from damaging the metal (see Illus. 3b).

Diagonal-cutting pliers, also called diagonal wire cutters, have a cutting jaw at an angle up to the point. Use them for cutting off both round and flat wire. There is a type that has a cutter on one jaw in combination with a round or flat jaw. These are less suitable for getting into tight places where it is necessary to snip off wire ends (Illus. 3c).

Metal-cutting shears, called plate shears, are necessary only for cutting thicker metals such as earring findings. A simple, very sharp scissors is sufficient for your sheet-silver cutting.

A rawhide or rubber mallet and a small anvil are handy for hammering and flattening. For wire-bending aids, you can use almost anything that is the right size and shape—a knitting needle, pencil, or yardstick, a bottle, etc. A bone folder is all that is necessary for embossing sheet silver. And finally, epoxy cement for glueing beads onto the metal.

A Looped-Wire and Bead Necklace

Materials
   18- or 20-gauge silver round wire
   20 beads, 12 light and 8 dark
   round-nose pliers
   diagonal-cutting pliers
   string
   tape measure or yardstick

The necklace in Illus. 4 is so easy to make from just one piece of silver wire, you might end up making dozens of them for friends and relatives.

Take a very long piece of string and place it around your neck. Decide what length you wish the large neckloop to be, remove the string and measure the length. An average size is 15″.

Now using the string again, follow Illus. 5 through Illus. 9 until you have formed three small loops and the neckloop, allowing

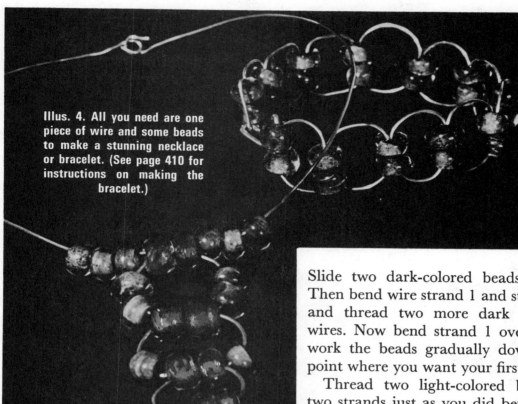

Illus. 4. All you need are one piece of wire and some beads to make a stunning necklace or bracelet. (See page 410 for instructions on making the bracelet.)

Slide two dark-colored beads on as shown. Then bend wire strand 1 and strand 2 together and thread two more dark beads on both wires. Now bend strand 1 over strand 2 and work the beads gradually downwards to the point where you want your first loop (Illus. 6).

Thread two light-colored beads onto the two strands just as you did before by pressing the upper ends together. Work these down in the same way to the point where you want loop #2 (Illus. 7). Thread two more dark beads on, cross the strands over again, and thread four light-colored beads on, two on each side, and complete loop #3 by threading on two more dark beads (Illus. 8).

Add the six light beads shown, three on each side, and bend your two strands into the neckloop shape. Make a simple clasp at the

at least 1½″ for clasping purposes. Undo your "string necklace" and measure the total length. It will probably be about 40″ long.

Cut a piece of wire at least 6″ longer than you need to allow for adjustments.

With your hands, bend the wire in the middle into the shape shown in Illus. 5.

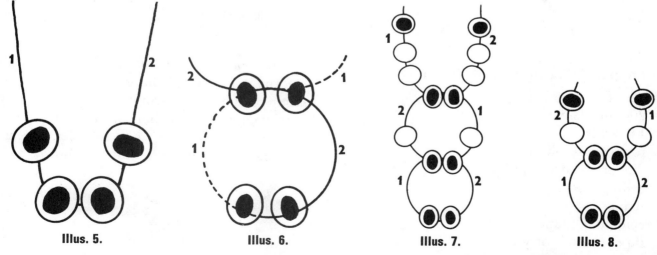

Illus. 5.   Illus. 6.   Illus. 7.   Illus. 8.

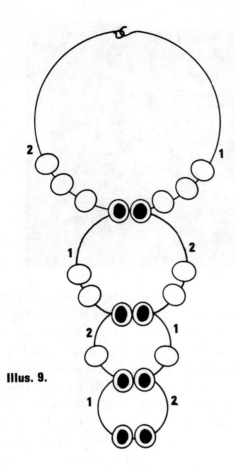

Illus. 9.

Although the bracelet in Illus. 4 has 24 beads and 12 loops, be a little less ambitious for your first wire and bead bracelet, or you will have to make loops that are too small to handle at this point. Be satisfied with 8 loops and 14 beads. Do not use more than two beads per "twist" unless they are very small.

Take your string and form 8 overlapping loops all stretched out in a line. Use tape to hold the loops together. Pick it up carefully and place it around your wrist. Adjust the loops as necessary—smaller or larger in order to fit. Take note of the two ends, undo the string and measure. An average length is 24″. Again, allow a little extra for clasping.

Now thread your beads onto the wire in the same way as with the necklace, crossing and threading two beads at a time. You will find your round-nose pliers most helpful to aid you with the bending. Actually, you can make a very simple device to help in your round bending if you wish, as shown in Illus. 11. This will help you whenever you want to make uniform rounded shapes.

end as shown in Illus. 10. Use the round-nose pliers for this bending procedure. Snip off any excess wire with your diagonal-cutting pliers.

Illus. 10.

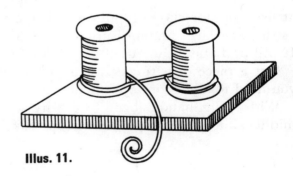

Illus. 11.

A Looped-Wire and Bead Bracelet

Materials
   20-gauge silver round wire
   14 beads
   round-nose pliers
   diagonal-cutting pliers
   rolling pin
   string
   cellophane tape
   tape measure or yardstick

Now, since your bracelet is still flat, in order to form it into wrist shape, use a wooden or plastic rolling pin to form it on. Work carefully, using your pliers and hands, until the desired shape is attained. For your bracelet, use the clasp shown in Illus. 12. Shape as shown.

Illus. 12.

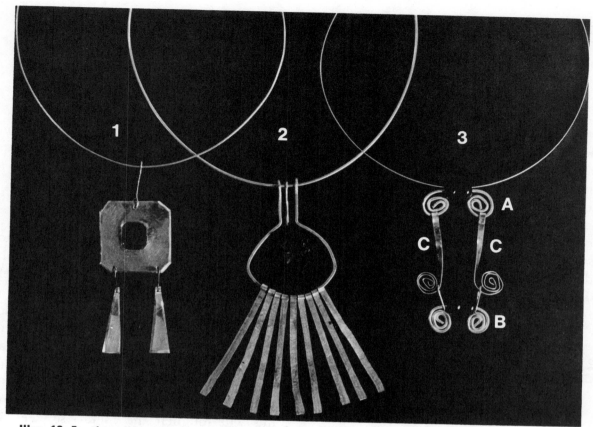

Illus. 13. For these three elegant neck adornments, see directions below for (1) and pages 412 and 413 for (2) and (3).

A Wire Neckloop and Jewelled
Silver Pendant

Materials

   18-gauge or lighter, silver round wire
   24-gauge silver round wire
   sheet silver 26 gauge or lighter
   a square bead, not too small
   string
   strong needle
   bone folder
   epoxy cement

This is neckloop (1) in Illus. 13.

Since this type of necklace looks best as a choker, measure off your neck length with your string and cut a corresponding piece of silver round wire. An average length is 15″ or 16″. The loop should be as close to a circle as possible, so shape your wire very carefully, holding one end with the flat-nose pliers and the other with the round-nose pliers. To achieve the best results, you might shape it around a half-gallon or gallon bottle, such as is used for mineral water or wine. Be sure you fill the bottle with liquid so it won't tip during the bending process, or enlist the aid of a friend to hold it steady. Make a simple clasp as in Illus. 10.

Next, make paper patterns for the square silver pendant and long triangular pieces attached to it. Make these fairly good-sized, say a 2″ square and 2″-long triangles. When you are satisfied with the proportions, outline the patterns on the sheet silver and cut. Pierce the square with a strong needle in three places as shown in Illus. 13. Pierce the triangles at the narrow ends.

Now try your hand at some simple embossing. When embossing, you work both sides of the silver, using a bone folder or wooden modelling tool (Illus. 14). If neither is handy, a nonmetallic letter opener would do as well.

Illus. 14. A typical wooden modelling tool.

Do your embossing on a support such as a hard rubber mat or thick felt mat. (A triple thickness of blotters will also serve the purpose.)

Using a grease pencil, sketch in a line all around the square. Our silver square has bevelled edges, achieved by simply cutting off the corners. However, for your first try at embossing, leave it square. Then with your tool, define the line on one side and then on the other as shown in Illus. 15. You may have

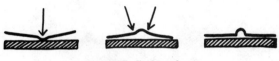

Illus. 15. Embossing.

to work both sides several times to achieve the desired result. Do the same with the triangles, remembering always to emboss on your mat. Do not press hard—a little experimental light pressure is advisable to start.

When you have finished, cut 1″-long pieces of the 24-gauge silver round wire and make the attachment pieces for the square and triangles. Bend these in the fashion shown in Illus. 16 which shows the right way and the wrong way to make this type of attachment loop. Before closing them over completely, insert the ends in the holes you pierced, as well as around the neckloop.

Illus. 16. A: Wrong. B: Right.

Now attach the decorative bead in the middle by simply glueing it on with epoxy cement, and you are finished!

A Neckloop with a Flat-Wire and Cameo Pendant

Materials

18-gauge silver round wire
18-gauge silver flat wire ⅛″ wide
large decorative bead, or cameo as shown
rawhide or rubber mallet (in a pinch you can wrap felt around an ordinary hammer)
anvil
epoxy cement
This is neckloop (2) in Illus. 13.
Make a choker-size neckloop.

To decide on the size of the wire which will enclose the cameo, use the string method as before—it should require approximately 10″ allowing for the two lengths attached to the neckloop. Use the silver round wire for this part and lay it on the anvil. With the mallet, tap *lightly* along its length until it has two flattened surfaces. Do not flatten it out completely. You will find it has stretched out somewhat. (A tip on hammering: excessive hammering will toughen the metal, so keep this in mind when you work.)

Illus. 17. Shaping wire.

In order to bend this wire into the shape shown, use any form you might have handy that is similar or make a form yourself. Take a block of wood, and hammer nails into your desired pattern as shown in Illus. 17. Then bend the wire around the nails until it has the shape you want. Be sure to snip the heads off the nails so that you can lift the wire off easily.

Before attaching this to the neckloop, make your flat-wire strands. Before cutting the individual pieces, decide how long they are to be. Since they will be attached to a curved surface, make them all the same length, and they will appear to form a similar curve (see Illus. 13). Suppose you choose 2″ for the length and 9 strands altogether, simply multiply, and cut an 18″-length of flat wire. Hammer this out as much as you please on your anvil. Then measure off each 2″ length and cut. Attach them by bending the ends over the finished part of the pendant and squeezing. Then attach the entire piece to the neckloop with simple bends as shown.

The large bead or cameo is hooked onto the neckloop with a piece of flattened round wire which, in turn, is glued onto the back of the cameo.

A Flat-Wire Neckloop with Spiral and Bead Pendant

Materials

18-gauge silver flat wire
18-gauge silver round wire
24-gauge silver round wire
4 large-eyed beads
very narrow string
round-nose pliers
flat-nose pliers

This is neckloop (3) in Illus. 13.

Form a choker-type neckloop as before, this time using the 18-gauge flat wire. Do not fashion a clasp immediately—leave the ends free until later on.

The three spiralled parts A, B, and C will be made separately and put together. A and B are made of round wire and C of flat wire.

Take your narrow string and make a form with spiralled ends as shown at A in Illus. 13 in proportion to the neckloop. Unravel and measure. Piece B will be similar but somewhat smaller; however, allow the same length for each. You can make tighter spirals for Part B, if you wish. Jot down the measurement, so you will not forget.

Two identical pieces of flat wire comprise Part C. Use a piece of string again to determine how long you want these pieces and make a note of it. They should be the same length, of course, or Part B will hang lopsided.

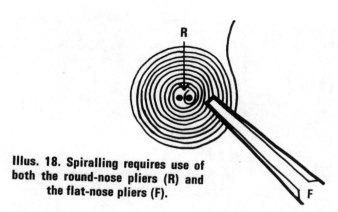

Illus. 18. Spiralling requires use of both the round-nose pliers (R) and the flat-nose pliers (F).

Cut your first piece of round wire. Then, with your round-nose pliers, grip one end, and with the aid of the flat-nose pliers, wrap a spiral around at least two times (Illus. 18). Now slip two beads on from the other end and proceed to wrap another, similar spiral at that end. Don't worry if they are not exactly alike—the distinction of hand-made jewelry is that it is rarely precision-wrought!

Make Part C in exactly the same way, forming somewhat tighter spirals and also adding two beads as shown.

Now cut your two pieces for Part C from the flat wire. Make your spirals as before and then, as in Illus. 19, using the round-nose pliers (R), twist the flat wire around the flat-nose pliers (F) a *quarter-turn* (90°) as shown.

You are now ready to attach the various pieces together. Take Part A and thread it onto the neckloop through the eyes of the beads until it is in the exact middle. Join Part C to Part A by inserting the two ends into the lower spirals and bending them over on the reverse side into hooks. Part B and Part C are joined together with the same 24-gauge wire loops which you used on page 411.

Make a clasp on the neckloop and wear your new creation with pride.

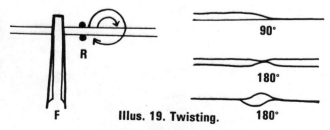

Illus. 19. Twisting.

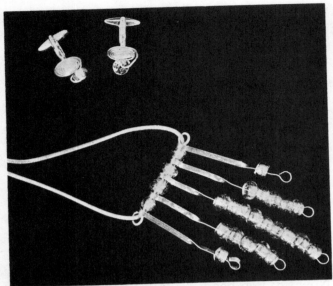

Illus. 20. Neckpiece and cuff links.

Neckpiece and Cuff Links

Materials

    28-gauge silver round wire
    22-gauge silver round wire
    18-gauge silver flat wire
    large, large-eyed beads (preferably wooden)
    leather thong (available at hobby and shoe
        repair shops)
    cuff-link findings
    mallet and anvil
    epoxy cement

To make the neckpiece, string four beads on a 3″ piece of 22-gauge round wire. Form closed loops on each end. Cut five pieces of the flat wire in three different lengths as shown. Twist each 90° with the pliers at different points—the shortest pieces, twist closer to the ends. String beads on as far as each twist will allow. Make closing loops on the ends. Then attach the assembly between the beads on the round wire with simple hooked-over ends. Pass a leather thong through the upper piece and merely tie it in back when you wear it.

Next, wind two pieces of 28-gauge wire into spirals, leaving about 1″ free on one end of each. Hammer them almost flat. Slip a bead on each, and twist the ends slightly back to hold them on. Glue the flattened spirals onto the cuff-link findings with epoxy cement.

Wire-and-Bead-Decorated Belt

Materials

    22-gauge round wire
    beads
    heavy velvet ribbon
    flat-nose pliers

Here is an elegant belt to wear on special occasions. The design easily can be adapted to matching accessories—bracelet, necklace, earrings. You are going to make a different kind of spiral now which you will also use in later projects.

Wrap a length of wire around a cylindrical object as shown in Illus. 21a, at least ten times, leaving 2½″ of straight wire on both ends. Remove, and with the flat-nose pliers, squeeze

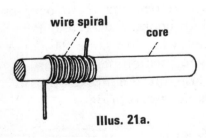

Illus. 21a.

Illus. 21. Wire-and-bead-decorated belt.

Illus. 22. Spiralled round-wire bottle collar.

out as shown. Twist all the ends together and attach to the ribbon.

The decorative hanging pieces are made with the 28-gauge wire. Take one piece, bend in two and twist carefully with your hands so that you create a "rope" or chain effect. Leave about $2\frac{1}{2}$" on each end and make spirals. Now, with the pliers, pull out the inner ends of these spirals and form tiny eyelet-like loops.

Cut two pieces of 28-gauge wire about 3" long. Thread one through each eyelet, place a bead on each end and form closing loops.

Cut two more pieces 2" long and thread one through the closing loops on the top of each beaded part. Make closing loops again. Then do the same with the other piece, attaching it to the bottom closing loops of the beaded parts. These two horizontal pieces will serve to hold the beaded parts stiff.

Attach the upper end of the twisted, rope-like part to the velvet ribbon also. Make two identical decorative pieces to hang on the sides, or vary as you wish.

A Wire-and-Bead Christmas Decoration
Materials
  18-gauge round wire
  22-gauge round wire
  large-eyed beads
  knitting needle
  round-nose pliers

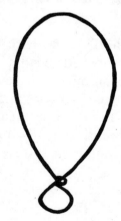

Illus. 23.

Shape a long oval loop with the 18-gauge wire in the size that you desire. Make a clasp as in Illus. 23.

Next, make the two spiral pieces in the

the coil until it assumes an elongated shape. Then pull the loops apart so that they fan out as shown. Press the two straight ends together, thread on a bead, and then form the ends into two "belt loops."

Make at least a dozen of these ornaments and slip on the velvet band. A simple bow or knot serves as an appropriate clasp.

Spiralled Round-Wire Bottle Collar
Materials
  20-gauge silver round wire
  28-gauge silver round wire
  small glass beads
  velvet ribbon
  round-nose pliers
  pencil

Make the large spring-like part by winding the 20-gauge wire tightly around a pencil. Do the same with the inner springy part but pull

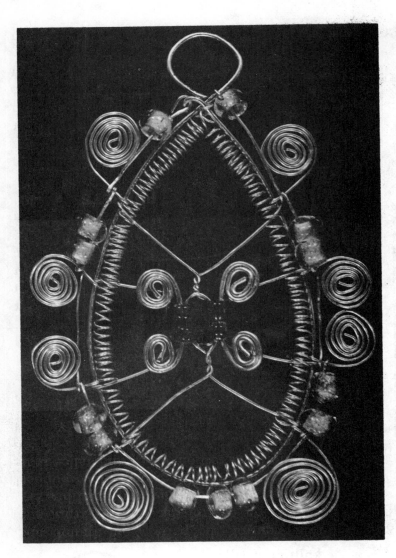

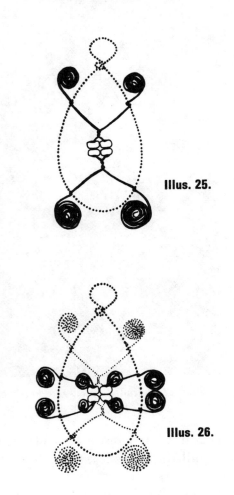

Illus. 24. You can adapt this lovely Christmas decoration to many uses. It is made of seven separate pieces joined together.

Illus. 25.

Illus. 26.

middle, each with two beads. (Be sure to use large-eyed beads because they will have to accommodate three pieces of wire.) Then take a length of wire and thread it through one pair of these beads, bend the ends and wrap them around the 18-gauge wire loop once. Make spirals with the remaining ends. Do the same with the other spiral and bead part. You should now have something that looks like Illus. 25.

Now take two more wires, pass one through each set of beads, and twist them a couple of times just above and below the beads. Attach the four ends as shown to the 18-gauge loop in the same way as before—wrap once around it and make spirals on the ends.

Then wrap 22-gauge wire around a knitting needle to form the large coiled part. Separate the loops a little by pulling on the ends of the wire. Bend into a long oval and rest it on the eight wire supports you just made so that it fits snugly within the 18-gauge loop. Hook onto the loop at the top.

The final step is to take a long piece of 22-gauge wire. Hook one end onto the clasp of the 18-gauge loop. Thread on a bead, wrap the wire once around the first spiral going counter-clockwise. Slip on two beads and go on to the next spiral. Continue in this manner until you come back to the beginning, and you'll have a beautiful and unique Christmas ornament.

Silver Gorget and Matching Earrings

Materials

26-gauge sheet silver
16-gauge, or heavier, round wire
24-gauge, or lighter, round wire
earring findings
scissors, paper and grease pencil
pliers and knitting needle
bone folder and embossing mat

Here you can achieve a medieval look by fashioning a silver gorget, originally a crescent-shaped piece of armour worn to protect the throat.

Make a paper pattern of the sheet silver crescent and measure it (using string for the wire pieces) around your neck. Allow for two tabs on each end.

Sketch your design on the paper. You need not use the design in Illus. 27, however, but keep it simple since this is a fairly large piece of silver and you would not want to spoil it.

Transfer your outline in grease pencil to the silver, as well as the design. Cut, not forgetting the tabs. Work lightly and carefully on your embossing with the bone folder, being sure to use the mat.

Form the wire pieces from the heavy round wire after measuring with string and the paper pattern. The two tabs will form the attachment, so do not tightly close the bottom wire loops.

Roll the tabs towards the back using a knitting needle until you have formed cylinders of a size that will accommodate the wire. Slip the wires through and squeeze tight.

Make matching earrings as shown (also using paper patterns) and hook onto ready-made findings of either the ear clip or screw-back type in the style called "pierced look." These have hooks for attaching dangles.

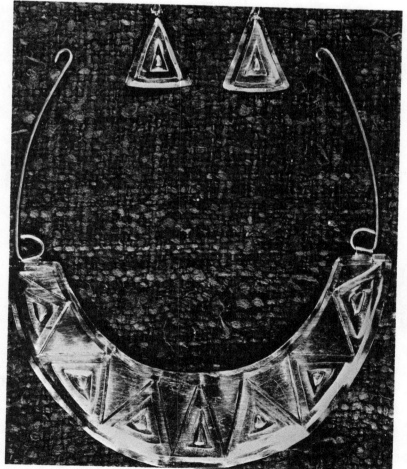

Illus. 27. A unique gorget and earrings made from silver sheet.

Illus. 28. Be sure to make tabs on each end for attaching the round wire.

TOYS

If you make your own toys, you will certainly feel a great sense of accomplishment—and you will enjoy both making them and playing with them. This section contains complete instructions for simple costumes, models and toys which you can make no matter what your age. The simplicity or complexity of the projects is only limited by your imagination.

Spanish Costume

Spanish Hat

For a costume party, or just for the fun of it, make a Spanish costume of hat, sword, and mask. First make a hat. Cut a disc about 12″ across from hard black paper. From its center, cut out a smaller disc. The large part will be the brim, and the smaller part the top of your hat. With tape, attach a strip of black paper about 4″ wide round the inner curve of the brim. Use as many pieces of tape as you need to keep the strip secure. Fasten the top, also taping from the inside. Attach a large elastic band or string to tie under your chin so the hat does not blow away.

Sword and Mask

Complete your Spanish costume with a sword and mask. Use black paper for the mask. Draw the design and then cut it out. Hold it in front of your face and make a small pencil mark where your eyes are. Cut the holes to fit over your eyes. Loop several elastic bands together and fasten the ends to the mask with staples or spread-fasteners.

Your sword can be a thin straight stick. Take a round cover from a box or a jar and make a cross-cut in the center. Pull the stick through and tape it to the sword top. Fasten a wire ring to your belt and wear the sword at your waist.

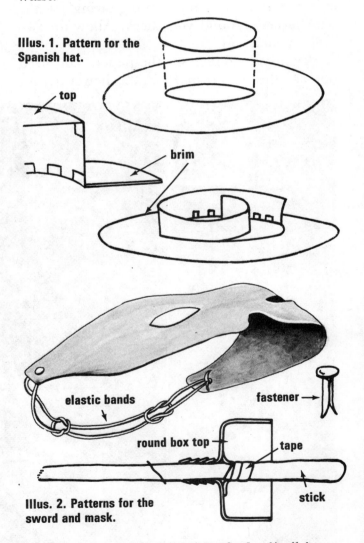

Illus. 1. Pattern for the Spanish hat.

top

brim

elastic bands

fastener →

round box top →

tape

stick

Illus. 2. Patterns for the sword and mask.

Condensed from the book, "101 Toys Children Can Make" by Robert and Katharine Kunz | © 1959 by Sterling Publishing Co., Inc., New York

Indian Hat

Here is another costume hat you can make yourself. Collect some bird feathers or cut them from colored paper. Cut a stiff paper strip, long enough to fit round your head. Cut notches at each end that fit into each other as shown in Illus. 3. Line up the feathers in a row on the inside and tape them down.

Tepee

The American Plains Indians lived in tepees —tents made of animal hide stretched over a frame of poles. You can make a small model of a tepee from paper.

Fold a large sheet of white paper into a cone. Tape it together from the inside. Cut the tip of the cone off as shown in Illus. 5. Gather some straight sticks, a little longer than the cone, and tape them on the inside. Their ends should extend through the opening on top of the cone. Tape two triangular pieces of paper

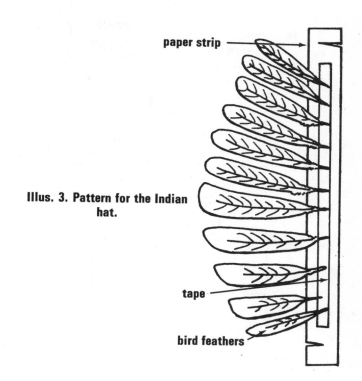

Illus. 3. Pattern for the Indian hat.

paper strip

tape

bird feathers

on the sides near the top, and attach a stick to each, as the picture shows. Cut a door in the lower part of the tepee and fold it open. With water colors, paint Indian designs on your tepee. If you make several different sized tepees, you can have an entire Indian village to play with.

Illus. 4. You will be able to form your own tribe with as authentic-looking an Indian hat as this!

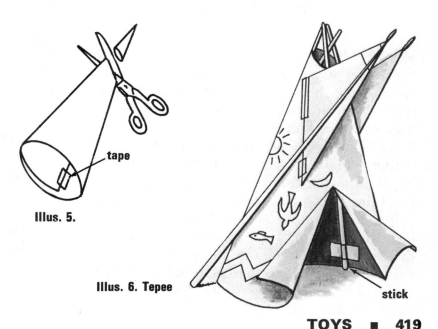

tape

Illus. 5.

Illus. 6. Tepee

stick

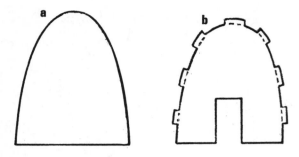

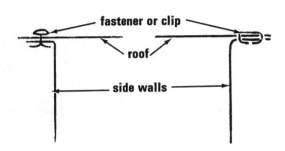

fastener or clip

roof

side walls

Illus. 7. Pattern pieces for the long house.

Long House

Another type of Indian dwelling is the Iroquois long house, made from bark, poles and sticks. You can make a model of a long house from cardboard and stiff paper.

Cut two pieces of cardboard in the shape pictured in Illus. 7a, and cut flaps in them. These form the front and back of the house. Bend the stiff paper to make the roof and sides and fasten the front and back flaps to it with metal fasteners or clips. Cut several holes in the center of the roof and a door in the front. Paint the house with water colors so it looks like the bark of a tree and posts. Or use split sticks for the posts, putting them on with tape.

Windmills

Tin-Plate Windmill

There are several different kinds of windmills. This type is often used to turn the water pump of a farmer's well. Make this one from a tin (foil) cake plate. With a pair of scissors, cut straight lines round the edge of the plate and bend all the blades in the same direction. Fasten a spool to the center of the plate with tacks from behind. Mount a wooden block on three long sticks. Then drive a long nail through the front of the spool and the plate into the wooden block. Put the windmill into the ground and watch it turn on windy days.

Box Windmill

The box windmill is commonly used on farms. You can make it with an empty milk container. Cut windows on the sides or paste colored paper on it. Make the roof from cardboard, and attach it with cellophane tape.

Cut the vanes or sails of the windmill from cardboard too, and fold it, following the pattern in Illus. 9. Put a knitting needle through the house, with a cork on the back

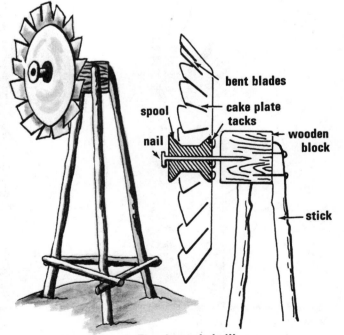

bent blades

spool

cake plate

tacks

nail

wooden block

stick

Illus. 8. Tin-plate windmill.

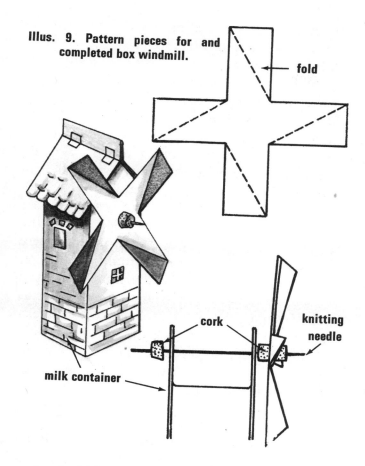

fold

cork

knitting
needle

milk container

one far away. Won't it be interesting to
discover where your bottle went? See Illus. 11.

Flower Vase

Bend a length of medium-weight wire, 12 to
18 inches long, into a design that pleases you.
Stretch one end into a hook and make a loop
at the top.

Decorate a small tin can with oil paint and
paint the wire too. Or, cut colored pictures
from a magazine and paste them on the can.
Make three small holes with a nail around the
top of the can and put pretty ribbon or cord
through them. Hang the cord from the hook
in the wire, and put the vase on the wall in
your room. When you put in water and
flowers, you have an unusual vase.

end to hold it in place (see Illus. 9). Put another
cork on the other end of the needle, slip the
sails on, and add a third cork in front. Leave
enough space between the corks and the container, as in the picture, and the sails will turn
in the wind.

Bottle Mail

When you were at the beach, did you ever
find a bottle with a letter in it? It's very exciting to see the bottle bobbing along on the
waves and find that it holds a note, maybe
written by someone many miles away.

Why don't you write a letter for someone
else to find? Put it in a bottle, and for more fun,
add a coin, a pencil or a tiny shell. Close it
tightly with a cork. Your bottle mail carrier
will be even more attractive if you put a
knitting needle, a nail or a wire in the cork.
Fasten a flag on it and send it out to sea.

If you put your name and address on your
letter, you may receive an answer from some-

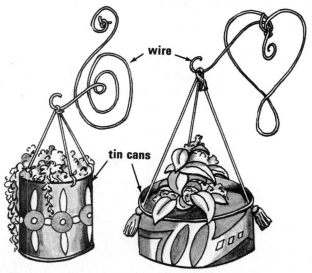

wire

tin cans

Illus. 10. This flower vase will brighten up any room.

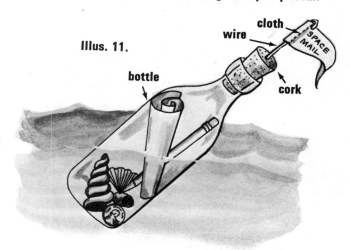

Illus. 11.

cloth

wire

SPACE MAIL

bottle

cork

shadow

light

white paper

Shadow Portrait

If you have an unused, empty picture frame, use that for the shadow portrait. Or make a frame by nailing four boards together. Tack a piece of white paper to the frame and hang it up.

Ask a friend to stand between the frame and a light (you can use a flash-light). The outline of his profile will be thrown on the white paper. With a pen or pencil, draw over it. Then trace the outline you have made on black paper, cut it out and paste it on strong cardboard. You can hang the shadow portrait on the wall of your room, or give it to someone as a gift.

Sun Clock

Before clocks were invented, people told time by sun dials. You can make a sun dial for your yard or garden very easily.

First get a pole that measures about 2 inches wide. Cut it about 4 feet long.

Have someone older sharpen one end with an axe and put it in the ground, in a spot where the sun usually shines. Then take a smooth board, 8 inches square, and nail it to the top of the pole. Put a knitting needle upright into the middle of the board.

Write the hours on the board when the sun is shining. You'll need a watch to put the numbers in the right place. Let's say you start at 9 o'clock in the morning. See where the needle casts its shadow and draw a dot where the shadow ends. Write the number 9 there. An hour later, see where the shadow is, and put in the dot and 10. And so on, as long as there is enough sun for the needle to have a shadow.

When you finish marking the hours around the board, you can tell the time by seeing at what hour the shadow points.

Jig-Saw Puzzle

Look through old magazines for colored pictures—landscapes or any other scenes you like. Cut one out and paste it on thin cardboard. Put it between thick books and press overnight. Then, with a sharp pair of scissors, cut the picture in many pieces, varying the shapes. Try to put the puzzle back together, or put the pieces in a flat box and give it to a friend. If you make one for a younger sister or brother, cut the picture into fairly large pieces so it will be easier to assemble.

knitting needle

board

pole

Illus. 13. A sun clock is an educational toy for you to make.

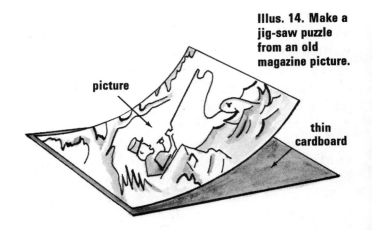

Illus. 14. Make a jig-saw puzzle from an old magazine picture.

picture

thin cardboard

the PROCESS is the thing

The Use of
Specific Crafts to
Make Different Things

COLD ENAMELLING

Smooth, shiny and colorful, an enamel glaze is one of the most beautiful finishes you can apply to a plain surface. And an enamel glaze is practical as well: scratch-resistant and heat-resistant, enamel protects as it decorates jewelry, trays, or pottery.

Not many craftsmen who work at home become involved with enamelling, because of the need for an expensive kiln in which to bake the enamel powder. But now, a product even better than enamel has been developed for craftsmen to use. It is a product that, when mixed in the proper proportions and allowed to harden, looks, feels and acts just like enamel—but you apply it without heat! Called "Boss Gloss™," the heatless enamel adheres to any surface, including those which cannot be enamelled by baking. Wood, clay, metal, glass, hard plastic—and even plastic foam—are only a few examples of the surfaces you can decorate with this one-step substance. Even children can safely apply an enamel-like finish to any surface with this non-toxic enamel. The discovery of this new innovative product is bound to have a profound effect on many crafts.

This heatless enamel is manufactured by California Titan Products, Inc., Santa Ana, California, and it is found in most art and craft supply shops. The heatless enamel comes in two containers. All you do is mix the two liquids together, brush or drip the mixture on any surface, and set the decorated object aside in a warm dry room until the enamel hardens. This usually takes a few days, the exact amount of time depending upon how thick a layer of enamel you apply. When the surface is hard, the heatless enamel is as solid and non-tacky as any baked glaze. The finish does not melt or scratch; it is water- and alcohol-proof; and it needs only occasional dusting to keep its surface shiny and attractive.

By mixing the heatless enamel yourself, you control the density of color and thickness of the medium. In one jar is the *Polymer* (numbered No. 1 on the jar), that part which gives the enamel its color. It is used in its liquid state. A wide variety of colors is available, including white, and by mixing the colors you can produce any unusual shade you require.

Clear Extender (No. 3) is a variation of Polymer (No. 1). It is thinner than Polymer

Illus. 1. A jar of Polymer, the component which gives color to the mixture.

Illus. 2. Clear Extender is a thinner, colorless form of Polymer.

Condensed from the book, "Enamel Without Heat" by Stephen J. Schilt and Donna J. Weir | © 1971 by Sterling Publishing Co., Inc., New York

Illus. 3. Without Curing Agent, the heatless enamel will not harden. Mix one part Curing Agent with three parts Polymer or Clear Extender for a permanent surface.

follow these proportions or the heatless enamel will not dry and harden properly.

The beautiful colors and glossy finish of heatless enamel resemble baked enamel glazes so closely that even experienced craftsmen are fooled. And you can decorate many objects—trays, dishes, jewelry, tiles, lamp shades, glasses, table tops.

Heatless enamel even coats surfaces which cannot be heated in a kiln. When you design with heatless enamel, you are not only creating beautiful ornaments, but enjoying hours of fun and colorful excitement as well.

and has no color. Use Clear Extender to thin the Polymer for easier flow and to lighten the color. You can also use Clear Extender by itself with Curing Agent (see below) to make a clear coating or an overglaze.

Curing Agent (No. 2) is the substance which combines with the Polymer or Clear Extender so the surface hardens. Also a liquid, Curing Agent must always be combined with Polymer and/or Clear Extender in the ratio of 1 to 3—that is, 1 part Curing Agent to every 3 parts Polymer or mixture of Polymer and Clear Extender or Clear Extender alone. *You must*

Decorating Plastic Foam

Plastic foam, commonly known in the United States by its trade name, Styrofoam, has challenged craftsmen who tried to decorate its surface. Most paints contain solvents which corrode the delicate foam, however, so that up until now only water paints have been used. Unfortunately, the finish of water paints is very flat, and the paint can only be applied in thin layers. Heatless enamel is a tremendous

Illus. 4. Decorate plastic foam with heatless enamel for an animal, storybook character, or other bizarre creature.

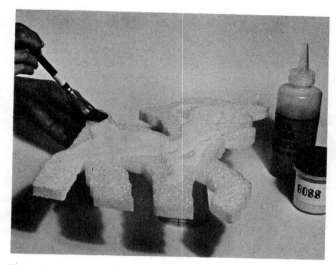

Illus. 5. To smooth the textured surface of the plastic foam, brush on a layer of Clear Extender mixed with Curing Agent and let dry for a day.

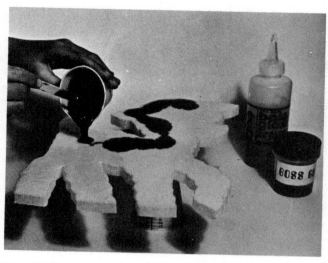

Illus. 6. When the layer of Clear Extender is dry, pour a mixture of colored Polymer and Curing Agent on the surface.

boon to would-be plastic foam decorators, since it contains no solvents which attack the foam, has a glossy finish, and can be applied in any thickness.

Buy some plastic foam in a craft shop or variety store. It is inexpensive and easy to cut with a knife or razor. Lightly sketch an outline on the plastic foam with a pencil, taking care not to press too hard. Cut around this outline with a knife in a holder or a single-edged razor blade. Plan your colors and, if you want a special shade, mix several colors of Polymer to make new tones. Place the plastic foam figure on a flat surface—the piece must be perfectly level or the glaze will not dry smooth.

If you do not want the bubbly surface of the plastic foam to show through colored glaze, coat the foam with Clear Extender. Pour 1 ounce of Clear Extender into a mixing cup (use either disposable paper or plastic cups, as the mixture sticks to all surfaces) and then add 2 teaspoons of Curing Agent. There are 6 teaspoons per ounce, so you are mixing Extender and Curing Agent in the proper ratio of 3 to 1. Mix the Clear Extender and Curing Agent together by stirring thoroughly with a stick or plastic spoon, but avoid stirring air into the

mixture. Allow the mixture to sit for at least 5 minutes, so that the two substances have a chance to combine completely. Use a paint brush to apply the clear mixture.

Allow this clear layer to dry for about a day. Heatless enamel dries according to schedule every time, so you can expect the following stages in the drying process:

First is the induction stage, which occurs right after mixing Polymer or Clear Extender with Curing Agent. The mixture is the same consistency as it was in the jar, either liquid or gel. After 1 to 3 hours, the compound becomes a thick, syrupy liquid. After 5 to 7 hours, the enamel is the consistency of taffy and you can no longer apply it with a brush. Instead, use a spatula or palette knife. In the gel stage, after 8 to 10 hours, the coating appears wet but it is gelled. If you touch the glaze now it stays where you push it. In the semi-cured stage, after 20 to 24 hours, the surface is fairly hard and can be gently handled. Complete curing of the surface takes about 7 days, but it is worth the wait: the surface is hard, scratch-resistant and permanent.

If you apply a first coat and want it to dry before you apply the second, leave it for a

Illus. 7. Push the Polymer to the edges of the piece with a stir stick. It is too thick to use easily with a brush.

while—preferably for 20 to 24 hours, but for at least 8 hours. Be careful when you finally touch it that you do not handle it too strongly or the layer will move.

For the colored layer, mix colored Polymer with Curing Agent in the same proportions you mixed Clear Extender—3 to 1. Pour or brush the mixture on the plastic foam shape and set the piece aside to harden. After a day, apply facial features (if your shape is an animal or a person) or other small details (if you have cut out an inanimate object). Use either a paint brush or a toothpick for fine areas. Leave the plastic foam piece in a warm dry room for about a week to allow it time to harden completely.

NOTE: If you leave a project to harden in a humid area (a steamy kitchen or a damp garage, for example), the surface of the glaze may be dulled with a "blush." To make sure the glaze dries to an attractive and clear finish, always place your projects in a dry room to harden. If a blush does form, apply a layer of Clear Extender to restore some of the shine. The true color, however, might not be restored.

For variety, outline the plastic foam and add details to the surface with narrow cord or braid. First apply the clear base coat and then, using white glue and a toothpick, attach the braid around the outside of the figure and to the face.

After attaching the braid, fill in each area

with glaze and let the piece dry overnight. For additional gloss, and to bring the surface of the glaze level with that of the braid, add an overglaze of Clear Extender all over the plastic foam.

At a loss as to what to do with your decorated plastic foam? Use smaller pieces as coasters—moisture does not soak through hardened heatless enamel—or a larger piece as a decorator tray for light-weight items. Make simple toys from plastic foam just as you

Illus. 8. To define areas of your plastic foam fellow, outline them with dark cord or braid.

would with wood: cut figures and add heatless enamel features with a brush. Glue the figures to sticks, for stick puppets, or simply let the heatless enamel harden and play with two-dimensional dolls. If you want to make a large project, construct a doll house for your plastic foam family. You do not need nails to fasten plastic foam, only glue—and instead of flat, dull paint, use shiny Boss Gloss for shingles on the roof, windows, doors, and even shrubbery around the base. Cut out seasonal shapes and add appropriate colors: a plastic foam Christmas tree, with a background of green heatless enamel and small red drops as festive ornaments, makes a lively addition to your holiday decorations. Make an Easter bunny, a pumpkin, a Valentine's Day heart.

Glaze on Clay and Natural Surfaces

Heatless enamel is so durable and non-porous that when you apply it to greenware (unbaked clay), you eliminate the need for baking. The glaze completely covers the surface and seals in moisture so the clay does not dry out and crack. A ceramic-like heatless enamel glaze is also perfectly suitable on

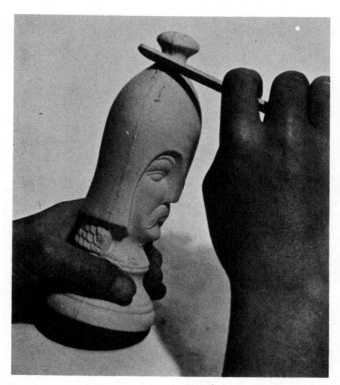

Illus. 10. Even if you have no ability in modelling, the unusual abstract shapes you can make benefit from a coat of color. Smooth the piece completely before you even mix the enamel.

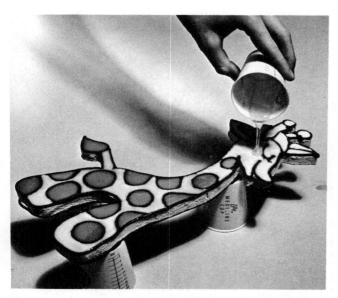

Illus. 9. For a level surface, pour Clear Extender mixed with Curing Agent on the colored areas until they are even with the raised braid.

bisqueware (baked clay), plaster of Paris, modelling clay, ceramic tiles and even papier mâché.

To decorate greenware, carefully trim and smooth the piece as if you were going to fire it in a kiln. Once you apply the heatless enamel, you cannot re-shape the clay under it, so be sure your piece is as smooth as you want it.

If the pottery is hollow—perhaps a bowl, vase or a figurine with a hollow base—glaze the inside first. Mix Polymer and Curing Agent together in the proportions of 3 to 1, and pour a small amount of the mixture into the hollow portion. Swirl the mixture around so the inside becomes coated with heatless enamel, and pour any extra out slowly. Heatless enamel does not keep, so either use it right away on another project, or discard it.

Allow the inside of your pottery to cure overnight, and then apply heatless enamel to the outside of the piece with a brush. Keep your

Illus. 11. Because the pottery is hard and heavy, it supports the pressure necessary to brush the glaze on. Use long, even strokes, and be careful to reach all corners of the surface.

brush strokes vertical and even. Use a liberal amount, but not so much that the mixture runs. You can always add a second coat later; in fact, on greenware and air-dried clay, a second coat is a good idea. Cover every portion except the bottom of the pottery with heatless enamel. Let the glaze harden for several days—

the longer the better—and gently place the piece upside-down in a large cup. Coat the bottom with heatless enamel and leave the pottery to harden completely.

Add other colors and designs to the pottery if you wish. You can drop heatless enamel from a toothpick or paint it on with a small paint brush, either before or after the first coat has dried. Shaped pottery usually does not need too much decoration other than a layer of glaze, since its beauty comes from the shape of the piece and the gloss of its surface. On flat shapes of air-dried clay, however, designs on the surface add much to the charm of the piece.

Other natural surfaces gain much appeal when you color them with heatless enamel. Add a face or interesting design to a smooth flat stone and use the finished piece as a paperweight, doorstop, or coffee-table knick-knack. Sea shells often have interesting shapes and need only a few highlights of color to emphasize a face or pattern in their texture. If you apply heatless enamel to wood, be sure the piece is clean of all sand and dust, and that it is smooth. Rub it with fine-grained sandpaper to make sure the surface is even. The same rules for mixing and drying hold when you decorate these natural surfaces with heatless enamel.

Transform plain ceramic tile which has

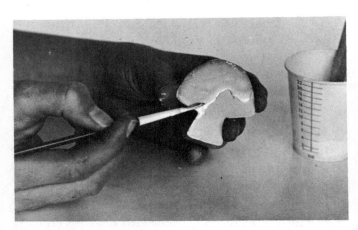

Illus. 12 (above). Brush heatless enamel on a small clay or stone shape to use as a paperweight, doorstop or other ornament. If you get some enamel on your hands or the table, wash it off before it hardens.

Illus. 13. Decorate insects, birds, and trees with preformed enamel drops for exact yet casual placement of color.

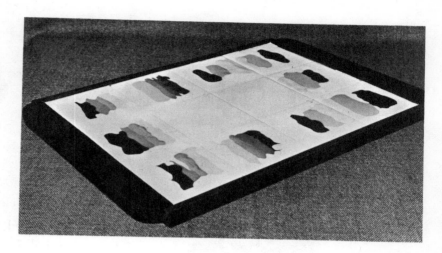

Illus. 14. Making a cheeseboard of tiles sounds more difficult than it really is. Color each tile separately—and simply—with heatless enamel, and then cement them together.

not been glazed (in bisque state) by decorating it with an enamel design (you can make your own tile from clay and cover its surface with heatless enamel). Use the individual tiles as trivets or coasters (heatless enamel resists heat and moisture) or glue several together and set them in a base for a cheeseboard or tray. A simple yet glamorous cheeseboard is shown in Illus. 14 and in color on page AA.

For the cheeseboard, decorate each tile separately, but be careful that when the tiles are placed next to each other, they fit together exactly. Consider each tile like a part of a mosaic or a patchwork quilt. You might even plan a picture, instead of an abstract design, but be sure to position every part of the picture on each tile in the exact position it belongs.

Use any decorating tricks for the tiles that you have learned so far: pour strips of one color on the tile, and add another color while the first is still wet. Make the colors bleed together by drawing one into the other with a toothpick. Or, to keep the colors distinct, allow the first strip to gel slightly before you pour the next.

Take advantage of the semi-cured stage of heatless enamel to add new designs.

After the decorated tiles are dry, make the wooden base to hold them. Buy a piece of plywood which is the size of all the tiles put together, in the shape you want the tray to be. Cover the plywood base with one or two layers of shellac, to waterproof the wood. Place the tiles on the plywood, but do not glue them in place yet. You might want to surround the tiles with wooden strips first. Use any wood which looks attractive to you. Shellac the strips for extra sheen if you want, and glue them to the plywood base with a strong, waterproof glue.

To attach the tiles to the tray permanently, use a cement made especially for clay tiles (your craft shop can supply you with one). Apply cement to both the plywood base and the back of the tile, and place the tile on the base. If there are any *interstices*—small spaces between the tiles—fill them in with cement. After the cement has dried, you can wash your cheeseboard, cut on it, and handle it as roughly as you would any store-bought tray.

Illus. 15. The tile is supported by two inverted paper cups to keep it level and away from the table. Pour or brush heatless enamel on the smooth surface.

COLD ENAMELLING ■ **431**

CURLING AND QUILLING

Illus. 1. The "bead" forming the eye of this rosette is a basic form you can adapt to many decorations.

There is probably no craft that uses fewer materials and tools than the age-old art of curling and quilling. Other than glue and a pair of scissors, you need only some material to work with. All of the decorations here are made from ribbon. However, the ribbon is very special and has characteristics that ordinary ribbon does not have. It is called Gaylord Glo-Tone Ribbon. (If you cannot locate it quickly in your local variety shop, write to the address on page 562.)

Glo-Tone comes in all colors of the rainbow (plus a few more!) in ½-inch, ¾-inch and 1¼-inch widths. It is flexible and tough, and can be rolled, bent, and creased without breaking or splitting. Because it has finished edges, there is no danger of ravelling or shredding. You can even make delicate fringes just a hairline apart by cutting with the grain. Also, you can actually cut a perfect round hole right in the middle of it. However, do be careful not to tear the cut ends.

Many of the decorations made with Glo-Tone can also be made with paper. Construction paper works best. However, always cut the paper strips with the grain. Experiment by rolling the paper first in one direction, then in the other. If the paper resists the rolling, you are going against the grain.

For creating with Glo-Tone, all-purpose glue or rubber cement is satisfactory. You will find that this ribbon is not stained by glue as happens with many ribbons. However, you do not need much adhesive so use it sparingly. If you wish, you can make a very wide ribbon by glueing two pieces together, slightly overlapping the edges.

Make a Necklace

You can make a *really* different necklace or bracelet quickly and easily from Glo-Tone ribbon. A basic form that you can use in many projects is a "bead." Cut a piece of ribbon approximately 8″ or 10″ long. Roll it up as tightly as you can and glue it so it cannot spring open. Until the glue dries, use a paper clip or a piece of masking or transparent tape

Condensed from the book, "Curling, Coiling and Quilling" by Inge Häslein and Rita Firschmann | © 1973 by Sterling Publishing Co., Inc., New York

to hold it in place. (Do not worry—the tape will not be permanently stuck to the ribbon, nor will it tear it.)

Make a number of these beads and string them together to make your necklace. Children will really enjoy making these, and they can adapt them to decorations for parties (Illus. 2), particularly if each bead is a different color.

Now that you have the "feel" of the ribbon, you can go on to making any number of decorative objects.

Animals

The winsome bunny in Illus. 3 would make an ideal decoration for Easter—or for any time of year. Make several in yellow and several in lilac or purple.

Start the bunny by making the oval body with 1½"-wide ribbon. Since all the parts will

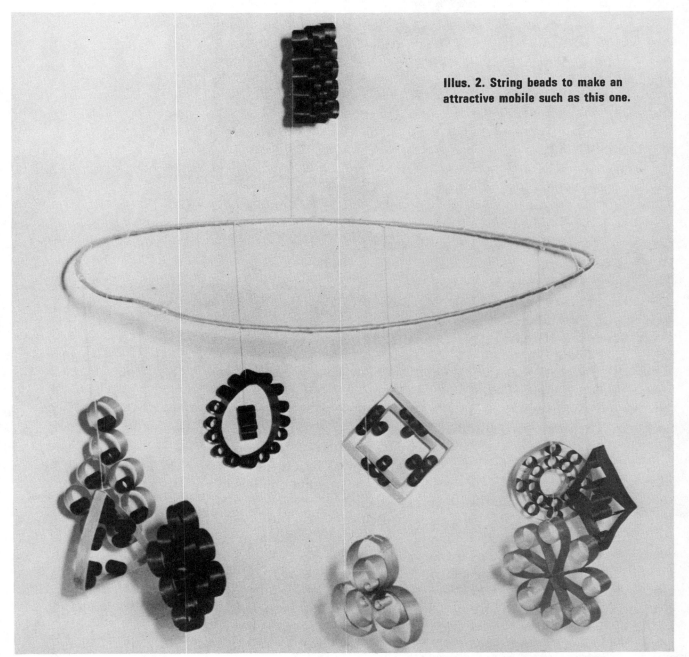

Illus. 2. String beads to make an attractive mobile such as this one.

Illus. 3. Bunny.

be attached to it, for extra strength, you might glue two pieces of ribbon together. Press together with your hands until the oval is formed. After glueing and taping together, from two strips of ½″-wide ribbon, form the two front paws. Glue together and then glue onto the body. Hold with paper clips. Make the loop for the tail with a 1¼″-strip. Glue and clip together. Then glue and clip the tail onto the body.

Wait till all of these parts are dry and then glue the body onto a double- or triple-thick strip of 1½″-ribbon. While this is drying, make the bunny head with 1½″-ribbon. Glue the two ends and clip or tape together. With ½″-strips, form the bunny ears in the same way as you did the paws. Glue each together and clip. When the head and ears are both dry, glue and clip the ears onto the back of the head. Compress with your hands to get an elongated effect.

Cut long, narrow fringes from the ribbon and glue on as whiskers. When everything is dry, glue the head onto the body and clip together. When all is firmly adhered, remove the clips.

A black cat with orange eyes and white whiskers makes a festive Halloween decoration (Illus. 4). Use ¾″-ribbon for all the parts. Begin by making the large body circle and glueing and clipping together. Then make two (or more) circles, decreasing in size, to fit inside the large one. When all are firmly dry, glue one inside the other.

Next, cut a very long strip for the tail. Bend over one end and then glue the tail and the circles together to a strip of double-thick ribbon as a base. The width of the base ribbon depends upon how tall you are making your cat. Put dabs of glue at each point that the tail touches a circle. Set aside to dry.

Make the head circle next. Then, tightly roll and glue two orange strips for the eyes.

Let dry. Take a strip of black ribbon, crease it in the middle and glue each end inside the head circle, with the crease pointing down, as a support for the eyes and whiskers. When this is firmly set, glue the orange eyes onto it.

To form the triangular ears, crease two strips into three equal parts. Then join the triangles by overlapping one side of each, and glueing together on the inside. The base will then be shorter than the two sides. Glue these onto the head, and clip. When all the parts of the head are dry, glue it onto the body and tail. Finally, cut some long white whiskers and place them across each other at an angle. Glue together and then glue onto the point of the crease of the strip that supports the eyes.

You can create the basic squirrel in Illus. 5 in the same way as you did the bunny and the cat. For the plumed tail, cut a $1\frac{1}{4}$″-ribbon into many long fringe-like strips, leaving approximately $1\frac{1}{2}$″ at one end to attach the tail to the body. To make the crest, first cut a slit through the top of the head. Then cut a piece of $1\frac{1}{2}$″-wide ribbon, the same length as the slit, and along one side of it, snip out a row of triangles, leaving at least $\frac{1}{4}$″ at the base. Smear glue along the base and insert into the slit on the head.

Illus. 4 (above). Black cat.

Illus. 5 (right). Squirrel.

Birds

You can make a whole treeful of the colorful birds as shown in Illus. 6. First, select a few dead twigs that you can pot attractively and which will look like a tree. For the base body, make one large circle and then a smaller one, and glue the smaller one inside the larger. The beak is made of a small piece of ribbon cut into a diamond shape and creased across the middle.

To make wings for these small birds, cut two slits in the top back of the body, about ¼″ apart and 1″ long (depending upon how big your birds are). Then cut out the wing shape in whatever form you want—notched, fringed, etc., from one piece of ribbon. Insert into the

Illus. 6. Birds in tree.

The tail feathers are made from several pieces of orange ribbon cut into fringes up to $\frac{1}{2}''$ from the ends and glued onto the body.

You can make his perch by glueing a strip of ribbon on a piece of wire bent into a circle. Then make a "bead" to use for a hanger. Slip heavy silk thread through the bead, glue the parrot on, and hang.

Insects

Since some of the most colorful creatures in the world are insects, Glo-Tone ribbon is ideal for bringing out their beauty. These small creations make perfect table decorations and

Illus. 7. Close-up of a bird in tree.

Illus. 8. Parrot.

slits, pull through, and adjust on both sides. Be sure to use a great variety of colors for your birds.

At first glance, the exotic parrot in Illus. 8 looks complicated, but actually, he takes very little time to put together. His elongated body is composed of several bent-over strips of bright green $\frac{1}{2}''$-ribbon, one inside the other, and his head consists of one long $\frac{1}{2}''$-wide strip rolled up and glued so that a small coil remains loose on the inside to serve as an eye. A bright yellow beak is simply pressed into shape and glued on.

CURLING AND QUILLING ■ **437**

Illus. 9. Snail and mushroom.

Illus. 10. Butterfly.

can be used to dress up ordinary place cards as shown in Illus. 11, as well as for pins or brooches.

The busy snail in Illus. 9 can be made in about two minutes! Simply take one long strip of ½″-blue ribbon, then roll one end round your finger, and glue the resulting bead. Clip together. Then with the remainder of the ribbon, make a series of circles of increasing sizes round the bead, glueing and clipping each together as you go.

Take two strips of yellow ½″-ribbon and glue them together about three quarters along their length, leaving two open ends as shown. Make two or three cuts along the upper strip, and curl the lower strip up. Glue the "shell" body onto the base.

The butterfly in Illus. 10 is made in several steps. First, take four pieces of 1¼″-wide red ribbon. Glue two pieces together on the long side, one slightly overlapping the other. This will form the left side of the butterfly. Then, glue the other two pieces together in the same way for the right side. Form the body by rolling a piece of ¾″-wide blue or green ribbon tightly together and then pulling out the ends a little.

Then, cut out the shapes of the wings in any way you wish from each of the two joined pieces, but make sure they match on both sides. Decorate them with tiny circles cut from a variety of different-colored pieces of ribbon. Glue each half onto the body, and insert two tiny strips of ribbon for antennae.

The tiny beetle on the place card in Illus. 11 has a bead body and a bead head. Use ¾″-ribbon for the body bead and ½″ for the head. Make the wings from two small pieces of ¾″-ribbon, cut to shape and decorated with small colored ribbon spots.

The wings of the dragonfly in Illus. 12 are

Illus. 11. Butterfly and beetle.

Illus. 12. Dragonfly.

made the same way as the butterfly wings. To make the long slender body, use a long piece of ½″-ribbon, and roll it tightly on an angle. Cut a ½″-piece of ribbon in half the long way, and roll as tightly as you can to form the tiny head. The antennae consist of one long sliver of ribbon inserted into the rolled head, and pulled through. Apply a dab of glue to the tail slivers and insert into the body.

Trees and Flowers

As a refuge for your insects and birds, you might want to make the tropical palm tree shown in Illus. 13, or a group of such trees. Simply roll loosely, and on an angle, a long strip of 1¼″-wide brown ribbon for the trunk. Cut a number of pieces of green ¾″-ribbon for the branches, and make a triple-thick green base. Insert the branches into the trunk. If they don't all fit, just cut the ends into points so they won't take up so much room. Glue the tree onto the base.

To create the big open flower in Illus. 14, make each part separately. Begin with dark red, $\frac{1}{2}$″-ribbon for the inner "petals." Simply compress a folded piece to get the crease, and then glue. Make the outer, yellow "petals" by merely looping strips over and glueing. Then glue all the red pieces inside the yellow ones and glue the various parts to each other near the middle of the flower. To hide the joined parts in the middle, cut out two large circles from $1\frac{1}{4}$″-ribbon and glue on each side as shown.

The large decorative flower in Illus. 15 is made from a number of strips of ribbon glued onto a circular piece of ribbon in the middle. To make them curl downwards as shown, simply wind each strip over your finger before glueing. Make small contrasting strips to form the "eye." The long stem is a piece of ribbon rolled in the same oblique way as for the tree trunk (Illus. 13), except it is rolled very tightly round a wooden dowel.

Illus. 14. Flower.

Illus. 15. Flower.

Illus. 13. Palm tree.

LACQUER AND CRACKLE

Crackle was first considered to be a natural "net-like, cracked pattern in a glaze or in glass." The concept altered slightly to include "*accidental* or *intended* fine cracks in a glaze." It is now possible to produce an authentic-looking crackle finish artificially not only on ceramic glaze, but also on other types of finishes.

Crackle is basically a sign of age and is very becoming on objects styled after their antique equivalents. We are all more or less familiar with this crackle effect, which is often common in old—and even new—ceramic pieces, on old paintings, antique furniture and other items that were at one time or another finished with lacquer or varnish.

These glaze-cracks occur on ceramic pieces when the clay body and the glaze shrink at different rates while cooling, so that the hardened glaze does not fit on the clay. On antique objects, on the other hand, the crackle originates spontaneously and in the course of time through the gradual volatilization—or evaporation—of the oil in the paint. Ultimately, of course, the fine, hairline cracks fill up with dust and dirt and thus become visible at a casual glance. Crackle is, then, actually nothing more than an indication of deterioration.

Opponents of deliberate crackle insist that one should not create artificially what requires generations of natural time to produce. Such an effect, they say, is a false one, and anything that is false is nothing but junk. But, nobody is corrupted simply by wishing to imitate an antique work of art, for a close examination clearly reveals that such things are not old, but have been antiqued by some modern method.

Crackle is, therefore, only a harmless technique for decorating things to get a charming, artistic effect. It helps bring prints of famous art works into harmony with their mountings.

Incidentally, you do not always have to fill the cracks with brown, grey, or another dust-imitating color, but you can also use such colors as orange, green, or even gold, for a striking effect in either setting off a background color, or, simply, in making an impression on the viewer.

Decorating Cardboard Boxes

You are now ready to choose your base—the object whose surface you want to crackle. For your first project, pick an inexpensive small box—one that you can easily experiment with. You can actually use any type of cardboard, from old scrap pieces decorated and glued onto another object, such as the hangers in Illus. 1, to new boxes bought especially to be crackled.

Applying Ground Color

If you use a new cardboard box, make sure you remove price tags or marks from the cardboard before you begin to work, because it will no longer be possible later on.

Cardboard or pasteboard boxes are usually cream-colored. If you want the ground—or base—to be a different color than cream, paint over it with water-based latex wall paint or, even better, with illustrator's tube colors,

Condensed from the book, "Lacquer & Crackle" by Hanny Nussbaumer | © 1972 by Sterling Publishing Co., Inc., New York

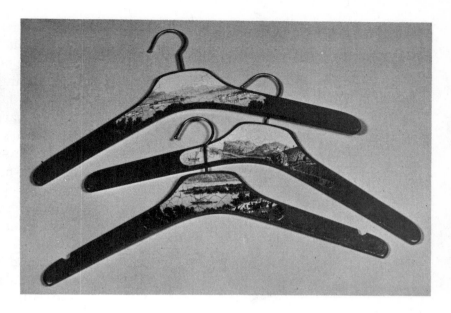

Illus. 1. Decorating old scraps of cardboard is just as much fun as using whole new boxes. The cardboard pieces glued onto these hangers are actually cut-out art prints, applied as described on page 448.

poster paint, tempera or gouache, which can be bought at an art supply shop. Add just enough water to whichever paint you choose so the paint is not too thick. Brush the paint on smoothly. Be sure not to make the paint too watery, or you will have to apply several coats. After the color dries, brush over it with clear shellac, using a 1″-, 1½″-, or 2″-wide varnish brush to "fix" (prevent the flaking of) the surface. Spray cans of fixatives are available at art supply shops.

To clean brushes used for water-based latex tube paints, poster paints, tempera or gouache, use soap and warm water.

Isolating the Medium

To prepare any medium for crackling, no matter what its shape, you have to isolate or "size" its surface. This means that you brush on a substance, called a sizing or size, which seals the surface.

To size the cardboard box—and, in fact, to size wood or parchment paper—you have a choice of one of three kinds of glue. The first is cellulose wallpaper paste, available in powder form at hardware and wallpaper stores. Stir one heaping tablespoonful of the powder into one pint of water, using a whisk or wire whip, egg beater or electric mixer. Stir briskly until

the paste has a uniform consistency. Let the paste stand for 15–20 minutes, then whip it briskly again. It is now ready for use.

NOTE: Mix cellulose wallpaper paste fresh everytime you use it, because it thickens very quickly.

The second type of glue is rabbit skin glue, which is available at art supply shops in the form of grains. Put four level tablespoonfuls of the grains into a tin can and add one pint of water. Let the mixture soak for several hours, and then place the container in a hot water bath. Keep the water hot, but not boiling, over a low heat until the glue dissolves. Stir from time to time. The glue is ready for use when the mixture is completely liquid. Rabbit skin glue made in this way keeps for about a month.

Your third choice of glue is a white glue (such as Elmer's Glue), sold for hobby purposes.

Illus. 2. Use a soft, flat hog bristle brush to apply glue sizing to the cardboard box.

Illus. 3. Lay a stick-on transfer in the still-wet coat of priming lacquer in the position you marked before you lacquered the cardboard box.

with a stick-on transfer picture. Lay the motif on the place you want it to be, and carefully mark the positions of the corners with pencilled dots. Using a varnish brush, apply a coat of priming lacquer, sometimes called body or flatting varnish, which is available at paint and hardware suppliers under various trade names. When buying priming lacquer, take care to choose a brand that is thin-flowing and which dries quickly. Let the priming lacquer begin to dry.

Stick-on transfer pictures may be single flowers, bouquets, beetles or, as in this case, birds, and have a protective layer of paper that prevents curling. Dampen one corner slightly and pull the two layers apart from there. Lay the picture, face down, protective paper *up*, on the still slightly wet coating of priming lacquer. Dab it carefully with a wet sponge, until you can push the thin sheet of paper away.

Some stick-on pictures—ships, coaches, and horses for example—frequently have a series of crossed lines on the back to make it easy to stick the picture down correctly. Use the crossed lines for this, but do not be influenced by the

This glue is milky white (it is made from casein), but dries clear. It may be thinned with water to a brushable consistency for glueing down paper or for applying to a surface as a size. For this project, it must be thinned with water. White glue keeps indefinitely and requires no special treatment for use.

Apply whichever sizing you decide on to the cardboard with a soft, flat, hog bristle brush, from sizes 2–6, depending on the dimensions of the box.

When the sizing is completely dry, apply a second coat in the same way. This prevents unsightly spots, caused by missed areas, from showing up later on. Be sure to pay close attention to the edges of the box, because if they are not sufficiently sized, later, the lacquer will penetrate under your design and cause ugly blotches.

Clean any brushes you use for glue sizing with warm water.

Attaching a Stick-On Transfer Picture

Now that the box is painted and sized, choose an attractive motif or design to apply. The matchbox in Illus. 3 has been decorated

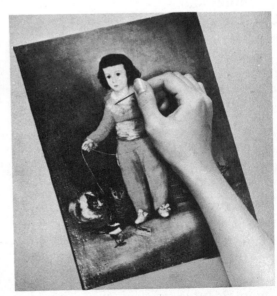

Illus. 4. Puncture with a needle any air bubbles that form on the stick-on transfer picture when you remove the protective paper.

picture showing through the protective paper. For this type of stick-on, take the picture by the thumb and forefinger in each upper corner, dip it in water until it is well soaked, and then lay it picture-side *down* on the still wet coating of priming lacquer. Press down carefully with a wet sponge until you can push the paper layer aside. If you see any bubbles marring the picture, stick them with a fine needle to let out the air. Press the picture flat with the wet sponge.

Another way to attach a stick-on transfer, instead of laying the picture on the wet coat of priming lacquer, is to brush the picture side with priming lacquer. Wait briefly, until the picture starts to dry and is tacky. Then, stick the picture directly onto the dry box. Press it carefully into place and dab it with a wet sponge to remove the protective paper.

The advantage of this method is that the picture can be applied to projects which require no coat of priming lacquer. The disadvantage is that occasionally traces of lacquer show along the edges of the picture.

The stamp box in Illus. 5 is decorated in still another way. Real postage stamps are set into the wet size coating, before any priming lacquer is applied.

Lacquer . . .

You have already used one coat of priming lacquer to attach the bird stick-on transfer to the matchbox. After that has dried completely for at least 12 hours, paint another coat of priming lacquer over the motif and ground color, with a broad, flat varnish brush. It is important to apply both coats of lacquer evenly, because the thickness of the lacquer layer will influence the crackle pattern. A thick coat results in deep, wide cracks and a thin coat in fine, hairline cracks.

Before you finish brushing on the lacquer, hold the box up to the light. Turn it this way and that so the light reflects on every part of the surface. If you see dull spots, they are spots you missed with your brush, so brush over them immediately. If the lacquer is almost dry

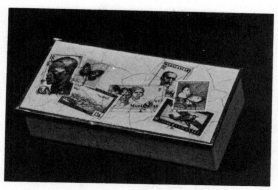

Illus. 5. Real stamps, set into the wet size coating, make an ideal and handy stamp-storage box.

and is tacky, you cannot brush over it any more or you will ruin the smoothness of the surface.

The second coat of priming lacquer must not dry completely. Let it get tacky, so that, when lightly touched with a finger, it shows a fingerprint. At room temperature, 65°–70°F (18.3°–21.1°C), this takes 2–3 hours.

Apply two coats of priming lacquer to the stamp box in this same manner. Clean a brush that has been used for lacquer with acetone or lacquer thinner. If the brush hardens with lacquer still in it, pour some thinner into a tin can and let the brush stand in it for several hours. Wash out the brush in warm, soapy water.

And Crackle!

Numerous brands of crackle medium, often having different constitutions and characteristics, are available. Make sure that both the priming lacquer and the crackle medium you buy are made by the same company and are designed to be used together! Crackle medium keeps about two months, but there is danger of deterioration after that.

Always work at room temperature. With a broad, flat brush, apply the crackle medium over the box in the manner shown in Illus. 6. Then, rub it with the palm of your hand, using light, circling movements, to consolidate the layer. Keep this up until the coat begins to dry, but is still slightly tacky. You must stop as soon as your finger begins to stick. If you do

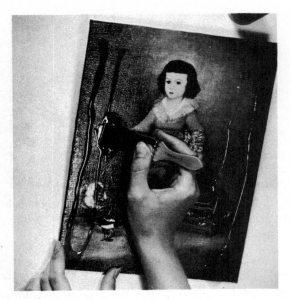

Illus. 6. Brush the crackle medium evenly over the surface with a broad, flat brush.

of linseed oil. Rub the color with a soft rag into the crackle with circling strokes until it adheres to the crackle (see Illus. 7). Let the box dry for at least 24 hours.

NOTE: Do not add linseed oil to red or green oil paint.

You can use different colors for accentuating the cracks—not only those which resemble dust—depending on the color of the background and the picture. On a dark green ground, for instance, use a light red or orange; on a black or dark brown ground, use a light grey, beige or yellow. Emerald green also produces a very striking effect.

Removing the Crackle Medium

The crackle medium is water-soluble. With a wet sponge, gently wipe the crackle medium

not put the project aside immediately, it will show finger marks.

The crackle begins to form after a short time, perhaps only a half hour. Hold the box up against the light and you should see the action taking place. Remember, though, that you will not see well-defined cracks until you apply color to the crackle.

If, however, within a half hour, you are unable to discover any sign of crackle taking place, or if the crackle appearing is too fine for your purpose, hold the project up to a heater or stove, or put it under an ordinary electric light bulb for a few minutes. This treatment forces the formation of the crackle.

If the crackle still does not appear, the fault is usually with the thickness and the drying time of the previously applied coats of lacquer.

Coloring the Crackle

A half hour after the crackle has completely formed, rub color into the fine network in order to make the network pattern stand out more clearly. You can let the project sit for a day or two before filling the cracks without harm to the effect.

Use tube oil colors, mixed with a few drops

Illus. 7. Choose an attractive color and apply it to the crackled surface with a soft cloth. After at least 24 hours, gently wipe the crackle off the box with a wet sponge. Some crackle mediums, such as "crackle-it," are not removed after you color them. In such cases, add a final coat of lacquer over the crackle.

off the box, leaving behind only the colored crackle pattern. This procedure is the high point, and your box, at last, sparkles with crackle.

For a final transparent, glossy effect, apply a coat of priming lacquer with a wide, flat brush. Use long strokes and cover the surface completely. Let the box dry, then fill with matches.

Book Coverings

Art Cards

A unique camouflage for a clumsy telephone book is the crackled book cover in Illus. 8. Artistic greeting cards or other kinds of cards make great book covers, because they mount easily on flat surfaces.

Search through your old Christmas cards, birthday cards and color postcards. Choose one large enough for the telephone book. Cut off any white borders with scissors or, for an especially straight edge, with a paper cutter. Many art cards do not have white borders, but they may have dog-eared or bent corners or small defects along the edges. Trim off any imperfections.

Paint and fix the telephone book's own cover in the same way you did the cardboard boxes (see pages 442 to 443). Choose a color which does not overpower, but which complements, the picture.

When the ground and the fixative are completely dry, prepare a sizing as instructed on page 443.

Place the art card in a tray of warm water and leave it there for 1 to 3 hours, depending on its thickness. Just before you remove the card from this water bath, size the painted book cover (see page 443).

Carefully take the card out of the water. Peel the softened back layer from the art print face (Illus. 9). Simply separate the layers at one corner and pull them apart.

While the picture is still wet, it must be glued to the telephone book, so press it down into the wet sizing coat. If both the card and the book

Illus. 8. You will certainly be proud of a handsome cover such as this on your battered old telephone book.

Illus. 9. Remove the art card from the water and carefully peel off the softened back layer.

LACQUER AND CRACKLE ■ 447

Illus. 10. Transform empty oatmeal or rolled oats boxes into original pencil holders or scrap baskets. Decorate each container with a different art card and then color the crackle appropriately to contrast with the ground color.

are dry, brush the reverse side of the picture with white glue and then glue it down. With a flat, soft brush, again size both the picture and the telephone book to keep them from spotting.

Put on the edging round the picture and the lettering beneath it with India ink on the sized surface.

When the edge and letters are dry, brush on two coats of priming lacquer and then the crackle medium as you did on page 445. In Illus. 8, the ground and the art card are covered with the same crackle and the same crackle color. Remove the crackle medium (see page 446) and brush on a final coat. You can use priming lacquer for a gloss effect, as you did for Illus. 3, or you can use a semi-gloss lacquer, for a silky lustre, or even a matt-finish lacquer for a matt or dull surface.

Art Prints

You can obtain art prints either from antique shops, book shops, stationers, or paint suppliers or from art calendars and magazines. Use only those prints that have a blank reverse side. With multi-layered paper called card stock, printing on the reverse side makes no difference, and such pictures are treated as art cards (see page 447). If the reverse side of a print on thin paper has any printing on it, however, do not use it. The printed material would eventually show through.

The address book in Illus. 11 has an artificial leather cover, onto which a piece of cream-colored cardboard is glued, and an art print applied.

Have your art print ready. The figures in Illus. 11 have actually been cut out from a larger print, but you can attach a whole print in the same way.

Mark the desired position of your print with pencil on the cardboard. Either attach the art print to the address book as if it were an art card (see page 447)—that is, into a wet size

Illus. 11. Enliven your address book with figures cut out from an art print or with a whole print which you especially admire. Add dates or words with India ink on the sized surface.

coat painted onto the address book, or follow another method. An effective way is to brush the back of the picture itself with sizing, using a soft, flat brush. Let it sit for a few moments. Then, take the two upper corners of the picture between thumb and forefinger of each hand and bring them into line with the two upper, pencilled marks on the piece of cardboard. Carefully stroke the picture downwards until the bottom corners also coincide with their respective pencil marks on the cardboard. Now brush the picture with sizing.

Wipe away any drops of sizing which gather on the edges of the picture with a wet sponge. Let the project dry.

As in the telephone book in Illus. 8, write the dates on this cover with India ink on the sized surface.

Follow the steps for priming lacquer and crackle on pages 445 to 446. Use only a thin layer of lacquer for the fine cracks in Illus. 11. Color the cracks brown as on page 446, apply a final coat—glossy or dull—and let the address book dry completely.

Parchment—Genuine and Imitation

Genuine parchment is the skin of a sheep, goat or other animal which is specially prepared to be written on. Imitation parchment paper is simply a paper imitation of genuine parchment. You must de-grease both parchment and parchment paper before you can lacquer and crackle them. To do this, moisten a cotton rag with ox gall, which can be bought from an art supply shop.

Size all parchment or parchment paper projects with white glue thinned with water (see page 443), because later, this helps the crackle formation.

Book Covers and Cases

The leather diary in Illus. 12 is smartly decorated with an imitation parchment art card. Attach the card and do the lacquer and crackle in the manner described on pages 445 to 446. A fine gold crackle color adds the final dignity to this handsome diary.

Art prints also make attractive motifs on parchment. See page 448 for instructions on

Illus. 12. Sometimes, you may not be satisfied with the crackle formation—even if it is elegant, fine gold crackle as on this diary cover. Just wash off the coat of crackle medium with a sponge dipped in warm water. After it is dry, brush the project again with priming lacquer—this is the third coat—and re-crackle. If you have already colored the cracks—on the whole project or only on a portion of it—first clean the color away with turpentine, then remove the crackle medium from the ruined part. Re-coat the entire project with priming lacquer and re-crackle only on the spoiled area.

Illus. 13. Use your imagination to create unique display items such as the imitation parchment photograph album above. Achieve an especially striking effect by using different sized cracks, contrastingly colored, on the background and on the print.

applying an art print. The photograph album in Illus. 13 has an imitation parchment cover on which an art print is placed. You can experiment with different types of cracks quite effectively on parchment. Lacquer and crackle as usual.

Lamp Shades

Many lamp shades are made of either genuine or imitation parchment. Combine creativity with thrift—use your imagination to make new shades from any old ones you are ready to throw out.

Each lamp shade in Illus. 14 has been beautifully restored with a cut-out from an art card. You can use related cut-outs or, for a more modern effect, totally contrasting ones. Size the shades and prepare the art cards as you did for cardboard (see page 443). Lacquer, crackle and then color according to your taste.

Chintz

Chintz, a cotton cloth often glazed with wax or some similar chemical substance, is usually imprinted with artistic designs which,

Illus. 14. Illuminate a room with this beautiful chandelier; decorate each shade elaborately with an art card and then lacquer and crackle.

when carefully cut out, are particularly suitable for crackle work. Chintz motifs—flowers, butterflies, birds or genre scenes (scenes from every-day life)—often have a printed frame or border. Naturally, you should not cut the frame off, because such borders look especially nice. Chintz is probably easier to handle than art prints on paper.

A chintz motif pressed onto the lamp shade in Illus. 15 adds life to an otherwise plain shade.

To apply a chintz cut-out to imitation parchment (or to cardboard), fix the surface and size the basket thoroughly with your choice of glue sizing (see page 443). Place the chintz motif in the *wet* size and press the cloth down. Brush over the cloth with the same glue sizing until the weave of the cloth is filled with glue.

For genuine parchment—and, incidentally, also for wood, sheet metal and glassware—first size the back of the cloth itself, and then lay the picture on a *dry* lamp shade. Wipe any excess sizing away from the edges with a wet sponge. Size the face of the picture evenly so that it will not feel rough when it is dry. Lacquer and crackle as always. The crackle is automatically finer on the chintz than on the parchment paper. Illus. 15 is trimmed with brocade.

Natural patina is a surface mellowing or softening. If you decorate a project with a reproduction of an antique painting, you get an especially nice effect if you narrow the contrast between the picture and the surface surrounding it. You can achieve this with an artfully applied patina.

If you do not want to use a picture motif for a particular lamp shade, simply tint it with a patina.

Use a tube oil color such as brown, which produces an authentic mellow coloring. If the oil paint is somewhat thick, add 3 or 4 drops of linseed oil, so that it flows smoothly. Do not add more than 3 or 4 drops, however, or the color will run too much. Mix well.

Illus. 15. A chintz motif perks up a rather plain parchment lamp shade. The crackle network is automatically finer on the chintz than on the parchment.

With a soft cloth, apply the color to the parchment gently, covering the surface with a circling motion. Use more or less pressure, depending on the intensity of the toning you want. Let the patina dry for 12 hours before you lacquer and crackle it. A single row of brocade trim is all you need to complete the project.

Wood as a Base

Wood is a wonderful, sturdy base on which to lacquer and crackle. Often, in fact, its natural color is attractive enough that a ground color is not necessary. If so, use sandpaper, #0, 2/0, 3/0, 4/0 or 6/0 depending on the wood, instead of paint to prepare the surface.

Book Ends

The book ends in Illus. 16 are natural wood color. If you buy new book ends, use sandpaper to sand off any stamped prices, numbers or trade-marks that there may be.

Size the book ends with clear shellac to close the pores of the wood. Use a soft, flat brush. Apply the shellac evenly, and not too thickly. Clean the brush with denatured alcohol.

NOTE: You can substitute one of the three glue sizings (see page 443) for the clear shellac to seal the wood.

When the shellac is dry, sand the book ends with fine grade sandpaper. If you are going to add any lettering, do so now with India ink.

The figures on the book ends are from art cards. Notice that they are cut out around the figures' outlines. If you do not separate the printed face from the paper underlayer when you glue it down, you get more of a relief effect. Brush the back side of the picture with white (Elmer's) glue and press it down where you want it. Do not apply sizing to the picture.

Brush on two coats of lacquer and crackle as usual. Color the cracks.

Letter Box

The wooden letter box in Illus. 17 is also natural wood color. The picture on the top is cut from chintz curtain material. Attach the picture as you did the chintz cut-out to genuine parchment (see page 450). Size the rest of the box with clear shellac, and let it dry. Lacquer and crackle. Even though the wood and chintz are evenly lacquered, do not be surprised when they crackle differently. Coarser cracks automatically result on the wood than on the chintz. Color the letter box cracks brown.

Illus. 17. The nature scene in this chintz cut-out is particularly realistic against the natural wood color of the box itself.

Sheet Metal Projects

Matchbox

The matchbox in Illus. 18 is made of metal. Clean bare or already primed metal—that is, painted or lithographed metal—with turpentine. It is advantageous, when you look for metal to crackle, to choose sheet metal ware that has already been primed or finished. However, if you use bare metal, paint it with synthetic resin (alkyd) enamel.

Clean any brushes you use for enamel with turpentine or sub-turps.

After metal is painted, no sizing is needed. The stick-on transfer picture in Illus. 18 is attached to the first coat of priming lacquer. Apply the second lacquer coat, the crackle and the color as shown on pages 445 to 446.

To remove crackle from the metal box, wash it off with cold water. Add a clear finish, glossy or not, with a wide, flat brush. Let the box dry and fill it with matches.

Metal Tray

Decalcomania is the process of permanently fixing a specially-prepared design (decal) to a surface. The metal tray in Illus. 19 is decorated

Illus. 18. Make a durable and waterproof container for your kitchen matches from a metal box.

with decals. A decal is different from a stick-on transfer, because it has only a thin covering. A decal is much easier to handle than a stick-on transfer. Decals are especially suitable for surfaces, such as trays, that have been grounded with a dark color. The decals' colors do not lose their intensity when attached to a dark background, as do the colors of stick-on transfers.

First, clean the metal tray with turpentine and then paint it. Let it dry. Then hold the

Illus. 19. Make original decals depicting characters from fairy tales. Crackle when the decal is absolutely dry. If something goes wrong when you crackle the scene, lay the tray in warm water until the coating strips off. Begin again. Crackled projects are washable, but do not leave them in warm water for a length of time.

decal, picture side up, by both upper corners, dip it for a few moments in water, and lay it face down on the dry tray. Press it down lightly with a wet sponge. As soon as you observe that the protective paper has loosened from the picture—a little side pressure on the picture will cause it to slip—press with your right thumb lightly on the upper right side of the decal and, with the other hand, carefully remove the paper backing. The decal is sturdier than the stick-on transfer, so do not worry about making mistakes. So long as it stays *wet*, the picture may be moved without trouble into its final position.

In craft and hobby shops, several products for home-made decals are now available. Essentially made of liquid plastic, these products allow you to make your own decals, preferably from color or black-and-white art prints on paper whose reverse side is blank. Such prints are available from art museums or

may be taken from calendars. The products can also be used on art cards and picture postcards if the soaking time is extended.

The liquid plastic is brushed on the face of the picture or print in one direction only and allowed to dry. A second coat is then brushed on in a crosswise direction and let dry. Continue in this manner until 4 to 6 alternating coats have been applied. Wash the brush immediately in warm, soapy water, as the dried film is insoluble.

When dry—after at least 6 hours—soak the plastic-coated print in water until the plastic film loosens from the paper. Strip the film and the picture away from the paper. Lay the picture on the tray, carefully press it down with a wet sponge, and allow it to dry.

Some home-decal products require that the peeled picture dry first. Then, coat the picture and the tray with the solution and mount the picture. Check carefully which type of product you buy.

Cover the metal tray with two coats of priming lacquer, crackle and color as usual. Remove the crackle as on page 446. Use a clear, heat- and alcohol-resistant finish, such as a polyurethane spar varnish, to ensure a long, well-protected life for your tray.

Glass and Ceramic Ware

You can achieve wonderful effects by treating glass or ceramics with lacquer and crackle. Glass is not porous and does not have to be sized, only scrubbed clean with a detergent and warm water. Rinse well and, preferably, let the glass air dry. A fan can be used to speed up the drying process.

A chintz cut-out, a stick-on transfer or a decal, as on the inside of the glass in Illus. 21, is perfect for application to glass.

Ceramic is often attractive enough by itself that no design other than a crackle network is necessary.

Quite a sophisticated possibility for crackle only is gold or silver crackle. Buy bronze

Illus. 20. One liquid you can use to create your own decals is "decal-it." Pour out the liquid along the edges of the art print or picture you wish to coat. Brush "decal-it" evenly— in one direction only—over the surface.

powder, bronzing liquid and poppy seed oil (used for thinning oil colors) from an art supply shop.

Place a half-teaspoonful of bronze powder in a tin lid, add a few drops of linseed oil, and stir with a match stick. Or, add bronzing liquid to the powder, stir, and put in an equal quantity of poppy seed oil.

You can also buy ready-mixed bronze powder, called "gold paint" or, if silver-colored, "aluminum paint." By the way, numerous other colors of bronze powder are available— red, blue, green and so on. Ask your paint dealer about them.

Clean any brushes you use for bronze powder with bronzing liquid.

Two-Color Crackle

A striking effect on a glass base is two-color crackle. Clean and dry the glass (page 454). Then brush on two coats of priming lacquer as usual. Crackle and color the first formed cracks as for any other project. Let it dry for 24 hours. Clean the glass with a wet sponge. Let it dry completely again. Now, apply another coat of priming lacquer. Do not let it dry completely, and apply a second coat of crackle medium. Fill the crackle with a second oil color. Complete the procedure as you do for single-color crackle.

Now that you are familiar with how to lacquer and crackle on various bases, experiment and see what unusual items you can create.

Illus. 21. Place a decal inside a glass for a conversation piece you will be proud to display. You may crackle the outside of the glass.

Illus. 22. Fantastic and intricate crackle patterns develop on undecorated ceramic ware.

MACRAMÉ

Tying knots has been important to men almost every day of their lives since civilization began. Modern man still finds knots essential for holding hundreds of items together. Before radio or even widespread literacy, sailors had little to do during their leisure time on board ship. With miles and miles of rope available to them, it was only natural that they would develop knot-tying into an intricate and decorative hobby, as well as a useful skill.

While knotting as an art reached its peak on board ship in the first half of the 19th century, the leisure time we have today has led to this ancient craft's revival. Macramé, the art of tying knots in decorative patterns, is popular once again. You can use almost any type of cord, rope or yarn in macramé: you should use thin and shiny cord for necklaces and belts, medium-weight yarn or twine for wall hangings, but you must use strong rope that will not break under stress for functional macramé —that is, knotted pieces that are meant to be used as well as admired. Rope made from many materials is available, each with its own special advantages and disadvantages.

Materials

The most important material you need for macramé is, of course, thread, rope or yarn. All yarns, woven fabrics and ropes are made of fibres. Vegetable fibres (Manila hemp and sisal) are mainly used, but sometimes animal fibres (wool, silk) and inorganic substances (synthetics, such as nylon and Dacron) are also wound into rope.

Manila hemp is grown mainly in the Philippine Islands. The fibres, which can be 10 or 12 feet long, are peeled from the leaves of the abacá plant.

Sisal comes mainly from Central America and East Africa. The white or yellow fibres are almost 5 feet long and come from a species of the agave plant.

Hemp is grown in central and southern

Illus. 1. Nylon silk.

Illus. 2. Manila hemp.

Illus. 3. First-grade three-strand hemp.

Condensed from the book, "Big-Knot Macramé" by Nils Strom and Anders Enestrom | © 1971 by Sterling Publishing Co., Inc., New York

Europe, America and Asia. The fibres sometimes grow up to 2½ feet long.

Flax, from which linen is made, is cultivated mainly in Europe. The fibres come from the stalk of the flax plant.

Jute is grown in India and Pakistan. The fibres are harvested from bushy plants which sometimes reach a height of 10 feet. The raw material is inexpensive, so jute is often used for sacks.

Coconut fibre is made from the hairy shells of coconut. The fibres are resistant to moisture, but are not very strong.

Cotton, which comes from the fibres growing on the cotton bush, is spun into yarn on machinery in mills. Rope made from cotton is only about half as strong as rope made from Manila hemp.

None of the materials in knotting are expensive. With just a small investment in the right kind of rope, you will soon be making original, useful, attractive objects.

The following two articles introduce you to two totally different types of macramé. *Macramé with Beads* includes those knots which you probably associate with macramé, whereas *Big-Knot Macramé* deals with much bigger, but just as attractive, knots.

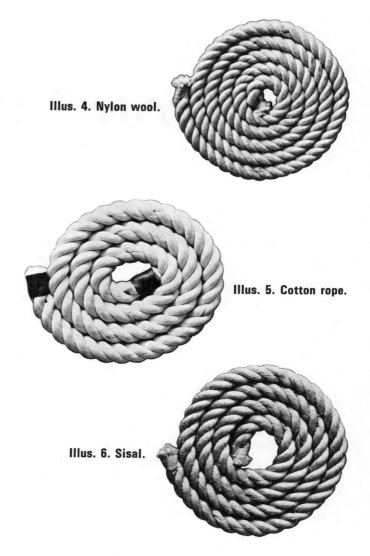

Illus. 4. Nylon wool.

Illus. 5. Cotton rope.

Illus. 6. Sisal.

MACRAMÉ WITH BEADS

Threading beads for necklaces, belts and other accessories is a popular craft, but did you ever think of incorporating the thread itself into the design? If you are going to attach the beads to a piece of cloth, you can embroider the thread around the beads to enhance their color and sparkle, at the same time as you secure them to the fabric (see the article *Beadcraft* on page 13). If, on the other hand, you are going to thread beads without a cloth backing, so they stand on their own as in a belt or necklace, you can knot and loop the thread around the beads with macramé knots. All sorts of delightful patterns, seemingly intricate yet really based on only a few simple stitches and knots, result as you experiment with the beads and string. Macramé and beadcraft, though they seem unrelated, have one very important thing in common: almost any design made with them is attractive.

The best part of decorating with beads and macramé knots is that you do not need any special equipment other than the beads and string. An occasional project may require something else—a covered bottle naturally needs a bottle to be covered—but in general, you need no more materials than the obvious ones. Use any cord, string or twine as long as it is not elastic or too soft. Do not use very fine threads, even for delicate pieces; the thread does not show up as much as it should, and the intricate knotting is hidden by the beads. Finally, gather an assortment of beads together —large ones with wide holes are best—to embellish and add sparkle to your work.

For this macramé you need a working base on which to anchor your knotting as you proceed. A firm pillow or the upholstered arm of a chair is suitable. Secure your knotting to this base with pins or thumb-tacks, so that as you knot you can pull tightly without dislodging the entire article you are making. Have on hand a pair of scissors, a variety of cord and twine, a tape measure and a crochet hook, to pull loose ends through to the wrong side of your work.

To determine how long to cut the cords, work a sample about 3 inches square, using the same pattern stitch and cord which you are going to use in your project. Divide the length of cord you used in the sample by 3, to determine how much cord you used in 1 square inch, and multiply that number by the number of square inches there will be in your finished project. If the design is a loose one with few knots, it might use strands only 3 times the length of the completed article (so you would cut cords 6 times the project's length, and fold them in half), while if your design is very dense it might require 5 or 6 times (doubled) the length of the project.

Double Knot

A double knot (abbr.: DK) is the knot most commonly used in macramé, and with just cause: it is very versatile, as you can make it either singly, in horizontal rows, or in diagonal rows. Follow the diagram in Illus. 1 for a single double knot, and in Illus. 2 for a horizontal double knot bar. To make a dia-

Condensed from the book, "Beads Plus Macramé" by Grethe La Croix | © 1971 by Sterling Publishing Co., Inc., New York

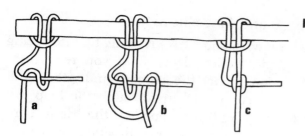

Illus. 1. Double knot (DK).

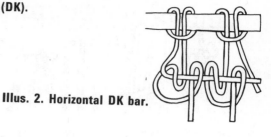

Illus. 2. Horizontal DK bar.

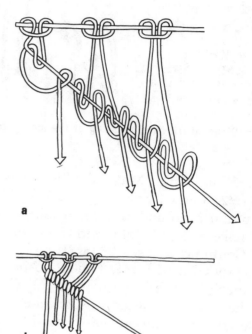

Illus. 3 a and b. Diagonal DK bar from left to right.

gonal double knot bar, slant the "knot bearer" (the cord around which the knots are made) at an angle and make double knots along its length. The diagram in Illus. 3 demonstrates how to make a diagonal double knot bar from left to right. You can make double knots and double knot bars in any direction: from left to right as illustrated, right to left, or a combination of both. By first making several diagonal bars in one direction, and then several in the reverse direction, you can create a loose, lacy pattern. The bars are connected by single strands of twine which are unadorned by knots.

Diagonal Double Knot Bars

There are two ways to make diagonal double knot bars (Diag. DK bars): open and closed. The difference is in how the ends of the bars are made. See Illus. 4 while you read these instructions. In open bars, you use cord #2 as the knot bearer (KB) in the first bar, and cord #3 then makes the first knot. In the second bar of an open bar set, cord #1 is the knot bearer, and #3 again makes the first knot. Thus both ends of the bars are "open."

To make a set of closed bars, use cord #1 as the KB in the first row, and start the knotting with cord #2. In the second bar, use #2 as the KB and start knotting with #3. At the end of this row, use #1 (which was the KB of the first row) as the last cord to knot. Thus both ends are "closed."

An attractive macramé pattern consists of two diagonal bars begun from opposite sides and forming a cross. Begin the diagonals from each side, using the end cords, #1 and #8 in

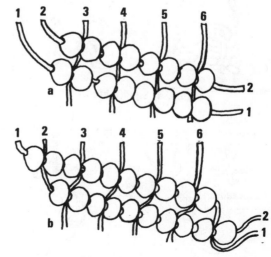

Illus. 4. In a: "open" bars. In b: "closed" bars.

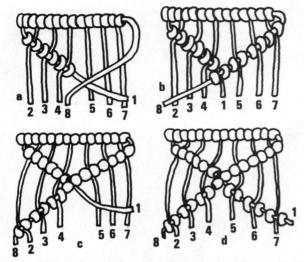

Illus. 5. Diagonal DK bars, crossing at the middle to form an "X".

Illus. 5, as KB's. Make double knots with cords #2, 3 and 4 around #1, and with cords #7, 6 and 5 around #8. Then take cord #1 and make a double knot with it around cord #8. Continue to use #8 as KB, and make knots around it with #4, 3 and 2. Using #1 as KB, make knots around it with #5, 6 and 7. You have made one cross. Continue making crosses this way for an easy, yet interesting, macramé design. Use the finished piece as a belt, bracelet, curtain tieback or wall hanging.

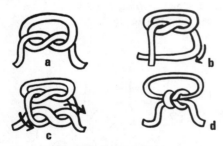

Illus. 6. Square knot.

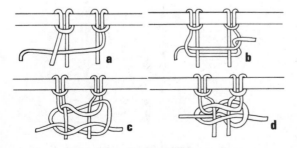

Illus. 7. Flat knot.

Square and Flat Knots

The square knot (SK) is made by interlacing two cords. Follow Illus. 6 as you read these instructions: place the left cord under the right. Bring the right cord up through the loop just made, and pull the end of the right cord through (a). Now, reverse direction: place the right cord (that is, what is *now* the right cord) under the left, and pull the left cord through the loop (b–c). Pull both ends evenly (d).

The square knot has several variations, the most common of which is the *flat knot* (FK). Make the flat knot in exactly the same way as the square knot, only tie each half knot around two cords. (See Illus. 7.) These cords do not form any part of the knot itself; they just hang and make the knot more prominent.

Many square or flat knots made one right after the other with the same two or four cords form a "sennit." Sennits are frequently used as transitional patterns between groups of diagonal and horizontal bars, while individual square and flat knots loosely connect strands for a lacy effect. Turn to the covered bottle on page 462 for an example of this type of knotting.

Simple Beaded Belt

Combining beads with the macramé knots you have learned is not difficult. The belt in Illus. 8 is a good project for you to start with: it uses both DK's and FK's, and looks much more intricate than it really is. The pleasing result will spur you on to make more complex articles.

The main portion of the belt is Diag. DK bars, while the thin portion is a sennit of FK's. Start the knotting by mounting cords on a foundation knot bearer (Fnd. KB) of a cord 6 inches long:

Step 1: Mount a cord about one third from the end of the 6-inch Fnd. KB.

Step 2: Slide a bead on the Fnd. KB from the longer side.

Step 3: Mount another cord next to this bead.

Step 4: Place another bead on the Fnd. KB.

Step 5: Take the inside strand of the cord you just mounted in Step 3 and loop it above and back to the Fnd. KB. Make a double knot with this cord on the Fnd. KB, so that the end of the cord hangs down as the fourth strand.

Step 6: Place another bead on the Fnd. KB.

Step 7: Mount another double cord next to this bead.

(When you have completed the belt, you will curl the ends of the Fnd. KB through the loop you made in step 5, and attach them with stitching to the wrong side. Do not do this until the knotting is completed, or you will not have a Fnd. KB to pin to your working base.)

Using the two outside strands as KB's, make Diag. DK bars towards the middle. You make two knots over each KB, as there are four strands besides the KB's. When the KB's meet in the center, do not knot them as you did on page 459. Instead, insert each through a bead, and then complete the cross by making two more knots on each KB. Before you make the last knot on each side, slide two beads on each strand. At this point in your work, there is one set of diagonal double knot bars with a bead in the center of the cross and two beads on each side. Make 13 crosses of the Diag. DK bars.

Place one bead on each of the KB's, and then make a DK on each KB with the two inside strands. Let the other two strands hang loose for the time being. The KB's are now the two strands in the middle of the belt. Using those strands which you just used to make the DK's, make successive FK's around the KB's. Make the sennit long enough so the belt is your waist measurement plus at least 4 or 5 inches.

When you have made the sennit long enough, place three beads on each of the inside cords (that is, the former KB's). Turn these ends away from the center, and stitch them to the underside of the sennit. Fasten the other two ends also with stitches, or pull them through nearby knots with a crochet hook.

The two strands still hang loose where the

Illus. 8. A belt made of macramé with beads. The construction is simple, but the results are unusual.

sennit begins. Pull these through one of the first FK's to the wrong side, and fasten with stitches. Do not forget to do the same to the ends of the Fnd. KB at the mounting.

To wear the belt, slip the sennit through the loop at the other end. Pull until it is as tight as you want, and then loop the sennit in and out of the first set of Diag. DK bars. The beads at the end of the sennit form a large knob which keeps the belt from unfastening.

Covered Bottle

Macramé is made of flexible cords, so you can knot around three-dimensional objects. A covered bottle is a simple project, besides being attractive and practical. You knot the cords right on the bottle itself, so the cover closely surrounds the glass shape. Rescue an

Illus. 9. Bottles covered with macramé and beads are among the most unique gift items you can give.

The Fnd. KB for a covered bottle is a cord. Thread a number of beads divisible by four on the cord (12 or 16 beads is customary, depending on the circumference of the bottle and the size of the beads) and tie the cord round the neck of the bottle or jar. Do not place too many beads on the Fnd. KB or there will not be enough space to mount the knotting cords. Mount one (double) cord between every two beads, as diagrammed in Illus. 10a. Now you are ready to begin the macramé knotting.

Every bead has two strands on each side of it. You are about to make FK sennits, which use *four* strands. Following Illus. 10b, pick up one strand (a) and bring it under the bead it is next to; then pick up the strand on the other side of the adjacent bead (d) and bring it to the first strand. These two strands, a and d, are those with which you tie the FK's, while the two middle strands, b and c, are those which hang through the middle of the sennit. Knot FK sennits as long as you want with each group of four cords.

Slip a clear bead on strands a and d of each set of four. Now re-group the sets of four in the following way: take strands d and a from adjacent groups of four and insert the ends into a dark bead, from opposite ends of the bead. These two strands are the center strands in the new group of four, while strand c, next to that d, and strand b, next to that a, are the outside strands which form knots. Tie FK sennits with the new groups of strands—lettered c–d–a–b—as long as you want.

ordinary wine bottle or a jar of an unusual shape from the garbage and decorate it for a sparkling and original ornament. The cover on the bottle in Illus. 9 is an easy design to make, and after practicing with its simple pattern, you should be inspired to try more intricate knots.

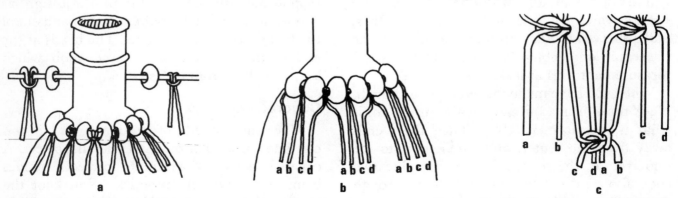

Illus. 10. In a: mounting cords on the Fnd. KB. In b: the four cords which make the first flat knot. In c: the four cords re-arranged to make the next flat knot.

After you have made these FK sennits, thread more beads on the strands as you just did, crossing the strands so that the original groups of four are back together. Tie FK's with a and d, and allow b and c to hang down the center of the sennit.

To form the criss-cross pattern on the bottle in Illus. 9, alternate your knotting threads, first making FK knots all round the bottle with a and d, and then switching to c and b. Add beads wherever it pleases you and make sennits rather than one knot if it looks attractive on your bottle.

Securing the strands on the bottom of the bottle is an important step in making this cover, for it holds them correctly in place on the entire bottle. Turn the bottle upside-down and hold it between your knees as you work. Tie strands from opposite sides of the bottle with square knots, but do not cut the ends off. Next, tie adjacent strands together, also with square knots. Continue tying square knots until every strand is connected to at least one other, and cut the ends off. When you make the knots, avoid large lumps, so the bottle can stand flat on a table. Glue the knots to the bottom of the bottle with a clear-drying glue if they do not lie flat against the glass.

Necklace

Jewelry which combines both sparkling beadwork and intricate knotting is the ultimate in ornate fashion accessories. To get started on this type of work, follow the instructions here to make the necklace on the left in Illus. 11. Examine the other designs closely if you want to copy the pieces here, or mount several cords and begin knotting an original pattern.

Illus. 11. Two examples of necklaces made with macramé and beads. Instructions for the necklace on the left begin on page 464.

If you do choose to make your own design, remember that symmetrical designs are usually most pleasing.

Instructions for necklace on left in Illus. 11: First make the long pieces for tying. Slip 13 beads on two long cords and slide the beads to the middle. Use four different shapes and/or colors of beads. Assign each type of bead a letter, and arrange them on the cords in the order of A–B–C–D–C–D–B–D–C–D–C–B–A.

Actually, any order is satisfactory, but when you use certain beads in specific places on the rest of the necklace, they will harmonize best if you begin with this order of beads. Alternate SK sennits with glass bars on each side of the 13 beads for the design on the ties.

Mount eight cords between the middle nine beads (there are, then, 16 strands for knotting). Make four FK sennits, two FK knots in each, with four groups of four strands each.

Slide an A bead on every strand which was a knotting strand (as opposed to a hanging strand). Make a sennit of two SK's with the two end strands on each side, and make three FK sennits of two FK's each with the 12 strands in the middle.

Slide an A bead on every hanging strand and make four FK sennits, each two FK's long.

Slide an A bead on every knotting strand. Make one SK with the two strands on each end, and divide the middle 12 strands into three groups of four strands. With each group, make one FK.

Let the middle four strands hang loose as you work with the six strands on each side. The directions here tell you how to work with one side, but naturally they apply to both sides. For the most symmetrical results, work both sides at the same time.

Slide a glass bar on the strand second from the end and one on the strand fifth from the end. The glass bars then have a strand on each side, as well as a strand through the center. Make one FK at the bottom of each glass bar, using only *one* hanging strand (the one which goes through the bar) instead of the usual two.

Slide an A bead on each of the first two strands from the end. Using the outside strand as KB, make a Diag. DK bar by tying DK's with the next two strands. Then, using what is *now* the outside strand, make another Diag. DK bar, tying knots with the next two strands (the second knotting strand is the KB of the first Diag. DK bar).

Place a D bead on the first and third strands. Make two more Diag. DK bars as before.

Slide one C bead on all three strands. Make one FK, with the middle strand hanging and the two on each side of it (#1 and #3) as knotting strands.

Separate the three strands by sliding five A beads on each. Tie a knot; then slide a C bead on each strand, and tie enough knots so the beads cannot slip off the strand. Clip off any excess string.

Now you are ready to complete the middle portion of the necklace. Taking the center four strands, slide three A beads on each of the outer strands of this group of four. Slide a B bead on the center two strands. Make two FK's with these four strands.

Repeat the last paragraph once. The middle portion should now be as long as the glass bars on the sides.

Pick up the three strands from each side which you left hanging after attaching the glass bars. Slide an A bead on the first and third of these three strands (on both sides of the center portion, of course). Make two Diag. DK bars with these three strands as you did before.

Now group all ten center strands together. Use the middle two strands as KB's for the first set of Diag. DK bars. Then use what have become the center strands as KB's for the *next* set of bars, and use the previous KB's as knotting strands. Do the same at the end of the second bar.

Slide one C bead on the middle two strands, and a D bead on each of the outer strands.

Using these outer strands as KB's, make three sets of closed Diag. DK bars towards the middle. Drop the KB of the first set of bars and pick up the next outer strand as KB as you did above.

Slide one A bead on the first two strands and one A bead on the next two strands. Make three sets of Diag. DK bars towards the middle again. When a KB from the left side reaches the middle, insert it through a C bead. Do the same from the right.

Let the ten strands hang loose. Knot the two middle ones once under the C bead. Tie a knot in each of the ten strands, then place an A bead on each. Then tie another knot, slide another A bead, and finish the strands with a large enough group of knots to prevent the beads from sliding off. Clip the ends of the strings.

Other Macramé Projects

There are virtually hundreds of things you can make with macramé knots: wall hangings, handbags, belts, bracelets, fringes for rugs or upholstered furniture, place mats—even vests, ties, skirts or free-standing sculptures. You should not need detailed instructions, because by now you are experienced enough with macramé and familiar with the appearance of the knots to be able to copy macramé objects by closely studying the pictures.

If you want to make only a small project, try one of the trinkets seen in Illus. 12. The eyeglass chain and pencil string use the same knotting technique: attach four strands of cord to the plastic caps which fit the ends of the eyeglasses and pencils (you can buy these in craft and hobby shops). Then thread beads on the strands, sometimes sliding the beads on all four, sometimes only on the middle two, and sometimes on each of the outer strands. Flat knots between the beads keep them from moving around on the cord.

The fancy piece attached to the watch, also in Illus. 12, is quite simple to make. Begin by mounting one cord on the watch handle, and then add beads and knots. To join more cords, mount them through the knots with the help of a crochet hook. Finish by making a small

Illus. 12. If you want to practice on a small project, try one of the ideas shown here. On the left, an eyeglass chain; in the middle, an ornament for a watch; on the right, a chain to hold a pencil.

loop of beads so you can hang the watch on a hook.

The girl in Illus. 13 is showing off the belt and bracelet she made herself. She mounted the knotting strands of the bracelet on a clasp which she purchased at a hobby store. When she had made the bracelet as long as she wanted it, she finished it off by making double knots with the knotting strands around the other end of the clasp. Then she turned the ends of the strands back through the beads and glued them there, and clipped off the excess string.

The belt is composed mainly of Diagonal and Horizontal DK bars. The girl mounted six cords on a Fnd. KB of cord, so she had 12 strands for knotting. To make the clasp of the belt, she threaded several beads on the ends of the Fnd. KB and looped the ends to make a

round clump of beads. She sewed the ends of the cords in place. If you have a needle with a large enough eye, you could thread the cord through the needle and run it on the underside of the belt through a few knots. A crochet hook can sometimes pull the cord through also.

Since there are beaded "buttons" at one end of the belt, there must be corresponding loops at the other end, to slip the beads through. When the belt is the proper length, finish off the four outer strands on each side of the belt by threading a needle with the cord and drawing it through a few knots. With the remaining four strands, make two SK sennits, long enough to circle the beaded buttons. Turn the sennits to the sides of the belt and fasten the ends on one of the ways described here.

These are only samples of the myriad of unique possibilities you can create with macramé and beads. Use any type of cord, string or twine, in any color, and decorate your knots with big or little beads. The ornaments you make are sure to be unusual, and you should be proud to give them as gifts or use them yourself.

Illus. 13. A belt or bracelet made from macramé and beads adds a sporty flair to a simple outfit. For a fancier ornament, use shiny cord and crystal beads.

BIG-KNOT MACRAMÉ

Big-knot macramé involves techniques that are quite unlike those you learned for macramé with beads. As you will see, the rope you use is much thicker and the knots much bigger. The results, more akin to the original sailor's knots, are different, but no less fun or satisfying to make.

To manipulate the rope you use for big-knot macramé, and to construct the projects in the section, you need to have some tools on hand. These are standard sailor's aids which make knot-tying easier. A *fid* is a tapering pin of wood that separates the strands of a piece of rope. It is handy when you want to insert rope between strands. You also need *cord* to whip the ends securely, *wax* to smooth and polish the cord, a *sailmaker's needle* for sewing sturdy ropes together, and a *sailmaker's palm*. This last instrument protects your hand while you push the needle through the thick rope.

Napkin Rings of Turk's-Head Knots

Easily twisted with just a small amount of rope, napkin rings can be fashioned from the popular Turk's-head knot, which twists the rope like a turban in one continuous ring. A Turk's-head knot can be either circular, to go round a napkin or scarf, or flat, for a mat under a hot dish. The napkin rings here are from three-ply Turk's-heads, but there are also four-ply, five-ply and multi-ply Turk's-heads.

Illus. 1. Napkin rings of three-ply Turk's-head knots and candle holders of five-ply knots decorate a casual table.

Condensed from the book, "Big-Knot Macramé" by Nils Strom and Anders Enestrom | © 1971 by Sterling Publishing Co., Inc., New York

Illus. 2. Wrap rope twice around napkin.

Illus. 3. Pull left twist over middle piece.

Illus. 4. Insert right end into loop.

Build the knot right around the napkin for the correct size. Begin by winding the rope around the napkin twice (Illus. 2). Use pins to hold the rope to the napkin and remove them as the knot takes form.

Make a loop (or "bight," as the sailors call it) with the left end over the middle piece of rope to form two crosses (see Illus. 3).

The right end (covered in black in Illus. 4 for a clearer picture) goes up and between the crosses in the loop. Pull the end through and wind it around the napkin. Bring it up on the front of the napkin, to the right of the rope already wound, and lay it over, then slip it under the two ropes (Illus. 5).

Make another loop over the middle turn, in the same direction as before, to form two new crosses. (Notice that the ends of the rope always

point up.) Just as in Illus. 4, put the right end into the loop, over one rope and under the next (Illus. 6). Illus. 7 shows the same end continuing, over and under above the cross you just made. The single-ply knot is complete in Illus. 10, where the ends of the rope meet.

Once you have made the basic knot, fill it in with more twists by following the path of the first twists with the ends of the rope. Continue until you have travelled round the knot three times and the ends of rope meet again. As you twist more rope, the Turk's-head knot tightens up and grips the napkin more firmly. After three trips round the knot with the rope, fasten the ends either by splicing, sewing or an overhand knot under the Turk's-head knot. Cut the ends so they cannot be seen.

If you remove the knot from the napkin

Illus. 5. Pull end through loop and towards back.

Illus. 6. Insert end into loop just formed.

Illus. 7. The end continues to the back side.

Illus. 8. Into another loop to the left . . .

Illus. 9. . . . then to the right again.

Illus. 10. Smooth the knot so it lies flat.

after one trip around with the rope, you can flatten it out and make a table mat instead of the circular ring. Insert the ends of the rope around the correct loops as you did when making the knot around a napkin. Use the mat under hot dishes, as a protective mat for vases, or as a decoration in a room with a nautical theme.

Candle Holders of Five-Ply Turk's-Head Knots

The candle holders in Illus. 1 are five-ply Turk's-head knots tightly wound around the base of the candles. At first glance this knot looks difficult, but its basic construction is not complicated. Besides, it is rewarding to make a knot that looks difficult. Make this knot directly on the object you want it to decorate (a lamp base, around candles for holders, or even around your wrist), or tie it first on another round object and remove it when finished.

To make tying the knot easier, two crosses have been numbered in the illustrations (1 and 2). The same crosses are numbered in all the pictures, so you can see where new loops have been added.

Make two turns around the cylinder and pin the end on the left to the base. Pull the middle piece of rope over the piece on the left. The crosses formed have been numbered 1 and 2 in Illus. 12b. Fasten the pieces of rope so that these crosses stay there. Now insert the right

Illus. 11. Continue weaving the end of the rope into the loops of the knot. When the knot is tripled, snip the ends and stitch them invisibly to the wrong side.

end (shown in black in Illus. 12c) of the rope from below between the two crosses—under the first piece of rope and over the second.

Draw the end upward around the cylinder (Illus. 13). Bring the black end from below and pass it between the two turns above cross 2. Draw the end around the object between those two turns and cross it over the turn on the right. Pin the rope here.

Insert the same end over, under and over

BIG-KNOT MACRAMÉ ■ 469

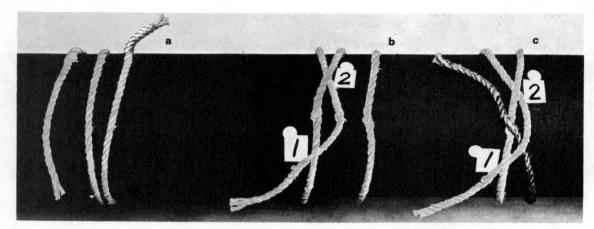

Illus. 12. In a, rope wrapped around. In b, first loop made. In c, end drawn through loop.

Illus. 13. Bring the end to the front.

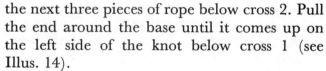

the next three pieces of rope below cross 2. Pull the end around the base until it comes up on the left side of the knot below cross 1 (see Illus. 14).

Draw the black end to the right of the knot, and pull it diagonally to the right, under and over the two pieces of rope it meets. Turn the end to the left and place it under, over, under, over, below cross 2. Turn the end around the base on the left until it comes up and meets the first end at cross 1. The first trip around the knot is completed.

Before you fill the knot in with rope, loosen the pins and even out the knot around the

Illus. 14. Continue winding end through loops.

Illus. 15. End goes over and under loops.

Illus. 16. First trip is complete.

Illus. 17. Knot is filled out.

cylinder. Be careful that you do not change the arrangement of ropes in the knot.

Double the knot, as begun in Illus. 16. Lay the same end of rope used for the first trip around the base to the right of the first round. As the knot fills out and tightens up, remove the pins. This knot, like the other Turk's-head knot, is usually tripled.

When you have gone around the knot three times (Illus. 17), remove the knot from its base and sew the ends invisibly to the back of the knot. Trim the excess ends, and you have a sturdy, practical knot you can use around many things.

Mats from Two-Dimensional Knots

Two-dimensional knots produce flat pieces of twisted rope which make sturdy mats. Place them in front of your doorway or inside the back door as a mat for wet clothing and snow equipment. Smaller, these two-dimensional knots are practical as trivets under hot pans, dishes, or pots. They are also very pretty twisted of gold braid and sewn to uniforms, overcoats, or lounging pajamas.

One mat you can construct is a Turkish mat from a prolonged knot. The prolonged knot is so named because it can be any length while its width remains the same. The mat here is about 20″ long and 8½″ wide, and requires 36 feet of 1″-rope for a mat that is tripled (that is, has three strands of rope around the knot). This mat is sometimes called a Turkish mat because of the prolonged knot's resemblance to a Turk's-head knot.

Make one loop about 6 feet from the end of

Illus. 18. Make two loops.

Illus. 19 (above). Wind a third loop.

Illus. 20 (right). Pull outside loops in direction of arrows.

Illus. 21. Make loops even.

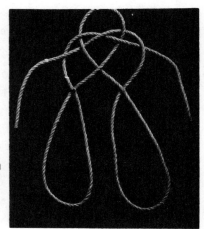

Illus. 22. Twist each loop.

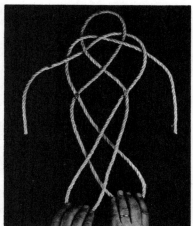
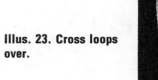

Illus. 23. Cross loops over.

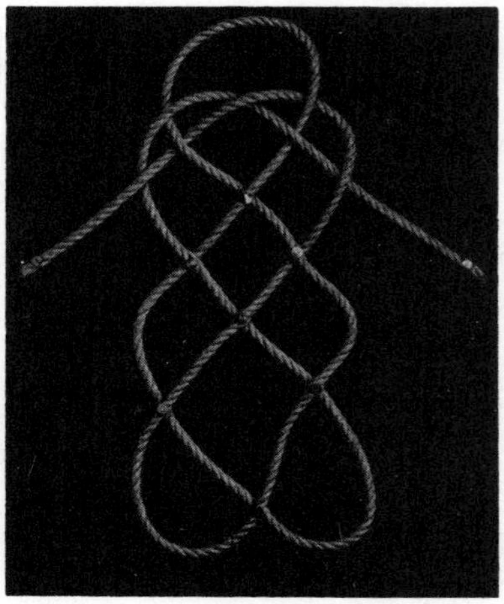

Illus. 24. Even loops again.

the rope, and then another loop on top of the first (see Illus. 18). Bring the right end under, over, under, over and under the five pieces of rope it meets in its trip around (Illus. 19). Turn the loops so the middle one is centered at the top and pull the loops on the sides down in the direction of the arrows in Illus. 20, for two extended loops about 20″ long.

Arrange the knot by evenly laying out the two loops (Illus. 21). Notice that they cross each other in the middle. Take the left loop and turn it to the right, so it crosses itself. Do the same with the right loop (both loops should turn to the right). With one loop in each hand, pass the right loop over the left one. Arrange the rope so it looks like Illus. 22—loops evenly spaced, crosses directly under each other.

Now use the ends of the rope again as indicated by the dark ends in Illus. 25. If the left end goes *under* a rope on the left, the right end must go *over* the corresponding piece on the right. When the ends meet at the bottom, the single-ply knot is complete. Now fill out the mat by doubling the single-ply knot with one of the ends. Triple the mat for extra strength and security. Carefully stitch the ends of the rope to the back so the mat lies flat.

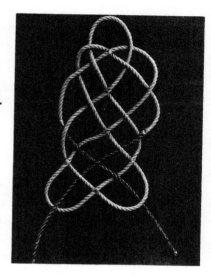

Illus. 25. Weave ends.

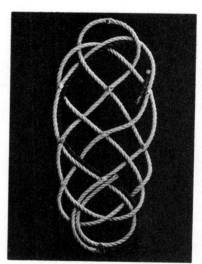

Illus. 26. Knot completed.

Illus. 27. Turkish mat.

NAPKIN FOLDING

Attractively folded table napkins can give even the plainest table setting or the most casual get-together for coffee a party look.

Do not be put off by the complicated appearance of some of the napkins. They are *all* easy to do. Some simply take a little longer than others, and as every busy host and hostess knows, time is of the essence. Therefore, the projects are more or less presented in the order of the time needed to make them. And, believe it or not, the time can actually be measured in seconds, not minutes!

Every folded napkin here is suitable for paper and some can also be made with linen. If you use paper, it is advisable to use the heavier 3-ply; however, you will find most paper napkins are the softer 1-ply. If, in using the very

soft paper, your productions tend to collapse, use two napkins together to give body. All of the folds, however, were tested on 1-ply paper napkins, and they all worked.

If you use linen, it helps if you add some starch in the laundering. If you are still not able to make sharp enough creases where necessary, try a little spray starch, and they will crease beautifully. When using linen, be sure to practice your folds first on paper napkins, so you won't spoil a freshly starched and ironed napkin. Then, when you start on the linen, you will know exactly what to do. A special note is made where linen is especially well suited for the folding.

Be sure after linen napkins are ironed flat that they are not put away folded or creased, so you won't have to re-iron before folding. In the case of paper napkins, the best way to get rid of the folds already in them is to run your fingernail *carefully* along the creases on the "mountain," or raised, side. This is also the easiest way to rip soft paper napkins, so do it very gently. Cloth, of course, should be ironed as flat as possible, especially on the edges.

You will find that paper napkins, because of the kind of soft, stretchy paper used to make them, rarely fold into perfectly lined-up squares, triangles, and so on; so, do not fuss over the initial folds. The napkins will come out looking better in the end than you might expect, even though the first folds might not be "true."

In the directions, the fold you are to make is represented by a dotted line, and arrows show

Illus. 1. Fan.

Condensed from the book, "Folding Table Napkins" by Marianne von Bornstedt and Ulla Prytz | © *1972 by Sterling Publishing Co., Inc., New York*

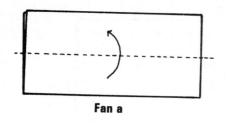

Fan a

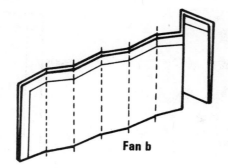

Fan b

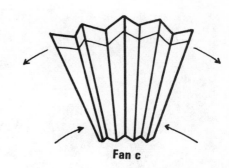

Fan c

Fan d

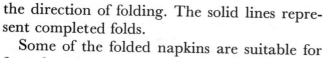

the direction of folding. The solid lines represent completed folds.

Some of the folded napkins are suitable for formal and semi-formal table service; others for informal, such as for brunch, after-dinner coffee, casual teas, buffets, snacks. There are also folds that will liven up children's parties. No matter what the occasion, you will find a unique and charming way to decorate your table with these festive folded napkins.

Fan

Fold (a) an open napkin double from bottom to top, and crease. Make another fold (a) from bottom to top. Make accordion pleats (b) from left to right. Depending upon the size of the napkin, make at least 6 pleats for a small one, 7 or 8, or more, for a larger napkin. Press pleats together firmly. Fan out the top (c) with one hand, holding the bottom pleats tightly together (c) with the other hand. Set on service plate (d). (If the Fan does not stand well enough to suit you, use two napkins together.)

Double Japanese Fan

Use together two napkins of the same size, but different colors.

After first fold (a) from bottom to top, fold two halves, one on each side, down from top to bottom (a). Make tight accordion pleats (b). Press together. Pull out valleys on both sides (c) using two open-ended pleats only. Leave closed, middle-pleated part standing upright (c). Press base and fan out top (d). Finished napkin should look like (e) from both sides.

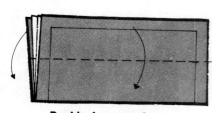

Double Japanese fan a

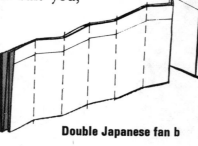

Double Japanese fan b

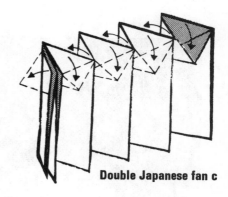

Double Japanese fan c

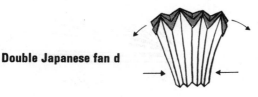

Double Japanese fan d

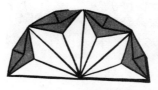

Double Japanese fan e

Illus. 2. Double Japanese fan.

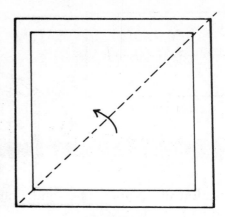

Festival a

Festival

Fold (a) open napkin diagonally from one corner to opposite corner, forming a triangle (b). Beginning at closed base, accordion-pleat (b) the triangle until it looks like (c). Then fold (c) across the middle. Press flat. The napkin will naturally fall into the shape shown in (d) when placed on plate. Or, tuck one half under service plate as in Illus. 3.

Festival b

Festival c

Illus. 3. Festival.

Festival d

Double Flute

Use two napkins of the same size but different colors (Illus. 4).

Lay one on the other so that there is a $\frac{3}{4}''$ margin on two sides (a). Fold (a) from lower left to upper right corner. There should now be an equal margin (b) on the two sides of the triangle. Roll (c) from wide base to point so that the napkin looks like a barber pole. Fold (d) across the middle and place in a glass.

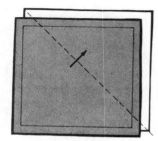

Double flute a

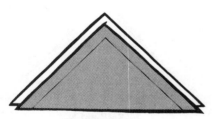

Double flute b

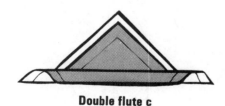

Double flute c

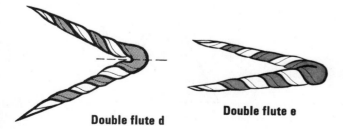

Double flute d   **Double flute e**

Illus. 4. Double flute.

Illus. 5. Sail. (This is also shown in color Illus. BB1 on page BB.)

Sail

Suitable for linen or paper napkins.

Fold (a) napkin into triangle from bottom to top. Roll up (b) from bottom to within 2″ of the top. Fold (c) from right to left. Set upright (d) on plate.

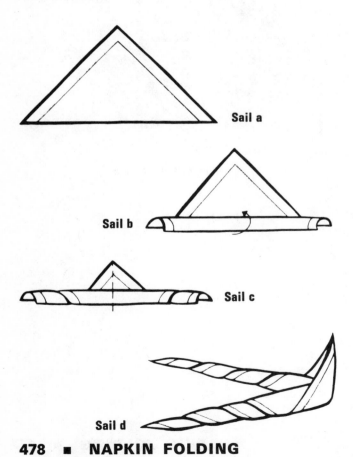

Sail a

Sail b

Sail c

Sail d

Sailboat

Fold (a) napkin twice to form ¼-size square, with open edges pointed down. Fold up (a) bottom point to meet top point. Fold in (b) sides to meet at the middle. Fold (c) bottom points back *under* and press flat. Fold back (d) napkin on the middle crease, so that it looks like (e). One by one, pull back (f) loose points so the napkin looks like (g).

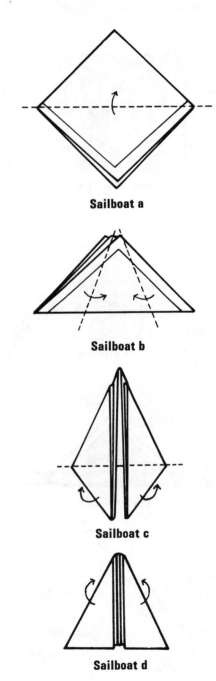

Sailboat a

Sailboat b

Sailboat c

Sailboat d

Illus. 6. Sailboat.

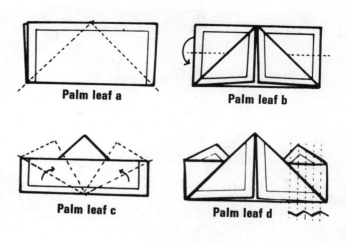

Palm leaf a

Palm leaf b

Palm leaf c

Palm leaf d

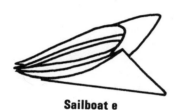

Sailboat e

Sailboat f

Sailboat g

Palm leaf e

the napkin. Turn back (c); then turn back the other corner. Turn the napkin over again. It should look like (d). Press all creases sharply. Accordion-pleat (d) from right to left. Make sure that one pleated fold is exactly in the middle of the napkin, or it will not stand straight when fanned out (e).

Palm Leaf

Suitable for paper or large linen napkins.

Fold (a) double from bottom to top. Fold (a) a single upper corner towards the middle; then other single upper corner towards the middle. Turn the napkin over. Fold down (b) entire top edge flush with bottom. Lift right-hand corner of this folded-down part and turn up (c), keeping a finger on the middle of

Illus. 7. Palm leaf.

Illus. 8. Buffet. (This is also shown in color Illus. BB3 on page BB.)

Buffet

Well suited to either linen or paper napkins. This fold can be done with either a single napkin or two same-sized, different-colored napkins. The instructions are for two napkins.

Fold (a) napkin twice into a $\frac{1}{4}$-size square, open edges on top and right side. Fold (a) down upper right corner in two thicknesses until the points are at the exact middle of the square (b). Fold (b, c) down twice more so that the napkin is cut by a diagonal. Fold (d) two more edges and tuck them into "pocket" at the middle. Fold (e) the two sides *under* so they meet in back. Place flatware inside the pocket.

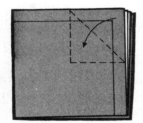

Buffet a

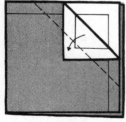

Buffet b

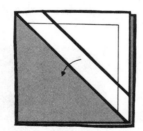

Buffet c

Buffet d

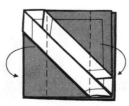

Buffet e

Buffet f

Rocket

Fold (a) napkin in half from bottom to top. Fold again (a) from bottom to top. Fold (b) two sides down so they meet in the middle. Turn (c) napkin over. Roll (d) each flap outward. Fold (e) rolls up so they meet in the middle. The napkin will look like (f). Turn over (g) and place on plate.

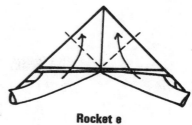

Rocket e

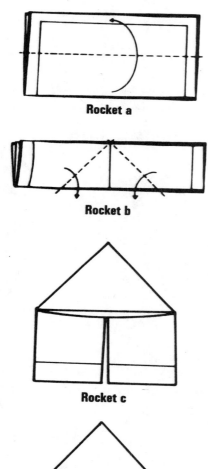

Rocket a

Rocket b

Rocket c

Rocket d

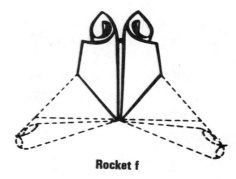

Rocket f

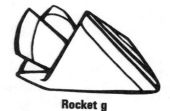

Rocket g

Illus. 9. Rocket.

Rabbit Ears

Suitable for starched linen and paper napkins.

Fold (a) open napkin from bottom to top and top to bottom so the two parts overlap exactly, forming three equal parts. Fold down (b) both top corners to meet in the middle. Fold up (c) both bottom corners to meet in the middle. Fold in (d) two lower sides to meet in the middle to look like (e). Turn napkin *over* and *upside-down* to look like (f). Fold up (f) lower triangle. Fold (g) napkin back on both sides of the middle. Fasten with staple at back. Pull rabbit ears apart a little. Spread base slightly to sit on plate.

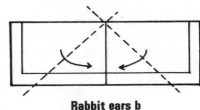

Rabbit ears b

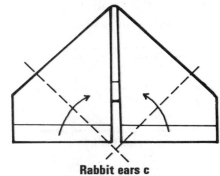

Rabbit ears c

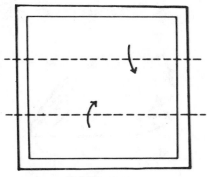

Rabbit ears a

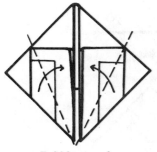

Rabbit ears d

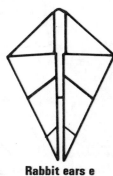

Rabbit ears e

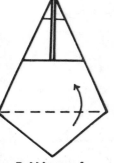

Rabbit ears f

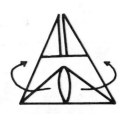

Rabbit ears g

Rabbit ears h

Illus. 10. Rabbit ears.

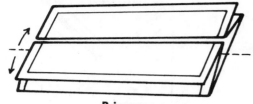

Princess a

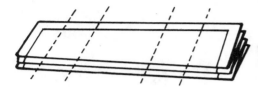

Princess b

Illus. 11. Princess. (This is also shown in color Illus. BB2 on page BB.)

Princess c

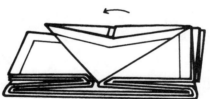

Princess d

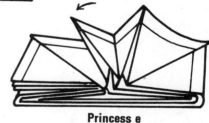

Princess e

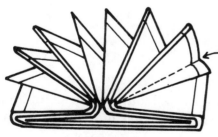

Princess f

Princess g

Princess

Suitable for paper or linen napkins.

Make two accordion pleats (a), one from the top, and one from the bottom, so they meet exactly in the middle. Fold back (a) each pleat along the exact middle so three open edges are on top (b). Accordion-pleat once (b) from both sides to meet in the middle (c). Fold top flap (d) into a triangle and press hard to crease. Make triangles (e) with each flap by reversing crease in the middle of each pleat (f), resulting in (g).

NAPKIN FOLDING ■ 483

Illus. 12. Water-lily.

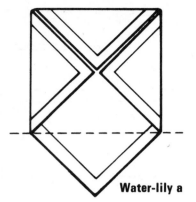

Water-lily a

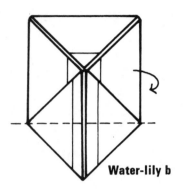

Water-lily b

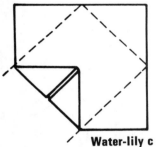

Water-lily c

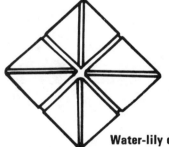

Water-lily d

Water-lily e

Water-lily f

Water-lily g

Water-Lily

Fold in (a) all four corners of an open napkin so they meet in the middle. Again fold in (b) all four new corners to join in the middle. Turn napkin over. Press flat. Fold up (c) corners to meet in the middle so it looks like (d). Press creases sharply. Hold in the middle with one hand, and, one by one, pull corner flaps on the underside up (e), punching in "mountain peaks," until all four corner flaps are up (f). Then pull single "leaf" parts up from underneath and fluff out (g). [Steps (e), (f), and (g) can also be done even more easily by placing (d) over a glass or cup before pulling.]

PEBBLE POLISHING

Pebble collecting, which was well known in our grandparents' day as a casual pastime, has come back into fashion lately in a big way. Unlike their grandmothers, who relied on skilled lapidaries to transform their finds into gems, today's collectors can polish and mount their pebbles easily, quickly and at little expense, thanks to the recent introduction of inexpensive tumble-polishing machines, epoxy resin and inexpensive jewelry findings, all of which are extremely simple to use.

If you already have a fair knowledge of the various kinds of pebbles that you may have picked up yourself, you probably do not need to do much research into the kinds of pebbles that do and do not polish well, which are hard and which are soft, which pebbles work well together in a tumble-polisher, etc. However, if you are ever in doubt, step into your nearest rock shop. For an intensive study of what pebbles to collect, where, and how to identify them, refer to the book from which this article was taken (see below).

To work efficiently, a tumble-polisher requires nothing more than connection to the household electricity, some pebbles, a suitable abrasive grit or polish and ordinary tap water. It will transform humble beach pebbles into highly polished gems with the minimum of care and attention. Epoxy resin is simply strong, permanent glue, and modern jewelry findings come in a variety of shapes and sizes.

Illus. 1. These are some of the items you can make with your polished pebbles.

Photo by Joe Rothstein

Condensed from the book, "Pebble Collecting and Polishing" by Edward Fletcher | © 1972 by Blandford Press Ltd., and © 1973 by Sterling Publishing Co., Inc., New York. Photographs in color section provided by Joe Rothstein

Illus. 2. Left, a natural quartz crystal; above right, a natural quartz crystal that has been sea-worn for centuries; below right, what a tumble-polisher will do to a natural quartz crystal in three weeks.

Tumble-Polishing Machines

You have certainly seen Nature's tumbler at work if you have stood on a beach and watched the rhythmical forces which are constantly at work near the water's edge. It is this same wearing-down-to-smoothness process which a tumble-polishing machine is designed to reproduce and speed up. Instead of the irresistible force of breaking waves, its energy derives from a small electric motor which turns rollers on which a barrel containing pebbles is placed. Inside the barrel, silicon carbide grits take the place of sands on the beach. As the barrel revolves, these grits wear down the roughened surfaces on each pebble to perfect smoothness. Unlike the sand on a beach, the grits in the tumbler can be carefully graded from very coarse to exceedingly fine. This means that the wearing-down process can be controlled and the smoothing process carried to a degree of perfection impossible to achieve with sand grains.

Polishing agents, introduced into the barrel during the final stages of the process, impart a mirror-finish to each pebble. Unlike wet beach pebbles, which lose their shine as soon as they dry out, correctly tumble-polished pebbles retain their beauty forever.

The first step is to acquire an efficient, reliable tumbling machine. Machines come in a wide variety of shapes and sizes; making the right choice can be tricky without some knowledge of the way in which the machine works and the job which each component in the machine must do.

A typical tumble-polisher consists of an electric motor which drives a pulley connected via a belt or some other method of drive to one of two parallel rollers. On these rollers a barrel containing the stones to be polished and a suitable abrasive or polish is made to revolve at a predetermined speed for a number of

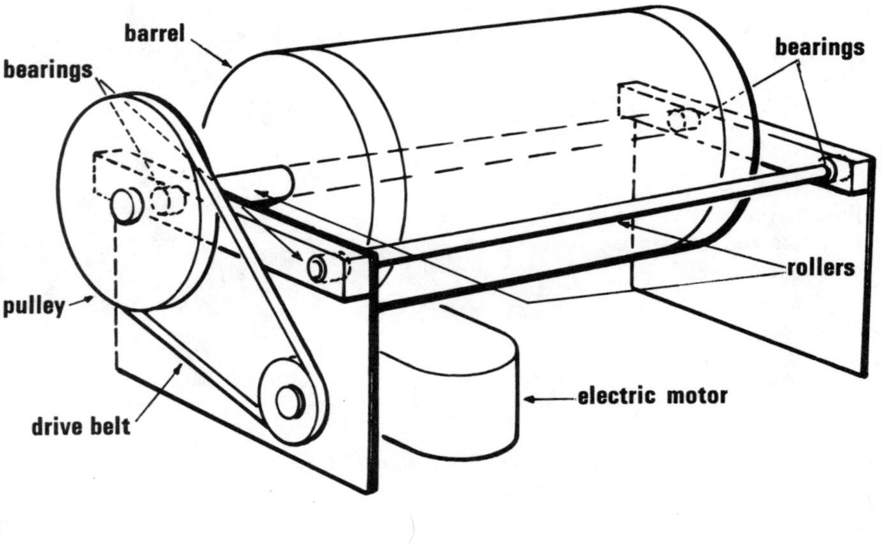

Illus. 3. A good tumble-polishing machine must: (1) have a reliable motor; (2) have a strong pulley and drive belt, or other driving method; (3) have tough, hard-wearing rollers; (4) have efficient bearings; (5) be easy to lubricate and maintain; (6) have a strong, leakproof, easy-to-clean barrel.

barrel

bearings

bearings

pulley

rollers

drive belt

electric motor

days. During this period the abrasives in the barrel are changed at regular intervals, each change being to a finer abrasive, until the polishing stage is reached and the pebbles are ready for making into jewelry.

The whole process takes several days and during that time the electric motor must run continuously. A twenty-day cycle, for example, requires 480 hours non-stop running on the part of the motor. So, it is of the utmost importance that the motor is reliable.

Let's look at five typical tumble-polishing machines with barrels of different sizes and consider their relative merits:

Tumble Capacity	Barrels	Advantages	Disadvantages
1½ lbs.	One, taking approximately 100 pebbles.	Inexpensive; easy to fill; very economical on grits and polish.	Can only tumble one load of hard or soft pebbles in one three-week cycle; limitation on pebble size.
3 lbs.	One, taking approximately 200 pebbles.	Will take *some* larger pebbles.	Can only tumble one load of hard or soft pebbles in one three-week cycle.
3 lbs.	Two, taking approximately 100 pebbles each.	Can polish hard and soft pebbles at the same time in separate barrels.	Limitations on pebble size.
6 lbs.	Three, one taking approximately 200 pebbles; two taking approximately 100 pebbles each.	Extremely versatile; large total capacity, but can also be used for tumbling small loads. Can grind hard and soft pebbles, and polish a third batch at the same time.	More expensive than any above.
12 lbs.	One, taking approximately 800 pebbles.	Will polish larger pebbles. Ideal for commercial use.	Difficult to fill owing to large capacity; can only tumble one load or hard or soft pebbles in one three-week period. Expensive.

Whatever your choice—large, small or in-between—you are strongly advised against metal barrels unless they are adequately lined on the inside with hard-wearing rubber. Chemical reactions which produce gas can be set up in an unlined metal barrel if it is filled with pebbles, water and abrasive and made to revolve for any length of time on a machine. If you *must* use metal, make absolutely sure that the lining seals off as much of the inner surface of the barrel as is possible from contact with grits, water and pebbles.

Plastic barrels are almost problem-free as far as gas is concerned. There is no reaction between acids and metal in plastic barrels and the small amount of gas which is generated by

Illus. 6. A large tumbler
with two, one-and-a-half-
pound barrels.

grinding pebbles in water is dissipated when the lid is removed for regular inspection of the pebbles during the polishing process. Some recently introduced barrels have safety valves built in to provide a suitable gas vent.

Perfect Polishing

The first important question to settle is where you are going to keep your machine. It makes a certain amount of noise so do not choose a bedroom. Next, consider where you least mind a bit of mess. Remember you will be filling and emptying the barrels with pebbles, water, grits, and polish many times during the machine's life.

Finally, has the spot you have selected a nearby electric outlet where you can safely plug in your machine? You do not want yards of cord lying around to be tripped over. Find a place at about table-top height where you can get at the machine comfortably to change grits, inspect barrels, oil bearings, etc. Last, make sure you wire it correctly and make the ground connection. Tumblers are perfectly safe to run from the household electricity supply but remember you are using water in the process. To disregard safety measures which the manufacturer has built into the machine would be very foolish.

Grits and Polish

Silicon carbide is a man-made abrasive substance which is extremely hard—many, many times harder than the toughest pebble. It also has the advantage of forming, when made, into wedge-shaped grains, which makes it an excellent grinding material.

When manufactured by heating and then crushing a mixture of silica sand, carbon, salt and sawdust, it is then graded by being passed through a series of fine mesh screens. The No. 80 grit with which almost all tumble-polishing starts gets its name from the fact that it has passed through a screen with 80 meshes to the inch.

You may buy two or three grades of silicon carbide, depending on the manufacturer's instructions. The coarse grit has the *lowest*

Illus. 7. Grinding and polishing compounds, ranging from very coarse (left) to finest (right).

number and the finer the grit, the higher its grade number. Some manufacturers recommend mixed grades which gradually break down inside the barrel and these are excellent if the manufacturer's instructions are followed.

The two most common polishes are cerium oxide and tin oxide and you should use whichever the manufacturer recommends.

These are not grinding materials. Their purpose is to add a permanent polish to the perfectly smooth pebbles you have produced in the earlier stages. No amount of polishing will remove any roughness you allow to remain on your pebbles after grinding. If there *is* roughness, you have not ground your pebbles long enough and you will merely waste polish if you do not put matters right by going back to an earlier grinding stage.

Last-Minute Checks

Your tumbler should have reached you in perfect condition, but you should check carefully before you switch on, especially if it reached you by mail. Check that it has been oiled and that the rollers are parallel and there are no obvious signs that the machine has received a severe blow in transit. There should be no loose wires hanging about and the belt should sit squarely in the grooves on the pulleys. If all seems well, plug in and switch on. The drive roller will turn much faster without a load and you should allow the machine to run for a few minutes like this. All moving parts should turn smoothly. If you hear odd scraping noises or if the rollers turn intermittently, something is wrong. Switch off at once and check your plug wiring and the manufacturer's instructions. If the machine does run smoothly, you can load your barrels.

Loading Your Barrels

Take the lid off one of your barrels and look inside. The inner walls should be perfectly smooth. If your barrels are metal and have rubber linings, make sure that the lining is correctly fitted and there are no bulges or loose seams. If the lid is fitted with a gasket or rubber seal, this too should be correctly seated.

You should have already sorted your pebbles into hard and soft groups, so start with your hard ones. Now is the time to discard badly cracked specimens. The first grind is tough

Illus. 8. Here is a good variety of pebbles, both in size and shape.

Illus. 9. This is a proper load for a barrel—approximately three quarters full. Overloading and underloading both result in failure.

and cracked specimens won't survive. For a one-and-a-half pound barrel you will need approximately one hundred pebbles, the largest not more than one inch across; the smallest approximately a quarter of an inch. Try to select a range of shapes—ovals, spheres, discs—because the grinding action is more efficient when different shapes are mixed together.

A three-pound barrel will require approximately two hundred pebbles and you will be able to include half a dozen larger specimens—up to a maximum size of two inches. Similarly, larger barrels will take more pebbles with a proportionate number of big ones. All, however, require a grading of sizes from large to small, with plenty of variety in shape. The tumbling action depends on there being sufficient space inside the barrel to allow the pebbles to fall, one over the next, as the barrel revolves.

Too much space and too few pebbles is just as bad as overfilling. If you do not put sufficient pebbles into the barrel, they do not ride up the walls to the point where tumbling commences. They slide back to the bottom and

all you get out of the barrel are badly polished, flattened discs. A little under three quarters full of pebbles of different shapes and sizes should be your aim. This applies to any size of barrel. Place the pebbles inside gently. Shake the barrel gently to settle them as you put them in and stop when you near the three-quarters-full point.

It is helpful to keep a simple progress chart so that you can record the dates and times you commence and finish different stages in the process, together with comments on results achieved. This information will prove invaluable when next you polish a batch of similar pebbles and you wish to try variations in grinding and polishing times in an effort to better your previous results. Keeping such records and retaining a few pebbles from each batch for comparisons will very soon lead you to perfection in polishing.

The First Grind

After loading your barrel with pebbles, add coarse silicon carbide. The amount of grit depends on the barrel's capacity. A one-and-a-half-pound barrel requires a heaping

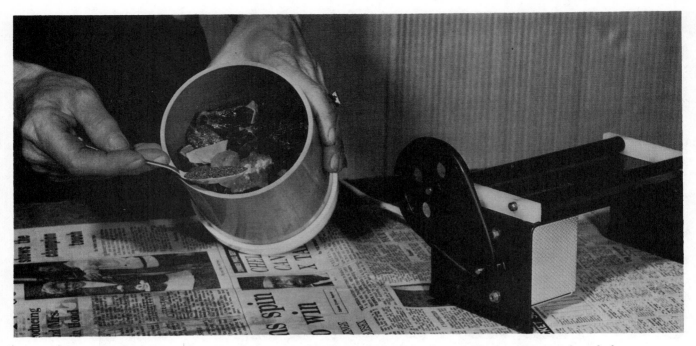

Illus. 10. Add the amount of coarse silicon carbide recommended by the manufacturer for your barrel size.

tablespoonful, while a three-pound barrel requires twice that amount. Check the manufacturer's instructions for other barrel sizes and act accordingly. Never put too much or too little grit into the barrel as this will upset the grinding process. Use a clean, dry spoon to measure the amount required and shake it evenly over the pebbles in the barrel.

Avoid contaminating the grits and polish, especially by getting any of the coarse grit into the finer material or polish. Use old metal cookie or tea canisters or similar containers as holders for your materials. Label the tins.

Next, run tap water into the barrel until it just covers the top of the pebbles. Don't *fill* the barrel with water. Stop as soon as you see the water cover the pebbles and put the lid on the barrel. You must replace the lid so that it forms a watertight fit on the barrel. Some lids will screw on; others will be a push fit; and some will be fixed by nuts and bolts. If grains of grit remain on the lid or the part of the barrel which comes into contact with the lid, they will not fit correctly. Wipe this area carefully before putting the lid in place and read the manufacturer's instructions for

achieving a watertight fit before putting the barrel on the rollers. When you have the lid on, wipe the outside of the barrel to remove water and grit and check that water is not leaking around the cap. If all is well, switch on the tumbler and place the barrel onto the turning rollers. The rollers will immediately slow down under the weight of the barrel but should settle down at once to a steady speed of revolution. Watch the barrel for a minute or two, checking for a steady rotation and no water leaks.

Listen to the sound of the pebbles as they grind. The pebbles should be tumbling or rolling one over the next as they near the top of the barrel in a continuous, rhythmical motion. If you hear bangs and knocks, or the sound of pebbles falling and hitting each other, something is wrong. You have not put sufficient pebbles into the barrel, or you have put too many of the wrong size. If you hear little or no movement you have put too many pebbles into the barrel and the tumbling action is not operating.

Now you must allow the barrel to turn on the rollers for the next twenty-four hours without interruption. When twenty-four hours has passed take the barrel off and carefully open the lid. You will probably find it easier to switch off the motor when removing the barrel during the first days, but you should soon get the knack of lifting the barrel cleanly and neatly from the rollers without stopping the machine—and replacing it just as expertly when you have finished your inspection.

You should see a dark grey liquid (slurry). Working over a sink, and with the tap turned on, carefully lift out half a dozen pebbles. Shake off as much of the slurry as possible before moving them clear of the barrel. Put the barrel to one side and run the pebbles you have removed under the tap to wash away all traces of the slurry. Now examine the washed pebbles carefully. Already they will feel smoother to your fingers, but they have a long way to go to perfection. Select one of the pebbles and dry it carefully. Now examine it under a good light and you will see the tiny pits and cracks on its surface.

Back into the barrel it must go, along with the others you removed. Wash the lid and the top of the barrel to remove all traces of grit and replace the lid as you did before. Once you are satisfied that you have a watertight seal, switch on the tumbler and replace the barrel on the rollers. Again, watch it for a minute or two to check for leaks. If all is well, wait another day and repeat the inspection.

You must decide when your pebbles are ready for the next stage. Fairly smooth beach pebbles composed mainly of quartz will take between three and six days to grind to the required smoothness. If you continue coarse grinding until the worst pebble in the barrel is perfectly smooth, the remainder will be too much reduced in size. Indeed, the smallest could be ground away completely if you allowed the first stage to go on too long.

When four or five of the half-dozen pebbles you remove for inspection satisfy you with their smoothness and blemish-free appearance, it is time to call a halt. Remove all the pebbles

Illus. 11. Add just enough water to cover the pebbles. Do it slowly so you will not have to pour off any excess or you will reduce the quantity of grit as well.

Illus. 12. At the end of the first stage, the pebbles should be perfectly smooth. Place them in a colander and wash thoroughly under running water.

from the barrel and place them in the sink with the tap running. (A colander is an excellent container for the pebbles.) Wash away all traces of grit. Never pour the sludge in the barrel down the drain. It will very quickly block your drains.

The Second Grind

Now, before the second grind, carefully weed out every pebble that has a bad pit, blemish, or crack. So little grinding takes place during the second stage that any deep imperfections cannot be removed. Next, check that your tumbler is working correctly, and that your barrel is absolutely clean and free from all traces of coarse grit, then load it once more to just less than three quarters full with pebbles. Add the correct amount of finer grit to the barrel and then cover the

pebbles with water again. Secure the cap, after carefully cleaning it, and place the loaded barrel onto the rollers once more.

This second stage in the tumbling process is the most important of all. During the first two or three days, the fine silicon carbide continues the grinding process begun by the coarse grit. Scratches and tiny imperfections are gradually worn away. It is at this point that the real work of the second stage begins. The fine grit starts to break down. It loses its power to remove scratches and pit marks and now prepares the pebble for the final polish. It is of great importance to continue the second stage until the pebbles are ready for polishing. If necessary, run this stage twice as long as the coarse grind.

Check progress daily by opening the barrel and carefully washing half a dozen pebbles before examining their surfaces. Look for absolute smoothness over the entire surface of each pebble. The smallest pitmarks will ruin the final polish, so examine your samples very, very carefully. At the end of this stage the pebbles should look exactly as they will when polished—except for their lack of shine. A matt finish probably best describes what you must aim for. You can begin to expect it five or six days after commencing your second stage.

If you think that your samples are ready, take a small piece of felt and soak it under the tap. Next, sprinkle half a teaspoonful of your polishing powder onto the wet felt. Take one of your sample pebbles firmly between finger and thumb and rub it vigorously backwards and forwards over the impregnated felt 40 or 50 times. Now, carefully dry the area of pebble you have polished and examine it in good light. Look for tiny pin pricks or scratches on the polished surface. If you see

even one, you must continue the second stage for at least another 24 hours before test-polishing another pebble. (However, under no circumstances should you add more fine grit to the barrel. Fresh silicon carbide would only scratch the pebbles.) If you are quite satisfied that the surface you have polished is perfect, the second stage is complete.

The Final Polish

You now have a batch of unpolished but perfectly smooth pebbles. Handle them very carefully at this stage. Don't pour them from one container to another. When washing them to remove every trace of silicon carbide, don't allow them to knock one against the other. The smallest scratch or chip will show up when they are polished.

Make sure that the barrel you are going to use is absolutely clean. Place the pebbles carefully inside, one at a time, until just under three quarters full. There will have been little

Illus. 13. Before the second grind, inspect the pebbles carefully for quality.

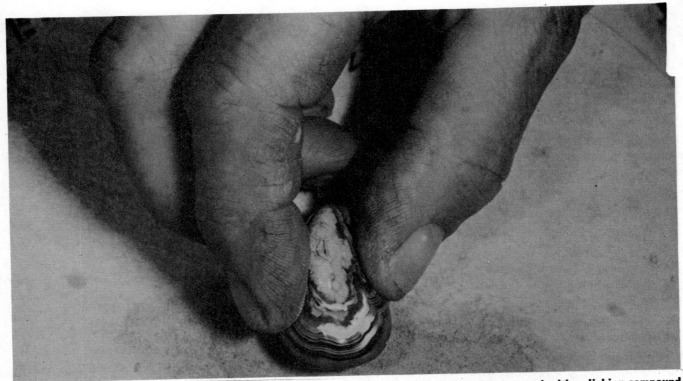

Illus. 14. After a few days on the second grind, test-polish one pebble on a piece of felt impregnated with polishing compound.

reduction in volume during the second stage because so little grinding takes place. If you had the correct load at the beginning of the second stage you should have just the right amount now.

Add the correct amount of polish to the barrel. Cover the pebbles with clean water, replace the cap, make sure that everything is clinically clean, and return the barrel to the rollers.

During this final stage pay particular attention to the sound of your pebbles as they tumble. A steady and rhythmical motion inside the barrel will produce the steady and rhythmical sound of pebbles tumbling one over the next. Any harsh banging or un-rhythmical striking of pebbles together is a sure sign that the tumbling action is not being carried out. If this is allowed to happen during the polishing stage, it will certainly produce cracks and scratches on the pebbles' surfaces.

The commonest cause of cracks and scratches at this stage is an insufficient load. With too few pebbles in the barrel, the load is thrown about violently, causing one pebble to strike against the next so harshly that cracks and scratches are the inevitable result. If you do hear irregular sounds during the first twenty-four hours of the polishing stage, remedy the situation at once.

Remove the barrel from the rollers, take off the lid, and add a small amount of wallpaper paste to the mixture, to thicken the liquid in the barrel so that it cushions the fall of each pebble. A *thin*-cream consistency is ideal. The addition of the paste will reduce the noise your pebbles make as they tumble. It also increases the time you must allow for the polish to do its work. A polishing stage of four days without paste might take seven days if paste is added. Do not add paste during the earlier grinding stages unless you are prepared to accept very long first and second stages.

Daily inspection of your pebbles is just as important at the polishing stage as it is during grinding so do not neglect it. The process should take from four to seven days to complete but only experience will tell you when the polish has done its work. Daily inspection, your log book, and experience will guide you. If you examine half a dozen pebbles each day and stop the process on the day you see no improvement on the previous day's polish, your results should be satisfactory.

The polishing powder leaves a film on the pebbles which is removed by placing the pebbles in the cleaned barrel, covering with water, and adding not more than half a tea-spoonful of detergent to break down the surface tension of the water. Run the barrel for four to eight hours, then remove the pebbles very carefully and wash off the detergent in running water. Place all the pebbles on a soft cloth and allow them to dry.

If you keep a careful log of all your tumbling for three or four months, you should certainly be able to achieve perfection at the end of that time. Experiment with longer or shorter runs, different amounts of grit and polish, and pebbles of different hardnesses. For quick guidance, following is a list of common faults and suggested causes.

Fault	Possible cause
Machine runs intermittently, or stops	Badly wired plug; lubrication of bearings not carried out; oil on drive belt or rollers.
Pebbles still rough after first and second grind	Overloaded barrel; insufficient grit; barrel slipping on rollers; hard and soft pebbles mixed.
Pebbles badly cracked after first grind	Underloaded barrel; poor specimens.
Inferior polish	Second stage grind not long enough; insufficient polish; hard and soft pebbles mixed in barrel.
Flats develop on pebbles	Underloaded barrel; speed of revolution too slow.
Leaking barrel	Caps not fitted correctly; grit particles not removed from cap or barrel.

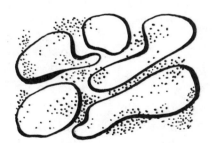

Illus. 15. A variety of shapes and sizes is the key to success when selecting pebbles or rocks for the tumbler. The small stones grind into the hollows of the large ones.

POTATO PRINTING

Illus. 1. This was made with a simple, triangular stencil.

You will be astonished at the variety and quality of prints you can attain from simple potato stamps. For instance, by limiting yourself to only one geometric form and one color you will recognize that the empty space—the unprinted area—really acts as a second color. Once you see this, you can begin to utilize more than one color and more than one form.

The value of potato printing is that it is a simple, economical way of decorating a variety of paper or fabric objects. You can print gift wrappings, napkins, aprons, blouses, neckties, greeting cards, stationery, and anything else your imagination seizes upon. The possibilities are unlimited. The materials you need are very easy to obtain and the technique is essentially a simple one.

Materials and Methods

Potatoes: First, peel and clean a few fresh, raw potatoes thoroughly. Have your colors handy.

Colors: For printing on paper, all water colors, tempera, and poster paints are suitable. You can also use lino-print colors. For fabric printing, use permanent colors.

Paper: You may use a variety of paper—absorbent paper, like typewriting paper, also unprinted newspaper (newsprint), transparent paper, light-colored cardboard, and so on.

Fabrics: Textiles such as cotton, linen, and silk give good printing results, but fabrics of coarse texture do not.

Other Equipment: You will need a sharp kitchen knife for shaping your potato stamp, or, for finer incisions, a razor blade in a holder. To apply colors, use a camel's-hair brush about $\frac{1}{2}''$ wide. If you use lino-print colors, use a small linoleum print roller to spread the color on a glass pane. Apply lino colors to the potato stamp either with the roller or by pressing the stamp against the painted glass. Keep a jar of water nearby to rinse the brushes.

Work Room: For working space, cover a table with newspaper to prevent staining.

Cutting the Stencil: Cut a potato into a handy

Condensed from the book, "Potato Printing" by Susanne Strose | © 1968 by Sterling Publishing Co., Inc., New York

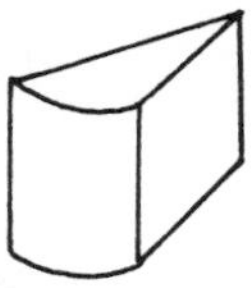

Illus. 2. Cut a triangular stencil like this . . .

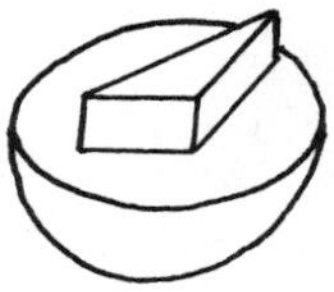

Illus. 3. . . . and not like this.

Illus. 4. For fine lines, cut your stencil like this . . .

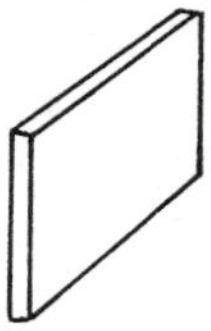

Illus. 5. . . . and not like this.

size so that you can grip it easily. Cut a whole piece of potato in the shape of your design so the potato stamps will print clearly and not overlap when placed side-by-side in the design (Illus. 2–Illus. 5).

The stamp, while it will give many impres-

sions, will not last indefinitely. You will have to cut fresh stencils each day and also a separate stencil for each color you apply, as the potato is porous and retains color.

Stencilling: Dip your brush into the paint and cover the flat stencilling surface of your stamp in even strokes. Whether you work with water color, tempera or lino color, always see to it that you apply your paint evenly to the stamp.

Just for fun, convert a rectangle or square to a different, simple form by cutting out a triangular shape.

Illus. 6 shows some of the many different designs hidden in such a modified pattern. You can improvise even more designs than those displayed here.

Lettering with Potatoes

Now, try to letter design stamps to reproduce the alphabet for monograms, and so on.

Cut large chunks of equal size out of your potatoes. Trace the letters on the surface area

Illus. 6. Various designs you can make by modifying a rectangle.

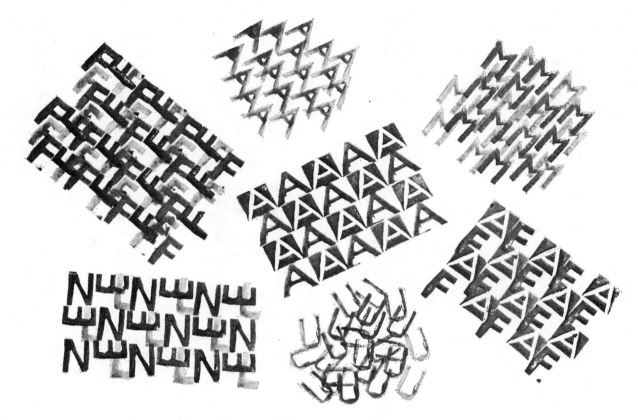

Illus. 7. Letters make interesting designs when printed.

Illus. 8. Printed papers make unique wrappings for a variety of items.

and remove all extraneous matter. Remember to cut all your letters in reverse, as reflected in a mirror. A "C" would be cut this way: Ɔ.

For variation in design, cut negative (or reverse) letters—that is, ones in which the surrounding area will print the color, leaving the letter itself white. You can easily achieve this by carving the letter deeply into the surrounding surface with a sharp tool, like a knife or razor blade.

If you want to print words with precision on a straight line, always use a ruler, and set the potato stamps in measures along its length.

Printed Papers

Paper stamped with small stars is an example of what you can use for Christmas wrapping. It is especially easy to glue your finished paper

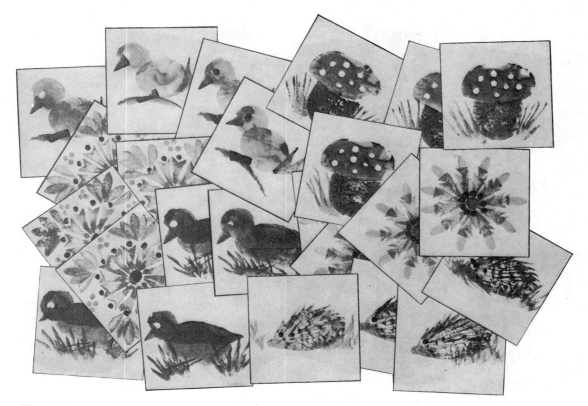

Illus. 9. Potato printing is a most suitable craft for making greeting cards or cards for various games.

Illus. 10. Delicate flowers are easy to print with potatoes.

to cartons and boxes. You can do the same on book jackets and album covers.

Covers for schoolbooks and exercise books are a bit more complicated if you intend to print the title over the already existing book cover, because you must adapt your own lettering in such a way that it does not clash with the underlying color and composition of the original. Several attempts may be necessary before you find the right one.

Flowers and Leaves

You can print bunches of flowers or tree leaves on postcards, onto the corners of napkins, or make up a calendar. Each month on the calendar could show a flower particular to that time of the year. You might print days and months in by hand underneath.

Printed Fabrics

For potato printing fabrics you need permanent colors which do not run or wash out in the laundry. Pour some color over a cloth you have folded several times; then spread the color carefully with a brush or knife. Now, press your potato stamps on this "stamp pad" and color them evenly.

Next, cover a drawing board with newspaper and fasten your fabric over it with thumbtacks. Stencil the fabric with your colored potato stamp. You must proceed with caution because spots and stains cannot be removed.

After you complete the coloring, take the material off the drawing board and iron it on the unprinted side. Now your fabric is colorfast and you can wash it without worrying that your work will fade or run.

Illus. 12. You can print on cloth to make anything from napkins and table mats, to aprons, smocks, bibs and scarves. You need much patience, however, to find and create the right patterns for such complicated items.

SCREEN PRINTING

The basic principle of screen printing, also called silk screen printing, is simple to understand: imagine a series of finely meshed screens of fabric stretched tightly over wooden frames. You either paint stencils on the screens with a special liquid, or cut them from stencil paper and attach them to the screens with an adhesive. Ink is rapidly forced through the screen with a rubber squeegee, similar to the implement which a window washer uses, to color both the screen and the printing surface beneath the screen. The stencils block the ink from coming through certain places on the screen, leaving portions of the printing surface free of ink. The pattern which is printed in the screen process is what you have stencilled as a design.

The visual effects you can obtain from screen printing are almost unlimited. You can make screen prints with sharp outlines and fine lines, simulating linoleum or wood block prints and pen-and-ink drawings. Or, by using liquid adhesives which you paint on the screen and then partially dissolve, you can produce a grained effect similar to a lithograph, with shading and soft edges round the areas of color. Even more versatility is possible because of the large number of materials on which you can make screen prints: paper and fabric are the most common, but with the proper inks, it is possible to print on wood, glass, leather, metal, plastic, and even foam rubber. And all in any number of different colors.

Illus. 1. In screen printing, soft areas of shading as well as solid areas with sharp edges are possible. "Child's Head" shows both techniques. You can also make sharp outlines and very fine lines.

The Frame and Screen

You can buy the equipment for screen printing already assembled in a variety of sizes. However, for greater flexibility, buy the frames by themselves. By placing push-pin hinges the same distance apart and in the exact same position on all your frames, you can easily remove and attach different-sized frames on a single printing base. With the complete printing unit, you are restricted to one frame. (You can also build a frame from scratch. For

Condensed from the book, "Screen Printing" by Heinrich Birkner | © 1971 by Sterling Publishing Co., Inc., New York

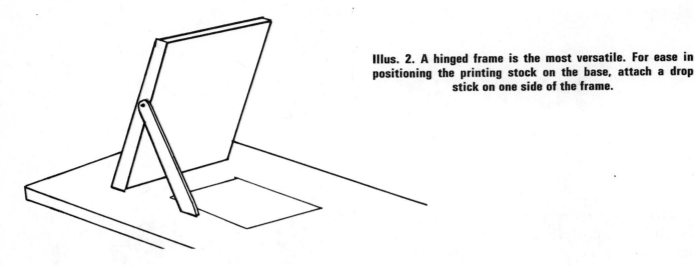

Illus. 2. A hinged frame is the most versatile. For ease in positioning the printing stock on the base, attach a drop stick on one side of the frame.

instructions see the book *Screen Printing*, by Heinrich Birkner, published by Sterling Publishing Co.)

You will need one more attachment on the hinged frame: a device to hold up the frame while you are positioning the printing stock on the base. The easiest method is to attach an arm or drop stick to one side of the frame (Illus. 2).

Making the Squeegee

The squeegee forces the ink through the finely meshed screen onto the stock. Like all the other equipment required for screen printing, squeegees can be bought in many shapes and sizes. The width of the design you are printing determines what size squeegee to use: the squeegee should be at least 1″ wider than the art. If it is too narrow, two strokes will be necessary and a streak will show where the strokes overlap.

If you cannot find the right size squeegee, you can make one fairly easily. You will need a rubber strip for the blade. If you can get white rubber, the chances of discoloring the printing inks are less than with black rubber. Polyurethane costs about three times what plain rubber does, but it is worth it—it has the correct amount of spring, wears down slowly, is easy to clean, and is unaffected by most paints and solvents. Polyurethane is manu-

factured in strips $2'' \times \frac{1}{4}''$ and $2'' \times \frac{3}{8}''$, and is sold by the inch. For squeegees which are longer than 1 foot, use the thicker polyurethane.

Buy three pieces of plywood, all the same length as the rubber strip. Two pieces should be about 3″ wide and one about 2″ wide, or wide enough so that 1″ of the rubber strip will extend beyond the plywood (see Illus. 3).

Sandwich the narrow piece of plywood between the other two pieces, flush at one side, and insert the polyurethane strip inside this sandwich so that about 1″ of it extends beyond the plywood. Join all the pieces with waterproof glue and short nails or tacks.

After many uses, the polyurethane blade will wear down, leaving a thicker deposit of

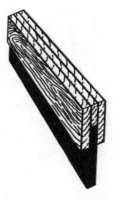

Illus. 3. A squeegee is very easy to make from three pieces of plywood and a rubber strip. If you want you can also attach a handle, although it is not necessary.

Illus. 4. Pull the squeegee across the screen in one long, straight, continuous motion towards you.

ink than you want on the print and a blurry outline of the subject. To sharpen the blade, rub the edge against a sheet of medium emery or garnet paper which is glued to a flat board.

Clean your squeegee after every use; paint that is allowed to dry on it will eventually corrode the polyurethane. When not using the squeegee, rest it flat on its side, not propped up on the blade end.

Making Stencils

This section details how to make and use four different kinds of stencils—cut-paper, hand-cut film, liquid block-out, and tusche-glue stencils.

The best place to make your stencils is in a well lit room, at room temperature. A nearby sink with running water is also necessary.

The Cut-Paper Stencil

This stencil produces a print with sharp, clear lines, since, as its name indicates, the

stencils are cut from paper. You can make either a positive print, where the design itself appears as color on the printing surface, or a negative print, where the background is color and the design itself is white.

Draw the outline of your design directly on the paper you will use as the stencil. Thin paper is best: newsprint (unprinted newspaper) is good, and poster paper is even better. Do not use coated paper, however. An important point to realize is that the thickness of the ink on the printing surface will be equal to the thickness of the paper stencil plus the screen. The printing surface is distant from the ink in the screen by this amount, so when the ink is forced through the screen, it fills up the thickness. A thick layer of ink, or impasto as it is called, sometimes looks attractive but it takes a long time to dry.

For cutting the stencil, a professional stencil-cutter's knife is worth the investment. It has a thin, narrow blade which makes very fine, detailed cuts. To keep the blade sharp, hone it on a fine-grain oil stone. Be very careful not to get oil on the screen.

Position the paper stencil on top of a sheet of paper or other printing stock and under the screen. The ink will then bind the paper stencil to the screen. (See page 514, "The Printing Process.")

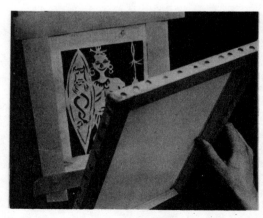

Illus. 5. Lay the cut-out on paper and cover it with the empty screen. The white figure is the silhouette that was cut and the black area is the paper.

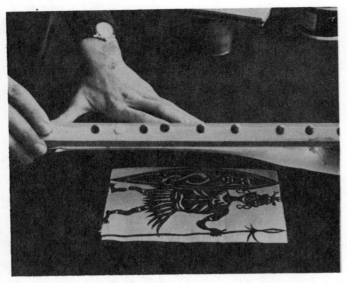

Illus. 6. When you lift the screen up after pulling your first proof, the paper stencil will adhere to the screen. The paper falling from the screen here is gummed paper which held the printing stock to the printing base (see Illus. 5).

Illus. 7. If you did not make a complete print, put the screen down again and try to cover the areas you skipped. Before you move the first piece of stock, mark the printing base with pencil or tape to show where the edges of the next paper must lie.

There are obvious advantages to this method of making stencils. Paper is usually available, and is easy to cut. Cleaning the screen of the stencil when you are finished printing is extremely easy: as you wash the screen with water to get rid of the ink, the paper stencil will come off also, and the screen will be ready for another stencil.

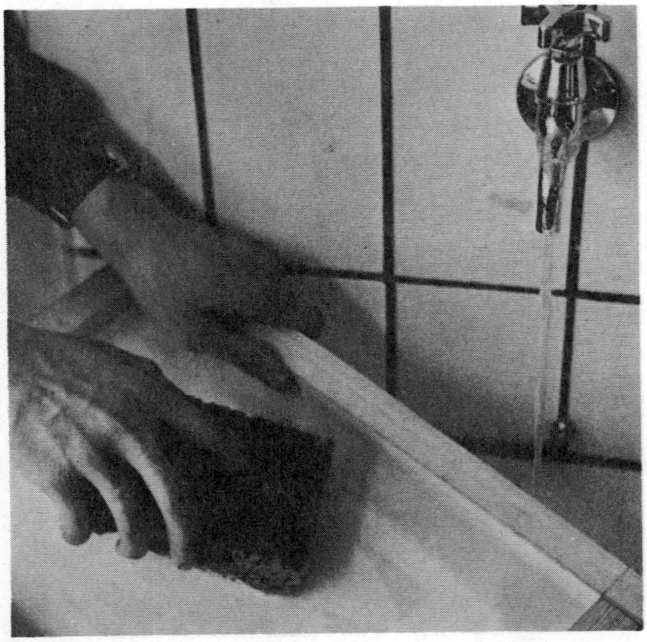

You cannot re-use paper stencils later; the entire print run must be made at one time. Also, some oil-based paints will be absorbed by the stencil, producing fuzzy lines after only about 50 prints. Still, for the beginning screen printer the cut-paper stencil is satisfactory.

The Hand-Cut Film Stencil

The hand-cut film stencil is made of special laminated paper sheets, available at craft shops, from which you cut your design. The sheets have two layers attached together with a temporary adhesive. The first layer is a thin, translucent stencil sheet, and the second layer is a thicker backing sheet made of tissue paper coated with wax. The stencil paper (sold under the brand names of Stenplex in England, and Nu-film or Profilm in the United States) is thin enough to be transparent, so you will be able to see your pencilled design through the paper.

Illus. 8. To clean the screen after using a cut-paper stencil, wash the ink off with water or another solvent. The stencil will fall off when there is no more ink to hold it.

Before you attach the stencil to the screen, you must prepare the screen. For silk screens, simply sponge with hot water and detergent, rinse with cold water, and set the screen aside to dry.

Cut a piece of the laminated sheet larger than your design by 1½″ on all sides. Lay this sheet over the design film-side up, and tape it at the edges, to keep it from moving. With a stencil-cutting knife, the same one you used for cut-paper stencils, cut around your design *through the top layer only.* Lift off each piece of the top layer as you cut it.

The method of fastening the stencil to the screen (the stencil itself consists of the remainder of the thin upper layer attached to the laminated backing sheet) depends on what

Illus. 10. After cutting the entire design, lift out the portions which are to be left open on the screen.

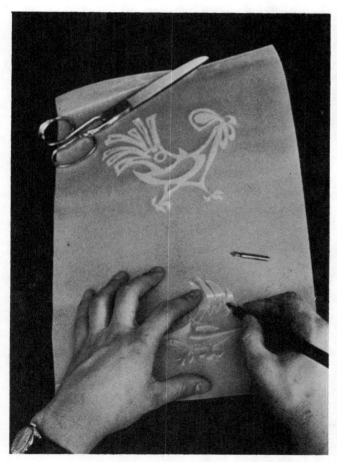

Illus. 9. Be sure your knife is sharp when cutting a film stencil. A dull blade will make you use too much pressure which presses the two layers together and hinders secure adhesion to the screen.

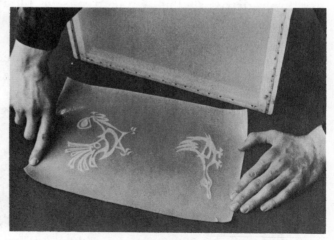

Illus. 11. Place the laminated sheet under the frame, making sure that it is positioned exactly. If there are any very large areas where the film has been removed, cut a small slit through the backing sheet. The slit allows air to escape.

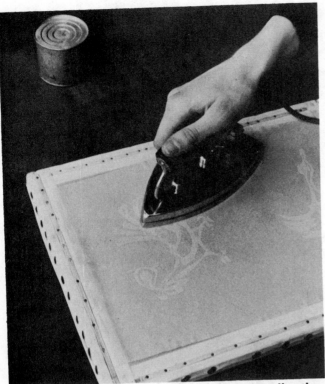

Illus. 12. Iron first through newsprint and then directly on the amber sheets. If you are working with green or blue sheets, use a combination of moisture and heat, or the manufacturer's special solvent.

Removing the amber film from the screen after printing is simple. Wash the printing ink completely from the screen (you can use water-based inks, since shellac is not soluble in water). Then flood the screen with alcohol, cover it with a sheet of clean newsprint, and let it soak for 15 minutes. The alcohol dissolves the shellac, so the stencil can be washed off after soaking. Rub the screen with cotton soaked in alcohol to make sure all the shellac is removed.

Blue and green film stencils adhere to the screen with water, because their glue is soluble in water. (Therefore, you cannot use these stencils with water-based inks.) To attach the blue stencil to the screen, dip a rag in cold water and squeeze it as dry as you can. Place the screen over the stencil and rub the inside of the screen with the damp rag, thus slightly moistening the stencil film. Lay a sheet of clean newsprint on the inside of the screen, and iron this quickly and lightly. The moisture and heat will melt the glue so it sticks to the screen. Remove the laminated backing sheet the same way as for an amber sheet.

type of laminated sheet you are using. These sheets come in different colors, indicating the different adhesives they contain. Amber sheets are of plasticized shellac, while green and blue sheets use water-soluble glues.

If you are using amber sheets, set your electric iron to the "silk" setting. Place the stencil attached to the backing sheet with the thin upper layer facing up on a sheet of cardboard or an ironing board, and lower the screen until it is in contact with the stencil. Cover the inside of the screen with clean newsprint. Iron with light pressure on the newsprint. Lift the newsprint occasionally until you can see the shellac melting into the mesh of the screen. Let the screen cool. Turn the screen over and carefully peel the backing sheet from the other layer, which is now attached to the screen. Then iron again, without the newsprint, until the stencil adheres completely.

Illus. 13. When the film is cool and dry, turn the screen over and slowly peel the backing paper off. If the film starts to come up with the backing paper, turn the screen over again and re-apply the film.

Illus. 14. A hand-cut film stencil was used to make this printed curtain (see "Cloth," page 520).

To fasten green stencils, put the green film, thin upper layer up, on the table and lower the screen on top of the film. Place heavy weights on each corner of the frame to hold it down firmly. Set up an electric fan or hair dryer to blow across the screen, and dip a rag into a mixture of alcohol and water. Wring the rag as dry as you can, and rub the inside of the screen with it. Do not go over the same place twice with the rag. When the screen turns a strong green, the glue has penetrated the mesh. Leave the fan or hair dryer blowing until the glue has dried, and peel off the backing.

Remove both blue and green films in the same way: clean the screen of ink with mineral spirits (paint thinner) or a solvent suitable to the ink you use. Mop the screen dry, and then hose the inside of the screen with hot water. Peel the stencil off, and sponge the screen with hot water and detergent to get rid of any remaining glue. Rinse with cold water and dry.

You can create unusual effects with film stencils by specially treating the stencil before you attach it to the screen. Use a wood burning tool to melt the edges of the stencil rather than a knife to cut it. The fuzzy edges which result will print blurry outlines, which resemble lithographs or charcoal drawings.

Save the scraps of film that you cut from the backing sheet. If you mix some film solvent with these scraps in a jar, you can use the solution to touch up weak spots in a stencil, or even to block out new areas on your screen with a brush. Once the film solution is painted on the screen and the solvent has evaporated, this stencil can be printed and then removed just like the stencils you cut and ironed to the screen.

The Liquid Block-Out Stencil

The liquid block-out stencil is quite simple to make: basically, you paint the part of the screen that is *not* to print with lacquer, shellac or glue, so that the liquid fills in the holes of the mesh screen and the ink cannot pass through. A fine mesh screen is important for sharp outlines, although you may sometimes prefer the soft edge obtained by using a looser mesh. When you apply the ink appropriate to your particular block-out liquid to the screen (water-based paints cannot be used with water-soluble glues, for example), the color goes

Illus. 16. To block out the narrow areas close to the design, use a pointed brush.

Illus. 15. To protect the art from being coated with liquid as you cover the screen, place a sheet of transparent paper between the screen and the art.

through the uncoated sections of the screen to the printing stock below.

Draw the design to be printed (called the "art") on light-colored paper with dark ink, so that its outlines clearly appear through the screen. Make the art small enough so there is a clear strip at least 2″ wide on each end of the screen for an "ink-carrying area," to get the squeegee moving easily.

Place the frame with its bottom or screen-side down, so that it rests on top of the art. Outline the art on the screen with a sharp, medium-soft pencil to indicate the areas that are to be covered by the lacquer. Then remove the art. Turn the frame over so the bottom of the screen is on top. Because the liquid you will use may drip through the screen, put a layer of newspaper on the base.

You are now ready to start applying the lacquer, shellac or glue. The liquid should not be so thin that it runs when you apply it to the screen; if it is too runny, leave it in a shallow bowl for a few minutes until it thickens. Start applying the lacquer with a flat bristle brush on the large open areas, but make the first coat a thin one so the lacquer does not immediately penetrate the screen. While this first coat is drying, use a pointed sable brush to coat the small spaces around the lines of the art.

Illus. 17. To make a shaded background such as this, apply a liquid block-out over the entire screen. Remove some of the substance by rubbing with a sponge moistened in solvent. Then apply the solid figures of the stencil.

Turn the frame over occasionally so you can catch any drops of lacquer that are hanging and paint them flat. After coating the frame thoroughly, leave it alone for about an hour to dry. Hold the frame up to a spotlight to make sure that no part has become porous during the drying. If you see pinholes, cover them with more lacquer. However, for special effects, you may want more pinholes: after the glue has dried, dampen a rag in the appropriate solvent and quickly run it over the screen. Some glue will be removed, leaving holes.

If you should slip and paint some lacquer in the wrong area, immediately try to wash it out with solvent. Once the stencil has dried it is almost impossible to remove lacquer from the screen. Use lacquer thinner for lacquer stencils; alcohol for shellac stencils; and

water for glue stencils. Wash that portion of the screen clean of any special remover so the ink you use is not affected by it.

The outside edges of the screen also need to be coated with lacquer, so that no ink can ooze between the screen and the frame during printing. Use your wide brush, and cover the places where the frame and screen meet to make sure it is impermeable.

The Tusche-Glue Stencil

Tusche is a waxy substance which does not dissolve in water, but does dissolve in paint thinner, turpentine or kerosene. You paint the design—the area that is to appear in color —on the screen with tusche, and then cover the entire screen with glue. When you dissolve the tusche with a solvent, the glue covering the tusche no longer has anything to cling to, and the design area is thus clean and free of any material. You must use oil-based inks with the tusche-glue type of stencil, since water dissolves glue.

Set the screen on top of your original art and fill in the proper areas of the screen with liquid tusche. To opaque an area completely, apply the tusche thickly; in some cases, it may be necessary to apply two coats, but let the undercoat dry first. Set the screen aside until the tusche is as dry as possible. Tusche rarely dries completely, but remains slightly sticky. When it reaches this state, you are ready to apply the glue.

Ordinary glue is perfectly suitable for the

Illus. 18. For added coverage, coat the sides of the screen with the block-out medium.

Illus. 19. Pour the tusche solvent on the screen, making sure it gets into all corners. Let it soak the tusche for about 15 minutes.

Illus. 20. Pour some tusche from the bottle into a bowl and let it thicken slightly. Then apply it thickly to the screen.

Illus. 21. If you poured a lot of solvent on the screen, pour the excess off before you begin to rub the screen.

tusche-glue stencil. Just be sure it is *water-soluble* and that it will not dissolve in paint thinner or kerosene. You may need to thin the glue; add small amounts of water until it can be easily spread.

Pour a little of the glue-water mixture on the border of the screen, not on the open screen. Use a piece of cardboard or matboard, or a wide brush, and spread the glue over the entire surface of the screen. Let the glue dry, and then hold the screen up to a spotlight to check for pinholes. The entire screen may need a second coat of glue.

After the glue has dried completely and you have filled in all the pinholes, you must dissolve the tusche with kerosene or thinner. Put a number of sheets of newsprint under the screen and pour the thinner over it. Leave the screen alone for a while (about 15 minutes) and then use a cloth to rub the areas where you painted the screen with tusche. The tusche will run into the newsprint; remove the top sheets occasionally for a new absorbent surface. Rub both sides of the screen until both the tusche and the glue which you applied over it have dissolved and no more black from the tusche appears on the newspaper.

If some spots of tusche cling to the screen, try rubbing the areas carefully with a small stiff brush. If the tusche does not dissolve at all in a certain area, it might be due to a thick layer of glue at that spot. Dab a few drops of water on the glue at the difficult places, to thin it slightly. Then apply more thinner and proceed in the usual way.

Dry the screen by rubbing both sides with a cloth. Make sure that all the glue is attached where you do not want ink to print, and that the tusche has been dissolved. Then the tusche-glue stencil is ready to print.

Illus. 22. Hold the screen up to a light to check for pinholes.

Silk Screen Inks and Aids

Special tacky inks are needed for silk screen printing, just as in every other printing technique. The distinctive feature of silk screen inks is their consistency: the inks must have body. The colors are therefore in an emulsion about the consistency of poster paint or thick cream

which prevents the ink from flowing too loosely on the screen, but at the same time makes it easy for the ink to be applied evenly to the screen. Silk screen inks also must not dry too quickly on the screen, as they would clog the mesh.

The base of the ink you are using, either water or oil and synthetic resins, is one of the factors which determines your choice of stencil: the ink and stencil must be opposite in nature, or neutral to each other. Water-based inks, for example, cannot be used with a block-out stencil of glue, since the glue dissolves in water. Yet amber film stencils cannot be loosened with water, so water-based inks are used with these stencils. The neutral shellac stencil is good for all types of inks, since shellac dissolves only with shellac thinner.

Besides water-based inks, you can buy a

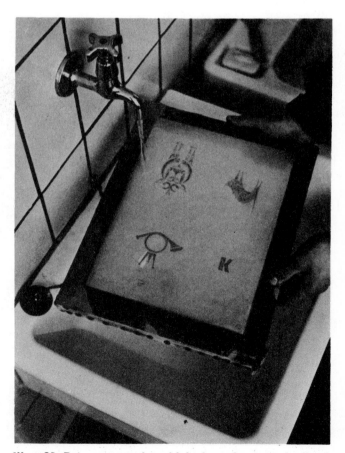

Illus. 23. Remove water-based inks from the screen by flooding the screen with warm water.

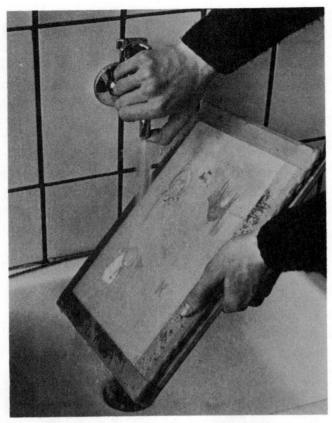

Illus. 24. If the warm water does not thoroughly remove the ink, and there are stubborn patches that have begun to dry in the screen, create a forceful jet of water by placing your finger over the faucet.

number of other special inks for all kinds of printing stocks. There are specialized inks for wood, glass, vinyl, hardboard and sheet metal, which make a scratchproof and weather-resistant surface. You can even give foam rubber an elastic and hard-wearing color.

The silk screen inks for textiles that you can buy today are excellent. The inks come in a wide variety of colors and you can mix them to obtain even more shades. When applied, the ink, being transparent, provides light shades, and by adding an extender you will print even more delicate veils of color. By overlapping these colors, you create new and surprising shades and effects, greenish blues and lavenders, for example. If you add white to the ink, however, it will become so opaque that you can print even black materials with bright colors. The ordinary "vat dyes" used by the

textile industry are not suitable for silk screening; because of their chemical composition, these dyes often need complicated treatments.

Never let textile ink dry in the screen. Print briskly, and clean the stencil immediately after you have made the last print. If the screen becomes clogged with dried ink, clean it only with a fine bristle brush and xylene, a chemical solvent. Take care that no ink gets on your clothes.

To prevent small prints, such as cards and signs, from sticking to the screen and causing unclear prints, buy an adhesive which you can spray on the base in small quantities before printing. It makes papers, cards and even small pieces of fabric stick to the base, rather than the screen, and does not leave any residue on the paper or fabric. After printing, you can easily peel the printing stock from the base.

The Printing Process
Mixing the Inks

First mix the inks in very small trial quantities on the sheet of glass. With the palette knife, take a little of the lighter colored

Illus. 25. Mix the inks on a glass sheet before you pull your first proof.

ink, and add the darker shades to it gradually, so you get to know the way the different colors combine with one another. The appearance of a color on glass is not always the color that will appear on your print, however. Brush a small sample of ink on the material that is to be printed, and leave it to dry. If your sample dries to a satisfactory color, mix a larger quantity of ink in the same proportions as the sample in one of the screw-top jars. Add a few drops of water or thinner to the mixture if necessary, until it has the right consistency—like thick cream. If the ink is too runny, the print will be blotchy and "bubbly." If the ink is too thick, the meshes of the screen are liable to clog.

Monochrome (One-Color) Printing

Spoon or pour the ink on one blocked-out end of the frame. Now, using a slight downward pressure, pull the squeegee towards you, running it quickly over the whole screen. As the screen must be completely covered with ink right from the start, immediately run the squeegee over the screen again in the reverse direction, unless you feel that the first application may be too thick.

While you hold the edge of the printed paper to prevent it from sticking to the screen, carefully raise the frame a little without changing its position to see from the side that all parts of the paper are uniformly printed. If they are not, lower the screen and apply the squeegee a third time. Occasionally, though rarely, you may need to do it four times.

Keep the squeegee at a constant pressure and speed as it pulls the ink; do not slow down as you reach the end. After a few prints, you should be able to judge exactly how to manipulate your equipment.

Polychrome (Multicolor) Printing

You should not try multicolor printing until you are fairly successful with printing in one color. Multicolor printing requires additional preparations.

Each separate color requires a separate stencil. If you have several screen and frame units, you can make all the stencils at the same time and thus reprint later if you want. If you have only one unit, you must make one stencil and print one color at a time.

On your original art, indicate with colored

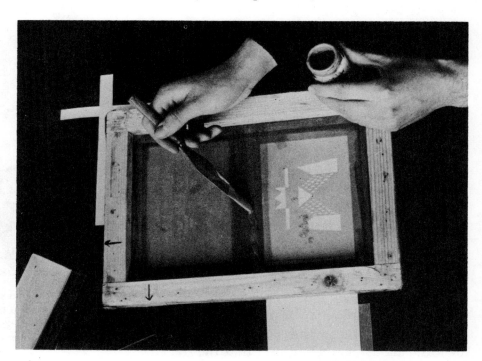

Illus. 26. Spoon ink onto the ink-carrying area. The upper portion of the screen here will be used for a second color.

Illus. 27. Before you remove the first proof, place register marks round the edges of the stock and the screen. Then every color will be printed in the same position on the paper as on the first print.

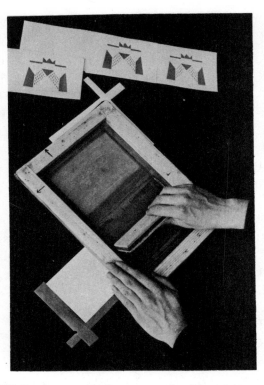

Illus. 28. You must press the squeegee hard in order to achieve the even, complete coverage shown in the prints drying here above the frame.

pencils which areas are to be in which color. Then place the screen over the art and proceed to make the appropriate stencil for your first color. (Always print the lightest color first.) When you print this color, mark the corners of the printing stock on the base with register guides so that you can replace the stock *exactly* in the same place when you print subsequent colors. Make the number of prints you will want, plus several additional ones (their use is explained below). Then remove the stencil and ink from the screen.

Place the cleaned screen over your original art and prepare the stencil for the second color. When you print the second color on the sheets, position them exactly, following the register guides. To pull a proof with the second color, coat the screen with ink and print on one of the extra sheets from the first run. (Use one of your poorer prints.) You may have to readjust the color or consistency of the ink. The fact that you made the second stencil by following the same art as the first ensures that the stencil

Illus. 29. If your frame is not hinged, it is not fastened to the base; therefore, you must register the frame as well as the paper. Outline the second color sections on tracing paper, and place the screen over this. Following the tracing paper, prepare the stencil.

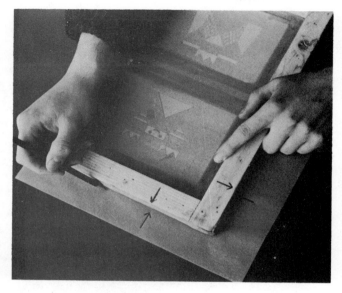

Illus. 30. After making the stencil, mark both the frame and the tracing paper so you will be able to replace the screen in the proper position. The tracing paper is necessary because it allows greater accuracy in positioning the frame unit.

Illus. 31. Remove the screen and slide your first print (with one color) under the tracing paper. Place register guides around the printing stock.

is in the right position on the screen, and your register guides guarantee that the screen and frame are correctly placed over the paper. Once everything is set up correctly, the second color is as easy to apply as the first.

For variation, try overlapping some colors

Illus. 32. Place the frame over the tracing paper by lining up the parts according to the marks you made. Slide the paper away and make register guides for the frame. Both stock and frame can now be removed or raised, and then replaced correctly.

to create new shades and tones. (You can also overlap by pouring two colors of the same type on the frame, side by side.) Experiment with different colors and varieties of inks on your printing stock before you print the series anyway, to be sure that your ink gives total coverage to your surface. Try different kinds of inks and different combinations of colors to see which give the most pleasing results.

Cleaning the Screen

After you are finished printing a series, you should clean both the ink and the stencil from the screen so you can re-use the screen later for another design.

First, remove the excess ink from the screen with a spatula or cardboard scraper and put it into the jar in which it was mixed. Label the jar and store it to use another time. If you have used a water-based ink, rinse the screen thoroughly with a jet of cold water, and then wash it in warm water with a little detergent. Rinse again with cold water and set the screen aside to dry.

For an oil-based ink, flood the screen with

paint remover or a special solvent purchased from your ink supplier. Let the screen soak in this solvent for 10 minutes. With a rag or a piece of cardboard remove as much ink as you can; then take a clean rag soaked in solvent and rub the screen. Wash it in warm water and detergent, scrubbing with a bristle brush if necessary. Rinse with warm water until the screen is clean.

The procedure for removing the stencil from the screen is included in the section explaining stencils (see page 505). Follow the special instructions that come with a particular stencil if you are using an unusual material.

Possibilities for Screen Printing

The possible uses of screen printing for decoration or design are endless. You can make greeting cards, stationery, posters, scarves, curtains, print dresses, shirts, colorful leather handbags or wallets; you can even print designs on wood, glass, metal, and plastic without much extra work.

Next time you need Christmas cards, or any other type of card, print your own personalized cards yourself. The easiest way is to buy a quantity of construction paper in an attractive

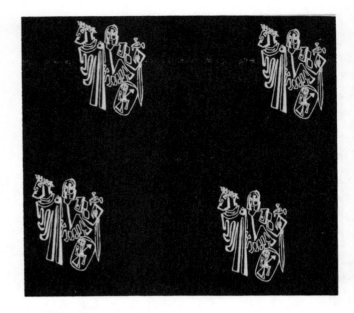

Illus. 33. The abstract motif on the left, which might have been inspired by Roman statesmen, is randomly repeated on the background above. Wallpaper, wrapping paper, curtains, and other large areas would be suitable for this design.

Illus. 34. The Nativity scene here by Wiltraud Jaspers was prepared from a simple block-out stencil, painted on the screen with a narrow brush.

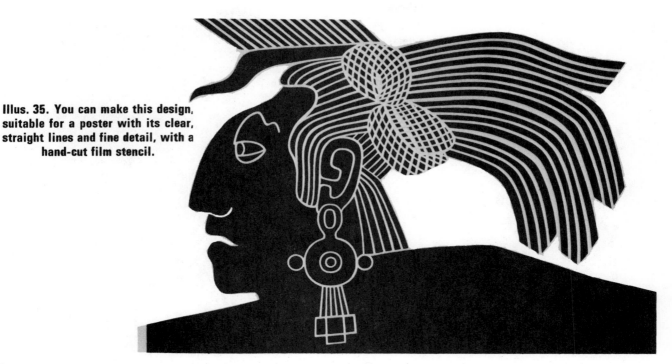

Illus. 35. You can make this design, suitable for a poster with its clear, straight lines and fine detail, with a hand-cut film stencil.

color and size, and either draw an original design or trace a photograph or painting. Any of the stencil methods discussed in this article are suitable, although the liquid brush-on or tusche-glue methods are preferable. First, print the cover design, and then, on the other side of the paper, the greeting and signature.

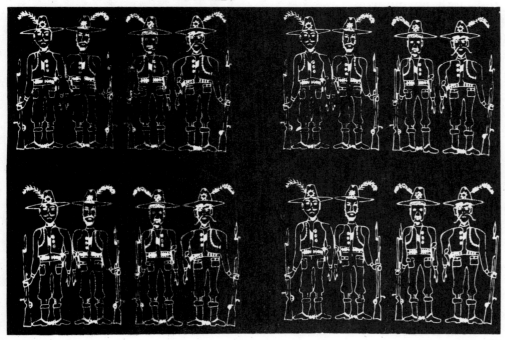

Illus. 36. The original art at the top was copied onto the screen and printed with white ink on a dark background to produce a regiment of moustached and feather-capped soldiers.

Illus. 37 (left). Decorative animal motifs are suitable for printing a design on cloth. To make the "repeat" design, simply lift and move the screen to a second place, and then make a new print.

Illus. 38 (right). An indigo motif covers the entire area of this silver-grey silk scarf.

Cloth

While most aspects of printing on cloth are the same as on paper, there are several specific requirements that you should consider.

You should be able to print successfully on almost any kind of fabric. Just be sure that your design and the weave of the cloth harmonize with each other. Bold subjects are well suited to coarse fabrics, while finely detailed designs would show up best on smooth, thin materials.

For a curtain or cover for a cushion, select a material with some body to it. There are various linen materials, both natural and man-made, which offer a wide selection. Because of the particularly beautiful texture of these fabrics, extremely large patterns are just as effective on them as small subjects. For dresses, blouses, tablecloths and napkins, you will want a fabric with a more flowing character. Try cotton or another soft material. Pure silk is undoubtedly the finest and most expensive material for silk screen prints, so do not attempt to print on it until you have some experience and feel sure of yourself.

Almost every kind of material has been

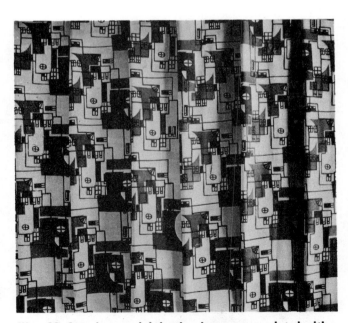

Illus. 39. Curtain material that has been screen printed with a pattern of lines, then accented by large solid areas of printed color.

Illus. 40. Three hand-made neckties of screen-printed fabric. The tie in the middle has a sharp tile-like pattern, while the other two, made from the same stencil, were printed with a repeat design purposely out of register.

Illus. 40. Three hand-made neckties of screen-printed fabric. The tie in the middle has a sharp tile-like pattern, while the other two, made from the same stencil, were printed with a repeat design purposely out of register.

refined in some way; usually, it is passed through a starch solution, stretched, and calendered. However, when the fibres are covered with the starch, the fabric can absorb only a limited amount of the silk screen inks. You must therefore remove the dressing before you print, so that the fibres can accept as much ink as possible.

For any material but natural silk, first rinse in cold water. Then wash briefly with a detergent made for fine fabrics, and rinse clean again. Next, add about a tablespoon of malt extract to a bucket of rinsing water, stir until the malt has completely dissolved, and soak the material in the malt solution overnight. The malt converts the starch into sugar, which you can then easily wash out of the fabric. Finally, rinse the material, let it dry, and iron it. Soaking in a malt solution is recommended for linen, cotton and man-made fibres. As a rule, natural silk has only a light dressing or none at all. Wash silk with a fine detergent, then rinse it and, before it dries, iron it smooth on the back of the material.

The liquid block-out method or tusche-glue method are again preferable for making stencils. One final note: before printing, stretch, and then pin the fabric to the printing base so it is tight and even.

Leather

Special dyes are available for printing on leather, and you can buy them in most craft and leather shops. Leather needs no special preparations, but make sure that the leather is clean, and be sure to use the right combination of paint, glue, and solvent. When printing, pin the leather to the table as you did for cloth. For ideas on using your printed leather, see the article, "Leathercrafting."

Other Surfaces

Glass, metal, plastic and wood are the materials to which the screen printer usually has difficulty adhering the ink. The smooth, non-porous surface, which looks tempting to decorate, is deceptive: the ink glides on the slippery finish with ease, but it peels off just as easily unless certain preventive steps are taken.

First remove all grease and oil from the surface. For most metals, commercial vinegar is a satisfactory cleaning agent which dissolves the grease but none of the metal. For wood, use turpentine to remove any protective lacquer coating. Alcohol is the best cleaning substance for glass. For plastics, however, the

Illus. 41. This pattern was printed in bright peacock blue on sand-colored silk, but would be very suitable for curtains or table cloths.

specific plastic you are printing on will determine the exact solvent, as well as the specific ink, you should use. Your ink and solvent supplier is the best source of information for anything regarding the adhesion of the ink to the printing surface.

Once you have thoroughly cleaned the material of all grease, you must choose the proper ink for this surface. To decide on the brand, category and color of ink, make a small smear of several inks on the cleaned surface. Allow at least 24 hours after printing before you evaluate the suitability of an ink for a particular surface. While the drying time of the ink is usually less than an hour, the extra time permits you to check adhesion of the ink to the surface.

To achieve permanent adhesion on metals, it is sometimes necessary to add a small amount of thinner to the ink. The thinner will in no way affect the screen or the drying time of the ink; it simply brings the ink into closer contact with the metal. Again, your crafts supplier is the best source of information for these materials.

SLAB CERAMICS

Make pottery without a potter's wheel and glaze without firing using the simple techniques and tools described here. You can form almost any shape with the slab method, and, with no more effort than is required to paint an object, give your creations a permanent glaze.

Illus. 1. Here is a sampling of the objects you can create using the slab method.

Materials

Almost any clay that is made specifically for modelling or throwing can be used for slab ceramics. It should contain *grog* (pre-fired particles of clay) to help prevent the clay from cracking when fired.

You will need some simple wooden modelling tools (available at craft and hobby shops), a needle-point tool (made by pushing the end of a sharp needle into a brush), a sponge to keep your hands wet and clean, a few bowls or cans for water, a rolling pin, and various cans, jars, pieces of wood, and so on, for forming the clay slabs.

You will also need texture tools to make designs in the clay. To make a simple texture tool, "groove" a design in a small piece of wood with a file (Illus. 2).

You can obtain interesting designs from Nature by pressing leaves, flowers and weeds into soft clay. Make other textures and designs by pressing burlap, textured wallpaper, wrinkled paper, or coins and nails into soft clay. Use any object with its own texture to achieve a variety of designs.

Carved plaster blocks are a particularly effective means of imprinting personalized

Condensed from the book, "Ceramics by Slab" by Joan and Anthony Priolo / © *1973 by Sterling Publishing Co., Inc., New York*

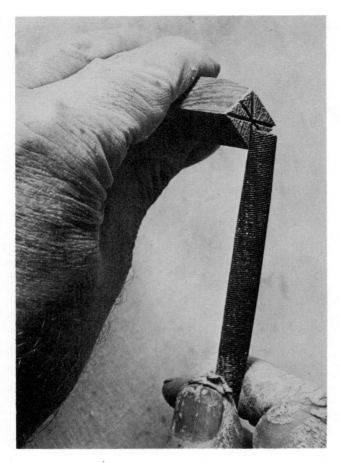

Illus. 2. You can make a simple "texture" tool yourself. Using a file, groove a design into a small piece of wood.

Illus. 3. Then press the texture tool into soft clay, and the result is an imprinted design which you can repeat or use with other texture tool impressions.

Illus. 4. You can use any textured object to decorate your slab creations. Here, a Nature design was made from a branch with the leaves on it.

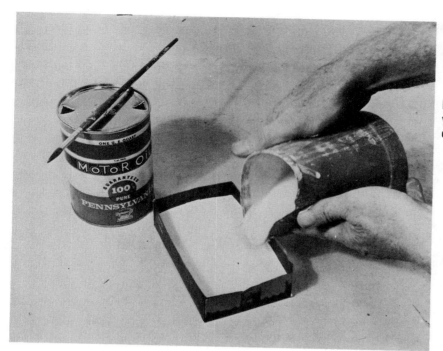

Illus. 5. For a more elaborate texture tool, you can make a plaster block quickly and easily. This method allows you to imprint initials, monograms or special crests.

designs, such as names, initials, etc. To make a plaster block, mix equal portions of water and plaster of Paris by weight. Stir mixture for one minute. Pour mixture into a cardboard box (greased with butter, motor oil, cooking oil, etc.) and let the plaster set until dry. Peel off the cardboard box. This one block can be cut into smaller blocks with a saw or knife. Any design can then be carved into one end of the block with a penknife or carving tool (Illus. 6).

Slip (liquid clay) is used as a cement to adhere one clay segment to another.

To make slip, allow a small amount of your clay to dry hard. Place the dried clay in a

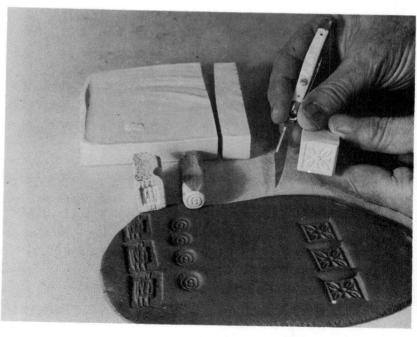

Illus. 6. From just one block of plaster, you can make a multitude of texture tools. An ordinary penknife will carve the plaster easily.

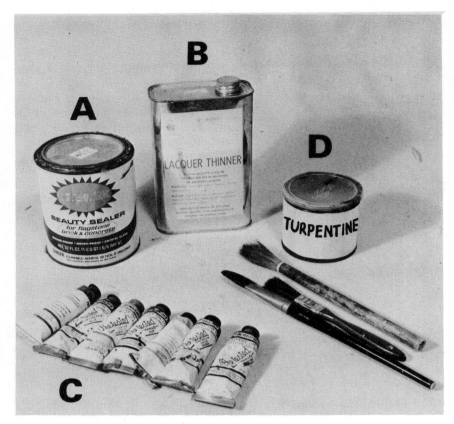

Illus. 7. Materials you need for glazing with slate and concrete sealer: (A) slate and concrete sealer; (B) lacquer thinner; (C) tube oil colors; (D) turpentine.

paper bag and crush it by gently hammering until the clay is broken into a powder. Pour the crushed clay into a can. Gradually add water and stir until a soft, buttery consistency is achieved.

For glazing, you need: slate and concrete sealer, a clear liquid available at hardware or paint shops that is inexpensive and dries quickly; tube oil paints of various colors; lacquer thinner; turpentine; and an ordinary paint brush (Illus. 7).

Techniques

Storing and Keeping Clay Workable

In order to keep your clay workable for a period of time (from several days to weeks), first spray the clay project with water; then wrap a wet cloth round the clay and cover with a plastic bag (Illus. 8). The wet cloth is not necessary if you plan to work on the clay the next day. You can also enclose a damp sponge in the bag.

Illus. 8. Keep your clay project in a workable state in a "damp closet," consisting of wet sponges and a plastic-bag covering.

526 ■ SLAB CERAMICS

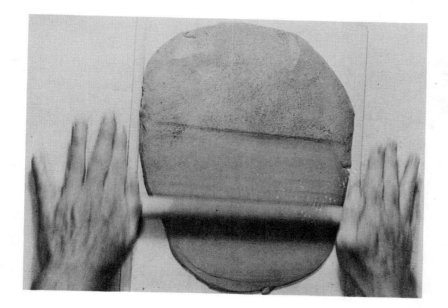

By spraying the clay with water at intervals and keeping it covered with a plastic bag, clay projects can be kept in a workable state indefinitely.

To keep finished flat surfaces, such as plaques and tiles, from curling, cover with a plastic sheet so that the work dries slowly.

Rolling out a Clay Slab

Cut off a desired amount of clay from the main block with a thin wire or string (wire or string will cut better than a knife because there is no drag).

Pat the clay into an even ball with your hands.

Start flattening out the ball of clay and keep flattening until it is too big to handle.

Place the flattened clay on newspaper or the non-slick side of oil cloth; or, better yet, on a piece of unsized canvas.

Use a rolling pin to roll out the clay pancake and make it smooth. If much rolling is necessary for the desired thickness, it is a good idea to lift the clay pancake from the canvas and replace it in a slightly different position to keep it from sticking to the canvas.

For an even thickness, place two sticks of wood (of the thickness desired for the clay) parallel to each other on either side of the clay.

When you use the rolling pin, the sticks will determine the thickness of the clay.

A general rule of thumb to follow is: Small items can be made with thin slabs of clay, but large items require thicker slabs.

Firing the Clay

Before you glaze your clay sculpture, it needs to be fired in a kiln. If you do not have a kiln, check with local craft and art shops. Many places will fire your pieces for a reasonable price.

Fire your pieces at 1700°–1850°F (927°–1010°C). Firing unglazed clay at this temperature is called *bisque-firing*.

Glazing

After your slab project has been bisque-fired, you will want to glaze it for color and waterproofing.

Ceramic glazes that require a second firing may, of course, be used. However, we would like to introduce you to a different type of glaze that is simple enough for anyone to apply, is completely waterproof, and does not require a firing.

This glaze is basically a slate and concrete sealer. Use the sealer directly from the can as a clear glaze or make any color glaze desired

SLAB CERAMICS ■ **527**

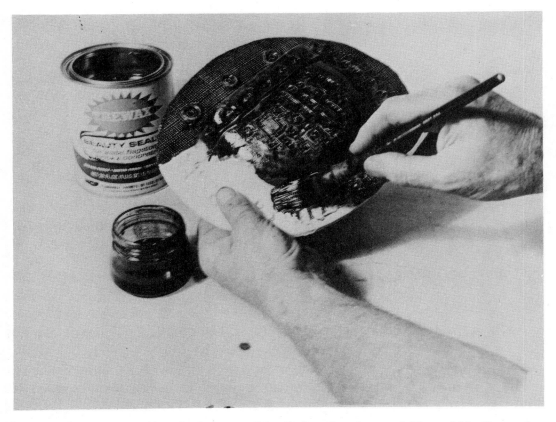

Illus. 10. Slate and concrete sealer is inexpensive, odorless, harmless, and dries quickly. Here a plaque is being glazed.

by adding a small amount of tube oil paint to the clear sealer.

Simply paint the clear or colored sealer on the fired piece with a paint brush. When the sealer has dried (one to two hours), your ceramic piece will be covered with a permanent glaze that is completely waterproof.

When glazing the inside of a pot that is to hold water, apply the sealer liberally to make sure all areas are well covered. To ensure maximum waterproofing, it is a good idea to apply two liberal coats of sealer. If the sealer is applied liberally and full strength, a shiny glaze will result. If a matt glaze is desired, thin the sealer with lacquer thinner. Use lacquer thinner also as a solvent for cleaning your glaze brushes.

Many color variations can be achieved by the texture of the ceramic piece itself, since the colored glaze will sink into any lines or crevices, making those areas darker.

Try using more than one color glaze on your piece. For example, let a second color glaze drip partially down over the first color glaze, or, apply one color glaze over another (such as green over blue) for a deeper, richer color.

Another easy and effective way to color your fired ceramic piece is to paint it with a thin wash of oil color and turpentine and then, when the wash has dried (a matter of minutes), glaze the entire piece with clear or tinted glaze. By using the oil color-turpentine wash, it is possible to shade one color into another, as in a painting.

While children especially will enjoy glazing their ceramic pieces with either sealer-glaze method because it is so easy, and results can be seen immediately, everyone, whether beginner or experienced, now can create a permanent, waterproof glaze of any desired color without a glaze firing by using slate and concrete sealer.

Illus. 11. Making coasters is as easy as making biscuits or cookies. Use a tin can of whatever size you want to cut out your basic coaster shape.

Illus. 12. Before shaping your coasters as on the left, first imprint a design on each using various texture tools. Remember, your coasters will have added interest if you vary the design a little on each.

Clay Coasters

For a beginning project, try making clay coasters. Roll some clay out flat, and use a can to cut out round shapes. Use various texture tools to press designs into the clay circles. To shape the flat clay circle into a coaster, cut a circle (same size as coaster) from a paper towel and place on the face of the clay circle to protect the design and prevent the clay from sticking to the glass. Place a small glass dish or bowl on top of the paper towel and press the edges of the clay circle against the dish to shape the coaster. Remove the paper towel and

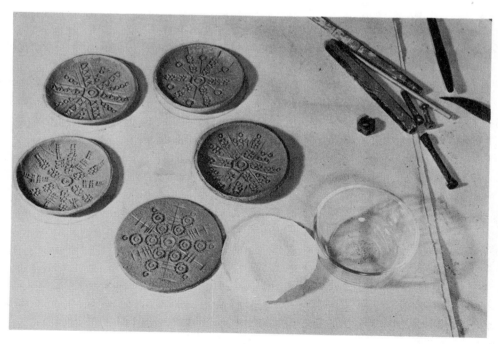

Illus. 13. Begin shaping your coasters by cutting out a circle of paper towelling the same size as the clay circles. The paper towel will keep the design from being smudged.

Illus. 14. Place the paper towel circle on a clay circle. Then take a glass bowl approximately the same size and press the edges of the clay up against the glass.

Illus. 15. Here are the finished coasters before being glazed. To see them in color turn to color Illus. FF4.

glass dish. A wet sponge finishes the edges. Now bisque-fire the coasters, and after they have cooled, glaze them. Color Illus. FF4 shows the finished product.

A Flower Plaque

Use a needle-point modelling tool to cut a flower pattern from a slab of rolled-out clay.

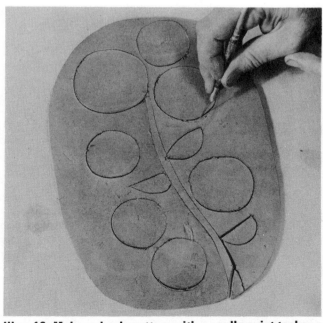

Illus. 16. Make a simple pattern with a needle-point tool on a slab of clay to begin your flower plaque.

Illus. 17. Remove each part of the design one by one. Form the petals over a light bulb, being sure to use paper towelling.

Illus. 18. Paint slip on each part of the flower arrangement and make designs through the slip with a wooden modelling tool. Attach the various parts to a slab of rolled-out clay with slip.

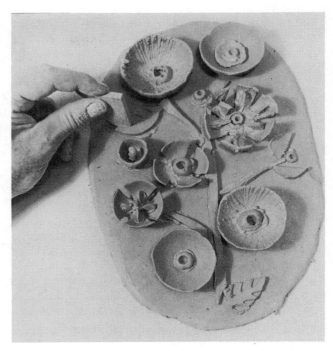

Illus. 19. Here, a texture tool is being used to make a leaf pattern. You can add all kinds of small buttons of clay to form "eyes" for your flowers. Then glaze your plaque.

Shape the flower petals by hand over a light bulb. (Be sure to put a piece of paper towel between the clay and the bulb.) Paint slip on the flower and make line designs by drawing with a wooden modelling tool through the slip. Attach flowers, stems, and leaves with slip to a slab of rolled-out clay. (It is a good idea, in this and all future projects, to roughen the clay where slip is to be painted with a wooden modelling tool, so the bond will be stronger.)

Paint small buttons of clay with slip and place in the middle of the flowers. Push the rounded end of a pencil into the clay buttons, attaching them securely and making a design. Press lines into the leaves with a texture tool. By using these simple steps, you can create a variety of flowers.

Clay Figures

Before starting a clay figure you might want to cut patterns from construction paper and experiment with various paper figures and animals. Then, when you have made a paper figure that is pleasing, cut the same pattern

from clay, and following the same prodecure, make a clay figure.

An Angel

Use a round bowl to cut a circle from a slab of rolled-out clay. Cut out a triangular section

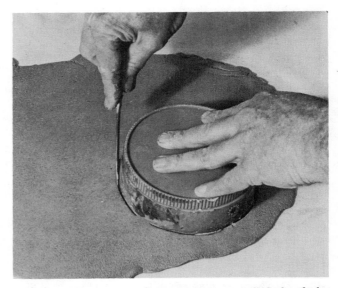

Illus. 20. Start your angel by cutting a round circle of clay using a tin can, bowl or other circular object as a guide.

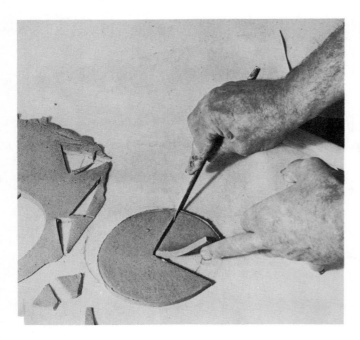

of the clay circle with a wooden modelling tool in order to form a cone shape for the body. Also cut shapes for the arms and wings. "Butter" the ends of the clay cone with slip and join together to form the body (Illus. 22). Smooth out the inside of the cone to make a stronger joint. Attach the arms and wings with slip. Model the head and also join to the body with slip. A face can be very simple with just a suggestion of features or as detailed as desired. For added interest, press in designs with the point of a pencil (Illus. 25). Fire and glaze.

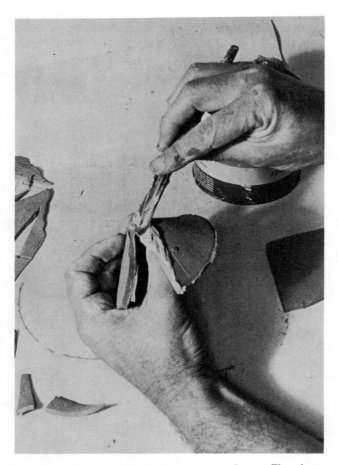

Illus. 22. Shape the clay into a cone as shown. Then butter the edges to be joined with slip. Be sure to handle the clay carefully.

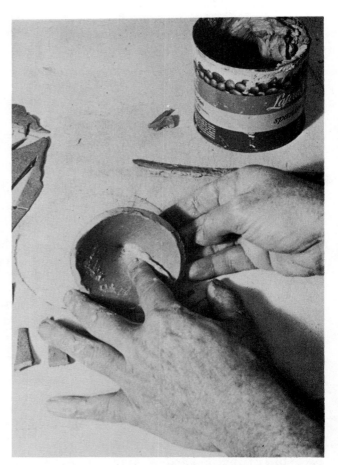

Illus. 23. Do not forget to smooth the joined line on the inside of the cone as well as on the outside. Now, cut out small wing and arm shapes and model a very simple head.

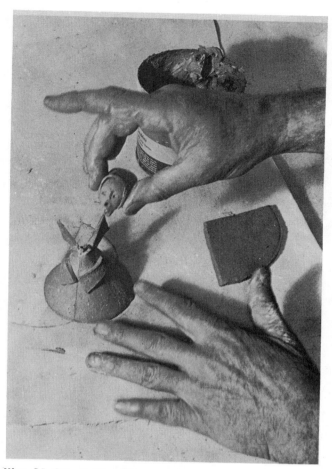

Illus. 24. Attach the wings, arms and head to the cone body with slip.

Illus. 25. Using a pencil point or other sharp tool, you can add small decorative touches to the finished angel.

Illus. 26. With glass bowls of different sizes, you can make any number of shallow clay bowls which you can put together like this.

A Clay Bowl

Turn a glass bowl upside-down. Cut a circle of paper towelling and place over the bowl (to prevent the clay from sticking). Form the clay over the paper towel and bowl. Trim off excess

Illus. 27. Again, use paper towelling between the clay and the glass to keep the clay from sticking. After forming the clay, trim off the excess and remove.

SLAB CERAMICS ■ 533

Illus. 28. Now, make a second bowl, but slightly deeper than the first. This will be the base. For a cut-away effect, outline three half moons on the second bowl as shown.

clay. Remove the clay bowl and paper towel. When making a deep bowl, it is a good idea to go through the forming process twice because the clay bowl will have marks and creases from the paper towel that should be smoothed out by hand, using slip. After smoothing, repeat the forming process, and trim off excess clay.

Now, make a second, smaller bowl in the same manner to form the base.

Now texture the bowls, if you wish, attach them with slip, fire, and glaze. Illus. 30 shows the finished bowl.

A bowl such as this also makes an ideal candleholder.

Illus. 29. After smoothing the edges of both bowls with a sponge and water, cut out the half moons from the second bowl to form the legs. "Paste" on small balls of clay with slip for decoration.

Illus. 30. Then attach the two sections together and your bowl is finished. Use this method to form a variety of "tiered" bowls such as this.

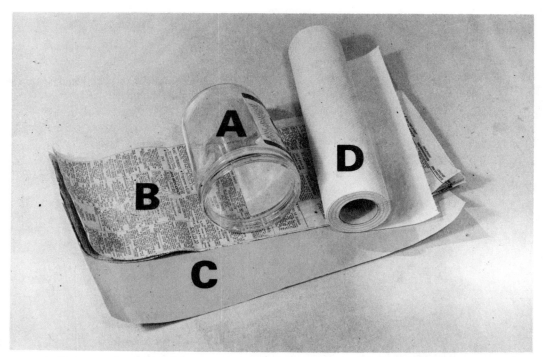

Illus. 31. These are the materials you need to make a round vase: (A) peanut-butter jar or any glass jar with a slight taper; (B) three or four sheets of newspaper cut to the height of the jar; (C) construction paper cut to the height of the jar; (D) paper towel.

A Round Vase

To begin, tape a sheet of newspaper round a tapered glass jar with transparent tape. Tape a piece of construction paper to itself over the newspaper layer. Do not tape this construction paper sleeve to the newspaper layer. The construction paper sleeve must move independently of the newspaper layer. (Although construc-

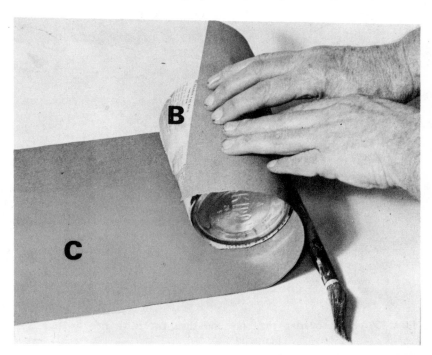

Illus. 32. Tape the first layer of the three or four sheets of newspaper to the jar using transparent tape.

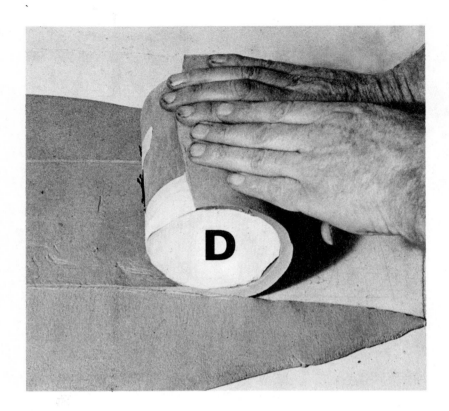

Illus. 33. Roll out a slab of clay and cut to the same height as the jar.

tion paper is used here, you can use newspaper for both layers.)

Then, press a piece of paper towelling round the bottom of the glass jar and partly up the sides. Hold in place with tape. Roll out a slab of clay and cut to the same height as the jar. Roll round the jar. (The paper towel will stick to the damp clay but will permit the

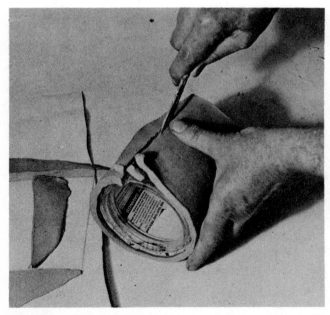

Illus. 34. First, overlap the clay and then cut it to fit perfectly.

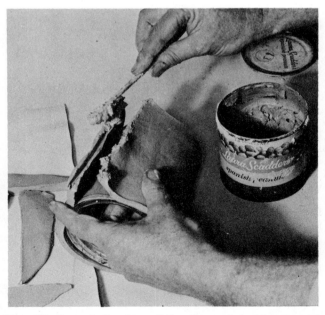

Illus. 35. Score both edges of the clay and then butter with slip.

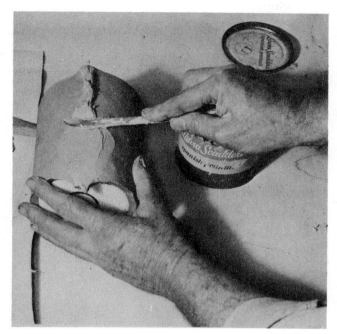

Illus. 36. Use a wooden modelling tool to press the edges together and make a completely smooth "join."

Illus. 37. After making the bottom for the vase, score and butter it. Note the glass jar inside the clay with the newspaper cushion between the glass and the clay.

glass jar to be removed later.) Overlap the rolled-out clay and cut for perfect fit (Illus. 34). Score and "butter" the edges of the clay with slip. Press the two "slipped" ends together

with a wooden modelling tool and smooth the seam. Cut a circle of clay for the bottom of the vase and score and "butter" the edges with slip. Press the bottom of the vase firmly in

Illus. 38. When you press the bottom in place, the glass jar inside keeps the clay from collapsing.

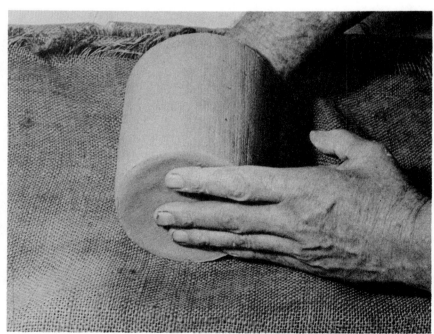

Illus. 39. With the glass jar still inside, you can begin your decorating. Here slip is painted on the vase and small balls of clay have been attached.

place, and use burlap to obtain an even texture all over the vase. (The glass jar inside prevents the clay vase from collapsing.) Paint slip on the vase for decoration.

Pull the glass jar out of the clay vase. The newspaper "cushion" which was taped to the jar remains adhered to the jar. The construction paper sleeve allows the newspapered jar to turn freely. With a little care, you can now remove the construction paper from the inside of the vase (see Illus. 40).

With just a little practice, you can form rectangular shapes from blocks of wood by using this same basic method.

A Bell that Rings

Among the other items that you can make with the glass-jar method is a bell that rings.

Illus. 40. When your decorating is complete, remove the glass jar from inside. The newspaper will come out readily since it is taped to the glass. Then remove the construction paper "sleeve."

Illus. 41. The finished vase. With this method, you can form many items, such as lamp bases, and so on.

the string and nut. In Illus. 44, a fired clay bell pull was added under the nut and two small, fired clay balls were threaded above the can.

Pull the assembled tin can inside the fired vase. Don't forget to make a hole in the vase (before firing) to pull the string through. See the finished bell, ready to ring, in color Illus. FF2.

Illus. 42. All that this bell needs is a touch of glaze. (See color Illus. FF2.)

After you make the vase, add strips of clay to form the bell shape (Illus. 43).

To make a bell out of the fired vase, you will need a tin can, a nut for a clapper, and a length of string. It is necessary to use a tin can for the bell when using low-fired bisque ware since only high-fired clay, such as porcelain has a natural ring to it.

Punch a hole in the tin can and thread with

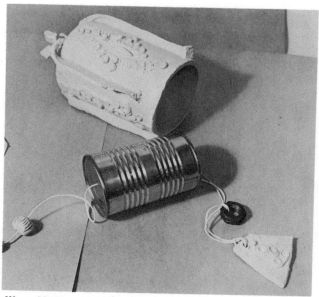

Illus. 43. To make your bell ring, you will need a tin can.

Illus. 44. The tin can is placed inside the bell after firing.

SLAB CERAMICS ■ **539**

appendix

IDEAS FOR DESIGNS

The design you choose to reproduce is as important—perhaps even more important—than the techniques you use to produce it. Throughout this book, you have been learning the basic techniques of crafts by imitating the instructional projects the editors have chosen. But, you do not have to copy other crafters' designs for attractive results. It is best, in fact, to start with a simple, original design and to use your own taste and the manual skills you have already acquired or are acquiring as you work. Your own creation may or may not be a better design than the one you copy, but at least it means that you are trying to do something on your own. Hundreds of simple, but effective and usable designs will come to you with a minimum of effort.

Keep in mind, first of all, that a design does not necessarily need to be identifiable by name as a horse, a building or a tree. These objects, of course, are potential inspirations for designs, but you can also search in a wider area for ideas to express yourself. Works of art, such as abstract paintings that you see in museums, scenes from magazines, children's coloring books, learn-to-draw art books, photographs, advertising lay-outs—almost anything you see may lead you to develop an abstraction or design which can serve as a basis for an original idea or new use of materials.

An excursion or "looking walk" is one of the most stimulating avenues for providing ideas for adults and children alike. Trips to a museum, pet shop, aquarium, park, farm, fruit market, flower nursery, firehouse and dairy could provide much food for creative thought. Examine things—feel the trunk of a tree, for example. Notice the color, shape and texture of objects you observe, and try to capture them in your designs.

Perhaps the looking walk will draw attention to the details of homes and buildings. You might stop and take a close look at one. Observe the interesting shingle patterns which adorn the roof, the flower garden, details of windows and front door.

Reading aloud a well chosen story can stimulate children to express ideas, as it allows each child to identify with the characters in the story. Be sure the incidents seem credible.

Phonograph records are an excellent source for exciting creativity because the background sounds and music produce a mood which can be captured artistically.

Sports events provide yet another source of inspiration for expression in art. Children perform in the gymnasium and playground, and they may depict their games in drawings. Students and adults are also spectators at exciting sports events, which would inspire some artwork.

Young children live in a comparatively small world, consisting of family, playmates, pets and teacher. Family activities hold special meaning for them and provide appropriate experiences to be expressed in art.

Children are not afraid to draw imaginary

Adapted from material written by Chester Jay Alkema and Ethel Jane Beitler and others

situations because they realize that objects cannot be drawn incorrectly. How can anyone criticize a drawing when it is not based on reality?

An older crafter might wish to base his or her imagined drawing on some exciting event. A young child might wish to portray himself as an adult. Perhaps he is a famous movie star, a rock and roll singer, a TV comedian, or a circus performer.

There is no bottom to the fund of material that you can use to promote creative art experiences derived from the world of fiction. And, there is no wrong way of interpreting fictional characters and events. Everyone conjures up images of stories when they read them —you gradually picture the place, the characters, and so on, as the story unfolds. It would be virtually impossible not to do so. Do not, however, restrict your sources to books— there are many phonograph records that have been made of children's classics, as well as more recent additions to children's literature.

Once you have read a story or a poem, immediately try to express it artistically and creatively. Remember though, not every kind of story is going to be suitable for creative work. You must exercise your discrimination to some extent. Try to choose a story where you can, to some degree at least, identify with the feelings and actions of the characters. Most classics are gems of human emotions—love, hate, jealousy, trust, distrust.

Holidays and festive events provide opportunities to express ideas. Valentine's Day, for example, would provide the perfect opportunity for children to create colorful valentines. A folded sheet of paper would permit the student to include a poem within the card. The card's cover might consist of a single valentine or a design composed of various-sized valentines. The felt-crafting or paper-crafting techniques might be used to imprint a lacy design around the valentine's edges.

The Christmas season provides another perfect opportunity to draw scenes which reflect

Illus. 1.

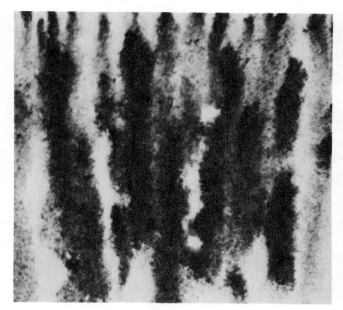

Illus. 2.

Illus. 3a.

the activities associated with the season. Drawings, dioramas, collages, felt or paper assemblages, for example, might reveal the family picking out a Christmas tree, decorating the tree, hanging the Christmas stockings, exchanging gifts, attending the Christmas church service, or eating Christmas dinner.

Suggestions

Following are photographs and drawings that should help you think of original designs. Once your eyes have been opened to what to look *for*, you will find a whole new world of things to look *at*.

Illus. 1 is a photograph of dried, caked earth which shows a casual, irregular development of lines which vary in thickness as well as direction.

Illus. 2 was made by pulling a brush loaded with black water color over a wet surface. The ink spread and left irregular edges which could inspire any number of projects.

Cut paper shapes of different sizes, shapes and colors and experiment with their arrangement. Pin them in place while you draw lines round them preparatory to utilizing the design for a craft (Illus. 3a and 3b).

Illus. 3b.

Illus. 4a.

Illus. 4b.

Illus. 4c.

Illus. 4 shows three different paper arrangements of dark and light cut-outs of the same design. The color relationships in your project do not have to be exactly the same as those in any of the experiments, but at least the trials can serve as inspiration for the colors you choose.

Illus. 5 shows a piece of plywood with an interesting grain-line design which you could interpret into an original creation.

Illus. 5.

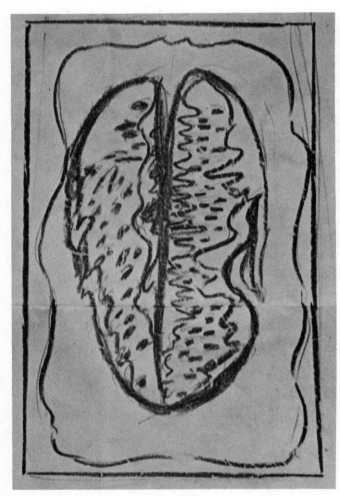

Illus. 6.

The rough sketch shown in Illus. 6 was inspired by the seeds and pulp of a cantaloupe. Visualize irregularity in the various parts of the design, rather than a strictly symmetrical treatment.

The rug in Illus. 7 was an experiment in the use of reverse colors and simple circular shapes which you can draw round cups, saucers, and plates, or with a compass. Sometimes, very precise and regular geometric shapes tend to give a more formal effect to a design, but semi-geometric shapes can produce an interesting design also.

Tempera paint experiments can also yield an endless variety of ideas. Illus. 8 was one such experiment.

The study of science affords many oppor-

Illus. 7.

tunities to correlate art or craft activities with new experiences. Children have a natural interest in animals, insects and plants. Animal antics might suggest humorous expression in a drawing. Both the microscope and the magnifying glass will prove indispensable in exploring science and art. View, for example, the veins of a leaf, the wing of an insect, the skin of a snake and stained specimens through the microscope. Try to see new lines, colors, textures, patterns and shapes. A whole new horizon is opened up. Try taking a "looking walk" with a magnifying glass in hand. Photomicrographs of nature's wonders also provide unlimited sources of ideas for designs. Illus. 9 shows a cross-section of a Buttercup root.

Illus. 8.

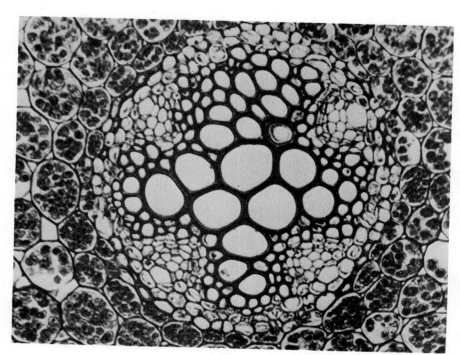

Illus. 9.

IDEAS FOR DESIGNS ■ 549

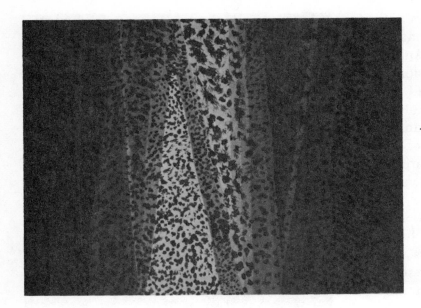

Illus. 10.

Illus. 11.

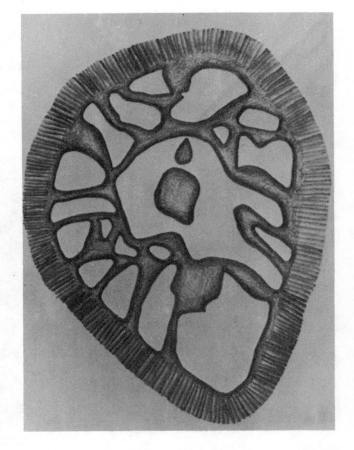

Other experiments may result in exciting compositions you could adapt for your projects. Brush and ink (Illus. 10), charcoal (Illus. 11), pencil (Illus. 12), and water color (Illus. 13) are four different media which are not too difficult to master. Illus. 14 shows a rug which was inspired by the water-color rendering of pecans.

Many times, slices of rocks, such as the agate in Illus. 15, give interesting suggestions for unusual creations.

Experiment with a variety of designs before deciding upon a specific pattern. Think about some of the techniques described and illustrated here and then plan your own. Decide which design you would like to reproduce for which craft. You might even use the same design to work with in several crafts—a single motif needlepointed, or worked into a crayon etching, or tole painted onto tinware, or cut out of paper, felt or leather might look entirely different and totally unique. Each medium and each technique alter the character of a design so much that overlapping is possible, perhaps even desirable.

Whichever design you choose, the most important thing about it, even more important than the design itself, is that *you* thought of it,

you planned it, and *you* will craft with it. What more satisfying creative experience could there be?

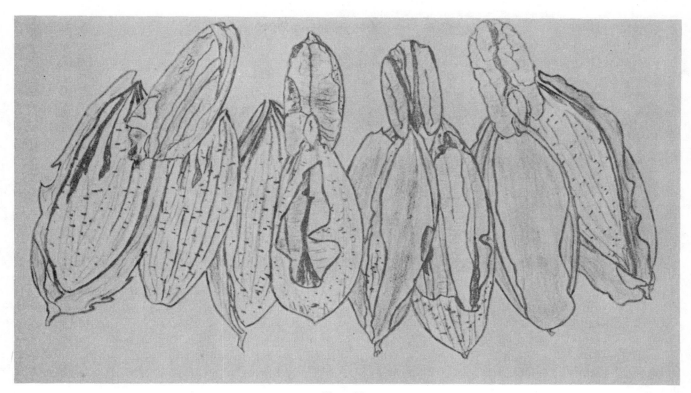

Illus. 12.

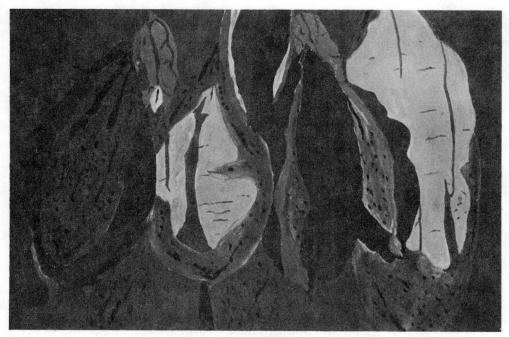

Illus. 13.

Illus. 14.

Illus. 15.

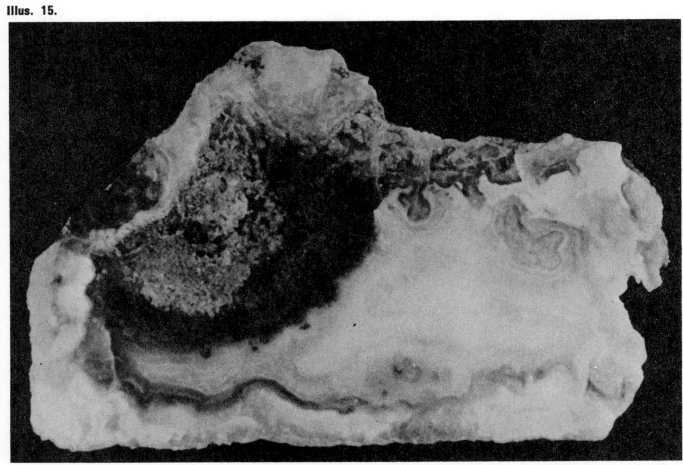

Illus. 16.

Illus. 17.

Illus. 18.

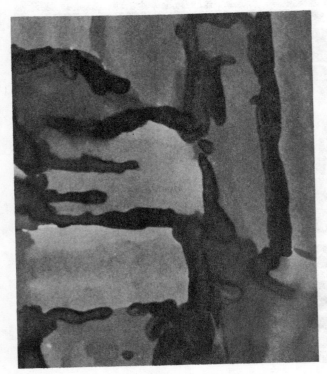

lus. 19.

Illus. 20.

Illus. 21.

Illus. 22.

Illus. 23.

Illus. 24.

Illus. 27.

Illus. 28.

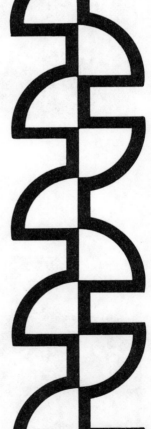

Illus. 29.

Illus. 30.

558 ■ **IDEAS FOR DESIGNS**

Illus. 31.

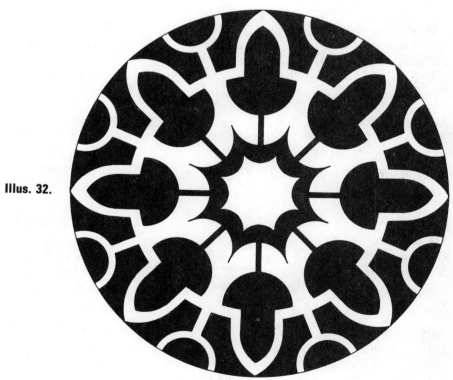

Illus. 32.

SUPPLIERS

Advance Process Supply Co.
400 N. Noble Street
Chicago, Illinois 60622
  Equipment and supplies for screen printing.

Aiko's
714 N. Wabash
Chicago, Illinois 60611
  Equipment and supplies for batiking; also, various papers.

Allcraft Tool and Supply Co.
215 Park Avenue
Hicksville, New York 11801
  Equipment and supplies for: metalworking, rock polishing, and wood carving.

American Art Clay Co., Inc.
4717 West 16th Street
Indianapolis, Indiana 46222
  Clay, kilns, and modelling tools.

American Handicrafts
P.O. Box 791
Fort Worth, Texas 76101
  Equipment and supplies for candle-making, felt crafting.

Art Handicrafts Co.
3512 Flatlands Avenue
Brooklyn, New York 11234
  Equipment and supplies for leathercrafting.

Barker Enterprises
15106—10th Avenue S.W.
Seattle, Washington 98166
  Equipment and supplies for candle-making.

Bead Game
505 N. Fairfax Avenue
Los Angeles, California 90036
  Beads.

Bergen Arts & Crafts
14 Prospect Street
Marblehead, Massachusetts 01945
  Equipment and supplies for: candle-making, batiking, jewelry-making, screen printing, weaving.

Dick Blick
P.O. Box 1267
Galesburg, Illinois 61401
  Equipment and supplies for: batik, ceramics, felt crafting, jewelry-making, macramé, paper crafting, plastic foam crafting, rock polishing, rug-making, screen printing, weaving, wood carving.

The Blue Mussel
478 Fifth Avenue South
Naples, Florida 33940
  Shells by the bag.

Bona Venture Supply Co.
17 Village Square
Hazelwood, Missouri 63042
  Equipment and supplies for: silk screen printing; also, balsa wood and clay.

The Brown Leather Co.
305 Virginia Avenue
Joplin, Missouri 64801
  All types of leather.

Burkart Bros., Inc.
6th Street & Highland Avenue
Verplanck, New York 10596
  Raw tinware (early American designs) for tole painting.

California Crafts Supply
1419 N. Central Park Avenue
Anaheim, California 92802
   Sheet metal; also, equipment and supplies for jewelry-making.

R. M. Catterson-Smith Limited
Exhibition Grounds
Wembley
ENGLAND
   Kilns.

CCM Arts and Crafts Inc.
9520 Baltimore Avenue
College Park, Maryland 20740
   Equipment and supplies for: batiking, beadcrafting, candle-making, ceramics, felt crafting, jewelry-making, leathercrafting, macramé, metal crafting, paper crafting, papier mâché, plastic foam crafting, rock polishing, rug-making, screen printing, weaving, wood carving; also, many types of balsa wood, inks, needles, paints, papers, string, thread, yarn, and general craft supplies.

Commonwealth Felt Co.
211 Congress Street
Boston, Massachusetts
   Felt.

William Condon & Sons Ltd.
Charlottetown
Prince Edward Island
CANADA
   Yarn for finger weaving.

Coulter Studio
138 E. 60th Street
New York, New York 10022
   Yarn for finger weaving.

Craftool Co.
1421 W. 240th Street
Harbor City, California 90710
   Equipment and supplies for wood carving (including wood blocks).

Craftools Inc.
1 Industrial Road
Wood-Ridge, New Jersey 07075
   Equipment and supplies for rock polishing; also, looms.

Craftsmen Potters Association of Great Britain
William Blake House, Marshall Street
London, W.1
ENGLAND
   Equipment and supplies for ceramics.

Craftsmen's Distributors Ltd.
1597 London Road
London, S.W.16
ENGLAND
   General craft supplies.

Craft Service
337 University Avenue
Rochester, New York 14607
   General craft supplies.

Crafts Unlimited
49 Shelton Street
London, W.C.2
ENGLAND
   Equipment and supplies for: batik, ceramics, lapidary, screen printing; also, general craft supplies.

Derby Lane Shell Center
10515 Gandy Boulevard
St. Petersburg, Florida 33702
   Shells by the bag.

Dharma Trading Co.
1952 University Avenue
Berkeley, California 94707
   Equipment and supplies for: knitting, crocheting, macramé, rug-making, weaving.

Durable Arts
P.O. Box 2413
San Rafael, California 94901
   Textile dyes for batiking and screen printing.

Economy Handicrafts
47–11 Francis Lewis Blvd.
Flushing, N.Y. 11361
  Equipment and supplies for: candle-making, ceramics, felt crafting, jewelry-making, leather-crafting, macramé, needlework, plastic foam crafting, rug-making, wood carving tools; also, beads yarn, and general craft supplies.

Fibrec, Inc.
2795 16th Street
San Francisco, California 94103
  Dyes for batik and screen printing.

Fleming Bottle & Jug Cutter, Inc.
Box 6157
Seattle, Washington 98188
  Bottle cutters.

Florida Supply House Ltd.
P.O. Box 847
Bradenton, Florida 33505
  Shells by the bag.

E. Friedlein & Co.
60 Minories
London, E.C.3
ENGLAND
  Shells.

Gaylord Specialties
225 Fifth Avenue
New York, New York 10010
  Gaylord Ribbon for quilling.

Gemex Co.
900 W. Los Vallecitos Blvd.
San Marcos, California 92069
  Equipment and supplies for: batiking, candle-making, felt crafting, jewelry-making, macramé, and needlework; also, beads and general craft supplies.

General Supplies Co.
526 Aviation Road
Fallbrook, California 92028
  Equipment and supplies for candle-making.

Gloria's Glass Garden
Box 1990
Beverly Hills, California 90213
  Beads.

Great Western Equipment Co.
3444 Main Street
Chula Vista, California 92011
  Materials and equipment for rock polishing.

C. R. Hill Co.
35 W. Grand River Avenue
Detroit, Michigan 48226
  Equipment and supplies for jewelry-making.

Homecraft Supplies
27 Trinity Road
London S.W.17
ENGLAND
  Equipment and supplies for leathercrafting.

House of Ceramics, Inc.
1011 N. Hollywood Street
Memphis, Tennessee 38108
  Equipment and supplies for ceramics.

International Candle House
349 Congress Street
Boston, Massachusetts 02210
  Equipment and supplies for candle-making.

Island Crafts
5735 14th Street W.
Bradenton, Florida 33507
  Equipment and supplies for: candle-making, macramé; also beads.

J. Johnson and Co.
33 Matinecock Avenue
Port Washington, New York 11050
  Equipment and supplies for wood carving.

Kraft Korner
5864 Mayfield Road
Cleveland, Ohio 44124
  Equipment and supplies for: macramé, jewelry-making, tole painting.

Leather and Handcrafts Ltd.
159 Symonds Street
Auckland 1,
NEW ZEALAND
   Equipment and supplies for: leathercrafting, plastic foam crafting; also, general craft supplies.

Lily Mills Co.
Shelby, North Carolina 28150
   Various types of hand looms (table and floor models), bobbin and warp winders, and yarns (cotton, wool, linen, novelty yarns, chenilles, and carpet yarns).

Macramé & Weaving Supply Co.
63 E. Adams
Chicago, Illinois 60093
   Equipment and supplies for macramé.

Mangelsen's
8200 J Street
Omaha, Nebraska 68127
   Equipment and supplies for: candle-making, macramé; also, beads, horseshoe nails, and general craft supplies.

Merribee Needlecraft Co.
2904 W. Lancaster
Ft. Worth, Texas 76107
   Equipment and supplies for needlework.

Miracle Cutter Co.
P.O. Box 280
Canby, Oregon 97013
   Bottle cutters.

A. Molokotos & Sons S.A.
Wool Spinning Mill, Tris Gefyres
Athens 907
GREECE
   Yarn for finger weaving.

Nasco House of Crafts
901 Janesville Avenue
Fort Atkinson, Wisconsin 53538
   Equipment and supplies for: batiking, ceramics, jewelry-making, paper crafting, rug-making, screen printing, weaving, wood carving.

National Artcraft Supply Co.
12217 Euclid Avenue
Cleveland, Ohio 44106
   Equipment and supplies for: jewelry-making, rock polishing.

Naz-Dar Co.
1087 N. North Branch Street
Chicago, Illinois 60622
   Equipment and supplies for screen printing.

The Needlewoman Shop
146–148 Regent Street
London W1R 6BA
ENGLAND
   Equipment and supplies for needlecrafting.

Harrison Neustadt
6 Benedict Avenue
Eastchester, New York 10709
   Rare and exotic wood scraps for jewelry and small carvings.

Paternayan Bros., Inc.
312 E. 95th Street
New York, New York 10028
   Yarn for finger weaving.

Pourette Mfg. Co.
6818 Roosevelt Way, N.E.
Seattle, Washington 98115
   Equipment and supplies for candle-making.

Prime Leather
30 Tottenham Street
London W.1
ENGLAND
   Equipment and supplies for leathercrafting.

Robin & Russ Handweavers
533 N. Adams Street
McMinnville, Oregon 97128
   Equipment and supplies for crocheting, knitting, macramé, rug-making and weaving.

K. R. Ruckstuhl, Inc.
P.O. Box 663
Provincetown, Massachusetts 02657
   Equipment and supplies for candle-making.

Sax Arts and Crafts
207 N. Milwaukee Street
Milwaukee, Wisconsin 53202
   Equipment and supplies for: batiking, beadcrafting, candle-making, ceramics, felt crafting, glass cutting, jewelry-making, leathercrafting, macramé, paper crafting, plastic foam crafting, rock polishing, rug-making, screen printing, weaving; also, balsa wood, dyes, inks, paints, sheet metal, wax, and general craft supplies.

Sy Schweitzer and Co., Inc.
P.O. Box 71, Gedney Station
White Plains, New York 10605
   Equipment and supplies for beadcrafting.

Sculpture House
38 East 30th Street
New York, New York 10016
   Equipment and supplies for ceramics.

Sippewissett Wax Works
Box 453
Seaside, California 93955
   Equipment and supplies for candle-making.

Skil-Crafts (a division of the Brown Leather Co.)
305 Virginia Avenue
Joplin, Missouri 64801
   Equipment and supplies for: beadcrafting, candle-making, ceramics, felt crafting, leathercrafting, paper crafting, plastic foam crafting, wood carving; also, general craft supplies.

S. & S. Arts and Crafts
Colchester, Connecticut 06415
   Equipment and supplies for: batiking, leathercrafting, paper crafting, rug-making, wood carving; also, clay, inks and threads.

Tandy Leather Co.
330 Fifth Avenue
New York, New York 10018
   Equipment and supplies for leathercrafting.
(Tandy Leather Co. also has retail outlets in many cities.)

Triarco Arts & Crafts
P.O. Box 106
Northfield, Illinois 60093
   Equipment and supplies for: batiking, candle-making, ceramics, jewelry-making, leathercrafting, paper crafting, plastic foam crafting, rug-making, screen printing, weaving, wood carving; also, general craft supplies.

Trinity Ceramic Supply, Inc.
9016 Diplomacy Row
Dallas, Texas 75235
   Clay.

Walco Products
1200 Zerega Avenue
Bronx, New York 10462
   Equipment and supplies for beadcrafting.

Walsall Saddlery
9 Murray Street
New York, New York 10007
   Horseshoe nails.

R. W. Williams Co.
The Sea, 525 N. Harbor Blvd.
San Pedro, California 90731
   Shells.

Vanguard Crafts Inc.
2915 Avenue J
Brooklyn, New York 11210
   Equipment and supplies for: batiking, ceramics, jewelry-making, rug-making, weaving.

X-Acto Inc.
48–41 Van Dam Street
Long Island City, New York 11101
   Equipment and supplies for: beadcrafting; tools for: leathercrafting, metal, paper, and wood.

Yarn Depot, Inc.
545 Sutter Street
San Francisco, California 94102
   Jute, straw, and a variety of yarns for: macramé, needlecraft, weaving.

BIBLIOGRAPHY

The following is a list of the books which were condensed for this volume. Refer to the books used for specific articles to further your knowledge of and skill in any crafts presented here. The books are listed alphabetically by title.

Alkema's Complete Guide to Creative Art for Young People
Alkema, Chester Jay
Sterling Publishing Co., Inc., 1972
Oak Tree Press Co., Ltd.

Balsa Wood Modelling
Warring, Ron
Sterling Publishing Co., Inc., 1973
Oak Tree Press Co., Ltd.

Bargello Stitchery
Christensen, Jo Ippolito and Ashner, Sonie Shapiro
Sterling Publishing Co., Inc., 1972
Oak Tree Press Co., Ltd.

Batik as a Hobby
Stein, Vivian
Sterling Publishing Co., Inc., 1969
Oak Tree Press Co., Ltd.

Beads Plus Macramé
La Croix, Grethe
Sterling Publishing Co., Inc., 1971
Oak Tree Press Co., Ltd.

Big-Knot Macramé
Enestrom, Anders and Strom, Nils
Sterling Publishing Co., Inc., 1971
Oak Tree Press Co., Ltd.

Cellophane Creations
Konijnenberg-De Groot, Jo
Sterling Publishing Co., Inc., 1972
Oak Tree Press Co., Ltd.

Ceramics by Slab
Priolo, Joan and Anthony
Sterling Publishing Co., Inc., 1973
Oak Tree Press Co., Ltd.

Colorful Glasscrafting
Eppens-van Veen, Jos H.
Sterling Publishing Co., Inc., 1973
Oak Tree Press Co., Ltd.

Coloring Papers
Strose, Susanne
Sterling Publishing Co., Inc., 1968
Oak Tree Press Co., Ltd.

Complete Crayon Book
   Alkema, Chester Jay
   Sterling Publishing Co., Inc., 1969
   Oak Tree Press Co., Ltd.

Crafting with Nature's Materials
   Alkema, Chester Jay
   Sterling Publishing Co., Inc., 1972
   Oak Tree Press Co., Ltd.

Creating from Scrap
   Frankel, Lillian and Godfrey
   Sterling Publishing Co., Inc., 1962
   Oak Tree Press Co., Ltd.

Creating Silver Jewelry with Beads
   Seitz, Marianne
   Sterling Publishing Co., Inc., 1971
   Oak Tree Press Co., Ltd.

Creating with Beads
   La Croix, Grethe
   Sterling Publishing Co., Inc., 1969
   Oak Tree Press Co., Ltd.

Creating with Flexible Foam
   Brouwer, Ab de
   Sterling Publishing Co., Inc., 1971
   Oak Tree Press Co., Ltd.

Creative Lace-Making with Thread and Yarn
   Fish, Harriet U.
   Sterling Publishing Co., Inc., 1972
   Oak Tree Press Co., Ltd.

Creative Paper Crafts in Color
   Alkema, Chester Jay
   Sterling Publishing Co., Inc., 1967
   Oak Tree Press Co., Ltd.

Cross Stitchery: Needlepointing with Yarns in a
Variety of Decorative Stitches
   Christensen, Jo Ippolito and Ashner, Sonie
      Shapiro
   Sterling Publishing Co., Inc., 1973
   Oak Tree Press Co., Ltd.

Curling, Coiling and Quilling
   Häslein, Inge and Frischmann, Rita
   Sterling Publishing Co., Inc., 1973
   Oak Tree Press Co., Ltd.

Enamel without Heat
   Schilt, Stephen J. and Weir, Donna J.
   Sterling Publishing Co., Inc., 1971
   Oak Tree Press Co., Ltd.

Felt Crafting
   Janvier, Jacqueline
   Sterling Publishing Co., Inc., 1970
   Oak Tree Press Co., Ltd.

Festive Food Decoration
   Ostrander, Sheila
   Sterling Publishing Co., Inc., 1969
   Oak Tree Press Co., Ltd.

Finger Weaving: Indian Braiding
   Turner, Alta R.
   Sterling Publishing Co., Inc., 1973
   Oak Tree Press Co., Ltd.

Flower Pressing
   Bauzen, Peter and Suzanne
   Sterling Publishing Co., Inc., 1972
   Oak Tree Press Co., Ltd.

Folding Table Napkins
   Bornstedt, Marianne von and Prytz, Ulla
   Sterling Publishing Co., Inc., 1972
   Oak Tree Press Co., Ltd.

Gadgets and Gifts for Girls to Make
Ostrander, Sheila
Sterling Publishing Co., Inc., 1962

Herb Magic and Garden Craft
Doole, Louise Evans
Sterling Publishing Co., Inc., 1972
Oak Tree Press Co., Ltd.

Hooked and Knotted Rugs
Beitler, Ethel Jane
Sterling Publishing Co., Inc., 1973
Oak Tree Press Co., Ltd.

Horseshoe-Nail Crafting
Carlbom, Hans
Sterling Publishing Co., Inc., 1973
Oak Tree Press Co., Ltd.

How to Make Things Out of Paper
Sperling, Walter
Sterling Publishing Co., Inc., 1961
Oak Tree Press Co., Ltd.

Ideas for Collage
Priolo, Joan B.
Sterling Publishing Co., Inc., 1972
Oak Tree Press Co., Ltd.

Junk Sculpture
LeFevre, Gregg
Sterling Publishing Co., Inc., 1973
Oak Tree Press Co., Ltd.

Lacquer and Crackle
Nussbaumer, Hanny
Sterling Publishing Co., Inc., 1972
Oak Tree Press Co., Ltd.

Leathercrafting
Petersen, Grete
Sterling Publishing Co., Inc., 1973
Oak Tree Press Co., Ltd.

Make Your Own Mobiles
Schegger, T.M.
Sterling Publishing Co., Inc., 1965
Oak Tree Press Co., Ltd.

Make Your Own Musical Instruments
Mandell, Muriel and Wood, Robert E.
Sterling Publishing Co., Inc., 1957

Making Paper Flowers
Strose, Susanne
Sterling Publishing Co., Inc., 1970
Oak Tree Press Co., Ltd.

Making Shell Flowers
Conroy, Norma M.
Sterling Publishing Co., Inc., 1972
Oak Tree Press Co., Ltd.

Model Boat Building
Lozier, Herb
Sterling Publishing Co., Inc., 1970
Oak Tree Press Co., Ltd.

Monster Masks
Alkema, Chester Jay
Sterling Publishing Co., Inc., 1973
Oak Tree Press Co., Ltd.

Needlepoint Simplified
Christensen, Jo Ippolito and Ashner, Sonie Shapiro
Sterling Publishing Co., Inc., 1971
Oak Tree Press Co., Ltd.

Nick-Nacks for Neatness
  Ostrander, Sheila
  Sterling Publishing Co., Inc., 1963

Off-Loom Weaving
  Bernstein, Marion H.
  Sterling Publishing Co., Inc., 1971
  Oak Tree Press Co., Ltd.

101 Best Nature Games and Projects
  Frankel, Lillian and Godfrey
  Sterling Publishing Co., Inc., 1959

101 Camping-Out Ideas and Activities
  Knobel, Bruno
  Sterling Publishing Co., Inc., 1961

101 Toys Children Can Make
  Kunz, Robert and Katharine
  Sterling Publishing Co., Inc., 1959

Original Creations with Papier Mâché
  Anderson, Mildred
  Sterling Publishing Co., Inc., 1967
  Oak Tree Press Co., Ltd.

Papier Mâché—and How to Use It
  Anderson, Mildred
  Sterling Publishing Co., Inc., 1965
  Oak Tree Press Co., Ltd.

Pebble Collecting and Polishing
  Fletcher, Edward
  Sterling Publishing Co., Inc., 1973
  Blandford Press, Ltd., 1972

Potato Printing
  Strose, Susanne
  Sterling Publishing Co., Inc., 1968
  Oak Tree Press Co., Ltd.

Puppet and Pantomine Plays
  Howard, Vernon
  Sterling Publishing Co., Inc., 1962
  Oak Tree Press Co., Ltd.

Puppet-Making
  Alkema, Chester Jay
  Sterling Publishing Co., Inc., 1971
  Oak Tree Press Co., Ltd.

Scissorscraft
  Grol, Lini
  Sterling Publishing Co., Inc., 1970
  Oak Tree Press Co., Ltd.

Screen Printing
  Birkner, Heinrich
  Sterling Publishing Co., Inc., 1971
  Oak Tree Press, Co., Ltd.

Spin, Dye and Weave Your Own Wool
  Duncan, Molly
  Sterling Publishing Co., Inc., 1972
  A. H. & A. W. Reed, Ltd., 1968

String Things You Can Create
  Saeger, Glen D.
  Sterling Publishing Co., Inc., 1973
  Oak Tree Press Co., Ltd.

Tall Book of Candle Crafting
  Guy, Gary
  Sterling Publishing Co., Inc., 1973
  Oak Tree Press Co., Ltd.

Tole Painting
  Fraser, B. Kay
  Sterling Publishing Co., Inc., 1971
  Oak Tree Press Co., Ltd.

Trapunto: Decorative Quilting
  Christensen, Jo Ippolito
  Sterling Publishing Co., Inc., 1972
  Oak Tree Press Co., Ltd.

Whittling and Wood Carving
  Hoppe, H.
  Sterling Publishing Co., Inc., 1969
  Oak Tree Press Co., Ltd.

INDEX

Letters indicate color pages